The Princeton Review

Practice

MCATs

BY JAMES L. FLOWERS, M.D.,
THEODORE SILVER, M.D.,
AND
THE STAFF OF THE PRINCETON REVIEW

FIRST EDITION

RANDOM HOUSE, INC.
NEW YORK

www.PrincetonReview.com

Princeton Review Publishing, L. L. C.
2315 Broadway
New York, NY 10024
E-mail: booksupport@review.com

All questions in the book were created by the authors.

MCAT is a registered trademark of the Association of American Medical Colleges, which does not
endorse this book.

ISBN 0-375-76456-9

Editor: Allegra Viner
Production Editor: Patricia Dublin
Additional Production: Steve Leduc
Production Coordinator: Stephanie Martin

ACKNOWLEDGMENTS

The Princeton Review would like to thank the following members of the MCAT Development Team for their work on Practice Test One: John Bahling, M.D.; Bethany Blackwell; Douglas Franzen, M.D.; Jacqueline Giordano; Meg Jay; Steven Leduc; Matthew B.A. Patterson, M.D.; Ephraim Tsalik, Ph.D.; Jennifer Wooddell; and Judene Wright.

CONTENTS

PART ◆ I

Introduction

Welcome

In April 1991, the Association of American Medical Colleges (AAMC) first administered the revised MCAT. At the same time (after two years of development), The Princeton Review introduced its comprehensive MCAT preparation course nationwide.

Since then, AAMC has made the MCAT progressively more difficult, due to the drastically increased number of medical school applicants in the mid-1990s. Throughout this, The Princeton Review has taken steps to ensure that their course reflects this stepped-up difficulty level.

In 1996, The Princeton Review and Hyperlearning, California's premiere MCAT prep company, took MCAT preparation to new heights by merging their programs—the combined course was billed as a "Test Prep Utopia" for premedical students, by the UCLA *Daily Bruin*. Now, the combined MCAT program has the largest, most up-to-date collection of MCAT materials available; the equivalent of over 30 MCATs.

Today, one out of every six students who take the MCAT takes our MCAT preparation course first. Students who take our course improve their MCAT scores by an average of 10 points. We are proud of our program, and of the accomplishments of our students.

This book is not a replacement for a full MCAT course—no book is. Instead, it is a valuable resource for students just beginning the MCAT preparation process who wish to diagnose their areas of strength and weakness. It is also a proven tool for students who have already invested the time required to master MCAT topics and are now looking for that extra edge.

Good Luck!

Introduction

HOW THIS BOOK IS ORGANIZED

Part I *describes the MCAT* and tells you how to prepare.

Parts II and IV present *full-length simulated MCATs* with answer keys and scoring grids.

Parts III and V *explain the answers* to the simulated tests that appear in Parts II and IV. For every question, we tell you why a particular answer is correct and why the others are wrong, so that you can understand your errors and correct them. For each of the writing samples, we provide a sample essay with grader commentary.

You'll get the most from this book if you pursue its parts fully and *in the appropriate order*. Read Part I (Introduction). Take the tests provided in Parts II and IV. Score yourself. Then identify your errors, strengths, and weaknesses by reading the explanations provided in Parts III and V.

WHAT IS THE MCAT?

The MCAT (Medical College Admission Test) is a seven-hour test that almost all American and Canadian medical schools use to help decide whether to admit or reject applicants. If you're planning to attend medical school, you will most likely need to take the MCAT. It can determine where you go—or whether you go at all.

WHO PRODUCES THE MCAT?

The MCAT is officially produced by the Association of American Medical Colleges (AAMC) in Washington, DC. The test is written and administered by American College Testing (ACT), and there is an office called the MCAT Program Office in Iowa City, Iowa, which handles questions about registration and administration for the MCAT.

WHAT'S THE MCAT LIKE, AND HOW MANY QUESTIONS DOES IT HAVE?

The MCAT is divided into four sections, as follows:

1. Physical Sciences (Physics and General Chemistry)

2. Verbal Reasoning

3. Writing Sample

4. Biological Sciences (Biology and Organic Chemistry)

Except for the Writing Sample section, the exam is entirely multiple-choice. All questions are followed by four choices (A, B, C, and D), and there is no penalty for guessing; a student's score is based only on the number of correct responses. No study aids of any kind—books, notes, scratch paper, formula sheets, or calculators—are permitted. The science sections of the MCAT apply first-year, college-level topics in Physics, General Chemistry, Biology, and Organic Chemistry to new—perhaps unfamiliar—situations.

PHYSICAL SCIENCES

The Physical Sciences section presents ten to eleven passages, each pertaining to physics and/or general chemistry. A science "passage" is a description of some physical situation or experiment, often accompanied by diagrams of experimental apparatus, data tables, graphs, and/or formulas. Each passage is followed by four to eight multiple-choice questions that concern the passage and the relevant science. In addition, the section presents fifteen questions that do not relate to any passage. We call these questions "free-standing." Altogether the Physical Sciences section has 77 questions, with a time limit of 100 minutes.

VERBAL REASONING

The Verbal Reasoning section consists of 60 questions with an 85-minute time limit. The section is composed of nine reading passages (450–600 words each) with five to ten questions following each one. Passages are excerpts from books or from articles published in magazines, newspapers, or journals. The subject matter is diverse, and includes history, sociology, psychology, political theory, social and literary criticism, anthropology, and general science. Most questions require recognition of the author's main idea and tone, as well as an understanding of the arguments used to establish and support his or her position. Simple retrieval of factual information contained in the passages makes up only a small percentage of the questions.

WRITING SAMPLE

After a one-hour lunch break, students return for the Writing Sample. This part of the exam requires the test taker to write two essays (with a time limit of 30 minutes for each one), each based on a brief philosophical or social statement. Students must address three specific writing tasks based on the topic provided: explain what the statement means, provide a counterexample to the statement, and provide criteria for determining when the statement is true and when it is not. There is no right or wrong answer. Two examples follow on the next page:

PART 1

A government cannot enforce a law if its citizens oppose it.

Write a unified essay in which you perform the following tasks. Explain what you think the above statement means. Describe a specific situation in which you believe a government can enforce a law if its citizens oppose it. Discuss what you think determines whether or not a government can enforce a law that the citizens oppose.

PART 2

No false statement can live indefinitely.

Write a unified essay in which you perform the following tasks. Explain what you think the above statement means. Describe a specific situation in which you believe a false statement can live indefinitely. Discuss what you think determines whether a false statement can or cannot live indefinitely.

BIOLOGICAL SCIENCES

The Biological Sciences section is structured the same way as the Physical Sciences section except the topics of the passages and questions are from Biology and Organic Chemistry.

HOW IS THE MCAT SCORED?

Approximately nine weeks after the test, students receive their score report by mail. (They can also get their scores online from the AAMC's official MCAT website, **www.aamc.org/students/mcat**, about seven weeks after the exam date.) The score report contains four scores, one for each section, plus the total numerical score of the three multiple-choice sections. The three multiple-choice sections are scored on a 1 to 15 scale (whole-number scores only), with 15 being the top. Scores of 10 or above (double-digit scores) are very good. Overall national averages are about 8. The Writing Sample is scored on a J through T letter scale, T being the highest. The average score is an O.

Here's a table that shows you how the MCAT is designed and scored.

Section	Number of Questions	Time Limit	Score Range
Physical Sciences	77	100 minutes	1–15
Verbal Reasoning	60	85 minutes	1–15
Writing Sample	2 essays	60 minutes (30 minutes per essay)	J–T
Biological Sciences	77	100 minutes	1–15

HOW CAN I PREPARE FOR THE MCAT?

According to the AAMC, the MCAT is designed to test scientific reasoning, critical thinking, and writing ability. AAMC says you should prepare for the science sections by reviewing your college textbooks and notes, and for the Verbal Reasoning and Writing sections through coursework in the humanities and writing.

While these things may be helpful, your best preparation for the MCAT is through *proper* study and practice. You must appreciate the difference between studying *science* and studying *science for the MCAT*. You must review the premedical sciences in a way that is systematically tailored *to the test*. Furthermore, you must study MCAT questions themselves. You should be wise to their design and schooled in *techniques* that can systematically lead to correct answers.

SHOULD I BUY THE PRACTICE MATERIALS THAT AAMC SELLS?

Yes, you probably should. AAMC MCAT practice materials are available for purchase at their official MCAT website, **www.aamc.org/students/mcat**.

REGISTERING FOR THE MCAT

MCAT registration is done online at the MCAT website, **www.aamc.org/students/mcat**.

You should also download a copy of the *MCAT Essentials* booklet (available for free as a PDF from the website); this booklet contains all the official information concerning MCAT registration and administration.

SOME MCAT STRATEGY TIPS FOR THE MUTLIPLE-CHOICE SECTIONS

1. Use process of elimination, and never leave an answer blank.

2. In the two Sciences sections, do all of the free-standing questions first. Since they do not rely on a passage, they tend to be quite straightforward. These independent questions appear in three groups of four to six questions each (for a total of fifteen) and almost always in the same places: There's a group after Passage IV, a second group after Passage VIII, and the final group at the very end of the section.

3. Don't do the passages in the order in which they are printed in the test booklet. For each of the three multiple-choice sections, first take a quick look through the passages and do them in whatever order you want: easier passages first, tougher passages later.

4. When taking practice tests leading up to the real thing, consider doing all of the passages in a single subject first. For example, in the Physical Sciences section, do all the Physics passages first, then all the G-Chem passages (or vice versa), and in the Biological Sciences section, do all the O-Chem passages first, then all the Biology passages (or vice versa). This approach may work better for you!

5. Consider skipping an entire passage—particularly in Verbal Reasoning—if you find it too difficult. Fill in answers for it, of course, but use the time that you'll save by maximizing your performance on the other passages.

6. Don't go looking for esoteric or exotic exceptions to rules that are taught in undergraduate-level science classes. MCAT questions are looking for straightforward answers. If you try to think of some strange exception to a basic rule that only a researcher in the field would have heard about, you're not only wasting time but you also probably won't pick the answer that the MCAT wants (so you won't get credit for your "brilliant" idea).

7. On the Physical Sciences section, always check your units. For example, if a question asks for energy, eliminate any answer choices whose units don't work out to be joules.

8. Don't waste time doing unnecessary mathematical computation. For example, if a question requires that you multiply 22.4 by 3.85, replace this messy calculation by the simple approximation $22 \times 4 = 88$.

9. Fill in the bubbles on your answer sheet in groups, not one question at a time. This saves a lot of valuable minutes. For example, bubble in your answers only after you've finished one or two passages. However, near the end of the section, as the time limit approaches, do fill in answers one at a time, to be sure that you get them all.

10. And finally, there's a helpful strategy that works surprisingly often, one you learned watching Sesame Street (get ready to sing): "One of these things is not like the others; three of these things are kinda the same…." Each MCAT question has four answer choices; if all else fails, find the three that are "kinda the same" and pick the one that's "not like the others" as your answer.

ARE THERE STRATEGIES AND TECHNIQUES FOR THE WRITING SAMPLE TOO?

Yes. In order to score well on your MCAT essays it's important to know how they are graded. An MCAT essay is normally read by two graders. Each grader spends about ninety seconds reading an essay. She then grades it "holistically." Holistic grading means that the reader does not make separate evaluations in terms of substance, organization, or grammar. Rather, she's supposed to keep all of these criteria in mind and then assign a grade based on an overall sense of the essay's quality.

Because the MCAT readers read each essay so quickly, first impressions count for a lot. Furthermore, if your essay is difficult to read or to understand, you will probably not get credit for many of your good ideas. Therefore, follow these guidelines.

1. Use clear, straightforward language. Don't use big words for their own sake; a fancy vocabulary is only impressive if you use the words correctly and appropriately.

2. Organize the essay to follow the structure of the question. Each question has three parts; the easiest approach is a three-paragraph essay. You must answer all three parts in order to get a good score.

3. Answer the question directly; don't go off on tangents.

Here is a sample question:

Consider this statement:
A society that is well educated will necessarily be free.
Write a unified essay in which you perform the following tasks: Explain what you think the above statement means. Describe a specific situation in which a well-educated society might not be free. Discuss what you think determines whether or not a well-educated society is free.

Response

Well-educated people will tend to seek social and political freedom. In this context, "freedom" means equality and the protection of civil rights. Furthermore, a totalitarian or tyrannical government will find it difficult to survive in the face of an informed and insightful public. As Victor Hugo said, "One can resist the invasion of armies but not the invasion of ideas." The intimate relationship between education and freedom is shown by the importance placed by the civil rights movement on school desegregation in the United States. The Brown v. Board of Education decision is seen as a landmark not only because of the belief that we can't be truly free without access to a good education, but also because the well educated are often the best equipped to carry on the fight for freedom.

However, the education afforded by a school depends on the objectives of those who select its curriculum. In some societies, a student might be "well educated" by that society's standards, and at the same time hold beliefs that are inconsistent with the idea and practice of freedom. In the former Soviet Union, for example, the educational system was very well developed and accessible to much of the population. In fact, many students came from other countries to take advantage of educational resources that were unavailable in their own nations. Soviet society was "well educated," and yet success within that educational system required students to accept or at least profess beliefs that most of us would see as inconsistent with the ideals of freedom. Another example would be the *madrasas* schools in Pakistan. These schools are available to poor students who do not have access to expensive private institutions. However, education in the *madrasas* is largely focused on the teaching of a fundamentalist interpretation of the Quran, to the exclusion of all other sources of knowledge. Pakistani society in one way is better educated because of the existence of these schools, and yet this kind of education does not foster freedom as we generally define it in the United States.

Therefore, when the curriculum is defined and controlled by a particular political or religious authority, education will reinforce the ideas of that authority. On the other hand, when the school system is less centralized and is open to a variety of influences, students will learn to question authority and to settle on their own goals and values. However, education does not come only through the school system. As we saw in Eastern Europe, the political system eventually broke down as people learned from the world around them that other ways of life were possible. If we take education to mean exposure to a variety of new ideas, then, Victor Hugo's statement holds true. In the long run, a truly well-educated people will work to create a more free society.

Note that this essay:

1. addresses all three of the assigned "tasks,"

2. is clearly organized, covering one task per paragraph, and

3. demonstrates a serious, professional tone and attitude.

These are the ingredients of a high-scoring MCAT essay.

WILL THIS BOOK GIVE ME EVERYTHING I NEED?

To be honest—probably not. Unless you're starting out as a top MCAT student, no *book* can fully prepare you for the MCAT—not this one or any other. If you're serious about earning a high MCAT score, you need a good teacher, powerful materials, personal contact, and *repeated opportunities to take simulated tests that are scored, analyzed, and returned.*

BUT THIS BOOK IS THE PLACE TO BEGIN

Find out where you stand and what you need. Set aside two full days and *take the simulated MCATs in this book.* Treat them seriously and subject yourself rigorously to MCAT test conditions:

- Start early in the morning, and for the whole day consider yourself absolutely unavailable for anything or anyone else.

- For each section give yourself only as much time as the instructions allow.

- Take the ten-minute breaks as indicated and take a full sixty-minute lunch hour between the Physical Science and Writing Sample sections of the test.

When you've finished the test, score yourself.

For each of the three multiple-choice sections, give yourself 1 point for each question you answered correctly. Then, use the scoring key on page 91, and derive your scaled scores for Physical Sciences, Verbal Reasoning, and Biological Sciences. (You can't score the Writing Sample, but we definitely want you to complete that section of the test anyway.)

Yes, then what?

If both your verbal and science scores are *10 or above*, you're in pretty good shape. Depending on your college grades and the medical school you want to attend, you might consider signing up for the MCAT without pursuing special preparation. Naturally, you should review any science that gives you trouble on our simulated test. Then, for a few weeks before you take the real test, sit down and address the sample tests and materials that AAMC provides. If that goes smoothly, take the MCAT as scheduled. You'll probably do well.

On the other hand, if your verbal and science scores are *9 or below*, you've got to raise them. That probably means you should consider a good MCAT course.

CHOOSING AN MCAT COURSE

Generally speaking, a *good* MCAT course will:

1. Provide you with teachers, teaching systems, and teaching materials that organize your work, maintain your attention, and monitor your progress day by day and week by week.

2. Thoroughly immerse you in physics, general chemistry, organic chemistry, biology, reading, and writing—in a way that is strategically designed for the MCAT.

3. Show you, systematically, how MCAT questions are structured and teach you how to select correct answers quickly by thinking like the test writers.

4. Give you repeated opportunities to take simulated MCATs that are quickly scored and returned to you for thorough review. Anyone who tries to prepare for the MCAT without repeated MCAT test taking might as well prepare for a driver's road test without ever getting behind a steering wheel. Hands-on practice with simulated MCATs is essential to raising scores.

Any course that fails to offer these four features is useless, no matter how many papers, booklets, or tapes it provides.

ENOUGH TALK — LET'S TAKE THE FIRST STEP

We've described the MCAT, and we've told you how to prepare for it. Now it's time to get started. Set aside a day and take the sample MCAT that's provided in Part II of this book. Use the answer sheets provided after each exam. Time yourself according to the standard MCAT testing day:

Morning

Physical Sciences:	1 hour, 40 minutes
Break:	*10 minutes*
Verbal Reasoning:	1 hour, 25 minutes
Lunch:	1 hour

Afternoon

Writing Sample (Part 1):	30 minutes
Writing Sample (Part 2):	30 minutes
Break:	*10 minutes*
Biological Sciences:	1 hour, 40 minutes

After you've taken each test, score yourself. Then, over the next few days, evaluate your performance carefully by reading the explanatory answers provided in Part III. They'll show you what you did right and what you did wrong. Next, repeat the process with the second practice MCAT provided in Part IV of this book and the answers and explanations provided in Part V. When you're all done you'll know just where you stand. You'll know where you're strong, you'll know where you're weak, and you'll be ready to plan your route toward a higher score.

From all of us at The Princeton Review, good luck.

PART ◆ II

MCAT Practice Test 1

PART II

MCAT Practice Test 1

Physical Sciences

Time: 100 Minutes

Questions 1 – 77

PHYSICAL SCIENCES

DIRECTIONS: Most questions in the Physical Sciences test are organized into groups, each preceded by a descriptive passage. After studying the passage, select the one best answer to each question in the group. Some questions are not based on a descriptive passage and are also independent of each other. You must also select the one best answer to these questions. If you are not certain of an answer, eliminate the alternatives that you know to be incorrect and then select an answer from the remaining alternatives. Indicate your selection by blackening the corresponding oval on your answer document. A periodic table is provided for your use. You may consult it whenever you wish.

PERIODIC TABLE OF THE ELEMENTS

1 H 1.0																	2 He 4.0
3 Li 6.9	4 Be 9.0											5 B 10.8	6 C 12.0	7 N 14.0	8 O 16.0	9 F 19.0	10 Ne 20.2
11 Na 23.0	12 Mg 24.3											13 Al 27.0	14 Si 28.1	15 P 31.0	16 S 32.1	17 Cl 35.5	18 Ar 39.9
19 K 39.1	20 Ca 40.1	21 Sc 45.0	22 Ti 47.9	23 V 50.9	24 Cr 52.0	25 Mn 54.9	26 Fe 55.8	27 Co 58.9	28 Ni 58.7	29 Cu 63.5	30 Zn 65.4	31 Ga 69.7	32 Ge 72.6	33 As 74.9	34 Se 79.0	35 Br 79.9	36 Kr 83.8
37 Rb 85.5	38 Sr 87.6	39 Y 88.9	40 Zr 91.2	41 Nb 92.9	42 Mo 95.9	43 Tc (98)	44 Ru 101.1	45 Rh 102.9	46 Pd 106.4	47 Ag 107.9	48 Cd 112.4	49 In 114.8	50 Sn 118.7	51 Sb 121.8	52 Te 127.6	53 I 126.9	54 Xe 131.3
55 Cs 132.9	56 Ba 137.3	57 La* 138.9	72 Hf 178.5	73 Ta 180.9	74 W 183.9	75 Re 186.2	76 Os 190.2	77 Ir 192.2	78 Pt 195.1	79 Au 197.0	80 Hg 200.6	81 Tl 204.4	82 Pb 207.2	83 Bi 209.0	84 Po (209)	85 At (210)	86 Rn (222)
87 Fr (223)	88 Ra 226.0	89 Ac† 227.0	104 Rf (261)	105 Db (262)	106 Sg (263)	107 Bh (262)	108 Hs (265)	109 Mt (267)									

	58 Ce 140.1	59 Pr 140.9	60 Nd 144.2	61 Pm (145)	62 Sm 150.4	63 Eu 152.0	64 Gd 157.3	65 Tb 158.9	66 Dy 162.5	67 Ho 164.9	68 Er 167.3	69 Tm 168.9	70 Yb 173.0	71 Lu 175.0
†	90 Th 232.0	91 Pa (231)	92 U 238.0	93 Np (237)	94 Pu (244)	95 Am (243)	96 Cm (247)	97 Bk (247)	98 Cf (251)	99 Es (252)	100 Fm (257)	101 Md (258)	102 No (259)	103 Lr (260)

GO ON TO THE NEXT PAGE.

Passage I (Questions 1–5)

Figure 1 shows a portion of the inner mechanism of a typical home smoke detector. It consists of a pair of capacitor plates which are charged by a 9-volt battery (not shown). The capacitor plates (electrodes) are connected to a sensor device, D; the resistor R denotes the internal resistance of the sensor. Normally, air acts as an insulator and no current would flow in the circuit shown. However, inside the smoke detector is a small sample of an artifically produced radioactive element, americium-241, which decays primarily by emitting alpha particles, with a half-life of approximately 430 years. The daughter nucleus of the decay has a half-life in excess of two million years and therefore poses virtually no biohazard.

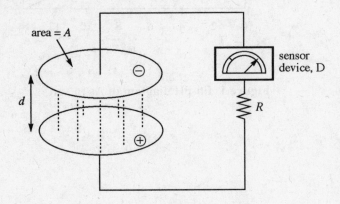

Figure 1 Smoke detector mechanism

The decay products (alpha particles and gamma rays) from the ^{241}Am sample ionize air molecules between the plates and thus provide a conducting pathway which allows current to flow in the circuit shown in Figure 1. A steady-state current is quickly established and remains as long as the battery continues to maintain a 9-volt potential difference between its terminals. However, if smoke particles enter the space between the capacitor plates and thereby interrupt the flow, the current is reduced, and the sensor responds to this change by triggering the alarm. (Furthermore, as the battery starts to "die out," the resulting drop in current is also detected to alert the homeowner to replace the battery.)

The capacitance of a parallel-plate capacitor is given by the equation

$$C = \varepsilon_0 \frac{A}{d}$$

Equation 1

where ε_0 is the universal permittivity constant, equal to 8.85×10^{-12} C^2/(N·m^2). Since the area A of each capacitor plate in the smoke detector is 20 cm^2 and the plates are separated by a distance d of 5 mm, the capacitance is 3.5×10^{-12} F = 3.5 pF.

1. If the capacitor plates were fully charged by the 9 V battery, what is the charge on the positive plate?

   A. 15.8 pC
   B. 31.5 pC
   C. 47.3 pC
   D. 63.0 pC

2. The sensor device D shown in Figure 1 performs its function by acting as:

   A. an ohmmeter.
   B. a voltmeter.
   C. a potentiometer.
   D. an ammeter.

3. Which of the following would decrease the capacitance of the capacitor in the detector?

   A. Placing a 1-mm-thick layer of polystyrene between the plates
   B. Moving the plates closer together
   C. Using smaller electrode plates
   D. Using a 6 V battery instead of a 9 V battery

4. What is the magnitude of the electric field between the electrodes when the plates are charged to a potential difference of 9 V?

   A. 0.045 V/m
   B. 0.9 V/m
   C. 45 V/m
   D. 1800 V/m

5. The current that exists in the circuit depicted in Figure 1 generates a weak magnetic field. Which of the following diagrams best illustrates the magnetic field $\vec{B}$ created by the current I in the wire?

   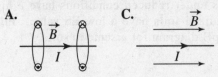

   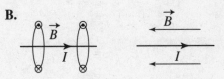

GO ON TO THE NEXT PAGE.

Passage II (Questions 6–11)

Arsenic, element 33, has been used for a variety of medicinal and industrial purposes, but is most widely known for its use as a poison. Inorganic forms are more toxic than organic forms, and trivalent forms are more toxic than both zero-valent or pentavalent forms.

Trivalent arsenic inhibits pyruvate dehydrogenase, an important enzyme used to create energy in cells, by binding to critical sulfhydryl groups on the molecule. One result is that fewer high-energy molecules (such as ATP) are created, resulting in widespread organ damage. Pentavalent arsenic resembles inorganic phosphate and thus can become incorporated into ATP, resulting in a molecule that does not deliver energy to critical body processes.

Treatment of acute arsenic poisoning requires consultation with a toxicologist experienced in the use of chelation therapy. Dimercaprol is an effective chelating agent that is administered intramuscularly in an oil suspension. It binds to arsenic-containing compounds and renders them inactive, as illustrated in Reaction 1:

$$\begin{array}{c} \text{SH} \\ | \\ \text{HOCH}_2\text{CHCH}_2\text{—SH} \end{array} + \text{AsO}_2^- $$

$$\downarrow$$

$$\begin{array}{c} \text{CH}_2\text{—S} \\ | \qquad\quad \text{As—O}^- \\ \text{HOCH}_2\text{CH—S} \end{array} + \text{H}_2\text{O}$$

Reaction 1

Arsenic compounds in soil are a contamination threat to water supplies. The acidity and oxidation state of soil are important considerations when assessing arsenic contamination. Acidity of soil is measured by standard pH scale, while the oxidation state of soil is measured on an Eh scale. Soils under reduced conditions have a high Eh value, and oxidized soils have a low Eh value. Figure 1 shows the Eh-pH diagram for arsenic in soil.

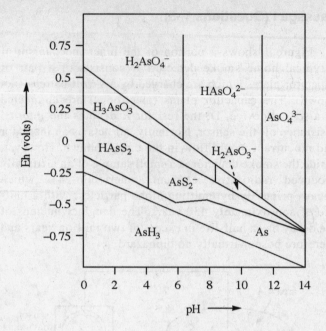

Figure 1 Eh-pH diagram of As in soil

6. Of the following, which is likely to be the *least* toxic?

A.

B.

C.

D.

GO ON TO THE NEXT PAGE.

7. Which of the following best describes the bond formed by dimercaprol to compounds of arsenic?

   A. Network covalent
   B. Ionic
   C. Coordinate covalent
   D. Metallic

8. Methylarsonic acid, $CH_3AsO(OH)_2$, is isolated in a laboratory analysis. What is its molecular shape?

   A. Square planar
   B. Seesaw
   C. Tetrahedral
   D. Trigonal bypyramidal

9. The role of dimercaprol in chelation therapy is best described as a:

   A. ligand that donates electron pairs.
   B. ligand that accepts electron pairs.
   C. Lewis acid that donates electron pairs.
   D. Lewis acid that accepts electron pairs.

10. Which of the following molecules are most likely to be appropriate for chelation therapy to treat toxic metal poisoning?

   A. I and II only
   B. I and III only
   C. II and III only
   D. I, II, and III

11. A sample of soil with suspected arsenic contamination has an Eh of 0.25 V and pH 6. Which of the following steps would be most effective in limiting potential toxicity?

   A. Alkalinizing the soil
   B. Aerating the soil
   C. Acidifying the soil
   D. Removing reducing agents from the soil

GO ON TO THE NEXT PAGE.

Passage III (Questions 12–17)

The batteries that start an automobile or power flashlights are devices that convert chemical energy into electrical energy. These devices use spontaneous oxidation–reduction reactions (called half-reactions) that take place at the electrodes to create an electric current. The strength of the battery, or electromotive force, is determined by the difference in electric potential between the half cells, expressed in volts. This voltage depends on which reactions occur at the anode and the cathode, the concentrations of the solutions in the cells, and the temperature. The cell voltage, E, at a temperature of 25°C and nonstandard conditions, can be calculated from the Nernst equation,

$$E = E° - \frac{0.0592}{n} \log_{10} Q$$

Equation 1

where $E°$ is the standard potential, n denotes the number of electrons transferred in the balanced half-reaction, and Q is the reaction quotient.

The lead storage battery used in automobiles is composed of six identical cells joined in series. The anode is solid lead, the cathode is lead dioxide, and the electrodes are immersed in a solution of sulfuric acid. As each cell discharges during normal operation, the sulfate ion is consumed as it is deposited in the form of lead sulfate on both electrodes, as shown in Reaction 1:

$$Pb(s) + PbO_2(s) + 4\,H^+(aq) + 2\,SO_4^{2-}(aq)$$

$$\downarrow$$

$$2\,PbSO_4(s) + 2\,H_2O(l)$$

Reaction 1

Each cell produces 2 V, for a total of 12 V for the typical car battery.

Unlike many batteries, however, the lead storage battery can be recharged by applying an external voltage. Because the redox reaction in the battery consumes sulfate ions, the degree of discharge of the battery can be checked by measuring the density of the battery fluid with a hydrometer. The fluid density in a fully charged battery is 1.2 g/cm^3.

Table 1 Standard Reduction Potentials at $T = 25°C$

Half-reaction	$E°$ (V)
$F_2(g) + 2e^- \rightarrow 2F^-(aq)$	+2.87
$Cl_2(g) + 2e^- \rightarrow 2Cl^-(aq)$	+1.36
$Cu^+(aq) + e^- \rightarrow Cu(s)$	+0.52
$Cu^{2+}(aq) + 2e^- \rightarrow Cu(s)$	+0.34
$Zn^{2+}(aq) + 2e^- \rightarrow Zn(s)$	−0.76
$Al^{3+}(aq) + 3e^- \rightarrow Al(s)$	−1.66
$Li^+(aq) + e^- \rightarrow Li(s)$	−3.05

12. Of the following, which one is the best reducing agent?

   A. Li^+
   B. Li
   C. Cl^-
   D. F^-

13. When a lead storage battery recharges, what happens to the density of the battery fluid?

   A. It decreases to 1.0 g/cm^3.
   B. It increases to 1.0 g/cm^3.
   C. It decreases to 1.2 g/cm^3.
   D. It increases to 1.2 g/cm^3.

GO ON TO THE NEXT PAGE.

14. In which of the following situations would a voltaic cell have the highest voltage?

A. When $Q < 1$
B. When $Q = 1$
C. When $Q > 1$
D. The cell voltage is independent of Q.

15. Which one of the following represents a galvanic cell?

A. $Zn(s) \mid Zn^{2+}(1\ M) \parallel Cu^{2+}(1\ M) \mid Cu(s)$
B. $Cu(s) \mid Cu^{+}(1\ M) \parallel Cu^{2+}(1\ M) \mid Cu(s)$
C. $Cl^{-}(1\ M) \mid Cl_2(g) \parallel Li^{+}(1\ M) \mid Li(s)$
D. $Zn(s) \mid Zn^{2+}(1\ M) \parallel Al^{3+}(1\ M) \mid Al(s)$

16. If the reaction in a concentration cell is spontaneous in the reverse direction, then:

A. $Q < K$, ΔG for the forward reaction is negative, and the cell voltage is positive.
B. $Q < K$, ΔG for the forward reaction is positive, and the cell voltage is negative.
C. $Q > K$, ΔG for the forward reaction is negative, and the cell voltage is positive.
D. $Q > K$, ΔG for the forward reaction is positive, and the cell voltage is negative.

17. People living in cold climates sometimes have trouble starting their cars on cold mornings. Frustrated drivers complain that the battery has "gone dead." If the temperature coefficient for voltage loss is -1.5×10^{-4} V/°C and the temperature drops by 40°C, is the battery "going dead" a logical explanation for the car not starting?

A. Yes, because the large temperature drop causes a significant drop in the intrinsic cell voltage.
B. Yes, because the internal resistance of the battery decreases as the temperature decreases.
C. No, because the large temperature drop does not by itself cause a significant drop in cell voltage.
D. No, because the internal resistance of the battery decreases as the temperature decreases.

GO ON TO THE NEXT PAGE.

Passage IV (Questions 18–23)

Zero-emission vehicles have long been recognized as a promising solution to the air pollution problems of the world's major metropolitan areas. Recently, electric cars powered by chemical energy stored in batteries have appeared on the commercial market. However, flywheels—rapidly spinning disks which can store up to four times more energy per unit weight—offer a better approach. Flywheels store energy in the form of rotational kinetic energy, and unlike lead–acid batteries, these "mechanical batteries" never need replacing, "recharge" faster than batteries, function equally well in hot or cold conditions, and are not composed of hazardous materials.

The rotational energy of a flywheel of radius R is given by the equation

$$KE_{rot} = \tfrac{1}{2}I\omega^2$$

Equation 1

where I is the flywheel's moment of inertia and v/R = ω is its angular speed. The moment of inertia, which quantifies an object's tendency to resist a change in its angular velocity (by analogy with mass, which quantifies an object's tendency to resist a change in its translational velocity), depends not only on the object's mass but also on how that mass is distributed about the axis of rotation. In particular, the more mass (on average) that is located farther from the axis, the greater the moment of inertia. For a cylindrical flywheel of uniform density with mass M and radius R (see Figure 1), the moment of inertia about the axis of symmetry through its center is given by the formula

$$I = \tfrac{1}{2}MR^2$$

Equation 2

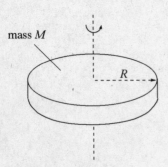

mass M

R

Figure 1 Flywheel

For a flywheel of a given size and shape, the amount of stored energy depends on its angular speed and the density of the material that the wheel is composed of. The density used is limited by the strength of the material, since more force is needed to move a material of greater density around its circular path. In theory, the amount of energy that can be stored is maximized when the ratio of the material's tensile strength, σ, to its density, ρ, is maximized, because then the flywheel could be "spun up" to higher angular speeds than could be tolerated by flywheels composed of weaker materials. (In practice, tiny defects in materials make the optimal design of flywheels a much more complex problem.) Currently, the largest σ/ρ ratios can be achieved by bonding together woven carbon fibers, which have tensile strengths greater than steel. Table 1 lists the tensile strengths and densities of some common materials.

Table 1 Tensile Strengths and Densities

Material	Tensile Strength σ (PA)	Density ρ (kg/m³)	σ / ρ (m² / s²)
Aluminum	2.2×10^8	2.7×10^3	8.1×10^4
Brass	4.7×10^8	8.6×10^3	5.5×10^4
Carbon fibers	6.9×10^9	1.7×10^3	4.1×10^6
Glass	1.0×10^9	5.0×10^3	2.0×10^5
Iron	3.0×10^8	7.8×10^3	3.8×10^4
Steel	1.9×10^9	8.0×10^3	2.4×10^5

Energy is stored in the wheel as it is first "spun up" using an electric motor connected to an electric power source. After disconnecting from the power source, the rotating flywheel can then be used to turn the same motor in the reverse direction, thereby generating electricity that can be used to power other electric motors that drive the car's wheels.

18. Four flywheels with the same dimensions are spinning with the same angular speed. According to Equation 1, the flywheel composed of which one of the following materials has the greatest rotational kinetic energy?

A. Aluminum
B. Brass
C. Carbon fibers
D. Steel

GO ON TO THE NEXT PAGE.

19. If all of the following wheels have the same mass and outer radius, which one has the greatest moment of inertia?

A.   C.

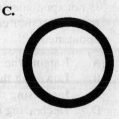

B.   D.

20. When compared to flywheels made of lower density materials, flywheels made of higher density materials tend to break apart at high angular speeds because:

A. the centrifugal force on any portion of the wheel is smaller.
B. the centripetal force on any portion of the wheel is smaller.
C. the inertia of any portion of the wheel is larger.
D. the radius of any portion of the wheel is smaller.

21. In theory, a flywheel constructed of which of the materials listed in Table 1 would be able to store the *least* amount of energy?

A. Aluminum
B. Brass
C. Glass
D. Iron

22. Which of the following best describes the energy transfers that take place starting at the power source and ending with the motion of a car powered by a flywheel system?

A. Chemical, electrical, kinetic
B. Electrical, kinetic, electrical
C. Chemical, kinetic, electrical, kinetic
D. Electrical, kinetic, electrical, kinetic

23. A flywheel of mass 400 kg and radius 0.5 m is rotating at an angular speed ω of 20 rad/s. What is the magnitude of the centripetal acceleration of a point on the outer rim of this wheel?

A. 100 m/s^2
B. 200 m/s^2
C. 400 m/s^2
D. 800 m/s^2

GO ON TO THE NEXT PAGE.

Questions 24 through 28 are **NOT** based on a descriptive passage.

24. Nitrogen has the highest oxidation number in which of the following compounds?

A. NH_3
B. NO_3^-
C. NO_2
D. N_2

25. A particle of mass 0.1 kg is moving at constant speed in a circular path of radius 50 cm. If the net force on the particle is 4 N, what is its kinetic energy?

A. 0.1 J
B. 0.5 J
C. 1 J
D. 2 J

26. An object is placed 6 cm from a convex lens whose radius of curvature is 4 cm. How far is the image from the lens?

A. 1.5 cm
B. 2.4 cm
C. 3 cm
D. 12 cm

27. Under standard conditions, the reaction

$$2\ NOCl(g) \rightarrow 2\ NO(g) + Cl_2(g) \qquad \Delta H = +77\ kJ$$

is not spontaneous. Which of the following changes to the reaction conditions could make this process spontaneous?

A. Raising the temperature
B. Lowering the temperature
C. Increasing the pressure
D. Decreasing the pressure

28. If an object is moving to the right along a straight line and at a constantly decreasing speed, then which one of the following must be true?

A. The object's velocity is parallel to its acceleration.
B. The net force on the object is directed to the right.
C. The object's momentum is directed to the left.
D. The total work performed on the object is negative.

GO ON TO THE NEXT PAGE.

Passage V (Questions 29–34)

A danger of mining operations is the collapse of tunnels or underground chambers, resulting in closed atmospheres for trapped workers. Significant efforts are made to provide emergency equipment that can sustain breathable air, focusing on oxygen generation and carbon dioxide removal.

Normal air at sea level (760 torr) contains 21% oxygen and 0.03% carbon dioxide. A typical human consumes about 2.7 L/hr of O_2 and generates about 2.3 L/hr of CO_2 during regular breathing. Maintaining O_2 partial pressure above 130 torr and CO_2 partial pressure below 30 torr is critical for survival. O_2 and CO_2 percentages in a closed atmosphere change over time according to the following formulas:

$$O_2\% = (\text{Initial } O_2\%) - \frac{NRt}{V}$$

Equation 1

$$CO_2\% = (\text{Initial } CO_2\%) + \frac{NRt}{V}$$

Equation 2

where R = O_2 consumption or CO_2 generation rate (in L/hr), t = time (in hr), V = floodable volume of compartment (in L), and N = the number of people in the compartment.

Oxygen candles can be burned to generate about 300 L/hr (1 atm) of emergency oxygen by the following reaction:

$$NaClO_3 + Fe \rightarrow NaCl + Fe_xO_y + O_2$$

Reaction 1

Carbon dioxide can be removed from a closed atmosphere with lithium hydroxide canisters by the following reaction:

$$2\,LiOH + CO_2 \rightarrow Li_2CO_3 + H_2O + heat$$

Reaction 2

Each canister can absorb approximately 40 kg of CO_2. Figure 1 shows the average absorption rate for one LiOH canister.

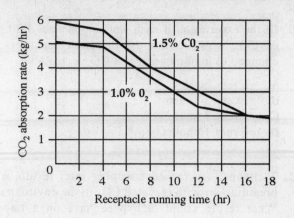

Figure 1 Average absorption rate for one LiOH canister

Experiment

A researcher investigates the effectiveness of oxygen candles and LiOH canisters on an experimental, enclosed mining shaft with the following characteristics:

P = 1 atm

Normal initial air composition

Floodable volume = 5.4×10^2 L

Number of trapped workers = 4

Regular breathing

Two LiOH canisters operating at a time

1 O_2 candle operating at a time

29. Which of the following would the researcher be *least* likely to observe as temperature and humidity increase in the experiment described in the passage?

   A. Decreased O_2 generation from candles
   B. Increased CO_2 clearance by LiOH canisters
   C. Increased compartment pressure
   D. Increased partial pressure of $H_2O(g)$

GO ON TO THE NEXT PAGE.

30. In the experiment, if each worker generates 1.5 kg/hr of CO_2, how often must the LiOH canisters be changed to maintain ambient CO_2 at 1.0%?

   A. Every hour
   B. Every 2 hours
   C. Every 7 hours
   D. Every 10 hours

31. Tachypnea (increased breathing rate) results from breathing air with elevated CO_2 in the environment. What result would tachypnea have on a trapped miner?

   A. Increased survival time from increased O_2 partial pressure
   B. Increased survival time from decreased O_2 consumption
   C. Decreased survival time from decreased CO_2 partial pressure
   D. Decreased survival time from increased O_2 consumption

32. If all the emergency atmosphere equipment in the experiment described in the passage were unavailable, about how long would the miners have before reaching a critical O_2 level?

   A. 4 days
   B. 6 days
   C. 8 days
   D. 10 days

33. Of the following actions, which one would likely be the most advantageous for survival in the experiment?

   A. Spreading the LiOH on blankets on the ground
   B. Digging to expand the floodable volume
   C. Burning the oxygen candles in a fire
   D. Partially flooding the compartment to raise compartment pressure

34. Suppose that after three days of being trapped in a shaft without emergency equipment, a miner is able to dig a very small hole that opens to the outside air. Which of the following will happen to the gases in the shaft?

   A. CO_2 will escape more rapidly than O_2, because it has a greater kinetic energy.
   B. CO_2 will escape more slowly than O_2, because it is moving against its concentration gradient.
   C. O_2 will escape more rapidly than CO_2, and the mole fraction of O_2 will increase.
   D. O_2 will escape more slowly than CO_2, and the mole fraction of CO_2 will decrease.

Passage VI (Questions 35–40)

The rate of a reaction is defined as the change in concentration per unit time. Usually, the disappearance of the reactants is monitored; however, it is also possible to quantify the reaction rate by measuring the appearance of products. Reaction rate must be experimentally determined. The rate of the reaction depends on the concentrations of reactants and products; as the reaction proceeds to completion, the rate slows, so that at equilibrium, the apparent rate of reaction is zero—the concentrations of all species remain constant.

Reactions physically occur when the reactants collide with sufficient energy to change their chemistry. The high-energy state of the reactants is called the activated complex. The higher the energy input required to bring about chemical change, the more slowly the reaction occurs. Two things can increase the rate of reaction. Increasing the temperature of the reactants or adding a catalyst increases the rate constant and the rate of the reaction. If the temperature of the reactants is increased, less energy is required to form the activated complex and the reaction proceeds more quickly. (The energy of the activated complex is a constant, but less energy input is required to raise the reactants to that energy level.) It is also possible to add a substance that will hold the reactants in a favorable configuration that encourages interaction resulting in chemical change, thereby lowering the activation energy. Such a substance is known as a catalyst.

Reaction order expresses the number of species involved in the activated complex of the rate-limiting step. First order reactions have only one species involved in the activated complex. In this case, the activated complex is a high-energy form of the reactant, such as a radical or ion, which is formed upon collision with another reactant molecule or the walls of the reaction container.

An example of a first order reaction is the thermal decomposition of dinitrogen pentoxide:

$$2\ N_2O_5\ (\text{in } CCl_4)\ \longrightarrow\ 4\ NO_2\ (\text{in } CCl_4)\ +\ O_2(g)$$

Reaction 1

This reaction is carried out in CCl_4 because both N_2O_5 and NO_2 are soluble, but O_2 is not. The reaction progress is monitored by measuring the volume of O_2 evolved. One hundred mL of a 2.0 M solution of N_2O_5 in CCl_4 is placed in a flask in a constant-temperature bath maintained at 45°C. The evolving gas is captured in a volumetric, mercury-filled manometer attached to the cork of the flask. Data collected at 200-minute intervals are plotted in Figure 1.

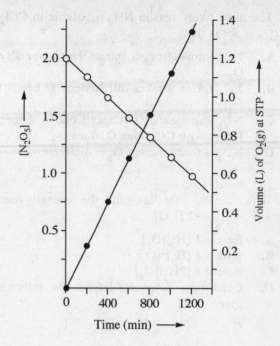

Figure 1 Gas data

35. Which one of the following is NOT a possible Lewis dot structure for N_2O_5?

A.

C.

B.

D.

36. What is the average rate of Reaction 1, the thermal decomposition of N_2O_5?

A. 4.2×10^{-4} M/min
B. 5.5×10^{-4} M/min
C. 8.4×10^{-4} M/min
D. 1.1×10^{-3} M/min

GO ON TO THE NEXT PAGE.

37. The most likely reason NO_2 is soluble in CCl_4 but O_2 is not is that:

    A. NO_2 forms stronger intramolecular bonds than O_2.

    B. NO_2 forms weaker intramolecular bonds than O_2.

    C. NO_2 experiences stronger London dispersion forces with CCl_4 than O_2 does.

    D. NO_2 is triatomic but O_2 is diatomic.

38. What is the rate law for the overall reaction $2 H_2 + O_2 \rightarrow 2 H_2O$?

    A.   Rate = k [H_2][O_2]

    B.   Rate = k [H_2]^2[O_2]

    C.   Rate = k [$2H_2$][O_2]

    D.   Cannot be determined from the information given

39. Monitoring which one of the following quantities would be *least* helpful in calculating the number of moles of NO_2 produced in Reaction 1?

    A.   Temperature of the system

    B.   Pressure of the system

    C.   Volume of reactant

    D.   Volume of products

40. What is the half-life of N_2O_5?

    A.   580 min

    B.   720 min

    C.   1180 min

    D.   2430 min

GO ON TO THE NEXT PAGE.

Passage VII (Questions 41–46)

The decay of a radioactive sample releases energy which can affect human tissue. Human tissue may be made to absorb radiation intentionally for diagnostic purposes, such as the use of radioactive iodine to study thyroid or kidney function or technetium to scan for a brain tumor. However, the exposure of human tissue to radiation may also be nondeliberate, such as that caused, for example, by naturally occurring sources such as cosmic rays impacting the atmosphere, radioactive elements in the ground, or potassium-40 in the diet, or by artificial sources in laboratories and nuclear power facilities. Radiation ionizes the atoms absorbing the energy, which can directly damage DNA strands in a cell; damage to DNA strands can also be caused by the attack of hydroxyl radicals produced by the ionization of water molecules in the cell.

If N_0 denotes the number of radioactive nuclei at time $t = 0$, then the number at any later time t is given by

$$N(t) = N_0 e^{-\lambda t}$$

Equation 1

The parameter λ is the *decay constant*, equal to $1/\tau$, where τ is the average lifetime (approximately 1.4 times the half-life) of a nucleus in the sample. The number of decays per unit time, called the *activity* and denoted by A, is

$$A = \lambda N(t)$$

Equation 2

The energy deposited by ionizing radiation per unit mass of body tissue is called the *absorbed dose*, D; the unit of absorbed dose is the *rad*. By definition, 1 rad is equal to 100 ergs per gram, where 1 erg is a non-SI unit of energy equal to 10^{-7} joule. Since 1.6×10^{-19} J = 1 eV, 1 rad is equivalent to 6.25×10^{10} MeV per kilogram.

The biological effect of radiation is not simply a matter of measuring the absorbed dose, however. Different types of radiation have different effects and are therefore assigned different *radiation weighting factors*. For example, β particles and γ-rays deliver their energy over a long path and thus deposit a relatively small amount over any small region; the radiation weighting factor, w_R, for these radiations is only 1. By contrast, the value of w_R for α particles is 20. So, to determine the overall effect of radiation on body tissue, the absorbed dose is multiplied by the weighting factor to give the *dose equivalent*:

$$DE = w_R D$$

Equation 3

When D is expressed in rads, the dose equivalent is given in *rems*.

The average dose equivalent due to naturally occurring background radiation averages about 0.2 rem per year. It is recommended that the general public limit their dose equivalent to 0.5 rem per year.

Table 1 Radiation Weighting Factors

Radiation	w_R
β^- particle, β^+ particle, X-ray, γ-ray	1
proton (> 2 MeV)	5
neutron (10–100 keV)	10
α particle	20

Table 2 Data for Selected Radioisotopes Used in Medical Diagnosis

Radioisotope	Half-life	Decay mode(s) and energies (in MeV)
^{18}F	2 hr	β^+ (0.6 MeV)
^{42}K	12 hr	β^- (3.5 MeV) γ (1.5 MeV)
^{58}Co	72 days	β^+ (0.5 MeV) γ (0.8 MeV)
^{99m}Tc	6 hr	γ (0.1 MeV)
^{131}I	8 days	β^- (0.6 MeV) γ (0.08 MeV)

41. After ^{131}I decays, what is the daughter nucleus?

A. ^{130}Te
B. ^{131}Te
C. ^{130}Xe
D. ^{131}Xe

GO ON TO THE NEXT PAGE.

42. A physician injects a patient with a small sample of $^{42}KCl(aq)$ in order to help her detect a tumor. How long must the patient wait until the activity drops to 5% of its initial value?

A. 32 hr
B. 40 hr
C. 52 hr
D. 64 hr

43. It can be inferred from the passage that compared to β particles, α particles of the same energy are:

A. less harmful, because they travel a shorter distance due to their greater mass.
B. less harmful, because they carry a smaller electric charge.
C. more harmful, because they deliver a greater absorbed dose.
D. more harmful, because they deposit larger amounts of energy over small regions.

44. If a sample of $Na^{18}F$ has an approximately constant activity of 10^9 decays/sec over a time interval of 1 minute, and all of the emitted radiation energy is absorbed by 2 kg of body tissue, what is the dose equivalent?

A. 0.3 rad
B. 0.3 rem
C. 0.6 rad
D. 0.6 rem

45. If all of the following radiations deposit 10^{12} MeV of energy to human tissue, which one would be most likely to cause the greatest harm?

A. 10 kg of tissue absorbing 50-keV neutrons
B. 40 kg of tissue absorbing α particles
C. 2 kg of tissue absorbing γ-rays
D. 10 kg of tissue absorbing 3-MeV protons

46. Compared to that of ^{58}Co, the decay constant λ of ^{131}I is:

A. smaller by a factor of 9.
B. smaller by a factor of (9/1.4).
C. larger by a factor of (9/1.4).
D. larger by a factor of 9.

Passage VIII (Questions 47–51)

The dissolution of a substance in a solvent affects the physical properties of the solvent, most notably the colligative properties: vapor-pressure depression, boiling-point elevation, freezing-point depression, and osmotic pressure. Knowledge of these properties can be used to determine the molar masses of unknown substances such as proteins and other biologically relevant molecules.

When a nonvolatile solute is added to a volatile solvent, the relative amounts of solvent molecules in contact with the surface decrease and fewer solvent molecules escape into the gaseous phase. This lowers the vapor pressure. For an ideal solution, the vapor pressure, P', is given by Equation 1, where X is the solvent mole fraction and P is the vapor pressure of the pure solvent:

$$P' = XP$$

Equation 1

One can use Equation 2 below to determine the free energy change ΔG associated with the transfer of a volatile solute to an ideal solution:

$$\Delta G = nRT \ln X$$

Equation 2

where n is the number of moles of solute being added, R is the universal gas constant (8.314 J/mol-K), and T is the temperature.

Since the presence of a solute lowers the vapor pressure, the boiling point is elevated. Equation 3 relates this new boiling point, T'_b, to the solvent mole fraction, X:

$$\Delta H_{vap}\left(1 - \frac{T'_b}{T_b}\right) = nRT'_b \ln X$$

Equation 3

where ΔH_{vap} is the enthalpy of vaporization and T_b is the boiling point of pure solvent. Based on this equation, the boiling-point elevation constant, k_b, can be determined:

$$k_b = \frac{RT_b^2 M}{1000\Delta H_{vap}}$$

Equation 4

where M is the molar mass of the solvent.

An equation of the same form as Equation 4 can be applied to determine k_f, the freezing-point depression constant. Table 1 lists the freezing points and freezing-point depression constants for a number of solvents.

Table 1 Solvent Data

Solvent	T_f (°C)	k_f
Benzene	5.5	5.12
Camphor	179.5	37.7
Carbon tetrachloride	−22.3	29.8
Chloroform	−63.5	4.68
Ethanol	−114.6	1.99
Naphthalene	80.5	6.90
Water	0.0	1.86

The last of the colligative properties, osmotic pressure, is also dependent on the number of dissolved particles and not on their nature. Osmotic pressure is defined as the pressure necessary to prevent the flow of solvent particles across a semipermeable membrane from a region of higher solvent concentration to a region of lower solvent concentration.

47. Which of the following best characterizes the process of vaporization?

    A.   Increase in entropy, increase in enthalpy
    B.   Increase in entropy, decrease in enthalpy
    C.   Decrease in entropy, increase in enthalpy
    D.   Decrease in entropy, decrease in enthalpy

48. Intravenous solutions must be isosmotic to blood (approximately 300 mM) to prevent damage to red blood cells. What mass of calcium chloride must be added to water to create 1 kg of solution isosmotic to blood?

    A.   11 g
    B.   33 g
    C.   37 g
    D.   111 g

GO ON TO THE NEXT PAGE.

49. Destructive distillation involves heating an organic substance in a closed container in the absence of oxygen. The destructive distillation of wood produces acetic acid (T_b = 117.9°C), methanol (T_b = 65.0°C), and acetone (T_b = 56.2°C). Which of these will be the first to be vaporized?

A. Acetic acid
B. Methanol
C. Acetone
D. It cannot be determined from the information given.

50. A hypertonic solution, X, separated from a hypotonic solution, Y, by a semipermeable membrane (permissive to water only) will result in all of the following after equilibration EXCEPT:

    I.   An increase in the melting point of Solution X.
    II.   An increase in the volume of Solution Y.
    III. An increase in the vapor pressure above Solution Y.

A. I only
B. I and II only
C. II and III only
D. I, II, and III

51. Of the following substances, which will provide the greatest protection against freezing?

A. 1 m ethanol (C_2H_6O)
B. 1 m potassium acetate ($KC_2H_4O_2$)
C. 1.5 m sucrose ($C_{12}H_{22}O_{11}$)
D. 0.5 m calcium chloride ($CaCl_2$)

GO ON TO THE NEXT PAGE.

Questions 52 through 56 are **NOT** based on a descriptive passage.

52. A block is attached to a spring and set into simple harmonic motion. Compared to the period of the oscillations of this block, the period of the oscillations of a block of greater mass attached to a spring with a larger spring constant would:

   A. be shorter.
   B. be longer.
   C. remain unchanged.
   D. Any one of the above is possible.

53. Of the following gases, which one deviates most from ideal behavior?

   A. He
   B. N_2
   C. NH_3
   D. H_2

54. An object of mass 500 grams is completely submerged in a fluid of specific gravity 2. If the object experiences a buoyant force of 25 N, what is its specific gravity?

   A. 0.1
   B. 0.25
   C. 0.4
   D. 0.5

55. Adding which one of the following would produce the greatest increase in the solubility of the sparingly soluble salt BaF_2?

   A. HCl
   B. NH_3
   C. KOH
   D. H_2CO_3

56.

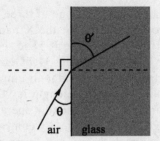

The figure above shows a ray of light in air striking the surface of a piece of glass. If n is the index of refraction of the glass, then which of the following equations is true?

   A. $\sin \theta = n \sin \theta'$
   B. $\cos \theta = n \cos \theta'$
   C. $n \sin \theta = \sin \theta'$
   D. $n \cos \theta = \sin \theta'$

GO ON TO THE NEXT PAGE.

Passage IX (Questions 57–61)

Both radar and ladar technologies are available to police departments to measure the speeds of vehicles. Police radar (radio detection and ranging) uses microwaves available in a variety of FCC-approved frequency bands, while ladar (laser detection and ranging) uses a laser beam in the upper-infrared frequency range.

Police radar devices use one of three different narrow bands of microwave radiation: the X band, centered at a frequency of 10.525 GHz; the K band, centered at 24.15 GHz; or the Ka band, centered at 34.7 GHz, where 1 GHz = 10^9 Hz. Ladar devices most commonly employ a laser which produces a beam whose wavelength is 904 nm. Although ladar devices are more accurate, the operator must aim the device at a single target vehicle. By contrast, radar devices have a larger beamwidth and can cover a wider area and several vehicles. Also, while most radar transmitters can be used in either stationary or moving modes (depending on whether the device is used in a stationary or moving police car), ladar transmitters are typically designed for stationary mode use only.

Police radar uses the Doppler effect to determine the speed of a vehicle. The device emits pulses of microwave radiation at its operating frequency, f; this incident radiation reflects off a moving vehicle, and the frequency of the reflected waves detected by the device, f_r, is recorded. If the radar device is used in stationary mode and is pointed directly at a target vehicle along its direction of travel, then the speed v_t of the target vehicle is given by the formula

$$v_t = \pm \, v\Delta f \, / \, 2f$$

Equation 1

where $\Delta f = f_r - f$ and v is the speed of the transmitted and reflected waves.

If the incident microwave beam makes an angle α with the direction of the target vehicle's velocity $\mathbf{v}_t$ (see Figure 1), then the device will measure the speed as $v_t \cos \alpha$; this is known as the *cosine effect*.

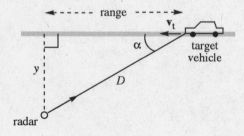

Figure 1 Radar model

The ladar device uses a different principle to determine the speed of a target vehicle. After it emits each brief pulse of light, the device measures the time required for the pulse to return after reflecting off the target. This alone determines the distance between the ladar device and the target vehicle. However, in a fraction of a second, the device sends out approximately one hundred pulses and can thus determine the change in distance to—and, consequently, the speed of—the target vehicle.

57. The frequency of the waves emitted by the ladar transmitter is most nearly:

A. 2.7×10^{13} Hz.
B. 3.3×10^{14} Hz.
C. 2.7×10^{15} Hz.
D. 3.3×10^{16} Hz.

58. When using a radar device in stationary mode, which of the following would tend to increase the error due to the cosine effect?

I. Measuring the target vehicle's speed at a closer range
II. Positioning the radar transmitter closer to the road
III. Using the Ka band rather than the X or K bands

A. I only
B. II only
C. I and II only
D. II and III only

GO ON TO THE NEXT PAGE.

59. A traffic officer is using a radar employing the X band in stationary mode, pointing the device directly at a target vehicle along its direction of travel. If the calculated value of Δf is −2800 Hz, then the target vehicle is:

A. approaching the officer at a speed of 40 m/s.
B. receding from the officer at a speed of 40 m/s.
C. approaching the officer at a speed of 50 m/s.
D. receding from the officer at a speed of 50 m/s.

60. Comparing radar and ladar transmitters, which one of the following is most likely true?

A. The ladar device has a greater accuracy since it transmits waves of a longer wavelength.
B. The radar transmitter is more prone to error in denser traffic conditions.
C. The radar device does not measure the distance to the target vehicle.
D. The ladar transmitter is more accurate since it emits light waves while the radar transmitter emits sound waves.

61. Suppose a ladar device emits light at an average rate of 500 pulses per second at an approaching target vehicle. The device measures the time interval between emission and reception of one of the pulses to be T_1 sec, and the time interval for the next pulse as T_2 sec. If c is the speed of light, which one of the following expressions gives the speed of the target vehicle?

A. $250(T_1 - T_2)c$
B. $250(T_2 - T_1)c$
C. $500(T_1 - T_2)c$
D. $500(T_2 - T_1)c$

GO ON TO THE NEXT PAGE.

Passage X (Questions 62–67)

The treatment of many gastrointestinal diseases was revolutionized by the development of drugs that block acid secretion in the stomach. Parietal cells in the stomach normally secrete protons in exchange for potassium ions as depicted in Figure 1. This maintains a pH of approximately 1.5 in the stomach lumen.

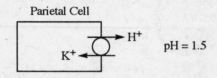

Figure 1 Proton–potassium exchange

Omeprazole is a medication that is a potent inhibitor of the H^+/K^+ exchange pump. The drug is a weak base with a pK_a of 1.6. After oral administration, it is absorbed primarily from the small intestine into the bloodstream. The properties of this compound cause it to accumulate in low-pH spaces, and it shows great organ specificity.

Following widespread use of omeprazole, it was discovered that many other oral medications, when used in conjunction, were less effective. Many oral medications are either weak acids or bases. When weak base medications reach the stomach, the amount of drug that is non-ionized or ionized can be predicted from the Henderson–Hasselbalch equation:

$$pH = pK_a + \log \frac{[B]}{[BH^+]}$$

Equation 1

where B denotes a weak base and BH^+ is its conjugate acid. Some drugs are absorbed in the stomach mostly in the non-ionized form, while others are only absorbed when dissolved in aqueous solution in the ionized form.

Ketoconazole is a powerful oral antifungal antibiotic absorbed into the bloodstream in the stomach. It is a weak base with a pK_a of 3, and it is only able to be absorbed in the ionized form. A researcher explores the relationship between stomach pH and ketoconazole absorption. The results are summarized in Figure 2.

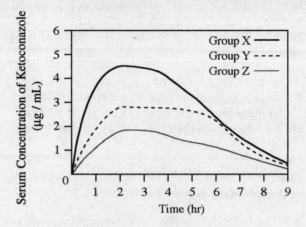

Figure 2 Experiment results

62. Under normal conditions, the value of $[H_3O^+]$ in the stomach is most nearly equal to which of the following?

    A. $1 \times 10^{-2}\ M$
    B. $3 \times 10^{-2}\ M$
    C. $1 \times 10^{-1}\ M$
    D. $3 \times 10^{-1}\ M$

63. Which of the following best explains why omeprazole specifically targets the stomach and not most other organs?

    A. The non-ionized form of the drug predominates in parietal cells.
    B. The ionized form of the drug becomes trapped within parietal cells.
    C. After ingestion, it is ionized in the stomach where it remains trapped.
    D. It effectively raises stomach pH, resulting in more of the drug becoming ionized for absorption.

GO ON TO THE NEXT PAGE.

64. What is the correct order of stomach pH values for the experimental groups in the passage?

A. Group X > Group Y > Group Z
B. Group Y > Group Z > Group X
C. Group Z > Group Y > Group X
D. Group X > Group Z > Group Y

65. A patient requiring oral therapy with ketoconazole is found to have achlorydia (neutral stomach pH). The most helpful intervention would be to administer ketoconazole:

A. with ginger ale (pH = 2).
B. with baking soda (NaH_2CO_3).
C. with omeprazole.
D. at a higher dose.

66. Approximately what percentage of omeprazole is ionized in blood (pH = 7.4)?

A. Less than 1%
B. 10%
C. 50%
D. Greater than 99%

67. Comparing ketoconazole and omeprazole, all of the following are true EXCEPT:

A. both are partially ionized in the stomach.
B. omeprazole has a weaker conjugate acid.
C. ketoconazole is a stronger base.
D. omeprazole has a higher K_a value.

GO ON TO THE NEXT PAGE.

Passage XI (Questions 68–72)

With regard to their electrical properties, solids are generally classified into one of three categories: conductors, insulators, or semiconductors. It is well known that metals, the prototype conductors, have a very high electrical conductivity because one or more electrons per atom in the crystal lattice of positive ions are not attached to any one ion; instead, they are free to roam through the lattice. These electrons, known as conduction electrons, are then free to respond to an applied electric field and drift through the metal; the result of this drift is electric current.

If we look at the situation more closely, we can understand not only why certain materials conduct electricity so easily, but also why other materials do not. When atoms are separated, any interaction between the electrons of one atom and those of the others is negligible. As a result, the electron energy levels are undisturbed, and we have the familiar case of discrete, quantized energy levels. However, as the atoms are brought closer together, the electrons interact and their energy levels split into many very closely spaced levels—so many, in fact, that even in a tiny crystal, the levels can be considered to be made up not of discrete values but of a continuous band of values.

The energies of the innermost electrons form completely filled energy bands. The valence electrons, however, are in an energy band—known as the valence band—which may be filled or partially filled. In addition, a conduction band is formed, consisting of energy levels available to electrons that are free to drift and conduct electricity. In a conductor, the conduction band and valence band overlap. As a result, there are some valence electrons which are automatically in the conduction band, as is the case with metals.

However, if the conduction band is empty and separated from the filled valence band by an energy gap, then valence electrons need to acquire sufficient energy to "jump" into the conduction band before the material can conduct electricity. The gap consists of energies which the electrons are forbidden to have; the size of this gap—the difference in energy between the top of the valence band and the bottom of the conduction band—is known as the *gap energy*, E_g. Table 1 lists the value of E_g for several different materials.

Table 1 Energy Gap Values

Crystal	E_g (eV)
PbSe	0.3
InAs	0.4
Si	1.1
GaAs	1.4
AgCl	3.2
ZnS	3.6
Diamond	5.4

In general, a material is called an insulator if the energy gap is greater than 3 eV, and a semiconductor if the energy gap is less than 3 eV. Semiconductors become more conducting as the temperature increases, since the electrons can acquire enough energy to jump the energy gap into the conduction band. At temperature T, the average kinetic energy of an electron is approximately kT, where k is the Boltzmann constant, 8.6×10^{-5} eV/K. Therefore, at room temperature, $T = 300$ K, the average energy of an electron is only about 0.025 eV, so there is insufficient energy to jump into the conduction band. At higher temperatures, however, electrons can acquire enough extra energy to jump the gap. In fact, at temperature T, the concentration of electrons in the conduction band is given by the equation

$$c(T) = Ae^{-T^*/T}$$

Equation 1

where A is a constant and $T^* = E_g/(2k)$.

68. A crystal composed of atoms of which of the following elements would be expected to have a partially filled conduction band, even at very low temperatures?

   A. Carbon
   B. Silicon
   C. Sodium
   D. Silver chloride

GO ON TO THE NEXT PAGE.

69. By how much would the temperature of a sample of zinc sulfide need to be increased to expect that virtually all of the electrons near the top of the valence band would jump to the conduction band?

A.   700 K
B.   2,100 K
C.   4,200 K
D.   42,000 K

70. If a constant electric field E were applied to a metal, what would be the change in velocity of a conduction electron (charge magnitude = e, mass = m) in the time t between collisions with the lattice ions?

A. eE/m
B. eEt/m
C. $2eE/m$
D. $2eEt/m$

71. Which one of the following statements concerning metals, insulators, and semiconductors is most likely true?

A.   As the temperature is increased, the resistivity of a metal increases but the resistivity of a semiconductor decreases.
B.   As the temperature is increased, the resistivity of a metal decreases but the resistivity of a semiconductor increases.
C.   Insulators typically have a smaller energy gap than semiconductors.
D.   Electrical conduction in insulators is due to the drift velocity of electrons while in the valence band.

72. Which of the following graphs best illustrates how the concentration of electrons in the conduction band of a semiconductor depends on temperature?

A.

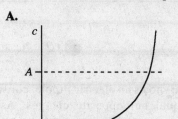

B.

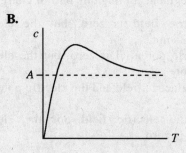

C.

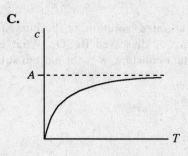

D.

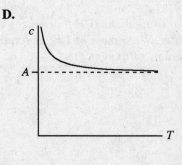

GO ON TO THE NEXT PAGE.

Questions 73 through 77 are **NOT** based on a descriptive passage.

73.

The figure above shows an electric dipole, consisting of a pair of equal but opposite charges. Assume that the electric potential decreases to zero as the distance from the charges increases. At the midpoint P of the line segment joining this pair of charges:

A. the electric field is zero, but the electric potential is not.
B. the electric potential is zero, but the electric field is not.
C. both the electric field and the electric potential are zero.
D. neither the electric field nor the electric potential is zero.

74. A one liter saturated solution of barium sulfate contains 2.5 mg of dissolved $BaSO_4$. What is the solubility product constant, K_{sp}, for barium sulfate?

A. 1.2×10^{-10}
B. 2.5×10^{-8}
C. 1.1×10^{-5}
D. 1.6×10^{-4}

75. The combustion of methane (CH_4) produces carbon dioxide and water. What mass of CH_4 is required to react with 96 grams of oxygen gas?

A. 12 g
B. 16 g
C. 24 g
D. 32 g

76. A string of length 60 m and fixed at both ends supports a standing wave. Including its endpoints, there are a total of five nodes along the string. What is the wavelength of the standing wave?

A. 10 m
B. 12 m
C. 15 m
D. 30 m

77. If a solution of NH_3 is titrated with HBr, then which of the following is true at the equivalence point?

A. The pH is greater than 7.
B. $[H_3O^+]$ is equal to $[OH^-]$.
C. The number of moles of H_3O^+ added is equal to the number of moles of OH^- initially present.
D. The salt formed is pH neutral.

STOP. IF YOU FINISH BEFORE TIME IS CALLED, CHECK YOUR WORK. YOU MAY GO BACK TO ANY QUESTION IN THIS SECTION.

STOP.

Verbal Reasoning

Time: 85 Minutes
Questions 78 – 137

VERBAL REASONING

DIRECTIONS: There are nine passages in the Verbal Reasoning test. Each passage is followed by several questions. After reading a passage, select the one best answer to each question. If you are not certain of an answer, eliminate the alternatives that you know to be incorrect and then select an answer from the remaining alternatives. Indicate your selection by blackening the corresponding oval on your answer document.

Passage I (Questions 78–83)

All things considered, the very problems inherent in the U.S.–Mexico relationship may provide possible avenues towards innovative resolution. Since at least the early part of this century the majority of
5 Mexican people have recognized the ugly truth about historical American exploitation of their country. The Mexican–American War, in which Colonel Travis and Davy Crockett made their heroic stand at the Alamo, still represents for many American schoolchildren the
10 fundamental American values of patriotism, valor, and freedom. Mexican schoolchildren, however, learn an entirely different truth: that the great imperialists to the north invaded sovereign Mexican territory and swallowed up vast parts of the country, including the
15 fabulously wealthy states of gold-laden California and oil-drenched Texas.

Over the years, "Uncle Sam" has become such a convenient and credible scapegoat that he is hauled out any time the Mexican government needs a likely
20 whipping boy to take popular heat off of some particularly outrageous domestic political betrayal. Indeed, a popular slogan often heard in Mexico, by which certain political figures have gained considerable popularity, is "*¡No a la deuda*!"—No to the debt!—
25 reflecting a belief that in the currency of exploited natural resources, Mexico long ago paid (and overpaid) to the United States whatever revenues it might have garnered from American loans.

Mexico does struggle with difficult social problems,
30 including among them the kind of grinding poverty which demoralizes and dehumanizes existence. On top of that, and in the face of a severe shortage of hard currency, Mexico still owes massive debts to foreign lenders. Unlike many other developing nations, however,
35 Mexico sits astride enormous reserves of crude oil. And therein, perhaps, lies a way forward.

Recently, some Mexican leaders have assumed considerable political risk in campaigning for a new relationship with the north. After all those generations
40 of deception by and distrust for the *americano*, to suggest that now the United States could be trusted to become a good neighbor, whose policy would shift from exploitation to partnership, requires a good deal of political leadership and personal courage.
45 Yet Mexican leaders desperately need debt relief. To conserve dwindling stores of dollars, they also need to marshal Mexico's resources towards rapid industrial development while at the same time providing some measure of socioeconomic respite to its long-suffering
50 people.

An agreement with Mexico to barter its outstanding debts to American financiers for large quantities of crude oil significantly discounted from the market price (possible only because Mexico is not an OPEC
55 member) would serve the vital interests of both nations. By paying with oil, Mexico could save scarce dollars for crucial domestic investment and essential social needs. Additionally, an influx of cheap petroleum into the U.S. market would exert considerable downward
60 pressure on domestic U.S. oil prices, resulting in an across-the-board multiplier effect on the economy. Both producer and consumer prices would fall, which would in turn reduce industrial costs, create thousands of new jobs, and inject a new boost of sustainable
65 consumer confidence and spending into the equation. Moreover, under the newly discounted price structure, a new federal tax on gasoline would hardly be noticed, and part of these increased revenues might be used to assist Mexico with environmental protection costs.

GO ON TO THE NEXT PAGE.

78. The author of the passage would probably most strongly *oppose*:

- **A.** a move to make Mexico an OPEC member.
- **B.** strict enforcement of existing environmental regulations in Mexico.
- **C.** extending further loans and credits to Mexico.
- **D.** development of Mexican industrial capacity.

79. Which of the following statements, if true, would most *undermine* the potential effectiveness of the author's proposal outlined in lines 51–55?

- **A.** The cheaper imported oil is, the weaker the incentive is to replace fossil fuels with alternatives such as wind and solar power.
- **B.** Mexico currently sells its oil to a wide variety of Latin American nations for a higher price than would be paid by the U.S. under the author's proposal.
- **C.** The influx of cheap imported oil into the U.S. market would have a stronger effect on producer prices than on consumer prices.
- **D.** A decline in industrial costs due to cheaper oil would allow most manufacturing plants to heavily invest in labor-saving machinery and to lay off a large percentage of their current work force.

80. The author's claim that increasing the U.S. market's petroleum supply will strengthen the economy suggests that the author:

    I.   believes that increased scarcity of a commodity will tend to increase the price of that commodity.

    II. is concerned about the environmental dangers of burning fossil fuels.

    III. sees new job creation as important to a healthy economy.

- **A.** II only
- **B.** I and III only
- **C.** II and III only
- **D.** I, II, and III

81. Which of the following is/are explicitly cited in the passage as contributing to the character of U.S.–Mexico relations?

    I.   Past military conflicts

    II. Past American exploitation of Mexican natural resources

    III. The resolve of some Mexican leaders to set aside "blame America" rhetoric

- **A.** I only
- **B.** III only
- **C.** II and III only
- **D.** I, II, and III

82. Which of the following findings, if true, would best support the author's assertion that if the policies outlined in the passage were followed, a federal tax on gasoline "would hardly be noticed" (line 67)?

- **A.** Mexican environmental protection efforts depend on U.S. assistance.
- **B.** Without the policy change, inflation would raise prices even more than a tax.
- **C.** With the new federal tax, the cost per gallon of gasoline would be lower than current gas prices.
- **D.** Gasoline price increases historically have had little impact on U.S. gas consumption.

83. According to the passage, the current popularity of the call "No to the debt!" is most directly a result of which of the following factors?

- **A.** Resentment created by the Mexican–American War
- **B.** Grinding poverty and hunger in Mexico's urban and rural areas
- **C.** The political ambitions of certain Mexican politicians
- **D.** Years of corrupt and irresponsible economic administration in Mexico

GO ON TO THE NEXT PAGE.

Passage II (Questions 84–91)

The genius of archaeology lies in its uncanny ability to recreate entire civilizations out of the most meager shards and dusty fragments of ancient lives. Inspiration for this imaginative act comes from many sources, 5 including the insights and self-discoveries brought about by archaeological role-playing. This novel technique penetrates centuries of oblivion by manufacturing replicas of artifacts found in communities buried long ago and figuring out what crucial purpose they served 10 in the daily needs and routines of those antecessor societies.

Archaeologists such as the University of Miami's Professor Knecht revive the artifacts of Cro-Magnon tribes by recreating the actual manufacturing process 15 likely employed in antiquity to create spearpoints out of deer antlers or animal bone. To be certain that the recreated spearpoints are as identical as possible to the originals recovered at sites, archaeologists test the aerodynamics, hardness, and power of their 20 reproductions. Because Cro-Magnon hunters often used an "atlatl" to hurl spears, role-players must take into account the increased velocity and improved aim achieved with that ancient device. The atlatl is a hooked stick which plugs into a hollowed-out pocket 25 at the bottom of a spear, and seems to have operated on a principle similar to that of the slingshot, adding heft and accuracy to the natural ability of a skilled hunter. Cro-Magnon ruins dating from 22,000 years ago have left evidence of functional atlatls. As they 30 test the conformity of their replicated spearpoints, archaeologists can approximate the additional force and velocity contributed by the atlatl by using an adjustable crossbow.

Archaeologists estimate that the Cro-Magnon, one 35 of the first *Homo sapiens*, populated Western Europe as early as 40,000 years ago, at the start of the Aurignacian period. Remnants of Cro-Magnon civilization have been traced from sites dating as recently as the Gravettian period, which began 12,000 years later. Over the course 40 of those 120 centuries, Cro-Magnon artisanry was not standing still; on the contrary, spearpoints recovered and replicated from later colonies are distinguished from earlier models by a relatively repair-friendly design and ready adaptability to different spears.

45 Their observations of reindeer and red deer jousts must have led the earliest Cro-Magnon hunters to imagine the advantages they might enjoy with weapons of the kind deer came by naturally. In the more immature artisanry, spearmaking pioneers split 50 antlers lengthwise in two and shaped them with wedges to fashion spearpoints with a split base. To fasten the finished point to a spear pole, artisans cut a cleft in the shape of a "U" into the shaft's end, and bound the point into the cleft with fibers from plants or animals. Then 55 they jammed a small wedge into the point's split base, forcing each side of the base into the wood of the shaft. The mechanical pressures acting on the shaft, point, and wedge, reinforced by the fibrous ligature, kept the weapon in one piece even through the accumulated 60 trauma of multiple hurls and successive hits. These weapons nevertheless were subject to damage and dulling, and the surviving examples found at sites indicate that repairs were, at best, improvisational and awkward.

65 Despite the difficulty of repairing these weapons, the split-based spearpoints must have proven fairly effective because they enjoyed eight thousand years of popularity with Cro-Magnon hunters. But 320 centuries ago, points shaped like lozenges displaced the earlier 70 forms. The new designs enabled hunters to resharpen their points efficiently, a feature that represented an economic and practical advance over the earlier split-based points, and one which in all likelihood was the cause of the eventual predominance of new round-based 75 or lozenge points.

84. The passage suggests that by re-creating the working techniques that reproduce ancient artifacts, archaeologists:

A. inspire fanciful reconstructions of the archaeological past.
B. establish the truth or falsity of ancient histories.
C. gain insight into the needs and desires of past cultures.
D. reinvent antiquity from contemporary perspectives.

GO ON TO THE NEXT PAGE.

85. Suppose several split-based spearpoints dating from the late Gravettian period were discovered in a perfect state of repair. How would this information affect the author's claims about the development of spearpoint design?

    A.   It would support the claim that round-based points replaced split-based points.

    B.   It would not significantly weaken the claim that Cro-Magnon weapons technology improved over time.

    C.   It would weaken the claim that split-based points were developed in the Aurignacian period.

    D.   It would weaken the claim that Gravettian Cro-Magnon weaponry was more advanced than that of Aurignacian Cro-Magnon.

86. Based on information in the passage, it is reasonable to conclude that during the Aurignacian period:

    A.   deer caused serious injuries with their antlers.

    B.   red deer were threatened with extinction.

    C.   reindeer were considered a prize game.

    D.   deer were regularly dehorned while still alive.

87. As used in the passage, the word *conformity* (line 30) most nearly means:

    A.   malleability.

    B.   similarity.

    C.   obedience.

    D.   endurance.

88. In describing the techniques by which Cro-Magnon artisans fastened points to their spears, the author cites all of the following factors EXCEPT:

    A.   fiber binding.

    B.   wedge pressure.

    C.   mechanical friction.

    D.   shaft cleft.

89. The passage suggests that before the development of the atlatl, hunters:

    A.   did not rely on spears as primary weaponry.

    B.   did not possess much natural ability.

    C.   had spearpoints which were difficult to sharpen.

    D.   were at a greater disadvantage with swiftly moving prey.

90. Which of the following findings, if true, would most support the value of the tests described in the second paragraph?

    A.   The replicated spearpoints are strong enough to withstand being trampled on, yet light enough to not cause the spear to wobble in flight.

    B.   The re-created spears fly smoothly with minimum deviation and maximum penetration of the target.

    C.   Climatic conditions in Gravettian Europe were similar to those in Western Europe today.

    D.   The re-created spearpoints, when thrown at animal carcasses, leave holes and splits in the bones similar to those found in bones unearthed from Cro-Magnon ruins.

91. According to the author, the difficulty in repairing some spearpoints:

    A.   initiated rapid development of better designs.

    B.   was an economic advantage because the spearpoints would eventually become obsolete.

    C.   decreased the efficacy of Cro-Magnon hunts.

    D.   was an inconvenient but not disabling defect.

GO ON TO THE NEXT PAGE.

Passage III (Questions 92–101)

Because scientific methodology requires that hypotheses be tested, the terminology employed by science must carry clear definitions that can be readily understood by all scientists in every language and
5 culture. Even if different languages use very different methods to represent the concepts of science, whether in pictographs, alphabetic characters, or binary codes, the concepts themselves must be considered universal. Once the concept has been distinguished from the
10 symbolic terminology which expresses it, the purposes of coherence and continuity make it essential to define those terms as precisely as possible, so that each linguistic or representative instance of the concept, as expressed by a particular language or culture, conveys
15 identical meaning.

There are two basic kinds of definitions used in scientific language. *Descriptive* definitions serve to assert or clarify the meaning of a given term as understood in common scientific use (for example,
20 "temperature" means the same as "degree of hotness or coldness"). A *stipulative* definition provides a particular meaning to a term, either by inventing a neologism (such as the word "quark" for a certain type of particle) or by applying a unique scientific meaning
25 to a familiar term (as in the "black hole" of deep-space science). Logicians call the term which is being defined the *definiendum*, and the term doing the defining is the *definiens*. In a descriptive definition, the definiens is said "to mean the same as" the definiendum, whereas
30 the definiens of a stipulative definition is "agreed to be the same thing as" the definiendum.

A scientific purist might insist that in any given scientific theory, every theoretical term must be defined. Such an obligation, however, leads quickly
35 into paradox: once we've arrived at a definiens for one term, it would then be necessary to formulate a second definiens to describe the first definiens, and then a third to define the second, ad infinitum. The problem arises in attempting to define these successive terms without
40 resorting to terms already defined, a challenge which leads quickly to a never-ending chain of definiendum and definiens. A brief illustration follows:

temperature = degree of hotness or coldness
hotness = relatively elevated temperature
45 coldness = temperature, but not hotness

To understand what "hotness" means, we substitute the definiens of the first definition for the term "temperature" in the second definition: "hotness" means "relatively elevated degree of hotness or coldness."
50 Holding apart the question of whether such a definition is even coherent, it should be at least apparent that we have now defined the word "hotness" in terms of

itself, a process which, though logical, does nothing to advance our original goal of understanding. Substituting
55 definitions in the same way in the third definition yields similar conundrums.

But even if we found a way to define each successive term without using any previously defined term, we would still face the necessity of defining the last definiens
60 in the system. Logically, the process, and therefore the system, would have an infinite number of terms, and ultimately no single term could ever be adequately defined, because each succeeding definiens would need to be defined in order to complete the definition of the
65 original definiendum. The only way out of this problem is to recognize the paradox and reject the purist's need for global definition. Some terms simply cannot be defined other than "by definition." Such terms are known commonly as "primary" terms or "axioms."

92. The main thesis of the passage is that:

- **A.** the defining process, fundamental to the scientific method, is self-limiting.
- **B.** definitions inevitably end in paradox.
- **C.** language cannot precisely define systems.
- **D.** science is a unique field of study.

93. In the first paragraph, the author suggests that science requires the sharing of ideas between scientists who speak different languages. It can be inferred that this requirement exists because science:

- **A.** cannot simply resort to primary terms to solve a logical paradox.
- **B.** involves concepts that transcend cultural and linguistic boundaries.
- **C.** has a set of primary analytical definitions.
- **D.** relies on universal codes and characters.

94. Which of the following claims is/are explicitly supported by a specific example in the passage?

- I. Scientific concepts are universal.
- II. Descriptive definitions state or explain meaning.
- III. Scientific purists demand that all terms be defined.

- **A.** I only
- **B.** II only
- **C.** II and III only
- **D.** I, II, and III

GO ON TO THE NEXT PAGE.

95. What does the author's discussion of testable hypotheses and their relation to language imply about science?

   A. Because linguistic differences lead distinct cultures to conceptualize science differently, hypothesis testing should vary from culture to culture.

   B. The scientific method requires controlled experiments.

   C. Scientific predictability knows no boundaries of culture or language.

   D. Any hypothesis may potentially be demonstrated or disproven anywhere in the world.

96. The author's reference to "pictographs, alphabetic characters, or binary codes" (line 7) is used in the passage primarily to:

   A. distinguish between concept and expression.

   B. emphasize the universality of scientific terms.

   C. clarify the purposes of coherence and continuity.

   D. provide a complete list of modes of expression.

97. According to the passage, which of the following sentences would be an example of a stipulative definition?

      I. A human being is a featherless biped.
     II. A parrot is a brightly plumed tropical bird skilled in verbal mimicry.
    III. A jackalope is a cross between a rabbit and an antelope.

   A. I only

   B. III only

   C. I and III only

   D. II and III only

98. The author argues in the last paragraph that because it would always be necessary to explain a previous definiens in terms of a subsequent definiens, no scientific system can make sense without the use of axioms. Which of the following, if valid, would most *weaken* this argument?

   A. Logical demonstration of a definiendum/definiens chain

   B. Demonstration that the paradox described by the author does not exist in all methodological systems

   C. Discovery of a consistent and coherent method of communicating concepts that does not require definitions of terms

   D. Refutation of the logic of scientific purism

99. The philosopher Carl Hempel has written that science answers human beings' "need to gain ever wider knowledge of...[themselves] and ever deeper understanding of the world...." If the author were to include that quote in the passage, it would most likely be used to:

   A. draw an analogy between science and the humanities.

   B. call for increased funding for scientific research.

   C. support the claim that science must be founded on universal concepts.

   D. support the arguments of scientific purists.

100. In discussing the relationship between terms and definitions, the author makes all of the following claims EXCEPT:

   A. The definiendum can mean the same as the definiens.

   B. Terms might be defined ad infinitum.

   C. All terms may be defined by descriptive definitions.

   D. Primary terms are required to avoid paradox.

101. In ordinary conversation, people often say that someone, something, or some experience is "beyond definition." Given the information provided in the passage, what question might this raise about definitions?

   A. Whether awareness of the type of paradox generated by the scientific purists' position occurs only in science, or in other modes of thought as well

   B. Whether most people really understand the logical process of scientific definition

   C. Whether stipulative or descriptive definitions are more applicable outside the realm of science

   D. Whether the human mind and the human heart ultimately defy logical description

GO ON TO THE NEXT PAGE.

Passage IV (Questions 102–106)

The long cherished American belief that one's privacy will be respected and preserved against invasion is being besieged on all sides. Historically subject to governmental and law enforcement abuses, the citizens
5 who drafted the United States Constitution included a provision in the Bill of Rights to protect the powerless from unwarranted intrusion by the powerful. The fourth amendment's guarantee of freedom from unwarranted "search and seizure," however, is far from absolute,
10 and the Supreme Court in recent years has continued to erode that protection.

With the Court's blessing, police departments all across the country now routinely post stop-and-check roadblocks, looking for everything from expired
15 inspection stickers and invalid registrations to alcohol breath and dilated pupils. Recently, the Supreme Court ruled that traffic patrol officers pulling motorists to the side of the highway are within the law in requiring that all passengers in the stopped car, not just the driver, exit
20 the vehicle. Although common sense tells us that under certain conditions a passenger left inside a vehicle could pose a serious threat to an officer discharging his lawful duties, the potential for abuse by some unscrupulous individuals wearing a uniform is worrisome.

25 Some observers believe that one factor strongly influencing the Court's degradation of the right to privacy is a revolutionary change in the way certain powerful segments of society look at the entire question of individual rights versus the legal, economic, and
30 information prerogatives of government and business. The unprecedented growth in the information industry's ability to store and retrieve data, and to make a healthy profit doing so, both motivates and facilitates that industry's efforts to bring extreme pressure to bear on
35 policymakers. A Supreme Court which allows greater governmental intrusion as a general rule essentially undermines the value society as a whole places on individual privacy and weakens its priority in the social dialogue, setting up a public mind-set and legislative
40 susceptibility exactly in line with industry objectives.

But it is the politicians, not the courts, who have the final responsibility for protecting citizens against private-sector violations of privacy, because constitutional protections generally apply only in
45 situations where the government is the offending party. When industry and big business are the organizations rooting around in private records, the courts can do nothing to rein them in without congressionally enacted statutory protections. Companies have a strong financial
50 incentive to violate citizens' privacy. For example, a recent *Time* magazine article reported that one-third of Fortune 500 corporations routinely pry into the private health histories of job applicants before hiring, with the goal of maximizing worker productivity and minimizing
55 company health insurance costs.

Unfortunately politicians hungry for campaign contributions are all too willing to embrace the advantages to businesses of unrestricted information flow (as enthusiastically outlined by industry lobbyists)
60 and to overlook the down side. And, in the absence of serious legislative concern for the privacy rights of individual citizens, there is little constraint on corporate willingness and power to rifle through personal records.

102. The author indicates that the framers of the U.S. Constitution:
   A. feared that powerful business interests might violate the privacy rights of individual citizens.
   B. were wary of governmental intrusion into the privacy of large corporations.
   C. believed that society needed to place a greater moral value on personal privacy.
   D. based its provisions in part on past experiences of governmental abuses.

103. The author of the passage would probably most strongly support legislation that:
   A. permitted police to check the fingerprints of every person stopped for a routine traffic violation.
   B. changed the Constitution to give the Supreme Court broader jurisdiction over non-governmental institutions.
   C. enabled citizens to limit access to their personal information.
   D. prohibited Internet users from flooding email boxes with junk advertisements.

GO ON TO THE NEXT PAGE.

104. According to the author, police departments in the United States:

> I. routinely abuse the increased latitude granted to them by the Supreme Court.
> II. have lobbied political leaders for the right to search passengers as well as the driver of a stopped car.
> III. may put individual officers in danger in the course of performing their jobs.

- **A.** I only
- **B.** III only
- **C.** I and III only
- **D.** II and III only

105. Which of the following findings, if true, would most support the author's contention in the fifth paragraph that politicians, in exchange for campaign contributions, are often willing to overlook invasions of privacy?

- **A.** Bills opposed by credit-reporting firms who had given heavily to politicians were defeated in Congress.
- **B.** The information industry donated 100 million dollars to the last congressional campaign.
- **C.** U.S. House representatives and senators regularly attend corporate-sponsored, expense-free conferences at 5-star resorts.
- **D.** Fortune-500 companies provide lavish hospitality tents for delegates to the major party political conventions.

106. The author indicates that which of the following bear or bears some responsibility for the erosion of privacy rights in the United States?

> I. Decreased corporate profits due to growing health insurance costs and rates
> II. Greater public tolerance of privacy violations, due in part to insufficient regard on the part of the Supreme Court for the protection of the less powerful
> III. Financial needs of electoral campaigns

- **A.** I only
- **B.** II only
- **C.** II and III only
- **D.** I, II, and III

GO ON TO THE NEXT PAGE.

Passage V (Questions 107–111)

Applauded by his admirers for breaking new ground in British theater and attacked by his critics for trampling on the sacred preserves of dramatic tradition, the playwright George Bernard Shaw, by
5 contrast, viewed himself as neither artistic pioneer nor cultural revolutionary. "I am an intellectual dustman," he liked to tell friends, "...an elucidator and tidier up." He acknowledged his eagerness to borrow ideas from other thinkers, and insisted that his creative gift lay in
10 scrupulously examining their intellectual and social implications and building on those foundations.

Nowhere was that propensity for seizing on the inventions of others more evident than in Shaw's presentation of the philosophy of the Life Force,
15 eloquently articulated in the play *Man and Superman* by the character Don Juan. Writing in an era of intellectual ferment, when Darwinian theory subjected established conceptions of humankind's origins and position in the universe to rigorous skepticism, Shaw could no more
20 defend those who absolutely denied the insights of Darwin's theories of evolution than he could endorse those who preached the existence of no God. Drawing on what he perceived to be undeniable elements inherent in both religion and biology, he discerned a vital and
25 purposeful intelligence driving—and giving meaning to—the evolutionary process of creation.

In contrast to conventional Western notions about divinity, Shaw's Life Force pretended no omnipotence and claimed no omniscience. Taking from human
30 science the method of "trial and error," Shaw applied the theological principle that humankind was made in God's image. He reasoned that humanity's means of discovering predictable truths about the nature of the universe, of acquiring scientific understanding, had
35 to derive from a creative power that operated in a like manner. This synthesis of scientific method and deistic doctrine led Shaw to the concept of a Life Force that pursues an absolute perfection and infallibility through a process of creative trial and error.

40 Shaw's philosophy thus accounts for the existence of evil in a world presumably directed by divine will. If the Life Force can achieve perfect truth only by testing imperfection and ruling out falsehood, then the existence and disclosure of evil is essential to the
45 realization of absolute good.

In *Man and Superman*, Don Juan declares that all forms of life contain the Life Force, which is itself their creator. Although there is an objective and design to the Life Force, its purpose is not yet readily apparent to
50 human consciousness, nor perhaps fully known even to itself. In its quest for perfection, the Life Force makes mistakes, and as a result evil occurs. As Dr. R. N. Roy has explained, in Shaw's universe, "evils are not meant for the punishment of sins; they are the survival of
55 errors originally well-intended."

Nothing matters to Shaw's Life Force other than moving toward the goal of perfection. As Don Juan makes explicit, progress refers to the attempts of "that raw force" to create "higher and higher [forms of life],
60 the ideal individual being completely self-conscious." The course evolution chose was a path from relative unconsciousness to conscious awareness, from "blind instinctiveness to self-understanding."

107. The central thesis of the passage is that:

A. Shaw's Life Force, a concept created through the synthesis of other ideas and doctrines, is a self-discovering and self-correcting power.

B. the Life Force intelligence is driven by a perfect plan and objective.

C. self-understanding is the highest form of meaning.

D. Shaw believed that earlier ideas of divinity were based on error and evil.

108. Which of the following exemplify the results of Shaw's gift for integrating old ideas with new ones, as cited in the passage?

    I. The view that the creation of evil results from mistakes made by a divine force

    II. The belief that God is uncertain about the way to final perfection

    III. The Darwinian theory of evolution

A. II only
B. I and II only
C. I and III only
D. I, II, and III

GO ON TO THE NEXT PAGE.

109. Shaw once said, "A lifetime of happiness! No man alive could bear it; it would be hell on earth." Based only on information provided in the passage, what would be the most reasonable interpretation of this statement?

    A.   Without mistakes and the suffering that comes from those mistakes, we cannot hope to learn how to achieve a good life.

    B.   Because of original sin, human beings do not deserve to live lives of true happiness.

    C.   Due to a perverse twist of human nature, some people are only truly happy when they are suffering.

    D.   Perfection is impossible, and we only make ourselves unhappy by trying to achieve it.

110. In the context of the passage, the word *disclosure* (line 44) most nearly means:

    A.   confession.

    B.   punishment.

    C.   acknowledgement.

    D.   isolation.

111. With which of the following statements would George Bernard Shaw most likely agree?

    A.   It is important to draw insight from both religion and science more for political than intellectual reasons.

    B.   Temporary concessions must be made to religious beliefs, so that the basic truth of Darwin's theories may eventually prevail.

    C.   Neither purely scientific nor purely theological viewpoints fully explain humanity's place in the world; an entirely distinct approach must be found.

    D.   The best plays neither ignore nor simply repeat the achievements of playwrights of the past.

GO ON TO THE NEXT PAGE.

Passage VI (Questions 112–117)

In our contemporary world so obsessed and controlled by science and technology, the idea of myth has fallen into disrepute. For most people, if one were to ask them, "myth" amounts to little more than superstition, wives'
5 tales, illusion, fantasy, or false conception. But the great ancient civilizations from which our own society evolved cherished fabulous tales of gods and heroes.

For the civilizations that produced them, myth occupied a place and served a function within the social
10 fabric reserved today for medicine, astrophysics, and cybernetics. Myth blazed like a beacon of clarity and reassurance in an uncertain and terrifying universe. Myth gave people a finite idea of their place in the scheme of things, taught them how to see themselves
15 in relation to forces beyond their control and how to survive and relate within a human society built on hierarchal power and often ruthless savagery.

The chasm of experience and time separating our lives at the third millennium from those who created
20 the classical myths in antiquity makes it difficult for us to comprehend the feelings of those to whom myth represented a living reality. We lack the testimony of the committed believers, who knew Athena's power as we know the atom's, who consulted the Delphic oracle as
25 we do the Hubble telescope, who deciphered the Muses' secret whispers as we decode the chromosomal helices. (For that matter, even the texts that have come down to us across the epochs are suspect, rescripted along the way by thousands of oral poets, censors, translators,
30 and politically correct intelligentsia of every stripe.)

Nevertheless, in certain far-flung corners of the globe, more or less impervious to the glitter, flash, and buzz of this Early Electronic Age, communities of humans who maintain their people's ancient knowledge
35 still practice the traditional rituals, still follow the folkloric customs. Anthropologists willing to shed their cosmetics of doctrine and costumes of theory might thus still gain a firsthand understanding of essential myth. For just as astronomers study astroradial photographs
40 of exploding supernovas to learn about the evolution of planets and the origins of organic life, so we might study modern aborigines to discover the strategies and insights of human consciousness in its primal attempts to process perceptual reality into cultural rules.

45 Prior to the work of Sir James Frazer, mythologists for the most part lined themselves up in one of two opposing camps. On one side were the naturalists, who believed that aboriginal peoples limited themselves to an elegiac worship of cosmology, investing the
50 sun, moon, stars, and climate with anthropomorphic identities. On the other side, the historicists argued that aboriginal myth amounted to nothing more than

historical chronicle, a fact-based record of past events.
55 Yet neither of these approaches does adequate justice to the fundamental power and function of myth in aboriginal societies.

By venturing into the field to live within aboriginal society, however, Bronislaw Malinowski, one of Frazer's disciples, penetrated the core of the matter.
60 His pioneering work in the Trobriand Islands led him to a comprehensive view of myth as "a vital ingredient of human civilization; not an idle tale, but a hard-worked active force; not an intellectual explanation or an artistic imagery, but a pragmatic charter of faith and
65 moral wisdom."

112. The author's primary purpose in the passage is to:

A. demonstrate the impossibility of understanding the function of myth in ancient society.

B. criticize the naturalist and historicist schools of thought for presenting inadequate visions of the place and power of myth.

C. explain the role of myth in ancient society and suggest ways of overcoming the problems involved in understanding that role.

D. explain why, given advances in science and technology, we no longer need myths to represent the roles we play in society and nature.

GO ON TO THE NEXT PAGE.

113. Suppose an original poetic text from the first century B.C. celebrating the heroic deeds of the god Apollo were discovered in an archaeological dig. How would this discovery affect the author's claim that we in modern society find it difficult to comprehend the meaning of myth in ancient societies?

A. It would refute the claim by indicating that data from living cultures can give us some insight into the role and power of myth.

B. It would support the claim, because rescripted texts are inadequate indicators of what myth meant to the people of that time.

C. It would be irrelevant to the claim, which is about mythological stories, not poetry.

D. It would not fully refute the claim, because even an original text does not recreate the living reality essential to cultural meaning.

114. In the passage, the author draws an analogy between:

A. naturalist and historicist approaches to understanding the role of myth in aboriginal society.

B. the role of science in the modern world and the place of myth in antiquity.

C. ancient gods and heroes and anthropomorphized cosmological entities in today's aboriginal cultures.

D. science and anthropology.

115. According to the passage, anthropologists can still gain understanding of the meaning and function of early human myth by:

A. developing computer models based on modern aboriginal communities.

B. applying contemporary theories and doctrines to interpret aboriginal social structures.

C. learning about the role played by myth in the lives of aborigines today.

D. adopting aboriginal traditions and truths as guiding moral precepts and analytical tools.

116. Which of the following statements, if true, would most *weaken* the author's argument that Malinowski's work in the Trobriands does justice to the true function of myth in that culture?

A. Sir James Frazer had as a primary goal the reconciliation of the naturalist and historicist schools.

B. The specific myths that define Trobriand society contain some images and themes found in no other ancient or modern cultures.

C. The presence of outside anthropological observers significantly changes the speech and behaviors of the members of the culture being observed.

D. Many well-respected anthropologists have rejected Malinowski's conclusions.

117. The author implies that the need ancient peoples had for myth's clarity and reassurance arose mainly from:

A. feelings of powerlessness and vulnerability.
B. an unstable social fabric.
C. ineffective medical techniques.
D. a finite sense of themselves.

GO ON TO THE NEXT PAGE.

Passage VII (Questions 118–126)

Every summer new cinematic box office records surpass those of the previous Christmas season's smash hits, as escalating production costs demand larger and larger opening weekend audiences. The studio publicity
5 machines, aided by film analysts in newspapers, television, and radio, bang the drums loudly for the latest big-budget releases. At the same time, directors, stars, and starlets parade across the television talk-show circuits to insure the investments in their most recent
10 productions and promote the continued prosperity of their careers. Yet almost regardless of a film's artistic merit (a concept which includes performance, direction, and production), it is the film consumers, as average ticket buyers are known to industry insiders,
15 who determine whether a given production is deemed "successful."

Moviegoers, both amateur and professional, cover a wide spectrum: from those who worship and obsess over celebrities, to those who thrill to a good story,
20 to those who spend hours and hours debating the subtleties of cinematic themes, extending even to those whose love for film informs and responds to a larger cultural perspective. This last class of moviegoers, the cultural critics, ought to be distinguished from those
25 who offer daily reviews in the mass media, because the foundations and motives of film criticism include certain defining elements which set it apart from the narrower activity of popular film analysis.

The film reviewer occupies a position central to the
30 ongoing viability of the medium, as an intermediary between an industry primarily concerned with efficient productivity and profitable distribution, and the international public whose interest provides the industry its monetary basis. Given the enormous volume of
35 global cinematic output, no single analyst can possibly review every film, and so the process of selecting films for popular commentary is, to some degree, subject to the limits of the industry's marketing system. Reviewers feel an obligation to address the general interests of
40 the viewing public, and so the presence of a highly bankable star in a movie will ensure a certain level of analytical attention, regardless of the perceived quality of the film. Similarly, a movie whose subject matter is directly relevant to a variety of topical concerns will
45 in and of itself generate public excitement, and media reviewers must respect that interest if for no other reason than to maintain their own visibility.

The cultural critic, on the other hand, tends to focus on larger social perspectives, and so is less
50 concerned with daily grosses and screen availability and competitive rankings and all the other urgent and momentary matters. Where the daily analyst may limit reviews to questions of relative enjoyability, star

power, and audience appropriateness, the cultural critic
55 expands the view to embrace historical, psychological, sociopolitical, and aesthetic issues. As essayist J. Aumont points out, the reviewer "informs and offers a judgment of appreciation"—thumbs up or thumbs down—while the critic is obliged to impart "the richness of the work
60 to as many people as possible" by "deconstructing the elements pertinent to the work" and illuminating "as many aspects as possible in the commentary." Fulfilling those objectives, Aumont argues, empowers the critic "to offer…an interpretation."

118. The central thesis of the passage is that:

  A. film reviewers, film consumers, and film studios all determine whether a movie will be successful or not.
  B. cultural critics offer deeper understandings of film aesthetics than do film reviewers.
  C. movie reviewers and cultural critics fulfill distinct functions in their discussions of film.
  D. film interpretation is a higher art than acting or directing.

119. The author cites Aumont's essay primarily for the purpose of:

  A. proving that reviewers contribute to the economic success of mass-market films.
  B. clarifying the distinction between a critic and a reviewer.
  C. elaborating on the topic of film interpretation.
  D. emphasizing the role of publicity in the film industry.

120. Based on the passage, a film critic who declares, "Without doubt, the best thing about that movie was the psychological development of character," most likely:

  A. would refuse to write about a high-budget film that included major stars in the cast.
  B. generally chooses to write about films that have received positive reviews from other critics.
  C. would not assume that a movie that had received few mass media reviews was not worth seeing.
  D. would enjoy this summer's smash hit.

GO ON TO THE NEXT PAGE.

121. Which of the following scenarios would be *least* likely, given the author's depiction of the relationship between film reviewers and the film industry?

    A. A heavily marketed movie with a close relationship to topical concerns receives very few mass media reviews.

    B. A film inspired by recent political events is judged by a cultural critic to have little relevance to the nature of modern technological society.

    C. A film intended for a limited "art house" audience unexpectedly becomes a popular success.

    D. A widely reviewed movie starring two celebrity actors makes little money at the box office and closes in two weeks.

122. The author of the passage most likely believes that:

    I.   film is as much an economic institution as an artistic one.

    II. positive reviews are crucial to a film's financial success.

    III. the critics' vision is central to a film's meaning.

    A. I only

    B. I and II only

    C. II and III only

    D. I, II, and III

123. Which of the following statements best expresses an assumption underlying the author's depiction of the daily film analysts' motivation for writing their reviews?

    A. Maintaining their own high public visibility is the most important factor in reviewers' choice of films.

    B. Daily film analysts do not primarily intend their reviews to illuminate core aspects of modern society by describing the qualities that tend to contribute to a movie's popular success.

    C. Cultural criticism can illustrate how core cultural patterns of a society are reproduced in the characters and plot lines of films.

    D. The more the industry spends on marketing and publicity, the more likely a reviewer is to give a favorable response in order to maintain status within the industry.

124. The author's claim at the end of the first paragraph that it is consumers who most powerfully determine a film's financial success or failure is supported in the passage in part through the observation that:

    A. most moviegoers have not cultivated a taste for cinematic art.

    B. film reviewers play a crucial role in the movie industry.

    C. people go to see movies for many different reasons, ranging from enjoyment of a good story to interest in cinematic themes and messages.

    D. escalating production costs force producers to cut back on artistic criteria.

125. In lines 60–61 the author cites Aumont's claim that critics work by "deconstructing the elements pertinent to the work." By *deconstructing*, Aumont most likely means:

    A. eliminating.

    B. building.

    C. explaining.

    D. demolishing.

126. Which of the following statements is NOT presented in the passage to help define the difference between a film critic and a film reviewer?

    A. Reviewers choose films partly based on the interests of the moviegoing public.

    B. Critics choose films to interpret in part based on the relevance of those films to larger social issues.

    C. Reviewers are concerned with maintaining professional standing.

    D. Critics are unconcerned with audience responsiveness to films.

GO ON TO THE NEXT PAGE.

Passage VIII (Questions 127–131)

For Marc Chagall, art served less as a mirror of reality than as the tangible construct of the artist's "chemistry": the combination of artistic craftsmanship, spirituality, and life experience. The dynamic synthesis
5 of these elements transformed previously blank canvas to vibrant artifact, giving birth to a dramatic testament of faith, morality, and beauty.

Forged in the brutal poverty and religious persecution of late 19th-century rural Russia, and hardened by
10 the hellish horrors of 20th-century warfare, Chagall's artistic visions manifest both the supremacy of the human spirit and the possibility of salvation through divine guidance. Acknowledging the mortal truth that "all life inevitably moves towards its end," Chagall
15 believed that he therefore "should illumine his life with the colors of love and hope"; love, according to the painter, constitutes the core principle of all religions. Given his formation and creed, it is not surprising that themes of suffering and loss interweave inextricably
20 with those of hope and redemption throughout Chagall's work.

Captivated since childhood by the Bible's epic sweep and moral depth, Chagall assimilated the grand, heroic histories his parents and grandparents read to
25 him from the Old Testament. Surrounded by the by-products of poverty—hunger, infirmity, disease, and despair—the artist's developing consciousness seized on those ancient mystic teachings as on a lifeboat in a raging storm. Powerless to overcome his community's
30 oppressors and vulnerable to the uncontrollable natural elements, the young painter sought refuge in an artistic vision in which myth and imagery transmuted to waking dream so vividly it bore the force of psychic visitation.

The intimate link between spiritual truth and the
35 vision and mission of the artist is starkly rendered in Chagall's 1917 painting *The Apparition*, in which the painter depicts himself at his easel, mesmerized and dumbfounded at the appearance of a heavenly angel before him. The French critic Fernand Hazere
40 observes that "the picture is a key that helps us to better understand Chagall's spiritual world and mission." In *The Apparition* the brightly glowing angel by its presence bestows on the artist (both on the canvas and in reality) the privileges and responsibilities of spiritual
45 ministry. Through his craft, then, the painter brings love and salvation to humankind.

This theme is reiterated in the painting *Jacob's Dream*. Here, Chagall shows Jacob in luminescent red at the center of the canvas. Jacob's head is tilted slightly
50 upwards and to the right, inclined away from a swirling maelstrom of purple, black, and plaintive yellow that

darkens the left side of the painting. That maelstrom, populated by vaguely human figures, reveals a hectic state of perilous imbalance and futility.

55 Jacob, glowing in his dream, seems impervious to all that sound and fury around him, charmed and strangely appeased by the cool blues and pure white that define the large, winged, celestial angel dominating the right half of the picture. Thus split between the fierce frenzy
60 of the bodily world and the tranquil reassurance of the spiritual, the canvas would seem a schizophrenic nightmare were it not for Jacob's confident, central presence as mediator. Refracted through the dreaming figure, Chagall's colors penetrate the schism, surprising
65 the dark, turbulent world with brave reverberations of grace and light.

127. The main idea of the passage is that:

    A. an artist's spiritual beliefs provide the most powerful influence on his or her artistic themes.

    B. Chagall could not have made great art without his early education in the Bible.

    C. Chagall saw himself as a spiritual mediator who could bring hope and love to the world through his art.

    D. genius emerges only through a life of genuine suffering.

128. According to the passage, how did Chagall's life experience affect his artistic vision?

    A. It led him to believe that the artist is powerless in the face of the suffering caused by war and disease.

    B. It prevented him from seeing reality and moving forward artistically.

    C. It led him to protest against the oppressive policies of the Russian state and to call for political reform.

    D. It inspired images of the artist guiding humanity through the turmoil of worldly existence toward redemption through love.

GO ON TO THE NEXT PAGE.

129. The passage suggests that Chagall's use of color in *Jacob's Dream* is related to his artistic themes in that:

  A. color instills a dynamic interaction among related parts of his composition.
  B. the theme of redemption in this work is subordinate to the emotional effect of the colors themselves.
  C. each artistic idea is color-coded throughout his work.
  D. primary colors like red and yellow usually symbolize hope, while dark colors represent chaos and fear.

130. The author quotes the French critic Fernand Hazere (lines 40–41) primarily for the purpose of:

  A. supporting his own interpretation of other scholarly works.
  B. relating modern French criticism to other critical approaches.
  C. further describing Chagall's artistic inspiration and purpose.
  D. calling into question the sincerity of Chagall's self-appointed missionary role.

131. In another essay, the author of the passage posits that for Chagall, the reality of art lies in its impact on the "eyes, hearts, and minds of those who view it." Which of the following interpretations of *Jacob's Dream* best exemplifies both this claim and the mission of the artist, as that mission is described in the passage?

  A. The central human figure represents a sinner torn between the temptations of bodily pleasures and the joy of spiritual redemption.
  B. Jacob represents the antithesis of the painter, as Jacob is mired in a maelstrom depicting hell while the painter wishes to deliver himself and others from suffering.
  C. The contrast between light and dark represents the eternal and irresolvable struggle between good and evil that defines human existence.
  D. Jacob represents the painter, who acts as an intercessor for humanity by bringing a message of hope to the world.

GO ON TO THE NEXT PAGE.

Passage IX (Questions 132–137)

Annual gas emissions of sulfur dioxide (SO_2) and nitrogen dioxide (NO_2) from North American coal-burning industries reach into the millions of tons. In the atmosphere, air oxidizes the sulfur dioxide to sulfur
5 trioxide (SO_3), which rain dissolves into sulfurous and sulfuric acid. Nitric (HNO_3) and nitrous (HNO_2) acids are formed from the reaction of water with nitrogen dioxide. In clouds, the aqueous phase reaction with hydrogen peroxide (H_2O_2) converts sulfur dioxide to
10 sulfuric acid (H_2SO_4). Eventually mild solutions of sulfuric and nitric acids precipitate as acid rain.

Despite a great deal of controversy, the United States government, deferring to its National Acid Precipitation Assessment Program (NAPAP), concluded in 1990 that
15 "there was no clear evidence" that acid rain causes damage to forest ecosystems. That evaluation, however, has been called into question by recent research focusing on the relation between acid rain and the cation exchange system, a natural buffering mechanism
20 that guards the ecosystem against injury from acid rain. Those studies demonstrate that not only have regulatory measures proved inadequate to control acid rain, in some cases they have contributed to a troubling new complication—depletion of the cation buffer.

25 The cation exchange system operates when acidic rain filters through soil containing negatively charged particles of decayed organic matter and clay, weakly bound to calcium and magnesium cations. These positively charged cations cannot compete with the
30 stronger attraction of acid rain's hydrogen ions, which displace them from their chemical bonds with the soil anions. Thus bound, the hydrogen atoms can neither further acidify groundwater nor produce harmful effects in the ecosystem through which the groundwater
35 flows.

The buffering system depends, however, on a stable supply of base cations in the soil. Once these positive ions have been mostly supplanted by acid rain's more strongly electrophilic hydrogen ions, the exchange
40 mechanism is exhausted and the buffer breaks down, allowing additional hydrogen ions to acidify the ecosystem. In regions of low soil cation concentration (whether from exchange exhaustion or natural deficiency), acidification produces sterilization of lakes
45 and streams, disruption of the reproductive cycles of aquatic life, injury to crops, and possibly thinning of forests.

Some analysts have linked the alarming reduction in the variety of amphibian species in the United States to
50 declines in waterway pH, either through direct acidic adulteration of reproductive biochemistry or by the toxic action of aluminum, which is also displaced from soil anions by acid rain. Liberation of soil aluminum by electrophilic hydrogen ions has also been cited
55 as a cause of plant root destruction and the resulting dramatic dieback of trees in Central Europe.

In response to these findings, most European governments have legislated and strictly enforced reductions in smokestack sulfur dioxide and nitrogen
60 oxides. Despite these controls, however, the pH of rainwater continues to register around pH 3.3—significantly more acidic than the norm.

To solve the riddle of rain acidity unabated by stringent emissions standards, researchers Hedin and
65 Likens looked at another, seemingly unrelated area of anti-pollution policy. They point out that in response to significant respiratory problems caused by microscopic dust in the atmosphere, industrialized countries have, for more than two decades, enforced restrictions on
70 particulate emissions. Because they are rich in calcium carbonate and magnesium carbonate, however, those very atmospheric particles, by dissolving in cloud droplets or by combining with SO_2 and NO_2, provide a natural neutralization of acid rain. Atmospheric dust
75 also replenishes the supply of soil cations, enabling the ecosystem's cation exchange to function on the ground.

Hedin and Likens found that atmospheric cations have dwindled sharply over the past three decades, by
80 49 percent in Britain's Hubbard Brook Experimental Forest and 74 percent in the forests of Sjoangen, Sweden. More significantly, they calculated that the reductions in atmospheric sulfur achieved through "clean air" laws closely parallel the observed decline in available cations,
85 indicating that at currently permissible emission levels the ecosystem will remain vulnerable to acid damage.

132. According to the passage, the levels of atmospheric cations in the Hubbard Brook Experimental Forest:

   A. were higher than levels in Sjoangen forests 30 years ago, and are lower now.
   B. have always been 25 percent lower than those in Sjoangen forests.
   C. declined by nearly 50 percent over the past three decades.
   D. dwindled from 74 percent to 49 percent.

GO ON TO THE NEXT PAGE.

133. The passage suggests that the 1990 NAPAP evaluation of acid rain is consistent with the United States government's decision to:

   A.   legislate emissions controls carefully crafted on the basis of scientific testimony.
   B.   warn coal-burning industries to reduce acid-producing emissions voluntarily.
   C.   fund ongoing university studies to monitor the effects of acid rain.
   D.   downplay environmentalists' concerns about damage to forests caused by acid rain.

134. According to the third paragraph of the passage, the role played by calcium and magnesium ions in the ecosystem's cation exchange mechanism is to:

   A.   give up their relatively weak anion bonds.
   B.   deplete the ecosystem's supply of cations.
   C.   bond soil anions in tight electrophilic linkage.
   D.   allow electrophilic hydrogen ions to acidify the soil.

135. Based on information in the passage, stringent regulations on emissions of sulfur dioxide and nitrogen oxides in Europe have:

   A.   proven ineffective because of inadequate inspections and enforcement.
   B.   reduced the acidity of rainwater by a significant factor.
   C.   added to the ongoing positive effects of earlier laws limiting particulate emissions.
   D.   likely been limited in their effect by other environmental regulations.

136. Hedin and Likens' research, as described in the passage, implies that societies determined to prevent environmental damage from rain acidification might find it necessary to:

   A.   maintain current limitations on sulfur dioxide and nitrogen oxides emissions.
   B.   eliminate current restrictions on particulate emissions.
   C.   balance the economic costs of pollution controls with the benefits.
   D.   consider potential unintended consequences of environmental regulations when formulating industrial policy.

137. According to the passage, acidification may cause all of the following EXCEPT:

   A.   respiratory problems.
   B.   crop injury.
   C.   stream and lake sterilization.
   D.   decline in the diversity of amphibian species.

STOP. IF YOU FINISH BEFORE TIME IS CALLED, CHECK YOUR WORK. YOU MAY GO BACK TO ANY QUESTION IN THIS SECTION.

STOP.

Writing Sample

Time: 60 Minutes
2 WS Items, Separately Timed
30 Minutes Each

WRITING SAMPLE

DIRECTIONS: This is a test of your writing skills. The test consists of two parts. You will have 30 minutes to complete each part.

If you finish writing on Part 1 before time is up, you may review your work on that part, but do not begin work on Part 2. If you finish writing on Part 2 before time is up, you may review your work only on that part of the test until the 30 minutes have expired.

Use your time efficiently. Before you begin writing each of your responses, read the assignment carefully to understand exactly what you are being asked to do in the three writing tasks. You may use the space beneath each writing assignment to make notes in planning each response.

Because this is a test of your writing skills, your response to each part should be an essay of complete sentences and paragraphs, as well organized and clearly written as you can make it in the time allotted. You may make corrections or additions neatly between the lines in your response, but do not write in the margins of the answer sheets.

There are six pages on which to write your responses, three pages for each part of the Writing Sample. You do not have to use all the pages, but to ensure that you have enough space for each essay, do not skip lines.

Essays that are illegible cannot be scored.

Start the 30 minute timing as you begin reading each Writing Sample item.

Part 1

Consider this statement:

In a democracy, the rights of the minority should take precedence over the desires of the majority.

Write a unified essay in which you perform the following tasks. Explain what you think the above statement means. Describe a specific situation in which the desires of the majority might take precedence over the rights of the minority. Discuss what you think determines whether the rights of the minority or the desires of the majority should take precedence.

Part 2

Consider this statement:

Advances in technology contribute to an increase in the standard of living.

Write a unified essay in which you perform the following tasks. Explain what you think the above statement means. Describe a specific situation in which advances in technology might <u>not</u> contribute to an increase in the standard of living. Discuss what you think determines whether or not advances in technology contribute to an increase in the standard of living.

Biological Sciences

Time: 100 Minutes

Questions 138 – 214

BIOLOGICAL SCIENCES

DIRECTIONS: Most questions in the Biological Sciences test are organized into groups, each preceded by a descriptive passage. After studying the passage, select the one best answer to each question in the group. Some questions are not based on a descriptive passage and are also independent of each other. You must also select the one best answer to these questions. If you are not certain of an answer, eliminate the alternatives that you know to be incorrect and then select an answer from the remaining alternatives. Indicate your selection by blackening the corresponding oval on your answer document. A periodic table is provided for your use. You may consult it whenever you wish.

PERIODIC TABLE OF THE ELEMENTS

1 H 1.0																	2 He 4.0
3 Li 6.9	4 Be 9.0											5 B 10.8	6 C 12.0	7 N 14.0	8 O 16.0	9 F 19.0	10 Ne 20.2
11 Na 23.0	12 Mg 24.3											13 Al 27.0	14 Si 28.1	15 P 31.0	16 S 32.1	17 Cl 35.5	18 Ar 39.9
19 K 39.1	20 Ca 40.1	21 Sc 45.0	22 Ti 47.9	23 V 50.9	24 Cr 52.0	25 Mn 54.9	26 Fe 55.8	27 Co 58.9	28 Ni 58.7	29 Cu 63.5	30 Zn 65.4	31 Ga 69.7	32 Ge 72.6	33 As 74.9	34 Se 79.0	35 Br 79.9	36 Kr 83.8
37 Rb 85.5	38 Sr 87.6	39 Y 88.9	40 Zr 91.2	41 Nb 92.9	42 Mo 95.9	43 Tc (98)	44 Ru 101.1	45 Rh 102.9	46 Pd 106.4	47 Ag 107.9	48 Cd 112.4	49 In 114.8	50 Sn 118.7	51 Sb 121.8	52 Te 127.6	53 I 126.9	54 Xe 131.3
55 Cs 132.9	56 Ba 137.3	57 La* 138.9	72 Hf 178.5	73 Ta 180.9	74 W 183.9	75 Re 186.2	76 Os 190.2	77 Ir 192.2	78 Pt 195.1	79 Au 197.0	80 Hg 200.6	81 Tl 204.4	82 Pb 207.2	83 Bi 209.0	84 Po (209)	85 At (210)	86 Rn (222)
87 Fr (223)	88 Ra 226.0	89 Ac† 227.0	104 Rf (261)	105 Db (262)	106 Sg (263)	107 Bh (262)	108 Hs (265)	109 Mt (267)									

	58 Ce 140.1	59 Pr 140.9	60 Nd 144.2	61 Pm (145)	62 Sm 150.4	63 Eu 152.0	64 Gd 157.3	65 Tb 158.9	66 Dy 162.5	67 Ho 164.9	68 Er 167.3	69 Tm 168.9	70 Yb 173.0	71 Lu 175.0
†	90 Th 232.0	91 Pa (231)	92 U 238.0	93 Np (237)	94 Pu (244)	95 Am (243)	96 Cm (247)	97 Bk (247)	98 Cf (251)	99 Es (252)	100 Fm (257)	101 Md (258)	102 No (259)	103 Lr (260)

GO ON TO THE NEXT PAGE.

Passage I (Questions 138–143)

The wall of the human eye is composed of three layers of tissue, an outer layer of tough connective tissue, a middle layer of darkly pigmented vascular tissue, and an inner layer of neural tissue. The outer layer is subdivided into the sclera, the white portion, and the cornea, the clear portion. The inner layer is more commonly known as the *retina* and contains several types of cells.

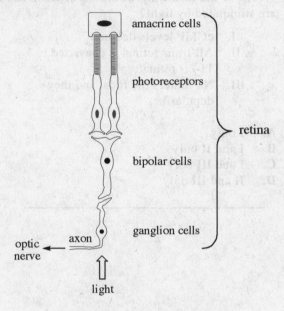

Figure 1 Retina structure

The photoreceptors of the retina include rods and cones which respond to light under different circumstances. Rods are more sensitive to light but cannot distinguish color; cones are less sensitive to light overall, but can respond to different wavelengths. Response to light involves visual pigments, which in all cases consist of a light-absorbing molecule called *retinal* (derived from vitamin A) bound to a protein called *opsin*. The type of opsin in the visual pigment determines the wavelength specificity of the retinal. The specific visual pigment in rod cells is called *rhodopsin*.

11-*cis* retinal

⇩ light

all-*trans* retinal

Figure 2 The two forms of retinal

In the absence of light, Na^+ channels in the membranes of rod cells are kept open by cGMP. The conformational change in retinal upon light absorption causes changes in opsin as well; this triggers a pathway by which phosphodiesterase (PDE) is activated. Active PDE converts cGMP to GMP, causing it to dissociate from the Na^+ channel and the channel to close. Until retinal regains its bent shape (helped by enzymes), the rod is unable to respond further to light.

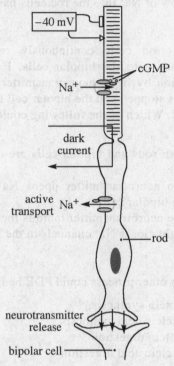

Figure 3 Rod cell in darkness

Visual defects can be caused by abnormal visual pigments or by misshapen eyeballs; for example, myopia (nearsightedness) is due to an eyeball that is too long, causing light rays from distant objects to focus in front of the retina so the image appears blurry.

GO ON TO THE NEXT PAGE.

138. Which of the following is NOT a possible explanation for why a person becomes temporarily blind upon walking into a dark movie theater on a sunny day?

A. The retinal in rod cells has not yet been converted to the 11-*cis* form.

B. The rod cells are already depolarized.

C. The cone cells require higher intensity light to be stimulated.

D. Flow of Na⁺ into the rod cells has stopped.

139. At rest, rod cells continuously release neurotransmitter onto the bipolar cells. However, upon stimulation by light, neurotransmitter release from the rod is stopped and the bipolar cell fires an action potential. Which of the following could best explain this?

A. Both rods and bipolar cells are depolarized at rest.

B. The neurotransmitter opens Na⁺ channels in the bipolar cell.

C. The neurotransmitter inhibits the bipolar cell.

D. Light closes Na⁺ channels in the bipolar cell.

140. In which other process could PDE be involved?

A. Protein synthesis

B. Nucleic acid synthesis

C. Protein digestion

D. Nucleic acid digestion

141. Vitamin A deficiency leads to a decrease in the ability to see in dim light. Poor night vision can be corrected by supplementation with this vitamin. Could supplementation with vitamin A also help correct the blurriness due to myopia?

A. No, myopic blurriness is not due to vitamin A deficiency.

B. No, vitamin A only helps synthesize rhodopsin and would have no effect on cones.

C. Yes, increased retinal synthesis would increase sharpness of vision.

D. Yes, myopic patients can see better in bright light.

142. The middle layer of the eyeball wall most likely contains:

A. bipolar cells.

B. photoreceptors.

C. blood vessels.

D. collagen fibers.

143. Which of the following would occur when rod cells are stimulated by light?

    I. cGMP levels decline.

    II. All-*trans* retinal is converted to 11-*cis* retinal.

    III. Na⁺ enters the rods, and they depolarize.

A. I only

B. I and II only

C. I and III only

D. II and III only

GO ON TO THE NEXT PAGE.

Passage II (Questions 144–147)

The small milkweed bug, *Lygaeus kalmii*, produces and emits a number of C_6-C_8 alkenals. Some of these small, fragrant, organic molecules are used to attract conspecific males or females for mating; thus, they act as sex pheromones. Others of the molecules are strongly malodorous and are used for defense.

Collaborating scientists in Brazil, the Netherlands, and Maryland have recently developed a method of noninvasive sampling and identification of these small organic molecules from live insects. This method involves the use of gas chromatography and mass spectrometry for the separation and identification of the components of the mixture of molecules involved in the sex- and defense-pheromone responses in *L. kalmii*. Several of the molecules identified in this manner are shown in Figure 1.

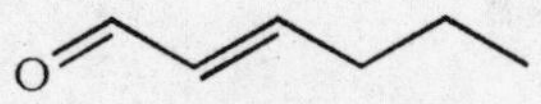

(*E*)-2-Hexenal

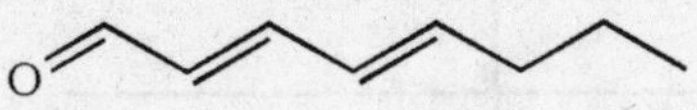

(*E,E*)-2,4-Octadienal

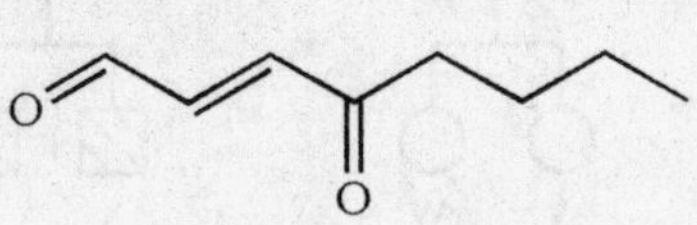

4-Oxo-(*E*)-2-octenal

Figure 1 Molecules identified using gas chromatography and mass spectrometry

In addition to its mass spectrum, Molecule A, shown below, was also identified by its ^{1}H NMR spectrum:

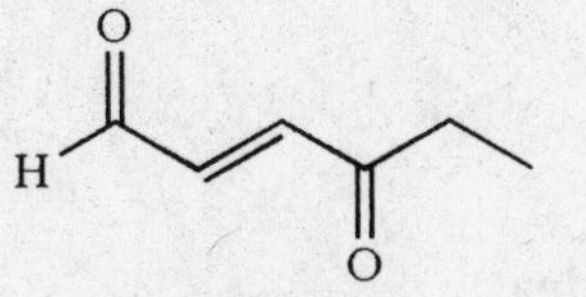

Molecule A

^{1}H NMR (CDCl$_3$): δ 9.68 (d, 1H); 7.26 (t, 1H); 7.18 (d, 1H); 2.98 (q, 2H); 1.11 (t, 3H) ppm

144. If a chemist were to react (*E,E*)-2-4-octadienal with NaBH$_4$ in ethanol and monitor the reaction by TLC, the spot corresponding to the product would be expected to have an R_f value that is:

A. less than that of the starting material.
B. equal to that of the starting material.
C. greater than that of the starting material.
D. greater than 1.

145. In which of the following reactions can (*E*)-2-hexenal NOT participate?

    I. Nucleophilic addition at C-1
    II. Conjugate addition at C-2
    III. Electrophilic addition at C-3

A. II only
B. III only
C. II and III only
D. I, II, and III

146. The ^{1}H NMR resonance at 2.98 ppm most likely corresponds to which set of protons on Molecule A?

A. A methyl group
B. A methylene group
C. An alkene proton
D. An aldehyde proton

147. If a chemist reacted 4-oxo-(*E*)-6-octenal with excess dimethylamine and monitored the reaction by IR spectroscopy, the diagnostic band showing conversion of starting material to the enamine product is the:

A. appearance of the C=N stretching frequency.
B. appearance of the C=C stretching frequency.
C. disappearance of the C=O stretching frequency.
D. disappearance of the C=C stretching frequency.

GO ON TO THE NEXT PAGE.

Passage III (Questions 148–154)

Cystic fibrosis (CF) is the most common inherited disease that is lethal in white populations and is associated with a defect in the cystic fibrosis transmembrane conductance regulator (CFTR) gene. CF is much more rare in other populations. Defects in the CFTR gene lead to thick, dehydrated mucous secretions, which may obstruct small bile ducts in the liver, air passages in the lungs, and exocrine gland ducts in the pancreas, and impair development of the vas deferens. The CFTR gene is large and susceptible to mutation at multiple sites, so there is much variability in the phenotypic expression of CF. The most severe complications of CF involve the lungs and pancreas. Mucus accumulation causes difficulty with breathing and recurrent pulmonary infections, particularly with gram-negative bacteria. Pancreatic involvement may cause both poor fat absorption and dysfunction of the endocrine pancreas.

A young couple, Josh and Raina, seek medical help for inability to conceive a child. An extensive workup on Raina, an East Indian woman, revealed short stature with normal reproductive organs and egg production. A workup of Josh, a Caucasian male, revealed a decreased sperm count secondary to a mutation on the CFTR gene. A pedigree analysis of their families is shown in Figure 1 below, detailing the inheritance patterns of both CF and achondroplasia. Achondroplasia is a common cause of dwarfism and is the result of a point mutation in the FGF receptor 3 gene. As a result of the mutation, the receptor is still translated, but adopts a constantly active conformation. People with achondroplasia are heterozygous for the defective allele, as homozygous fetuses are not viable.

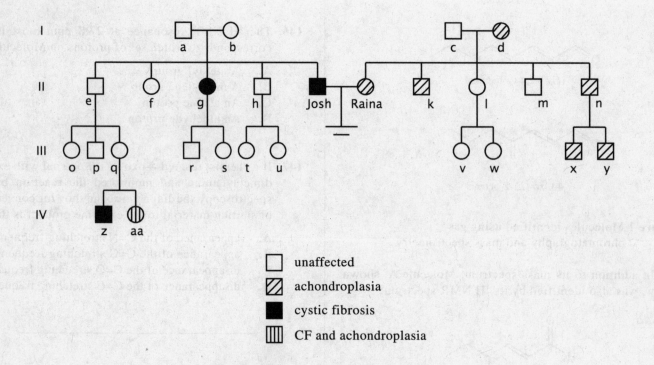

Figure 1 Family pedigree of Josh and Raina

GO ON TO THE NEXT PAGE.

148. What are the most likely patterns of inheritance for CF and achondroplasia?

   A.   CF: X-linked recessive
           Achondroplasia: autosomal dominant
   B.   CF: autosomal dominant
           Achondroplasia: autosomal recessive
   C.   CF: spontaneous mutation only
           Achondroplasia: X-linked recessive
   D.   CF: autosomal recessive
           Achondroplasia: autosomal dominant

149. If the frequency of the CF allele in a randomly mating population is 0.02, what is the frequency of individuals who do NOT manifest symptoms of CF?

   A.   0.0004
   B.   0.9604
   C.   0.98
   D.   0.9996

150. Achondroplasia can be seen in an individual without a family history of the disease, such as in Individual IV-aa in the pedigree in Figure 1. This is not the case with cystic fibrosis. If Individual IV-aa had a son with Individual II-k, what is the probability that their living son would be a carrier for CF and NOT have achondroplasia?

   A.   1/8
   B.   1/6
   C.   1/4
   D.   1/3

151. According to the passage, which of the following may be associated with CF?

     I.   Recurrent lung infection with bacteria that have a thick layer of peptidoglycan
    II.   Deficiency in fat-soluble vitamins, such as vitamin A and vitamin E
   III.   Inability to appropriately lower glucose levels after a meal

   A.   I only
   B.   II only
   C.   II and III only
   D.   I, II, and III

152. All of the following statements regarding the digestive system of cystic fibrosis patients are true EXCEPT:

   A.   Flow of bile produced in the gallbladder may be prevented due to obstruction of small bile ducts.
   B.   Damage to exocrine tissue within the pancreas may hinder the secretion of lipases.
   C.   Secretions from both the salivary gland and pancreas are important for starch digestion.
   D.   CF patients may have a normal digestive system.

153. Suppose that Josh and Raina are eventually able to conceive, and Raina gives birth to a boy. What is the probability that their son will have either CF or achondroplasia?

   A.   0%
   B.   25%
   C.   50%
   D.   100%

154. The mutation responsible for achondroplasia is most likely associated with:

   A.   a frameshift in the reading frame of the messenger RNA.
   B.   the insertion of a new amino acid with different electrostatic properties compared to the original amino acid.
   C.   a deletion of one base pair at the 5′ end of the FGF gene.
   D.   the insertion of the same amino acid into the growing polypeptide, allowed by the degeneracy of the genetic code.

GO ON TO THE NEXT PAGE.

Passage IV (Questions 155–160)

Pressure during diving is of concern to divers, since air obeys Boyle's law:

$$V \propto 1/P$$

Equation 1

assuming constant temperature and moles of gas. The pressure exerted by a column of water 10 m deep is equal to 1 atmosphere. At very high oxygen partial pressures, such as are found in the lungs during diving, the amount of oxygen dissolved in the blood increases markedly (see Figure 1). This can lead to acute oxygen poisoning, which includes symptoms such as dizziness, visual disturbances, nausea, twitching of muscles, and, in extreme cases, seizures. The symptoms of acute oxygen poisoning are thought to be caused by the excessive production of free radicals that, among other effects, oxidize and damage the fatty acids that are found in the membranous structures of cells.

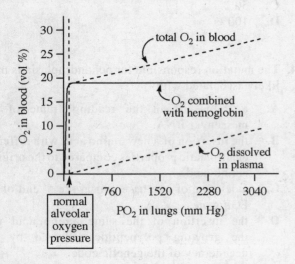

Figure 1 Total O_2 in the blood at very high PO_2 levels

Mark is a relatively inactive person who enjoys vacationing in locations that have a wide variety of dangerous sports in which to participate. Two years ago he went on vacation in Hawaii and went diving. Last year he went to Vancouver and went skiing. When diving and skiing he noticed changes in his heart and ventilation rates as shown in Tables 1 and 2.

Table 1 Heart and Ventilation Rates on First Day of Vacation

Location	Heart rates (beats/min)		Ventilation rates (resp/min)	
	At rest	Active	At rest	Active
Hawaii	80	115	14	20
Vancouver	90	150	30	40

Table 2 Heart and Ventilation Rates Two Weeks after Onset of Vacation

Location	Heart rates (beats/min)		Ventilation rates (resp/min)	
	At rest	Active	At rest	Active
Hawaii	80	82	14	19
Vancouver	90	130	25	35

155. Free-radical production during acute oxygen poisoning would most likely have the greatest effect on the:

A. stomach.
B. brain.
C. cornea and lens of the eye.
D. liver.

156. Normal total lung capacity at sea level is approximately 6 L. Mark inhales maximally at the surface of the water, then, without exhaling, dives to a depth of 10 m. At this depth the volume of air in his lungs is approximately:

A. 3 L.
B. 6 L.
C. 9 L.
D. 12 L.

GO ON TO THE NEXT PAGE.

157. "Blood doping" is the intravenous injection of packed red blood cells, usually prior to athletic competition. Mark plans to vacation in Vancouver this year, and intends to "dope his blood" prior to his visit. Blood doping could have which of the following effects (compared to his prior visit to Vancouver with no blood doping)?

    I.   Decreased ventilation rate
   II.   Increased resistance to blood flow
  III.   Decreased heart rate

A.   I only
B.   II only
C.   I and II only
D.   I, II, and III

158. After 2 hours of diving at an average depth of 12 m, Mark produced a much larger volume of urine than normal. This is most likely due to:

A.   increased blood pressure leading to increased filtration rate.
B.   decreased blood pressure leading to osmotic movement of water out of cells.
C.   increased blood pressure leading to an increase in ADH production.
D.   increased blood pressure leading to the release of aldosterone.

159. Mark found that during his trip to Vancouver his appetite increased significantly and he ingested a larger quantity of food; however, he did not gain any weight. A quick calculation showed that the increase in appetite could not be accounted for by an increase in work during skiing compared to diving. All of the following could be reasons for Mark's increased appetite EXCEPT:

A.   decreased Krebs cycle activity due to decreased PO_2.
B.   increased glycolysis due to anaerobic respiration.
C.   increased beta-oxidation of fatty acids due to increased activity.
D.   decreased oxidative phosphorylation due to high altitude.

160. During Mark's diving lesson his instructor told him to exhale as he rose to the surface to prevent lung collapse. Lung collapse during ascension is typically due to a rupture of the lung wall which permits air to enter the pleural cavity. The rupture of the lung wall is most likely due to:

A.   decreased water pressure leading to an increase in intrapleural pressure.
B.   expansion of the air in the lungs according to Boyle's law.
C.   decreased water pressure leading to a rapid outward expansion of the rib cage.
D.   increased lung air pressure according to Boyle's law.

GO ON TO THE NEXT PAGE.

Questions 161 through 165 are **NOT** based on a descriptive passage.

161. Which of the following could NOT be a possible genotype in the ovum of a human female?

- **A.** 23-X
- **B.** 24-XX
- **C.** 22-O
- **D.** 23-Y

162. Local anesthetics, such as lidocaine or Novocain, block voltage-gated sodium channels in nerve cells. Effects would include:

- I. Loss of resting membrane potential
- II. Blocking of action potential transmission
- III. Loss of repolarization

- **A.** I only
- **B.** II only
- **C.** I and II only
- **D.** I, II, and III

163. New-onset poliomyelitis has been eradicated from the Western Hemisphere due to an aggressive vaccination agenda. Currently, it is recommended that children be vaccinated against polio by receiving three doses of Inactivated Polio Vaccine (IPV) at ages 2 months, 4 months, and 6 months. Which of the following is the mostly likely mechanism IPV uses to confer immunity?

- **A.** IPV stimulates a humoral immune response, which leads to B cells producing antibody and a set of memory B cells directed against the polio virus.
- **B.** IPV infects respiratory cells, and portions of the viral coat are presented to CD8$^+$ killer T cells, marking the respiratory cells for destruction.
- **C.** Portions of the polio virus coat are presented by Antigen Presenting Cells to CD4$^+$ helper T cells, leading to production of memory neutrophils.
- **D.** IPV is phagocytosed by macrophages, then presented to B cells via MHC class I.

164. What is the most stable intermediate species during the conversion of 2-iodo-3-methylbutane to an alcohol via reaction with water?

A.

$$\left[H_2O \overset{\delta^+}{-\!-\!-} \overset{}{\underset{\underset{H_3C \quad H}{}}{C}} \overset{\delta^-}{-\!-\!-} I \right]^{\ddagger}$$

C.

$$\left[H_2O -\!-\!- \overset{\oplus}{\underset{\underset{H_3C \quad H}{}}{C}} -\!-\!- I \right]^{\ddagger}$$

B.

D.

165. With which of the following organelles would the mRNA for the estrogen receptor be associated?

- I. Ribosomes
- II. Rough ER
- III. Golgi apparatus

- **A.** I only
- **B.** I and II only
- **C.** II and III only
- **D.** I, II, and III

GO ON TO THE NEXT PAGE.

Passage V (Questions 166–170)

Dyes are ionizable, aromatic compounds that absorb visible light due to the presence of a highly conjugated system of *p* orbitals. The observed color is one that is complementary to the wavelength of light absorbed by the molecule (complementary color pairs are red/green, orange/blue, and yellow/violet). Dyes bind to the materials to be colored, such as fabrics or paper, through inter- and intramolecular interactions, including hydrogen bonds, ionic interactions, covalent bonds, and coordinate covalent bonds. The stronger the interaction between dye molecule and fiber, the more permanent the color will be. When a dye covalently bonds to a fiber, it becomes a part of the fabric itself and cannot be washed away.

Two of the most common dye types are mordant dyes and direct dyes. A *mordant* is a polyvalent metal ion (usually Al^{3+} or Fe^{3+}) that forms a coordination complex with certain dyes. Mordants chelate to the fabric as well as the dye molecule, thereby improving their colorfastness. Mordant dyes are primarily used on protein-based fibers such as wool, silk, angora, and cashmere since the mordant can bind to the constituent amino acids of these fibers. *Direct* dyes are typically charged molecules, and interact with the material to be dyed through ionic forces or hydrogen bonding. As such they tend to bleed more than mordant dyes. Direct dyes are more commonly used on cellulose fibers such as cotton, linen, or hemp.

Azo dyes, a subclass of direct dyes, may be used in a dyeing technique in which an insoluble azo compound is produced directly onto or within a fiber. This is achieved by treating the fiber first with a diazonium component, followed by a coupling component. With suitable adjustment of dyebath conditions the two components react to produce the required insoluble azo dye. The coupling reagent used in the final step is typically a molecule containing either a phenolic hydroxyl group or an arylamine. The synthesis of methyl orange, an azo dye, is shown in Figure 1.

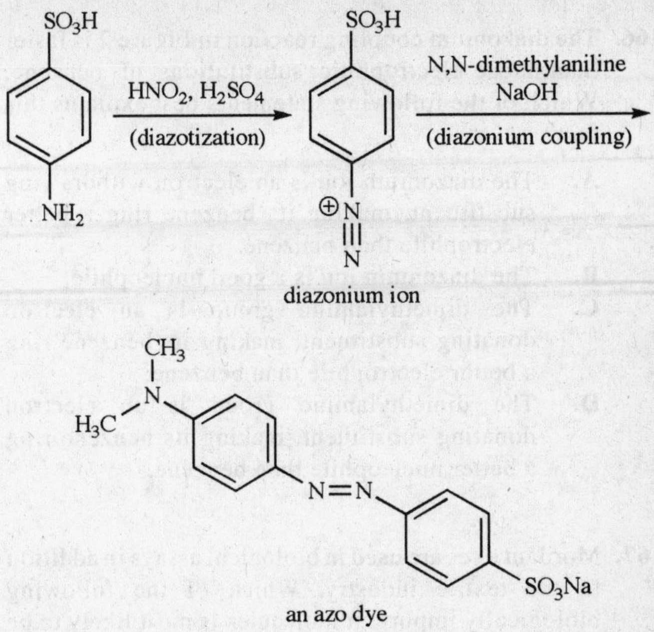

Figure 1 Synthesis of methyl orange

Figure 2 below represents the mechanism of the diazonium coupling reaction in the synthesis of methyl orange.

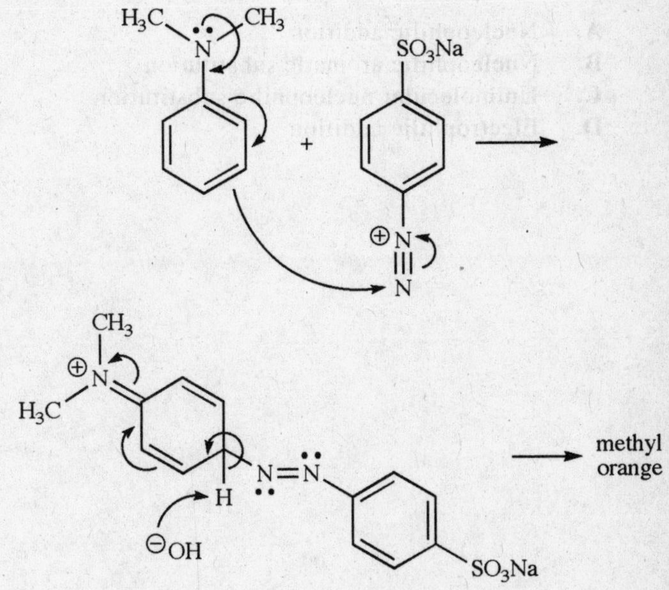

Figure 2 Mechanism of diazonium coupling

GO ON TO THE NEXT PAGE.

166. The diazonium coupling reaction in Figure 2 is faster than most electrophilic substitutions of benzene. Which of the following statements best explains this fact?

    A. The diazonium ion is an electron withdrawing substituent, making its benzene ring a better electrophile than benzene.

    B. The diazonium ion is a good nucleophile.

    C. The dimethylamino group is an electron donating substituent, making its benzene ring a better electrophile than benzene.

    D. The dimethylamino group is an electron donating substituent, making its benzene ring a better nucleophile than benzene.

167. Mordant dyes are used in biological assays in addition to the textile industry. Which of the following biologically important molecules is most likely to be labeled by a mordant dye?

    A. Glycogen
    B. Chromatin
    C. Cholesterol
    D. Starch

168. What type of reaction is the second step in the synthesis of methyl orange?

    A. Nucleophilic addition
    B. Nucleophilic aromatic substitution
    C. Unimolecular nucleophilic substitution
    D. Electrophilic addition

169. A chemist conducts a competition experiment in which she treats the diazonium ion in Figure 1 with a 1:1 molar ratio of N,N-dimethylaniline and benzenesulfonic acid in an attempt to synthesize a mixture of methyl orange and another azo dye.

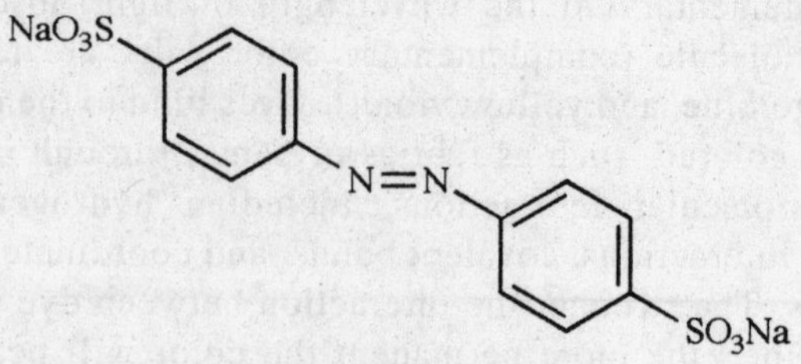

Compound A

Which of the following reasons explain(s) why Compound A (shown above) is NOT the major product of this experiment?

    I. Benzenesulfonic acid is a poorer nucleophile than N,N-dimethylaniline.

    II. The sulfonic acid substituent is a meta director.

    III. Benzenesulfonic acid is more sterically hindered than N,N-dimethylaniline.

    A. I only
    B. II only
    C. I and II only
    D. II and III only

170. How many signals would appear in the ^{13}C NMR spectrum of Compound A shown in Question 169?

    A. 2
    B. 4
    C. 8
    D. 12

GO ON TO THE NEXT PAGE.

Passage VI (Questions 171–176)

The development of sexual characteristics depends upon various factors, the most important of which are hormonal control, environmental stimuli, and the genetic makeup of the individual. The hormones that contribute to the development include the steroid hormones estrogen, progesterone, and testosterone, as well as the pituitary hormones FSH (follicle-stimulating hormone) and LH (luteinizing hormone).

To study the mechanism by which estrogen exerts its effects, a researcher performed the following experiments using cell culture assays.

Experiment 1:

Human embryonic placental mesenchyme (HEPM) cells were grown for 48 hours in Dulbecco's Modified Eagle Medium (DMEM), with media change every 12 hours. Upon confluent growth, cells were exposed to a 10 μg per mL solution of green fluorescent-labeled estrogen for 1 hour. Cells were rinsed with DMEM and observed under confocal fluorescent microscopy.

Experiment 2:

HEPM cells were grown to confluence as in Experiment 1. Cells were exposed to Pesticide A for 1 hour, followed by the 10 μg/mL solution of labeled estrogen, rinsed as in Experiment 1, and observed under confocal fluorescent microscopy.

Experiment 3:

Experiment 1 was repeated with Chinese Hamster Ovary (CHO) cells instead of HEPM cells.

Experiment 4:

CHO cells injected with cytoplasmic extracts of HEPM cells were grown to confluence, exposed to the 10 μg/mL solution of labeled estrogen for 1 hour, and observed under confocal fluorescent microscopy.

The results of these experiments are given in Table 1.

Table 1 Detection of Estrogen
(+ indicates presence of estrogen)

Experiment	Media	Cytoplasm	Nucleus
1	+	+	+
2	+	+	+
3	+	+	+
4	+	+	+

After observing the cells in each experiment, the researcher bathed the cells in a solution containing 10 μg per mL of a red fluorescent probe that binds specifically to the estrogen receptor only when its active site is occupied. After 1 hour, the cells were rinsed with DMEM and observed under confocal fluorescent microscopy. The results are presented in Table 2.

Table 2 Observed Fluorescence and Estrogen Effects
(G = green, R = red)

Experiment	Media	Cytoplasm	Nucleus	Estrogen effects observed?
1	G only	G and R	G and R	Yes
2	G only	G only	G only	No
3	G only	G only	G only	No
4	G only	G and R	G and R	Yes

Based on these results, the researcher determined that estrogen had no effect when not bound to a cytosolic, estrogen-specific receptor.

The researcher also repeated Experiment 2 using Pesticide B, an estrogen analog, instead of Pesticide A. Results from other researchers had shown that Pesticide B binds to the active site of the cytosolic estrogen receptor (with an affinity 10,000 times greater than that of estrogen) and causes increased transcription of mRNA.

171. The results summarized in Table 1 can best be explained by which of the following?

   A. The plasma membrane and nuclear membrane have estrogen-specific protein channels.
   B. Estrogen can cross the plasma membrane by simple diffusion and crosses the nuclear membrane through the nuclear pores.
   C. Estrogen is derived from amino acids and therefore crosses all membranes by facilitated diffusion.
   D. Estrogen is derived from cholesterol and therefore crosses all membranes by simple diffusion.

172. Pesticide A most likely functions as:

   A. an agonist.
   B. an inhibitor.
   C. a lipase.
   D. a receptor.

GO ON TO THE NEXT PAGE.

173. When the researcher performed Experiment 2 using Pesticide B instead of Pesticide A, which of the following fluorescence and estrogen effects did the researcher most likely observe?

- **A.** *Media:* green and red
  Cytoplasm: green and red
  Nucleus: green and red
  Estrogen effects: no
- **B.** *Media:* green only
  Cytoplasm: green and red
  Nucleus: green and red
  Estrogen effects: no
- **C.** *Media:* green only
  Cytoplasm: green and red
  Nucleus: green and red
  Estrogen effects: yes
- **D.** *Media:* green only
  Cytoplasm: green and red
  Nucleus: green only
  Estrogen effects: no

174. Which of the following graphs would best illustrate the binding of estrogen (E) to its receptor in the presence of its analog, Pesticide B?

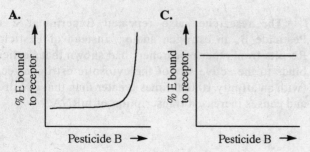

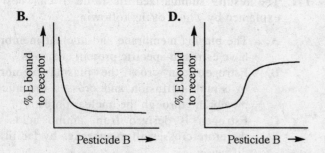

175. The difference in the results of Experiments 3 and 4 can best be explained by the presence of estrogen receptor in which of the following?

- **A.** Nuclei of CHO cells
- **B.** Cytoplasm of CHO cells
- **C.** Nuclei of HEPM cells
- **D.** Cytoplasm of HEPM cells

176. If Experiment 2 were repeated, but this time exposing the cells first to Pesticide A and then to Pesticide B before exposing them to the green fluorescent-labeled estrogen and the red fluorescent probe, which of the following statements will most likely be true?

- **A.** Pesticide A and Pesticide B bind to the same site on the estrogen receptor.
- **B.** Estrogen effects would be observed.
- **C.** Only green fluorescence would be observed.
- **D.** Both green and red fluorescence would be observed.

GO ON TO THE NEXT PAGE.

Passage VII (Questions 177–182)

When first viewing cells through a microscope, early scientists hypothesized that the mitochondria might have originally been separate organisms that are now living symbiotically within eukaryotic cells. As the science of microscopy advanced and other organelles were discovered, this view fell by the wayside. The discovery of an independent mitochondrial genome and observations of mitochondrial replication independent of cellular division brought the endosymbiotic theory back to the forefront.

Most of the proteins contained in and utilized by mitochondria are encoded by nuclear DNA and imported into the mitochondria. However, mitochondria have small circular dsDNA genomes very similar to bacterial or plasmid genomes. In humans, mitochondrial DNA (see Figure 1) is about 16,500 bp and may vary from mitochondrion to mitochondrion within a single cell. Mitochondria carry out their own DNA replication, transcription, and protein synthesis in the mitochondrial matrix.

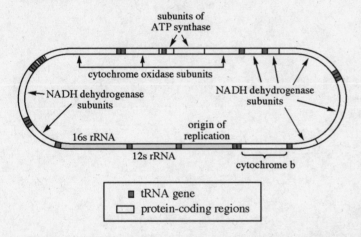

Figure 1 Organization of the mitochondrial genome

Leber's Hereditary Optic Neuropathy ("Leber's" for short) is a disease that results in a rapid loss of vision. It usually begins in adolescence and can result in total blindness due to degeneration of the optic nerve. Leber's runs in families and has long been suspected as having a genetic cause. However, there are two puzzling aspects to the disorder. First, the disorder is highly variable, causing complete blindness in some people and only minor loss of vision in others. Second, only women pass the disorder along to their children. The children of men with Leber's never inherit the disorder, but the children of women with Leber's do.

An investigator wondered whether there was a chance that Leber's might be due to a problem with mitochondria, since the cells of the optic nerve have some of the highest energy requirements of any nervous tissue. Using restriction enzymes to analyze fragments of mitochondrial DNA, he discovered that Leber's patients have a point mutation in their mtDNA that normal patients do not. This change affects a protein in the electron transport chain, causing it to function less efficiently than the unaffected protein.

177. Which one of the following does NOT support the theory that mitochondria were once separate organisms that were incorporated into eukaryotic cells?

- **A.** Mitochondria isolated from some species of yeast are able to survive outside of the yeast cell.
- **B.** Scientists have discovered a family of purple cyanobacteria that are very similar to mitochondria in structure and function but live independently.
- **C.** The mitochondrial genome is double-stranded DNA.
- **D.** The mitochondrial "alphabet" of anticodons for translation is read differently from the "alphabet" of nuclear DNA.

GO ON TO THE NEXT PAGE.

178. A woman with Leber's disease has two sons in their mid-twenties. One became completely blind over time, while the other exhibited only minor symptoms. Because of their disability, the sons have lived at home their entire lives. Which of the following would best explain the difference in severity?

- **A.** One son is homozygous recessive for Leber's, and the other is heterozygous.
- **B.** Different mitochondria in the egg have different genomes, and the severity of the disease depends on the number of mutant mitochondria present in the zygote.
- **C.** The disease has a significant environmental component that determines its severity.
- **D.** One son inherited a mutant X chromosome from the mother, while the other inherited a wild-type X.

179. In order for mitochondria to synthesize a protein, the nucleus must encode which of the following?

- I. RNA polymerase
- II. DNA polymerase
- III. Ribosomes

- **A.** I only
- **B.** I and II only
- **C.** I and III only
- **D.** II and III only

180. Although mitochondria are found in every cell throughout the body, mutations in mitochondrial DNA typically only affect a few cell types, such as neurons or muscle cells. Which of the following could be a possible explanation for this?

- **A.** Not all cells possess mitochondria, and only cell types that do are affected.
- **B.** Cell types that are not affected have nuclear genes for the mutated mitochondrial protein.
- **C.** Affected cell types have had nuclear genes for DNA repair enzymes deleted.
- **D.** Mutations in electron transport proteins are more significant in cell types that have high energy requirements.

181. Leber's is most likely caused by what type of mutation?

- **A.** Deletion
- **B.** Insertion
- **C.** Missense
- **D.** Nonsense

182. Mitochondrial ribosomes are:

- **A.** made from 16s and 12s subunits.
- **B.** encoded in the nucleus.
- **C.** made from 50s and 30s subunits.
- **D.** usually found in the cytosol.

GO ON TO THE NEXT PAGE.

Passage VIII (Questions 183–187)

Polypropylene is a versatile synthetic polymer used in the production of bottles, upholstery, carpet fibers, sewing thread, and rope. It is an example of a chain growth or addition polymer, which is produced by a successive lengthening of a reactive intermediate. The addition of an initiator to the double bond of propylene forms a free radical, which subsequently reacts in a propagation step with another propylene molecule, as shown in Figure 1. Each new radical reacts successively with another propylene molecule to lengthen the chain.

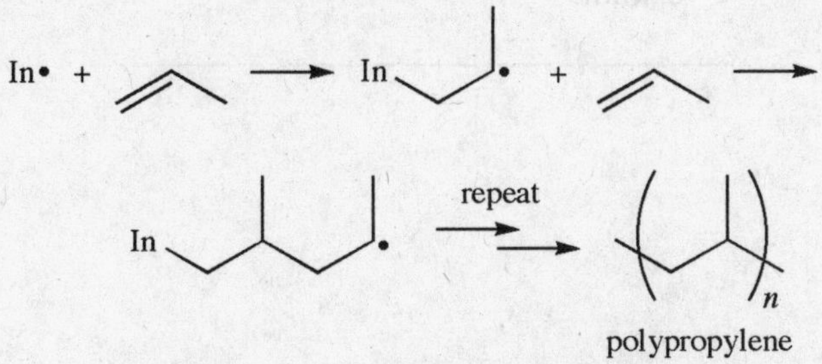

Figure 1 Radical polymerization

Polypropylene can also be produced by a cationic mechanism using a Lewis acid initiator, and monomers such as acrylonitrile, also known as cyanoethene, can be used to produce polymers via an anionic intermediate. The type of intermediate is dependent upon the electronic properties of the substituents present on the monomer units.

Polymerization of substituted alkenes leads to structures with numerous stereocenters on the backbone of the polymer. Unless special measures are taken, the configuration of each stereocenter will be random, producing an *atactic* polymer. Through use of the Ziegler–Natta catalyst, polypropylene and other polymers can be produced in both the *isotactic* form in which all substituents are on the same side of the chain, or in the *syndiotactic* form, in which the positions of the substituents alternate sides.

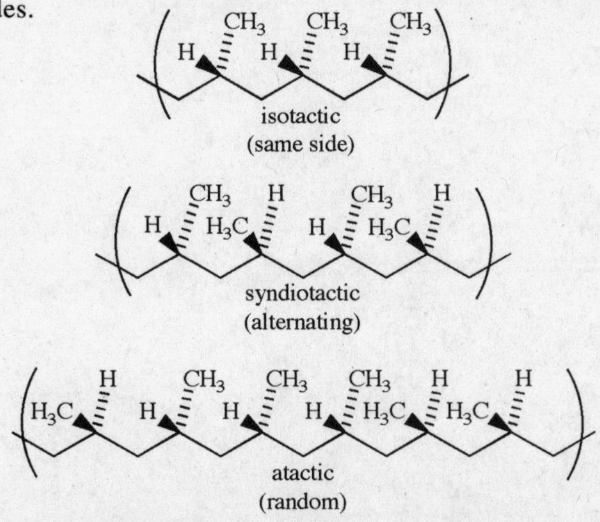

Figure 2 Polypropylene isomers

These isomeric forms have somewhat different properties, and therefore different uses. Isotactic and syndiotactic polymers tend to have higher melting points and are more resilient than their atactic forms.

Natural rubber and gutta-percha are natural polymers formed by the polymerization of 2-methyl-1,3-butadiene. These molecules differ only by the E/Z geometry of their double bonds. While natural rubber is soft and tacky, gutta-percha is harder and more brittle. Rubber can be made more durable by introducing sulfur, which will cross link the backbone chains through disulfide bonds in a process called vulcanization.

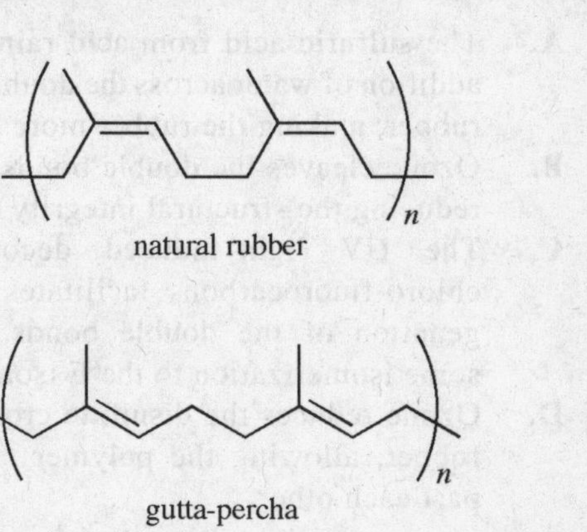

natural rubber

gutta-percha

Figure 3 Natural polymers formed by polymerization of 2-methyl-1,3-butadiene

183. Which of the following compounds should one expect to find in the largest quantity upon treatment of 1,4-dimethyl-1-cyclohexene with bromine and ultraviolet light?

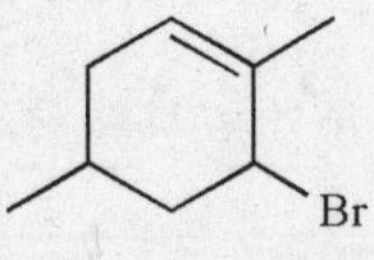

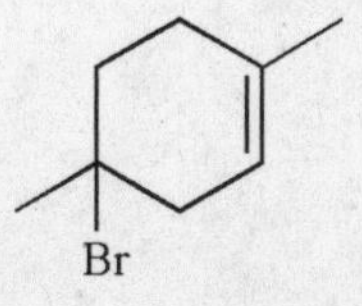

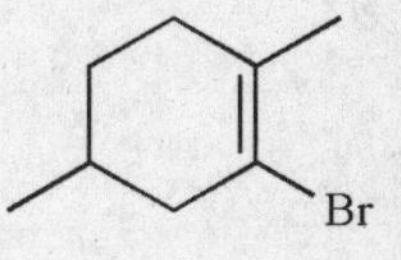

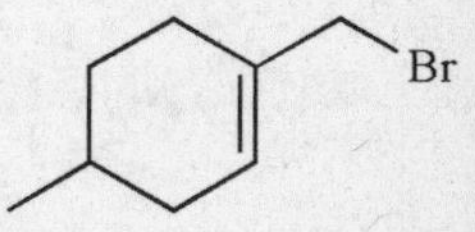

GO ON TO THE NEXT PAGE.

184. Which of the following reagents would most likely be used as the radical initiator in the polymerization of polypropylene?

- **A.** Sodium borohydride
- **B.** Potassium hydroxide
- **C.** Benzoyl peroxide
- **D.** Phosphorus trichloride

185. Radial tires have sidewalls made of natural rubber, and tend to crack and weather rapidly near cities with high levels of industrial pollutants. What is the best explanation for this observation?

- **A.** The sulfuric acid from acid rain catalyzes the addition of water across the double bonds of the rubber, making the rubber more hydrophilic.
- **B.** Ozone cleaves the double bonds in the rubber, reducing the structural integrity of the tire.
- **C.** The UV light–induced decomposition of chloro-fluorocarbons facilitates radical halogenation of the double bonds, allowing for some isomerization to the E isomer.
- **D.** Ozone reduces the disulfide cross-links of the rubber, allowing the polymer chains to slide past each other.

186. The reactive intermediate most likely involved in the polymerization of methylpropenoate is a:

- **A.** carbanion, because the electron donating group will destabilize the negative charge on the intermediate.
- **B.** carbocation, because the electron donating group will stabilize the positive charge on the intermediate.
- **C.** carbocation, because the electron withdrawing group will stabilize the positive charge on the intermediate.
- **D.** carbanion, because the electron withdrawing group will stabilize the negative charge on the intermediate.

187. Compared to their stereoisomers, gutta-percha and isotactic polypropylene have higher melting points because they:

- **A.** have larger dipole–dipole interactions because of the orientation of their substituents.
- **B.** have stronger London dispersion forces since each strand can overlap with the next more easily due to the orientation of their substituents.
- **C.** have stronger London dispersion forces due to their greater molecular weights.
- **D.** can hydrogen bond, whereas their isomers cannot.

GO ON TO THE NEXT PAGE.

188. Regarding embryogenesis, which of the following sequence of events is in correct order?

A. Implantation—cleavage—gastrulation—neurulation—blastulation

B. Blastulation—implantation—cleavage—neurulation—gastrulation

C. Implantation—blastulation—gastrulation—cleavage—neurulation

D. Cleavage—blastulation—implantation—gastrulation—neurulation

189. What is the major product of the following Diels–Alder reaction?

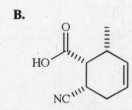

A.

B.

C.

D.

190. An embryo with a karyotype of 45 XO would develop:

A. normal male genitalia.

B. male genitalia without functioning testes.

C. normal female genitalia.

D. undifferentiated genitalia (hermaphrodite).

191. A chemist measured the following rate data for the reaction between 2-chloroheptane and potassium cyanide:

Trial	$[E^+]$	$[Nuc^-]$	Reaction Rate
1	$1.12 \times 10^{-3}\ M$	$1.12 \times 10^{-3}\ M$	$1.50 \times 10^{-3}\ Ms^{-1}$
2	$5.60 \times 10^{-4}\ M$	$1.12 \times 10^{-3}\ M$	$7.50 \times 10^{-4}\ Ms^{-1}$
3	$5.60 \times 10^{-4}\ M$	$4.48 \times 10^{-3}\ M$	$3.00 \times 10^{-3}\ Ms^{-1}$

What is the mechanism of the formation of the product?

A. S_N1, because the reaction rate doubled when the alkyl halide concentration doubled.

B. S_N1, because the reaction rate remained unchanged regardless of the cyanide concentration.

C. S_N2, because the reaction rate doubled when the alkyl halide concentration doubled.

D. S_N2, because the reaction rate quadrupled when the cyanide concentration quadrupled.

192. Some genetic disorders produce men who lack both vas deferens due to developmental failure. It is most likely true that the ejaculatory fluid of these men would be:

A. alkaline, fructose-rich, and lack spermatozoa.

B. acidic, fructose-rich, and lack spermatozoa.

C. alkaline, fructose-deficient, and have a very low spermatozoa count.

D. acidic, protein-deficient, and contain poorly functioning spermatozoa.

GO ON TO THE NEXT PAGE.

Passage IX (Questions 193–199)

When oxygen binds to hemoglobin, usually one electron is transferred from the heme iron to molecular oxygen, creating a ferric–superoxide complex (Fe^{3+}–O_2^{-}). Most of the oxygen is subsequently released as molecular oxygen but occasionally a superoxide ion (O_2^{-}) is released. This leaves a ferric iron atom (Fe^{3+}) in the heme group. This oxidized form of hemoglobin is called *methemoglobin*. The ferric heme of methemoglobin is unable to bind oxygen. In addition, the oxygen affinity of any accompanying ferrous hemes in the hemoglobin tetramer is increased; as a result, oxygen delivery to the tissues is impaired. Methemoglobin is normally present in the blood in small amounts, typically less than 3%. Methemoglobin is usually reduced back to hemoglobin by cytochrome b5 reductase (which contains a non-covalently bound FAD+ group) through an NADH-dependent reaction. Methemoglobinemia results when methemoglobin levels become abnormally high. This can occur when there is increased methemoglobin production, decreased clearance of methemoglobin, or both. Early symptoms include cyanosis (blue skin color), headache, fatigue, and dizziness, and can progress to respiratory depression, loss of consciousness, shock, and death as methemoglobin levels rise.

A second biochemical pathway, using NADPH as the reducing agent, can be used to reduce methemoglobin. Administration of external agents such as methylene blue can increase this pathway 4–5 times over its normal activity. NAD+ and NADP+ differ only in the presence of an extra phosphate on the adenosine ribose of NADP+. This difference has little to do with redox activity, but is recognized by substrate-binding sites of enzymes. This second pathway is dependent on the *hexose monophosphate shunt* to produce NADPH, which can be generated from glucose-6-phosphate through the *oxidative branch*; see Figure 1.

The formation of NADPH is an important early step in the synthesis of many biomolecules. NADPH functions as a reducing agent in various synthetic (anabolic) pathways, including that for fatty acids. In contrast, NAD+ serves as the electron acceptor in catabolic pathways. The *non-oxidative branch* of the hexose monophosphate shunt first converts ribulose-5-phosphate into ribose-5-phosphate, which can be made into nucleotides or deoxynucleotides; thus, this series of reactions is also known as the *pentose phosphate pathway*. The non-oxidative branch can continue through a series of reversible reactions to convert ribose-5-phosphate into other carbohydrates which can be shunted to numerous anabolic and catabolic pathways (Figure 2).

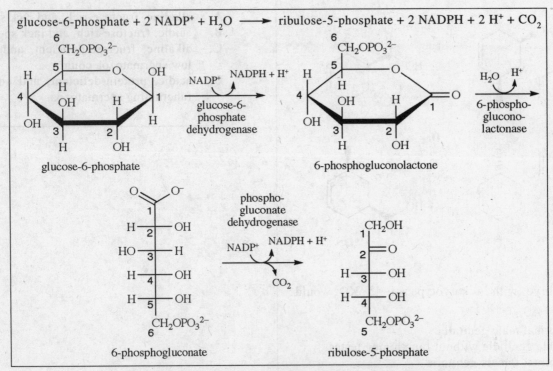

$$glucose\text{-}6\text{-}phosphate + 2\ NADP^+ + H_2O \longrightarrow ribulose\text{-}5\text{-}phosphate + 2\ NADPH + 2\ H^+ + CO_2$$

Figure 1 Oxidative branch of the hexose monophosphate shunt

I.	ribose-5-phosphate ⇌ ribulose-5-phosphate ⇌ xylulose-5-phosphate
II.	ribose-5-phosphate + xylulose-5-phosphate ⇌ sedoheptulose-7-phosphate + glyceraldehyde-3-phosphate
III.	sedoheptulose-7-phosphate + glyceraldehyde-3-phosphate ⇌ fructose-6-phosphate + erythrose-4-phosphate
IV.	xylulose-5-phosphate + erythrose-4-phosphate ⇌ fructose-6-phosphate + glyceraldehyde-3-phosphate

Figure 2 Non-oxidative branch of the hexose monophosphate shunt

GO ON TO THE NEXT PAGE.

193. What role does methylene blue serve in treating methemoglobinemia?

A. It oxidizes $NADP^+$ to NADPH to reduce Fe^{2+} to Fe^{3+}.
B. It oxidizes NADPH to $NADP^+$ to reduce Fe^{2+} to Fe^{3+}.
C. It oxidizes $NADP^+$ to NADPH to reduce Fe^{3+} to Fe^{2+}.
D. It oxidizes NADPH to $NADP^+$ to reduce Fe^{3+} to Fe^{2+}.

194. Why is it important that enzymes can recognize the difference between NAD^+ and $NADP^+$?

A. It allows for separation of catabolic and anabolic pathways.
B. NAD^+ is regenerated in the Krebs cycle; $NADP^+$ is generated through the HMP shunt.
C. NADPH serves as a control element for some enzymes; NADH does not.
D. NAD^+ reacts more quickly than $NADP^+$.

195. If a cell is low on energy, which molecule is most likely to be produced via the HMP shunt?

A. Ribose-5-phosphate
B. Glyceraldehyde-3-phosphate
C. NADPH
D. Sedoheptulose-7-phosphate

196. In the graph below, which line depicts the effect of methemoglobin on the normal (N) hemoglobin O_2-saturation curve?

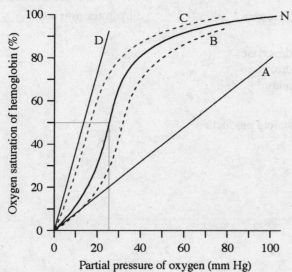

A. A
B. B
C. C
D. D

197. The enzymes of the HMP shunt are highly sensitive to feedback inhibition. Which one of the following provides the most likely explanation for this?

A. The HMP shunt is a rarely used pathway and needs to be tightly regulated.
B. All enzymes are highly sensitive to feedback inhibition.
C. Feedback inhibition is a very effective way to regulate enzyme activity.
D. It would be inefficient to produce excess precursor molecules when they are not needed for biosynthesis.

198. Radiolabeling studies have shown that the HMP shunt is much more active in adipose tissue than in skeletal muscle. This is because:

A. muscle tissue utilizes more energy than adipose tissue.
B. muscle tissue lacks the enzymes for the HMP shunt.
C. adipose tissue requires NADPH to create fatty acids.
D. adipose tissue produces more energy than muscle tissue.

199. How many carbon atoms does erythrose-4-phosphate have?

A. 3
B. 4
C. 5
D. 6

GO ON TO THE NEXT PAGE.

Passage X (Questions 200–204)

Typically, modern culture separates the sexes into two categories: men and women. However, there are some cultures today that recognize three sexes, as depicted in the 1997 documentary *Guevote* by Rolando Sanchez. This movie illustrates life in a small village in the Dominican Republic where 2% of the population is classified as "pseudo-hermaphroditic." These people appear to be female at birth, but they develop male secondary sexual characteristics at puberty, including growth of a penis and development of a scrotum. Most of these children are the product of consanguineous relationships and have been labeled by the villagers as "guevedoche." These individuals have a deficiency of the enzyme 5-α-reductase, which converts testosterone to dihydrotestosterone (DHT). The human penis, scrotum, and prostate require DHT for development. The guevedoche have an increased ratio of testosterone to DHT, but other hormones and enzymes responsible for sexual development are found at relatively normal levels.

Early in gestation, both male and female fetuses contain undifferentiated Müllerian ducts (potential fallopian tubes, uterus, and upper vagina) and Wolffian ducts (potential epididymis, vas deferens, and ejaculatory ducts). XY fetuses and XX fetuses are sexually indistinguishable throughout the first seven weeks of life. By week 8 interstitial (Leydig) cells in the collection of fetal germ cells begin secreting testosterone, which stimulates Wolffian duct differentiation and the development of male genitalia. Also at week 8, the fetal sustenacular (Sertoli) cells begin secreting Müllerian Inhibitory Factor (MIF), which leads to degeneration of the Müllerian ducts. If the fetus fails to produce testosterone, the Müllerian ducts develop and the Wolffian ducts degenerate, yielding classically female genitalia. Figure 1 below shows the production of testosterone from cholesterol.

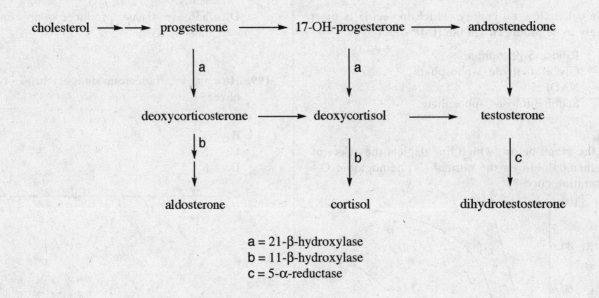

a = 21-β-hydroxylase
b = 11-β-hydroxylase
c = 5-α-reductase

Figure 1 Pathway of steroid production

GO ON TO THE NEXT PAGE.

200. Guevedoche children will develop a penis, scrotum with testicles, and other secondary male characteristics when they reach puberty. Initially perceived as females at birth, some are found to be males before puberty when an ultrasound of masses in their abdomen reveals undescended testicles and the absence of a uterus or fallopian tubes. Based on this information, it is most likely true that guevedoche children:

- **A.** produce MIF at normal levels.
- **B.** produce MIF at greatly elevated levels.
- **C.** produce MIF at greatly reduced levels.
- **D.** do not produce any MIF.

201. Guevedoche lack the ability to make 5-α-reductase *in utero*, and therefore do not develop a penis, scrotum, or prostate at that time. However, these male organs develop as they reach puberty. Which of the following is the most likely explanation for this phenomenon?

- **A.** The penis and scrotum that develop during adolescence are actually labial and clitoral swellings resulting from overexpression of the genes for the estrogen receptor.
- **B.** Because of a lack of 5-α-reductase, testosterone levels are greatly elevated, leading to masculinization of female external genitalia.
- **C.** There are two genes on separate chromosomes for 5-α-reductase, and while one gene is normally expressed *in utero*, the other is not expressed until puberty.
- **D.** Because of a lack of 5-α-reductase, testosterone levels are elevated throughout childhood; then, at puberty, when testosterone and estrogen levels both increase even further, secondary male sex organs appear as a result of overdevelopment of the Wolffian ducts.

202. The higher than normal frequency of guevedoche in the Dominican Republic is the direct product of consanguineous relationships (relationships between close blood relatives). Which type of inheritance pattern is most consistent with increased phenotypic expression of a rare disease arising as a result of inbreeding within a population?

- **A.** X-linked dominant
- **B.** Autosomal dominant
- **C.** Mitochondrial inheritance
- **D.** Autosomal recessive

203. The genital organs of the guevedoche that develop at puberty are derivatives of the mesodermal germ layer. Which of the following is/are also derivatives of the mesodermal germ layer?

- I. Skeletal muscle
- II. Liver
- III. Kidney

- **A.** I only
- **B.** II only
- **C.** I and III only
- **D.** II and III only

204. Deficiency of the 21-β-hydroxylase enzyme is an autosomal recessive disease that is the leading cause of congenital adrenal hyperplasia. Based on Figure 1, which of the following is *least* likely to be a symptom of 21-β-hydroxylase deficiency?

- **A.** Increased levels of 17-hydroxyprogesterone in the serum
- **B.** Affected females presenting with an enlarged clitoris, male pattern baldness, and early puberty
- **C.** Elevated levels of serum potassium with elevated levels of urine sodium
- **D.** Affected males presenting with severe hypertension in early childhood

GO ON TO THE NEXT PAGE.

Passage XI (Questions 205–209)

Carbonyl groups in the linear form of carbohydrates can react with primary amines to form imines (Schiff bases). A spontaneous two-step isomerization known as the *Amadori rearrangement* can then convert the imine to the more stable ketoamine.

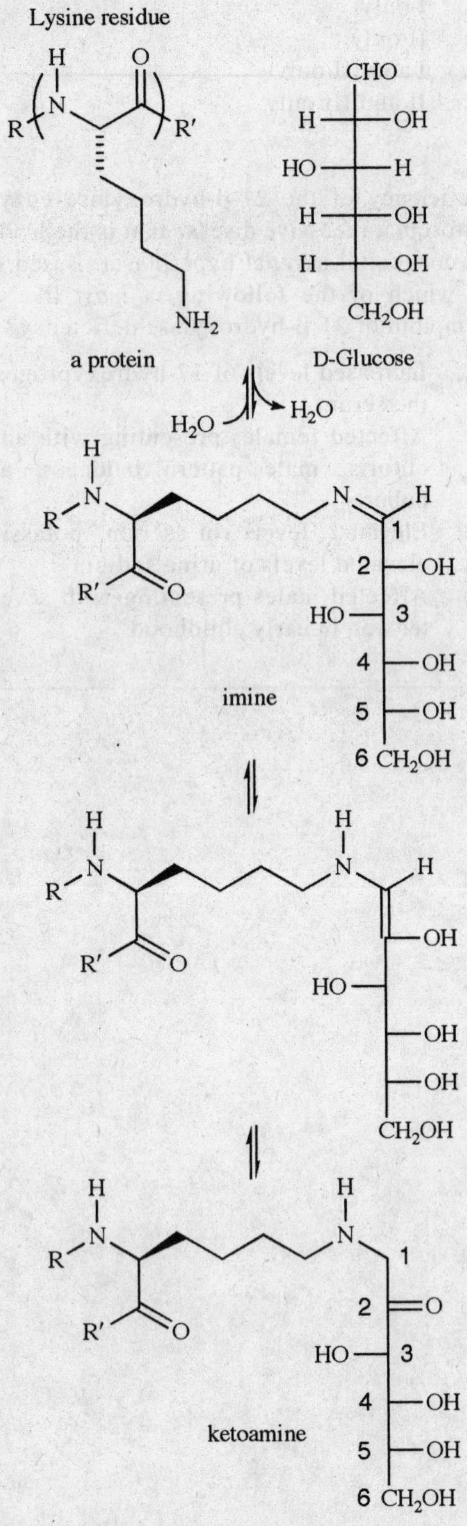

Figure 1 Amadori rearrangement

This reaction occurs within the human body between natural carbohydrates (such as glucose) and primary amines in proteins (such as the lysine side chain).

This spontaneous chemical modification of proteins can inhibit enzymatic activity, protein folding, and protein assembly, as well as generate covalent protein cross-links, leading to a host of deleterious effects. This reaction becomes especially prevalent when glucose levels are high, and it is thought to be one of the mechanisms of long-term cardiovascular and ocular degeneration in diabetic patients.

GO ON TO THE NEXT PAGE.

205. Which of the following is the most likely intermediate in the conversion of glucose to the imine in Figure 1?

A.

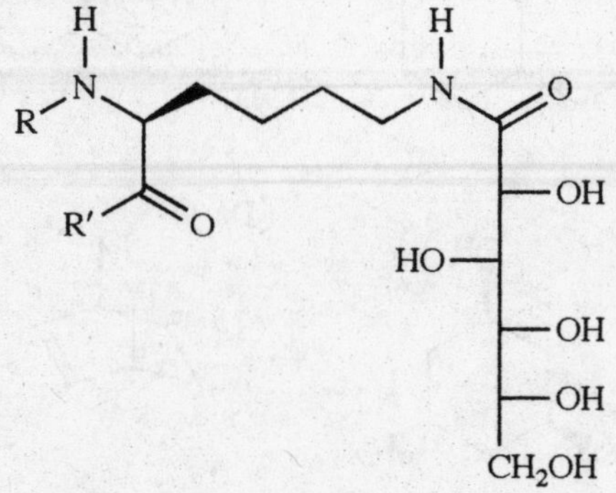

B.

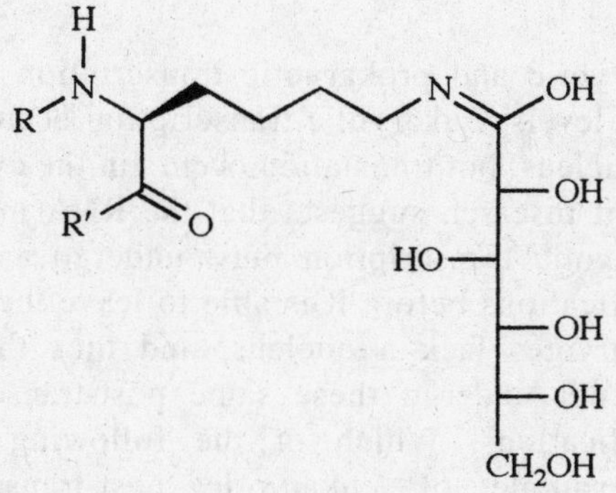

C.

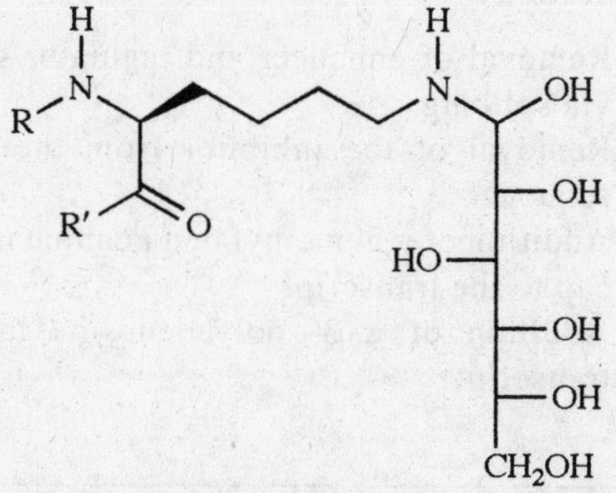

D.

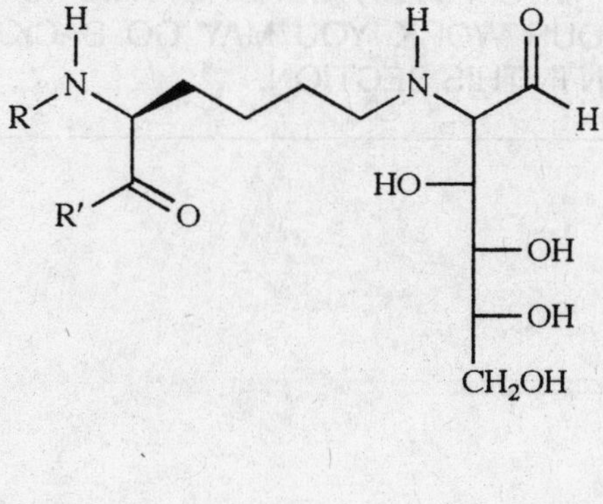

206. The imine and ketoamine shown in Figure 1 are best described as:

A. resonance forms.
B. tautomers.
C. conformational isomers.
D. diastereomers.

207. Following formation of the ketoamine in Figure 1, which carbon stereocenter is most likely to undergo racemization?

A. C-3
B. C-4
C. C-5
D. C-6

208. What other nucleophiles present in proteins might form Schiff bases with glucose?

A. Any cysteine side chain
B. Any glycine side chain
C. The C-terminal amino acid
D. The N-terminal amino acid

209. When treated with Benedict's reagent, the ketoamine formed after lysine reacts with glucose will show:

A. a positive Benedict's test, because the product is a reducing sugar.
B. a negative Benedict's test, because the product is not a reducing sugar.
C. a positive Benedict's test, because the product is not a reducing sugar.
D. a negative Benedict's test, because the product is a reducing sugar.

GO ON TO THE NEXT PAGE.

Questions 210 through 214 are **NOT** based on a descriptive passage.

210. Infants born prematurely are at increased risk of death from respiratory distress syndrome due to their inability to produce enough surfactant. Which of the following is the normal anatomical pathway of the respiratory system?

A. Larynx—pharynx—trachea—bronchioles—bronchi—alveoli

B. Pharynx—trachea—larynx—bronchi—bronchioles—alveoli

C. Pharynx—larynx—trachea—bronchi—bronchioles—alveoli

D. Larynx—pharynx—bronchi—trachea—bronchioles—alveoli

211.

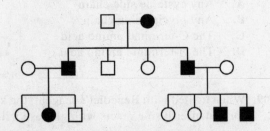

For the pedigree shown above, assume that persons who married into the family do not possess the disease-causing allele. If those with the disease are represented by shaded squares or circles, what is the inheritance pattern of the disease?

A. Mitochondrial

B. X-linked recessive

C. Autosomal recessive

D. Autosomal dominant

212. Which of the following acetylating conditions will convert diethylamine into an amide at the fastest rate?

A. Acetic acid / HCl

B. Acetic anhydride

C. Acetyl chloride

D. Ethyl acetate

213. Which one of the following could have a nonzero optical activity?

A.

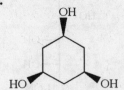

C.

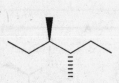

B.

D.

214. Eukaryotic and prokaryotic transcription differ on many levels. Eukaryotic transcription occurs within the nucleus, but translation occurs in the cytoplasm. Recent research suggests that the RNA made from eukaryotic transcription must undergo a series of modifications before it is able to leave the nucleus. Prokaryotes lack a nucleus, and thus their RNA does not undergo these same post-transcriptional modifications. Which of the following is NOT an example of eukaryotic post-transcriptional modification?

A. Removal of enhancer and regulator sequences via splicing

B. Removal of the inhibitor from the repressor sequence

C. Addition of a 5′ methylated guanine nucleotide cap to the transcript

D. Addition of a 3′ polyadenosine tail to the transcript

STOP. IF YOU FINISH BEFORE TIME IS CALLED, CHECK YOUR WORK. YOU MAY GO BACK TO ANY QUESTION IN THIS SECTION.

STOP.

MCAT PRACTICE TEST SCORE CONVERSION CHARTS

Estimated Scaled Score	Physical Sciences Raw Scores
15	74–77
14	72–73
13	68–71
12	66–67
11	61–65
10	56–60
9	52–55
8	46–51
7	41–45
6	33–40
5	27–32
≤4	0–26

Estimated Scaled Score	Verbal Reasoning Raw Scores
15	60–60
14	59–59
13	55–58
12	52–54
11	48–51
10	44–47
9	40–43
8	37–39
7	34–36
6	28–33
5	26–27
≤4	0–25

Estimated Scaled Score	Biological Sciences Raw Scores
15	76–77
14	73–75
13	69–72
12	66–68
11	62–65
10	56–61
9	51–55
8	46–50
7	41–45
6	36–40
5	33–35
≥4	0–32

The Princeton Review

Diagnostic MCAT Form ○ Side 1

1. YOUR NAME:
(Print)

Last   First   M.I.

SIGNATURE: _____ **DATE:** ___/___/___

HOME ADDRESS: _____
(Print)
Number and Street

City   State   Zip

E-MAIL: _____

SCHOOL: _____

PHONE NO.: _____
(Print)

CLASS OF: _____

Completely darken bubbles with a No. 2 pencil. If you make a mistake, be sure to erase mark completely. Erase all stray marks.

► **IMPORTANT:** Please fill in these boxes exactly as shown on the back cover of your test book.

YOUR NAME
First 4 letters of last name | FIRST INIT | MID INIT

(bubbles Ⓐ through Ⓩ for each column)

TEST CODE
(bubbles 0–9)

TEST FORM

SEX
○ MALE
○ FEMALE

OTHER
1 Ⓐ Ⓑ Ⓒ Ⓓ Ⓔ
2 Ⓐ Ⓑ Ⓒ Ⓓ Ⓔ
3 Ⓐ Ⓑ Ⓒ Ⓓ Ⓔ

PHONE NUMBER
(bubbles 0–9)

DATE OF BIRTH

MONTH	DAY	YEAR
○ JAN		
○ FEB		
○ MAR		
○ APR		
○ MAY		
○ JUN		
○ JUL		
○ AUG		
○ SEP		
○ OCT		
○ NOV		
○ DEC		

(answer bubbles A B C D)

1–27, 28–54, 55–77

OpScan iNSIGHT™ forms by Pearson NCS EM-255327-1:654321   Printed in U.S.A.

© The Princeton Review Mgt. L.L.C. 2004

The Princeton Review
Diagnostic MCAT Form ○ Side 2

SECTION 2

SECTION 3

78 Ⓐ Ⓑ Ⓒ Ⓓ
79 Ⓐ Ⓑ Ⓒ Ⓓ
80 Ⓐ Ⓑ Ⓒ Ⓓ

81 Ⓐ Ⓑ Ⓒ Ⓓ
82 Ⓐ Ⓑ Ⓒ Ⓓ

83 Ⓐ Ⓑ Ⓒ Ⓓ
84 Ⓐ Ⓑ Ⓒ Ⓓ

85 Ⓐ Ⓑ Ⓒ Ⓓ
86 Ⓐ Ⓑ Ⓒ Ⓓ
87 Ⓐ Ⓑ Ⓒ Ⓓ

88 Ⓐ Ⓑ Ⓒ Ⓓ
89 Ⓐ Ⓑ Ⓒ Ⓓ
90 Ⓐ Ⓑ Ⓒ Ⓓ

91 Ⓐ Ⓑ Ⓒ Ⓓ
92 Ⓐ Ⓑ Ⓒ Ⓓ

93 Ⓐ Ⓑ Ⓒ Ⓓ
94 Ⓐ Ⓑ Ⓒ Ⓓ

95 Ⓐ Ⓑ Ⓒ Ⓓ
96 Ⓐ Ⓑ Ⓒ Ⓓ
97 Ⓐ Ⓑ Ⓒ Ⓓ

98 Ⓐ Ⓑ Ⓒ Ⓓ
99 Ⓐ Ⓑ Ⓒ Ⓓ
100 Ⓐ Ⓑ Ⓒ Ⓓ

101 Ⓐ Ⓑ Ⓒ Ⓓ
102 Ⓐ Ⓑ Ⓒ Ⓓ

103 Ⓐ Ⓑ Ⓒ Ⓓ
104 Ⓐ Ⓑ Ⓒ Ⓓ

105 Ⓐ Ⓑ Ⓒ Ⓓ
106 Ⓐ Ⓑ Ⓒ Ⓓ
107 Ⓐ Ⓑ Ⓒ Ⓓ

108 Ⓐ Ⓑ Ⓒ Ⓓ
109 Ⓐ Ⓑ Ⓒ Ⓓ
110 Ⓐ Ⓑ Ⓒ Ⓓ

111 Ⓐ Ⓑ Ⓒ Ⓓ
112 Ⓐ Ⓑ Ⓒ Ⓓ

113 Ⓐ Ⓑ Ⓒ Ⓓ
114 Ⓐ Ⓑ Ⓒ Ⓓ

115 Ⓐ Ⓑ Ⓒ Ⓓ
116 Ⓐ Ⓑ Ⓒ Ⓓ
117 Ⓐ Ⓑ Ⓒ Ⓓ

118 Ⓐ Ⓑ Ⓒ Ⓓ
119 Ⓐ Ⓑ Ⓒ Ⓓ
120 Ⓐ Ⓑ Ⓒ Ⓓ

121 Ⓐ Ⓑ Ⓒ Ⓓ
122 Ⓐ Ⓑ Ⓒ Ⓓ

123 Ⓐ Ⓑ Ⓒ Ⓓ
124 Ⓐ Ⓑ Ⓒ Ⓓ

125 Ⓐ Ⓑ Ⓒ Ⓓ
126 Ⓐ Ⓑ Ⓒ Ⓓ
127 Ⓐ Ⓑ Ⓒ Ⓓ

128 Ⓐ Ⓑ Ⓒ Ⓓ
129 Ⓐ Ⓑ Ⓒ Ⓓ
130 Ⓐ Ⓑ Ⓒ Ⓓ

131 Ⓐ Ⓑ Ⓒ Ⓓ
132 Ⓐ Ⓑ Ⓒ Ⓓ

133 Ⓐ Ⓑ Ⓒ Ⓓ
134 Ⓐ Ⓑ Ⓒ Ⓓ

135 Ⓐ Ⓑ Ⓒ Ⓓ
136 Ⓐ Ⓑ Ⓒ Ⓓ
137 Ⓐ Ⓑ Ⓒ Ⓓ

138 Ⓐ Ⓑ Ⓒ Ⓓ
139 Ⓐ Ⓑ Ⓒ Ⓓ
140 Ⓐ Ⓑ Ⓒ Ⓓ

141 Ⓐ Ⓑ Ⓒ Ⓓ
142 Ⓐ Ⓑ Ⓒ Ⓓ

143 Ⓐ Ⓑ Ⓒ Ⓓ
144 Ⓐ Ⓑ Ⓒ Ⓓ

145 Ⓐ Ⓑ Ⓒ Ⓓ
146 Ⓐ Ⓑ Ⓒ Ⓓ
147 Ⓐ Ⓑ Ⓒ Ⓓ

148 Ⓐ Ⓑ Ⓒ Ⓓ
149 Ⓐ Ⓑ Ⓒ Ⓓ
150 Ⓐ Ⓑ Ⓒ Ⓓ

151 Ⓐ Ⓑ Ⓒ Ⓓ
152 Ⓐ Ⓑ Ⓒ Ⓓ

153 Ⓐ Ⓑ Ⓒ Ⓓ
154 Ⓐ Ⓑ Ⓒ Ⓓ

155 Ⓐ Ⓑ Ⓒ Ⓓ
156 Ⓐ Ⓑ Ⓒ Ⓓ
157 Ⓐ Ⓑ Ⓒ Ⓓ

158 Ⓐ Ⓑ Ⓒ Ⓓ
159 Ⓐ Ⓑ Ⓒ Ⓓ
160 Ⓐ Ⓑ Ⓒ Ⓓ

161 Ⓐ Ⓑ Ⓒ Ⓓ
162 Ⓐ Ⓑ Ⓒ Ⓓ

163 Ⓐ Ⓑ Ⓒ Ⓓ
164 Ⓐ Ⓑ Ⓒ Ⓓ

165 Ⓐ Ⓑ Ⓒ Ⓓ
166 Ⓐ Ⓑ Ⓒ Ⓓ
167 Ⓐ Ⓑ Ⓒ Ⓓ

168 Ⓐ Ⓑ Ⓒ Ⓓ
169 Ⓐ Ⓑ Ⓒ Ⓓ
170 Ⓐ Ⓑ Ⓒ Ⓓ

171 Ⓐ Ⓑ Ⓒ Ⓓ
172 Ⓐ Ⓑ Ⓒ Ⓓ

173 Ⓐ Ⓑ Ⓒ Ⓓ
174 Ⓐ Ⓑ Ⓒ Ⓓ

175 Ⓐ Ⓑ Ⓒ Ⓓ
176 Ⓐ Ⓑ Ⓒ Ⓓ
177 Ⓐ Ⓑ Ⓒ Ⓓ

178 Ⓐ Ⓑ Ⓒ Ⓓ
179 Ⓐ Ⓑ Ⓒ Ⓓ
180 Ⓐ Ⓑ Ⓒ Ⓓ

181 Ⓐ Ⓑ Ⓒ Ⓓ
182 Ⓐ Ⓑ Ⓒ Ⓓ

183 Ⓐ Ⓑ Ⓒ Ⓓ
184 Ⓐ Ⓑ Ⓒ Ⓓ

185 Ⓐ Ⓑ Ⓒ Ⓓ
186 Ⓐ Ⓑ Ⓒ Ⓓ
187 Ⓐ Ⓑ Ⓒ Ⓓ

188 Ⓐ Ⓑ Ⓒ Ⓓ
189 Ⓐ Ⓑ Ⓒ Ⓓ
190 Ⓐ Ⓑ Ⓒ Ⓓ

191 Ⓐ Ⓑ Ⓒ Ⓓ
192 Ⓐ Ⓑ Ⓒ Ⓓ

193 Ⓐ Ⓑ Ⓒ Ⓓ
194 Ⓐ Ⓑ Ⓒ Ⓓ

195 Ⓐ Ⓑ Ⓒ Ⓓ
196 Ⓐ Ⓑ Ⓒ Ⓓ
197 Ⓐ Ⓑ Ⓒ Ⓓ

198 Ⓐ Ⓑ Ⓒ Ⓓ
199 Ⓐ Ⓑ Ⓒ Ⓓ
200 Ⓐ Ⓑ Ⓒ Ⓓ

201 Ⓐ Ⓑ Ⓒ Ⓓ
202 Ⓐ Ⓑ Ⓒ Ⓓ

203 Ⓐ Ⓑ Ⓒ Ⓓ
204 Ⓐ Ⓑ Ⓒ Ⓓ

205 Ⓐ Ⓑ Ⓒ Ⓓ
206 Ⓐ Ⓑ Ⓒ Ⓓ
207 Ⓐ Ⓑ Ⓒ Ⓓ

208 Ⓐ Ⓑ Ⓒ Ⓓ
209 Ⓐ Ⓑ Ⓒ Ⓓ
210 Ⓐ Ⓑ Ⓒ Ⓓ

211 Ⓐ Ⓑ Ⓒ Ⓓ
212 Ⓐ Ⓑ Ⓒ Ⓓ

213 Ⓐ Ⓑ Ⓒ Ⓓ
214 Ⓐ Ⓑ Ⓒ Ⓓ

IF YOU NEED MORE SPACE, PLEASE CONTINUE ON THE NEXT PAGE.

STOP here for Part 1. Do not turn to the next page until told to do so.

**DO NOT WRITE
ON THIS
PAGE**

IF YOU NEED MORE SPACE, PLEASE CONTINUE ON THE NEXT PAGE.

STOP here for Part 2. Do not return to Part 1.

PART

PART ◆ III

MCAT Practice Test 1:
Answers and Explanations

MCAT PRACTICE TEST 1 ANSWER KEYS

PHYSICAL SCIENCES

1	B	11	A	21	D	31	D	41	D	51	B	61	A	71	A
2	D	12	B	22	D	32	C	42	C	52	D	62	B	72	C
3	C	13	D	23	B	33	A	43	D	53	C	63	B	73	B
4	D	14	A	24	B	34	C	44	B	54	C	64	C	74	A
5	B	15	A	25	C	35	B	45	A	55	A	65	A	75	C
6	B	16	D	26	C	36	A	46	D	56	B	66	A	76	D
7	C	17	C	27	A	37	C	47	A	57	B	67	B	77	C
8	C	18	B	28	D	38	D	48	A	58	A	68	C		
9	A	19	C	29	B	39	C	49	C	59	B	69	D		
10	A	20	C	30	D	40	C	50	C	60	C	70	B		

VERBAL REASONING

78	A	88	C	98	C	108	B	118	C	128	D
79	D	89	D	99	C	109	A	119	B	129	A
80	B	90	D	100	C	110	C	120	C	130	C
81	D	91	D	101	A	111	D	121	A	131	D
82	C	92	A	102	D	112	C	122	B	132	C
83	C	93	B	103	C	113	D	123	B	133	D
84	C	94	B	104	B	114	B	124	B	134	A
85	B	95	D	105	A	115	C	125	C	135	D
86	A	96	A	106	C	116	C	126	D	136	D
87	B	97	B	107	A	117	A	127	C	137	A

BIOLOGICAL SCIENCES

138	B	148	D	158	A	168	A	178	B	188	D	198	C	208	D
139	C	149	D	159	C	169	C	179	A	189	B	199	B	209	A
140	D	150	D	160	B	170	B	180	D	190	C	200	A	210	C
141	A	151	C	161	D	171	D	181	C	191	D	201	C	211	D
142	C	152	A	162	B	172	B	182	A	192	A	202	D	212	C
143	A	153	C	163	A	173	C	183	A	193	D	203	C	213	A
144	A	154	B	164	B	174	B	184	C	194	A	204	D	214	B
145	C	155	B	165	A	175	D	185	B	195	B	205	C		
146	B	156	A	166	D	176	C	186	D	196	C	206	B		
147	C	157	D	167	B	177	C	187	B	197	D	207	A		

ANSWERS AND EXPLANATIONS

PHYSICAL SCIENCES

Questions 1–77

Passage I (Questions 1–5)

1. If the capacitor plates were fully charged by the 9 V battery, what is the charge on the positive plate?

   A. 15.8 pC
   B. 31.5 pC
   C. 47.3 pC
   D. 63.0 pC

   B By definition, $Q = CV = (3.5 \text{ pF})(9 \text{ V}) = 31.5$ pC.

2. The sensor device D shown in Figure 1 performs its function by acting as:

   A. an ohmmeter.
   B. a voltmeter.
   C. a potentiometer.
   D. an ammeter.

   D The passage states that the alarm sounds when the sensor device detects a drop in current. Therefore, the sensor performs its function by measuring current; it is an ammeter.

3. Which of the following would decrease the capacitance of the capacitor in the detector?

   A. Placing a 1-mm-thick layer of polystyrene between the plates
   B. Moving the plates closer together
   C. Using smaller electrode plates
   D. Using a 6 V battery instead of a 9 V battery

   C Choice A is wrong since the insertion of a dielectric always increases the capacitance. Choice B is wrong since a decrease in d implies an increase in C (note Equation 1 in the passage). Choice D has no effect on the capacitance, so the answer must be choice C: a smaller A implies a smaller C (again, note Equation 1).

4. What is the magnitude of the electric field between the electrodes when the plates are charged to a potential difference of 9 V?

   A. 0.045 V/m
   B. 0.9 V/m
   C. 45 V/m
   D. 1800 V/m

   D Using the equation $V = Ed$, we find that $E = V/d = (9 \text{ V})/(5 \times 10^{-3} \text{ m}) = 1.8 \times 10^3$ V/m.

5. The current that exists in the circuit depicted in Figure 1 generates a weak magnetic field. Which of the following diagrams best illustrates the magnetic field $\vec{B}$ created by the current I in the wire?

   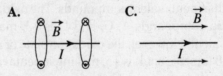

   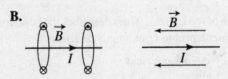

   B The magnetic field lines created by a straight wire are circles which wrap around the wire; this eliminates choices C and D. Furthermore, the direction of the magnetic field lines obeys the right-hand rule. Grasping the wire in your right hand with your thumb pointing in the direction of the conventional current I (which in this case means to the right), your fingers curl out of the plane of the page above the wire and into the plane of the page below the wire.

Passage II (Questions 6–11)

6. Of the following, which is likely to be the least toxic?

A.

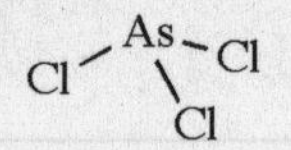

B.

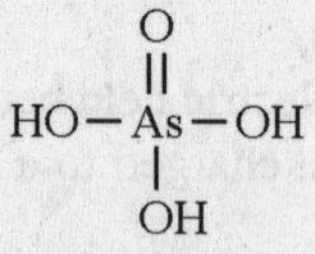

C.

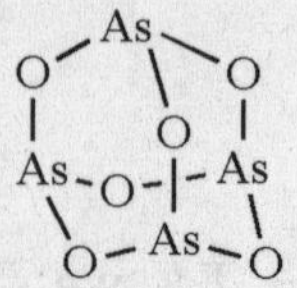

D.

B The passage states that trivalent compounds are more toxic than pentavalent compounds. The oxidation state of As in compounds A, C, and D is +3, making them all trivalent. However, the oxidation state of As in compound B (arsenic acid) is +5, making it pentavalent and thus less toxic.

7. Which of the following best describes the bond formed by dimercaprol to compounds of arsenic?

A. Network covalent
B. Ionic
C. Coordinate covalent
D. Metallic

C The bond between S and As is covalent, so eliminate choices B and D. Network covalent bonds are connected in a lattice of covalent bonds such as diamond or quartz. Dimercaprol is a chelator (Lewis base) that donates full electron pairs to form coordinate covalent bonds, so C is the best choice.

8. Methylarsonic acid, $CH_3AsO(OH)_2$, is isolated in a laboratory analysis. What is its molecular shape?

A. Square planar
B. See-saw
C. Tetrahedral
D. Trigonal bipyramidal

C In this compound, As has no lone pairs and is surrounded by four electron groups, as indicated by the structure shown below.

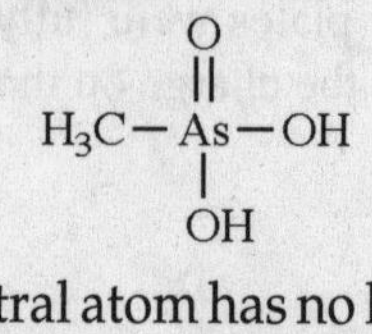

Because the central atom has no lone pairs, the shape cannot be square planar or see-saw (eliminating choices A and B). And since the central atom is surrounded by four electron groups, not five, the shape must be tetrahedral (choice C), not trigonal bipyramidal (choice D).

9. The role of dimercaprol in chelation therapy is best described as a:

A. ligand that donates electron pairs.
B. ligand that accepts electron pairs.
C. Lewis acid that donates electron pairs.
D. Lewis acid that accepts electron pairs.

A Lewis bases, or ligands, donate electron pairs and Lewis acids accept electron pairs, so eliminate choices B and C. Dimercaprol donates electron pairs to effectively bind arsenic compounds, so A is the best choice.

10. Which of the following molecules are most likely to be appropriate for chelation therapy to treat toxic metal poisoning?

$C_{17}N_4O_2H_{22}$

I   II   III

A. I and II only
B. I and III only
C. II and III only
D. I, II, and III

A Compound I, succimer, has two S moieties with lone pairs of electrons available to donate and form a stable ring around a metal compound. Compound II, penicillamine, has an S moiety and N moiety, each with a lone pair of electrons available for donating to form a stable ring around a metal compound. (In fact, both I and II are compounds used in chelation therapy.) Compound III, sildenafil, has an S and N moiety, but the S has no lone pairs to donate. This would be an ineffective chelator.

11. A sample of soil with suspected arsenic contamination has an Eh of 0.25 V and pH 6. Which of the following steps would be most effective in limiting potential toxicity?

A. Alkalinizing the soil
B. Aerating the soil
C. Acidifying the soil
D. Removing reducing agents from the soil

A At this Eh and pH, the most likely form of arsenic, according to Figure 2 in the passage, would be $H_2AsO_4^-$. This is a pentavalent form. Adding oxygen via aeration (lowers Eh), acidifying the soil (lowers pH), or removing reducing agents from the soil (lowers Eh), would all steer conditions toward H_3AsO_3. This is a trivalent, and thus more toxic form of arsenic. Alkalinizing the soil would maintain pentavalent forms.

Passage III (Questions 12–17)

12. Of the following, which one is the best reducing agent?

A. Li^+
B. Li
C. Cl^-
D. F^-

B The best reducing agent will be the species that is most easily oxidized. Li^+, which is already oxidized, cannot act as a reducing agent, eliminating choice A. The oxidations of Li, Cl^-, and F^- are the reverse of the corresponding reduction reactions in Table 1. Since the reduction of Li^+ to Li has the lowest reduction potential, the oxidation of Li to Li^+ is the most favorable of the three oxidations reactions left to consider, implying that Li is the best reducing agent of the choices given. Intuitively, it's a far stronger reducing agent than Cl^- or F^- due to the ease with which lithium will lose its single valence-shell electron to become a closed-shell cation. Halogen anions, such as Cl^- and F^-, do not readily donate electrons, since by doing so, they would lose their acquired closed-shell configuration.

13. When a lead storage battery recharges, what happens to the density of the battery fluid?

A. It decreases to 1.0 g/cm^3.
B. It increases to 1.0 g/cm^3.
C. It decreases to 1.2 g/cm^3.
D. It increases to 1.2 g/cm^3.

D The passage states that the density of the fluid in a fully charged battery is 1.2 g/cm^3. Since the density *decreases* as the battery is being *discharged* (because sulfate ions are being consumed), the fluid density must *increase* when the battery is *recharging*.

14. In which of the following situations would a voltaic cell have the highest voltage?

    A.   When $Q < 1$
    B.   When $Q = 1$
    C.   When $Q > 1$
    D.   The cell voltage is independent of Q.

A According to the Nernst equation, E will be greatest when the log term is most negative (subtracting a *negative* quantity from $E°$ will cause E to be *greater* than $E°$). Since log Q is negative when $0 < Q < 1$, the answer here is A.

15. Which one of the following represents a galvanic cell?

    A. $Zn(s) \mid Zn^{2+}(1\ M) \parallel Cu^{2+}(1\ M) \mid Cu(s)$
    B. $Cu(s) \mid Cu^{+}(1\ M) \parallel Cu^{2+}(1\ M) \mid Cu(s)$
    C. $Cl^{-}(1\ M) \mid Cl_2(g) \parallel Li^{+}(1\ M) \mid Li(s)$
    D. $Zn(s) \mid Zn^{2+}(1\ M) \parallel Al^{3+}(1\ M) \mid Al(s)$

A A galvanic cell is one in which the chemical reaction occurs spontaneously to produce an electron flow and will have a positive E_{cell}. In the cell diagram, the anode (where oxidation occurs) is written to the left of the double vertical line, and the cathode (where reduction occurs) is written to the right. The cell in choice A, then, has the oxidation of Zn to Zn^{2+} at the anode [potential $= -(-0.76\ V) = +0.76\ V$], and reduction of Cu^{2+} to Cu at the cathode [potential $= +0.34\ V$], giving an overall cell voltage of $E_{cell} = +0.76\ V + 0.34\ V = +1.10\ V$. Since $E_{cell} > 0$, this must be the galvanic cell. The overall voltages of the cells diagrammed in choices B, C, and D are all negative and are therefore not galvanic cells (they are electrolytic cells).

16. If the reaction in a concentration cell is spontaneous in the reverse direction, then:

    A. $Q < K$, ΔG for the forward reaction is negative, and the cell voltage is positive.
    B. $Q < K$, ΔG for the forward reaction is positive, and the cell voltage is negative.
    C. $Q > K$, ΔG for the forward reaction is negative, and the cell voltage is positive.
    D. $Q > K$, ΔG for the forward reaction is positive, and the cell voltage is negative.

D The reaction quotient Q, like the equilibrium constant K, is expressed as the concentrations of products divided by the concentrations of the reactants. Q, however, describes the ratio of products to reactants at any time during the course of the reaction, not just at equilibrium. Given that the reaction will proceed toward equilibrium, if a reaction is proceeding in the reverse direction, then Q must be greater than K (meaning that there are more products and less reactants at this time than at equilibrium). This eliminates choices A and B. If the reaction is spontaneous in the reverse direction, then it is nonspotaneous in the forward direction, so ΔG for the forward reaction must be positive, implying that the cell voltage is negative.

17. People living in cold climates sometimes have trouble starting their cars on cold mornings. Frustrated drivers complain that the battery has "gone dead." If the temperature coefficient for voltage loss is $-1.5 \times 10^{-4}\ V/°C$ and the temperature drops by 40°C, is the battery "going dead" a logical explanation for the car not starting?

    A.   Yes, because the large temperature drop causes a significant drop in the intrinsic cell voltage.
    B.   Yes, because the internal resistance of the battery decreases as the temperature decreases.
    C.   No, because the large temperature drop does not by itself cause a significant drop in cell voltage.
    D.   No, because the internal resistance of the battery decreases as the temperature decreases.

C The voltage change due to a 40°C drop in temperature is $(-1.5 \times 10^{-4}\ V/°C)(40°C) = -0.006\ V$, which is insignificant (it's only a 0.05% decrease). Therefore, A is wrong. Also, choices B and D do not answer the question; the answer must be C. The reason batteries don't work when it's cold is that the viscosity of the electrolyte increases as the temperature decreases, which significantly reduces the conductivity of the solution. The ions move much more slowly, the resistance of the fluid increases, and the power ouput of the battery decreases. When the temperature rises again, the viscosity returns to normal, and the battery recovers.

Passage IV (Questions 18–23)

18. Four flywheels with the same dimensions are spinning with the same angular speed. According to Equation 1, the flywheel composed of which one of the following materials has the greatest rotational kinetic energy?

- A. Aluminum
- B. Brass
- C. Carbon fibers
- D. Steel

B Since all the wheels have the same ω, the wheel with the greatest I will have the greatest kinetic energy, because $KE_{rot} = (1/2)I\omega^2$. Since all the wheels have the same dimensions, the equation $I = (1/2)MR^2$ implies that the wheel with the greatest mass will have the greatest I. But again, because the dimensions are the same, the wheel with the greatest mass will be the one with the greatest density. This is brass, according to Table 1.

19. If all of the following wheels have the same mass and outer radius, which one has the greatest moment of inertia?

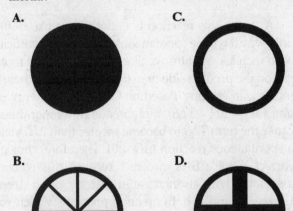

A.

C.

B.

D.

C The passage states that "the more mass on the average that is located farther from the axis [of rotation], the greater the moment of inertia." Since each wheel has the same overall mass, Wheel C has the most mass located farther from the axis (which, as in Figure 1, is perpendicular to the face of the wheel, through its center).

20. When compared to flywheels made of lower density materials, flywheels made of higher density materials tend to break apart at high angular speeds because:

- A. the centrifugal force on any portion of the wheel is smaller.
- B. the centripetal force on any portion of the wheel is smaller.
- C. the inertia of any portion of the wheel is larger.
- D. the radius of any portion of the wheel is smaller.

C The greater the density of the material, the greater the mass (or, equivalently, the inertia) of any portion, or "chunk," of the wheel. If the molecular bonds are not strong enough to provide the necessary centripetal force to move the "chunk" in a circular path, the material breaks. (Each "chunk" has the tendency to move in a straight line due to its inertia.)

21. In theory, a flywheel constructed of which of the materials listed in Table 1 would be able to store the *least* amount of energy?

- A. Aluminum
- B. Brass
- C. Glass
- D. Iron

D The passage states, "In theory, the amount of energy that can be stored is maximized when the ratio $[\sigma/\rho]$ is maximized...." Therefore, it is reasonable to conclude that the amount of energy that can be stored is *minimized* when this ratio is *smallest*. Of the materials listed in Table 1, iron has the smallest σ/ρ ratio.

22. Which of the following best describes the energy transfers that take place starting at the power source and ending with the motion of a car powered by a flywheel system?

- A. Chemical, electrical, kinetic
- B. Electrical, kinetic, electrical
- C. Chemical, kinetic, electrical, kinetic
- D. Electrical, kinetic, electrical, kinetic

D Because the end of the transfer is the motion of the car, the sequence must end with kinetic energy, so eliminate choice B, and since the transfer begins at the power source (which is an *electric* power source, as stated in the last paragraph of the passage), eliminate choices A and C. The answer must be D, consistent with the description in the last paragraph of the passage.

23. A flywheel of mass 400 kg and radius 0.5 m is rotating at an angular speed ω of 20 rad/s. What is the magnitude of the centripetal acceleration of a point on the outer rim of this wheel?

A. 100 m/s^2
B. 200 m/s^2
C. 400 m/s^2
D. 800 m/s^2

B Centripetal acceleration is $v^2/R = (\omega R)^2/R = \omega^2 R$. Therefore, $a_c = \omega^2 R = (20 \text{ rad/s})^2(0.5 \text{ m}) = 200 \text{ m/s}^2$.

Free-Standing Questions (24–28)

24. Nitrogen has the highest oxidation number in which of the following compounds?

A. NH_3
B. NO_3^-
C. NO_2
D. N_2

B The oxidation state of nitrogen in NH_3 is -3 because each hydrogen is $+1$ and the molecule is neutral. The oxidation number of nitrogen in NO_3^- is $+5$ because each oxygen is -2 and the molecule has an overall charge of -1. The oxidation state of nitrogen in NO_2 is $+4$ because each oxygen is -2 and the molecule is neutral. The oxidation number of nitrogen in N_2 is 0 because N_2 is the elemental form of nitrogen. Therefore, nitrogen has the highest oxidation number in NO_3^-.

25. A particle of mass 0.1 kg is moving at constant speed in a circular path of radius 50 cm. If the net force on the particle is 4 N, what is its kinetic energy?

A. 0.1 J
B. 0.5 J
C. 1 J
D. 2 J

C The net force on an object undergoing uniform circular motion is the centripetal force, mv^2/r. If this equals 4 N, then $mv^2 = (4 \text{ N})r$. Since we are given that $r = 0.5$ m, we find that $mv^2 = 2$ J. Therefore, $KE = (1/2)mv^2 = (1/2)(2 \text{ J}) = 1 \text{ J}$.

26. An object is placed 6 cm from a convex lens whose radius of curvature is 4 cm. How far is the image from the lens?

A. 1.5 cm
B. 2.4 cm
C. 3 cm
D. 12 cm

C If the radius of curvature of the lens is 4 cm, then its focal length is $f = (1/2)R = 2$ cm. Substituting $f = 2$ cm and $o = 6$ cm into the lens equation, $1/o + 1/i = 1/f$, we find that $i = 3$ cm.

27. Under standard conditions, the reaction

$$2 \text{ NOCl}(g) \rightarrow 2 \text{ NO}(g) + \text{Cl}_2(g) \qquad \Delta H = +77 \text{ kJ}$$

is not spontaneous. Which of the following changes to the reaction conditions could make this process spontaneous?

A. Raising the temperature
B. Lowering the temperature
C. Increasing the pressure
D. Decreasing the pressure

A Since this reaction is endothermic ($\Delta H > 0$), the only way it will be spontaneous is if there is a sufficiently high increase in entropy. Since there are more moles of gas on the product side than the reactant side, there is an increase in entropy. Based on Gibbs' Free Energy equation ($\Delta G = \Delta H - T\Delta S$), a high enough temperature will cause the term $T\Delta S$ to become greater than ΔH, yielding a spontaneous reaction ($\Delta G < 0$). Therefore, choice A is correct. Choice B is incorrect because this reaction is associated with an increase in entropy, not a decrease. Choices C and D both mention pressure, which would not impact on the thermodynamics of this reaction. Pressure plays a role in reaction kinetics and equilibrium.

28. If an object is moving to the right along a straight line and at a constantly decreasing speed, then which one of the following must be true?

A. The object's velocity is parallel to its acceleration.
B. The net force on the object is directed to the right.
C. The object's momentum is directed to the left.
D. The total work performed on the object is negative.

D The object described in the question has a velocity that is directed to the right but whose acceleration is directed in the opposite direction, to the left (since it is slowing down); this eliminates choice A. Because the acceleration is always parallel to the net force (by Newton's second law, $\mathbf{F}_{net} = m\mathbf{a}$), $\mathbf{F}_{net}$ points to the left, eliminating choice B. Finally, because the momentum $\mathbf{p}$ is equal to $m\mathbf{v}$, the object's momentum is always parallel to its velocity; since $\mathbf{v}$ is directed to the right, so is $\mathbf{p}$; this eliminates choice C. The answer must be D. An object that is losing speed is losing kinetic energy, so ΔKE is negative; by the work–energy theorem, $W_{total} = \Delta KE$, W_{total} must also be negative.

Passage V (Questions 29–34)

29. Which of the following would the researcher be *least* likely to observe as temperature and humidity increase in the experiment described in the passage?

 A. Decreased O_2 generation from candles
 B. Increased CO_2 clearance by LiOH canisters
 C. Increased compartment pressure
 D. Increased partial pressure of $H_2O(g)$

B Oxygen candles are self-sustaining from the exothermic oxidation of Fe. Both H_2O and increased temperature would not favor the forward reaction (eliminates A). Likewise, increased T and H_2O will not favor the forward reaction of LiOH canisters (B is correct). In a closed container with constant V, as T increases, P increases (eliminates C). H_2O is generated from LiOH and respiration, increasing the partial pressure of H_2O vapor (eliminates D).

30. In the experiment, if each worker generates 1.5 kg/hr of CO_2, how often must the LiOH canisters be changed to maintain ambient O_2 at 1.0%?

 A. Every hour
 B. Every 2 hours
 C. Every 7 hours
 D. Every 10 hours

D The CO_2 generated by four workers is (4)(1.5 kg/hr) = 6 kg/hr. If two canisters are in operation, then each is responsible for half the load, or 3 kg/hr. At this rate, the canisters must be changed every 10 hours (according to Figure 1) to maintain ambient CO_2 at 1.0%.

31. Tachypnea (increased breathing rate) results from breathing air with elevated CO_2 in the environment. What result would tachypnea have on a trapped miner?

 A. Increased survival time from increased O_2 partial pressure
 B. Increased survival time from decreased O_2 consumption
 C. Decreased survival time from decreased CO_2 partial pressure
 D. Decreased survival time from increased O_2 consumption

D Anything that increases breathing rate in a closed atmosphere will be bad for survival (eliminates A and B) because more O_2 is consumed (D is correct) and more CO_2 is generated. The partial pressure of CO_2 will rise with time (eliminates C).

32. If all the emergency atmosphere equipment in the experiment described in the passage were unavailable, about how long would the miners have before reaching a critical O_2 level?

 A. 4 days
 B. 6 days
 C. 8 days
 D. 10 days

C Rearranging Equation 1 in the passage to solve for critical O_2 time gives

$$t = \frac{V}{RN}(O_2\%_{initial} - O_2\%_{crit})$$

From the passage, a partial pressure of 130 torr is critical for O_2, which corresponds to (130 torr/760 torr)(100%) = 17% at 1 atm. So, plugging in this value of $O_2\%_{crit}$, along with the values of $O_2\%_{initial}$, V, R, and N given in the passage, we find that

$$t = \frac{V}{RN}(O_2\%_{initial} - O_2\%_{crit})$$

$$= \frac{5.4 \times 10^2 \text{ L}}{2.7 \frac{L}{hr} \cdot 4}(21\% - 17\%)$$

$$= 200 \text{ hr}$$

$$\approx 8 \text{ days}$$

33. Of the following actions, which one would likely be the most advantageous for survival in the experiment?

A. Spreading the LiOH on blankets on the ground
B. Digging to expand the floodable volume
C. Burning the oxygen candles in a fire
D. Partially flooding the compartment to raise compartment pressure

A Spreading LiOH increases surface area, rate, and efficiency of CO_2 removal (A is best). Changing V would slightly change both O_2 and CO_2 partial pressures (not one preferentially), and require increased exertion (B) or risk of exposure (D). Fires in enclosed spaces consume valuable O_2, negating the use of candles (C is wrong).

34. Suppose that after three days of being trapped in a shaft without emergency equipment, a miner is able to dig a very small hole that opens to the outside air. Which of the following will happen to the gases in the shaft?

A. CO_2 will escape more rapidly than O_2, because it has a greater kinetic energy.
B. CO_2 will escape more slowly than O_2, because it is moving against its concentration gradient.
C. O_2 will escape more rapidly than CO_2, and the mole fraction of O_2 will increase.
D. O_2 will escape more slowly than CO_2, and the mole fraction of CO_2 will decrease.

C At the same temperature, CO_2 and O_2 have the same average kinetic energy (A is wrong). Graham's law states that relative escape velocities of gas molecules are inversely proportional to the square root of their masses: $v_1/v_2 = \sqrt{m_2/m_1}$. CO_2 escapes more slowly, but moves down its concentration gradient to the outside air where CO_2% would be lower (B is wrong). O_2 escapes more rapidly, but relatively more O_2 will come into the chamber to establish equilibrium, thus raising the mole fraction of O_2 inside the sfaft (C is correct). Although the mole fraction of CO_2 decreases with time, O_2 escapes more rapidly (D is wrong).

Passage VI (Questions 35–40)

35. Which one of the following is NOT a possible Lewis dot structure for N_2O_5?

A.

C.

B.

D.

B The structure shown in B cannot be correct because the net charge on the structure is –2, but N_2O_5 is a neutral molecule.

36. What is the average rate of Reaction 1, the thermal decomposition of N_2O_5?

A. 4.2×10^{-4} M/min
B. 5.5×10^{-4} M/min
C. 8.4×10^{-4} M/min
D. 1.1×10^{-3} M/min

A The concentration of N_2O_5 drops from 2.0 M to 1.0 M in approximately 1,200 min. Since the coefficient of N_2O_5 in the balanced reaction is 2 (see Reaction 1),

$$\text{rate} = -\frac{1}{\text{coeff of }X} \cdot \frac{\Delta[\text{reactant }X]}{\Delta t}$$
$$= -\frac{1}{2} \cdot \frac{(1.0-2.0)\,M}{1200\text{ min}}$$
$$= 4.2 \times 10^{-4}\,M/\text{min}$$

37. The most likely reason NO_2 is soluble in CCl_4 but O_2 is not is that:

A. NO_2 forms stronger intramolecular bonds than O_2.
B. NO_2 forms weaker intramolecular bonds than O_2.
C. NO_2 experiences stronger London dispersion forces with CCl_4 than O_2 does.
D. NO_2 is triatomic but O_2 is diatomic.

C Recall that solubility depends on intermolecular associations between solute and solvent; therefore, choices A and B are eliminated since they refer to intramolecular (covalent) bonds. Choice D can be eliminated because the number of atoms is not important. Choice C must be correct since it is the only statement that discusses intermolecular forces.

38. What is the rate law for the overall reaction $2 H_2 + O_2 \rightarrow 2 H_2O$?

- A. Rate = $k [H_2][O_2]$
- B. Rate = $k [H_2]_2[O_2]$
- C. Rate = $k [2H_2][O_2]$
- D. Cannot be determined from the information given

D The passage states that reaction rate laws must be empirically determined. Without empirical data, it is not possible to determine the rate law.

39. Monitoring which one of the following quantities would be *least* helpful in calculating the number of moles of NO_2 produced in Reaction 1?

- A. Temperature of the system
- B. Pressure of the system
- C. Volume of reactant
- D. Volume of products

C Since the oxygen produced is a gas and its volume is being measured in a manometer, the number of moles can be calculated using the Ideal-Gas law: $n = PV/(RT)$. Therefore, it is important to measure the pressure, volume, and temperature of $O_2(g)$, but not the volume of reactant.

40. What is the half-life of N_2O_5?

- A. 580 min
- B. 720 min
- C. 1180 min
- D. 2430 min

C The half-life is the time required for half of the substance to disappear. Looking at the graph in Figure 1, the time required for N_2O_5 to drop from a concentration of 2.0 M to 1.0 M is approximately 1200 min.

Passage VII (Questions 41–46)

41. After ^{131}I decays, what is the daughter nucleus?

- A. ^{130}Te
- B. ^{131}Te
- C. ^{130}Xe
- D. ^{131}Xe

D According to Table 2, ^{131}I decays by β^- emission; that is, the nucleus transforms a neutron into a proton and an electron (and an antineutrino, which is of no concern here) and then emits the electron. As a result, the daughter nucleus has 1 more proton but the same mass number. Therefore, the daughter is ^{131}Xe. The nuclear reaction is

$$^{131}_{53}I \rightarrow {}^{131}_{54}Xe + {}^{0}_{-1}e^-$$

42. A physician injects a patient with a small sample of $^{42}KCl(aq)$ in order to help her detect a tumor. How long must the patient wait until the activity drops to 5% of its initial value?

- A. 32 hr
- B. 40 hr
- C. 52 hr
- D. 64 hr

C Equation 2 tells us that the activity is proportional to the number of radioactive nuclei present at any time, and according to Table 2, the half-life of ^{42}K is 12 hours. Therefore, since the number of radioactive nuclei present drops by 1/2 every 12 hours, so will the activity. Consider the sequence 100% → 50% → 25% → 12.5% → 6.25% → 3.125%, where each arrow represents the passage of one half-life. Since 5% is between 6.25% and 3.125%, a time interval of between 4 and 5 half-lives—that is, a time interval between 48 hours and 60 hours—will be required for the activity to drop to 5% of its initial value. Only choice C falls in this range.

43. It can be inferred from the passage that compared to β particles, α particles of the same energy are:

    A. less harmful, because they travel a shorter distance due to their greater mass.

    B. less harmful, because they carry a smaller electric charge.

    C. more harmful, because they deliver a greater absorbed dose.

    D. more harmful, because they deposit larger amounts of energy over small regions.

D Because α particles have a much greater radiation weighting factor than β particles do, α particles are intrinsically more harmful to biological systems; this eliminates choices A and B. (Choice B could also be eliminated since α particles carry a *greater* electric charge than β particles.) Choice C is a trap: all things being equal, α particles would deliver the same *absorbed dose*, but it's the *dose equivalent* that most directly measures the biological effect of radiation. The passage states that "β particles . . . deposit a relatively small amount [of energy] over any small region," and β particles have the lowest weighting factor. Since α particles have the highest weighting factor, we can infer that, in contrast to β particles, α particles deposit *larger* amounts of energy over small regions.

44. If a sample of $Na^{18}F$ has an approximately constant activity of 10^9 decays/sec over a time interval of 1 minute, and all of the emitted radiation energy is absorbed by 2 kg of body tissue, what is the dose equivalent?

    A. 0.3 rad

    B. 0.3 rem

    C. 0.6 rad

    D. 0.6 rem

B First, eliminate choices A and C; the question asks for dose equivalent, which is expressed in rems, not rads. Since Table 2 tells us that each decay of ^{18}F emits a β⁺ particle with an energy of 0.6 MeV, the total energy delivered in 1 minute by this sample is

$$\frac{10^9 \text{ decays}}{\text{sec}} \cdot \frac{0.6 \text{ MeV}}{\text{decay}} \cdot \frac{60 \text{ sec}}{\text{min}} \cdot 1 \text{ min} = 3.6 \times 10^{10} \text{ MeV}$$

Dividing this by 2 kg gives the absorbed dose:

$$D = \frac{3.6 \times 10^{10} \text{ MeV}}{2 \text{ kg}} = \frac{1.8 \times 10^{10} \text{ MeV}}{\text{kg}}$$

Converting this to rads, we get

$$(1.8 \times 10^{10} \tfrac{\text{MeV}}{\text{kg}}) \cdot \frac{1 \text{ rad}}{(6.25 \times 10^{10} \tfrac{\text{MeV}}{\text{kg}})} = \frac{1.8}{6.25} \text{ rad} \approx 0.3 \text{ rad}$$

Finally, since $w_R = 1$ for β⁺ particles, the dose equivalent of 0.3 rad by β⁺ particles is 0.3 rem, choice B.

45. If all of the following radiations deposit 10^{12} MeV of energy to human tissue, which one would be most likely to cause the greatest harm?

    A. 10 kg of tissue absorbing 50-keV neutrons

    B. 40 kg of tissue absorbing α particles

    C. 2 kg of tissue absorbing γ-rays

    D. 10 kg of tissue absorbing 3-MeV protons

A Here we use the data given in Table 1. The radiation most likely to cause the greatest harm is the one that delivers the greatest dose equivalent. In each case, the absorbed dose D is equal to the total absorbed energy, $E = 10^{12}$ MeV, divided by the appropriate mass of body tissue; then, multiplying this result by the weighting factor gives the dose equivalent, $DE = w_R \cdot D$. We find that

    choice A: $DE = 10 \cdot E/10 \;\;= E$
    choice B: $DE = 20 \cdot E/40 \;\;= E/2$
    choice C: $DE = 1 \cdot E/2 \;\;\;\;\;= E/2$
    choice D: $DE = 5 \cdot E/10 \;\;\;= E/2$

Clearly, then, the radiation described in choice A delivers the greatest dose equivalent.

46. Compared to that of ^{58}Co, the decay constant λ of ^{131}I is:

    A. smaller by a factor of 9.

    B. smaller by a factor of (9/1.4).

    C. larger by a factor of (9/1.4).

    D. larger by a factor of 9.

D According to Table 2, the half-life of ^{131}I (8 days) is 9 times less than the half-life of ^{58}Co (72 days). Because we're told that the average lifetime τ is proportional to the half-life, it follows that the value of τ for ^{131}I is also 9 times less than that of ^{58}Co. But the decay constant λ is the *reciprocal* of τ, so the value of λ for ^{131}I is 9 times greater than that of ^{58}Co.

Passage VIII (Questions 47–51)

47. Which of the following best characterizes the process of vaporization?

    A. Increase in entropy, increase in enthalpy
    B. Increase in entropy, decrease in enthalpy
    C. Decrease in entropy, increase in enthalpy
    D. Decrease in entropy, decrease in enthalpy

A Vaporization is the process of transforming a liquid into a gas. Molecules are going from a more ordered liquid state to a more disordered gaseous state, increasing entropy (C and D are incorrect). Heat must be added to the system to break the intermolecular forces that keep the substance in the liquid state. Adding heat, an endothermic process, increases the enthalpy of the system (B is incorrect).

48. Intravenous solutions must be isosmotic to blood (approximately 300 mM) to prevent damage to red blood cells. What mass of calcium chloride must be added to water to create 1 kg of solution isosmotic to blood?

    A. 11 g
    B. 33 g
    C. 37 g
    D. 111 g

A Blood is mostly water ($\rho = 1000$ kg/L), so molarity is roughly equal to molality (0.3 M). Osmolarity is determined by the number of osmotically active particles. $CaCl_2$ has three osmotically active particles per molecule dissolved. To produce a 0.3 M solution, we need to make a 0.1 M calcium chloride solution. The molecular mass of $CaCl_2$ is about 111 g/mol. To make a 0.1 M solution in 1 kg of solution (≈ 1 liter), we need 0.1 mol (Molarity = moles/liter); 0.1 mol multiplied by 111 g/mol is approximately 11 grams (choice A).

49. Destructive distillation involves heating an organic substance in a closed container in the absence of oxygen. The destructive distillation of wood produces acetic acid ($T_b = 117.9°C$), methanol ($T_b = 65.0°C$), and acetone ($T_b = 56.2°C$). Which of these will be the first to be vaporized?

    A. Acetic acid
    B. Methanol
    C. Acetone
    D. It cannot be determined from the information given.

C Boiling point is the temperature at which vapor pressure is equal to external pressure. Since external pressure will be the same throughout the destructive distillation process, the substance to vaporize first will be the one that has the lowest T_b. A low T_b indicates that the intermolecular attractive forces in the liquid state are relatively weak, which creates a relatively high vapor pressure at any given temperature. Since acetone has the lowest boiling point, it will vaporize first, making C the correct answer.

50. A hypertonic solution, X, separated from a hypotonic solution, Y, by a semipermeable membrane (permissive to water only) will result in all of the following after equilibration EXCEPT:

    I. An increase in the melting point of Solution X.
    II. An increase in the volume of Solution Y.
    III. An increase in the vapor pressure above Solution Y.

    A. I only
    B. I and II only
    C. II and III only
    D. 1, II, and III

C A hypertonic solution has a higher osmotic pressure than the surrounding solution; a hypotonic solution has a lower osmotic pressure. To reach equilibrium, there will be a net flow of water from the hypotonic (Y) to the hypertonic (X) solution. This decreases the concentration of solute in X and increases it in Y. A lower solute concentration in X will increase the melting point (I is true and thus eliminated). Since water is flowing from Y to X, the volume of Y will decrease (II is false and thus correct here). As water leaves Y, the solute concentration increases and the vapor pressure decreases (III is false and thus correct here).

51. Of the following substances, which will provide the greatest protection against freezing?

    A. 1 *m* ethanol (C_2H_6O)
    B. 1 *m* potassium acetate ($KC_2H_4O_2$)
    C. 1.5 *m* sucrose ($C_{12}H_{22}O_{11}$)
    D. 0.5 *m* calcium chloride ($CaCl_2$)

B The best protection against freezing will be given by the substance that lowers the T_f by the greatest amount. This is determined by the number of dissolved particles. One molal ethanol gives 1 molal of dissolved particles. One molal potassium acetate gives 2 molal particles (one K^+ and one acetate). Sucrose does not dissociate and therefore yields 1.5 molal particles. Finally, 0.5 molal calcium chloride will produce a 1.5 molal solution (one Ca^{2+} and two Cl^-). Therefore, the highest molality of dissolved particles is found in choice B.

Free-Standing Questions (52–56)

52. A block is attached to a spring and set into simple harmonic motion. Compared to the period of the oscillations of this block, the period of the oscillations of a block of greater mass attached to a spring with a larger spring constant would:

    A. be shorter.
    B. be longer.
    C. remain unchanged.
    D. Any one of the above is possible.

D The period of oscillations of a block attached to a spring is given by the equation $T = 2\pi(m/k)^{1/2}$, where m is the mass of the block and k is the spring constant. If m and k are *both* increased, the ratio m/k could increase, decrease, or remain the same, so T could increase, decrease, or remain the same.

53. Of the following gases, which one deviates most from ideal behavior?

    A. He
    B. N_2
    C. NH_3
    D. H_2

C Deviations from ideal behavior occur due to atomic size and intermolecular attractive forces, which affect the measured volume and pressure, respectively.

All the gases are relatively small and are unlikely to differ significantly in their effects on volume. However, they are not equivalent in their respective intermolecular attractive forces. Helium, nitrogen, and hydrogen experience London dispersion forces. But ammonia (choice C) experiences hydrogen bonding, which is far stronger than London attractions and more likely to impact on gas behavior.

54. An object of mass 500 grams is completely submerged in a fluid of specific gravity 2. If the object experiences a buoyant force of 25 N, what is its specific gravity?

    A. 0.1
    B. 0.25
    C. 0.4
    D. 0.5

C Let the mass, density, and volume of the object be m, ρ, and V, respectively. If the object is completely submerged, then by Archimedes' principle, the buoyant force it feels is $\rho_{fluid}Vg$. But $V = m/\rho$, so we have $\rho_{fluid}(m/\rho)g = 25$ N. Plugging in $\rho_{fluid} = 2000$ kg/m³, m = 0.5 kg, and $g = 10$ N/kg, we find that $\rho = 400$ kg/m³. Therefore, the object's specific gravity is 0.4.

55. Adding which one of the following would produce the greatest increase in the solubility of the sparingly soluble salt BaF_2?

    A. HCl
    B. NH_3
    C. KOH
    D. H_2CO_3

A BaF_2 will eventually reach equilibrium between the solid and aqueous state: $BaF_2(s) \leftrightarrow Ba^{2+}(aq) + 2\ F^-(aq)$. To increase the solubility of BaF_2, we want to stress this equilibrium to shift it to the right. Consider choice A, HCl. It will dissociate in solution into H^+ and Cl^-. Since HF is a weak acid, most of the dissolved F^- will combine with H^+. Thus, according to Le Chatelier's principle, this will shift the BaF_2 equilibrium to the right, allowing for a greater solubility. Choices B and C describe a weak and strong base, respectively. These will decrease the $[H^+]$, which would leave more F^- in solution. Consequently, the solubility of BaF_2 will not change. Choice D is a weak acid and will therefore raise the $[H^+]$ to a lesser extent than HCl, so A is the best choice.

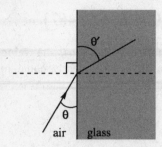

56. The figure above shows a ray of light in air striking the surface of a piece of glass. If n is the index of refraction of the glass, then which of the following equations is true?

    A. $\sin \theta = n \sin \theta'$
    B. $\cos \theta = n \cos \theta'$
    C. $n \sin \theta = \sin \theta'$
    D. $n \cos \theta = \sin \theta'$

B Note that the angles θ and θ' are not defined with respect to the normal of the surface; instead θ is the complement of the angle of incidence and θ' is the complement of the angle of refraction. By Snell's law, with $n = 1$ for air, we have $\sin \theta_1 = n \sin \theta_2$, where θ_1 is the angle of incidence and θ_2 is the angle of refraction. Because $\sin \theta_1 = \cos \theta$ and $\sin \theta_2 = \cos \theta'$, Snell's law in this case becomes $\cos \theta = n \cos \theta'$.

Passage IX (Questions 57–61)

57. The frequency of the waves emitted by the ladar transmitter is most nearly:

    A. 2.7×10^{13} Hz.
    B. 3.3×10^{14} Hz.
    C. 2.7×10^{15} Hz.
    D. 3.3×10^{16} Hz.

B The ladar emits infrared waves, which travel at the speed of light, $c = 3 \times 10^8$ m/s. Using the fundamental equation $\lambda f = v$, with $\lambda \approx 900 \times 10^{-9}$ m and $v = c$, we find that $f = c/\lambda = (3 \times 10^8$ m/s$)/(900 \times 10^{-9}$ m$) \approx 3.3 \times 10^{14}$ Hz.

58. When using a radar device in stationary mode, which of the following would tend to increase the error due to the cosine effect?

    I. Measuring the target vehicle's speed at a closer range
    II. Positioning the radar transmitter closer to the road
    III. Using the Ka band rather than the X or K bands

    A.   I only
    B.   II only
    C.   I and II only
    D.   II and III only

A The speed measured by the radar is $v_t \cos \alpha$, where v_t is the target vehicle's true speed. The error will be increased if $\cos \alpha$ is reduced, which occurs if α is increased. Referring to Figure 1 in the passage, for a fixed y, the smaller the range, the larger the angle α; therefore Item I is true. However, decreasing y would reduce α, so Item II is false. Finally, the frequency of the emitted microwave radiation would have no effect here, so Item III is false. Therefore, the answer is A.

59. A traffic officer is using a radar employing the X band in stationary mode, pointing the device directly at a target vehicle along its direction of travel. If the calculated value of Δf is –2800 Hz, then the target vehicle is:

    A.   approaching the officer at a speed of 40 m/s.
    B.   receding from the officer at a speed of 40 m/s.
    C.   approaching the officer at a speed of 50 m/s.
    D.   receding from the officer at a speed of 50 m/s.

B First, the fact that Δf is negative implies that f_r is less than f, so the target vehicle must be moving away from the officer (remember that the Doppler effect predicts that relative motion away produces a decrease in frequency). This observation alone eliminates choices A and C. To determine the actual value of v_t, we use Equation 1, with $v = c$ and $f \approx 10.5$ GHz (X band):

$$v_t = -\frac{c\Delta f}{2f} \approx -\frac{(3 \times 10^8 \text{ m/s})(-2800 \text{ Hz})}{2(10.5 \times 10^9 \text{ Hz})}$$

$$= \frac{(3 \times 10^8 \text{ m/s})(7 \cdot 400 \text{ Hz})}{21 \times 10^9 \text{ Hz}}$$

$$= 40 \text{ m/s}$$

60. Comparing radar and ladar transmitters, which one of the following is most likely true?

A. The ladar device has a greater accuracy since it transmits waves of a longer wavelength.

B. The radar transmitter is more prone to error in denser traffic conditions.

C. The radar device does not measure the distance to the target vehicle.

D. The ladar transmitter is more accurate since it emits light waves while the radar transmitter emits sound waves.

C Choice A is wrong since IR waves have a shorter wavelength than microwaves do. Choice B is wrong, since the passage states that the ladar must be aimed at a single target vehicle; therefore, it is the ladar, not the radar, that would be more prone to error in denser traffic conditions. Choice D is wrong since the radar does not emit sound waves—it emits microwaves. The answer must be C. While the ladar measures the time between emission and reception of its light pulse, and thus determines the distance to the target vehicle, the radar device measures the reflected wave frequency only.

61. Suppose a ladar device emits light at an average rate of 500 pulses per second at an approaching target vehicle. The device measures the time interval between emission and reception of one of the pulses to be T_1 sec, and the time interval for the next pulse as T_2 sec. If c is the speed of light, which one of the following expressions gives the speed of the target vehicle?

A. $250(T_1 - T_2)c$
B. $250(T_2 - T_1)c$
C. $500(T_1 - T_2)c$
D. $500(T_2 - T_1)c$

A Since the target vehicle is *approaching* the ladar device, T_2 will be less than T_1; thus $T_2 - T_1$ is negative. This eliminates choices B and D since speed is never negative. If T is the round-trip time for a pulse, then the round-trip distance traveled by the pulse is cT; this means that the (one-way) distance to the target is $(1/2)cT$. So, in the time between the pulses, the target vehicle has moved a distance $(1/2)cT_1 - (1/2)cT_2 = (1/2)(T_1 - T_2)c$. Dividing this change in position by the time Δt between pulses gives the speed of the car. Since the ladar emits pulses at an average rate of 500 per second, we conclude that the time interval between pulses is $\Delta t = 1/500$ sec. Therefore, the speed of the car is $250(T_1 - T_2)c$.

Passage X (Question 62–67)

62. Under normal conditions, the value of $[H_3O^+]$ in the stomach is most nearly equal to which of the following?

A. $1 \times 10^{-2}\ M$
B. $3 \times 10^{-2}\ M$
C. $1 \times 10^{-1}\ M$
D. $3 \times 10^{-1}\ M$

B $[H_3O^+]$ can be approximated from the pH of the stomach, given in the passage as 1.5. Since pH = −log $[H_3O^+]$, if pH = 1.5, then $[H_3O^+]$ must be between 10^{-2} and 10^{-1}, so the answer must be B. In general, if the pH is between n and $n + 1$, where n is a whole number, then $[H_3O^+]$ will be between $10^{-(n+1)}$ and 10^{-n}.

63. Which of the following best explains why omeprazole specifically targets the stomach and not most other organs?

A. The non-ionized form of the drug predominates in parietal cells.

B. The ionized form of the drug becomes trapped within parietal cells.

C. After ingestion, it is ionized in the stomach where it remains trapped.

D. It effectively raises stomach pH, resulting in more of the drug becoming ionized for absorption.

B The passage states that omeprazole is primarily absorbed in the small intestine (eliminating C). The pH of the stomach is 1.5 and the pK_a of omeprazole is 1.6. Using the Henderson–Hasselbalch equation (Equation 1 in the passage), we get

$$pH - pK_a = \log \frac{[B]}{[BH^+]} \quad \Rightarrow$$

$$1.5 - 1.6 = \log \frac{[B]}{[BH^+]} \quad \Rightarrow$$

$$-0.1 = \log \frac{[B]}{[BH^+]}$$

Because the left side of the equation is negative, the ratio $[B]/[BH^+]$ must be less than 1, so $[BH^+]$ is slightly greater than $[B]$. The ionized form of the drug predominates at low pH (eliminates A and D), and it is unable to passively diffuse out of the low pH environment of the parietal cell.

64. What is the correct order of stomach pH values for the experimental groups in the passage?

- **A.** Group X > Group Y > Group Z
- **B.** Group Y > Group Z > Group X
- **C.** Group Z > Group Y > Group X
- **D.** Group X > Group Z > Group Y

C If absorption of ketoconazole is related to pH, then the pH order from the graph must be X > Y > Z or Z > Y > X (eliminates B and D). Ketoconazole has a pK_a of 3, and is absorbed only in the ionized form. From Equation 1, we find that

$$pH - pK_a = \log \frac{[B]}{[BH^+]}$$

So, to maximize the ionized form, pH must be as low as possible. If absorption in Group X is the best, that means the stomach is most acidic, or has the lowest pH (eliminates A).

65. A patient requiring oral therapy with ketoconazole is found to have achlorydia (neutral stomach pH). The most helpful intervention would be to administer ketoconazole:

- **A.** with ginger ale (pH = 2).
- **B.** with baking soda (NaH_2CO_3).
- **C.** with omeprazole.
- **D.** at a higher dose.

A As in the preceding question, the absorption of ketoconazole is maximized when stomach pH is minimized. NaH_2CO_2 is a base, and omeprazole will also raise pH (eliminates B and C). A is a better choice than D, since it will lower stomach pH.

66. Approximately what percentage of omeprazole is ionized in blood (pH = 7.4)?

- **A.** Less than 1%
- **B.** 10%
- **C.** 50%
- **D.** Greater than 99%

A Again, using Equation 1, we can calculate that

$$pH - pK_a = \log \frac{[B]}{[BH^+]} \Rightarrow$$

$$7.4 - 1.6 = \log \frac{[B]}{[BH^+]} \Rightarrow$$

$$5.8 = \log \frac{[B]}{[BH^+]}$$

This shows that [B] is about 6 orders of magnitude higher than [BH⁺], so far less than 1% will be ionized in the blood.

67. Comparing ketoconazole and omeprazole, all of the following are true EXCEPT:

- **A.** both are partially ionized in the stomach.
- **B.** omeprazole has a weaker conjugate acid.
- **C.** ketoconazole is a stronger base.
- **D.** omeprazole has a higher K_a value.

B Both omeprazole and ketoconazole have pK_a values greater than the pH of the stomach, so they will get ionized there (eliminates A). Choice C is eliminated since the higher the pK_a, the stronger the base. Because $pK_a = -\log K_a$, the higher the K_a, the lower the pK_a (eliminates D). The answer must be B: the weaker the base, the stronger its conjugate acid.

Passage XI (Questions 68–72)

68. A crystal composed of atoms of which of the following elements would be expected to have a partially filled conduction band, even at very low temperatures?

  A. Carbon
  B. Silicon
  C. Sodium
  D. Silver chloride

C A crystal with a partially filled conduction band, even at very low temperatures, must be a conductor. Choice C, sodium, is a metal, and thus an excellent conductor, so this is the best answer here. Diamond is a crystal of carbon, and according to Table 1, it has an energy gap of 5.4 eV and thus is definitely an insulator, eliminating choice A. Choices B and D are also listed in Table 1, with energy gaps which classify them as a semiconductor and insulator, respectively.

69. By how much would the temperature of a sample of zinc sulfide need to be increased to expect that virtually all of the electrons near the top of the valence band would jump to the conduction band?

  A. 700 K
  B. 2,100 K
  C. 4,200 K
  D. 42,000 K

D The passage states that the average energy of an electron at temperature T is kT. Therefore, to acquire enough energy to jump into the gap, the temperature would need to be high enough to ensure that $kT \geq E_g$. According to Table 1, the energy gap for zinc sulfide (ZnS) is 3.6 eV, so the minimum temperature necessary would be $(3.6 \text{ eV})/(8.6 \times 10^{-5} \text{ eV/K}) = 42{,}000 \text{ K}$.

70. If a constant electric field E were applied to a metal, what would be the change in velocity of a conduction electron (charge magnitude = e, mass = m) in the time t between collisions with the lattice ions?

  A. eE/m
  B. eEt/m
  C. $2eE/m$
  D. $2eEt/m$

B The electric force on the electron would have magnitude eE, and thus impart an acceleration a of eE/m. Since $\Delta v = at$, the change in velocity in time t would be eEt/m. Note that choices A and C have units of acceleration, not velocity, so they can be eliminated immediately.

71. Which one of the following statements concerning metals, insulators, and semiconductors is most likely true?

  A. As the temperature is increased, the resistivity of a metal increases but the resistivity of a semiconductor decreases.
  B. As the temperature is increased, the resistivity of a metal decreases but the resistivity of a semiconductor increases.
  C. Insulators typically have a smaller energy gap than semiconductors.
  D. Electrical conduction in insulators is due to the drift velocity of electrons while in the valence band.

A As the temperature is increased, the conductivity of a semiconductor increases, so its resistivity decreases; this eliminates choice B. The passage states that the energy gap for insulators is more than 3 eV, while for semiconductors, it is less than 3 eV; therefore, insulators have a larger energy gap than semiconductors, eliminating choice C. Finally, D is wrong, since it is the drift of conduction electrons—that is, electrons in the conduction band, not the valence band—that account for electrical conduction. Therefore, by process of elimination, the answer must be A. (Note: Metals have a practically "infinite" supply of conduction electrons, and as the temperature is increased, the greater random thermal motion of these electrons and the lattice ions produces more and more frequent collisions, reducing the drift velocity—and thus the conductivity.)

72. Which of the following graphs best illustrates how the concentration of electrons in the conduction band of a semiconductor depends on temperature?

A.

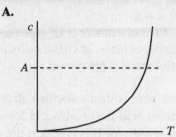

B.

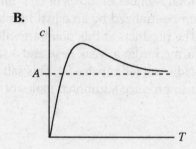

C.

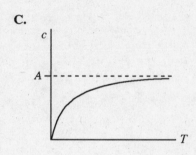

D.

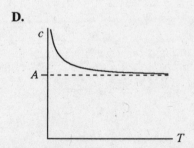

C The concentration of electrons in the conduction band is given by Equation 1, $c(T) = Ae^{-T^*/T}$. Note that as T increases, $e^{-T^*/T}$ approaches $e^0 = 1$, so c approaches (but never equals) the value A. This eliminates choices A and B. Since the number of electrons in the conduction band must increase as the temperature increases (because the electrons in the valence band can eventually acquire enough thermal energy to jump the gap), the graph of $c(T)$ must increase to A; this eliminates choice D.

Free-Standing Questions (73–77)

73. $-Q \bigcirc\!-\!-\!-\!-\!\underset{P}{-\!-}\!-\!-\!-\!-\!\bullet +Q$

The figure above shows an electric dipole, consisting of a pair of equal but opposite charges. Assume that the electric potential decreases to zero as the distance from the charges increases. At the midpoint P of the line segment joining this pair of charges:

A. the electric field is zero, but the electric potential is not.

B. the electric potential is zero, but the electric field is not.

C. both the electric field and the electric potential are zero.

D. neither the electric field nor the electric potential is zero.

B At the point P, the electric field vector due to the left-hand source charge points to the left and the electric field vector due to the right-hand source charge *also* points to the left. Therefore, the net electric field at P is not zero, eliminating choices A and C. Now, the electric potential at a distance r from a point charge q is kq/r. If the distance between the charges is d, then P is at a distance of $r = d/2$ from each charge. In this case, then, the total electric potential at point P is $k(-Q)/r + kQ/r = 0$, so the answer is B.

74. A one liter saturated solution of barium sulfate contains 2.5 mg of dissolved $BaSO_4$. What is the solubility product constant, K_{sp}, for barium sulfate?

A. 1.2×10^{-10}
B. 2.5×10^{-8}
C. 1.1×10^{-5}
D. 1.6×10^{-4}

A $BaSO_4$ dissociates into Ba^{2+} and SO_4^{2-}, so $K_{sp} = [Ba^{2+}][SO_4^{2-}] = x^2$, where $x = [Ba^{2+}]$. Since the molar mass of $BaSO_4$ is approximately $137.3 + 32 + 4(16) = 233$ g/mol, its molar solubility is

$$x = \frac{2.5 \times 10^{-3} \text{ g}}{L} \cdot \frac{1 \text{ mol } BaSO_4}{233 \text{ g}} = 1.1 \times 10^{-5} \tfrac{\text{mol } BaSO_4}{L}$$

Therefore, $K_{sp} = x^2 = (1.1 \times 10^{-5})^2 = 1.2 \times 10^{-10}$.

75. The combustion of methane (CH_4) produces carbon dioxide and water. What mass of CH_4 is required to react with 96 grams of oxygen gas?

    A.   12 g
    B.   16 g
    C.   24 g
    D.   32 g

C The balanced reaction is $CH_4 + 2\,O_2 \rightarrow CO_2 + 2\,H_2O$. Thus, 1 mole of CH_4 is needed for every 2 moles of O_2. Because O_2 has a molar mass of $2(16) = 32$ g/mol, 96 g of O_2 is equivalent to 3 moles. Therefore, 1.5 moles of CH_4 will be required. The molar mass of CH_4 is $12 + 4(1) = 16$ g/mol, so 1.5 moles would have a mass of $(1.5)(16\text{ g}) = 24$ g.

76. A string of length 60 m and fixed at both ends supports a standing wave. Including its endpoints, there are a total of five nodes along the string. What is the wavelength of the standing wave?

    A.   10 m
    B.   12 m
    C.   15 m
    D.   30 m

D The first harmonic standing wave has two nodes (just the two fixed endpoints of the string), the second harmonic has three nodes, the third harmonic has four nodes, and the fourth harmonic has five nodes. Therefore, the standing wave described in this question is the fourth harmonic. The wavelength of the nth harmonic standing wave for a string fixed at both ends is $\lambda_n = 2L/n$. With $L = 60$ m and $n = 4$, this formula gives us $\lambda_4 = 2(60\text{ m})/4 = 30$ m.

77. If a solution of NH_3 is titrated with HBr, then which of the following is true at the equivalence point?

    A.   The pH is greater than 7.
    B. $[H_3O^+]$ is equal to $[OH^-]$.
    C.   The number of moles of H_3O^+ added is equal to the number of moles of OH^- initially present.
    D.   The salt formed is pH neutral.

C When a weak base is titrated with a strong acid, the equivalence point will occur at a pH less than 7 (eliminates A). The reason for this is that at the equivalence point, the total number of moles of OH^- initially present have been neutralized by an equal number of moles of H_3O^+. The products at this point are salt and water. The salt formed from a weak base and a strong acid will be an acidic salt (eliminates D). This salt combines with water to produce additional moles of H_3O^+ (eliminates B).

ANSWERS AND EXPLANATIONS

VERBAL REASONING

Questions 78–137

Passage I (Questions 78–83)

78. The author of the passage would probably most strongly *oppose*:

- **A.** a move to make Mexico an OPEC member.
- **B.** strict enforcement of existing environmental regulations in Mexico.
- **C.** extending further loans and credits to Mexico.
- **D.** development of Mexican industrial capacity.

A The author states in the last paragraph that Mexico could enter into the described agreement with the U.S. only because it is not an OPEC member. Therefore, one can infer that out of the four choices given, the author would be most opposed to the idea of Mexico joining OPEC (choice A). Nothing in the passage suggests that the author would oppose strict enforcement of environmental rules (choice B). On the contrary, the author says that increased revenues might be used to assist the Mexicans with environmental protection costs. There is no evidence in the passage that under this new trade relationship Mexico would have the same problems with loans and credits as in the past, so the author would not strongly oppose choice C. The author recognizes that Mexico needs to "marshal [its] resources towards rapid industrial development" (lines 45–46) and proposes his oil-for-debt plan as a way to achieve that goal, which eliminates choice D.

79. Which of the following statements, if true, would most *undermine* the potential effectiveness of the author's proposal outlined in lines 51–55?

- **A.** The cheaper imported oil is, the weaker the incentive is to replace fossil fuels with alternatives such as wind and solar power.
- **B.** Mexico currently sells its oil to a wide variety of Latin American nations for a higher price than would be paid by the U.S. under the author's proposal.
- **C.** The influx of cheap imported oil into the U.S. market would have a stronger effect on producer prices than on consumer prices.
- **D.** A decline in industrial costs due to cheaper oil would allow most manufacturing plants to heavily invest in labor-saving machinery and to lay off a large percentage of their current work force.

D If the cost savings described by the author in the last paragraph would also stimulate manufacturing industries to replace a large number of workers with machines, it is likely that there would not be a significant net increase in jobs in the United States. Thus, choice D goes furthest toward undermining the potential effectiveness of the proposal.

The author never advocates the replacement of fossil fuels with alternative sources, so the fact that replacement might become less likely (choice A) has no impact on the author's proposal. The author admits that Mexico would be selling oil to the U.S. at a discounted price (lines 51–55), and choice B does not include enough information to show that selling oil to other nations at a higher price would be problematic. The author's proposal states that both producer and consumer prices would be lowered (line 62) but does not assume that both would fall by the same amount, or that consumer prices would fall more. Therefore, choice C has no effect on the author's argument.

80. The author's claim that increasing the U.S. market's petroleum supply will strengthen the economy suggests that the author:

    I.   believes that increased scarcity of a commodity will tend to increase the price of that commodity.

    II.   is concerned about the environmental dangers of burning fossil fuels.

    III. sees new job creation as important to a healthy economy.

    A.   II only
    B.   I and III only
    C.   II and III only
    D.   I, II, and III

B In lines 58–60, the author argues that the availability of cheap Mexican oil would depress domestic oil prices. If decreased scarcity (increased availability) would decrease prices, we can infer that increased scarcity (decreased availability) would increase prices. Therefore, Item I is true. The author mentions the costs of environmental protection measures at the end of the passage, but does not specifically discuss damage due to burning oil or other fossil fuels. Item II is false. One of the author's goals in implementing his proposal is to create "thousands of new jobs" which would then boost consumer confidence and increase spending (lines 62–65). Item III reflects this goal and is, therefore true. Answer choice B is correct.

81. Which of the following is/are explicitly cited in the passage as contributing to the character of U.S.–Mexico relations?

    I.   Past military conflicts

    II.   Past American exploitation of Mexican natural resources

    III. The resolve of some Mexican leaders to set aside "blame America" rhetoric

    A.   I only
    B.   III only
    C.   II and III only
    D.   I, II, and III

D In the first paragraph, the author cites the Mexican–American War as a factor in U.S.–Mexico relations, so Item I is true. The author refers to U.S. exploitation of Mexican resources at the end of the second paragraph, making Item II true. Item III is also true. The author describes these leaders in the beginning of the fourth paragraph. Choice D is correct.

82. Which of the following findings, if true, would best support the author's assertion that if the policies outlined in the passage were followed, a federal tax on gasoline "would hardly be noticed" (line 67)?

    A.   Mexican environmental protection efforts depend on U.S. assistance.
    B.   Without the policy change, inflation would raise prices even more than a tax.
    C.   With the new federal tax, the cost per gallon of gasoline would be lower than current gas prices.
    D.   Gasoline price increases historically have had little impact on U.S. gas consumption.

C The author claims that "under the newly discounted price structure" a new "tax on gasoline would hardly be noticed" (paragraph 5). If the after-tax price-per-gallon were still lower than current prices, most consumers would have no way of knowing that the price would have been even lower without the tax. Therefore, the effects of the tax would not be noticeable. Choice C supports this reasoning. There is no connection drawn by the author, nor in this finding, between the protection of the environment in Mexico and how noticeable the new tax might be (choice A). Choice B gives no reason to believe the tax would not be noticed. If the proposal were implemented, there would not be inflation but there would be an additional tax. What would happen without the proposal is irrelevant to evaluating the effects of the tax included within the proposal. The fact that people might continue to buy as much gasoline after the imposition of a tax does not indicate that they would not notice the tax in the first place (choice D).

83. According to the passage, the current popularity of the call "No to the debt!" is most directly a result of which of the following factors?

A. Resentment created by the Mexican–American War

B. Grinding poverty and hunger in Mexico's urban and rural areas

C. The political ambitions of certain Mexican politicians

D. Years of corrupt and irresponsible economic administration in Mexico

C In lines 22–24, the author states that some political figures have "gained considerable popularity" by advocating debt nullification. Choice C correctly identifies Mexican politicians as a force in the popularity of the slogan. While historical resentment (choice A) may be a distant contributing factor, this resentment is not given as a direct cause of calls for voiding the national debt. The author does not describe Mexican economic policy as corrupt, and so choice D is not supported. In paragraph 3, the author refers to "the kind of grinding poverty which demoralizes and dehumanizes existence," but does not link those social and economic problems directly with the suggestion that Mexico nullify its debts. Therefore, choice B is also incorrect.

Passage II (Questions 84–91)

84. The passage suggests that by recreating the working techniques that reproduce ancient artifacts, archaeologists:

A. inspire fanciful reconstructions of the archaeological past.

B. establish the truth or falsity of ancient histories.

C. gain insight into the needs and desires of past cultures.

D. reinvent antiquity from contemporary perspectives.

C Choice C is supported by the discussion in paragraph 1, in which the author refers to firsthand experience gained by "role-playing" as the basis for discovering "the daily needs and routines" of ancient societies. Choice D is inconsistent with the passage. Archeologists, as described in this passage, attempt to experi-

ence and understand aspects of life as it was lived at the time, not view it from their own contemporary perspective (see paragraphs 1 and 2). In paragraph 1, the author says that the inspiration for archaeological insights comes from re-creating ancient artifacts "and figuring out what crucial purpose they served." Therefore, the reconstructions are not described as "fanciful" (choice A), nor are they created to test the accuracy of ancient histories that have already been written (choice B).

85. Suppose several split-based spearpoints dating from the late Gravettian period were discovered in a perfect state of repair. How would this information affect the author's claims about the development of spearpoint design?

A. It would support the claim that round-based points replaced split-based points.

B. It would not significantly weaken the claim that Cro-Magnon weapons technology improved over time.

C. It would weaken the claim that split-based points were developed in the Aurignacian period.

D. It would weaken the claim that Gravettian Cro-Magnon weaponry was more advanced than that of Aurignacian Cro-Magnon.

B Choice B is correct. The discovery of some split-based points would not significantly undermine the author's claim that the manufacture of lozenge-shaped points "displaced the earlier forms" (lines 69–71). A hunter from the later period may still have used a point from the old model, or the points that were found may have been discarded, used or unused, when the new points became available. While this finding does not strengthen the author's claim, it does not give enough information to weaken it either. Choice D is the opposite of the correct choice, B. The existence of early-model spearpoints in the Gravettian (later) period does not significantly undermine the claim that a different technology existed in that time. Alternatively, just because a point may have been made in a later period does not show that the model was not developed in an earlier period (choice C). The discovery of a split-based spearpoint from a later time period gives no support for the claim that split-based points were replaced by round or lozenge-shaped points (choice A).

86. Based on information in the passage, it is reasonable to conclude that during the Aurignacian period:

    A. deer caused serious injuries with their antlers.
    B. red deer were threatened with extinction.
    C. reindeer were considered a prize game.
    D. deer were regularly dehorned while still alive.

A Choice A is correct. In lines 46–49, the author writes that "observations of...deer jousts must have led Cro-Magnon hunters to imagine the advantages they might enjoy with weapons of the kind deer came by naturally." The author then describes how the Cro-Magnon fashioned deer antlers into weapons of their own. This implies that they saw and appreciated the kinds of wounds antlers can inflict. Choice B is too extreme. Although Cro-Magnon use of antlers for spearpoints suggests that they may have hunted deer for their antlers, nothing in the passage implies the threat of extinction. In fact, for all we know from the passage, the Cro-Magnon may have used antlers from deer that died of natural causes. Choice C is incorrect. The author gives no indication that reindeer were valued more than red deer, or that usefulness for weapons making was the most valuable or prized characteristic of potential game or prey. Nothing in the passage suggests whether or not deer were killed before their horns were taken (choice D).

87. As used in the passage, the word *conformity* (line 30) most nearly means:

    A. malleability.
    B. similarity.
    C. obedience.
    D. endurance.

B The purpose of this section of the passage is to describe how archeologists manufactured spearpoints to be identical to the ones found in archeological digs. That is, they made spearpoints that conformed or were similar to the size, shape, and hardness of the originals. When you replace "conformity" with "similarity" (choice B) in the passage, it makes sense in the context of the author's discussion in that paragraph. A malleable substance is one that is easily shaped or molded.

While malleability of antlers is certainly an issue in the passage, it is not the issue in this part of the passage, so choice A can be eliminated. While conformity (choice C) may mean obedience in another context, it is not relevant to the author's discussion in the passage. The archeologists were not testing how durable or lasting their re-creations were, but rather how similar they were in "aerodynamics, hardness and power." Choice D is incorrect, because while endurance or durability may be related to hardness, it is not the direct concern of the scientists described in the passage.

88. In describing the techniques by which Cro-Magnon artisans fastened points to their spears, the author cites all of the following factors EXCEPT:

    A. fiber binding.
    B. wedge pressure.
    C. mechanical friction.
    D. shaft cleft.

C This is an EXCEPT question; the correct answer will NOT be cited in the passage. Choices A, B, and D are mentioned in the passage. In lines 52–55, the author writes that Cro-Magnon artisans fastened a "finished point to a spear pole...and bound the point into the cleft with fibers from plants or animals" (lines 52–55; choice A); the artisans "jammed a small wedge into the point's split base.... The mechanical pressures...kept the weapon in one piece...." (lines 55–60; choice B); and that "artisans cut a cleft in the shape of a 'U' into the shaft's end, and bound the point into the cleft...." (choice D). The author mentions mechanical pressures, but never talks about "mechanical friction" (lines 53–55; choice C) as a way of fastening spearpoints to a shaft. Thus, choice C is the only choice not cited in the passage and is, therefore, correct.

89. The passage suggests that before the development of the atlatl, hunters:

   A. did not rely on spears as primary weaponry.

   B. did not possess much natural ability.

   C. had spearpoints that were difficult to sharpen.

   D. were at a greater disadvantage with swiftly moving prey.

D If the atlatl improved speed and aim, hunters before its invention would have been at a disadvantage compared to those hunting after, so choice D is correct. The passage states that atlatls have been found dating from 22,000 years ago. The author implies that Cro-Magnon spear-making dates from the early Aurignacian period, which began 40,000 years ago (paragraph 3). Therefore, spears were used long before the earliest indication of the use of the atlatl. Given that no other weapons are mentioned in the passage, we have no reason to conclude that spears were not a primary weapon in the earlier period and, therefore, can eliminate choice A. In paragraph 2, the passage states that the atlatl added "heft and accuracy to the natural ability of a skilled hunter," and nowhere indicates that Cro-Magnon hunters lacked natural ability (choice B). Choice C is also incorrect. The passage states that "points shaped like lozenges with rounded bases" came into use "three hundred twenty centuries [32,000 years] ago," and represented "new designs" that "enabled hunters to resharpen their points efficiently" (paragraph 5). Because the earliest found atlatls date from 22,000 years ago (paragraph 2), the best available evidence indicates that the spearpoints that were easier to sharpen predated the atlatls by some 10,000 years.

90. Which of the following findings, if true, would most support the value of the tests described in the second paragraph?

   A. The replicated spearpoints are strong enough to withstand being trampled on, yet light enough not to cause the spear to wobble in flight.

   B. The re-created spears fly smoothly with minimum deviation and maximum penetration of the target.

   C. Climatic conditions in Gravettian Europe were similar to those in Western Europe today.

   D. The re-created spearpoints, when thrown at animal carcasses, leave holes and splits in the bones similar to those found in bones unearthed from Cro-Magnon ruins.

D Remember: The purpose of the tests is "to be certain that the re-created spearpoints are as identical as possible to the originals recovered at sites" (lines 16–18). We do not know from the passage that the findings noted in choice A or choice B are true of the original spearpoints. These findings do not support the value or usefulness of the tests and are, therefore, incorrect. Nothing in the passage tells us that climatic conditions are relevant to the accuracy of these tests, so we can eliminate choice C. Choice D indicates that the re-created spears have an effect on bone that is similar to damage done to bones in the time of Cro-Magnon hunters. It gives further evidence that the re-creation was reasonably accurate and is, therefore, the correct answer.

91. According to the author, the difficulty in repairing some spearpoints:

   A. initiated rapid development of better designs.
   B. was an economic advantage because the spearpoints would eventually become obsolete.
   C. decreased the efficacy of Cro-Magnon hunts.
   D. was an inconvenient but not disabling defect.

D We can eliminate choice B because we know nothing from the passage about the Cro-Magnon economy, nor do we know that spearpoints were sold or bartered, or that anyone would benefit from their obsolescence. In lines 66–69 the author writes, "Despite the difficulty of repairing these weapons, the split-based spearpoints must have proven fairly effective, because they enjoyed eight thousand years of popularity with Cro-Magnon hunters." Eight thousand years of popularity hardly indicates "rapid development of better designs," so choice A is incorrect. We can eliminate choice C, because the passage states that the new points were easier to resharpen, not that they were more effective in hunting than the older model. This leaves choice D. The fact that the spearpoints were difficult to repair did not mean that they were not useful. Choice D is correct.

Passage III (Questions 92–101)

92. The main thesis of the passage is that:

   A. the defining process, fundamental to the scientific method, is self-limiting.
   B. definitions inevitably end in paradox.
   C. language cannot precisely define systems.
   D. science is a unique field of study.

A In paragraph 1, the author argues for the necessity of clear, consistent, and universally accepted scientific definitions. The rest of the passage explains that if we require, as do the purists, that every term be defined, we end up in the impossible position of requiring an infinite string of definitions (see in particular paragraph 5). By arguing for the necessity of axioms or self-defined terms to put an end to this chain (see lines 65–69), the author claims that the system is self-limiting. This makes choice A correct.

While the author does describe the claim that every scientific term be further defined as leading to paradox (lines 32–38), he does not go so far as to claim that all definitions end in paradox. Even if true, choice B still would be too narrow to be the main point of the passage. Choice C can be eliminated because the author argues that some specific terms in science cannot be defined with a definiens, not that language cannot define systems in general. The author does not compare science to other fields of study as suggested in choice D. The purpose of the passage is to discuss a particular issue involved in scientific definitions, not to argue for the uniqueness of science.

93. In the first paragraph, the author suggests that science requires the sharing of ideas between scientists who speak different languages. It can be inferred that this requirement exists because science:

   A. cannot simply resort to primary terms to solve a logical paradox.
   B. involves concepts that transcend cultural and linguistic boundaries.
   C. has a set of primary analytical definitions.
   D. relies on universal codes and characters.

B In the first paragraph the author argues that science must be founded on "clear definitions that can be readily understood by all scientists in every language and culture" and that scientific concepts "must be considered universal." This indicates that scientific concepts are not specific to particular cultures or languages, which makes choice B correct.

Choice A contradicts the author's discussion of using "primary terms" to solve the logical paradox of successive definitions in the sciences (lines 65–69). Choice D contradicts information in paragraph 1, which states that specialized (not universal) characters and codes are used to express universal concepts. We can eliminate choice C because the author mentions "primary terms," not "primary analytical definitions." Even if the two terms were interchangeable, the need for primary terms is related not to the need to share ideas, but to the paradox of infinite definitions described in paragraphs 3–5.

94. Which of the following claims is/are explicitly supported by a specific example in the passage?

    I.   Scientific concepts are universal.
    II. Descriptive definitions state or explain meaning.
    III. Scientific purists demand that all terms be defined.

    A. I only
    B. II only
    C. II and III only
    D. I, II, and III

B Remember: We are looking for statements that are supported by example(s) in the passage. Item I is false. While the author states that scientific concepts "must be considered universal," no specific example of their universality is given (see paragraph 1). At the beginning of paragraph 2, the definition of the word "temperature" is given as an example of descriptive definitions explaining meaning. So, Item II is supported by an example in the passage and is, therefore, true. While the author does claim that purists demand definitions, no specific example is given to support this. Thus, Item III is false. Only Item II is true, so answer choice B is correct.

95. What does the author's discussion of testable hypotheses and their relation to language imply about science?

    A. Because linguistic differences lead distinct cultures to conceptualize science differently, hypothesis testing should vary from culture to culture.
    B. The scientific method requires controlled experiments.
    C. Scientific predictability knows no boundaries of culture or language.
    D. Any hypothesis may potentially be demonstrated or disproved anywhere in the world.

D In the first paragraph, the author states that "concepts" must have "identical meaning" regardless of the culture of the scientific worker in order to facilitate hypothesis testing, a requirement of scientific methodology. Because scientific concepts and the scientific method are universal, any scientist or laboratory anywhere in the world might test and prove, or disprove, any given hypothesis. This agrees with choice D.

Choice A contradicts the discussion in paragraph 1. The author states that linguistic differences lead different cultures to express ideas or hypotheses differently, but that there must be agreement on the ideas or concepts themselves as well as on how to test them. Be careful not to use outside knowledge when considering answer choices. Nothing in the passage talks about controlled experiments (choice B). We can eliminate choice C because the author does not discuss predictability.

96. The author's reference to "pictographs, alphabetic characters, or binary codes" (line 7) is used in the passage primarily to:

    A. distinguish between concept and expression.
    B. emphasize the universality of scientific terms.
    C. clarify the purposes of coherence and continuity.
    D. provide a complete list of modes of expression.

A The list of different modes of expression is given to illustrate the difference between concept (universal) and expression (variable) and reinforce the main idea of the first paragraph—that concepts or ideas must be the same in every culture. Choice A is correct.

Choice B contradicts the passage (see lines 5–7 and 12–14) and conflicts with the reference in the question stem, which emphasizes the variability of scientific terms, in contrast to the universality of scientific concepts. Choice C is the right answer to the wrong question. The author makes the references listed in the question stem in order to illustrate some of the different (nonproblematic) ways in which different languages represent concepts, not in order to explain why we need coherence and continuity in those concepts. Choice D is too strong. These three modes of expression are given as examples, not as a complete list.

97. According to the passage, which of the following sentences would be an example of a stipulative definition?

- I. A human being is a featherless biped.
- II. A parrot is a brightly plumed tropical bird skilled in verbal mimicry.
- III. A jackalope is a cross between a rabbit and an antelope.

- **A.** I only
- **B.** III only
- **C.** I and III only
- **D.** II and III only

B We can refer to the discussion of stipulative and descriptive definitions in paragraph 2 to answer this question. Items I and II are false. Note that they are very similar, but no choice includes both I and II. Item I describes aspects of a human being, rather than providing a term that is equivalent to "human being"; Item II describes aspects of a parrot, rather than providing a term that is equivalent to "parrot." Item III fits the author's characterization of a stipulative description given in paragraph 2. A cross between a rabbit and an antelope is a jackalope; this definition does not just describe certain qualities of a jackalope, it provides an equivalent to the term "jackalope." Only Item III is true, making answer choice B correct.

98. The author argues in the last paragraph that because it would always be necessary to explain a previous definiens in terms of a subsequent definiens, no scientific system can make sense without the use of axioms. Which of the following, if valid, would most *weaken* this argument?

- **A.** Logical demonstration of a definiendum/definiens chain
- **B.** Demonstration that the paradox described by the author does not exist in all methodological systems
- **C.** Discovery of a consistent and coherent method of communicating concepts that does not require definitions of terms
- **D.** Refutation of the logic of scientific purism

C Choice C is correct. If it were true that there was a way of communicating and agreeing on scientific concepts without definitions, axioms would no longer be needed. Note that we do not need to know specifically what that "nondefinitional system" would involve for

choice C to weaken the author's argument—the question stem tells us to take it as true that such a system exists.

Choice A does not weaken the author's argument—it strengthens it. The author himself demonstrates a logical definiendum/definiens chain in order to prove the need for axioms (paragraphs 3 and 4). Choice D also strengthens the author's argument. The definitional paradox described by the author in paragraphs 3 and 4 itself refutes the claim of the purists by showing that their approach is logically incoherent. Choice B is too broad. The argument made in the passage applies only to science. The fact that this paradox may not exist in other (nonscientific) fields has no significant impact on the author's specific claims.

99. The philosopher Carl Hempel has written that science answers human beings' "need to gain ever wider knowledge of...[themselves] and ever deeper understanding of the world...." If the author were to include that quote in the passage, it would most likely be used to:

- **A.** draw an analogy between science and the humanities.
- **B.** call for increased funding for scientific research.
- **C.** support the claim that science must be founded on universal concepts.
- **D.** support the arguments of scientific purists.

C In the first paragraph, the author discusses the need to achieve universal agreement on scientific concepts so that we can test hypotheses; that is, so that we can uncover scientific meaning or truths. This can be related to Hempel's characterization of science as a quest for deeper understanding. Of the four answers, choice C is the only claim that is both made in the passage and directly relevant to the new information in the question.

Choices A and B are outside the scope of the passage. Be careful not to make assumptions or use outside knowledge. The author never discusses, directly or indirectly, the humanities, nor does he mention funding. We can eliminate choice D because the author rejects, not supports, the purists' claims (paragraph 5); the correct answer must be consistent with both the new information in the question and the argument presented in the passage.

100. In discussing the relationship between terms and definitions, the author makes all of the following claims EXCEPT:

A. The definiendum can mean the same as the definiens.

B. Terms might be defined ad infinitum.

C. All terms may be defined by descriptive definitions.

D. Primary terms are required to avoid paradox.

C This is an EXCEPT question—we are looking for a claim that the author DOES NOT make. In paragraph 5, the author states that some terms "cannot be defined, other than by definition." Furthermore, in his discussion of descriptive and stipulative definitions (paragraph 2) the author never indicates that all words potentially have a descriptive definition (choice C). Choice C is correct.

In paragraph 2, the author explains that in descriptive definitions "the term being defined" is the definiendum and "the term doing the defining is the definiens." He writes, "for example, 'temperature' means the same as 'degree of hotness or coldness.'" Therefore, the author does make the claim stated in answer choice A. Choice B is supported in paragraphs 3 and 4 by the author's discussion of a situation in which a chain of definitions might be required "ad infinitum" (lines 34–42). In paragraph 5, the author states that the only way out of the problem is to "reject the purist's need for global definition" and accept the use of "'primary' terms or 'axioms'" (choice D).

101. In ordinary conversation, people often say that someone, something, or some experience is "beyond definition." Given the information provided in the passage, what question might this raise about definitions?

A. Whether awareness of the type of paradox generated by the scientific purists' position occurs only in science, or in other modes of thought as well

B. Whether most people really understand the logical process of scientific definition

C. Whether stipulative or descriptive definitions are more applicable outside the realm of science

D. Whether the human mind and the human heart ultimately defy logical description

A The author notes that logical paradox occurs when one attempts to define terms ad infinitum, that is, beyond the ability of language to define them (paragraphs 3–5). The question stem raises the point that in various everyday situations people find themselves confounded by the need to express perceptions in language that seems inadequate. Therefore, the new information in the question might raise the issue of whether or not definitional paradoxes arise in nonscientific, as well as scientific, contexts, making choice A correct.

Both choices B and C can be eliminated based on the new information in the question stem, which is not specific to scientific definitions, but refers instead to more everyday situations. Choice B addresses people's understanding of "scientific definition," which is too narrow. Choice C can be eliminated, because the new information in the question stem has no direct relevance to the specifics of descriptive and stipulative definitions. In addition, a statement that something is "beyond definition" tells us nothing about the comparative applicability of either type of definition. Choice D is too broad. The question stem and the passage discuss cases in which terms or things cannot be defined. Choice D raises the question of whether our minds and hearts "defy logical description," a much more sweeping issue.

Passage IV (Questions 102–106)

102. The author indicates that the framers of the U.S. Constitution:

   A.   feared that powerful business interests might violate the privacy rights of individual citizens.

   B.   were wary of governmental intrusion into the privacy of large corporations.

   C.   believed that society needed to place a greater moral value on personal privacy.

   D.   based its provisions in part on past experiences of governmental abuses.

D In lines 3–5, the author writes that the citizens who drafted the Constitution were "historically subject to governmental and law enforcement abuses." This supports choice D. Choices A, B, and C are not supported in the passage. Even though the author discusses current problems involving business interests and individual privacy, she does not indicate that the framers foresaw these problems (choice A). The privacy of corporations (choice B) is not an issue in the passage. The framers were concerned with protecting the powerless (see paragraph 1), not the powerful. Finally, the author does not suggest that the framers believed society as a whole placed insufficient importance on the issue of privacy (choice C). In fact, she writes that the importance of preserving privacy rights is a "long cherished American belief" (lines 1–3).

103. The author of the passage would probably most strongly support legislation that:

   A.   permitted police to check the fingerprints of every person stopped for a routine traffic violation.

   B.   changed the Constitution to give the Supreme Court broader jurisdiction over nongovernmental institutions.

   C.   enabled citizens to limit access to their personal information.

   D.   prohibited Internet users from flooding email boxes with junk advertisements.

C The author argues that individual privacy is "besieged by all sides" (lines 1–3), and that some of the main culprits are the information industry and big business who go "rooting around in private records"

(lines 46–49). Therefore, we can infer that the author would support legislation that allowed individuals to limit outsiders' access to those individuals' personal information. Choice C is correct.

In paragraph 2, the author reports Supreme Court decisions allowing traffic officers to "require that all passengers in the stopped car...exit the vehicle" and finds "the potential for abuse by some unscrupulous" officers to be "worrisome." Given this view, and the general tone of the passage, it is unlikely that the author would support further intrusion on individual privacy by condoning universal fingerprint checks at routine traffic stops (choice A). In paragraphs 2 and 3 the author argues that recent Supreme Court decisions have degraded the right to privacy. Especially given the negative tone of the author's discussion of the Court, there is no evidence in the passage that the author would support giving it greater jurisdiction or power (choice B). There is nothing in the passage to indicate that the author would seek to restrict junk email (choice D), even though the reader's own feelings might make this a tempting choice. Furthermore, the problem discussed by the passage is the collection, not the dissemination, of information.

104. According to the author, police departments in the United States:

   I.   routinely abuse the increased latitude granted to them by the Supreme Court.

   II.   have lobbied political leaders for the right to search passengers as well as the driver of a stopped car.

   III.   may put individual officers in danger in the course of performing their jobs.

   A.   I only

   B.   III only

   C.   I and III only

   D.   II and III only

B Item I is too strong. While abuses may occur (paragraph 2), the author does not indicate that they happen routinely. While the right to "search passengers as well as the driver of a stopped car" was granted by the Court (paragraph 2), we are not told of any lobbying efforts by police departments for this right. Therefore, Item II is false. While the author emphasizes the potential for abuse on the part of the police, she admits that "a passenger left inside a vehicle could pose a serious threat to an officer discharging his lawful duties" (lines 20–23). This supports Item III. Only Item III is true, which makes answer choice B correct.

105. Which of the following findings, if true, would most support the author's contention in the fifth paragraph that politicians, in exchange for campaign contributions, are often willing to overlook invasions of privacy?

    A. Bills opposed by credit-reporting firms who had given heavily to politicians were defeated in Congress.

    B. The information industry donated 100 million dollars to the last congressional campaign.

    C. U.S. House representatives and senators regularly attend corporate-sponsored, expense-free conferences at 5-star resorts.

    D. Fortune-500 companies provide lavish hospitality tents for delegates to the major party political conventions.

A See paragraphs 4 and 5. If bills opposed by the credit-reporting industry (an industry that could be seen as invading privacy by collecting and disseminating personal financial information) were also opposed by politicians to whom these firms had given money, the author's argument would be strengthened. Choice A is correct.

Choice B does not provide enough information to strengthen the author's argument. The fact that the industry donated money does not by itself show that politicians responded by supporting legislation allowing the invasion of privacy. Compare this answer to choice A, which gives more evidence that the politicians may in fact be influenced by contributions. Choices C and D can also be eliminated. While the author claims that "there is little restraint on corporate willingness to rifle through personal records" (lines 62–64), she does not say that all corporations intrude upon individual privacy. We do not know whether or not corporations from the information industry are among the sponsors of the conferences mentioned in choice C. Furthermore, as in option B, there is no specific trade-off mentioned in choice C or D.

106. The author indicates that which of the following bear or bears some responsibility for the erosion of privacy rights in the United States?

    I.   Decreased corporate profits due to growing health insurance costs and rates

    II.   Greater public tolerance of privacy violations, due in part to insufficient regard on the part of the Supreme Court for the protection of the less powerful

    III.   Financial needs of electoral campaigns

    A. I only

    B. II only

    C. II and III only

    D. I, II, and III

C Item I is false. While the author does mention corporate investigations into job applicants' medical records "with the goal of maximizing worker productivity and minimizing company health insurance costs" (lines 50–55), we don't know from the passage that increased health insurance costs have decreased corporate profits. Be careful not to use outside knowledge or personal opinion. Item II is supported in the second half of paragraph 3. Item III is also supported by the passage. In paragraph 3, the author places blame on the ability of the information industry to "bring extreme pressure to bear on policymakers," and in paragraph 5, she states that "politicians hungry for campaign contributions are all too willing to embrace the advantages to businesses of unrestricted information flow." Both Item II and Item III are correct, so answer choice C is correct.

Passage V (Questions 107–111)

107. The central thesis of the passage is that:

- **A.** Shaw's Life Force, a concept created through the synthesis of other ideas and doctrines, is a self-discovering and self-correcting power.
- **B.** the Life Force intelligence is driven by a perfect plan and objective.
- **C.** self-understanding is the highest form of meaning.
- **D.** Shaw believed that earlier ideas of divinity were based on error and evil.

A Choice A is correct. The first paragraph discusses how Shaw built his own ideas through a synthesis of the insights of others. The rest of the passage describes how a synthesis of elements of religion and biology (paragraphs 2 and 3) resulted in his concept of a Life Force that through trial and error (paragraph 3) seeks perfection through greater self-understanding (paragraphs 3–6).

Choices B and D are too narrow to be central theses. In addition, choice B conflicts with the author's repeated assertion that Shaw's Life Force is not perfect; rather, it seeks perfection through trial and error. And, nothing in the author's description of Shaw's beliefs indicates that Shaw held the view of earlier ideas of divinity stated in answer choice D (see paragraphs 2 and 3). Choice C is too broad. The passage is specifically about Shaw; the correct answer needs to be as well. In addition, while Shaw may have believed choice C to be true (see lines 56–63), the author of the passage is describing Shaw's beliefs, not advocating them.

108. Which of the following exemplify the results of Shaw's gift for integrating old ideas with new ones, as cited in the passage?

- I. The view that the creation of evil results from mistakes made by a divine force
- II. The belief that God is uncertain about the way to final perfection
- III. The Darwinian theory of evolution

- **A.** II only
- **B.** I and II only
- **C.** I and III only
- **D.** I, II, and III

B Item I is true. The author states that this belief arose out of a combination of scientific trial and error with the idea that humanity is made in God's image (paragraphs 3–5). Item II is also true. The author states that the Life Force's purpose is "perhaps [not] fully known even to itself" (lines 48–51). Shaw's concept of the Life Force is a result of Shaw's "synthesis of scientific method" or trial and error and "deistic doctrine" (lines 36–39). The author indicates that the Life Force is Shaw's conception of God (see in particular lines 27–32). Item III is false. The "Darwinian theory of evolution," mentioned in paragraph 2, is not the result of Shaw's gift for integrating ideas; it is one idea that was integrated with others to create the concept of the Life Force. Item I and Item II are true, making answer choice B correct.

109. Shaw once said, "A lifetime of happiness! No man alive could bear it; it would be hell on earth." Based only on information provided in the passage, what would be the most reasonable interpretation of this statement?

- **A.** Without mistakes and the suffering that comes from those mistakes, we cannot hope to learn how to achieve a good life.
- **B.** Because of original sin, human beings do not deserve to live lives of true happiness.
- **C.** Due to a perverse twist of human nature, some people are only truly happy when they are suffering.
- **D.** Perfection is impossible, and we only make ourselves unhappy by trying to achieve it.

A Choice A is consistent both with the quote in the question stem and with information in the passage. The author states that Shaw's Life Force seeks to achieve self-understanding or perfect truth through trial and error, as do people here on Earth (paragraph 3). Mistakes, then, and the suffering they cause, have a vital role to play in our quest for a better existence. And, an entirely happy life would be a life without progress. A is the only choice that is supported by the passage.

Choices B, C, and D are not supported by the passage. There is no indication that Shaw believed either in original sin or that human beings do not deserve happiness (choice B). In fact, the concept of a Life Force, in whose image we are made according to Shaw (lines 30–32), involves the idea that we can evolve towards perfection (lines 56–63), an idea that is inconsistent with the concept of original sin. While choice C may be true in real life, there is nothing in the passage that describes this type of masochism. Choice D is inconsistent with the author's description of the Life Force, whose goal is to move towards and finally achieve perfection (paragraph 6)

110. In the context of the passage, the word *disclosure* (line 44) most nearly means:

- **A.** confession.
- **B.** punishment.
- **C.** acknowledgement.
- **D.** isolation.

C If we replace "disclosure" with "acknowledgement" (choice C) in the cited line, it fits with the main idea of that paragraph and with the theme of the passage as a whole; through trial and error, the Life Force makes mistakes that result in evil, but then recognizes and corrects those mistakes in its quest for perfect truth. Choice C is correct.

In the context of the passage (paragraphs 4 and 5), evil results from errors. If the Life Force makes a mistake it does not confess the error (choice A), but recognizes and corrects it. The only time punishment (choice B) is mentioned is in paragraph 5: "evils…are not meant for the punishment of sins: they are the survival of errors originally well intended" (lines 53–55). The author rules out the issue of punishment, either of evil or by evil. Choice D does not make sense in the context of the passage. Evils must be recognized, not isolated.

111. With which of the following statements would George Bernard Shaw most likely agree?

- **A.** It is important to draw insight from both religion and science more for political than intellectual reasons.
- **B.** Temporary concessions must be made to religious beliefs, so that the basic truth of Darwin's theories may eventually prevail.
- **C.** Neither purely scientific nor purely theological viewpoints fully explain humanity's place in the world; an entirely distinct approach must be found.
- **D.** The best plays neither ignore nor simply repeat the achievements of playwrights of the past.

D If Shaw, a playwright, sees himself not as a revolutionary or pioneer, but as someone who builds on the ideas of others (lines 4–11), we can infer that he would agree that theater should build on but not blindly repeat the past (choice D).

There is no mention of Shaw's political ideas or goals in the passage, so we can eliminate choice A. In paragraph 2 the author writes, "Shaw could no more defend those who absolutely denied the insights of Darwin's theories than he could endorse those who preached the existence of no God." The passage consistently illustrates that Shaw believed both theological and scientific thought had value; he synthesized the two rather than siding with one or the other, which makes choice B incorrect. Choice C is half right (the first half) but half wrong. Shaw synthesized or combined ideas from science and religion, rather than taking a completely distinct or independent path. From the beginning of the passage, Shaw is described as someone who likes to "borrow ideas from other thinkers," and that "his gift lay in scrupulously examining their intellectual and social implications and building on those foundations" (paragraph 1).

Passage VI (Questions 112–117)

112. The author's primary purpose in the passage is to:

    A. demonstrate the impossibility of understanding the function of myth in ancient society.

    B. criticize the naturalist and historicist schools of thought for presenting inadequate visions of the place and power of myth.

    C. explain the role of myth in ancient society and suggest ways of overcoming the problems involved in understanding that role.

    D. explain why, given advances in science and technology, we no longer need myths to represent the roles we play in society and nature.

C The author discusses the role of myth in ancient society and the difficulties involved in understanding that role (paragraphs 1–3). He then describes how we can at least partially overcome those difficulties by studying modern aboriginal cultures in which myth still plays a central role (paragraphs 4–6). Choice C is correct.

Choice A is too strong. The author states that we *can* gain *some* understanding of what myth meant to ancient societies by learning about the meaning and role of myth in modern aboriginal cultures (paragraphs 4 and 6). Choices B and D are too narrow. The inadequacies of the naturalist and historicist schools of thought (choice B) are discussed only in the fifth paragraph. And, while the author does discuss how myth has been replaced by science in modern society (choice D) in paragraphs 1–3, he makes this point in order to explain why we have trouble today understanding the role myth has played in the past.

113. Suppose an original poetic text from the first century B.C. celebrating the heroic deeds of the god Apollo were discovered in an archaeological dig. How would this discovery affect the author's claim that we in modern society find it difficult to comprehend the meaning of myth in ancient societies?

    A. It would refute the claim by indicating that data from living cultures can give us some insight into the role and power of myth.

    B. It would support the claim, because rescripted texts are inadequate indicators of what myth meant to the people of that time.

    C. It would be irrelevant to the claim, which is about mythological stories, not poetry.

    D. It would not fully refute the claim, because even an original text does not recreate the living reality essential to cultural meaning.

D The author indicates that our fundamentally different way of seeing the world, and our lack of access to those who created ancient myth, make it difficult for us to fully understand the meaning of myth in ancient society (paragraph 3). Therefore, although this newly discovered text would not have the problem of having been rescripted over time (lines 27–30), the difficulty of escaping our own cultural context and assumptions would still exist. Therefore, the discovery of an ancient text would not fully refute the author's argument that we find it difficult to understand the role that myth played in the distant past. Choice D is correct.

Choices A and B misrepresent the new information in the question stem. An original text from the first century B.C. could not be called data from a living culture, nor is an original text "rescripted." Choice C is incorrect, because the author never indicates that myths cannot be told through poetry.

114. In the passage, the author draws an analogy between:

    A.   naturalist and historicist approaches to under-standing the role of myth in aboriginal society.

    B.   the role of science in the modern world and the place of myth in antiquity.

    C.   ancient gods and heroes and anthropomorphized cosmological entities in today's aboriginal cultures.

    D.   science and anthropology.

B The author argues that science performs the same function today as myth performed for ancient societies. For example, the author writes, "For the civilizations that produced them, myth occupied a place and served a function within the social fabric reserved today for medicine, astrophysics, and cybernetics" (lines 8–11). This supports the analogy in choice B.

Drawing an analogy involves showing similarities. Choice A is incorrect because naturalist and historicist approaches are contrasted, not compared, with each other (paragraph 5). Similarly, while both science and anthropology (choice D) are mentioned, the author does not compare or show similarities between the two. In paragraph 5, the author asserts that the naturalists believed aboriginal peoples worshiped anthropomorphized cosmological entities, but the author rejects the naturalist view. Therefore, we cannot say that the author draws an analogy between ancient gods and heroes on one side, and entities that may not even exist in today's aboriginal culture on the other side. We can eliminate choice C.

115. According to the passage, anthropologists can still gain understanding of the meaning and function of early human myth by:

    A.   developing computer models based on modern aboriginal communities.

    B.   applying contemporary theories and doctrines to interpret aboriginal social structures.

    C.   learning about the role played by myth in the lives of aborigines today.

    D.   adopting aboriginal traditions and truths as guiding moral precepts and analytical tools.

C The author suggests that it is necessary to "study modern aborigines to discover the strategies and insights of human consciousness in its primal attempts to process perceptual reality into cultural rules" (lines 41–44). Furthermore, he points out that "by venturing into the field,...Malinowski...penetrated the core of the matter" (lines 57–59). Choice C is correct.

Choice A contradicts the author's implication that in order to gain an understanding of early human myth it is necessary to distance oneself from "the glitter, flash, and buzz of this Early Electronic Age" (paragraph 4). Choice B directly contradicts statements made in the passage. The author explicitly declares that understanding may be achieved by "anthropologists willing to shed their cosmetics of doctrine and costumes of theory." Furthermore, in paragraph 3 the author indicates that one problem we have in understanding ancient myth is that we find it difficult to see past our modern experience and assumptions. Finally, the author does refer to the need "to discover the strategies and insights" of those who live by myth (lines 41–44), and mentions the "faith and moral wisdom" it contains for them (lines 61–65). But he stops short of advocating the adoption of aboriginal traditions and truths as effective guidelines for our own time (choice D).

116. Which of the following statements, if true, would most *weaken* the author's argument that Malinowski's work in the Trobriands does justice to the true function of myth in that culture?

    A.   Sir James Frazer had as a primary goal the reconciliation of the naturalist and historicist schools.

    B.   The specific myths that define Trobriand society contain some images and themes found in no other ancient or modern cultures.

    C.   The presence of outside anthropological observers significantly changes the speech and behaviors of the members of the culture being observed.

    D.   Many well-respected anthropologists have rejected Malinowski's conclusions.

C If Malinowski's very presence in a culture would change how the people of that culture spoke and behaved, it would cast doubt on any conclusions Malinowski drew from his observations. Therefore, if choice C were true, Malinowski may not in fact have "penetrated to the core of the matter" (paragraph 6) of the true role of myth in human civilization. Choice C weakens the author's argument.

Although Malinowski was Frazer's disciple (lines 58–59), he did not necessarily follow Frazer's lead in every respect. While choice A would cast doubt on the validity or depth of Frazer's interpretation of myth (given that the author rejects both the naturalist and historicist schools), it doesn't directly undermine either Malinowski or the author's interpretation of Malinowski's work. Choice B does not weaken the author's arguments, because neither the author nor Malinowski claims that the specifics of myths are the same in every culture. Rather, they both argue that myth as a whole plays a central, defining role in ancient and aboriginal societies, not all societies. Finally, the fact that not all respected anthropologists agree with Malinowski is not enough to weaken either his claims or the author's interpretation of those claims (choice D). The author himself mentions anthropologists from two opposing camps (historicists and naturalists) who would disagree; for all we know, they may be well respected by their colleagues.

117. The author implies that the need ancient peoples had for myth's clarity and reassurance arose mainly from:

    A.   feelings of powerlessness and vulnerability.

    B.   an unstable social fabric.

    C.   ineffective medical techniques.

    D.   a finite sense of themselves.

A In paragraph 2, the author writes, "Myth blazed like a beacon of clarity and reassurance in an uncertain and terrifying universe. Myth…taught [people] how to see themselves in relation to forces beyond their control, and how to survive and relate within a human society built on hierarchical power and often ruthless savagery." This supports answer choice A.

While ancient society is described as "hierarchical," ruthless, and savage (lines 15–17), it is not depicted as unstable (choice B). Choice C is a trap. The author's statement that medicine is one thing that has replaced myth in our modern society (lines 8–10) is not enough information to infer that medical techniques were ineffective in ancient times, or that lack of good medical care contributed to the need for myth. Be careful not to use outside knowledge. Choice D confuses cause and effect. Myth "gave people a finite sense of their place in the scheme of things" (lines 13–14); it did not arise out of a finite sense of self.

Passage VII (118–126)

118. The central thesis of the passage is that:

    A.   film reviewers, film consumers, and film studios all determine whether a movie will be successful or not.

    B.   cultural critics offer deeper understandings of film aesthetics than do film reviewers.

    C.   movie reviewers and cultural critics fulfill distinct functions in their discussions of film.

    D.   film interpretation is a higher art than acting or directing.

C The first half of the passage is generally concerned with the commercial aspects of film, and the role that movie reviewers play. The second half of the passage focuses on the role of the cultural film critics, and demonstrates their distinct function. Choice C incorporates both of these aspects of the passage and, as such, captures the author's central thesis.

Choices A and B, while supported in the passage, are too narrow to be the central thesis. In particular, choice A leaves out the author's contrast between reviewers and cultural critics (paragraphs 3 and 4). Choice B leaves out the author's discussion of the role played by reviewers in the film industry (paragraph 3). Choice D is too extreme. While the passage does describe actors' and directors' efforts to sell their movies (lines 13–14), the author does not go so far as to suggest that acting or directing themselves are lesser arts.

119. The author cites Aumont's essay primarily for the purpose of:

- **A.** proving that reviewers contribute to the economic success of mass-market films.
- **B.** clarifying the distinction between a critic and a reviewer.
- **C.** elaborating on the topic of film interpretation.
- **D.** emphasizing the role of publicity in the film industry.

B The quotes from Aumont in paragraph 4 specifies a distinction between a reviewer who offers a " 'judgment of appreciation'—thumbs up or thumbs down" and a critic who considers " 'the richness of the work' " leading to " 'an interpretation.' " Choice B is correct.

Choice A is the right answer to the wrong question. The author argues this point earlier in the passage (see lines 29–39), not in the context of Aumont's analysis in the last paragraph. While the idea of interpretation is introduced in paragraph 4, the primary purpose of the author's discussion of Aumont is not to elaborate on the topic (choice C), but to assert it in the first place. In addition, the claim that critics interpret films is offered in support of the more central argument about the distinction between reviewers and critics. Choice D is incorrect. While the role of publicity is part of the author's contrast between reviewers and critics (paragraph 4), this point is made earlier in the passage. The contrast drawn by Aumont is more specifically between reviewers who focus on appreciation (or lack thereof), and critics who offer their interpretation of the deeper meanings of the film.

120. Based on the passage, a film critic who declares, "Without doubt, the best thing about that movie was the psychological development of character," most likely:

- **A.** would refuse to write about a high-budget film that included major stars in the cast.
- **B.** generally chooses to write about films that have received positive reviews from other critics.
- **C.** would not assume that a movie that had received few mass media reviews was not worth seeing.
- **D.** would enjoy this summer's smash hit.

C Choice C is supported by the passage. If a person appreciates aspects like psychological development (as critics tend to, according to the author), he or she may look beyond celebrity of the actors or topical plots. Therefore, this critic may find value in films that are overlooked by reviewers, who tend to focus on the most highly publicized movies (paragraph 3).

The idea that a film critic's interest in a movie would not be primarily sparked by big budget or bankable stars does not mean that he/she would refuse to write about such films. Furthermore, the author of the passage never suggests that big-budget movies with big stars cannot also raise "historical, psychological, sociopolitical, and aesthetic issues," interests attributed to the film critic in lines 54–56. Therefore, choice A is incorrect. The author does not discuss whether or not one critic's interest in a film is dependent on whether or not the film has been written about (positively or negatively) by other critics (choice B). And, while critics may often choose to write about less well known movies, they may or may not enjoy more popular movies (choice D).

121. Which of the following scenarios would be *least* likely, given the author's depiction of the relationship between film reviewers and the film industry?

- **A.** A heavily marketed movie with a close relationship to topical concerns receives very few mass media reviews.
- **B.** A film inspired by recent political events is judged by a cultural critic to have little relevance to the nature of modern technological society.
- **C.** A film intended for a limited "art house" audience unexpectedly becomes a popular success.
- **D.** A widely reviewed movie starring two celebrity actors makes little money at the box office and closes in two weeks.

A The author argues that reviewers' choices of films to analyze are strongly and positively affected by topicality and marketing (paragraph 3). Therefore, one would expect a topical, heavily marketed film to receive many, not few, mass media reviews. Choice A is correct.

Choice B has no direct relevance to the author's argument about film reviewers (the choice refers to cultural critics, not reviewers; the question asks about reviewers). Furthermore, the author does not suggest that cultural critics will find contemporary social relevance in all films with a contemporary theme. Choice C is incorrect, because the passage does not claim that only mass marketed films can become hits. We can eliminate choice D because while the author would expect this film to be widely reviewed (lines 40–42), he does not claim that reviews are a guarantee of success. There is no reason, based on the passage, to think that such a movie is a guaranteed box-office success.

122. The author of the passage most likely believes that:

- I. film is as much an economic institution as an artistic one.
- II. positive reviews are crucial to a film's financial success.
- III. the critics' vision is central to a film's meaning.

- **A.** I only
- **B.** I and II only
- **C.** II and III only
- **D.** I, II, and III

B Item I is supported in paragraphs 1 and 3. Item II is also true. The author states that the "film reviewer occupies a position central to the ongoing viability of the medium, as an intermediary between [the] industry… and the international public whose interest provides the industry its monetary basis" (lines 29–34). From this we can conclude that films rely to a great extent on positive reviews for their box-office success. Item III is false, because the passage does not suggest that critics create meaning, only that they interpret it. Items I and II are true, making answer choice B correct.

123. Which of the following statements best expresses an assumption underlying the author's depiction of the daily film analysts' motivation for writing their reviews?

- **A.** Maintaining their own high public visibility is the most important factor in reviewers' choice of films.
- **B.** Daily film analysts do not primarily intend their reviews to illuminate core aspects of modern society by describing the qualities that tend to contribute to a movie's popular success.
- **C.** Cultural criticism can illustrate how core cultural patterns of a society are reproduced in the characters and plot lines of films.
- **D.** The more the industry spends on marketing and publicity, the more likely a reviewer is to give a favorable response in order to maintain status within the industry.

B The author contrasts reviewers or "daily analysts" with cultural critics. The former cover narrower ground, expressing "judgments of appreciation," while the latter delve into the deeper social, psychological, and artistic significance and meaning of films (paragraph 4). This contrast involves the assumption that reviewers do not primarily intend to analyze or interpret films on these deeper levels. Therefore, choice B is correct.

Choice A is too extreme (notice the word "most" in the statement). While a reviewer's public visibility is listed as a factor (see lines 45–47), the author does not prioritize it over all other factors. Choice D is too strong. While marketing will affect what films a reviewer chooses to review (paragraph 3), the author does not imply or assume that these reviews will be favorable. Finally, choice C is not directly relevant to the motivation of reviewers (who are distinguished from cultural critics).

124. The author's claim at the end of the first paragraph that it is consumers who most powerfully determine a film's financial success or failure is supported in the passage in part through the observation that:

    A.   most moviegoers have not cultivated a taste for cinematic art.

    B.   film reviewers play a crucial role in the movie industry.

    C.   people go to see movies for many different reasons, ranging from enjoyment of a good story to interest in cinematic themes and messages.

    D.   escalating production costs force producers to cut back on artistic criteria.

B In lines 29–34, the author argues that reviewers play a crucial role in the movie industry as an intermediary between those producing the films and those paying to see them. If reviewers' "thumbs up or thumbs down" to the public (lines 56–58) is so important to the industry, it adds support to the author's statement that consumers determine the financial success of a movie. Choice B is correct.

Remember, the correct answer needs to be both supported by the passage and relevant to the topic raised in the question. Choices A and C satisfy only part of the requirement. Choice A is too extreme and is not relevant to the topic of the question. The author indicates that various facets of movies appeal to different filmgoers, but he does not say that the public's lack of artistic taste

determines a film's success at the box office. Choice C is not relevant to the question. The author acknowledges moviegoers' wide range of motivations in paragraph 2, but this does not lend support specifically to the author's argument about the role played by consumers in a film's financial success. Choice D is too strongly worded. While the author implies that escalating costs do lead to intensified publicity campaigns (lines 1–7), the passage does not indicate that this happens at the expense of artistic merit, or that producers are forced to prioritize costs over merit. Furthermore, even if this were supported by the passage, it would give no direct support to the issue cited in the question.

125. In lines 60–61 the author cites Aumont's claim that critics work by "deconstructing the elements pertinent to the work." By *deconstructing*, Aumont most likely means:

    A.   eliminating.

    B.   building.

    C.   explaining.

    D.   demolishing.

C The author writes in the last paragraph that a critic provides an interpretation of the film through analyzing its different aspects. If we reword the sentence as, "explaining the elements pertinent to the work," it makes sense in the context of that section of the passage. Choice C is correct.

The critic does not remove or eliminate (choice A) the elements, but instead "illuminates" them. "Deconstruct" in this context means to take apart, explain, and interpret. If we reword the sentence as "building the elements pertinent to the work," it implies that the critic him- or herself creates the elements that make up a film, rather than interprets them. Choice B doesn't work. Finally, the author does not suggest that by interpreting a film's elements, a cultural critic destroys or damages ("demolishes," choice D) the film in any way.

126. Which of the following statements is NOT presented in the passage to help define the difference between a film critic and a film reviewer?

- **A.** Reviewers choose films partly based on the interests of the movie-going public.
- **B.** Critics choose films to interpret in part based on the relevance of those films to larger social issues.
- **C.** Reviewers are concerned with maintaining professional standing.
- **D.** Critics are unconcerned with audience responsiveness to films.

D Remember, you are looking for the statement that DOES NOT meet the criterion in the question stem. The author does not imply that critics do not care about how an audience responds to a film. In addition to being too extreme, the statement in choice D is not used by the author to help "define the difference between a film critic and a film reviewer." Choice D is the correct answer.

In lines 38–40, the author states, "reviewers feel an obligation to address the general interests of the viewing public" (choice A). The ideas in choice B and choice C are also used to contrast critics with reviewers. In lines 48–49, "the cultural critic tends to focus on larger social perspectives," and writes analyses that "embrace historical, psychological, sociopolitical and esthetic issues" (lines 54–56; choice B). In lines 45–47, the author notes that daily reviewers (unlike critics) often write reviews "if for no other reason than to maintain their own visibility" (choice C).

Passage VIII (Questions 127–131)

127. The main idea of the passage is that:

- **A.** an artist's spiritual beliefs provide the most powerful influence on his or her artistic themes.
- **B.** Chagall could not have made great art without his early education in the Bible.
- **C.** Chagall saw himself as a spiritual mediator who could bring hope and love to the world through his art.
- **D.** genius emerges only through a life of genuine suffering.

C The theme in choice C is reiterated throughout the passage. In particular, the second and third paragraphs describe how Chagall, faced with the suffering he experienced and saw around him, came to believe in the primacy of hope and love. Paragraphs 4–6 describe his vision of the "spiritual ministry" of the artist. At the end of paragraph 4 the author states, "Through his craft, then, the painter brings love and salvation to humankind." Choice C is correct.

Choice A is too broad to be the main idea of this passage. While this may be true of Chagall, the author does not suggest that it is true of all artists. Choice D is also too broad to be the main point and is not supported by the passage. While Chagall's genius was formed in part through his suffering (paragraphs 2 and 3), the author does not argue that this is the only way his genius could have emerged. In addition, the passage is specifically about Chagall, not all artists or individuals. Choice B is too extreme to be supported by the passage (the author describes the influence of the Bible on Chagall, but does not indicate that he could not have been a great artist without it). Furthermore, even if it were supported, it would be too narrow to be the main idea.

128. According to the passage, how did Chagall's life experience affect his artistic vision?

    A. It led him to believe that the artist is powerless in the face of the suffering caused by war and disease.

    B. It prevented him from seeing reality and moving forward artistically.

    C. It led him to protest against the oppressive policies of the Russian state and to call for political reform.

    D. It inspired images of the artist guiding humanity through the turmoil of worldly existence toward redemption through love.

D Choice D is correct. In paragraphs 2 and 3 the author describes how Chagall's experience of turmoil and suffering inspired him to turn to themes of love, hope, and redemption. The author states that for Chagall, "the painter brings love and salvation to humankind" through his work (lines 45–46). The image of the painter as a guide appears in *The Apparition* (lines 42–46).

Choice A contradicts the passage. Far from powerless, the artist in Chagall's artistic vision "brings love and salvation to humankind" (lines 45–46). We can eliminate choice B, because although the author states that Chagall's work was not "a mirror of reality" (lines 1–4), Chagall's life certainly did not prevent him from seeing reality. Rather, his life experience inspired him to create an artistic vision and philosophy that sought to provide hope to a suffering world (paragraphs 2, 4, and 6). Furthermore, there is no negative tone or criticism in the passage to indicate that the author believes Chagall failed to progress artistically. Finally, the passage never mentions political protest or calls for reform (choice C). Chagall's idea of salvation, as described, was spiritual, not political.

129. The passage suggests that Chagall's use of color in *Jacob's Dream* is related to his artistic themes in that:

    A. color instills a dynamic interaction among related parts of his composition.

    B. the theme of redemption in this work is subordinate to the emotional effect of the colors themselves.

    C. each artistic idea is color-coded throughout his work.

    D. primary colors like red and yellow usually symbolize hope, while dark colors represent chaos and fear.

A Support for choice A is found in paragraphs 5 and 6. The author describes the "swirling maelstrom of purple and black and plaintive yellow" on the left of the painting, and the "cool blues and pure white that define...the right half of the picture." Split between these two halves defined by a contrast in color, Chagall's canvas achieves a dynamic interaction between these separate parts, as "through the dreaming figure, Chagall's colors penetrate the schism, surprising the dark, turbulent world with brave reverberations of grace and light."

Choice B mistakes the relationship described in the passage; Chagall's use of color facilitated his expression of the themes of suffering and redemption (see paragraphs 5 and 6). The word "subordinate" in particular makes choice B wrong. While the author interprets the meaning of the colors in the canvases described in the passage (see paragraphs 5 and 6), she does not argue that every idea is always coded to the same color in all Chagall's works (choice C). Choice D is inconsistent with the author's description of *Jacob's Dream*, in which yellow is used in the dark and chaotic side of the painting (lines 50–52). Furthermore, the author does not generalize about Chagall's use of colors in other paintings.

130. The author quotes the French critic Fernand Hazere (lines 40–41) primarily for the purpose of:

A. supporting his own interpretation of other scholarly works.

B. relating modern French criticism to other critical approaches.

C. further describing Chagall's artistic inspiration and purpose.

D. calling into question the sincerity of Chagall's self-appointed missionary role.

C Choice C is correct. In paragraph 4, the author uses Hazere's comment transitionally to emphasize the point that Chagall's spiritual understanding led him to recognize his "privileges and responsibilities" as an artist.

Choices A, B, and D are incorrect. The author of the passage presents no interpretations of other scholarly works (choice A), nor does she criticize Chagall in any way in the passage, or call into question his sincerity (choice D). In addition, the author of the passage does not discuss French criticism generally, or compare it to other approaches (choice B). The fact that Hazere is French is not a significant issue in the passage.

131. In another essay, the author of the passage posits that for Chagall, the reality of art lies in its impact on the "eyes, hearts, and minds of those who view it." Which of the following interpretations of *Jacob's Dream* best exemplifies both this claim and the mission of the artist, as that mission is described in the passage?

A. The central human figure represents a sinner torn between the temptations of bodily pleasures and the joy of spiritual redemption.

B. Jacob represents the antithesis of the painter, as Jacob is mired in a maelstrom depicting hell while the painter wishes to deliver himself and others from suffering.

C. The contrast between light and dark represents the eternal and irresolvable struggle between good and evil that defines human existence.

D. Jacob represents the painter, who acts as an intercessor for humanity by bringing a message of hope to the world.

D Choice D is consistent with the information in the question as well as with the author's interpretation of the painting and the main idea of the passage as a whole. The author writes, "through his craft, the painter brings love and salvation to humanity" (lines 45–46). This theme which characterizes *The Apparition* is "reiterated in the painting *Jacob's Dream*" (lines 47–48), where Jacob acts as "mediator" between "the fierce frenzy of the bodily world and the tranquil reassurance of the spiritual" (lines 59–63). The meaning or reality of Chagall's art, then, lies in its redemptive and inspirational effect on those who view it.

In paragraphs 5 and 6, the central figure represents a mediator or redeemer who looks towards the light, not a sinner, and the "bodily world" is described as "plaintive," chaotic, dark, and full of "fierce frenzy," not as pleasurable. Therefore, choice A is incorrect. Choice B is inconsistent with the passage. In paragraph 4–6, the author suggests that Jacob represents the painter who is moving himself and his viewers away from darkness and chaos, not the "antithesis of the painter." Choice C is not supported in the passage. According to the author, Chagall saw his painting as a way to redeem (bring communion to) humanity. In paragraph 4, the author writes, "Through his craft, then, the author brings love and salvation to humankind." At the end of the passage, she writes, "Refracted through the dreaming figure [of Jacob as mediator], Chagall's colors penetrate the schism, surprising the dark, turbulent world with brave reverberations of grace and light." It follows that the author would not accept an interpretation based on an irresolvable conflict.

Passage IX (Questions 132–137)

132. According to the passage, the levels of atmospheric cations in the Hubbard Brook Experimental Forest:

    A. were higher than levels in Sjoangen forests 30 years ago, and are lower now.
    B. have always been 25 percent lower than those in Sjoangen forests.
    C. declined by nearly 50 percent over the past three decades.
    D. dwindled from 74 percent to 49 percent.

C Choice C is correct. The author reports that "over the past three decades" cations in the Hubbard Brook facility dropped "by 49 percent," while those in Sjoangen fell by "74 percent" (lines 78–81). Nothing in the passage compares their relative levels either 30 years ago or now. That is, the percentage by which each dropped tells us nothing about whether the total amount in one area is or was higher than the total amount in another area, so choice A can be eliminated. Choice B is a trap based in part on the fact that the difference between 74 and 49 is 25. The passage compares the percentage by which each declined, not their total amounts. All we know is that the Swedish forests now have a lesser percentage (26%, if they have declined by 74%) of their original atmospheric cations than has Hubbard Brook (51%, if it has declined by 49%). We do not know what the original levels were, or which one was higher. Choice D misuses the numbers in a way that is not supported by the passage.

133. The passage suggests that the 1990 NAPAP evaluation of acid rain is consistent with the United States government's decision to:

    A. legislate emissions controls carefully crafted on the basis of scientific testimony.
    B. warn coal-burning industries to reduce acid-producing emissions voluntarily.
    C. fund ongoing university studies to monitor the effects of acid rain.
    D. downplay environmentalists' concerns about damage to forests caused by acid rain.

D The author notes that both the NAPAP and the U.S. government concluded that "there was no clear evidence" (lines 12–16) that acid rain causes ecosystem damage. This supports choice D.

See paragraphs 1 and 2. There is no mention of emissions controls enacted in the United States in paragraph 2 or in the rest of the passage, so we can eliminate choice A. While the author does discuss sulfur dioxide and nitrogen dioxide emissions from "North American coal-burning industries," she makes no reference to warnings to the coal industry issued by the U.S. government. So, we can eliminate choice B. Because the author refers to "recent research" which "called into question" the 1990 NAPAP conclusions, one might assume (without evidence from the passage) that the government funded additional studies of the problem. But there is nothing in the passage that supports this choice, C; as far as we know, the government continued to deny that there was a serious problem.

134. According to the third paragraph of the passage, the role played by calcium and magnesium ions in the ecosystem's cation exchange mechanism is to:

    A. give up their relatively weak anion bonds.
    B. deplete the ecosystem's supply of cations.
    C. bond soil anions in tight electrophilic linkage.
    D. allow electrophilic hydrogen ions to acidify the soil.

A In lines 27–32, the author explains that "weakly bound...calcium and magnesium cations...cannot compete with the stronger attraction of acid rain's hydrogen ions, which displace them from their chemical bonds with soil anions." This supports choice A.

Choices B, C, and D conflict with information provided in the passage. Paragraph 4 explains that it is not calcium and magnesium cations that deplete the ecosystem (choice B), but the constant assault of "acid rain's more strongly electrophilic hydrogen ions" by which "the exchange mechanism is exhausted." In lines 26–32, the author notes that calcium and magnesium bonds with soil anions are relatively weak, not "tight" (choice C), and break down readily in the presence of the "more strongly electrophilic hydrogen ions." Finally, the passage states that as long as the supply of calcium and magnesium cations in the soil remains undepleted, these ions prevent (not allow) acidification of the soil by hydrogen ions (choice D).

135. Based on information in the passage, stringent regulations on emissions of sulfur dioxide and nitrogen oxides in Europe have:

- **A.** proven ineffective because of inadequate inspections and enforcement.
- **B.** reduced the acidity of rainwater by a significant factor.
- **C.** added to the ongoing positive effects of earlier laws limiting particulate emissions.
- **D.** likely been limited in their effect by other environmental regulations.

D In paragraph 7, the author says that "for more than two decades...restrictions on particulate emissions" have reduced the levels of "atmospheric dust particles which...provide a natural neutralization of acid rain." This suggests that regulations limiting the emission of microscopic dust particles have reduced the amount of particles available in the atmosphere and soil to neutralize acid rain and allows us to eliminate choice C and accept choice D.

In paragraph 6, the author discusses legislated reductions in smokestack emissions, and says that "despite those controls" the acidity of rainwater "continues to register...significantly higher than the norm." He implies that the controls are in place, and that ineffective enforcement is not the problem, making choice A incorrect. Choice B can be eliminated, because the author states, "rainwater continues to register around pH 3.3—significantly more acidic than the norm."

136. Hedin and Likens' research, as described in the passage, implies that societies determined to prevent environmental damage from rain acidification might find it necessary to:

- **A.** maintain current limitations on sulfur dioxide and nitrogen oxides emissions.
- **B.** eliminate current restrictions on particulate emissions.
- **C.** balance the economic costs of pollution controls with the benefits.
- **D.** consider potential unintended consequences of environmental regulations when formulating industrial policy.

D See paragraphs 6–8. The author argues that current regulatory policy has had the unintended effect of weakening the cation buffer and so leaving the ecosystem "vulnerable to acid damage." To prevent further damage, nations would need to take all potential effects of industrial policy into account. Choice D is correct.

The passage states that current limitations are ineffective in reducing acid rain, perhaps because of the counterbalancing effect of reduction in particulate emissions (paragraph 7). The author ends the passage with the statement that, "at currently permissible emission levels the ecosystem will remain vulnerable to acid damage." Therefore, the passage gives no direct support for maintaining controls at current levels (choice A). Choice B is unlikely, because although Hedin and Likens identify restrictions on particulate emissions as a contributor to the exhaustion of the cation buffer system, to argue that governments should replenish the buffer by permitting increased dust particle emissions would be to ignore the "significant respiratory problems caused by microscopic dust in the atmosphere" which initially compelled "industrialized countries" to impose those restrictions (paragraph 7). Finally, although choice C offers an argument frequently heard in current political discussion, nothing in the passage touches on the question of the economic costs of pollution controls. Be careful not to draw on outside knowledge.

137. According to the passage, acidification may cause all of the following EXCEPT:

- **A.** respiratory problems.
- **B.** crop injury.
- **C.** stream and lake sterilization.
- **D.** decline in the diversity of amphibian species.

A In lines 67–70, the author cites microscopic dust, not acidification, as a cause of respiratory problems. Therefore, choice A is the correct answer to this EXCEPT question. Lines 44–47 state that acidification produces "injury to crops" (choice B) and "sterilization of lakes and streams" (choice C). Lines 48–52 note that acidification produces a "reduction in the variety of amphibian species" (choice D).

ANSWERS AND EXPLANATIONS

WRITING SAMPLE

Note: There is no single "correct" or "best" answer to any particular writing sample question. The essays provided in this section are possible responses; they display the characteristics of a top-scoring essay.

Part 1

In a democracy, the rights of the minority should take precedence over the desires of the majority.

When we hear the word "democracy," a phrase that often comes to mind is "majority rule." While the principle of majority rule certainly structures our electoral system in the United States, a true democracy has to go beyond simply counting up votes and installing the most popular candidate. Ideas such as the guarantee of civil rights and equal protection under the law have to be included in our vision of a democratic system. In the realm of civil rights, the freedom of speech is especially important, as citizens who are not allowed to speak freely and to hear a variety of dissenting opinions from others cannot participate effectively in a representative system. Once we begin censoring speech that the majority finds offensive, we step onto a slippery slope that may eventually lead to a disappearance of the right to free speech itself. In a well-known case many years ago, the ACLU successfully defended the right of Neo-Nazis to march through Skokie, Illinois, a largely Jewish suburb of Chicago. Many claimed that this presented a clear exception to the right to free speech, as no one could legitimately defend the marchers' ideas. However, the ACLU convincingly argued that no matter how offensive and indefensible the speech, we can't silence it simply because it violates most peoples' beliefs. In this case, the desire of the majority was to shut down the march, but the right of the minority to speak should have and did take precedence.

However, in some extreme cases, the rights of a minority of the population must lose out in service of the needs and desires of the nation as a whole. In times of war, when the security of the nation is at risk, the government is justified in violating certain individual civil rights. Not only our right to free speech but even our right to bodily autonomy and self-defense can be legitimately suspended. For example, during the Vietnam War, young men were drafted into military service, often against their will. Those who defend the draft argue that when the security of the nation is at stake, individuals may be required to make great sacrifices, even to give their lives in order to make the nation safe. Thus the desire of the majority for national security may override the right of some individuals to protect and ensure their own personal security. While many would argue that North Vietnam did not pose a real threat to the U.S., most would accept that if a war is in fact just and necessary, citizens can be called upon to die for their country. Yet this sacrifice will be required of only a minority of citizens; most will be able to go about their lives with little significant disruption. Of course, for something so fundamental as civil rights to be suspended, the danger must be real. During WWII the government interned Japanese Americans in concentration camps, with the rationale that these citizens posed a threat to national security. It has become clear since then that no such threat existed and that the internment was unjustified, even though it was in line with the fears and desires of the non-Japanese majority at the time.

Overall, then, the rights of a minority can only be suspended in the face of a clear and concrete threat. Furthermore, this suspension of rights must be temporary. If it generalizes into an ongoing policy, placing permanent restrictions or unequal burdens on certain classes of citizens, the democratic system itself will eventually fail. Democracy provides us with great gifts, but it also comes with certain duties; one duty we have as citizens is to tolerate the existence and the opinions of those with whom we disagree, even of those we find repugnant. Only if the minority acts in a way that threatens our lives (either on an individual or on a societal level), or if a minority must be sacrificed to preserve the nation as a whole, can we take the rights of that minority away. In fact, in the long run the majority is also protected when we protect minority rights. The danger of the slippery slope is a real one. The more we accept limitations on the rights of others, the greater the likelihood that one day we will wake up to discover our own freedoms have disappeared.

Part 2
Advances in technology contribute to an increase in the standard of living.

Back in the 1800s, Thomas Carlyle said, "Man is a tool-using animal. Without tools he is nothing, with tools he is all." This is even more true today. We live in the "Age of Technology," where almost every aspect of our lives is shaped and defined by the tools and machines we use. While in the past a significant advance in technology may have occurred once or twice in a century, now things change radically within the space of a few years. Two decades ago, personal computers were rare. Now, almost every aspect of our lives depends on access to computer technology. For the most part, as technology improves, so does our quality of life. It is difficult to imagine living in a time when it took months to travel across the nation, when it took weeks to get news about events in other countries, or when it took an entire day to do a load of laundry by hand. We even get impatient at the idea of spending an hour cooking a meal in the oven when we could instead accomplish the same result in 10 minutes with a microwave. Technology usually allows us to accomplish tasks more easily and more quickly. In many ways, then, our standard of living is higher today because our daily chores not only involve less hard physical labor, but can also be done more quickly, freeing up time to be spent on more enjoyable activities. We also can enjoy technology more directly; resources such as DVD and MP3 players and the Internet make it easier to entertain ourselves.

However, in recent years an unexpected consequence of technological advances has become more and more apparent. Labor-saving technology is supposed to free us to spend more time doing what we enjoy. However, Americans are working more and more hours on the job; we now have the longest work week and the fewest days of vacation of any nation in the world. How can this be, given that we are also one of the most technologically advanced nations in the world? While economic and social changes play a role in this, we can also see that the more accessible we are to our job through email and cell phones, the more of our "free time" we are expected to spend working. In the past, once an employee left the workplace, he or she was "off the clock." Now, even people with relatively low status and low-paying jobs are often expected to check and respond to work-related email at home and to be available by cell phone for work-related discussions after hours. According to statistics tracking increases in stress-related conditions, we are not working more because we enjoy it, but because we have to. When people can spend more of their time working due to technological advances, they are more likely to be required to do so by their employer.

Therefore, when technology allows us to accomplish an existing task more quickly and easily, it improves our standard of living both by reducing the drudgery involved in daily life and by allowing us to do more of the things that we enjoy. However, when technological advances create new tasks and responsibilities, it works in the opposite direction. When work can infiltrate every nook and cranny of our lives, the quality of our lives suffers. Winning the forty-hour work week was one of the major successes of the labor movement in the twentieth century. That forty-hour week has now largely disappeared. We may be defined as human beings in part by our ability and desire to use tools, as Carlyle said, but we shouldn't be defined only by our productive capacity in the workplace. Technological evolution is now much more rapid than socioeconomic evolution; society needs to catch up and restructure the workplace so that technology is a resource but not a burden.

ANSWERS AND EXPLANATIONS

BIOLOGICAL SCIENCES

Questions 138–214

Passage I

138. Which of the following is NOT a possible explanation for why a person becomes temporarily blind upon walking into a dark movie theater on a sunny day?

    A. The retinal in rod cells has not yet been converted to the 11-*cis* form.
    B. The rod cells are already depolarized.
    C. The cone cells require higher intensity light to be stimulated.
    D. Flow of Na^+ into the rod cells has stopped.

B When in bright light (such as outside on a sunny day) virtually all of the retinal in rod cells is in its all-*trans* form. Once it is converted back to its 11-*cis* form by the enzymes in the rod cells, it is almost immediately straightened again by light; this straightening is referred to as "bleaching." Thus, in bright light the majority of the rods are inactive (bleached) and are unable to respond upon first entering a darkened theater (choice A is a possible explanation and can be eliminated). The passage states that cone cells are less sensitive to light, and the relatively dim light of a movie theater is not enough to stimulate them (choice C is a possible explanation and can be eliminated). If Na^+ flow into the rods has been stopped, it is because the cells have been activated by light (bleached) and cannot respond (choice D is a possible explanation and can be eliminated). However, rod cells are normally depolarized at rest (when not responding to light). In the absence of light, cGMP keeps the Na^+ channel open, and Na^+ flows into the cell, down its gradient, causing the cell to be depolarized. When light strikes the retinal, a series of events occur that cause the channel to close, which stops Na^+ from entering. This causes the stimulated rod cell to hyperpolarize. So, if the rod cells are already depolarized, that means they are at rest and are ready to respond to light. This cannot be a possible explanation for the temporary blindness, making choice B the correct answer choice.

139. At rest, rod cells continuously release neurotransmitter onto the bipolar cells. However, upon stimulation by light, neurotransmitter release from the rod is stopped and the bipolar cell fires an action potential. Which of the following could best explain this?

    A. Both rods and bipolar cells are depolarized at rest.
    B. The neurotransmitter opens Na^+ channels in the bipolar cell.
    C. The neurotransmitter inhibits the bipolar cell.
    D. Light closes Na^+ channels in the bipolar cell.

C If the neurotransmitter were inhibitory, then its continuous release from the rod cell in the absence of light would prevent the bipolar cell from firing action potentials. Then, when light strikes the rod cell and the release of neurotransmitter is stopped, the bipolar cell is no longer inhibited and can fire action potentials. If the bipolar cell were also depolarized at rest (the time during which neurotransmitter is released), then the cessation of transmitter release would cause the cell to hyperpolarize and prevent an action potential from occurring (choice A is wrong). If the neurotransmitter opened Na^+ channels in the bipolar cell, then its release during rest would cause action potentials, not the other way around (choice B is wrong). There is no reason to assume that light has any effect on a bipolar cell; in any case, if light did close Na^+ channels in the bipolar cell, the cell would stop firing action potentials (choice D is wrong).

140. In which other process could PDE be involved?

    A. Protein synthesis
    B. Nucleic acid synthesis
    C. Protein digestion
    D. Nucleic acid digestion

D Phosphodiesterase is an enzyme that breaks phosphodiester bonds, such as are found in nucleic acids. Thus, PDE could be involved in the breakdown (digestion) of nucleic acids (choice D is correct and B is wrong). Recall that nucleotide monomers are held together with phosphodiester bonds to form the nucleic acid polymer. Proteins are polymers of amino acids, held together by peptide bonds, upon which PDE has no effect (choices A and C are wrong).

141. Vitamin A deficiency leads to a decrease in the ability to see in dim light. Poor night vision can be corrected by supplementation with this vitamin. Could supplementation with vitamin A also help correct the blurriness due to myopia?

    A. No, myopic blurriness is not due to vitamin A deficiency.
    B. No, vitamin A only helps synthesize rhodopsin and would have no effect on cones.
    C. Yes, increased retinal synthesis would increase sharpness of vision.
    D. Yes, myopic patients can see better in bright light.

A Myopia (nearsightedness) is caused by a misshapen eyeball (in this case it's too long). Vitamin A is a precursor to retinal, which is part of the visual pigment; however, vitamin A supplementation cannot change the shape of the eyeball, and so would have no effect on the blurriness of myopia. Retinal (derived from vitamin A) is found in both rods and cones (choice B is wrong), and increased retinal synthesis would increase sharpness of vision by increasing the ability of the photoreceptors to respond to light, however this is irrelevant since in myopia, bad photoreceptors are not the problem (choice C is wrong). Anybody can see better in bright light since cones are activated, but again, this is irrelevant to the question (choice D is wrong).

142. The middle layer of the eyeball wall most likely contains:

    A. bipolar cells.
    B. photoreceptors.
    C. blood vessels.
    D. collagen fibers.

C The first paragraph of the passage describes the wall of the eye, and the middle layer is described as being pigmented (colored) and vascular (contains blood vessels). Photoreceptors and bipolar cells are essentially specialized neurons and would be found in the retina (the inner layer; choices A and B are wrong). Collagen fibers are strong fibers found in connective tissue and would most likely be found in the tough outer layer of the eyeball (choice D is wrong).

143. Which of the following would occur when rod cells are stimulated by light?

    I.   cGMP levels decline.
    II.   All-*trans* retinal is converted to 11-*cis* retinal.
    III. Na$^+$ enters the rods, and they depolarize.

    A. I only
    B. I and II only
    C. I and III only
    D. II and III only

A When rod cells are stimulated by light, 11-*cis* retinal is converted to the all-*trans* form (Statement II is false), opsin is activated, transducin is activated, PDE is activated, and cGMP levels fall (Statement I is true). In the absence of cGMP, the Na$^+$ channels close, Na$^+$ stops entering the rod cell, and the cell hyperpolarizes (Statement III is false).

Passage II (Questions 144–147)

144. If a chemist were to react (E,E)-2-4-octadienal with NaBH$_4$ in ethanol and monitor the reaction by TLC, the spot corresponding to the product would be expected to have an R_f value that is:

    A. less than that of the starting material.
    B. equal to that of the starting material.
    C. greater than that of the starting material.
    D. greater than 1.

A The product of the reduction reaction is an alcohol, which is more polar than the starting aldehyde. More-polar compounds do not travel as far on TLC plates as less-polar compounds do, and therefore have smaller R_f values.

145. In which of the following reactions can (E)-2-hexenal NOT participate?

    I. Nucleophilic addition at C-1
    II. Conjugate addition at C-2
    III. Electrophilic addition at C-3

    A. II only
    B. III only
    C. II and III only
    D. 1, II, and III

C Nucleophilic addition at C-1, the carbonyl carbon, is one of the two major types of reactions that carbonyl compounds undergo. Since Item I is false, choice D is eliminated. Conjugate addition, or Michael addition, must occur at the beta carbon to the carbonyl, which would be C-3, not C-2. Since Item II is true, choice B is eliminated. Even though carbon–carbon double bonds typically react as nucleophiles, since this π bond is conjugated to the carbonyl, the beta carbon has a partial positive charge due to resonance. Therefore, an electrophile will not add to C-3, but as already stated, a nucleophile would in a conjugate addition.

146. The ^{1}H NMR resonance at 2.98 ppm most likely corresponds to which set of protons on Molecule A?

    A. A methyl group
    B. A methylene group
    C. An alkene proton
    D. An aldehyde proton

B Since the resonance at 2.98 ppm integrates for 2 H and is a quartet, it must represent two equivalent protons with three neighboring protons. It must therefore be the methylene (CH$_2$) group.

147. If a chemist reacted 4-oxo-(E)-6-octenal with excess dimethylamine and monitored the reaction by IR spectroscopy, the diagnostic band showing conversion of starting material to the enamine product is the:

    A. appearance of the C=N stretching frequency.
    B. appearance of the C=C stretching frequency.
    C. disappearance of the C=O stretching frequency.
    D. disappearance of the C=C stretching frequency.

C The dimethylamine will react with the carbonyl carbons of both the aldehyde and ketone, and the C=O stretch will disappear. The new bonds formed are carbon–nitrogen single bonds and carbon–carbon double bonds. Therefore, A is false (the question states an enamine forms, not an imine). Choice B can be eliminated because there is already a C=C in the starting material, so formation of a new C=C will not register in the IR spectrum. The nitrogen cannot add to the C=C since it is not conjugated to the ketone, eliminating D.

Passage III (Questions 148–154)

148. What are the most likely patterns of inheritance for CF and achondroplasia?

    A. CF: X-linked recessive
        Achondroplasia: autosomal dominant
    B. CF: autosomal dominant
        Achondroplasia: autosomal recessive
    C. CF: spontaneous mutation only
        Achondroplasia: X-linked recessive
    D. CF: autosomal recessive
        Achondroplasia: autosomal dominant

D Remember to answer the three basic questions before tackling any pedigree problem, and remember that in pedigrees showing two different conditions, the three questions must be answered separately for each condition. First, is the condition/disease caused by a dominant allele or a recessive allele? If the disease skips generations it is most likely recessive. Based on this, we can conclude that CF is recessive and achondroplasia is dominant (choices B and C are wrong). Second, is the disease allele carried on an autosome or on one of the sex chromosomes? If significantly more men than women are affected, the disease is most likely sex-linked. Based on the pedigree, we can conclude that both CF and achondroplasia are autosomal (choice D is correct and A is wrong). Since both conditions are autosomal, the third question ("If sex-linked, is the disease carried on the X chromosome or the Y chromosome?") is irrelevant and unnecessary in this case.

149. If the frequency of the CF allele in a randomly mating population is 0.02, what is the frequency of individuals who do NOT manifest symptoms of CF?

    A. 0.0004
    B. 0.9604
    C. 0.98
    D. 0.9996

D This is a Hardy–Weinberg question and requires use of the phenotypic frequency equation $p^2 + 2pq + q^2 = 1$. Here, p represents the frequency of the dominant allele, and q represents the frequency of the recessive allele. CF is an autosomal recessive disorder, so for individuals to express CF, they must be homozygous recessive, or qq (= q^2). The question states that the frequency of the CF allele is 0.02, so $q = 0.02$ and thus $q^2 = 0.0004$. But remember, these are the affected individuals, so the frequency of *unaffected* individuals is $1 - 0.0004 = 0.9996$.

150. Achondroplasia can be seen in an individual without a family history of the disease, such as in Individual IV-aa in the pedigree in Figure 1. This is not the case with cystic fibrosis. If Individual IV-aa had a son with Individual II-k, what is the probability that their living son would be a carrier for CF and NOT have achondroplasia?

    A. 1/8
    B. 1/6
    C. 1/4
    D. 1/3

D The chance that this child is a CF carrier is 100% (probability = 1), because the mother (IV-aa) is homozygous recessive for CF (she has CF) and the father (II-k) is most likely homozygous dominant (wild-type normal). CF does not appear anywhere in his family, the passage states that it is rare in general, and especially in non-Caucasian populations, so this is a safe assumption. All children born to this couple would be heterozygous with respect to CF and would be carriers. For achondroplasia however, this child has only a 1/3 chance of being unaffected. The passage states that homozygous dominant fetuses are nonviable (die *in utero*). Individual IV-aa has achondroplasia, but her mother does not, so IV-aa must be heterozygous. A similar situation applies to II-k, who has achondroplasia and whose father does not. Let A be the mutant allele and a the wild type (normal) allele. The possible progeny of this cross are shown in the Punnett Square below. Only three of four progeny will be viable, and 2/3 of these will be heterozygous and express the disorder; 1/3 will not have the disease. Finally, the question asks, what is the probability of both of these events occurring in the same child (carrier of CF and not have achondroplasia)? The Rule of Multiplication applies: prob (A and B) = prob (A) × prob (B). The probability of their son carrying CF and not having achondroplasia is $1 \times 1/3 = 1/3$.

		mother	
		A	**a**
father	**A**	AA (lethal)	Aa
	a	Aa	aa (unaffected)

151. According to the passage, which of the following may be associated with CF?

    I.   Recurrent lung infection with bacteria that have a thick layer of peptidoglycan

    II.   Deficiency in fat-soluble vitamins, such as vitamin A and vitamin E

    III. Inability to appropriately lower glucose levels after a meal

  A. I only
  B. II only
  C. II and III only
  D. I, II, and III

C The passage states that CF patients have recurrent infections with Gram-negative bacteria (which have a thin layer of peptidoglycan and an outer membrane). Therefore, Statement I is false since it refers to Gram-*positive* bacteria. Statement II is true: CF patients can have difficulty absorbing fats, and this could lead to problems absorbing the fat-soluble vitamins. Statement III is also true: dysfunction (abnormal function) of the endocrine pancreas could lead to difficulties with insulin release (among the other hormones secreted by the pancreas), which would lead to an inability to reduce blood glucose levels after eating.

152. All of the following statements regarding the digestive system of cystic fibrosis patients are true EXCEPT:

  A. Flow of bile produced in the gallbladder may be prevented due to obstruction of small bile ducts.
  B. Damage to exocrine tissue within the pancreas may hinder the secretion of lipases.
  C. Secretions from both the salivary gland and pancreas are important for starch digestion.
  D. CF patients may have a normal digestive system.

A Bile is produced by the liver and is only stored in the gallbladder (choice A is not true and is the correct choice). Part of the exocrine function of the pancreas is to release digestive enzymes, such as lipases, into the small intestine. Damage to this tissue could prevent or hinder the release of these enzymes, and this may contribute to the difficulty seen in fat absorption (choice B is a true statement and can be eliminated). Starch digestion begins in the mouth, where salivary amylase breaks starch into polysaccharides. These polysaccharides are then broken down into disaccharides in the duodenum by pancreatic amylase. Note that this is true for anyone, CF patient or not (choice C is true and can be eliminated). Some CF patients may be completely normal with respect to the digestive system; the passage states that the CFTR gene is large and the gene can be mutated many different ways, leading to different CF phenotypes (choice D is true and can be eliminated).

153. Suppose that Josh and Raina are eventually able to conceive, and Raina gives birth to a boy. What is the probability that their son will have either CF or achondroplasia?

  A. 0%
  B. 25%
  C. 50%
  D. 100%

C For CF we can assume that because CF is rare, people not related to others with CF are most likely wild type (normal, non-carriers). Raina, as an East Indian and unrelated to Josh, is even more unlikely than a Caucasian to be a carrier of a CF mutation; it is safe to assume that she is homozygous dominant (normal) as far as CF is concerned. Josh, however, has CF, so his CF genotype is homozygous recessive. All of their children would be carriers of the CF allele, but would not be affected, so the probability of a child of theirs having CF is 0%. Regarding achondroplasia: since Josh does not express achondroplasia, it can be assumed he does not have the defective allele; remember that this disorder is caused by a dominant allele, so to be normal, one must be homozygous recessive. Raina, however, does express achondroplasia, so she must have at least one dominant allele for that disorder. And since her father did not have the disease (homozygous recessive), he must have passed on a recessive allele to Raina; Raina must then be heterozygous for achondroplasia. The probability of a child expressing achondroplasia, then, depends solely on Raina. Josh can only donate a recessive allele, and Raina has a 50% chance of donating the dominant allele that would cause the disease in their child. The question asks for the probability that their son has either disease. Using the Rule of Addition, prob (A or B) = prob (A) + prob (B) – prob (A and B), we find that the probability of their son having either CF or achondroplasia is 0% + 50% – (0% × 50%) = 50%.

154. The mutation responsible for achondroplasia is most likely associated with:

  A. a frameshift in the reading frame of the messenger RNA.
  B. the insertion of a new amino acid with different electrostatic properties compared to the original amino acid.
  C. a deletion of one base pair at the 5′ end of the FGF gene.
  D. the insertion of the same amino acid into the growing polypeptide, allowed by the degeneracy of the genetic code.

B According to the passage, achondroplasia results from a point mutation in the gene that encodes the FGFR3. It is important to note that the protein encoded by the FGFR3 gene is still translated and functional (although it adopts a different conformation that is constantly active). Thus it is very unlikely that a frameshift mutation is the cause of this defect. This type of mutation is usually the result of insertions or deletions of bases *not* in multiples of three. Altering the reading frame of the transcript virtually always results in a truncated protein (due to a premature stop codon) or a polypeptide with a radically different amino acid sequence compared to the normal protein. In either case, the protein is not functional (choices A and C are wrong). It is possible that an identical amino acid is inserted into the growing polypeptide, even though there is a point mutation in the gene. While each codon is specific for only one amino acid, there may be more than one codon that corresponds to the same amino acid. However, if an identical amino acid were inserted into the growing polypeptide, the resulting protein would be no different from the normal protein; this would be a silent mutation. Clearly, since the FGFR3 in achondroplastic individuals is constantly active, there must be some difference (in other words, the mutation is *not* silent, choice D is wrong). Protein function often depends on the electrostatic properties within its constitutive amino acids. For example, enzymatic activity often depends on positively or negatively charged residues that line the active site of an enzyme; these residues are used to stabilize reaction transition states. Changing an amino acid to one with a different charge may change the structural or functional properties of the protein (choice B is correct). Although not presented in the passage, the point mutation usually replaces an arginine residue (positively charged) with a glycine residue (neutral).

Passage IV (Questions 155–160)

155. Free-radical production during acute oxygen poisoning would most likely have the greatest effect on the:

- A. stomach.
- B. brain.
- C. cornea and lens of the eye.
- D. liver.

B The passage states that free radicals damage the fatty acids in the membranous structures of cells. Nervous tissue (e.g., the brain, choice B) is especially susceptible to damage due to free radicals because of its high lipid content (myelin). Note that the eye may be a tempting choice because it can be considered part of the nervous system, but the cornea and lens of the eye are not specifically nervous tissue (choice C is wrong). Damage to the membranes of stomach and/or liver cells would be bad, but would not be as devastating to function as damage to the membranes and myelin of the brain (choices A and D are wrong).

156. Normal total lung capacity at sea level is approximately 6 L. Mark inhales maximally at the surface of the water, then, without exhaling, dives to a depth of 10 m. At this depth the volume of air in his lungs is approximately:

- A. 3 L.
- B. 6 L.
- C. 9 L.
- D. 12 L.

A At 10 m, Mark is exposed to 2 atmospheres of pressure (1 atmosphere from the water plus 1 atmosphere from the air above the water). Since, according to Boyle's Law, pressure and volume are inversely proportional, the volume of a quantity of air at 2 atmospheres will be half the volume of that air at 1 atmosphere. If Mark's lungs held a volume of 6 L when the pressure is 1 atmosphere (at sea level), then they will hold a volume of 3 L when the pressure is 2 atmospheres (at 10 m below the surface).

157. "Blood doping" is the intravenous injection of packed red blood cells, usually prior to athletic competition. Mark plans to vacation in Vancouver this year, and intends to "dope his blood" prior to his visit. Blood doping could have which of the following effects (compared to his prior visit to Vancouver with no blood doping)?

- I. Decreased ventilation rate
- II. Increased resistance to blood flow
- III. Decreased heart rate

- A. I only
- B. II only
- C. I and II only
- D. I, II, and III

D One of the reasons Mark's ventilation rate increased on his previous trip to Vancouver is that the PO_2 of oxygen at high altitudes is lower than at sea level. To compensate for the reduced oxygen in the atmosphere, ventilation rate increases. However, increasing the number of red blood cells circulating in the system by "doping the blood" increases the amount of hemoglobin that can bind oxygen, and reduces the need for rapid ventilation. Statement I is true, and choice B can be eliminated. The increased number of red cells increases the blood volume and viscosity, and this increases resistance to flow. Statement II is also true and choice A can be eliminated. Finally, due to the increased oxygen-carrying capacity of the blood, the heart does not have to pump blood around the body as fast, and the heart rate decreases. The increased blood pressure can also contribute to this. Statement III is also true, and choice C is eliminated. Note that due to the increased viscosity of the blood, the heart has to work harder—in other words, *contractility* is increased, but this is not the same thing as an increased heart *rate*.

158. After 2 hours of diving at an average depth of 12 m, Mark produced a much larger volume of urine than normal. This is most likely due to:

    A. increased blood pressure leading to increased filtration rate.

    B. decreased blood pressure leading to osmotic movement of water out of cells.

    C. increased blood pressure leading to an increase in ADH production.

    D. increased blood pressure leading to the release of aldosterone.

A Diving increases blood pressure considerably (choice B is wrong). Since filtration in the kidney depends strictly on blood pressure, an increase in pressure leads to an increase in filtration rate and an increase in urine volume (choice A is correct). This is, in fact, one of the primary means of regulating blood pressure; if blood pressure increases, more urine is produced, which decreases the blood volume and decreases the blood pressure. Aldosterone and ADH work together to regulate blood pressure, but they are released when blood pressure decreases, not increases (choices C and D are wrong). By way of review, aldosterone increases sodium reabsorption, which increases blood osmolarity, which increases ADH production, which increases water reabsorption, which increases blood volume, which increases blood pressure.

159. Mark found that during his trip to Vancouver his appetite increased significantly and he ingested a larger quantity of food; however, he did not gain any weight. A quick calculation showed that the increase in appetite could not be accounted for by an increase in work during skiing compared to diving. All of the following could be reasons for Mark's increased appetite EXCEPT:

    A. decreased Krebs cycle activity due to decreased PO_2.

    B. increased glycolysis due to anaerobic respiration.

    C. increased beta-oxidation of fatty acids due to increased activity.

    D. decreased oxidative phosphorylation due to high altitude.

C The question states that the increase in appetite is *not* due to increased work; choice C is not true, and therefore the correct answer choice. Mark's increase in appetite is most likely due to the fact that at high elevations there is less oxygen available for aerobic respiration (choices

A and D can be reasons for the increased appetite and can be eliminated), thus the body relies more heavily on anaerobic respiration (glycolysis alone) to produce ATP (choice B can be a reason and is thus eliminated). Because anaerobic respiration is inefficient, Mark must eat more food to compensate.

160. During Mark's diving lesson his instructor told him to exhale as he rose to the surface to prevent lung collapse. Lung collapse during ascension is typically due to a rupture of the lung wall which permits air to enter the pleural cavity. The rupture of the lung wall is most likely due to:

    A. decreased water pressure leading to an increase in intrapleural pressure.

    B. expansion of the air in the lungs according to Boyle's Law.

    C. decreased water pressure leading to a rapid outward expansion of the rib cage.

    D. increased lung air pressure according to Boyle's Law.

B Just as air volume decreases when water pressure increases on the way down in a dive, air volume will increase as water pressure decreases on the way up in a dive. Thus if a breath of air is taken prior to ascension, and that breath is not exhaled on the way up, that volume of air will rapidly expand to the point where the lung wall can be damaged. There is no reason to assume that decreased water pressure would increase intrapleural pressure; if anything, absolute intrapleural pressure would decrease as well (relative intrapleural pressure would remain the same; choice A is wrong). Decreasing water pressure may allow the rib cage to expand outward, but it is unlikely that this expansion would be so dramatic and so fast as to damage the lungs (choice C is wrong). Again, water pressure decreases during ascension, which means that lung air pressure decreases as well (this is what allows the volume of air in the lungs to expand; choice D is wrong).

Free-Standing Questions (161–165)

161. Which of the following could NOT be a possible genotype in the ovum of a human female?

   A. 23-X
   B. 24-XX
   C. 22-O
   D. 23-Y

D Female oogonia (diploid cells) typically have two X chromosomes (genotype 46-XX). During meiosis, these divide into haploid ova, which typically have only one X chromosome and a genotype of 23-X (choice A is a possible—in fact, the normal—genotype and can be eliminated). If the chromosomes fail to separate properly (non-disjunction), you can find either both X chromosomes (24-XX) or neither X chromosome (22-0) in a mature ovum (choices B and C are possible—although abnormal—genotypes and can be eliminated). However, fertile females do not carry Y chromosomes and cannot generate ova containing this chromosome (choice D is not possible and is the correct answer choice).

162. Local anesthetics, such as lidocaine or Novocain, block voltage-gated sodium channels in nerve cells. Effects would include:

   I.   Loss of resting membrane potential
   II. Blocking of action potential transmission
   III. Loss of repolarization

   A. I only
   B. II only
   C. I and II only
   D. I, II, and III

B Blocking the voltage-gated sodium channels would prevent transmission of action potentials (Item II is true). It would not, however, affect the RMP because that is maintained by the Na^+/K^+ ATPase and the K^+ leak channels (Item I is false). Repolarization is a function of voltage-gated potassium channels and would not be affected by blocking the voltage-gated Na^+ channels (Item III is false).

163. New-onset poliomyelitis has been eradicated from the Western Hemisphere due to an aggressive vaccination agenda. Currently, it is recommended that children be vaccinated against polio by receiving three doses of Inactivated Polio Vaccine (IPV) at ages 2 months, 4 months, and 6 months. Which of the following is the mostly likely mechanism IPV uses to confer immunity?

   A. IPV stimulates a humoral immune response, which leads to B cells producing antibody and a set of memory B cells directed against the polio virus.
   B. IPV infects respiratory cells, and portions of the viral coat are presented to $CD8^+$ killer T cells, marking the respiratory cells for destruction.
   C. Portions of the polio virus coat are presented by Antigen Presenting Cells to $CD4^+$ helper T cells, leading to production of memory neutrophils.
   D. IPV is phagocytosed by macrophages, then presented to B cells via MHC class I.

A Most vaccines stimulate the humoral branch of the immune system to confer immunity. Essentially, the vaccination provokes the primary immune response. This response is technically unnecessary except for the production of memory cells. If the real virus (antigen) ever appears, the immune system would initiate the secondary immune response via these memory cells. This is a much faster and stronger response which destroys the threat before symptoms can develop. The question text states that the virus is inactivated, therefore it cannot infect cells (choice B is wrong). IPV probably is phagocytized by macrophages. They would present the viral proteins to helper T cells (not B cells, choice D is wrong) via MHC II (not MHC I, choice D is still wrong). The helper Ts would secrete chemicals to enhance proliferation of B cells and killer Ts. They do not lead to the production of "memory neutrophils"—in fact, no such things exist. Neutrophils are part of the nonspecific body defense systems (choice C is wrong).

164. What is the most stable intermediate species during the conversion of 2-iodo-3-methylbutane to an alcohol via reaction with water?

A.

$$\left[\begin{array}{c} \overset{\delta^+}{H_2O} ---\overset{\textstyle C}{\underset{H_3C \quad H}{|}}--- \overset{\delta^-}{I} \end{array} \right]^{\ddagger}$$

C.

$$\left[\begin{array}{c} H_2O ---\overset{\textstyle \oplus}{\underset{H_3C \quad H}{C}}--- I \end{array} \right]^{\ddagger}$$

B.

D.

B Transition states, as shown in choices A and C, are the highest energy species during a reaction, and can therefore be eliminated. This substitution should be an S_N1 mechanism because of solvolysis conditions. When the iodide leaves, a secondary carbocation intermediate is formed, then rearranges to the more stable tertiary carbocation via hydride shift.

165. With which of the following organelles would the mRNA for the estrogen receptor be associated?

   I.   Ribosomes
   II.   Rough ER
   III. Golgi apparatus

  A. I only
  B. I and II only
  C. II and III only
  D. I, II, and III

A The estrogen receptor is a cytosolic protein; since all protein translation occurs on ribosomes, Item I is true. However, only proteins that are ultimately secreted, embedded in the plasma membrane, or associated with lysosomes are translated by ribosomes attached to the rough ER, so Item II is false. Finally, mRNA is not associated with the Golgi apparatus (which is used to sort and package proteins made on the rough ER), so Item III is false.

Passage V (Question 166–170)

166. The diazonium coupling reaction in Figure 2 is faster than most electrophilic substitutions of benzene. Which of the following statements best explains this fact?

  A. The diazonium ion is an electron withdrawing substituent, making its benzene ring a better electrophile than benzene.
  B. The diazonium ion is a good nucleophile.
  C. The dimethylamino group is an electron donating substituent, making its benzene ring a better electrophile than benzene.
  D. The dimethylamino group is an electron donating substituent, making its benzene ring a better nucleophile than benzene.

D The aromatic ring is always the nucleophile in electrophilic aromatic substitution (EAS) reactions; therefore choice C must be eliminated. While A is a true statement, it does not answer the question. The N_2^+ group is electron withdrawing due to its positive charge, so the benzene ring it is attached to will be less nucleophilic—more electrophilic—than benzene. However, this benzene ring is not involved in the diazonium coupling reaction since it is the nitrogen atom that is attacked by the π electrons of the coupling reagent. Choice B can also be eliminated, because the N_2^+ group has a positive charge, making it a good electrophile.

167. Mordant dyes are used in biological assays in addition to the textile industry. Which of the following biologically important molecules is most likely to be labeled by a mordant dye?

  A. Glycogen
  B. Chromatin
  C. Cholesterol
  D. Starch

B The passage states that mordants bind well with amino acid residues. Therefore, choices A and D can be eliminated, since they are sugar polymers, and choice C can be eliminated because cholesterol is a lipid. Chromatin is the only biomolecule that contains amino acids.

168. What type of reaction is the second step in the synthesis of methyl orange?

 A. Nucleophilic addition
 B. Nucleophilic aromatic substitution
 C. Unimolecular nucleophilic substitution
 D. Electrophilic addition

A The diazonium ion has a triple bond, while the product azo dye has only a double bond between the nitrogen atoms. Since one π bond has been broken, this must be an addition reaction, eliminating choices B and C. The aromatic ring that adds to the N_2^+ group is a nucleophile, making this a nucleophilic addition.

169. A chemist conducts a competition experiment in which she treats the diazonium ion in Figure 1 with a 1:1 molar ratio of N,N-dimethylaniline and benzenesulfonic acid in an attempt to synthesize a mixture of methyl orange and another azo dye.

Compound A

Which of the following reasons explain(s) why Compound A (shown above) is NOT the major product of this experiment?

 I.   Benzenesulfonic acid is a poorer nucleophile than N,N-dimethylaniline.
 II. The sulfonic acid substituent is a meta director.
 III. Benzenesulfonic acid is more sterically hindered than N,N-dimethylaniline.

 A. I only
 B. II only
 C. I and II only
 D. II and III only

C The sulfonic acid substituent is a deactivating group and therefore pulls electron density away from the benzene ring. This inductive effect makes the ring less nucleophilic than the N,N-dimethylaniline which is activated by the amino group. Since Item I is true, eliminate choices B and D. All deactivators with a partial positive charge on the atom directly attached to the aromatic ring are meta directors, so Item II is true, making choice A incorrect.

170. How many signals would appear in the ^{13}C NMR spectrum of Compound A shown in Question 169?

 A. 2
 B. 4
 C. 8
 D. 12

B Because the molecule is symmetrically substituted (para substituents on both rings) and the substituents are the same on both benzene rings, there are only 4 different types of carbon atoms in the molecule.

Passage VI (Questions 171–176)

171. The results summarized in Table 1 can best be explained by which of the following?

    A. The plasma membrane and nuclear membrane have estrogen-specific protein channels.
    B. Estrogen can cross the plasma membrane by simple diffusion and crosses the nuclear membrane through the nuclear pores.
    C. Estrogen is derived from amino acids and therefore crosses all membranes by facilitated diffusion.
    D. Estrogen is derived from cholesterol and therefore crosses all membranes by simple diffusion.

D Estrogen is derived from cholesterol and is therefore lipid soluble; it does not require channels to cross membranes (so choices A and C are wrong). Choice B may be true, but choice D is a better answer since estrogen, being lipid soluble, does not need to cross through the pores.

172. Pesticide A most likely functions as:

    A. an agonist.
    B. an inhibitor.
    C. a lipase.
    D. a receptor.

B The results presented in Table 2 show that there are no estrogen effects observed when Pesticide A is present, so it cannot be acting as either an agonist (choice A is wrong) or a receptor (choice D is wrong) for estrogen. While a lipase might prevent the effects of estrogen by destroying estrogen itself (estrogen is essentially a lipid), this is clearly not the case with Pesticide A, as the presence of estrogen is still observed (choice C is wrong). The best choice is B. Pesticide A is acting as an inhibitor that prevents binding of estrogen to its receptor and thus prevents its effects.

173. When the researcher performed Experiment 2 using Pesticide B instead of Pesticide A, which of the following fluorescence and estrogen effects did the researcher most likely observe?

    A. *Media:* green and red
       Cytoplasm: green and red
       Nucleus: green and red
       Estrogen effects: no
    B. *Media:* green only
       Cytoplasm: green and red
       Nucleus: green and red
       Estrogen effects: no
    C. *Media:* green only
       Cytoplasm: green and red
       Nucleus: green and red
       Estrogen effects: yes
    D. *Media:* green only
       Cytoplasm: green and red
       Nucleus: green only
       Estrogen effects: no

C Green and red fluorescence can be observed only when the active site of the estrogen receptor is bound. Since there is no estrogen receptor in the media, choice A is incorrect. Because the passage states that Pesticide B binds the receptor and results in increased transcription of mRNA, we can deduce that green and red fluorescence (i.e., bound receptor) will be observed in both the cytoplasm and the nucleus (choice D is wrong), and also that estrogen effects (increased transcription) will be observed (choice C is correct and B is wrong).

174. Which of the following graphs would best illustrate the binding of estrogen (E) to its receptor in the presence of its analog, Pesticide B?

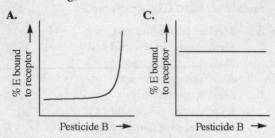

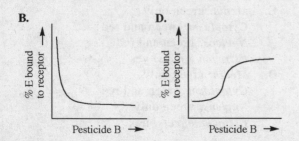

B Pesticide B and estrogen compete for binding at the active site of the estrogen receptor. Therefore, as the concentration of Pesticide B increases, the percentage of estrogen bound to receptor decreases. Only the graph in choice B illustrates this behavior.

175. The difference in the results of Experiments 3 and 4 can best be explained by the presence of estrogen receptor in which of the following?

 A. Nuclei of CHO cells
 B. Cytoplasm of CHO cells
 C. Nuclei of HEPM cells
 D. Cytoplasm of HEPM cells

D There is no estrogen receptor present in either the nuclei or the cytoplasm of the CHO cells, because only green fluorescence is observed in Experiment 3 (so choices A and B are wrong). Since only HEPM cytoplasm was injected into the CHO cells in Experiment 4, the receptor must be located there.

176. If Experiment 2 were repeated, but this time exposing the cells first to Pesticide A and then to Pesticide B before exposing them to the green fluorescent-labeled estrogen and the red fluorescent probe, which of the following statements will most likely be true?

 A. Pesticide A and Pesticide B bind to the same site on the estrogen receptor.
 B. Estrogen effects would be observed.
 C. Only green fluorescence would be observed.
 D. Both green and red fluorescence would be observed.

C Pesticide A does not bind to the active site of the receptor; if it did, both green and red fluorescence would be observed in Table 2, Experiment 2 (eliminating choice A). Since the cells are exposed to Pesticide A first, Pesticide A would inhibit the binding of Pesticide B to the active site; therefore, green and red fluorescence would not both be observed, and no estrogen effects would be observed (eliminating choices B and D).

Passage VII (Questions 177–182)

177. Which one of the following does NOT support the theory that mitochondria were once separate organisms that were incorporated into eukaryotic cells?

    A. Mitochondria isolated from some species of yeast are able to survive outside of the yeast cell.

    B. Scientists have discovered a family of purple cyanobacteria that are very similar to mitochondria in structure and function but live independently.

    C. The mitochondrial genome is double-stranded DNA.

    D. The mitochondrial "alphabet" of anticodons for translation is read differently from the "alphabet" of nuclear DNA.

C If mitochondria can live outside of their "host" cells, this suggests that they were once independent organisms (choice A supports the endosymbiotic theory and can be eliminated). Other independent organisms with similar structure and function as mitochondria suggest the existence of a common evolutionary precursor; this supports the idea of mitochondria as independent organisms (choice B can be eliminated). If the anticodon sequences were read differently in mitochondria (for example, if UGA is read as "stop" in eukaryotes but as *Trp* by mitochondria), this would suggest that they were independent organisms. In fact, the genetic code *is* different in mitochondria. This suggests that the mitochondrial genome evolved separately from the nuclear genome of the "host" cell (choice D supports the endosymbiotic theory and can be eliminated). However, the simple fact that mitochondrial DNA is double stranded does not suggest that mitochondria were originally separate organisms. One could argue that their dsDNA genome is nuclear DNA that was incorporated into the mitochondria (choice C does not support the theory and is the correct choice).

178. A woman with Leber's disease has two sons in their mid-twenties. One became completely blind over time, while the other exhibited only minor symptoms. Because of their disability, the sons have lived at home their entire lives. Which of the following would best explain the difference in severity?

    A. One son is homozygous recessive for Leber's, and the other is heterozygous.

    B. Different mitochondria in the egg have different genomes, and the severity of the disease depends on the number of mutant mitochondria present in the zygote.

    C. The disease has a significant environmental component that determines its severity.

    D. One son inherited a mutant X chromosome from the mother, while the other inherited a wild-type X.

B As described in the passage, several mitochondrial genotypes exist side-by-side in an individual cell, including in an egg. Mitochondria are not carefully separated by the mitotic spindle, so a mixture of mitochondria is randomly split between two daughter cells during mitosis (or meiosis). The variability seen among patients with Leber's can be explained by the percentage of defective mitochondria carried by an individual. Clinical studies revealed that individuals suffering from Leber's-induced blindness carried more than 70% defective mitochondria, while those with milder forms had no more than 30%. While this may not have been immediately apparent, the other answer choices can be eliminated. Since both sons lived at home their entire lives, they were both subjected to the same environment, so environmental effects could not play a role in determining severity (choice C is wrong). The passage states that the children of men with Leber's never inherit the disorder, so it cannot be caused by a recessive allele or by a mutation on the X chromosome. If it were, men with Leber's could potentially pass it on to their children (choices A and D are wrong). The reason it is strictly maternally inherited is because all organelles of the zygote come from the egg; thus, all mitochondria come from the mother.

179. In order for mitochondria to synthesize a protein, the nucleus must encode which of the following?

I.   RNA polymerase
II. DNA polymerase
III. Ribosomes

A.   I only
B.   I and II only
C.   I and III only
D.   II and III only

A In order to synthesize proteins, only RNA polymerase and ribosomes are needed (Item II is false, and choices B and D can be eliminated). Figure 1 shows that mitochondrial DNA codes for rRNA, so mitochondria do not need to import ribosomes (Item III is false, and choice C can be eliminated). RNA polymerase is essential for transcription, and since it is not coded for in the mitochondrial genome, it must be imported (Item I is true, and choice A is the correct choice). Note that the mitochondrial genome also encodes tRNA and some of the electron transport proteins. As discussed in the first question in this passage, mitochondria read anticodons differently and therefore provide their own tRNAs.

180. Although mitochondria are found in every cell throughout the body, mutations in mitochondrial DNA typically only affect a few cell types, such as neurons or muscle cells. Which of the following could be a possible explanation for this?

A.   Not all cells possess mitochondria, and only cell types that do are affected.
B.   Cell types that are not affected have nuclear genes for the mutated mitochondrial protein.
C.   Affected cell types have had nuclear genes for DNA repair enzymes deleted.
D.   Mutations in electron transport proteins are more significant in cell types that have high energy requirements.

D The mitochondrial genome codes for only a few proteins (see Figure 1), most of which are part of the electron transport chain. Thus a mutation in one of these proteins lowers the efficiency of the electron transport chain. Cells with low energy needs are not affected by this decreased efficiency, but cells with high energy needs (such as nerve or muscle cells) are unable to produce enough energy. As cells die due to lack of energy, the remaining cells must work harder and therefore require more energy,

causing more cells to die. This explains the slow onset and progressive nature of Leber's. As stated in the question, all cells in the body (and in fact all eukaryotic cells in general) have mitochondria (choice A is wrong). All cell types in an organism have the same nuclear DNA, so if there were a replacement or repair gene, all cells would have it and would be affected (or not affected) in the same way (choice B is wrong). There is no reason to assume that nuclear genes have been deleted, and why would this occur only in these cell types? In fact, it is highly unusual for DNA to be deleted at all; it is much more likely that the genes are simply turned off, and again, there is no reason this would occur only in these cell types (choice C is wrong).

181. Leber's is most likely caused by what type of mutation?

A.   Deletion
B.   Insertion
C.   Missense
D.   Nonsense

C The mutation is described in the text as a point mutation, not an insertion or deletion (choices A and B are wrong). In any case, insertions or deletions would shift the reading frame and lead to seriously dysfunctional proteins. Since the mutation leads to a protein with altered function, it must be a missense mutation (choice C is correct). Nonsense mutations create stop codons that truncate translation early and usually lead to dysfunctional proteins (choice D is wrong).

182. Mitochondrial ribosomes are:

A.   made from 16s and 12s subunits.
B.   encoded in the nucleus.
C.   made from 50s and 30s subunits.
D.   usually found in the cytosol.

A Figure 1 shows that the mitochondrial genome, not the nuclear genome, encodes the ribosomal proteins (choice B is wrong), and that these proteins are 12s and 16s (choice A is correct). Prokaryotes have 50s and 30s subunits (choice C is wrong). Mitochondrial ribosomes are found in the matrix of the mitochondria, not in the cytosol (choice D is wrong).

Passage VIII (Questions 183–187)

183. Which of the following compounds should one expect to find in the largest quantity upon treatment of 1,4-dimethyl-1-cyclohexene with bromine and ultraviolet light?

A.

C.

B.

D.

A The major product arises from the most stable radical intermediate. The vinyl radical that gives rise to the molecule in choice C cannot be stabilized effectively by either induction or resonance. The tertiary radical that leads to the molecule in choice B is stabilized by induction, but the resonance stabilization of the allylic radicals in both A and D is stronger. In D, there will be primary and secondary allylic resonance structures, whereas in A there are two secondary allylic structures, making it the most stable of all.

184. Which of the following reagents would most likely be used as the radical initiator in the polymerization of polypropylene?

    A. Sodium borohydride
    B. Potassium hydroxide
    C. Benzoyl peroxide
    D. Phosphorus trichloride

C Peroxides are often used to initiate radical reactions because the O–O bond is so weak and cleaves homolytically.

185. Radial tires have sidewalls made of natural rubber, and tend to crack and weather rapidly near cities with high levels of industrial pollutants. What is the best explanation for this observation?

    A. The sulfuric acid from acid rain catalyzes the addition of water across the double bonds of the rubber, making the rubber more hydrophilic.
    B. Ozone cleaves the double bonds in the rubber, reducing the structural integrity of the tire.
    C. The UV light induced decomposition of chloro-fluorocarbons facilitates radical halogenation of the double bonds, allowing for some isomerization to the E isomer.
    D. Ozone reduces the disulfide cross-links of the rubber, allowing the polymer chains to slide past each other.

B Ozonolysis cleaves carbon–carbon double bonds, leaving either aldehydes or ketones as products. Breaking the chain of the polymer will make the material weaker. Addition of a reagent across the double bond as in A will have no effect because the chain will remain intact. The isomerization suggested in choice C does not break the chain or significantly alter the structure. Since ozone is an oxidizing agent, it cannot reduce disulfide bonds.

186. The reactive intermediate most likely involved in the polymerization of methylpropenoate is a:

    A. carbanion, because the electron donating group will destabilize the negative charge on the intermediate.
    B. carbocation, because the electron donating group will stabilize the positive charge on the intermediate.
    C. carbocation, because the electron withdrawing group will stabilize the positive charge on the intermediate.
    D. carbanion, because the electron withdrawing group will stabilize the negative charge on the intermediate.

D The passage states that the substituent on the alkene affects the identity of the preferred intermediate in the polymerization reaction. Since an ester group is electron withdrawing, it can stabilize a negative charge on the alpha carbon, making a carbanion the best suited intermediate.

187. Compared to their stereoisomers, gutta-percha and isotactic polypropylene have higher melting points because they:

    A. have larger dipole–dipole interactions because of the orientation of their substituents.

    B. have stronger London dispersion forces since each strand can overlap with the next more easily due to the orientation of their substituents.

    C. have stronger London dispersion forces due to their greater molecular weights.

    D. can hydrogen bond, whereas their isomers cannot.

B Since both polypropylene and gutta-percha are hydrocarbons, they are nonpolar molecules and can neither hydrogen bond nor participate in dipole–dipole interactions. Since the passage makes no mention of molecular weights of the polymers, and since the major difference between the isomers in question is stereochemistry and orientation of substituents, choice B is better than choice C.

Free-Standing Questions (188–192)

188. Regarding embryogenesis, which of the following sequence of events is in correct order?

    A. Implantation—cleavage—gastrulation—neurulation—blastulation

    B. Blastulation—implantation—cleavage—neurulation—gastrulation

    C. Implantation—blastulation—gastrulation—cleavage—neurulation

    D. Cleavage—blastulation—implantation—gastrulation—neurulation

D After the ovum is fertilized, it begins the process of embryogenesis. First, it undergoes many cycles of mitosis (*cleavage*) to form a ball of cells called the morula. Next, through the process of *blastulation*, the morula develops a central cavity (hollows out) around an inner mass of the cells; this entire structure is called a blastula. This blastula is *implanted* in the uterus before undergoing *gastrulation*, differentiation of the three primary germ layers of an embryo (called a gastrula at this stage). Finally, the gastrula begins forming its nervous system through the process of *neurulation*. The correct sequence of events is shown in choice D.

189. What is the major product of the following Diels–Alder reaction?

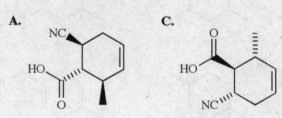

    A.   **C.**

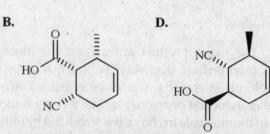

    B.   **D.**

B The substituents of the dienophile must maintain their stereochemistry. Since the cyano group and the carboxylic acid start out on the same side of the double bond, they must end up on the same side of the ring. (Choices A and C are the same molecule, and must therefore be eliminated.)

190. An embryo with a karyotype of 45 XO would develop:

    A. normal male genitalia.

    B. male genitalia without functioning testes.

    C. normal female genitalia.

    D. undifferentiated genitalia (hermaphrodite).

C The Y chromosome directs the production of testes, which secrete testosterone and Müllerian Inhibiting Factor (MIF), which leads to the development of male genitalia. In the absence of a Y chromosome (XX, XO, XXX, or any other karyotype) female genitalia, both internal and external, are the default.

191. A chemist measured the following rate data for the reaction between 2-chloroheptane and potassium cyanide:

Trial	$[E^+]$	$[Nuc^-]$	Reaction Rate
1	$1.12 \times 10^{-3}\ M$	$1.12 \times 10^{-3}\ M$	$1.50 \times 10^{-3}\ Ms^{-1}$
2	$5.60 \times 10^{-4}\ M$	$1.12 \times 10^{-3}\ M$	$7.50 \times 10^{-4}\ Ms^{-1}$
3	$5.60 \times 10^{-4}\ M$	$4.48 \times 10^{-3}\ M$	$3.00 \times 10^{-3}\ Ms^{-1}$

What is the mechanism of the formation of the product?

A. S_N1, because the reaction rate doubled when the alkyl halide concentration doubled.

B. S_N1, because the reaction rate remained unchanged regardless of the cyanide concentration.

C. S_N2, because the reaction rate doubled when the alkyl halide concentration doubled.

D. S_N2, because the reaction rate quadrupled when the cyanide concentration quadrupled.

D The reaction rate changes with a change in both electrophile and nucleophile concentrations. Therefore, A and B can be eliminated since the reaction cannot be first order. Choice C will be true for all S_N1 *and* S_N2 reactions, so D is the best answer.

192. Some genetic disorders produce men who lack both vas deferens due to developmental failure. It is most likely true that the ejaculatory fluid of these men would be:

A. alkaline, fructose-rich, and lack spermatozoa.
B. acidic, fructose-rich, and lack spermatozoa.
C. alkaline, fructose-deficient, and have a very low spermatozoa count.
D. acidic, protein-deficient, and contain poorly functioning spermatozoa.

A The vas deferens only delivers the sperm component of semen. The alkalinity and the fructose components come from the seminal vesicles, prostate gland, and bulbourethral glands. Since only the vas deferens is absent, only the sperm component would be affected, and sperm would be absent from the semen (choices C and D are wrong). The fluid would still be alkaline and fructose rich (choice A is correct and B is wrong).

Passage IX (Question 193–199)

193. What role does methylene blue serve in treating methemoglobinemia?

A. It oxidizes $NADP^+$ to NADPH to reduce Fe^{2+} to Fe^{3+}.

B. It oxidizes NADPH to $NADP^+$ to reduce Fe^{2+} to Fe^{3+}.

C. It oxidizes $NADP^+$ to NADPH to reduce Fe^{3+} to Fe^{2+}.

D. It oxidizes NADPH to $NADP^+$ to reduce Fe^{3+} to Fe^{2+}.

D Although the passage does not specifically describe its role, the function of methylene blue can be deduced from what needs to happen to methemoglobin. Methemoglobin is Fe^{3+} and needs to be reduced (gain one or more electrons) to Fe^{2+} (choices A and B are wrong). If Fe^{3+} must be reduced, then NADPH must be oxidized to $NADP^+$ (choice C is wrong).

194. Why is it important that enzymes can recognize the difference between NAD^+ and $NADP^+$?

A. It allows for separation of catabolic and anabolic pathways.

B. NAD^+ is regenerated in the Krebs cycle; $NADP^+$ is generated through the HMP shunt.

C. NADPH serves as a control element for some enzymes; NADH does not.

D. NAD^+ reacts more quickly than $NADP^+$.

A Redox reagents are needed for both anabolic and catabolic pathways; by separating reagents for each pathway, reactions can be more carefully regulated. Using the same reagents for both pathways might cause reverse reactions to occur as concentrations of products increased. Choice B is a true statement but does not answer the question. Both NADPH and NADH can, in a way, act as "control elements"; the passage describes reactions as being "NADH-dependent," and implies NADPH-dependence in others (choice C is wrong). The passage does not mention reaction rates for either reagent (choice D is wrong).

195. If a cell is low on energy, which molecule is most likely to be produced via the HMP shunt?

    A.   Ribose-5-phosphate
    B.   Glyceraldehyde-3-phosphate
    C.   NADPH
    D.   Sedoheptulose-7-phosphate

B A cell that is low on energy would direct its biochemical pathways towards glycolysis and the Krebs cycle. Of the molecules listed in the answer choices, glyceraldehyde-3-phosphate is the most direct entry point to glycolysis (it is produced when 1,6-bisphosphofructose is split in half). A cell low on energy will not be synthesizing macromolecules, so it does not need ribose (to make nucleotides, choice A is wrong) or NADPH, which is used in various anabolic reactions (choice C is wrong). One can argue that sedoheptulose-7-phosphate is made at the same time G-3-P is made. However, S-7-P is an intermediate in the HMP shunt—it cannot enter glycolysis (choice B is better than choice D).

196. In the graph below, which line depicts the effect of methemoglobin on the normal (N) hemoglobin O_2-saturation curve?

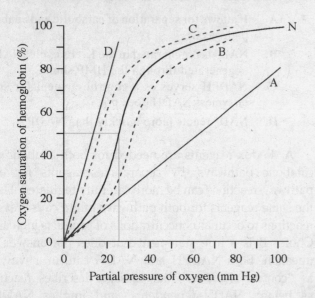

    A.   A
    B.   B
    C.   C
    D.   D

C Oxygen binding in hemoglobin is cooperative and displays a sigmoidal curve (choices A and D are wrong). The ferric (Fe^{3+}) heme is unable to bind oxygen at all, and the passage states that the remaining ferrous (Fe^{2+}) hemes in the tetramer have an increased oxygen affinity. Line C shows a "left shift," the result of the increased oxygen affinity of the ferrous hemes, as described in the passage. Line B shows a "right shift," indicating a reduced oxygen affinity (choice B is wrong).

197. The enzymes of the HMP shunt are highly sensitive to feedback inhibition. Which one of the following provides the most likely explanation for this?

    A.   The HMP shunt is a rarely used pathway and needs to be tightly regulated.
    B.   All enzymes are highly sensitive to feedback inhibition.
    C.   Feedback inhibition is a very effective way to regulate enzyme activity.
    D.   It would be inefficient to produce excess precursor molecules when they are not needed for biosynthesis.

D Cells are nothing if not efficient. ATP and reducing agents are valuable commodities and will not be used wastefully to produce molecules that aren't needed. If biosynthesis is not required, NADPH will not be used in that way. As described in the passage, the HMP shunt is very important for biosynthetic reactions and is used more frequently than "rarely" (choice A is wrong). While most enzymes are highly sensitive to feedback inhibition, not all of them are (choice B is wrong). Choice C is true but does not answer the question.

198. Radiolabeling studies have shown that the HMP shunt is much more active in adipose tissue than in skeletal muscle. This is because:

    A.   muscle tissue utilizes more energy than adipose tissue.
    B.   muscle tissue lacks the enzymes for the HMP shunt.
    C.   adipose tissue requires NADPH to create fatty acids.
    D.   adipose tissue produces more energy than muscle tissue.

C One of the reasons for the existence of the HMP shunt is to produce NADPH, an important reducing agent in biosynthetic (anabolic) pathways. Thus, tissues involved in biosynthesis, such as adipose tissue which synthesizes and stores fat (choice C is correct), would be expected to run the HMP shunt more than non-biosynthetic tissues (such as muscle). While muscle tissue uses more energy than adipose tissue, it would just burn more glucose and have a more active TCA cycle than adipose (note that these would be catabolic pathways—choice A is a true statement but does not explain the reason for the more active HMP shunt in adipose tissue). Muscle tissue would still have the appropriate enzymes for the HMP shunt—it still needs to make nucleotides, etc.; it just wouldn't be running that pathway as much (choice B is wrong). Adipose tissue does not produce much energy. It stores potential energy as fat, and can release fatty acids into the bloodstream for other cells to break down so that they can produce energy. Muscle tissue is a much greater producer of energy (which it uses very quickly for contraction, choice D is wrong).

199. How many carbon atoms does erythrose-4-phosphate have?

    A. 3
    B. 4
    C. 5
    D. 6

B Erythrose-4-phosphate has to have at least 4 carbons because the phosphate group is on the 4th carbon. Consider Figure 2. Reaction II shows two 5-carbon molecules (ribose and xylulose, 10 carbons total) combining to form sedoheptulose and glyceraldehyde (still 10 total carbons). Reaction III shows these 10 carbons combining to form fructose and erythrose. Since the number of carbons on both sides of the equation must be the same, and since we know fructose has 6 carbons, erythrose must have 4. This is confirmed by Reaction IV, which shows a 5-carbon molecule (xylulose) plus erythrose combining to produce fructose (6 carbons) and glyceraldehyde (3 carbons). Erythrose must have 4 carbons to keep the equation balanced, with 9 carbons on each side.

Passage X (Questions 200–204)

200. Guevedoche children will develop a penis, scrotum with testicles, and other secondary male characteristics when they reach puberty. Initially perceived as females at birth, some are found to be males before puberty when an ultrasound of masses in their abdomen reveals undescended testicles and the absence of a uterus or fallopian tubes. Based on this information, it is most likely true that guevedoche children:

    A. produce MIF at normal levels.
    B. produce MIF at greatly elevated levels.
    C. produce MIF at greatly reduced levels.
    D. do not produce any MIF.

A As stated in the passage, the uterus and fallopian tubes are derived from the Müllerian ducts. The absence of these organs indicates that MIF must be present (choice D is wrong), and at least at normal levels (choice C is wrong). There is no reason to assume that MIF levels would be greatly elevated, and in fact the passage states that while the testosterone-to-DHT ratio is elevated, the other hormones and enzymes are found at normal levels (choice A is correct and B is wrong).

201. Guevedoche lack the ability to make 5-α-reductase *in utero*, and therefore do not develop a penis, scrotum, or prostate at that time. However, these male organs develop as they reach puberty. Which of the following is the most likely explanation for this phenomenon?

    A. The penis and scrotum that develop during adolescence are actually labial and clitoral swellings resulting from overexpression of the genes for the estrogen receptor.
    B. Because of a lack of 5-α-reductase, testosterone levels are greatly elevated, leading to masculinization of female external genitalia.
    C. There are two genes on separate chromosomes for 5-α-reductase, and while one gene is normally expressed *in utero*, the other is not expressed until puberty.
    D. Because of a lack of 5-α-reductase, testosterone levels are elevated throughout childhood; then, at puberty, when testosterone and estrogen levels both increase even further, secondary male sex organs appear as a result of overdevelopment of the Wolffian ducts.

C Guevedoche lack the ability to convert testosterone to DHT in utero, and therefore are unable *at that time* to develop the external male genitalia that depend on DHT for development (specifically the penis, prostate, and scrotum). There are actually two types of 5AR: type I 5AR is the product of a gene on Chromosome 5, and type II 5AR is the product of a gene on Chromosome 2. The mutation that leads to the guevedoche phenotype is found in type II 5AR; this gene is normally expressed in the penile, prostatic, and scrotal tissues *in utero*. However, other tissues (specifically scalp and skin) begin to express the gene for type I 5AR at puberty. The 5AR produced at puberty converts testosterone to DHT, and the DHT then binds to receptors on the tissues of the penis, scrotum, and prostate cells, causing them to develop (C is correct). Guevedoche have what *appears* to be labial swelling and an enlarged clitoris at birth, but these are actually just underdeveloped scrotal and penile tissues, which will develop further once levels of 5AR rise at puberty. In any case, expression levels of the estrogen receptor are not mentioned in the passage (choice A is wrong). The passage states that other hormones are found at normal levels, so testosterone levels can be expected to be normal (choices B and D are wrong). Only the *ratio* of testosterone to DHT is elevated, not the absolute level. Note also that the Wolffian ducts develop into the epididymis, vas deferens, and ejaculatory ducts, not the penis or scrotum (choice D is wrong).

202. The higher than normal frequency of guevedoche in the Dominican Republic is the direct product of consanguineous relationships (relationships between close blood relatives). Which type of inheritance pattern is most consistent with increased phenotypic expression of a rare disease arising as a result of inbreeding within a population?

   A. X-linked dominant
   B. Autosomal dominant
   C. Mitochondrial inheritance
   D. Autosomal recessive

D Dominant disorders are typically not rare (they usually show increased phenotypic expression) because they are caused by a dominant allele. An offspring need only receive one allele from one affected parent to express the disease. For example, suppose a man heterozygous for a dominant disorder (*Aa*) marries an unaffected woman (*aa*). The offspring all have a 50% probability of inheriting the dominant allele from their father and thus of being affected by the disorder themselves. This is true for both autosomal disorders and X-linked disorders (choices A and B are wrong). Mitochondrial disorders are strictly maternally inherited, since the organelles of the zygote come only from the ovum. Thus, expression of this type of disorder does not change if a woman enters into a consanguineous relationship; the probability her offspring will inherit the disease depends only on her (choice C is wrong). However, recessive disorders are typically rare because they require a homozygous recessive genotype in order to be expressed, with one recessive allele coming from each of the parents. If mating is totally random, the frequency of a recessive disorder in a population is related to the frequency of the recessive allele; for example, if $q = .001$ ($p = .999$), then the frequency of affected individuals (qq) is only .000001, or 1 in 1 million. This number is the same from generation to generation, assuming mating stays random. Now consider what happens when mating is not random, and is consanguineous. We will use the same allele frequencies and to look at two generations. Assume the first-generation parents were not consanguineous; they chose each other randomly. The probability of one of them being a carrier is $2pq$. The probability of the father or the mother being a carrier is $2pq + 2pq$, or $4pq$. The probability that the carrier passes the recessive allele on to a son is $1/2$, and the probability that the carrier passes the recessive allele on to a daughter is also $1/2$. Now suppose the son and daughter mate and produce offspring. If they are both heterozygous, the probability of them having an affected child is $1/4$. So the total probability of an affected child from a consanguineous relationship is:

(probability original father is heterozygous + probability original mother is heterozygous)
× probability the recessive allele is passed to a son
× probability the recessive allele is passed to a daughter
× probability son and daughter have an affected offspring

$$= (2pq + 2pq) \times 1/2 \times 1/2 \times 1/4 = 4pq/16$$
$$= pq/4 = .000999/4 \approx 1/4000$$

This is a considerably greater probability than 1 in 1 million from the randomly mating population. Thus, consanguineous relationships (inbreeding) lead to increased expression of rare disorders. This is why this type of relationship is regulated legally, and is taboo in many cultures.

203. The genital organs of the guevedoche that develop at puberty are derivatives of the mesodermal germ layer. Which of the following is/are also derivatives of the mesodermal germ layer?

   I.   Skeletal muscle
   II. Liver
   III. Kidney

   A. I only
   B. II only
   C. I and III only
   D. II and III only

C The parts of the body derived from the mesoderm comprise primarily the connective tissues and the non-glandular organs. These include the muscles (Item I is true), the blood vessels and heart, the lymphatic system, the bones, the urinary organs (except for the bladder, Item III is true), and the reproductive organs. Digestive system glands (e.g., the liver and pancreas) are derived from endoderm (Item II is false).

204. Deficiency of the 21-β-hydroxylase enzyme is an autosomal recessive disease that is the leading cause of congenital adrenal hyperplasia. Based on Figure 1, which of the following is *least* likely to be a symptom of 21-β-hydroxylase deficiency?

   A. Increased levels of 17-hydroxyprogesterone in the serum
   B. Affected females presenting with an enlarged clitoris, male pattern baldness, and early puberty
   C. Elevated levels of serum potassium with elevated levels of urine sodium
   D. Affected males presenting with severe hypertension in early childhood

D 21-β-hydroxylase deficiency will lead to a lack of both aldosterone and cortisol due to the inability to synthesize these hormones, as well as increased levels of the substrates for this enzyme, namely progesterone and 17-OH-progesterone (choice A is likely to be a symptom and can be eliminated). The increased levels of 17-OH-progesterone will lead to the shunting of the pathway towards production of androgens, such as testosterone, which will lead to masculinization of female genital organs (choice B is likely to be a symptom and can be eliminated). The lack of cortisol interrupts the negative feedback pathway with ACTH and is the cause of the adrenal hyperplasia (enlargement of the adrenal glands in an effort to synthesize cortisol). The lack of aldosterone prevents reabsorption of sodium from the urine and secretion of potassium into the urine; consequently urine levels of sodium will increase, and serum levels of potassium will increase (choice C is likely to be a symptom and can be eliminated). However, the normal secretion of aldosterone and subsequent Na⁺ reabsorption is one of the primary means of regulating blood pressure. The reabsorption of sodium is followed by a reabsorption of water, as well as an increase in blood osmolarity and subsequent ADH secretion. The secretion of ADH causes even more water reabsorption, this time at the collecting duct of the nephron. The reabsorption of water increases blood volume and pressure. Thus, the lack of aldosterone due to the 21-β-hydroxylase deficiency would prevent the above from occurring, and would result in low blood pressure (choice D is not a possible symptom and is the correct answer choice).

Passage XI (Questions 205–209)

205. Which of the following is the most likely intermediate in the conversion of glucose to the imine in Figure 1?

A.

B.

C.

D.

C The passage states that imines are formed from primary amine nucleophiles and aldehyde or ketone electrophiles. The first step involves formation of a new C–N bond between the nitrogen and the carbonyl carbon. After proton transfer from nitrogen to the alkoxide oxygen, the structure in choice C is formed. Choice A, an amide, can be formed only from an amine and a carboxylic acid derivative, while B is an amide analog of the keto–enol tautomerism that occurs in ketones and aldehydes. Choice D shows reaction at the alpha carbon of the aldehyde, which is not electrophilic.

206. The imine and ketoamine shown in Figure 1 are best described as:

A. resonance forms.
B. tautomers.
C. conformational isomers.
D. diastereomers.

B The imine and ketoamine are structural isomers in a rapid equilibrium, and are therefore tautomers. Resonance forms involve the movement of only electrons, not atoms, eliminating A. Choice C is false because conformational isomers have all the same connectivities of atoms. These molecules are not diastereomers because they do not differ at any stereocenters.

207. Following formation of the ketoamine in Figure 1, which carbon stereocenter is most likely to undergo racemization?

A. C-3
B. C-4
C. C-5
D. C-6

A Choice D can be eliminated since C-6 is not a stereocenter. Racemization involves the inversion of configuration of a stereocenter. C-3 will be easily racemized since the alpha proton is acidic. When the enolate of the ketone is formed, it can be reprotonated from either side of the double bond, forming both *R* and *S* configurations at that carbon.

208. What other amino-acid nucleophiles present in proteins might form Schiff bases with glucose?

    A. Any cysteine side chain
    B. Any glycine side chain
    C. The C-terminal amino acid
    D. The N-terminal amino acid

D The passage states that primary amines are needed to form imines. The N-terminal amino acid of a protein will have a primary amino group. The C-terminal amino acid has a free carboxylic acid group, eliminating choice C. Cysteine has a sulfur in its side chain, and glycine has no side chain.

209. When treated with Benedict's reagent, the ketoamine formed after lysine reacts with glucose will show:

    A. a positive Benedict's test, because the product is a reducing sugar.
    B. a negative Benedict's test, because the product is not a reducing sugar.
    C. a positive Benedict's test, because the product is not a reducing sugar.
    D. a negative Benedict's test, because the product is a reducing sugar.

A Benedict's test is a test for the presence of aldehydes and ketones, and a positive test indicates that the carbonyl functional group has reduced the copper reagent. Because the ketoamine still has a free carbonyl group, the reagent will show a positive test.

Free-Standing Questions (210–214)

210. Infants born prematurely are at increased risk of death from respiratory distress syndrome due to their inability to produce enough surfactant. Which of the following is the normal anatomical pathway of the respiratory system?

    A. Larynx—pharynx—trachea—bronchioles—bronchi—alveoli
    B. Pharynx—trachea—larynx—bronchi—bronchioles—alveoli
    C. Pharynx—larynx—trachea—bronchi—bronchioles—alveoli
    D. Larynx—pharynx—bronchi—trachea—bronchioles—alveoli

C Air enters the respiratory pathway via the nose or mouth, continues through the *pharynx* (commonly called the throat), the *larynx* ("voice box"), the *trachea*, the right and left primary *bronchi*, which branch into the *bronchioles*, which lead to the *alveoli*, where gas exchange occurs.

211.

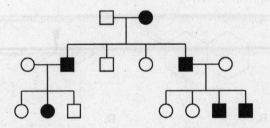

For the pedigree shown above, assume that persons who married into the family do not possess the disease-causing allele. If those with the disease are represented by shaded squares or circles, what is the inheritance pattern of the disease?

    A. Mitochrondrial
    B. X-linked recessive
    C. Autosomal recessive
    D. Autosomal dominant

D The pattern cannot be mitochondrial because the father in the second generation passed it to his daughter (choice A is wrong). It cannot be X-linked recessive. The mother in the first generation is affected by the disorder, so if it were X-linked recessive, she would have to be homozygous recessive for the bad X. In that case the only X she would have available to donate to her children would be a recessive X, and all of her sons would inherit the disorder. Since she passed it on to only two of her three sons, it cannot be X-linked recessive (choice B is wrong). It cannot be autosomal recessive because the affected parents in the second generation married "wild types" that do not possess the disease-causing allele, but still passed this disorder along to their children (choice C is wrong). Therefore, it must be autosomal dominant.

212. Which of the following acetylating conditions will convert diethylamine into an amide at the fastest rate?

    A. Acetic acid / HCl
    B. Acetic anhydride
    C. Acetyl chloride
    D. Ethyl acetate

C Acetyl chloride is an acid chloride, the most reactive of carboxylic acid derivatives.

213. Which one of the following could have a nonzero optical activity?

A.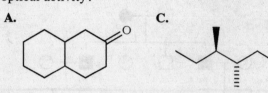

C.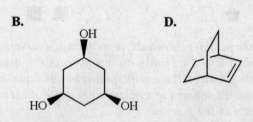

B.

D.

A Choices B and D have no stereocenters and therefore cannot be chiral. Choice C is a meso compound and will be optically inactive as well. The ketone (choice A) is the only compound that is chiral and, therefore, optically active.

214. Eukaryotic and prokaryotic transcription differ on many levels. Eukaryotic transcription occurs within the nucleus, but translation occurs in the cytoplasm. Recent research suggests that the RNA made from eukaryotic transcription must undergo a series of modifications before it is able to leave the nucleus. Prokaryotes lack a nucleus, and thus their RNA does not undergo these same post-transcriptional modifications. Which of the following is NOT an example of eukaryotic post-transcriptional modification?

A. Removal of enhancer and regulator sequences via splicing
B. Removal of the inhibitor from the repressor sequence
C. Addition of a 5′ methylated guanine nucleotide cap to the transcript
D. Addition of a 3′ polyadenosine tail to the transcript

B There are three modifications of the primary RNA transcript in eukaryotes: removal of introns (often enhancer and regulator sequences) and splicing together of exons, the addition of a 5′ methylguanine cap, and the addition of a 3′ poly-A tail (choices A, C, and D are examples of post-transcriptional modification and can be eliminated). However, removal of an inhibitor from a repressor sequence occurs at the pre-transcriptional level, and typically involves the removal of a DNA-binding protein from a regulatory sequence on DNA (choice B is not post-transcriptional and is the correct answer choice).

PART ◆ IV

MCAT Practice Test 2

PART

IV

MCAT Practice Test 2

Physical Sciences

Time: 100 Minutes

Questions 1 – 77

PHYSICAL SCIENCES

DIRECTIONS: Most questions in the Physical Sciences test are organized into groups, each preceded by a descriptive passage. After studying the passage, select the one best answer to each question in the group. Some questions are not based on a descriptive passage and are also independent of each other. You must also select the one best answer to these questions. If you are not certain of an answer, eliminate the alternatives that you know to be incorrect and then select an answer from the remaining alternatives. Indicate your selection by blackening the corresponding oval on your answer document. A periodic table is provided for your use. You may consult it whenever you wish.

PERIODIC TABLE OF THE ELEMENTS

1 H 1.0																	2 He 4.0
3 Li 6.9	4 Be 9.0											5 B 10.8	6 C 12.0	7 N 14.0	8 O 16.0	9 F 19.0	10 Ne 20.2
11 Na 23.0	12 Mg 24.3											13 Al 27.0	14 Si 28.1	15 P 31.0	16 S 32.1	17 Cl 35.5	18 Ar 39.9
19 K 39.1	20 Ca 40.1	21 Sc 45.0	22 Ti 47.9	23 V 50.9	24 Cr 52.0	25 Mn 54.9	26 Fe 55.8	27 Co 58.9	28 Ni 58.7	29 Cu 63.5	30 Zn 65.4	31 Ga 69.7	32 Ge 72.6	33 As 74.9	34 Se 79.0	35 Br 79.9	36 Kr 83.8
37 Rb 85.5	38 Sr 87.6	39 Y 88.9	40 Zr 91.2	41 Nb 92.9	42 Mo 95.9	43 Tc (98)	44 Ru 101.1	45 Rh 102.9	46 Pd 106.4	47 Ag 107.9	48 Cd 112.4	49 In 114.8	50 Sn 118.7	51 Sb 121.8	52 Te 127.6	53 I 126.9	54 Xe 131.3
55 Cs 132.9	56 Ba 137.3	57 La* 138.9	72 Hf 178.5	73 Ta 180.9	74 W 183.9	75 Re 186.2	76 Os 190.2	77 Ir 192.2	78 Pt 195.1	79 Au 197.0	80 Hg 200.6	81 Tl 204.4	82 Pb 207.2	83 Bi 209.0	84 Po (209)	85 At (210)	86 Rn (222)
87 Fr (223)	88 Ra 226.0	89 Ac† 227.0	104 Rf (261)	105 Db (262)	106 Sg (263)	107 Bh (262)	108 Hs (265)	109 Mt (267)									

*	58 Ce 140.1	59 Pr 140.9	60 Nd 144.2	61 Pm (145)	62 Sm 150.4	63 Eu 152.0	64 Gd 157.3	65 Tb 158.9	66 Dy 162.5	67 Ho 164.9	68 Er 167.3	69 Tm 168.9	70 Yb 173.0	71 Lu 175.0
†	90 Th 232.0	91 Pa (231)	92 U 238.0	93 Np (237)	94 Pu (244)	95 Am (243)	96 Cm (247)	97 Bk (247)	98 Cf (251)	99 Es (252)	100 Fm (257)	101 Md (258)	102 No (259)	103 Lr (260)

GO ON TO THE NEXT PAGE.

Passage I (Questions 1–5)

Three common types of radioactive decay are listed below. These processes occur in a fission reactor that uses U-235 as a fuel. Fission of such uranium atoms will occur if they are struck by a high-energy neutron.

Gamma Rays

Gamma rays (γ) are high-energy photons. These particles carry away excess energy when a nucleus moves to a lower energy level. The following reaction is one possible outcome when U-235 is struck by a high-energy neutron:

$$^{235}_{92}U + ^{1}_{0}n \rightarrow ^{92}_{36}Kr + ^{141}_{56}Ba + 3^{1}_{0}n + ^{0}_{0}\gamma$$

There are many other massless and chargeless particles that can carry energy away from a nucleus. A neutrino (ν) is such a particle.

Alpha Decay

Some nuclei can spontaneously emit alpha particles ($^{4}_{2}\alpha$), which are the nuclei of helium atoms.

A nucleus of U-235 will split when struck by a high-speed neutron. However, this process creates many more high-speed neutrons than it consumes. To keep the reaction from running out of control, most reactors contain control rods that are made of a material that will absorb the excess neutrons. Boron can be used to absorb high-energy neutrons and instead produce low-energy alpha particles.

$$^{10}_{5}B + ^{1}_{0}n \rightarrow ^{11}_{5}B$$

$$^{11}_{5}B \rightarrow ^{7}_{3}Li + ^{4}_{2}\alpha$$

Beta Decay

A beta particle (β) is an energetic electron. When a nucleus emits a beta particle, it will lose one neutron and gain one proton. Although the probability is very small, U-235 could emit a beta particle and decay to an isotope of neptunium.

$$^{235}_{92}U \rightarrow ^{235}_{93}Np + ^{0}_{-1}\beta$$

(Note: proton mass = 1.0073 amu; electron rest mass = 9.11×10^{-31} kg; 1 amu = 931 MeV; 1 eV = 1.6×10^{-19} J.)

1. Two helium nuclei fuse and release energy in the form of photons. What type of energy is lost by the nuclei and transferred into the photons?

    A. Kinetic
    B. Radiant
    C. Mass
    D. Electromagnetic

2. $^{236}_{90}Th$ emits two beta particles and two alpha particles. Which of the following nuclei results?

    A. $^{226}_{87}Fr$
    B. $^{226}_{88}Ra$
    C. $^{228}_{88}Ra$
    D. $^{224}_{86}Rn$

3. One-half of a Tl sample decays to Pb in 3.1 minutes through the emission of beta particles. If an initially pure sample of Tl contains 7 g of lead after 9.3 minutes, what was the approximate mass of the original sample?

    A. 7 g
    B. 8 g
    C. 28 g
    D. 32 g

4. An element decays to an isotope of itself, releasing alpha and beta particles. In terms of the number of particles released, the ratio of alpha particles to beta particles is which of the following:

    A. 1/2
    B. 1
    C. 2
    D. 4

5. How many photons, each of energy 2.8 MeV, can be produced when 1 gram of matter is converted to energy?

    A. 2×10^{26}
    B. 2×10^{32}
    C. 2×10^{35}
    D. 4×10^{35}

GO ON TO THE NEXT PAGE.

Passage II (Questions 6–10)

In an experimental procedure, particles were sent into a magnetic field perpendicular to the field's direction. The figure below shows the paths of three particles, X, Y, and Z, that were sent into the field.

The magnetic field is directed into the page, which is signified by the symbol ⊗ for vector **B**.

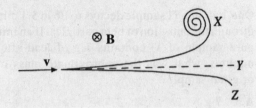

When moving through a magnetic field, any charged particle experiences a force whose magnitude is given by:

$$F = qvB\sin\theta$$

The angle θ is the angle between the direction of the particle's motion and the orientation of the magnetic field. The variables q, v, and B represent the magnitudes of the charge on the particle, the velocity of the particle, and the magnetic field strength, respectively.

When a relatively low energy particle is sent into a magnetic field, it travels a spiral path that decays in a circular fashion, as shown for particle X in the figure above. The motion is circular in nature because the principal force affecting the particle is perpendicular to the direction of its motion.

6. A series of charged particles are fired into the magnetic field. Which of the following best describes the magnitude of the force acting on the particle as θ is increased from 0° to 90°?

   A. It remains constant.
   B. It decreases at a rate that is proportional to θ.
   C. It increases at a rate that is proportional to θ.
   D. It increases at a rate that is not proportional to θ.

7. Particle W, a proton (not shown), is given an initial velocity of 3×10^4 m/s in the direction of path Y. If the magnetic field strength is 5.2 T, what is the initial force felt by particle W?

   A. 5×10^{-15} N, down
   B. 5×10^{-15} N, up
   C. 2.5×10^{-14} N, down
   D. 2.5×10^{-14} N, up

8. If particle Y were given an additional velocity component into the page, with a magnitude equal to the magnitude of its original velocity in the direction of path Y, the force felt by the particle would:

   A. decrease by a factor of 4.
   B. decrease by a factor of 2.
   C. remain the same.
   D. increase by a factor of 2.

9. Observing paths followed by particles X and Z, an experimenter would be justified in concluding that the two particles:

   A. have charges of equal magnitude.
   B. are negatively charged.
   C. are oppositely charged.
   D. are positively charged.

10. Which of the following diagrams represents the force **F** experienced by a positively charged particle traveling with velocity **v** through a magnetic field **B**?

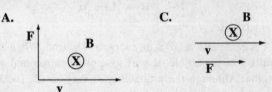

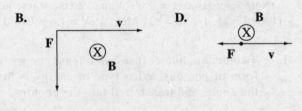

Passage III (Questions 11–15)

Reaction 1 was allowed to proceed under controlled conditions, and the concentration of reactant A was measured at regular intervals until the reactants and products came to equilibrium.

$$A\ (aq) \rightleftarrows B\ (aq) + C\ (aq)$$
$$\Delta H = 150\ kJ$$
Reaction 1

The rate for this reaction is a measure of how fast reactants disappear or products form. Reaction 1 was determined to be a first-order reaction, and the following rate law governs its rate:

$$Rate = k[A]$$

where k is the rate constant for the reaction. This value, *k of reactant*, is constant for any given temperature, but increases with increasing temperature. For most reactions, it nearly doubles for every 10°C by which temperature is increased.

The rate of Reaction 1 at any point in its progress can also be determined experimentally by tracking the change in concentration of reactants or products over time (t):

$$Rate = -\Delta[A]/\Delta t = \Delta[B]/\Delta t = \Delta[C]/\Delta t$$

Figure 1 depicts a change in the concentration of A as the reaction proceeded at 25°C and 1 atm pressure in a chamber containing 2 liters of solution. The process was later repeated in a chamber whose temperature was maintained at 65°C.

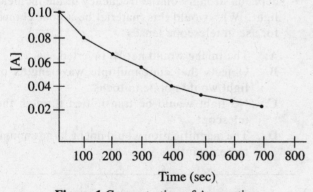

Figure 1 Concentration of A over time

11. Based on the passage, what should be the approximate initial rate of Reaction 1 at 65°C?

- A. 2×10^{-4} mol/s
- B. 3×10^{-3} mol/s
- C. 6×10^{-3} mol/s
- D. 2×10^{-2} mol/s

12. Based on the passage, how many moles of A have disappeared from the solution after 600 seconds have elapsed?

- A. 0.06 moles
- B. 0.07 moles
- C. 0.14 moles
- D. 0.16 moles

13. If Reaction 1 is run at 65°C and a graph analogous to that of Figure 1 is drawn to depict the reaction rate, how will the curve of the new graph differ from that of Figure 1?

- A. The new curve will descend more steeply.
- B. The new curve will descend less steeply.
- C. The new curve will be identical to the first line.
- D. The new curve will be horizontal.

14. How would increasing the temperature at which the reaction takes place affect the rates of the forward and reverse reactions and the eventual equilibrium?

- A. It would increase the rate of the forward reaction, decrease the rate of the reverse reaction, and shift the equilibrium toward the formation of products.
- B. It would decrease the rate of the forward reaction, increase the rate of the reverse reaction, and shift the equilibrium toward the formation of reactants.
- C. It would increase the rate of the forward reaction, increase the rate of the reverse reaction, and shift the equilibrium toward the formation of products.
- D. It would increase the rate of the forward reaction, increase the rate of the reverse reaction, and shift the equilibrium toward the formation of reactants.

15. If the initial concentration of A is doubled, what will be the effect on the initial rate of reaction and the rate constant?

- A. The rate of reaction and the rate constant will double.
- B. The rate of reaction and the rate constant will not change.
- C. The rate of reaction will double and the rate constant will not change.
- D. The rate of reaction will not change and the rate constant will double.

GO ON TO THE NEXT PAGE.

Passage IV (Questions 16–21)

The prototypical astronomical telescope is designed as shown in Figure 1 below.

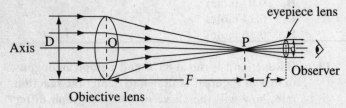

Figure 1 Telescope design

The objective lens, O, has a long positive focal length. The incident parallel rays emanating from the object to be visualized enter from the left and traverse the objective lens. The eyepiece is located nearer to the observer. It has a short positive focal length and acts as a magnifying glass.

The magnification created by a telescope is given by the ratio of the focal length of the objective lens F to the focal length of the eyepiece f. For the telescope pictured above, F is equal to 40 cm and f is equal to 2 cm. The lenses are made of glass with a refractive index of 1.5.

The focal lengths F and f of the objective lens and eyepiece, respectively, coincide at point P. The image formed by the objective lens is real and inverted. This image then acts as the object for the eyepiece, which transforms it into an enlarged virtual image that remains inverted. The inversion is of little practical consequence because the astronomical telescope is normally used to study distant objects.

16. What would be the effective magnification of the telescope in Figure 1 if someone were to accidentally use the objective lens as the eyepiece?

    A. 0.02
    B. 0.05
    C. 2
    D. 20

17. An investigator works with a telescope that is equipped with a variety of removable lenses. Among the following combinations, the investigator will achieve greatest magnification with:

    A. an objective with a large focal length and an eyepiece with a large focal length.
    B. an objective with a small focal length and an eyepiece with a small focal length.
    C. an objective with a large focal length and an eyepiece with a small focal length.
    D. an objective with a small focal length and an eyepiece with a large focal length.

18. An object is to be observed using only the eyepiece lens. If the object lies at a distance of 1.5 cm from the eyepiece lens, the image will be located:

    A. 1 cm from the eyepiece.
    B. 2 cm from the eyepiece.
    C. 3 cm from the eyepiece.
    D. 6 cm from the eyepiece.

19. What is the power of the eyepiece of the telescope in Figure 1?

    A. 2 diopters
    B. 5 diopters
    C. 20 diopters
    D. 50 diopters

20. If the eyepiece lens were replaced with a lens composed of a material with a refractive index greater than 1.5, which of the following would be expected to occur?

    A. The magnification of the telescope would increase.
    B. The magnification of the telescope would be unchanged.
    C. The magnification of the telescope would decrease.
    D. The effect on the magnification cannot be determined.

21. A certain material has an index of refraction which depends strongly on the frequency of the incident light. Why would this material be a poor choice for use in telescope lenses?

    A. The image would not be inverted.
    B. Objects that emit multiple wavelengths of light would not be in focus.
    C. No light would be transmitted through the telescope.
    D. The magnification would not be large enough to be useful.

GO ON TO THE NEXT PAGE.

Questions 22 through 27 are **NOT** based on a descriptive passage.

22. An object of mass m is sliding down a frictionless ramp that is elevated at an angle of 60°. What is the magnitude of the object's acceleration parallel to the ramp?

A. $g \cos 60°$
B. $g \sin 60°$
C. $mg \cos 60°$
D. $mg \sin 60°$

23. Which of the following electronic configurations belongs to a diamagnetic element in its ground state?

A. $1s^2 2s^1$
B. $1s^2 2s^2 2p^1$
C. $1s^2 2s^2 2p^4$
D. $1s^2 2s^2 2p^6$

24. A constant current of 5 amperes is passing through a 10-ohm resistor. How much energy is dissipated in the resistor over the course of 10 seconds?

A. 250 J
B. 500 J
C. 1000 J
D. 2500 J

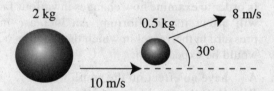

25. An object of mass 2 kg, moving horizontally at 10 m/s, collides with a smaller object, initially at rest, of mass 0.5 kg. After the collision, the smaller object moves with velocity 8 m/s at an angle of 30° above the horizontal. What is the vertical speed of the larger object after the collision?

A. 0.25 m/s
B. 0.5 m/s
C. 1 m/s
D. 2 m/s

26. The pressure of a gas at a temperature of 27°C is measured to be P. If the temperature is increased to 127°C while all other factors are kept constant, what will be the new pressure of the gas?

A. 1/5 P
B. 3/4 P
C. 4/3 P
D. 5P

27. As an ideal fluid flowing in a cylindrical pipe through a constant pressure differential moves from a region of larger diameter to a region of smaller diameter, which of the following will occur?

A. Flow rate will remain constant and fluid velocity will increase.
B. Flow rate will remain constant and fluid velocity will remain constant.
C. Flow rate will increase and fluid velocity will increase.
D. Flow rate will increase and fluid velocity will remain constant.

Passage V Questions (28–33)

Human teeth are covered by a layer of enamel that serves to protect them. This enamel is composed of the mineral *hydroxyapatite*, whose empirical formula is $Ca_5(PO_4)_3OH(s)$.

When tooth decay occurs, hydroxyapatite is dissolved into the saliva, as shown in the following reaction:

$$Ca_5(PO_4)_3OH(s) \rightleftarrows 5Ca^{2+}(aq) + 3PO_4^{3-}(aq) + OH^-(aq).$$
Reaction 1

The forward reaction represents tooth decay. However, the reverse reaction normally occurs at a faster rate than does the forward reaction, and under normal conditions, teeth do not decay in saliva.

The consumption of food with a large sugar content promotes tooth decay because the digestion of sugar, which begins in the mouth, produces acid. Acid, in turn, affects the equilibrium of Reaction 1.

Fluoride is used to fight tooth decay because it can replace hydroxide in the enamel formation process to form a compound called *fluorapatite*, $Ca_5(PO_4)_3F(s)$, which undergoes this reaction:

$$Ca_5(PO_4)_3F(s) \rightleftarrows 5Ca^{2+}(aq) + 3PO_4^{3-}(aq) + F^-(aq).$$
Reaction 2

The fluoride ions produced in Reaction 2 are much less likely to react in an acidic environment than are the hydroxide ions produced in Reaction 1.

28. The process of tooth decay is most likely to occur in saliva maintained at which of the following pOH values?

   A. 8.0
   B. 7.0
   C. 6.0
   D. 5.0

29. The oxidation state of calcium in the hydroxyapatite molecule is:

   A. −1
   B. 0
   C. +1
   D. +2

30. Fluorapatite is more resistant to tooth decay than is hydroxyapatite because compared to hydroxide ion, the fluoride ion is:

   A. a stronger base that interacts less with hydrogen ions in saliva.
   B. a weaker base that interacts less with hydrogen ions in saliva.
   C. a stronger base that reacts more with hydrogen ions in saliva.
   D. a weaker base that reacts more with hydrogen ions in saliva.

31. The presence of acid in saliva acts to promote tooth decay because acid in saliva will:

   A. increase the hydroxide concentration.
   B. increase the hydroxyapatite concentration.
   C. decrease the hydroxide concentration.
   D. decrease the calcium concentration.

32. If observing Reaction 1 in a laboratory, adding which of the following would have the least effect on its equilibrium?

   A. 0.5 mol of sulfuric acid
   B. 1 mol of hydrochloric acid
   C. 0.33 mol of nitric acid
   D. 0.33 mol of phosphoric acid

33. Reaction 2 is examined under controlled conditions in order to examine how changes in various factors will affect its equilibrium. An increase in the pressure in the vessel in which the reaction occurs would be expected to:

   A. have no effect on the equilibrium.
   B. shift the equilibrium to the right.
   C. shift the equilibrium to the left.
   D. prevent the reaction from occurring.

GO ON TO THE NEXT PAGE.

Passage VI (Questions 34–39)

A researcher conducted two experiments designed to examine the principles of projectile motion. In both experiments, effects due to the air were negligible.

Experiment 1

In eight trials, a projectile was launched from ground level at an initial speed of 20 m/s. With each trial, the angle of elevation was varied. Maximum height, horizontal distance, and flight time were recorded in Table 1.

Table 1 Trial Results

Trial	Angle of Elevation	Flight Time (sec)	Height (m)	Distance (m)
1	10°	0.7	0.6	13.7
2	20°	1.4	2.3	25.7
3	30°	2.0	5.0	34.6
4	40°	2.6	8.3	39.4
5	50°	3.1	11.7	39.4
6	60°	3.5	15.0	34.6
7	70°	3.8	17.7	25.7
8	80°	3.9	19.4	13.7

Experiment 2

In five repeated trials, a projectile was launched horizontally—with 0° angle of elevation—from a platform raised 50 m above a level surface. With each trial, the projectile's initial speed was varied. Flight time and horizontal distance were recorded in Table 2.

Table 2 Trial Results

Trial	Speed (m/s)	Flight Time (sec)	Distance (m)
1	10	3.2	32
2	20	3.2	64
3	30	3.2	96
4	40	3.2	128
5	50	3.2	160

34. In the absence of air resistance, which of the following quantities remains constant throughout the flight of a projectile?

    I.   Horizontal speed
    II. Momentum
    III. Acceleration

A. I only
B. II only
C. I and II only
D. I and III only

35. In which trial of Experiment 1 did gravity do the greatest amount of work during the projectile's descent?

A. Trial 1
B. Trial 4
C. Trial 5
D. Trial 8

36. If a ninth trial of Experiment 1 had been performed, and the projectile had traveled a horizontal distance of 28 m, its initial angle of elevation could have been:

A. 22°.
B. 28°.
C. 32°.
D. 38°.

37. In Trial 3 of Experiment 1, what was the ratio of the projectile's kinetic energy at impact to its kinetic energy at launch?

A. $1\sqrt{2}$
B. 1
C. $\sqrt{2}$
D. 2

38. What was the approximate speed of the projectile in Trial 3 of Experiment 2 as it impacted the ground?

A. 30 m/s
B. 44 m/s
C. 53 m/s
D. 62 m/s

39. If Experiment 2 were performed a second time, with the initial height set at 125 m, what would be the expected flight time for the projectiles?

A. 5 sec
B. 6 sec
C. 7 sec
D. 8 sec

GO ON TO THE NEXT PAGE.

Passage VII (Questions 40–45)

A student attempts to identify the metals involved in several oxidation–reduction reactions of the form:

$$Y^{2+}(aq) + Z(s) \rightarrow Y(s) + Z^{2+}(aq)$$
Reaction 1

The student examines three separate galvanic cells, all of which are designed as shown in Figure 1.

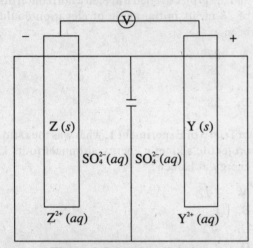

Figure 1 Galvanic cell design

The student has been told that all half-reactions occurring in the cells are listed in Table 1.

Table 1 Half-Reactions

Half-Reaction	E(V)
$Ba^{2+}(aq) + 2e^- \rightarrow Ba(s)$	-2.9
$Mg^{2+}(aq) + 2e^- \rightarrow Mg(s)$	-2.4
$Be^{2+}(aq) + 2e^- \rightarrow Be(s)$	-1.9
$Mn^{2+}(aq) + 2e^- \rightarrow Mn(s)$	-1.2
$Zn^{2+}(aq) + 2e^- \rightarrow Zn(s)$	-0.8
$Cd^{2+}(aq) + 2e^- \rightarrow Cd(s)$	-0.4

Experiment 1

The voltmeter is connected to one cell of the electrodes and registers a potential difference of 0.5 V.

Experiment 2

The voltmeter is connected to the electrodes of a second cell and registers a potential difference of 0 V.

Experiment 3

The voltmeter is connected to the electrodes of a third cell and registers a potential difference of 1.6 V.

40. Regarding the reaction taking place in Experiment 1, which of the following statements must be true?

   A. The free-energy change is positive.
   B. The free-energy change is negative.
   C. The free energy does not change.
   D. The free-energy change is equal to the voltage.

41. If it is known that Z(s) for Experiment 1 is solid magnesium, the student should determine that the identity for Y(s) is:

   A. barium.
   B. beryllium.
   C. zinc.
   D. cadmium.

42. Which of the following could be the identities of $Y^{2+}(aq)$ and Z(s) in Experiment 2?

   A. $Be^{2+}(aq)$ and Mn(s)
   B. $Mg^{2+}(aq)$ and Ba(s)
   C. $Cd^{2+}(aq)$ and Zn(s)
   D. $Zn^{2+}(aq)$ and Be(s)

43. The student conducts a fourth experiment by connecting a voltmeter to the electrodes of another galvanic cell. If the voltmeter reads 0.6 V, what conclusion can the student draw?

   A. Neither half-reaction is present in Table 1.
   B. At least one of the half-reactions is not present in Table 1.
   C. At least one of the half-reactions is present in Table 1.
   D. Both half-reactions are present in Table 1.

44. Among the species listed in Table 1, which is the strongest reducing agent?

   A. $Cd^{2+}(aq)$
   B. Cd(s)
   C. $Ba^{2+}(aq)$
   D. Ba(s)

45. The positive electrode in Figure 1 is the:

   A. anode, where reduction takes place.
   B. anode, where oxidation takes place.
   C. cathode, where reduction takes place.
   D. cathode, where oxidation takes place.

Passage VIII (Questions 46–50)

When an object falls through a fluid, it experiences a frictional force tending to oppose its downward motion. This force's magnitude depends on the object's speed, size, and shape, and the fluid's viscosity.

For a small sphere falling through a viscous fluid, the frictional force is given by the formula $F_f = 6\pi\eta r v$, where η is the viscosity of the fluid, r is the radius of the sphere, and v is the speed of the sphere.

As the sphere falls through the fluid, it experiences a downward force due to its weight mg. This downward force will be countered by the frictional force F_f and by the buoyant force F_b exerted by the fluid. When the sum of all the forces acting on the falling object is equal to zero, the object is said to have reached terminal velocity.

The following table gives values for the viscosity and density of various fluids under standard conditions.

Table 1 Viscosity and Density

Fluid	Viscosity (N-s/m^2)	Density (kg/m^3)
Air	1.8×10^{-5}	1.3
Water	1.0×10^{-3}	1,000
Glycerin	8.3×10^{-1}	1,260
Ethyl alcohol	1.2×10^{-3}	800

46. What is the frictional force on a sphere of glycerin of radius 1 cm falling at a speed of 1.6 m/s through water?

- **A.** 3×10^{-5} N
- **B.** 3×10^{-4} N
- **C.** 2.5×10^{-3} N
- **D.** 2.5×10^{-2} N

47. For an object descending through fluid, which of the following best describes the change in frictional force as the object's speed increases?

- **A.** Linear and increasing
- **B.** Linear and decreasing
- **C.** Constant
- **D.** Quadratic and increasing

48. Two spherical drops with equal radii fall through the air. One is composed of glycerin and the other of ethyl alcohol. Which would be expected to reach the greater terminal velocity?

- **A.** Ethyl alcohol, because it has the lower viscosity
- **B.** Ethyl alcohol, because it has the lower density
- **C.** Glycerin, because it has the higher viscosity
- **D.** Glycerin, because it has the higher density

49. Which of the following will affect the buoyant force experienced by a solid object falling through a fluid?

- **A.** Density of the object
- **B.** Density of the fluid
- **C.** Speed of the object
- **D.** Viscosity of the fluid

50. If an object is at rest inside a container of fluid (not at the top or bottom), then:

- **A.** the object and fluid have equal densities.
- **B.** the object and fluid have equal viscosities.
- **C.** the frictional force exceeds the object's weight.
- **D.** this situation is impossible.

GO ON TO THE NEXT PAGE.

Questions 51 through 55 are **NOT** based on a based on a descriptive passage.

51. A chamber at constant temperature contains 10 moles of helium gas and 1 mole of neon gas. Which of the following is NOT true?

   A. The average speed of the helium atoms is greater than the average speed of the neon atoms.
   B. The partial pressure due to the helium atoms is greater than the partial pressure due to the neon atoms.
   C. The total mass of helium present in the chamber is greater than the total mass of neon present in the chamber.
   D. The average kinetic energy of the helium atoms is greater than the average kinetic energy of the neon atoms.

52. Which of the following subatomic particles would experience the greatest force when exposed to an electric field?

   A. An alpha particle
   B. A beta particle
   C. A proton
   D. A neutron

53. A student prepares a 1 molal aqueous solution of each of the following salts. Which solution will show the greatest boiling point elevation?

   A. $NaCl(aq)$
   B. $MgCl_2(aq)$
   C. $NaNO_3(aq)$
   D. $MgSO_4(aq)$

54. An object of specific gravity 0.4 and volume 0.5 m^3 is floating in a fluid of specific gravity 2. What percentage of the object's volume lies above the surface of the fluid?

   A. 20%
   B. 40%
   C. 60%
   D. 80%

55. Samples of which of the following molecules will exhibit the strongest intermolecular interactions?

   A. O_2
   B. N_2
   C. CO_2
   D. H_2O

GO ON TO THE NEXT PAGE.

Passage IX (Questions 56–62)

Solar energy offers several advantages over the combustion of fossil fuels. Chief among these are the facts that its supply is virtually unlimited and that it need not produce hazardous waste products. One disadvantage of solar energy is the inconsistency of its availability. Figure 1 illustrates a device designed to store solar energy through the use of a reversible chemical process.

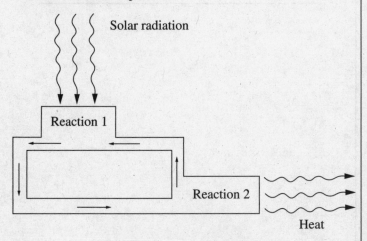

Figure 1 Solar energy device

$$2\ SO_3(g) \rightarrow 2\ SO_2(g) + O_2(g)$$
$$\Delta H = 198\ kJ$$
Reaction 1

Reaction 1 is endothermic and occurs at high temperatures.

$$2\ SO_2(g) + O_2(g) \rightarrow 2\ SO_3(g)$$
$$\Delta H = -198\ kJ$$
Reaction 2

Reaction 2 is exothermic and occurs only in the presence of a catalyst.

The device is closed to the outside, and gas is circulated around the system. Energy is stored in the endothermic process of Reaction 1 and can be later released by initiating the exothermic process of Reaction 2.

56. Solar radiation with which of the following properties will make the most energy available in storage by the device?

  A. A long wavelength
  B. A high velocity
  C. A high frequency
  D. A long period of vibration

57. Reaction 1 occurs spontaneously at high temperatures. The most probable cause for this phenomenon is that at high temperatures:

  A. increasing entropy compensates for increasing enthalpy.
  B. increasing entropy compensates for decreasing enthalpy.
  C. decreasing entropy compensates for increasing enthalpy.
  D. decreasing entropy compensates for decreasing enthalpy.

58. The heat of formation of $SO_3(g)$ is –396 kJ/mol. What is the heat of formation of $SO_2(g)$?

  A. –396 kJ/mol
  B. –297 kJ/mol
  C. –198 kJ/mol
  D. –495 kJ/mol

59. How many moles of sulfur dioxide would be needed to generate enough energy to power a 60 W light bulb for one week straight, assuming 100% efficiency?

  A. 6.1 mol
  B. 15.3 mol
  C. 183 mol
  D. 367 mol

GO ON TO THE NEXT PAGE.

60. One of the advantages of the solar energy conversion device is that the energy can be stored indefinitely and released when desired. That is because:

   A. all of the reactants and products are in the gas phase.
   B. the endothermic reaction takes place only at high temperatures.
   C. the exothermic reaction takes place only in the presence of a catalyst.
   D. the exothermic reaction releases more energy than is stored by the endothermic reaction.

61. The formation of oxygen gas in Reaction 1 would be promoted by:

   A. increasing the pressure of the reaction chamber.
   B. decreasing the pressure of the reaction chamber.
   C. increasing the concentration of sulfur dioxide in the reaction chamber.
   D. decreasing the concentration of sulfur trioxide in the reaction chamber.

62. If 1 mole of oxygen gas is consumed by Reaction 2 over the course of 1 hour, what is the power of the conversion device?

   A. 3 W
   B. 22 W
   C. 55 W
   D. 330 W

GO ON TO THE NEXT PAGE.

Passage X (Questions 63–68)

A mass undergoing undamped simple harmonic motion caused by a spring on a frictionless surface will obey the law of conservation of energy. An apparatus is set up as shown in Figure 1.

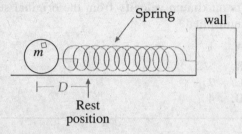

Figure 1 Model of apparatus at rest

The oscillation of the mass is set in motion by displacing the mass an initial distance D from the rest position of the spring system, as shown in Figure 1, and then releasing it from rest.

As oscillation proceeds, the total energy of the mass and spring is unchanged. Its value depends on the initial displacement, D, the distance between the spring's resting position and the point at which oscillation is begun. The energy of the system undergoes conversion between kinetic energy of the mass and elastic potential energy of the spring.

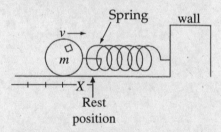

Figure 2

The speed v of a mass m undergoing undamped oscillation can be found at any distance X from rest if the spring constant k and the initial displacement D are known:

$$v = \sqrt{\frac{k}{m}\left(D^2 - X^2\right)}$$

Equation 1

63. Which of the following graphs best relates E, the total energy of the spring and mass system, to the initial displacement, D, from rest position?

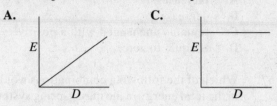
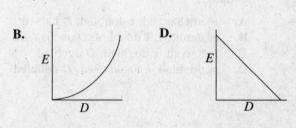

64. If the mass, while moving to the left at a distance X to the left of the rest position, collided elastically with a block and transferred all of its momentum to the block, how much kinetic energy would the block have?

A. $1/2\ kX^2$
B. $kD^2 - kX^2$
C. kX^2
D. $1/2\ kD^2 - 1/2\ kX^2$

65. Which of the following changes to the system would produce the greatest increase in the block's speed at a given displacement from the resting position?

A. Increasing the mass of the block and the spring constant of the spring
B. Decreasing the mass of the block and the spring constant of the spring
C. Increasing the mass of the block and decreasing the spring constant of the spring
D. Decreasing the mass of the block and increasing the spring constant of the spring

GO ON TO THE NEXT PAGE.

66. As the block moves through the point shown in Figure 2, the magnitude of its acceleration:

    A. increases.
    B. decreases.
    C. remains unchanged with a positive value.
    D. is equal to zero.

67. Which of the following combinations would result in the total energy in the mass–spring system being doubled?

    A. m unchanged, k doubled, D halved
    B. m doubled, k doubled, D unchanged
    C. m halved, k doubled, D doubled
    D. m doubled, k unchanged, D doubled

68. The mass is now placed between two identical springs, each attached to a wall at the other end, such that the total energy of the system is 0 when the mass is midway between the walls. Now, if the mass were displaced a distance D from the rest position and released, by what factor would its maximum velocity from the original setup be multiplied?

    A. 1
    B. $\sqrt{2}$
    C. 2
    D. 4

GO ON TO THE NEXT PAGE.

Passage XI (Questions 69–73)

According to the Bohr model of the hydrogen atom, the energy levels of the electron in a hydrogen atom are quantized. As the electron orbits the hydrogen nucleus, it is restricted to specific orbitals and their associated energy levels. The energy of an electron in a hydrogen atom is given by the expression:

$$E_n = -E_g\left(\frac{1}{n^2}\right)$$

Equation 1

where E_g is equal to 2.18×10^{-18} J, and n is the principal quantum number associated with the electron. By convention, an orbiting electron has a negative energy value to signify that its energy is lower than that of a free electron.

When an electron within a hydrogen atom moves from one energy level to another, the change in energy is given by the equation:

$$\Delta E = E_g\left(\frac{1}{n_i^2} - \frac{1}{n_f^2}\right)$$

Equation 2

where n_i and n_f are the initial and final quantum numbers, respectively. When the atom absorbs energy and the electron moves to a higher energy level, ΔE has a positive value. When the atom releases energy and the electron moves to a lower energy state, ΔE has a negative value.

An atom releases energy in the form of electromagnetic radiation whose frequency is given by the equation:

$$\Delta E = hf$$

where f is the frequency of the radiation and h is Planck's constant, equal to 6.63×10^{-34} J-sec.

Some of the electromagnetic radiation emitted by a hydrogen atom falls in the visible spectrum. Figure 1 shows a line emission spectrum for hydrogen.

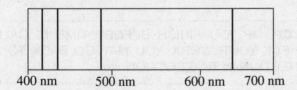

Figure 1 Hydrogen emission

69. What is the energy of an electron occupying the third quantum level ($n = 3$) of a hydrogen atom?

   A. -1.96×10^{-17} J
   B. -2.42×10^{-19} J
   C. -6.54×10^{-18} J
   D. -7.27×10^{-19} J

70. Which of the lists below could represent the wavelengths of the electromagnetic radiation emitted by hydrogen atoms?

   A. 410 nm, 434 nm, 486 nm, 580 nm
   B. 410 nm, 434 nm, 486 nm, 656 nm
   C. 410 nm, 486 nm, 580 nm, 656 nm
   D. 410 nm, 486 nm, 628 nm, 656 nm

71. When an electron moves, within a hydrogen atom, from the third quantum level ($n = 3$) to the second quantum level ($n = 2$), which of the following is true?

   A. ΔE will be positive and a photon will be emitted.
   B. ΔE will be positive and a photon will be absorbed.
   C. ΔE will be negative and a photon will be emitted.
   D. ΔE will be negative and a photon will be absorbed.

72. A photon of which of the following wavelengths will have the highest energy?

   A. 400 nm
   B. 500 nm
   C. 600 nm
   D. 700 nm

73. An increase in an electron's quantum number will produce:

   A. increased stability and increased energy.
   B. increased stability and decreased energy.
   C. decreased stability and decreased energy.
   D. decreased stability and increased energy.

GO ON TO THE NEXT PAGE.

Questions 74 through 77 are **NOT** based on a descriptive passage.

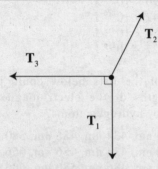

74. The figure above (not drawn to scale) shows three cables under tension, all connected to a common point and in static equilibrium. If $T_1 = 12$ N and $T_2 = 13$ N, what is the magnitude of $\mathbf{T}_3$?

   A. 1 N
   B. 5 N
   C. 12.5 N
   D. 25 N

75. Barium fluoride is a slightly soluble salt with $K_{sp} = 1.7 \times 10^{-6}$. If the concentration of barium ions in a saturated aqueous solution is equal to 4.3×10^{-3} M, what is the concentration of fluoride ions in the solution?

   A. 4.0×10^{-4} M
   B. 2.0×10^{-2} M
   C. 4.0×10^{-2} M
   D. 2.0×10^{-1} M

76. An object of mass m is tied to a string of length r. The object is whirled around and maintained in a circular path by the tension T in the string. Which of the following graphs best represents the change in v as the path's radius, r, is changed?

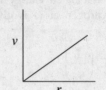
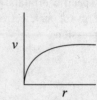
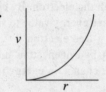
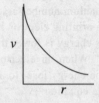

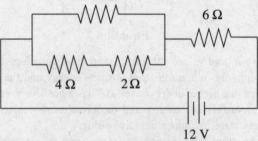

77. In the circuit above, what is the current through the 6-ohm resistor?

   A. 1.5 A
   B. 1.75 A
   C. 2 A
   D. 2.5 A

STOP. IF YOU FINISH BEFORE TIME IS CALLED, CHECK YOUR WORK. YOU MAY GO BACK TO ANY QUESTION IN THIS SECTION.

Verbal Reasoning

Time: 85 Minutes
Questions 78 – 137

VERBAL REASONING

DIRECTIONS: There are nine passages in the Verbal Reasoning test. Each passage is followed by several questions. After reading a passage, select the one best answer to each question. If you are not certain of an answer, eliminate the alternatives that you know to be incorrect and then select an answer from the remaining alternatives. Indicate your selection by blackening the corresponding oval on your answer document.

Passage I (Questions 78–83)

Federal law requires that states articulate guidelines for establishing the size of child support awards to be paid by a noncustodial parent to a custodial parent. The law was enacted in response to a widespread percep-
5 tion that many states lacked meaningful criteria through which child support awards were to be established. In enacting the law, Congress has been generally concerned that child support orders might be either inadequate or unjust. Congress has found that some awards are eco-
10 nomically inadequate to facilitate basic child rearing. Others reflect a pattern of inconsistency wherein two noncustodial parents similarly situated might find themselves paying very different child support awards.

As to the matter of inadequacy, a recent study showed
15 that the nation's noncustodial parents would have paid more than $30 billion in a recent fiscal year if support awards took realistic account of the cost of child rearing. Census data, however, indicate that only $10.1 billion was due in that year and, moreover, that only $7.1 bil-
20 lion was actually paid. The situation thus revealed an adequacy gap of $20 billion and a compliance gap of $3 billion. Without congressional action, the adequacy gap would likely increase. The compliance gap is likely to increase regardless.

25 It is a matter of fundamental fairness that like parties should be treated alike, and as individuals, most state judges are fairly consistent in the standards and criteria they apply in setting child support awards. Yet studies show that within a given state, judges do not necessar-
30 ily exhibit similar patterns in setting their awards. The quality of life for a separating couple and their children will depend on the judge who sets the support award rather than on preestablished criteria. It was found that in Colorado, one parent might be required to make a support
35 payment equal to 6 percent of income, while a similarly situated parent before another court might be required to pay a full third of his or her income.

As the new federal law takes hold, states face a choice regarding the model on which they wish to base their criteria.
40 The "flat rate" model imposes on all paying parents a payment equal to a flat percentage of income, adjusted for the number of children at issue. Rates might be, for example, 8 percent for one child, 15 percent for two children, and 20 percent for three children. Under such a flat rate
45 structure, all paying parents with one child would pay 8 percent of their income in support. The actual rates, of course, would depend on the states.

Conversely, the "income shares" model embodies the idea that each child should receive that percentage of to-
50 tal parental income as would have been received had the parents not separated. Each parent, in turn, is expected to contribute out of his or her income pro rata according to his or her contribution to total income. Suppose, for example, a separating couple has one child. Spouse A
55 is the custodial spouse and has an income of $20,000. Spouse B has an income of $60,000, which makes for a total parental income of $80,000. Twenty-five percent of the total derives from Spouse A and 75 percent from Spouse B. If the court determined that the child would
60 ordinarily enjoy the benefit of 20 percent of the total income ($16,000), the parents would be required to provide that amount pro rata. Spouse A would be expected to contribute 25 percent ($4,000), and Spouse B would pay 75 percent ($12,000).

65 Flat rate and income shares awards reflect different values and thus lead to different awards. Where two children live with a payee spouse and the payee spouse has no income, Wisconsin's flat rate approach, for example, would require monthly payments of $186 from a payor
70 spouse whose monthly income is $600. In the same situation, the income shares approach would require a monthly payment of $90. Because the approach to guidelines may differ from state to state, such guidelines will not bring about parity in support orders across state lines.

GO ON TO THE NEXT PAGE.

78. Which of the following statements is most supported by the passage?

    A. The compliance gap measures the court costs of child support proceedings unpaid by litigants and covered by state budgets.

    B. The adequacy gap measures the court costs of child support proceedings unfunded by state budgets and covered by federal assistance.

    C. The compliance gap measures the child support dollar amount awarded in courts and unpaid by parents.

    D. The adequacy gap measures the child support dollar amount awarded in courts and unpaid by parents.

79. The author cites research to support which of the following claims?

    I. Judges do not always rely on the same criteria when setting child support awards, even within the same state.

    II. Fairness dictates that noncustodial spouses in comparable circumstances should be treated alike.

    III. The "compliance gap" is likely to increase.

    A. I only

    B. I and II only

    C. II and III only

    D. I, II, and III

80. Which of the following is most analogous to the relationship between the flat rate and income shares models described in the passage?

    A. Local telephone charges at a monthly flat rate or a rate based on the amount of monthly usage

    B. Long-distance telephone rates based on a flat rate per minute or based on mileage between the call origination phone and the call destination phone

    C. Monthly loan interest at a fixed rate or at a variable rate

    D. An income tax system based on a single tax rate or on a graduated rate that escalates with income

81. Which of the following conclusions can justifiably be drawn from the author's discussion of judges?

    A. Individual judges are inconsistent in the criteria they apply.

    B. Judges often set awards according to capricious standards.

    C. The amount of child support may be different depending on the judge who awards it.

    D. If each state were to establish set criteria for child support awards, noncustodial parents would be treated fairly by the courts.

82. Which of the following statements, if true, would most strengthen the position of those who oppose leaving child support legislation up to the individual states?

    A. State governments should protect the "life, liberty, and pursuit of happiness" of the nation's children.

    B. Divorced individuals often do not live in the same part of the country as their former spouses.

    C. The federal government can best evaluate statistical variations in the cost of living index from state to state.

    D. The federal government has a constitutional obligation to ensure due process of law for all persons, including those involved in divorce proceedings.

83. A recent theory suggests that children of divorced spouses whose custodial parent received regular and sufficient child support payments will score higher on scales measuring self-esteem and self-confidence than those whose parents do not comply with court-ordered support. Social workers who accept this theory would be LEAST likely to support which of the following?

    A. Support groups at the local level that help parents who do not meet child support obligations deal with the resulting psychological issues

    B. Support groups at the local level for custodial parents and their children who do not receive regular and sufficient child support

    C. Federal regulations that make it more difficult for parents to avoid compliance with court-ordered support judgments

    D. State laws requiring automatic deductions from payroll checks of parents convicted of failing to pay child support

GO ON TO THE NEXT PAGE.

Passage II (Questions 84–90)

As the largest land animal on the planet, the elephant is a potent symbol of the animal kingdom, distinguished by its size, prehensile trunk, ivory tusks, and enormous ears. In the West, where the elephant is an exotic creature
5 known only from books, movies, circuses, and zoos, its image suffers distortion and even exploitation. Whether romanticized or trivialized, the elephant is rarely presented in its complex reality. But in Africa, where humans and elephants—or their respective ancestors—have
10 coexisted for a million years or more, the elephant is known in fuller dimensions. It has been a source of food, material, and riches; a fearsome rival for resources; and a highly visible, provocative neighbor. Inevitably it has had an impact on artistic imagination. Even in areas
15 where the elephant has now vanished, it persists as a symbol in expressive culture. As interpreted in African sculpture, masquerade, dance, and song, its image undergoes a startling range of transformations. But no matter how it is represented, its size and power are the features
20 most likely to be dramatized, for they not only inspire respect, but also stand, for better or worse, as emblems for human values.

The elephant is, of course, only one creature within the vast drama of intricate relationships that link the
25 animal world with the human one. It should not be isolated from the hierarchy of fauna that give it context not just in actuality but also in its symbolic life. In its symbolic functions, it is at times interchangeable with other creatures, depending on culture and circumstance:
30 Qualities ascribed to the elephant in one instance may be given to the leopard or duiker in another. Even within a single culture, the meanings ascribed to it can shift. Or it may be just one of an array of animals treated more or less equally, much like those of the biblical Noah's
35 ark—a theme that has been explored in glass paintings from Senegal, thorn carvings from Nigeria, and popular paintings from Ethiopia.

The elephant may be considered as a microcosm—a large one, to be sure. By virtue of its sheer size and prom-
40 inence, the roles it plays in art and historical processes are magnified. In the broader terms of the macrocosm, one might ask how humans relate to their environment and the fauna they share it with, and above all, how they interpret that relationship. In Africa as elsewhere, people
45 represent their relationship to animals in multiple ways, and their complex experience of it can be read in the symbolic language of their respective cultures. Although elephant imagery may have its origins in actual observation, it is just as often a product of the imagination,
50 and African depictions of the elephant have as much to say about human society as about the animal itself. Ultimately, historical events, social responsibilities, religious beliefs, and political relationships are the primary subjects of elephant imagery.

55 For some, this may appear problematic. Within the scientific community, finding *human* traits in *animals* is often seen as sentimental anthropomorphizing, even though it is, according to Levi-Strauss, a fundamental activity of the human mind. On the other hand, finding *animal* traits
60 in *humans* tends to be seen outside the scientific community as pernicious and degrading. Mary Midgley puts it quite succinctly:

Unquestionably there does remain a nonscientific but powerful tendency to resent and fear all
65 close comparison between our own species and any other. Unquestionably we often tend to feel— at times extremely strongly—that the gap between our own species and all others is enormous.

Yet in African cultures, the perception of this "enor-
70 mous gap" provokes much thoughtful and creative response. Of all creatures, the elephant—so huge, so remote, and yet so apparently human—most dramatizes the gap between the species. Donal Cosentino, surveying the elephant in oral traditions, sees it as the Gray Planet,
75 whose sightings are full of mystery and portent. But the phenomenon is by no means confined to oral literature; indeed, many visual representations are driven by the impulse to mediate the breach between worlds.

84. The passage suggests that Africans' long-standing coexistence with elephants has caused them to regard elephants primarily with:

A. appreciation.
B. contempt.
C. fear.
D. reverence.

85. Suppose that the elephants in a particular region of Africa were to disappear. How would this new information affect the author's claims about the animal's impact on the artistic product of humans living in the area?

- **A.** Owing to their scarcity, talismanic objects carved from elephant tusks would acquire considerable value as magical totems.
- **B.** Communities would barter their local products for cultural works and artisan crafts from communities that remained physically close to elephants.
- **C.** The dance and song of the local inhabitants would gradually lose all traces of elephant imagery.
- **D.** Elephant imagery would continue to play an important role in the local culture.

86. Suppose it is discovered that muralists in a number of African communities portrayed jaguars as provisioners of food, material, and wealth; as dangerous competitors for resources; and as dramatically inspirational cohabitants. How would this information affect the author's claims about the interchangeability of symbolic function?

- **A.** It would support the claim that culture and circumstance help determine which qualities are ascribed to which animals.
- **B.** It would support the claim that some people believe the gap between animals and humans to be enormous.
- **C.** It would weaken the claim that Senegalese glass paintings are comparable in their imagery to Noah's ark.
- **D.** It would weaken the claim that the elephant may be viewed as a microcosm.

87. The claim that elephant imagery in African culture reveals information about Africans' social lives is based mainly on:

- **A.** western European cultural analysis.
- **B.** African representations of the microcosm and macrocosm.
- **C.** Nigerian thorn carvings.
- **D.** Ethiopian popular art.

88. Levi-Strauss and Mary Midgley are cited in the passage in order to support the point that:

- **A.** African cultures tend to anthropomorphize to a much greater degree than European cultures.
- **B.** science scholars have systematically identified a number of human qualities in animals.
- **C.** the human capacity to liken human characteristics to animal traits is a complex and contradictory phenomenon.
- **D.** anthropological scholars have achieved a general consensus of opinion with regard to anthropomorphism.

89. According to the passage, a gap exists between all of the following EXCEPT:

- **A.** African and Western versions of elephant imagery.
- **B.** the size of an elephant and its symbolic import.
- **C.** actual elephants and elephant imagery.
- **D.** the perspective of the elephant as a microcosm and as a macrocosm.

90. It can be inferred from the passage that humans view their relationship to animals:

- **A.** in nearly universal symbols across different cultures.
- **B.** in varied ways that depend on each culture's symbolic forms.
- **C.** in superficial and simplistic terms.
- **D.** in more practical than symbolic terms.

GO ON TO THE NEXT PAGE.

Passage III (Questions 91–96)

Since the early days of the scientific study of computers, researchers have been fascinated by the subspecialty of artificial intelligence (AI). The notion that a non-organic information processor might independently ac-
5 complish certain tasks theretofore deemed unachievable without the direct involvement of a living human intelligence enthralled pioneers in the field.

Rudimentary efforts to teach computers language translation relied solely on word equivalences pro-
10 grammed in the computer's dictionary and linked to automated syntax substitution. With this approach, however, the sentences generated usually defied grammatical, syntactical, and logical sense. The problem for programmers lay in the difference between the human mind's
15 free understanding of the linguistic meaning contained in words [and] the computer's confinement in the linguistic symbols themselves. As investigators developed techniques for programming computer comprehension of human vocal commands, however, they learned to com-
20 municate semantic significance to artificial intelligence even in the absence of semiotic input.

In the area of game strategy, computers have realized considerably more success than in language translation. [For example,] over the years, computerized tactical
25 chess programs have evolved with such expertise and proficiency that the only human beings who can now prevail over them are among the international elite masters of the game.

Symptomatic evaluation and differential defect iden-
30 tification occur in artificial intelligence in much the same manner as in human intelligence. Computers can be programmed with the entire scope of relevant expert knowledge. Expert knowledge programs differ from simple databases in that the latter consist only of pieces
35 of information for the computer to search (e.g., lists of names, addresses, and telephone numbers), whereas the former include a set of rules as well, which serve to direct the computer's search according to interactive inputs.

In these rule-based searches, initial gross analysis is
40 achieved by cueing the artificial memory with a specific array of symptoms. Through a process of reductive elimination informed by operator responses to a rule-based question series, the computer generates a set of possible diagnoses consistent with the encoded symptomatic pro-
45 file and ranked according to programmed probability. This kind of expert defect analysis, in which specific compartments of memory within an extensive body of knowledge are accessible to the computer's search only on the basis of compliance with logical rules of inclusion
50 and exclusion, today represents an area of significant accomplishment for artificial intelligence.

A strategic approach to problem solving is essential to the ability to provide professional-caliber counsel. The ability to include or exclude knowledge compartments
55 from an ongoing processor search endows artificial intelligence with a trait something akin to human judgment and analytical discretion, and is achieved by organizing the elements of expert knowledge within categorical frames. The particular elements comprising each framed category
60 within a larger knowledge base bear some shared relation to a specific input event or data constellation: that is, they form an encapsulated informational object. In this regard, frames are not unlike traditional databased tuples or file archives, with the essential difference, however, that
65 framed memory accessibility derives from data linkage, itself regulated and encapsulated according to procedural production syllogisms.

Linkage between and among frames proceeds in accordance with the restrictions of analytical logic:
70 IF a particular data requirement is fulfilled, THEN a specified frame of memory is made accessible to the computer. The study of coherent linkage of knowledge frames through syllogistic requisites has led computer scientists to the invention of semantic or neural networks.

75 In neural networks, data constellations or elements are stored as nodes, integral knowledge objects interconnected by definitive informational relationships. Even more sophisticated applications can equip the computer with the ability to derive its own rules of linkage—and
80 relative regulatory influence among contrasting and/or complementary rules—in accordance with its individual input experience base. (For instance, a node labeled "implement of silverware" might relate to identical probability to the particular elements "knife," "fork," and
85 "spoon." However, the computer might be programmed to learn that a greater probability should be linked to "fork" if the silverware object is pronged, or to "spoon" if it is curved.) Neural network learning programs are currently undergoing development in [a variety of] areas.

GO ON TO THE NEXT PAGE.

91. The passage suggests that the facet of artificial intelligence that particularly intrigued early computer scientists was the fact that:

A. a mechanical apparatus could be taught to translate human languages.
B. a computer could learn to accomplish thinking tasks completely independently of any live human being.
C. a machine might be able perform tasks that required intelligence without the immediate participation of humans.
D. a machine could teach human beings artificial modes of mental activity.

92. According to the passage, artificial intelligence programmers initially approached language translation by:

A. providing computers with independent memory of diverse systems of semiotic linguistic representation.
B. liberating computers from confinement in semantic-free meaning.
C. eliminating from translation programs languages with similar vocabulary and parallel syntax.
D. teaching computers to recognize a word-based message connected to a programmed syntax replacement.

93. The author implies that in relation to playing games:

A. computers will never be able to master the game of chess as well as humans.
B. chess is the only game in which computers can effectively compete with humans.
C. computer learning has been generally more effective in the area of game playing than in language translation.
D. computers usually prevail over human opponents in chess, except against internationally elite linguists.

94. According to passage information, computer defect analysis functions differently from simple data retrieval in that:

A. it incorporates a program of guidelines to selectively retrieve stored data.
B. it excludes reductive elimination as a retrieval tool.
C. it requires detailed inputs as retrieval prompts.
D. there is no essential difference between the two processes.

95. Discussing the relation of analytical logic to artificial intelligence, the author states that:

A. coherent linkage of knowledge frames occurs independently of IF/THEN propositions.
B. syllogistic procedures define tuple-based information retrieval.
C. syllogistic principles provide the basis for connecting integral knowledge objects.
D. it is impossible to arrange tuples for medical diagnosis as logically correlated objects.

96. For which of the following statements regarding neural networks does the passage offer the most support?

A. Established informational relationships are generally inadequate to bridge nodal synapses.
B. Established informational relationships are wholly unaffected by inputted information.
C. For computers to construct neural links between information nodes, human operators must provide programmed rules of relative probability.
D. Through empirical learning methods, computers can decide and apportion weighted linkage.

GO ON TO THE NEXT PAGE.

Passage IV (Questions 97–102)

Just as an embryo retraces much of the human evolutionary past, the budding artist reinvents the first stages of art. Soon, however, he or she completes that process and begins to respond to the culture around him
5 or her. Even children's art is subject to the taste and outlook of the society that shapes his or her personality. In fact, we tend to judge children's art according to the same criteria as adult art—only in appropriately simpler terms—and with good reason, for if we examine
10 its successive stages, we find that the youngster must develop all the skills that go into adult art: coordination, intellect, personality, imagination, creativity, and aesthetic judgment. Seen this way, the making of a youthful artist is a process as fragile as growing up itself, and one that
15 can be stunted at any step by the vicissitudes of life. No wonder that so few continue their creative aspirations into adulthood.

Given the many factors that feed into it, art must play a very special role in the artist's personality. Sigmund
20 Freud, the founder of modern psychiatry, conceived of art primarily in terms of sublimation outside of consciousness. Such a view hardly does justice to artistic creativity, since art is not simply a negative force at the mercy of our neuroses, but a positive expression that integrates diverse
25 aspects of personality. Indeed, when we look at the art of the mentally ill, we may be struck by its vividness; but we instinctively sense that something is wrong because the expression is incomplete.

Artists sometimes may be tortured by the burden of
30 their genius, but they can never be truly creative under the thrall of psychosis. The imagination is one of our most mysterious facets. It can be regarded as the connector between the conscious and the subconscious, where most of our brain activity takes place. It is the very glue that
35 holds together our personality, intellect, and spirituality. Because the imagination responds to all three, it acts in lawful, if unpredictable, ways that are determined by the psyche and the mind. Thus, even the most private artistic statements can be understood on some level, even if only
40 an intuitive one.

The imagination is important, as it allows us to conceive of all kinds of possibilities in the future and to understand the past in a way that has real survival value. It is a fundamental part of our makeup. The ability to
45 make art, in contrast, must have been acquired relatively

recently in the course of human evolution. The record of the earliest art is lost to us. Human beings have been walking the earth for some two million years, but the oldest prehistoric art that we know of was made only
50 about 35,000 years ago, though it was undoubtedly the culmination of a long development no longer traceable. Even the most "primitive" ethnographic art represents a late stage of development within a stable society.

Who were the first artists? In all likelihood, they were
55 shamans. Like the legendary Orpheus, they were believed to have divine powers of inspiration and to be able to enter the underworld of the subconscious in a deathlike trance. But, unlike ordinary mortals, they were then able to return to the realm of the living. Even today, the artist
60 remains a magician whose work can mystify and move us—an embarrassing fact to civilized people, who do not readily relinquish their veneer of rational control.

In a larger sense, art, like science and religion, fulfills our innate urge to comprehend ourselves and the
65 universe. This function makes art especially significant and, hence, worthy of our attention. Art has the power to penetrate to the core of our being, which recognizes itself in the creative act. For that reason, art represents its creator's deepest understanding and highest aspirations;
70 at the same time, the artist often plays an important role as the articulator of our shared beliefs and values.

97.   The main idea of the passage is that:

A.   artists serve as mediators between our daily reality and the world of the unconscious.

B.   as human society has evolved and become more sophisticated, so has human artistic expression.

C.   artistic expression reflects the psychological processes and makeup of its creator.

D.   the essential appeal of art is its power to mystify.

98.   In the context of the passage, the word "genius" (line 28) refers primarily to:

A.   the recognition and appreciation of an artist's ability by critics and the public at large.

B.   the psychological sensitivity to reality that an artist develops.

C.   the intellectual attainments of individual artists.

D.   the neurotic and psychotic manifestations of artistic perception.

GO ON TO THE NEXT PAGE.

99. The passage implies that art relates to its audience:

    A.   by delivering both a personal and a universal communication from artist to audience.

    B.   less intensely today because, no longer associated with magic, its power to mystify and to move has dwindled.

    C.   by providing insight into another's creativity only, while science and religion allow us to comprehend ourselves and the universe.

    D.   irrespective of an audience's emotional and spiritual needs.

100. The passage suggests that the ability to create art:

    A.   evolved before the imagination evolved.

    B.   evolved primarily as a survival skill.

    C.   has been documented to exist as early as two million years ago, when humans first inhabited the Earth.

    D.   was the result of a long developmental process that occurred within stable societies.

101. According to the passage, why is art embarrassing to some people who pride themselves on their civilized rationality?

    A.   Art's essential mystery frustrates those who like to appear cultivated.

    B.   Art makes many social sophisticates feel ignorant.

    C.   Art's simultaneous universality and individual relevance seems paradoxical to some who pride themselves on their logical powers.

    D.   Art is able to access the most fundamental and private essence of the self.

102. The author's discussion of Sigmund Freud's view of art and artists most supports the claim that:

    A.   art represents an integrative psychological function rather than an uncontrolled psychic expression.

    B.   art, which sublimates psychological ambiguity, is superior to that which generates mystery.

    C.   successful psychotherapy would enable an artist to sublimate the need for artistic expression.

    D.   development of individual artistic consciousness retraces much of humans' evolutionary past.

GO ON TO THE NEXT PAGE.

Passage V (Questions 103–112)

Assigning the label of structuralist to the totality of literary criticism born of theoretical speculation usually reflects an uninformed perspective rather than a malicious one, although even within this ignorant reductionism we
[5] find a useful presupposition:...that structuralism's crucial facets are common to and inherent in each of those theoretical literary strategies that represent a significant uprooting of the critical enterprise from its traditional homeground. Nevertheless, this precept does not usually motivate those
[10] literary commentators who tend to view theoretical strategies as manifestations of opposition to the established criteria of the New Criticism...which itself generally focuses on a humanistic consideration of human affairs through the lens of common values and shared ethical assumptions...
[15] as expressed by a given artist's aesthetic and medium. Such opposition...seeks to undermine and subjugate literature by denying its ontological mission and, under the theoretical academic guise of interdisciplinary scholarship, by supplanting its uniquely interpretive text with a multitude
[20] of diverse, alien, and/or tangential discourses: a usurpation, according to these commentators, which negates the existence of a given work's discrete essence, devalues the critic's elucidative task, and ultimately defiles the artist's creative act.

[25] Theoretical inclusiveness, however, is not a purpose wholly uncelebrated by the New Criticism. Indeed, Wellek and Warren's classic critical overview, *Theory of Literature*, represents New Criticism as a sophisticated and multilateral...[application] of the critic's imaginative
[30] powers in the service of textual exegesis. Their scholarly commitment to humanism stood as a bulwark against academic and epistemological usurpation by natural science, and against...[its] empirical method of inquiry;... New Critics honored aesthetic sensibility and artistic
[35] expression as fundamental aspects of the human experience...necessary and sufficient in their own right.

When theoretical, "structuralist" critics apply social-scientific modes of reasoning to literature—say, concentrating on themes of class conflict in Steinbeck's *Of Mice*
[40] *and Men*, or deploying feminist ideology in a discussion of women's plight throughout Shakespeare's dramatic opus—traditionalists feel the call anew to defend literature from intellectual violation by extra-literary predators.

[45] Interdisciplinary theoreticians, infiltrating literary study with the methods and objectives of the social sciences, abandon the concerns and interests of thematic aestheticism...[in favor] of a configurative analysis focused not on the structures and processes integral to the
[50] work's operation, but rather on those external to it. For traditionalists, this exterior theoretical approach amounts to intellectual desertion and cultural betrayal, and raises the fundamentalist, anti-intellectual specter of literature's cremation.

[55] The "global," multifaceted "inclusivity" of interdisciplinary theory, then, seemingly proposes an intensively bounded dominion, apportioning validity to virtually any discursive or ideological critical advocacy, while excluding and consigning to the margins only those approaches
[60] committed to a humanistic, universalist exploration of the artistic object itself! Such narrowly defined legitimacy nicely conforms with the reactionary apartheidism espoused and embraced by the fashionable tenets of identity politics, the doctrines and proponents of which are seen
[65] by traditionalists as the disinformation and dupes of a... resurgent, unscrupulous segregationalist agenda. In this perspective, identity apartheidism collaborates with reactionary fundamentalism, instilling its disciples with an obsessive dependence on restriction and taboo.

[70] Whereas the underlying objective of deconstruction implies the systematic repudiation of literature's enterprise, reducing meaning and emotion to semiotics and mechanics, traditionalists remain committed to diversely interpretive excursions, providing they remain integral
[75] to—and not intrusive on—the literary work itself. Thus, a feminist scholar who discovers the painful horrors of women's oppression explicitly...[described] in the shadow of artistically perfected and objectively glorified female images will be applauded by traditionalists for remaining
[80] faithful to the literary text, even as she or he delineates an oppressive element of intoxicating poetic beauty, and of the critical canon so bedazzled by the latter as to be blinded to the former.

103. The author's claim that "structuralist" criticism represents an attempt to "uproot the critical enterprise" rests on the New Critics' belief that:

A. the complexities of theoretical disciplines should inform all literary commentary.

B. theoretical foundations are totally useless to the task of literary criticism.

C. the essential mission of literature unmasks disguises of similitude and dissimilitude.

D. literary criticism should focus primarily on the literary work.

GO ON TO THE NEXT PAGE.

104. The author most likely believes that New Critics view their opponents as undermining and subjugating literature by:

    A. placing a fundamental emphasis on humanistic interpretation.

    B. utilizing external discourses as the basis for the critical endeavor.

    C. negating the usurpation of literature's unique discourse.

    D. rejecting interdisciplinary methodology as a basis for discourse.

105. According to the passage, empirical reasoning represents:

    A. a diversion for traditionalist literary critics.

    B. a threat to "structuralist" critics.

    C. a rebuttal to feminist extrapolations of 18th-century novels.

    D. a mode of analysis antithetical to traditional literary concerns.

106. Based on information in the passage, students who are drawn to a humanistic interpretive approach:

    A. ignore the metatextual domains of the literary universe.

    B. reject the traditionalist school of literary criticism.

    C. are excluded by the theoretical structuralists.

    D. are animated by the nihilistic exclusivity of ideological analysis.

107. Based on information in the passage, "inclusivity" as conceived by theoretical advocates conforms with:

    A. an identity politics unwittingly serving reactionary forces.

    B. an identity politics serving to liberate its disciples from restriction and taboo.

    C. a universalist humanism tending to embrace multicultural perspectives.

    D. a universalist humanism working to defuse reactionary apartheidism.

108. The author implies that the underlying objectives of deconstruction inevitably distort literary expression because they:

    A. can never effectively negate the humanistic principles of literary criticism.

    B. infer a semiotic relationship to the mechanics of novelistic form.

    C. impart meaning to a narrative's emotional content.

    D. reject inherent meaning and motive as appropriate subjects for critical consideration.

109. The author cites Wellek and Warren in order to support the claim that:

    A. traditional criticism is not entirely exclusive.

    B. authors should use their imaginative powers to serve textual exegesis.

    C. structuralism's "inclusivity" violates humanism.

    D. criticism should focus on the values explicitly described in the text itself.

110. Of which of the following critical approaches would a traditionalist most likely approve?

    A. A psychoanalytic analysis of T. S. Eliot as revealed by images used in "The Wasteland."

    B. A study of racial and identity politics that influenced the writing of Richard Wright's *Native Son*.

    C. An analysis of the structure and characterization within Steinbeck's *Of Mice and Men*.

    D. A feminist scholar's focus on the oppressive conditions that led to the female images in Sylvia Plath's poetry.

GO ON TO THE NEXT PAGE.

111. The author argues that structuralist analysis poses an anti-intellectual threat to literature's existence. Which of the following circumstances, if true, would LEAST strengthen the argument?

A. A multidisciplinary committee urges that the Literature faculty be dispersed among other Humanities and Social Science departments.

B. An associate dean of Academic Affairs proposes that Literature course offerings be cut in half.

C. A feminist critic of Chaucer's poetry offers his course through the Women's Studies department.

D. A Freudian critic of James Joyce's novels offers her course through the Literature department.

112. Suppose a course description in a college bulletin promises "an in-depth literary examination of the novels of William Faulkner and Mark Twain." Students later find that the course focuses nearly exclusively on themes of cultural injustice. Based on your reading of the passage, this new information would probably lead the author to:

A. support a student who accused the professor of false advertising.

B. organize a boycott of the course the following semester.

C. publish an article defending the professor's academic freedom.

D. oppose a dean who suggested moving the course to the Political History department.

Passage VI (Questions 113–118)

The primary function of formal science education, whether precollege or college, is to ensure a steady supply of scientists and science-related professionals, including, of course, science educators. Everything else
5 done in science education, regardless of its educational worth or numbers of students involved, turns out to be secondary to this goal. Not that this is its avowed purpose, of course. Science educators persistently try to persuade themselves, and the community at large, to
10 believe that there is a loftier purpose to science education, namely, to educate the general public—to achieve widespread scientific literacy—and indeed many educators have visions of such an ideal. But the reality behind such grand objectives is that the practical goal of
15 producing future scientists must (and does) come first. Urging students into science as a profession is clearly part of the responsibility of science educators, but one must bear in mind that here we are dealing with only about 5 to 10 percent of high school students. To face
20 the issue squarely, it is obvious that science departments, whether in our schools or colleges, are no different from most other disciplines in seeking to increase the enrollment of nonmajors in their courses; their underlying motive is more to attract critical masses of faculty and adequate
25 equipment budgets for research than to satisfy some compelling educational need of the general (nonscience) student.

The competition is keen in most faculties to be included in the distribution requirements for all students,
30 and equally acute in most science departments to design courses that will attract these students regardless of whether such courses will have a lasting effect on them. Think for a moment if the science departments in our high schools had to justify their existence by serving only the
35 10 percent or so who claim to be science-bound, or if our college science departments served only its majors. Most science departments would collapse for lack of a critical mass of faculty, and the training of science professionals would have to be given over to a relatively few special-
40 ized state or national high schools and colleges. Many university science departments survive only by virtue of the "point credits" they earn through their introductory courses. How else to account for such promotional course titles as Physics for Poets, Kitchen Chemistry, Biology
45 for Living, etc.

The mistake we make is in assuming that because some, perhaps even many, of our students perform well in school science, they have achieved a measure of scientific literacy that will serve them as adults... Most science
50 teachers leave their classes feeling that they have communicated successfully with some nonscience students, and most likely they have. But the end effect of this is a delusion. Good school performance, even a reasonable level of scientific literacy while one is a student, provides no
55 assurance that the individual will retain enough science when he or she becomes a responsible adult, presumably contributing to the overall good of society.

Here lies the crux of the matter. Whatever we may do to turn students on to science, to make them acutely
60 aware of the world around them, and get them to at least appreciate what the scientific enterprise is about, if not so much science itself, we are guided in the schools by immediate feedback rather than long-term retention. After all, to be pragmatic about it, having literate students
65 who turn out to be scientific illiterates as adults does not do much for society. We know that the staying power of science courses is very poor, but what is particularly depressing is the fact that although most students lapse back into scientific illiteracy soon after they graduate,
70 they nevertheless think they are reasonably literate in science.

113. The author's claim that science educators must set "practical goal[s]" before aspiring to loftier objectives (lines 13–15) is supported by which of the following observations?

A. There is a relative lack of competition from other departments for the science majors' interest.
B. General students seek large numbers of science courses.
C. Science departments seek large numbers of science faculty.
D. Society has a compelling need to achieve widespread scientific literacy.

GO ON TO THE NEXT PAGE.

114. The passage suggests that one of the main purposes of teaching general science to masses of students is to:

    A. enable large numbers of citizens to participate intelligently in a scientifically oriented economy.
    B. provide an understanding of empirical methodology to all students as an essential problem-solving skill.
    C. familiarize nonscience majors with newly challenging ethical issues generated by scientific technology.
    D. justify the maintenance of a large academic and research establishment in science.

115. Given the information in the passage, most nonscience majors who study general science in either high school or college will most likely:

    A. enroll in pseudo-scientific courses such as "Physics for Poets," etc.
    B. do so to meet course distribution and "point credits" requirements.
    C. subscribe to popular science periodicals after graduation.
    D. retain little science knowledge after graduation.

116. Based on information in the passage, if science departments taught fewer "promotional course[s]" (line 43) to undergraduates, which of the following outcomes would likely occur?

    A. Colleges and universities would produce significantly higher numbers of scientifically literate graduates.
    B. All students would graduate with significantly greater scientific literacy.
    C. Science departments might risk decreased budgetary support from administrations.
    D. Nonscience departments might be overwhelmed by increasing student enrollments.

117. The author suggests that restricting high school science departments to only science majors would result in:

    A. the demise of many high school science departments.
    B. the proliferation of specialized state or national high schools.
    C. improved high school science curricula.
    D. better utilization of academic resources.

118. Suppose the majority of high school graduates were found to demonstrate an educated interest in science and science-related issues fifteen years post graduation. This new information would most *challenge* the claim that:

    A. schools are guided more by immediate feedback than by long-term results.
    B. most scientifically illiterate graduates believe themselves to be scientifically knowledgeable.
    C. having literate students who become scientifically illiterate adults does not do much for society.
    D. the staying power of science courses is very poor.

Passage VII (Questions 119–124)

According to newspaper accounts, certain activist participants in the recent community antiviolence summit appeared to indict the entire "Western Civilization value system" as the prime reason behind "a scarcity of mo-
5 rality" among adolescents from economically deprived environments, and as a major cause of the recent, insane escalation of deadly violence among the community's youth. To lay the blame for such terror at the feet of "Western Civilization values" is not only inflammatory,
10 it is also so poorly conceived and even irresponsible as to be called fatuous. Because it seems improbable that the summit participants quoted in the article are capable of hurling such ignorant slurs, the most probable explanation for the story is that the comments were quoted out
15 of context.

But let us consider the larger theme: If there really exists such an ethical system as so-called "Western Civilization values" (as opposed to, say, human values), it must revolve around the concept of individual rights exercised
20 within a "team" context of family and community, and based on biblical religious and/or ethical-humanist ideals. In such a system, self-worth and peer esteem derive from the setting of constructive goals, and the application of creative, individual effort and "team play" cooperation
25 toward their realization.

In this system of beliefs, self-improvement and community empowerment through education and moral commitment are highly prized, and genuine compassionate concern for one's fellow being—particularly for the poor,
30 the infirm, the defenseless, and the bereft—is regarded as especially noble. Recognition of individual dignity, regardless of a person's socioeconomic status, is given primary importance under this value system, and respect is earned and granted on the basis of character, convic-
35 tion, and courage, and not because of twisted "macho" acts of reckless mayhem.

How can such "Western Civilization values" be viewed as somehow unnatural and inappropriate for, or alien to, the citizens of our society and communities? That some
40 folks of various and diverse cultural backgrounds might distort those values to the point of extreme greed, apathy, or violence toward others is not the fault of the value system itself, but of those individuals' inadequate understanding of the ethical concepts involved.

45 Nonetheless, no one can argue that "Western Civilization"—a quasisociological designation mangled beyond recognition by some rhetorician's delusions—any more than any other quasigeocultural conglomeration, is always successful at fulfilling the ideals of their value
50 system. (As the Book of Genesis relates, for example, when paranoid jealousy and obsessive hate overwhelmed Joseph's brothers and drove them to cast him into a ditch and sell him in chains to slave traders, they were betraying—not affirming—Old Testament values.) Still,
55 people who sell illegal, addictive narcotics to children, adolescents, or pregnant and nursing women, or who illegally distribute, sell, and use handguns and semiautomatic weapons in the street, or who believe that violence and deadly force are appropriate responses to emotional
60 quarrels, personal tiffs, and differences of opinion, can no more be said to be representative of "Western Civilization values" than can those ancient nobles and mercenaries who participated for profit in the inexcusable sale of their own neighboring tribesfolk as slaves be considered
65 representative of their continental values, controversial as such a reflection might appear.

Similarly, and more important, those relatively few but fearsome young people who seem determined to destroy their own neighborhoods, and—in the process—their own
70 lives, together with the lives of their neighbors, or those older folks who foster and empower such deadly notions of self-aggrandizement and peer reputation, are no more representative of the economically deprived than Jack the Ripper is representative of Western values.

119. The author suggests which of the following to be true of "Western Civilization values"?

A. They are superior to the value systems of other cultural groups.

B. They are entirely inappropriate as moral guidelines for other cultural groups.

C. Their imposition on economically deprived communities is responsible for maladaptive behaviors among some adolescents.

D. They contain many elements accepted across many cultures.

GO ON TO THE NEXT PAGE.

120. The author states that remarks of summit speakers who blamed "Western Civilization values" for antisocial behavior among today's youth:

A. imply that "Western Civilization values" teach inequality and injustice.
B. should have been censored.
C. were probably imprecisely reported.
D. have led to a general decline in moral civility.

121. With which of the following statements would the author most likely agree?

A. "Western Civilization" is a term more useful to sociology than to everyday reality.
B. "Western Civilization" is useful only as a rhetorical term.
C. "Western Civilization" refers to a distinct geographical group.
D. "Western Civilization" refers to a distinct cultural group.

122. The author suggests that the true reason(s) for antisocial behavior among some adolescents is/are:

   I. the principle that respect is earned on the basis of character.
   II. the distortion of a humanistic value system.
   III. the negative influence of some more mature members of society.

A. I only
B. II only
C. II and III only
D. I, II, and III

123. Among the following, the author *most* likely believes that some of the responsibility for urban social maladies is due to:

A. "Western Civilization values."
B. non–"Western Civilization values."
C. ancient mercenaries of diverse backgrounds.
D. people who sell guns on the streets.

124. The author argues that "Western Civilization values" are founded on true belief, personal bravery, and moral action. Which of the following findings, if true, would most *weaken* the author's contention?

A. Most Americans believe that violence is the most appropriate way to resolve personal disputes.
B. Many Americans learn moral commitment as a part of their religious training.
C. Most Americans believe that bravery is the most important of all values.
D. Most Americans believe that bravery, honesty, and commitment are the keys to a civilized society.

Passage VIII (Questions 125–130)

African art includes houses, masks, costumes, uniforms, and the decorations that adorn clothing. We cannot understand it without first abandoning some conventional notions. African art goes beyond monuments and that
5 which one might observe in a museum.

The mbari house is filled with sculptures and probably represents a religious offering. The construction of the house is conducted in ritualistic fashion, and once built, the house and its sculptures are never maintained.
10 They are permitted to deteriorate and to become once again a part of the ground from which they came. Typically, a mbari house contains upwards of seventy sculptures. Usually the sculptures depict significant deities of the community. The front of a mbari house, for example,
15 will usually feature the sculpted figure of the goddess of the earth. The sculpture is a veritable complex showing not only the goddess herself, but also her children seated nearby. Her servants, too, are figured in poses that clearly illustrate their function as her guards. Away from the
20 front of the house, other sculptures are usually found. These may assume a variety of forms. They may represent gods or depict human figures of myth or history.

Close to the Ivory Coast, there lives a tribe called "Dan." The Dan are inveterate mask makers and have
25 what amounts to a mask-making club that they call "poro." Masks play a significant role in the operation of Dan society. Members of poro tend to hold functional political offices, and they generally regulate community affairs. They wear masks while executing their functions,
30 and community regard for the masks aids them in their work as does the anonymity that the mask provides. For example, the Dan have developed a mask that represents justice or judging, and the community judge, a member of poro, wears the mask when performing his official func-
35 tion. Other functionaries called on to perform unpopular tasks are similarly protected by anonymity when they wear the masks that represent their offices.

The Yoruba Gelade is another mask-making group. Gelade refers to a mysterious group of persons who de-
40 vote themselves to the appeasement of gods whom they believe to be the sponsors of witchcraft. Gelade masks are costumes and nothing more. They are worn by masqueraders who don them in connection with performances and cult activities. The masks themselves represent a diverse
45 number of personages with whom the Yoruba are familiar. Some masks represent merchants. Others represent motorists, hunters, physicians, and in general, the varied array of characters to whom the Yoruba are exposed. The Gelade give performances in which they use the masks
50 to partake of social commentary. In this respect, then, the masks constitute graphic art, and the performances constitute literature.

One should not try to understand African art by resorting to the usual classifications and subdivisions. The
55 classifications "fine art," "decorative art," and "craft" do not do it justice. The African culture differs from the European in that artwork is not separate from utilitarian objects. The designation "African art" describes elaborately adorned eating utensils, simple furniture, clothing,
60 usable pottery, and basketry. African art is thus an "art of life."

125. What is the main idea of the passage?

   A. African art serves as a barrier between the artist class and the community.
   B. African art is essentially inaccessible to students of Western art.
   C. African art participates in diverse functional ways in the community's daily life.
   D. Western art is divorced from the community's daily functioning.

126. To emphasize the idea that African art is unlike Western art, the author explicitly cites all of the following information EXCEPT:

   A. structures housing African art are built according to ritual practices and laws.
   B. once completed, some African sculptures are allowed to crumble and rot.
   C. African sculptures often depict historical heroes.
   D. African art includes common objects of daily household use.

127. The term "literature" (line 52) is used in the sense of:

   A. an unbound collected body of tribal writings.
   B. a catalogue of religious sculptures and myths.
   C. family stories passed down through generations of oral tradition.
   D. cultural narratives based on tribal values and beliefs.

GO ON TO THE NEXT PAGE.

128. Which of the following circumstances, if true, would most *challenge* the notion that the Dan poro masks serve to protect their wearers while executing official duties in the community?

A. Members of the poro are selected through a democratic process rather than on the basis of clan affiliation.

B. Community officers are chosen in tribal electoral campaigns instead of designated from within the poro.

C. The poro's mask-making activities begin to consume twice the amount of time it had previously.

D. The poro gradually evolves into a guild of craftspersons that institutes bylaws and secret oaths.

129. Based on the passage, it is reasonable to conclude that the masks of the Dan tribe differ from those of the Yoruba Gelade in that a Dan mask:

A. might accurately describe the role of the person who wears it.

B. is rarely designed by the person who wears it.

C. is designed to mollify the cult of magic practitioners.

D. has a special relationship to social function.

130. If a member of the Yoruba community were kidnapped and transported to a Dan village, one might reasonably expect that in participating in the daily activities of the Dan:

A. the Yoruban might confuse ceremony with commentary.

B. the Yoruban might confuse governance with utilitarianism.

C. the Yoruban might confuse reality with the unconscious.

D. the Yoruban might confuse reality with criticism.

Passage IX (Questions 131–137)

Before the sun evolved into the Earth-sustaining and life-giving body that it is today, it underwent the same process of stellar formation by which other stars come into being. Astronomers generally divide that formative
[5] process into three recognizable phases, distinguished from each other on the basis of the star's approximate diameter and other physical characteristics. Our sun presently occupies the third, or "main sequence" phase, which will likely come to an end some five billion years
[10] from now, when, obliterating the inner planets, it will transform into a "red giant."

As a "G-dwarf" class star some 4.8 billion years old, the sun's current, main sequence diameter is roughly 700-thousand kilometers. In its first phase, the "protosun"
[15] measured some 150 million kilometers—equal to one Astronomical Unit (AU)—in diameter. As an intermediate phase T-Tauri class star, the sun's diameter contracted to 28,000 thousand kilometers. An ongoing process of "dense hydrogen cloud collapse" powers this transfor-
[20] mative contraction of stars, producing, in the case of the sun, a main sequence G-dwarf star approximately one-eighth its original size.

Although astronomers previously believed that proto-stellar hydrogen clouds obey a "power law" of molecular
[25] distribution—by which the vast majority of molecular material would coalesce around a hyperdense center—recent investigations have rather shown that Gaussian (bell-shaped) rules prevail. Applying high-resolution as-troradiometry in wavelengths of less than a millimeter,
[30] Ward-Thompson et al. concluded that the density at the center of protostellar hydrogen clouds is significantly lower than previously estimated. One interesting side-light to this discovery, detailed by Myhill and Boss, dem-onstrates that the absence of such a Gaussian distribution
[35] would make the creation of binary star systems—so-called "double" stars—virtually impossible.

As recently as four years ago, astrophysicists be-lieved that binary star systems represented an exceptional
[40] astrophysical phenomenon. The recognition of Gaussian distributions of hydrogen in the protostellar dense clouds, however, set the molecular stage for a universe where star pairs predominate over single suns. Given the requisite angular momentum and a gravitational energy more than
[45] twice its thermal energy (below 10 Kelvin), Boss calcu-lated that the cloud's gravitational collapse will result in a "fragmentation" of protostellar material, ultimately yielding two protostars bound together by mutual gravi-tational attraction—a protobinary system. Because such
[50] forces and energies are more the norm than otherwise in protostellar dense hydrogen cloud formations, double stars should far outnumber singles.

Spectroscopic measurements of the periodic Doppler shift of all G-dwarf stars within 72 light-years from the
[55] Earth, in fact, validate those findings. Duquennoy and Mayor determined that in a sample of 164 representative G-dwarfs in our galaxy, companion systems occurred at a frequency nearly twice that of lone stars. Spectroscopy also revealed that multiple stars—triples or quadruples—
[60] appeared much less frequently than binaries, about one-seventh and one-thirtieth as often, respectively.

Richard Muller et al. have suggested that even our sun represents one-half of a binary system with a separation distance so enormous as to make the doubles essen-
[65] tially invisible and unknown to each other. Such a vast separation would mean that the sun and its companion orbit each other once approximately every thirty million years. As the sun's companion unleashes gravitational disturbances on every perihelion approach, comet show-
[70] ers from the farthest ranges of the solar system could tumble down to Earth, conceivably resulting in planetary extinctions every thirty million years, such as that which exterminated the dinosaurs. Because no detectable star lies close enough to the sun to enforce gravitational orbit,
[75] however, most astrophysicists doubt the plausibility of Muller's solar-pair hypothesis.

131. According to the passage, modern scientists believe that star formation involves all of the following EXCEPT:

   A. processes that tend to form star pairs more often than single stars.

   B. separation of protostellar material to yield protostars.

   C. diminution in size facilitated by Gaussian rules.

   D. the aggregation of molecular matter around a highly dense core.

GO ON TO THE NEXT PAGE.

132. The author refers to spectroscopic measurements in order to support the claim that:

    A. quadruples occur more often than triples.
    B. triples occur less often than singles.
    C. singles occur more often than doubles.
    D. doubles occur less often than triples.

133. Compared to a star in the main sequence phase, a T-Tauri star is, according to the passage:

    A. younger and larger.
    B. younger and smaller.
    C. older and larger.
    D. older and smaller.

134. According to the passage, the "power law" of molecular distribution is challenged by the observation that:

    A. our own sun is a G-dwarf class star.
    B. many stars are formed as pairs.
    C. protostars have centers of very high density.
    D. astroradiometry may be employed in extremely small wavelengths.

135. Which of the following is evidence used by the author to support the claim that our own sun is probably not part of a star pair?

    A. The other star of the pair would have to exist outside our own galaxy.
    B. Comet showers are known to occur with a frequency greater than once every thirty million years.
    C. The other star of the pair would cause the extinction of most of Earth's animal species.
    D. Investigations reveal no star sufficiently close to the sun to exert significant gravitational force on it.

136. According to the passage, the termination of the phase now occupied by our sun will cause some planets to:

    A. become red giants.
    B. enter their main sequence phase.
    C. shrink in diameter.
    D. disappear.

137. The discovery that star formation is governed not by the "power law" but by Gaussian rules might best be analogized to the finding that:

    A. a given disease spreads not directly from one patient to another but by an insect bite, which explains why a person could contract the disease without exposure to an afflicted patient.
    B. left-handedness corresponds not to a longer life span but to a shorter life span, which explains the fact that left-handed persons tend to have a greater facility for artistic and verbal creativity.
    C. the first carts and wagons tended to break apart on encountering bumps, which led to the installation of springs and, later, shock absorbers.
    D. certain isolated societies have no concept of property or ownership, which explains why such peoples never developed weapons of mass destruction.

STOP. IF YOU FINISH BEFORE TIME IS CALLED, CHECK YOUR WORK. YOU MAY GO BACK TO ANY QUESTION IN THIS SECTION.

Writing Sample

Time: 60 Minutes
2 WS Items, Separately Timed
30 Minutes Each

WRITING SAMPLE

DIRECTIONS: This is a test of your writing skills. The test consists of two parts. You will have 30 minutes to complete each part.

If you finish writing on Part 1 before time is up, you may review your work on that part, but do not begin work on Part 2. If you finish writing on Part 2 before time is up, you may review your work only on that part of the test until the 30 minutes have expired.

Use your time efficiently. Before you begin writing each of your responses, read the assignment carefully to understand exactly what you are being asked to do in the three writing tasks. You may use the space beneath each writing assignment to make notes in planning each response.

Because this is a test of your writing skills, your response to each part should be an essay of complete sentences and paragraphs, as well organized and clearly written as you can make it in the time allotted. You may make corrections or additions neatly between the lines in your response, but do not write in the margins of the answer sheets.

There are six pages on which to write your responses, three pages for each part of the Writing Sample. You do not have to use all the pages, but to ensure that you have enough space for each essay, do not skip lines.

Essays that are illegible cannot be scored.

Start the 30 minute timing as you begin reading each Writing Sample item.

Part 1

Consider this statement:

Trial by jury ensures a fair verdict.

Write a unified essay in which you perform the following tasks. Explain what you think the above statement means. Describe a specific situation in which trial by jury might <u>not</u> ensure a fair verdict. Discuss what you think determines whether or not trial by jury ensures a fair verdict.

Part 2

Consider this statement:

The greater the fear of failure, the lower the likelihood of success.

Write a unified essay in which you perform the following tasks. Explain what you think the above statement means. Describe a specific situation in which fear of failure might <u>not</u> decrease the likelihood of success. Discuss what you think determines whether or not fear of failure decreases the likelihood of success.

Biological Sciences

Time: 100 Minutes
Questions 138 – 214

BIOLOGICAL SCIENCES

DIRECTIONS: Most questions in the Biological Sciences test are organized into groups, each preceded by a descriptive passage. After studying the passage, select the one best answer to each question in the group. Some questions are not based on a descriptive passage and are also independent of each other. You must also select the one best answer to these questions. If you are not certain of an answer, eliminate the alternatives that you know to be incorrect and then select an answer from the remaining alternatives. Indicate your selection by blackening the corresponding oval on your answer document. A periodic table is provided for your use. You may consult it whenever you wish.

PERIODIC TABLE OF THE ELEMENTS

1 H 1.0																	2 He 4.0
3 Li 6.9	4 Be 9.0											5 B 10.8	6 C 12.0	7 N 14.0	8 O 16.0	9 F 19.0	10 Ne 20.2
11 Na 23.0	12 Mg 24.3											13 Al 27.0	14 Si 28.1	15 P 31.0	16 S 32.1	17 Cl 35.5	18 Ar 39.9
19 K 39.1	20 Ca 40.1	21 Sc 45.0	22 Ti 47.9	23 V 50.9	24 Cr 52.0	25 Mn 54.9	26 Fe 55.8	27 Co 58.9	28 Ni 58.7	29 Cu 63.5	30 Zn 65.4	31 Ga 69.7	32 Ge 72.6	33 As 74.9	34 Se 79.0	35 Br 79.9	36 Kr 83.8
37 Rb 85.5	38 Sr 87.6	39 Y 88.9	40 Zr 91.2	41 Nb 92.9	42 Mo 95.9	43 Tc (98)	44 Ru 101.1	45 Rh 102.9	46 Pd 106.4	47 Ag 107.9	48 Cd 112.4	49 In 114.8	50 Sn 118.7	51 Sb 121.8	52 Te 127.6	53 I 126.9	54 Xe 131.3
55 Cs 132.9	56 Ba 137.3	57 La* 138.9	72 Hf 178.5	73 Ta 180.9	74 W 183.9	75 Re 186.2	76 Os 190.2	77 Ir 192.2	78 Pt 195.1	79 Au 197.0	80 Hg 200.6	81 Tl 204.4	82 Pb 207.2	83 Bi 209.0	84 Po (209)	85 At (210)	86 Rn (222)
87 Fr (223)	88 Ra 226.0	89 Ac† 227.0	104 Rf (261)	105 Db (262)	106 Sg (263)	107 Bh (262)	108 Hs (265)	109 Mt (267)									

*	58 Ce 140.1	59 Pr 140.9	60 Nd 144.2	61 Pm (145)	62 Sm 150.4	63 Eu 152.0	64 Gd 157.3	65 Tb 158.9	66 Dy 162.5	67 Ho 164.9	68 Er 167.3	69 Tm 168.9	70 Yb 173.0	71 Lu 175.0
†	90 Th 232.0	91 Pa (231)	92 U 238.0	93 Np (237)	94 Pu (244)	95 Am (243)	96 Cm (247)	97 Bk (247)	98 Cf (251)	99 Es (252)	100 Fm (257)	101 Md (258)	102 No (259)	103 Lr (260)

GO ON TO THE NEXT PAGE.

Passage I (Questions 138–142)

Organisms use metabolic reactions to derive free energy from the oxidation of fuel molecules. In eukaryotic cells, metabolism includes the process of oxidative phosphorylation. This process occurs on the mitochondrial respiratory chain and forms ATP by transferring electrons from NADH and FADH$_2$ to oxygen. The mitochondrial respiratory chain, with inhibitors, is illustrated in Figure 1.

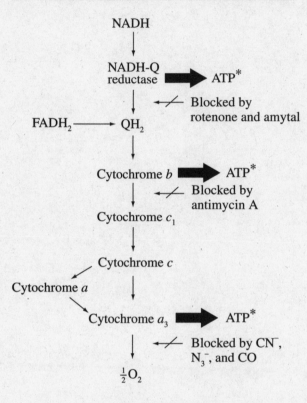

Figure 1 Motochondrial respiratory chain

* Note: ATP synthetase is the enzyme complex which synthesizes ATP from ADP + P$_i$, utilizing the energy of the proton gradient generated by the electron transport chain.

To elucidate the site inhibited by rotenone, an organic insecticide, researchers carried out the following protocols:

- Mitochondrial extracts containing intact respiratory chains were exposed to rotenone in the presence of NADH and FADH$_2$.

- Oxygen consumption before and after organic insecticide administration was measured, and mitochondrial cytochrome structure was analyzed by X-ray crystallography.

It was found that the inhibited structure was cytochrome b, which possesses the heme-containing center pictured in Figure 2.

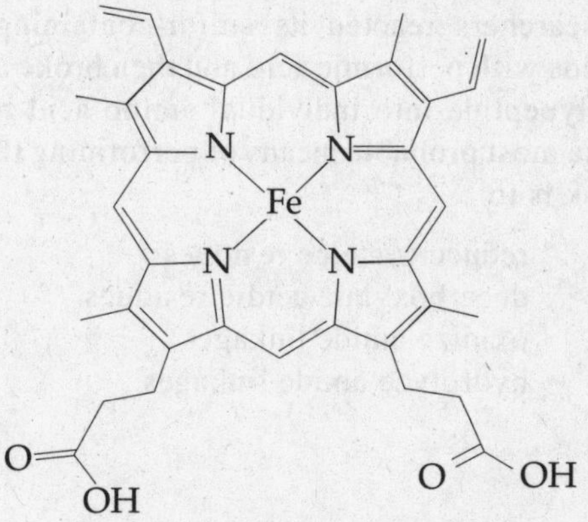

Figure 2 Heme-containing center

There was a significant drop in oxygen consumption upon administration of rotenone.

138. An uncoupler of oxidative phosphorylation such as dinitrophenol allows the mitochondrial respiratory chain to proceed without subsequent ATP synthesis, by neutralizing the proton gradient. Specifically, this is done by transporting protons along their concentration gradient across the inner mitochondrial membrane. Which of the following is an uncoupler of ATP synthesis?

A. NADH-Q reductase
B. FADH$_2$
C. Antimycin A
D. None of the above

139. Substance X is known to noncompetitively inhibit NADH-Q reductase. A high cellular concentration of which of the following phosphorus-containing compounds would allow the cell to partially continue oxidative phosphorylation despite the addition of Substance X?

A. FADH$_2$
B. NADPH
C. ADP
D. NADH

GO ON TO THE NEXT PAGE.

140. The heme-containing structure of cytochrome *b* in Figure 2 above possesses how many chiral centers?

A. 3
B. 2
C. 1
D. 0

141. To further characterize cytochrome *b*, the researchers reacted its sulfur-containing amino acids with performic acid and then broke apart the polypeptide into individual amino acid residues. The most probable means of performing this latter task is to:

A. reduce cysteine residues.
B. decarboxylate acidic residues.
C. oxidize amide linkages.
D. hydrolyze amide linkages.

142. The heme portions of cytochrome molecules are able to transfer electrons among themselves because of:

A. thioether linkages.
B. pi-electron delocalization.
C. enol-intermediate racemization.
D. shortened bond length.

GO ON TO THE NEXT PAGE.

Passage II (Questions 143–147)

A milk inspector was randomly sent by the state Food and Drug Administration to a dairy plant to sample containers of both raw and pasteurized milk to certify that milk production was being conducted under sanitary conditions. Milk contamination may be the result of several types of bacterial growth. The first organism to flourish in milk is usually *Streptococcus lactis*, which ferments the sugar lactose to lactic acid. The chemical environment produced by fermentation is conducive to the growth of the non–spore-forming, gram-positive organism *Lactobacillus experimentalis*, which then predominates. Facultatively anaerobic, spore-forming bacteria such as *Streptococcus faecalis* may also be present. Fresh milk, which contains emulsified fat droplets, tends to be anaerobic and has a pH of about 7. Pasteurization is the most common procedure that kills non–spore-forming pathogenic bacteria. The FDA's laboratory conducted the examination according to the procedure below:

1. Take ten samples of raw and ten samples of pasteurized milk.

2. Shake each sample vigorously to obtain a homogeneous sample of milk.

3. Using a pipette, transfer 10 mL of each sample of milk to a total of twenty sterilized test tubes.

4. Heat the tubes and hold at 50°C for fifteen minutes in a water bath and then add sufficient melted vaspar to form a 1/2-inch layer above the milk in each tube.

5. Incubate all tubes at 37°C for three days.

6. Make thin smears of milk broth and stain with methylene blue and Gram stain.

143. Which of the following best describes the appearance of *Lactobacillus experimentalis* when stained and then viewed under a light microscope?

A. Spherical
B. S-shaped
C. Rodlike
D. Asymmetrical

144. The proliferation of *Lactobacillus* in milk samples indicates:

A. high lactose concentration.
B. a drop in the pH.
C. predominance of spore-forming bacteria.
D. the absence of *Streptococcus faecalis*.

145. If one of the raw milk samples were slowly heated to 100°C and then held at that temperature for fifteen minutes, which of the following graphs would best represent resulting spore-forming and non–spore-forming bacterial populations during this time period?

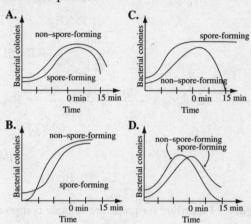

146. The Gram-staining procedure used in the laboratory enables the inspector to:

A. identify bacterial species present in the incubate.
B. distinguish between aerobic and anaerobic organisms.
C. differentiate pathogenic from nonpathogenic colonies.
D. distinguish between bacteria whose peptidoglycan layer lies outside the cell membrane or within the periplasmic space.

147. Which of the following environmental factors will negatively impact the growth of *Streptococcus faecalis*?

I. A decrease in the nutritional content of the milk
II. The process of pasteurization
III. A decrease in ambient oxygen concentration

A. I only
B. I and II only
C. II and III only
D. I, II, and III

Passage III (Questions 148–153)

The figure illustrates a procedure used in the preparation of organic compounds from alkyl halides. These compounds are useful intermediates for the synthesis of a variety of organic products.

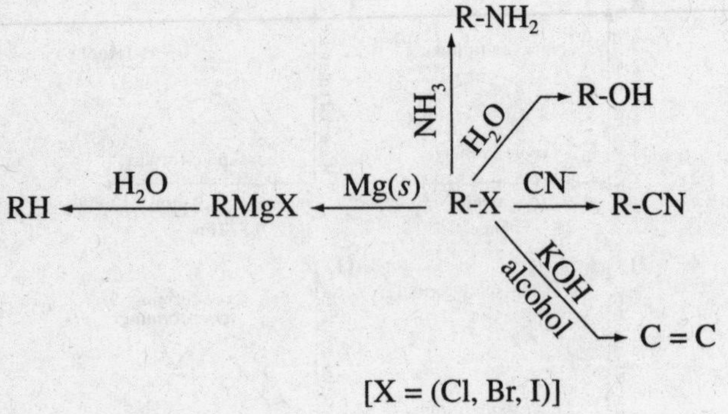

$[X = (Cl, Br, I)]$

Figure 1 Procedure for preparing organic compounds

148. When alkyl halides react with potassium hydroxide to yield alkene derivatives, the potassium hydroxide acts as:

A. an acid.
B. a base.
C. a proton donor.
D. a reductant.

149. If one were to substitute heavy water (D_2O) in the last steps of the Grignard reaction as shown above, the reaction would lead to the synthesis of:

A. R-R.
B. R-OD.
C. R-D.
D. R-H.

150. Alkyl halides are not usually prepared by direct halogenation of alkanes because:

A. alkanes are not very reactive compounds.
B. alkanes have low boiling points.
C. alkanes are converted to alkenes by halogenation.
D. alkanes do not dissolve in polar solutions.

151. The addition of a peroxy acid to the alkene product shown in Figure 1 would lead to the formation of:

A. a *cis*-diol product.
B. an epoxide and a carboxylic acid.
C. a dihaloalkane.
D. an alcohol via acid-catalyzed hydration of the alkene.

152. Alkyl halides are often insoluble in water because:

A. they are hydrophilic.
B. they are ionic compounds.
C. they contain large aliphatic groups.
D. they contain electron-withdrawing groups.

153. Distinction between alcohols may be accomplished using all of the following EXCEPT:

A. boiling point determination.
B. density determination.
C. observation of a strong and broad stretch from 3600–3200 cm^{-1} on IR spectroscopy.
D. melting point determination.

GO ON TO THE NEXT PAGE.

Questions 154 through 158 are **NOT** based on a descriptive passage.

154. An *eclipsed* conformation of *n*-butane is illustrated below, in the figure on the left. Which of the circled positions in the figure on the right corresponds to the terminal methyl group placed in the *anti* conformation?

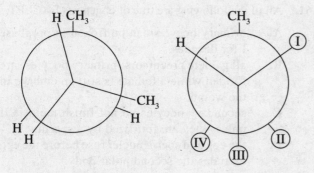

- **A.** I
- **B.** II
- **C.** III
- **D.** IV

155. When lettuce is placed in deionized water, it remains crisp because:

- **A.** the cells lose H_2O.
- **B.** the cells swell with H_2O.
- **C.** the stomates close in response to excess water.
- **D.** the chloroplasts generate greater levels of ATP.

156. Which statement below most accurately describes the characteristic features of striated muscle cells?

- **A.** Striated muscle cells are stimulated by the autonomic nervous system and contain few mitochondria.
- **B.** Striated muscle cells are mononucleate and arranged in syncytial bundles.
- **C.** Striated muscle cells have alternating A-bands and I-bands arranged in a transverse pattern.
- **D.** Striated muscle cells are similar to smooth muscle cells except that they lack internal stores of calcium.

157. Sickle-cell anemia is a blood disorder due to a point mutation in a single gene and is inherited as an autosomal recessive trait. If a woman who is heterozygous for this disorder and a man who is homozygous dominant have a son, then the son most likely has:

- **A.** full-blown sickle-cell anemia.
- **B.** sickle-cell trait, a carrier disease.
- **C.** the same chance of inheriting the sickle-cell gene as his sister.
- **D.** no signs or symptoms of the disease.

158. Consider the reaction below:

$$CH_3CH_2CH_2OH \xrightarrow[CH_2Cl_2]{PCC} CH_3CH_2CHO$$

Which of the following observations about the infrared spectrum of the reaction mixture would indicate that the reaction shown above occurred?

- **A.** The disappearance of a broad and strong stretch at 1700 cm^{-1}
- **B.** The appearance of a sharp stretch between 3000 and 2850 cm^{-1}
- **C.** The appearance of a sharp and strong stretch at 1700 cm^{-1}
- **D.** The appearance of a broad and strong stretch between 3600 and 3200 cm^{-1}

GO ON TO THE NEXT PAGE.

Passage IV (Questions 159–163)

Physiological changes during the human menstrual cycle are affected by levels of sex hormones. The following procedure measured the secretion of estrogens during the menstrual cycle and during pregnancy and menopause.

Test subjects with approximately equal weights and levels of daily activity were chosen. Pregnant subjects were tested at the 160th day of the gestational period or at term. Another group of subjects was tested after showing postmenopausal signs and symptoms for at least two months prior to testing. Menstruating subjects were tested either at the onset of menstruation, at the peak of ovulation, or at the luteal maximum. The luteal maximum represents the greatest amount of estrogen secretion during the second half of the menstrual cycle.

During the test period, urine samples were taken every four hours. Urinary levels of five naturally occurring estrogens were measured using the Kober test. The Kober test produces a pink color in the presence of estrogens, including the oxidative product estriol. The results of the procedure are shown in Table 1, with the value of estrogen levels averaged for each test group.

Table 1 Test Results

Estrogen Excreted per 24 Hours					
Time Measurement	Estriol	Estrone	Estradiol	16-Epiestriol	16α-Hydroxy-estrone
Onset of menstruation	7 μg	6 μg	3 μg	*	*
Ovulation peak	28 μg	21 μg	10 μg	*	*
Luteal maximum	23 μg	15 μg	8 μg	*	*
Pregnancy, 160 days	8 mg	0.8 mg	0.3 mg	*	*
Pregnancy, term	31 mg	2.5 mg	0.85 mg	0.80 mg	1.8 mg
Postmenopause	4.3 μg	3.0 μg	0.7 μg	*	*

159. On the basis of urinary excretion as shown in Table 1, which two subject test groups showed the greatest level of estrogen output?

    I. Onset of menstruation
    II. Ovulation peak
    III. Pregnancy, 160 days
    IV. Pregnancy, term

  A. I and III
  B. I and IV
  C. II and III
  D. III and IV

160. From Table 1, which variable would prove to be the best marker for the term stage of normal pregnancy, as indicated by the Kober test?

  A. The oxidation of estradiol
  B. The presence of estriol
  C. The presence of 16α-hydroxyestrone
  D. A positive Kober reaction

161. All of the following are true of oogenesis EXCEPT:

  A. primary oocytes can be frozen in prophase I for decades.
  B. all gamete precursors (primary oocytes) are formed while a female is still an embryo in the womb.
  C. secondary oocytes do not finish meiosis II unless they are fertilized by a sperm.
  D. the egg and sperm nuclei fuse before the egg extrudes the second polar body.

162. According to the passage, what change in the ratio of estrone to estradiol is expected to occur as women enter postmenopause?

  A. The ratio increases, because estradiol levels decrease relatively more than estrone levels decrease.
  B. The ratio increases, because estradiol levels decrease while estrone levels are unaffected.
  C. The ratio is unchanged, because both estrogen hormone levels decrease in the postmenopausal period.
  D. The ratio decreases, because estrone levels decrease more than estradiol levels.

163. Researchers further studied estrogen levels in subjects at the luteal minimum of estrogen secretion and at the 210th day of pregnancy. Which findings would NOT indicate a trend similar to that found during the original procedures?

  A. The levels of estriol are greater than the levels of estradiol in both pregnant and luteal minimum groups.
  B. The levels of estradiol are lower than those of estrone in the pregnant group.
  C. The estrone levels are elevated in the pregnant group compared with the luteal minimum group.
  D. The ratio of 16-epiestriol levels between the pregnant and luteal minimum groups is 1:2.

Passage V (Questions 164–169)

The stomach is composed of circular, oblique, and longitudinal layers of smooth muscle. Like all tubular structures, it has an internal space termed the *lumen*. Its glands, composed of secretory cells, contribute to gastric juices in the lumen. Parietal cells produce hydrochloric acid, which gives the gastric juices an approximate pH of 1.0. Parietal cells also secrete intrinsic factor, which is necessary for vitamin B$_{12}$ absorption. Chief cells produce pepsinogen, and mucous cells contribute soluble and insoluble forms of mucus. The mucus lubricates the stomach, to protect its internal walls from mechanical injury and to shield its mucosal lining from digestion by acid and enzyme activity. Endocrine cells called G cells secrete the hormone gastrin, which stimulates acid secretion. Figure 1 illustrates acid secretion by the parietal cells of the stomach.

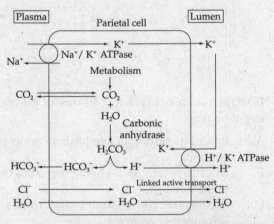

Figure 1 Acid secretion by parietal cells

An H$^+$/K$^+$ ATPase located on the luminal surface of the parietal cells facilitates secretion of H$^+$ ions into the lumen against their concentration gradient, with Cl$^-$ ions actively secreted in conjunction with them. For every H$^+$ ion secreted into the lumen, one HCO$^-_3$ ion is secreted into the plasma.

Acetylcholine, gastrin, and histamine stimulate gastric acid secretion. These substances have a synergistic effect. Parasympathetic stimulation promotes gastric motility and gastric acid secretion. These effects are inhibited by several factors, including low pH within the gastric juice and high levels of the hormone secretin (which, among other effects, normally *inhibits* pepsin secretion).

164. All of the following statements regarding pepsinogen are true EXCEPT that:

- **A.** it is an inactive zymogen.
- **B.** gastric acid facilitates conversion of pepsinogen to the active enzyme pepsin.
- **C.** it is secreted by gastric chief cells.
- **D.** it initiates the digestion of lipids.

165. According to Figure 1, which ion shows lower concentration in gastric secretions than in plasma?

- **A.** Potassium
- **B.** Chloride
- **C.** Hydrogen
- **D.** Sodium

166. Hydrogen and chloride ions in the stomach draw water into the lumen so that gastric secretions are isotonic to plasma. This form of movement is most appropriately termed:

- **A.** active transport.
- **B.** passive transport.
- **C.** osmosis.
- **D.** facilitated transport.

167. Studying the gastric activities of a volunteer, a group of researchers monitor the stomach's venous blood and report a transitory period during which it is highly basic. With which of the following is the period of basicity most likely associated?

- **A.** Active acid secretion
- **B.** Reduced gastrin secretion
- **C.** Active secretin secretion
- **D.** Reduced pepsinogen secretion

168. Carbonic acid that is produced by the parietal cell is formed from:

- **A.** carbon dioxide and hydrogen ion with facilitation by carbonic anhydrase.
- **B.** carbon dioxide and hydrogen ion with facilitation by ATPase.
- **C.** carbon dioxide and water with facilitation by carbonic anhydrase.
- **D.** carbon dioxide and water with facilitation by ATPase.

169. Which of the following pharmacological agents would most likely stimulate gastric motility?

- **A.** An agent that mimics the action of secretin
- **B.** An agent that acts as a terminal parasympathetic transmitter
- **C.** An agent that blocks parasympathetic transmission
- **D.** An agent that acts as a sympathetic transmitter

GO ON TO THE NEXT PAGE.

Passage VI (Questions 170–175)

Neurons within the brain stem synthesize and release serotonin to serotonergic cells throughout areas of the central nervous system. Targets of the neurotransmitter include the nearby amygdala, hypothalamus, and midbrain regions, together with the more remote cortex. A product of tryptophan metabolism and the precursor of melatonin, serotonin plays a role in regulating sleep, mood, aggressive behavior, memory, appetite, and cognition.

The methamphetamine derivative MDMA, popularly called Ecstasy, acts on serotonin pathways by destroying axons that release serotonin. Damage to axons is thought to be directly related to dosage. Some affected axons are later able to regenerate, but they may forge new connections instead of reestablishing their original ones.

An experiment was performed in which squirrel monkeys and rats were administered theoretically recreational doses of MDMA and their brains were examined twelve to eighteen months later. Results indicated that regrowth of affected axons reinstated previous synaptic connections in rats. In squirrel monkeys, however, reconnections presented a pattern that differed from that shown by the rats. The extent of axonal restoration in the monkeys also differed, depending on the connecting target. Results from the study are presented in Table 1.

Table 1 Axonal Resoration 12–18 Months after MDMA Administration

Serotonergic target	Rat	Squirrel monkey
Amygdala	++	+++
Hypothalamus	++	+++
Cortex	++	+

Axonal regrowth from brain stem to brain targets:

+	less than number of original connections
++	equal to number of original connections
+++	surpasses number of original connections

170. Serotonin is derived from:
A. an amino acid.
B. an enzyme.
C. another neurotransmitter.
D. a hormone.

171. Among the following, which graph best describes the degree of axonal degeneration as a function of MDMA dose?

A.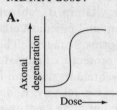

C.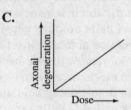

B.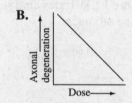

D.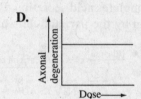

172. If MDMA is found to produce insomnia, the reason might be that:

A. it inhibits serotonin synthesis in brain stem neurons.
B. it destroys serotonin-containing axons in the brain stem.
C. it competes for serotonin binding sites on serotonergic neurons.
D. it causes degeneration of cell bodies of serotonin-producing neurons.

GO ON TO THE NEXT PAGE.

173. The most likely explanation for the differences in axonal regeneration to the three connecting targets, as demonstrated by the squirrel monkey results on Table 1, is that:

- **A.** excessive axonal repair to the amygdala and hypothalamus inhibits reconnection to the cortex.
- **B.** dendrites of neurons in the cortex can compensate for axonal deficiencies.
- **C.** longer axonal projections regenerate more easily than do shorter ones.
- **D.** shorter axonal projections regenerate more easily than do longer ones.

174. A drug that prevented the reuptake of serotonin would most likely:

- **A.** produce an action potential in the presynaptic neuron by binding to receptors on the axonal membrane.
- **B.** reduce the intensity of an action potential in the postsynaptic neuron.
- **C.** prevent the postsynaptic neuron from undergoing frequent action potentials.
- **D.** increase the amount of stimulation received by dendrites of the postsynaptic neuron.

175. All of the following statements correctly describe events associated with synaptic transmission of a nerve impulse EXCEPT:

- **A.** mitochondria supply the ATP needed for synthesis of neurotransmitter.
- **B.** neurotransmitters are released into the synaptic cleft in direct response to an action potential.
- **C.** calcium is actively sequestered in direct response to an action potential.
- **D.** neurotransmitters bind to receptors on the postsynaptic membrane and cause a change in permeability of the membrane.

GO ON TO THE NEXT PAGE.

Questions 176 through 180 are **NOT** based on a descriptive passage.

176. Within the cell, protein turnover reflects a balance between the rates of protein synthesis and degradation. For a given eukaryotic protein, the rate of synthesis is most tightly regulated by which of the following factors?

   A. The amount of heterochromatin available for transcription
   B. The number of mRNA transcripts available for translation
   C. The amount of RNA polymerase bound at the Pribnow box promoter site
   D. The amount of RNA-dependent RNA polymerase available for transcription

177. The likelihood of a given allele's sudden predominance within a small, isolated population independent of adaptive advantage is best attributed to:

   A. the Hardy-Weinberg law.
   B. genetic drift.
   C. adaptive radiation.
   D. survival of the fittest.

178. If 1-propanol is subjected to ^{1}H NMR, the protons on the methyl group will be split into a:

   A. singlet.
   B. doublet.
   C. triplet.
   D. quadruplet.

179. Which of the following represents an effect of antidiuretic hormone (ADH) on the renal nephron?

   A. It increases water loss by reducing the permeability of the collecting duct to water.
   B. It reduces water loss by increasing the permeability of the collecting duct to water.
   C. It reduces water loss by increasing the permeability of the loop of Henle to water.
   D. It increases water loss by reducing the permeability of the loop of Henle to water.

180. A man whose mother is a carrier for color-blindness and whose father was color-blind has a male child with a normal female. What are the chances that the male child will be color-blind?

   A. 0%
   B. 25%
   C. 50%
   D. 100%

Passage VII (Questions 181–186)

In studying the effects of molecular substituents on the acidity of carboxylic acids, researchers have compared equilibrium reactions for the deprotonation of a number of dicarboxylic acids. A standard reaction for comparison purposes is the deprotonation of malonic acid.

$$HOOCCH_2COOH + H_2O \leftrightarrows HOOCCH_2COO^- + H_3O^+$$

Reaction 1

The equilibrium constant for Reaction 1 is symbolized as K_1. The anion in Reaction 1 can be further deprotonated; the equilibrium constant for this reaction is symbolized as K_2, a value substantially smaller than the original K_1.

$$HOOCCH_2COO^- + H_2O \leftrightarrows {}^-OOCCH_2COO^- + H_3O^+$$

Reaction 2

The ratios of K_1 and K_2 are determined under equilibrium conditions and do not apply to nonequilibrium conditions.

Table 1 lists the values of K_1 and K_2 for several dicarboxylic acids.

Table 1 K Values

Compound	Formula	K_1	K_2
Oxalic acid	HOOC–COOH	5400×10^{-5}	5.2×10^{-5}
Malonic acid	HOOCCH$_2$COOH	140×10^{-5}	0.2×10^{-5}
Succinic acid	HOOC(CH$_2$)$_2$COOH	6.4×10^{-5}	0.23×10^{-5}
Maleic acid	HOOCCH=CHCOOH	1000×10^{-5}	0.055×10^{-5}
Fumaric acid	HOOCCH=CHCOOH	96×10^{-5}	4.1×10^{-5}

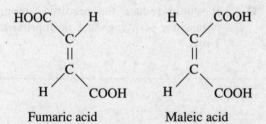

Fumaric acid   Maleic acid

181. Based on the passage, one could estimate a dicarboxylic acid's K_1 value by determining:

    A.   its concentration in a nonequilibrium mixture.

    B.   the stability of the anion form versus the stability of the acid.

    C.   its tendency to undergo decarboxylation.

    D.   its crystallization structure.

182. Glutaric acid is a dicarboxylic acid with the formula $HOOC(CH_2)_3COOH$. This acid is most likely to have a K_1 constant closest in value to which substance listed in the table?

    A.   Fumaric acid

    B.   Maleic acid

    C.   Succinic acid

    D.   Oxalic acid

183. If equal concentrations of succinic acid, malonic acid, and maleic acid were heated in a weakly basic solution, which of the following products would NOT be expected to be found at equilibrium?

    A. $HOOCCH_2COO^-$

    B. $HOOC(CH_2)_2COO^-$

    C. $HOOCCH=CHCOO^-$

    D. $HOOC–COOH$

184. Based on information in the passage, it would be difficult to estimate K_2 for a molecule with the formula $HOOCCH_2CHCOO^-$ because:

    A.   a compound substituted with an amino group cannot be compared directly to succinic acid.

    B.   it cannot exist in the deprotonated form.

    C.   it must form an insoluble compound.

    D.   it represents an unstable compound.

185. In an aqueous mixture known to contain only maleic and fumaric acids, the proportion of maleic to fumaric can best be determined by:

    A.   radioactive tagging of the corresponding alkene.

    B.   hydration of the anion solution.

    C.   acidification of the solution.

    D.   nuclear magnetic resonance spectroscopy of the mixture.

186. The value of K_1 of the dicarboxylic compound glutamic acid is larger than the K_1 of glutaric acid because:

    A.   glutamate is readily convertible into a nonpolar zwitterion.

    B.   the deprotonated form of glutamic acid is less stable than the glutarate anion.

    C.   glutamate is an acidic amino acid.

    D.   glutamic acid is a stronger acid than glutaric acid.

GO ON TO THE NEXT PAGE.

Passage VIII (Questions 187–191)

Catalases are a group of functionally and structurally similar iron-containing enzymes especially prominent in erythrocytes and in the lysosomes and peroxisomes of the liver. They constitute one of a number of groups of enzymes that catalyze the decomposition of hydrogen peroxide to water and oxygen:

$$2H_2O_2 \rightarrow 2H_2O + O_2$$

Hydrogen peroxide arises from photorespiration and degradation of cellular waste products. It is highly toxic to cells, producing free radicals which attack nucleic acids and proteins. Catalase is important to cell survival due to its rapid elimination of hydrogen peroxide. Catalase is a high-turnover enzyme; a single catalase molecule reacts with up to five million substrate molecules per minute.

Experiment

In a first trial, hydrogen peroxide was titrated with potassium permanganate in the absence of catalase. In a second trial, hydrogen peroxide was again tritrated with potassium permanganate after the addition of catalase. The following observations were made.

Finding 1 (Trial 1)

28 mL of potassium permanganate was required to titrate 5 mL of 0.005 M hydrogen peroxide to water.

Finding 2 (Trial 2)

Three minutes after the addition of catalase, the amount of potassium permanganate required for titration was one-third of the amount required in the absence of catalase.

Finding 3 (Trial 3)

Data obtained for the first fifteen minutes following addition of catalase indicated a nearly constant rate of hydrogen peroxide decomposition, evidenced by a decline in the amount of permanganate required for titration.

187. The substrate in the experiment is:

    A.   catalase.
    B.   potassium permanganate.
    C.   hydrogen peroxide.
    D.   water.

188. The primary function of lysosomes is to:

    A.   sequester degradative enzymes from the cytoplasm.
    B.   store water and other materials.
    C.   digest worn cells and organelles.
    D.   modify secretory enzymes before they are sent from the cell.

189. With reference to the experiment, which of the following did NOT occur during the three-minute period following the introduction of catalase?

    A.   The substrate bound to the enzyme.
    B.   A substrate-enzyme complex was formed.
    C.   The reaction proceeded.
    D.   A new enzyme was synthesized.

190. Reduction of temperature would have which of the following effects on the second trial?

    A.   It would impair catalase activity.
    B.   It would enhance catalase activity.
    C.   It would prevent regeneration of the catalase at the conclusion of the reaction.
    D.   It would convert the catalase to an inorganic catalyst.

191. Extreme high temperature would have which of the following effects on the second trial?

    A.   It would increase the required amount of potassium permanganate to approximately 18 mL.
    B.   It would increase the required amount of potassium permanganate to approximately 28 mL.
    C.   It would maintain the required amount of potassium permanganate at approximately 9 mL.
    D.   It would reduce the required amount of potassium permanganate to approximately 1 mL.

Passage IX (Questions 192–197)

Cholesterol is a steroid widely found in animal tissues. It is a major component of human gallstones and egg yolks. Cholesterol is an important intermediate in the biosynthesis of steroid hormones such as testosterone and estradiol. It has received much popular attention because of its association with atherosclerosis or "hardening of the arteries."

Cholesterol

192. How many chiral centers does the above cholesterol molecule feature?

- **A.** 7
- **B.** 6
- **C.** 5
- **D.** 4

193. What is the product of the reaction shown below?

A.

B.

C.

D.

194. When cholesterol reacts with CH_3COOH, it forms:

- **A.** a carboxylic acid and water.
- **B.** a carboxylic acid and an alcohol.
- **C.** an ester and water.
- **D.** an ester and an alcohol.

195. A student believes that cholesterol will readily undergo electrophilic addition when reacted with hydrogen (H_2). Is the belief reasonable?

- **A.** Yes, because cholesterol is a conjugated diene.
- **B.** Yes, because cholesterol may undergo a hydrogenation reaction.
- **C.** No, because cholesterol is not aromatic.
- **D.** No, because electrophilic addition of H_2 requires catalysis.

196. Which of the following is the most probable product when cholesterol undergoes ozonolysis?

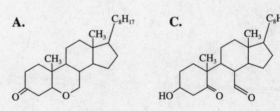

A.

C.

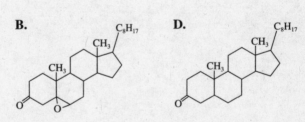

B.

D.

GO ON TO THE NEXT PAGE.

197. Suppose an investigator attempts to produce 5-cholestene-3-one from cholesterol. Which of the following infrared spectroscopic findings would inform the investigator that the reaction has occurred?

Cholesterol → Jones' reagent → 5-Cholestene-3-one

A. The disappearance of OH absorption from the reactant

B. The disappearance of the carbonyl group in the product

C. The disappearance of a double bond from the reactant

D. The disappearance of a methyl group from the reactant

Passage X (Questions 198–203)

Spiral cleavage is a feature of most developing mollusks, all annelids, turbellarian flatworms, and nemertean worms. Unlike radial cleavage, in which cell division is in parallel or perpendicular orientation to the animal-vegetal axis of the egg, spiral cleavage involves cell division at oblique angles, so that daughter cells form a spiral. Viewed from the animal pole of the embryo, the upper ends of the mitotic spindle alternate from a clockwise orientation to a counterclockwise one. Cytoplasmic factors in the oocyte determine the orientation of the cleavage plane to the left or to the right.

In snails, shell coiling is either right-handed or left-handed, with each orientation developing as a mirror image of the other (Figure 1). The rotation of coiling is consistent for all members of a species. However, mutations produce individuals that display an orientation opposite to that which is normal for their species. The reverse orientation in mutants originates at the second cell division of cleavage, when one mitotic spindle shows abnormal positioning.

Researchers have identified a single pair of alleles that control the direction of snail shell coiling. By mating rare left-handed coil mutants of the snail *Lymnaea peregra* with wild-type snails, they determined that the right-handed allele (D) was dominant to the left-handed allele (d). It is the genotype of the mother, however, but not of the developing offspring, that determines the direction of cleavage in the offspring.

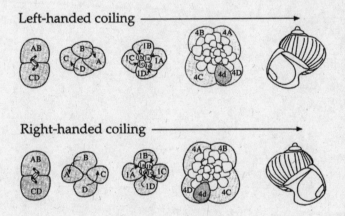

Figure 1 Coiling

198. Which of the following does NOT occur at the same time that the mitotic spindle assembles in the dividing cell?

  A. Chromosomes condense and become visible when viewed with a microscope.
  B. The nuclear membrane begins to disintegrate.
  C. Chromosomes line up along the cell's equator.
  D. Centrioles divide and each one moves to an opposite pole of the cell.

199. The mating shown below would create offspring that exhibit which of the following shell-coiling patterns?

  DD (male) × dd (female) → Dd (offspring)

  A. All right-coiling
  B. All left-coiling
  C. 50% right-coiling and 50% left-coiling
  D. Cannot be determined from the information provided

200. In mammals, oogenesis involves:

  A. two divisions that ultimately produce one haploid ovum.
  B. two divisions that ultimately produce four haploid ova.
  C. one division that ultimately produces one haploid ovum.
  D. one division that ultimately produces two haploid ova.

201. When scientists injected a low-molecular-weight yellow dye into a single cell of a sixteen-cell mollusk embryo, they discovered that the dye was confined to that cell and its progeny. When they injected the dye into a single cell of a thirty-two-cell embryo, they located the dye in that cell as well as in adjacent cells. Based on these findings, it is most reasonable to conclude that communication between cells of a developing mollusk embryo develops at the:

  A. zygote stage.
  B. neurula stage.
  C. gastrula stage.
  D. blastula stage.

GO ON TO THE NEXT PAGE.

202. Members of a given species:

    A. have identical genotypes.

    B. have identical phenotypes.

    C. are unable to breed with one another to produce viable offspring.

    D. are unable to produce fertile offspring with members of another species.

203. If, with regard to a particular population of *Lymnaea peregra*, all conditions for operation of the Hardy-Weinberg Law are fully satisfied, then, over time, the prevalence in the population of the left-handed (d) allele would most likely:

    A. increase significantly.

    B. decrease significantly.

    C. increase significantly and then decrease significantly.

    D. remain relatively constant.

Passage XI (Questions 204–208)

Isopropyl alcohol is a colorless liquid with an odor characteristic of alcohols. It melts at −89.5°C and boils at 82.5°C. The compound is soluble in water, ethanol, and ether. It is often used as a disinfectant and as a skin-cooling agent, called "rubbing alcohol." Many alcohols are made commercially by the hydration of alkenes. Isopropyl alcohol is prepared by reacting propylene ($CH_3CH=CH_2$) with a strong acid such as sulfuric acid, followed by treatment with water.

The initial step is shown below:

$$CH_3-CH=CH_2 + H^+ + HSO_4^- \longrightarrow \text{Intermediate} + HSO_4^-$$

The reaction of the intermediate with water then yields isopropyl alcohol.

$$\text{Intermediate} + H_2O \longrightarrow CH_3-\overset{\displaystyle OH}{\underset{\displaystyle H}{C}}-CH_3 + H^+$$

204. In the preparation of isopropyl alcohol, what is the role of sulfuric acid?

A. It acts as a catalyst.
B. It increases the pH of the solution.
C. It ionizes the alkene.
D. It causes a reduction of the alkene.

205. How many chiral centers are featured within the isopropyl alcohol molecule?

A. 0
B. 1
C. 2
D. 3

206. What property of isopropyl alcohol makes it most useful as a skin-cooling agent?

A. It forms hydrogen bonds.
B. It is weakly acidic.
C. It is relatively volatile.
D. It acts as a proton acceptor.

207. Between isopropyl alcohol and *n*-propanol, which compound likely has the higher boiling point?

A. *N*-propanol, because it has the higher molecular weight
B. *N*-propanol, because it is a straight chain alcohol
C. Isopropyl alcohol, because its density is higher than that of *n*-propanol
D. Isopropyl alcohol, because its carbon chain branches

208. All of the following are isomers of isobutyl alcohol EXCEPT:

A. $(CH_3)_3COH$.
B. $CH_3CH_2COCH_3$.
C. $CH_3CH_2CH_2CH_2OH$.
D. $CH_3CHOHCH_2CH_3$.

GO ON TO THE NEXT PAGE.

Questions 209 through 214 are **NOT** based on a descriptive passage.

209. On a single human gene, a researcher discovers a point mutation in which one nucleotide residue has been substituted for another. She further discovers that transcription of the affected gene alters the resulting messenger RNA codon, but that the altered codon does not affect the polypeptide produced when the messenger RNA undergoes translation. Among the following, the most likely explanation for the unchanged polypeptide is that:

    A. the point mutation did not impair the efficacy of DNA polymerases.

    B. the point mutation did not impair the efficacy of RNA polymerases.

    C. the point mutation caused a shift in the ribosomal reading frame.

    D. the genetic code is degenerate.

210. All of the following statements about RNA polymerase and DNA polymerase are true EXCEPT:

    A. RNA polymerase normally catalyzes the addition of a thymine subunit to a nascent RNA strand.

    B. RNA polymerase normally catalyzes the elongation of a nascent polymer in the 5' to 3' direction.

    C. DNA polymerase is not affected by the presence of upstream regulatory elements.

    D. DNA polymerase normally catalyzes the elongation of a nascent polymer in the 5' to 3' direction.

211. A virus that employs reverse transcriptase to carry out its infective cycle within a host cell has as its nucleic acid core:

    A. RNA.

    B. DNA.

    C. either RNA or DNA.

    D. neither RNA nor DNA.

212. Formation of ATP from ADP and inorganic phosphate occurs via:

    A. hydrolysis, which involves the removal of a molecule of water.

    B. hydrolysis, which involves the addition of a molecule of water.

    C. dehydration synthesis, which involves the removal of a molecule of water.

    D. dehydration synthesis, which involves the addition of a molecule of water.

213. Which of the following ovarian cell organelles will show the greatest levels of activity during the secretion of estrogen?

    A. Lysosomes

    B. Smooth ER

    C. Golgi apparatus

    D. Ribosomes

214. During the replication of a human chromosome, the lagging strand:

    A. acts as a template for the leading strand.

    B. must undergo semidiscontinuous synthesis due to antiparallel orientation of the DNA double helix.

    C. undergoes frequent mutations because base-pairing tends to lag behind base-pairing on the leading strand.

    D. undergoes nucleotide addition by DNA polymerase at the 5' end of the growing chain.

STOP. IF YOU FINISH BEFORE TIME IS CALLED, CHECK YOUR WORK. YOU MAY GO BACK TO ANY QUESTION IN THIS SECTION.

STOP.

MCAT PRACTICE TEST SCORE CONVERSION CHARTS

Estimated Scaled Score	Physical Sciences Raw Scores
15	74–77
14	72–73
13	68–71
12	66–67
11	61–65
10	56–60
9	52–55
8	46–51
7	41–45
6	33–40
5	27–32
≤4	0–26

Estimated Scaled Score	Verbal Reasoning Raw Scores
15	60–60
14	59–59
13	55–58
12	52–54
11	48–51
10	44–47
9	40–43
8	37–39
7	34–36
6	28–33
5	26–27
≤4	0–25

Estimated Scaled Score	Biological Sciences Raw Scores
15	76–77
14	73–75
13	69–72
12	66–68
11	62–65
10	56–61
9	51–55
8	46–50
7	41–45
6	36–40
5	33–35
≥4	0–32

The Princeton Review

Diagnostic MCAT Form ○ Side 1

1. YOUR NAME:
(Print)

Last   First   M.I.

SIGNATURE:

DATE:

HOME ADDRESS:
(Print)

Number and Street

City   State   Zip

E-MAIL:

SCHOOL:

PHONE NO.:
(Print)

CLASS OF:

IMPORTANT: Please fill in these boxes exactly as shown on the back cover of your test book.

Completely darken bubbles with a No. 2 pencil. If you make a mistake, be sure to erase mark completely. Erase all stray marks.

TEST FORM

TEST CODE

SEX
○ MALE
○ FEMALE

OTHER
1 Ⓐ Ⓑ Ⓒ Ⓓ Ⓔ
2 Ⓐ Ⓑ Ⓒ Ⓓ Ⓔ
3 Ⓐ Ⓑ Ⓒ Ⓓ Ⓔ

YOUR NAME
First 4 letters of last name | FIRST INIT | MID INIT

DATE OF BIRTH
MONTH | DAY | YEAR
JAN
FEB
MAR
APR
MAY
JUN
JUL
AUG
SEP
OCT
NOV
DEC

PHONE NUMBER

The Princeton Review
Diagnostic MCAT Form ○ Side 2

SECTION 2

78 Ⓐ Ⓑ Ⓒ Ⓓ
79 Ⓐ Ⓑ Ⓒ Ⓓ
80 Ⓐ Ⓑ Ⓒ Ⓓ

81 Ⓐ Ⓑ Ⓒ Ⓓ
82 Ⓐ Ⓑ Ⓒ Ⓓ

83 Ⓐ Ⓑ Ⓒ Ⓓ
84 Ⓐ Ⓑ Ⓒ Ⓓ

85 Ⓐ Ⓑ Ⓒ Ⓓ
86 Ⓐ Ⓑ Ⓒ Ⓓ
87 Ⓐ Ⓑ Ⓒ Ⓓ

88 Ⓐ Ⓑ Ⓒ Ⓓ
89 Ⓐ Ⓑ Ⓒ Ⓓ
90 Ⓐ Ⓑ Ⓒ Ⓓ

91 Ⓐ Ⓑ Ⓒ Ⓓ
92 Ⓐ Ⓑ Ⓒ Ⓓ

93 Ⓐ Ⓑ Ⓒ Ⓓ
94 Ⓐ Ⓑ Ⓒ Ⓓ

95 Ⓐ Ⓑ Ⓒ Ⓓ
96 Ⓐ Ⓑ Ⓒ Ⓓ
97 Ⓐ Ⓑ Ⓒ Ⓓ

98 Ⓐ Ⓑ Ⓒ Ⓓ
99 Ⓐ Ⓑ Ⓒ Ⓓ
100 Ⓐ Ⓑ Ⓒ Ⓓ

101 Ⓐ Ⓑ Ⓒ Ⓓ
102 Ⓐ Ⓑ Ⓒ Ⓓ

103 Ⓐ Ⓑ Ⓒ Ⓓ
104 Ⓐ Ⓑ Ⓒ Ⓓ

105 Ⓐ Ⓑ Ⓒ Ⓓ
106 Ⓐ Ⓑ Ⓒ Ⓓ
107 Ⓐ Ⓑ Ⓒ Ⓓ

108 Ⓐ Ⓑ Ⓒ Ⓓ
109 Ⓐ Ⓑ Ⓒ Ⓓ
110 Ⓐ Ⓑ Ⓒ Ⓓ

111 Ⓐ Ⓑ Ⓒ Ⓓ
112 Ⓐ Ⓑ Ⓒ Ⓓ

113 Ⓐ Ⓑ Ⓒ Ⓓ
114 Ⓐ Ⓑ Ⓒ Ⓓ

115 Ⓐ Ⓑ Ⓒ Ⓓ
116 Ⓐ Ⓑ Ⓒ Ⓓ
117 Ⓐ Ⓑ Ⓒ Ⓓ

118 Ⓐ Ⓑ Ⓒ Ⓓ
119 Ⓐ Ⓑ Ⓒ Ⓓ
120 Ⓐ Ⓑ Ⓒ Ⓓ

121 Ⓐ Ⓑ Ⓒ Ⓓ
122 Ⓐ Ⓑ Ⓒ Ⓓ

123 Ⓐ Ⓑ Ⓒ Ⓓ
124 Ⓐ Ⓑ Ⓒ Ⓓ

125 Ⓐ Ⓑ Ⓒ Ⓓ
126 Ⓐ Ⓑ Ⓒ Ⓓ
127 Ⓐ Ⓑ Ⓒ Ⓓ

128 Ⓐ Ⓑ Ⓒ Ⓓ
129 Ⓐ Ⓑ Ⓒ Ⓓ
130 Ⓐ Ⓑ Ⓒ Ⓓ

131 Ⓐ Ⓑ Ⓒ Ⓓ
132 Ⓐ Ⓑ Ⓒ Ⓓ

133 Ⓐ Ⓑ Ⓒ Ⓓ
134 Ⓐ Ⓑ Ⓒ Ⓓ

135 Ⓐ Ⓑ Ⓒ Ⓓ
136 Ⓐ Ⓑ Ⓒ Ⓓ
137 Ⓐ Ⓑ Ⓒ Ⓓ

SECTION 3

138 Ⓐ Ⓑ Ⓒ Ⓓ
139 Ⓐ Ⓑ Ⓒ Ⓓ
140 Ⓐ Ⓑ Ⓒ Ⓓ

141 Ⓐ Ⓑ Ⓒ Ⓓ
142 Ⓐ Ⓑ Ⓒ Ⓓ

143 Ⓐ Ⓑ Ⓒ Ⓓ
144 Ⓐ Ⓑ Ⓒ Ⓓ

145 Ⓐ Ⓑ Ⓒ Ⓓ
146 Ⓐ Ⓑ Ⓒ Ⓓ
147 Ⓐ Ⓑ Ⓒ Ⓓ

148 Ⓐ Ⓑ Ⓒ Ⓓ
149 Ⓐ Ⓑ Ⓒ Ⓓ
150 Ⓐ Ⓑ Ⓒ Ⓓ

151 Ⓐ Ⓑ Ⓒ Ⓓ
152 Ⓐ Ⓑ Ⓒ Ⓓ

153 Ⓐ Ⓑ Ⓒ Ⓓ
154 Ⓐ Ⓑ Ⓒ Ⓓ

155 Ⓐ Ⓑ Ⓒ Ⓓ
156 Ⓐ Ⓑ Ⓒ Ⓓ
157 Ⓐ Ⓑ Ⓒ Ⓓ

158 Ⓐ Ⓑ Ⓒ Ⓓ
159 Ⓐ Ⓑ Ⓒ Ⓓ
160 Ⓐ Ⓑ Ⓒ Ⓓ

161 Ⓐ Ⓑ Ⓒ Ⓓ
162 Ⓐ Ⓑ Ⓒ Ⓓ

163 Ⓐ Ⓑ Ⓒ Ⓓ
164 Ⓐ Ⓑ Ⓒ Ⓓ

165 Ⓐ Ⓑ Ⓒ Ⓓ
166 Ⓐ Ⓑ Ⓒ Ⓓ
167 Ⓐ Ⓑ Ⓒ Ⓓ

168 Ⓐ Ⓑ Ⓒ Ⓓ
169 Ⓐ Ⓑ Ⓒ Ⓓ
170 Ⓐ Ⓑ Ⓒ Ⓓ

171 Ⓐ Ⓑ Ⓒ Ⓓ
172 Ⓐ Ⓑ Ⓒ Ⓓ

173 Ⓐ Ⓑ Ⓒ Ⓓ
174 Ⓐ Ⓑ Ⓒ Ⓓ

175 Ⓐ Ⓑ Ⓒ Ⓓ
176 Ⓐ Ⓑ Ⓒ Ⓓ
177 Ⓐ Ⓑ Ⓒ Ⓓ

178 Ⓐ Ⓑ Ⓒ Ⓓ
179 Ⓐ Ⓑ Ⓒ Ⓓ
180 Ⓐ Ⓑ Ⓒ Ⓓ

181 Ⓐ Ⓑ Ⓒ Ⓓ
182 Ⓐ Ⓑ Ⓒ Ⓓ

183 Ⓐ Ⓑ Ⓒ Ⓓ
184 Ⓐ Ⓑ Ⓒ Ⓓ

185 Ⓐ Ⓑ Ⓒ Ⓓ
186 Ⓐ Ⓑ Ⓒ Ⓓ
187 Ⓐ Ⓑ Ⓒ Ⓓ

188 Ⓐ Ⓑ Ⓒ Ⓓ
189 Ⓐ Ⓑ Ⓒ Ⓓ
190 Ⓐ Ⓑ Ⓒ Ⓓ

191 Ⓐ Ⓑ Ⓒ Ⓓ
192 Ⓐ Ⓑ Ⓒ Ⓓ

193 Ⓐ Ⓑ Ⓒ Ⓓ
194 Ⓐ Ⓑ Ⓒ Ⓓ

195 Ⓐ Ⓑ Ⓒ Ⓓ
196 Ⓐ Ⓑ Ⓒ Ⓓ
197 Ⓐ Ⓑ Ⓒ Ⓓ

198 Ⓐ Ⓑ Ⓒ Ⓓ
199 Ⓐ Ⓑ Ⓒ Ⓓ
200 Ⓐ Ⓑ Ⓒ Ⓓ

201 Ⓐ Ⓑ Ⓒ Ⓓ
202 Ⓐ Ⓑ Ⓒ Ⓓ

203 Ⓐ Ⓑ Ⓒ Ⓓ
204 Ⓐ Ⓑ Ⓒ Ⓓ

205 Ⓐ Ⓑ Ⓒ Ⓓ
206 Ⓐ Ⓑ Ⓒ Ⓓ
207 Ⓐ Ⓑ Ⓒ Ⓓ

208 Ⓐ Ⓑ Ⓒ Ⓓ
209 Ⓐ Ⓑ Ⓒ Ⓓ
210 Ⓐ Ⓑ Ⓒ Ⓓ

211 Ⓐ Ⓑ Ⓒ Ⓓ
212 Ⓐ Ⓑ Ⓒ Ⓓ

213 Ⓐ Ⓑ Ⓒ Ⓓ
214 Ⓐ Ⓑ Ⓒ Ⓓ

**DO NOT WRITE
ON THIS
PAGE**

IF YOU NEED MORE SPACE, PLEASE CONTINUE ON THE NEXT PAGE.

IF YOU NEED MORE SPACE, PLEASE CONTINUE ON THE NEXT PAGE. ➡

STOP here for Part 2. Do not return to Part 1.

PART V

MCAT Practice Test 2:
Answers and Explanations

MCAT PRACTICE TEST 2 ANSWER KEYS

PHYSICAL SCIENCES

1	C	11	B	21	B	31	C	41	B	51	D	61	B	71	C
2	C	12	C	22	B	32	D	42	A	52	A	62	C	72	A
3	B	13	A	23	D	33	A	43	B	53	B	63	B	73	D
4	A	14	C	24	D	34	D	44	D	54	D	64	D	74	B
5	A	15	C	25	C	35	D	45	C	55	D	65	D	75	B
6	D	16	B	26	C	36	A	46	B	56	C	66	B	76	C
7	D	17	C	27	A	37	B	47	A	57	A	67	B	77	A
8	C	18	D	28	A	38	B	48	D	58	B	68	B		
9	C	19	D	29	D	39	A	49	B	59	D	69	B		
10	A	20	A	30	B	40	B	50	A	60	C	70	B		

VERBAL REASONING

78	C	88	C	98	B	108	D	118	D	128	B
79	A	89	B	99	A	109	A	119	D	129	A
80	D	90	B	100	D	110	C	120	C	130	D
81	C	91	C	101	D	111	C	121	B	131	D
82	B	92	D	102	A	112	A	122	C	132	B
83	A	93	C	103	D	113	C	123	D	133	A
84	A	94	A	104	B	114	D	124	A	134	B
85	D	95	C	105	D	115	D	125	C	135	D
86	A	96	D	106	C	116	C	126	C	136	D
87	B	97	C	107	A	117	A	127	D	137	A

BIOLOGICAL SCIENCES

138	D	148	B	158	C	168	C	178	C	188	C	198	C	208	B
139	A	149	C	159	D	169	B	179	B	189	D	199	B	209	D
140	D	150	A	160	C	170	A	180	A	190	A	200	A	210	A
141	D	151	B	161	D	171	C	181	B	191	B	201	D	211	A
142	B	152	C	162	A	172	B	182	C	192	A	202	D	212	C
143	C	153	C	163	D	173	D	183	D	193	C	203	D	213	B
144	B	154	C	164	D	174	D	184	A	194	C	204	A	214	B
145	C	155	B	165	D	175	C	185	D	195	D	205	A		
146	D	156	C	166	C	176	B	186	D	196	C	206	C		
147	A	157	C	167	A	177	B	187	C	197	A	207	B		

ANSWERS AND EXPLANATIONS

PHYSICAL SCIENCES

Questions 1–77

Passage I (Questions 1–5)

1. Two helium nuclei fuse and release energy in the form of photons. What type of energy is lost by the nuclei and transferred into the photons?

    A. Kinetic
    B. Radiant
    C. Mass
    D. Electromagnetic

C The question describes a nuclear fusion reaction. Nuclear fusion (and fission) reactions illustrate the equivalency of mass and energy as described by Einstein's famous equation, $E = mc^2$. This nuclear fusion reaction converts mass to energy in the form of electromagnetic radiation.

2. $^{236}_{90}$Th emits two beta particles and two alpha particles. Which of the following nuclei results?

    A. $^{226}_{87}$Fr

    B. $^{226}_{88}$Ra

    C. $^{228}_{88}$Ra

    D. $^{224}_{86}$Rn

C Write the reaction as follows, with $^{A}_{Z}$X denoting the daughter nucleus:

$$^{236}_{90}\text{Th} \rightarrow {}^{A}_{Z}\text{X} + 2\,^{0}_{-1}\beta + 2\,^{4}_{2}\alpha$$

Both the mass numbers (superscripts) and the charges (subscripts) must balance, so

$$236 = A + 2(0) + 2(4) \Rightarrow A = 228$$
$$90 = Z + 2(-1) + 2(2) \Rightarrow Z = 88$$

Therefore, $^{A}_{Z}\text{X} = {}^{228}_{88}\text{Ra}$, since the periodic table shows that element number 88 is radium (Ra).

3. One-half of a Tl sample decays to Pb in 3.1 minutes through the emission of beta particles. If an initially pure sample of Tl contains 7 g of lead after 9.3 minutes, what was the approximate mass of the original sample?

    A. 7 g
    B. 8 g
    C. 28 g
    D. 32 g

Time/minutes	Fraction remaining
0	1
3.1	1/2
6.2	1/4
9.3	1/8

B Since beta particles have negligible mass, you can assume that the mass of the Pb that appears is equal to the mass of the Tl that decays. That means 7 g of Tl decayed. Since Tl has a half-life of 3.1 minutes, 9.3 minutes represents three half-lives. In three half-lives, 7/8 of the original sample decays. Simple algebra reveals that:

$$(7/8)x = 7\text{g} \Rightarrow x = 8\text{g}$$

4. An element decays to an isotope of itself, releasing alpha and beta particles. In terms of the number of particles released, the ratio of alpha particles to beta particles is which of the following:

A. 1/2
B. 1
C. 2
D. 4

A Because the element decayed to an isotope of itself, its atomic number did not change. Alpha decay decreases the atomic number by two. Beta decay increases atomic number by one. Atomic number will be unchanged only if there are two beta decays for every alpha decay.

5. How many photons, each of energy 2.8 MeV, can be produced when 1 gram of matter is converted to energy?

A. 2×10^{26}
B. 2×10^{32}
C. 2×10^{35}
D. 4×10^{35}

A Photons have energy but no mass. When a question concerns the conversion of mass to energy, remember Einstein's formula:

$$E = mc^2$$
$$E = (.001 \text{ kg})(3 \times 10^8 \text{ m/s})^2$$
$$E = 9 \times 10^{13} \text{ J}$$

Next, determine how many photons correspond to 9×10^{13} J of energy:

$(9 \times 10^{13} \text{ J}) \times (1 \text{ photon} / 2.8 \text{ MeV}) \times (1 \text{ eV} / 1.6 \times 10^{-19} \text{ J}) \times (1 \text{ MeV} / 10^6 \text{ eV}) = 2 \times 10^{26}$ photons

Passage II (Questions 6–10)

6. A series of charged particles are fired into the magnetic field. Which of the following best describes the magnitude of the force acting on the particle as θ is increased from 0° to 90°?

A. It remains constant.
B. It decreases at a rate that is proportional to θ.
C. It increases at a rate that is proportional to θ.
D. It increases at a rate that is not proportional to θ.

D The force increases from 0 at $\theta = 0$ to qvB at $\theta = 90°$. This rate is not proportional to θ, but rather to $\sin \theta$.

7. Particle W, a proton (not shown), is given an initial velocity of 3×10^4 m/s in the direction of path Y. If the magnetic field strength is 5.2 T, what is the initial force felt by particle W?

A. 5×10^{-15} N, down
B. 5×10^{-15} N, up
C. 2.5×10^{-14} N, down
D. 2.5×10^{-14} N, up

D Using the equation given in the passage, we find that

$$F = qvB \sin \theta$$
$$= (1.6 \times 10^{-19} \text{C})(3 \times 10^4 \text{ m/s})(5.2 \text{ T})\sin 90°$$
$$= 2.5 \times 10^{-14} \text{ N}$$

By the right-hand rule, if the particle is positively charged and moves with velocity **v** to the right through a magnetic field **B** that points into the page, then the force **F** acting on the particle will point *upward*.

8. If particle Y were given an additional velocity component into the page, with a magnitude equal to the magnitude of its original velocity in the direction of path Y, the force felt by the particle would:

A. decrease by a factor of 4.
B. decrease by a factor of 2.
C. remain the same.
D. increase by a factor of 2.

C A velocity directed *into the page* is parallel to the direction of the magnetic field, and angle θ is zero. Applying the equation provided in the passage shows that the force associated with such a velocity is zero. That, in turn, means that the added velocity would bring no change to the force felt by the particle.

9. Observing paths followed by particles X and Z, an experimenter would be justified in concluding that the two particles:

    A. have charges of equal magnitude.
    B are negatively charged.
    C. are oppositely charged.
    D. are positively charged.

C The magnetic field force causes the two particles to move in opposite directions. That can only mean that their charges are opposite; one is positive and the other negative.

Choice A is wrong. The charge magnitude does not explain the particles' divergent paths.

10. Which of the following diagrams represents the force **F** experienced by a positively charged particle traveling **v** with velocity through a magnetic field **B**?

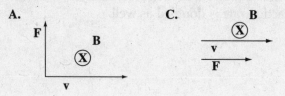

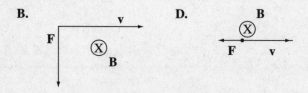

A The particle experiences a force that is perpendicular to both the particle's velocity and the field lines, so choices C and D are wrong. Correctly apply the right-hand rule to choose between choices A and B, and you will decide on choice A.

Passage III (Questions 11–15)

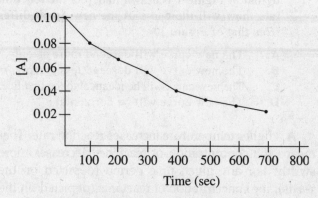

Figure 1 Concentration of A over time

11. Based on the passage, what should be the approximate initial rate of Reaction 1 at 65°C?

    A. 2×10^{-4} mol/s
    B. 3×10^{-3} mol/s
    C. 6×10^{-3} mol/s
    D. 2×10^{-2} mol/s

B The passage states that rate very nearly doubles for each increase of 10°C, so an increase of 40°C would result in an increase of about a factor of 16. The initial rate at 25° was 2×10^{-4} mol/s, so the approximate rate at 65° would be 32×10^{-4} mol/s, or 3×10^{-3} mol/s.

12. Based on the passage, how many moles of A have disappeared from the solution after 600 seconds have elapsed?

    A. 0.06 moles
    B. 0.07 moles
    C. 0.14 moles
    D. 0.16 moles

C After 600 seconds, the approximate concentration is 0.03 mol/L, so there are about 0.06 mol left in solution. Initially the concentration was 0.10 mol/L, which corresponds to 0.20 mol in solution. Thus, 0.14 mol have disappeared after 600 seconds.

13. If Reaction 1 is run at 65°C and a graph analogous to that of Figure 1 is drawn to depict the reaction rate, how will the curve of the new graph differ from that of Figure 1?

    A. The new curve will descend more steeply.
    B. The new curve will descend less steeply.
    C. The new curve will be identical to the first line.
    D. The new curve will be horizontal.

A Higher temperature increases reaction rate. That means the concentration of reactants decreases more swiftly. For any given time period (depicted on the x-axis), the concentration of reactants (depicted on the y-axis) will experience a greater fall. The curve's slope steepens.

14. How would increasing the temperature at which the reaction takes place affect the rates of the forward and reverse reactions and the eventual equilibrium?

    A. It would increase the rate of the forward reaction, decrease the rate of the reverse reaction, and shift the equilibrium toward the formation of products.
    B. It would decrease the rate of the forward reaction, increase the rate of the reverse reaction, and shift the equilibrium toward the formation of reactants.
    C. It would increase the rate of the forward reaction, increase the rate of the reverse reaction, and shift the equilibrium toward the formation of products.
    D. It would increase the rate of the forward reaction, increase the rate of the reverse reaction, and shift the equilibrium toward the formation of reactants.

C For this reaction, enthalpy change, ΔH, is positive and the reaction, therefore, is endothermic; it absorbs heat from the surroundings. You might think of heat as belonging to the left side of the equation:

$$\text{heat} + A \rightleftarrows B + C$$

Adding heat to the reaction system drives the equilibrium to the right and increases equilibrium concentrations of the products. Increased temperature also increases the rate constant for both the forward reaction *and* the reverse reaction, which causes reaction rate to increase as well.

15. If the initial concentration of A is doubled, what will be the effect on the initial rate of reaction and the rate constant?

    A. The rate of reaction and the rate constant will double.
    B. The rate of reaction and the rate constant will not change.
    C. The rate of reaction will double and the rate constant will not change.
    D. The rate of reaction will not change and the rate constant will double.

C The rate constant does not change with concentration of the reactant (although it does change with temperature). As you learn at the beginning of the passage (and from your own review of chemical kinetics), rate = k [A], which means that rate is directly proportional to the concentration of reactant(s). If the initial concentration of substance A is doubled, then the initial reaction rate is doubled as well.

Passage IV (Questions 16–21)

16. What would be the effective magnification of the telescope in Figure 1 if someone were to accidentally use the objective lens as the eyepiece?

A. 0.02
B. 0.05
C. 2
D. 20

B If the roles of the lenses were reversed, the magnification would be f/F (instead if F/f), which equlas 2/40, or 0.05.

17. An investigator works with a telescope that is equipped with a variety of removable lenses. Among the following combinations, the investigator will achieve greatest magnification with:

A. an objective with a large focal length and an eyepiece with a large focal length.
B. an objective with a small focal length and an eyepiece with a small focal length.
C. an objective with a large focal length and an eyepiece with a small focal length.
D. an objective with a small focal length and an eyepiece with a large focal length.

C The passage's last paragraph tells you that magnification is equal to the fraction: F (focal length of objective lens)/f (focal length of eyepiece). Magnification is greatest when that fraction is greatest. Fractions, of course, increase with an increasing numerator and a decreasing denominator. Choice C represents a fraction with a large numerator and a small denominator.

18. An object is to be observed using only the eyepiece lens. If the object lies at a distance of 1.5 cm from the eyepiece lens, the image will be located:

A. 1 cm from the eyepiece.
B. 2 cm from the eyepiece.
C. 3 cm from the eyepiece.
D. 6 cm from the eyepiece.

D Apply the lens equation:

$$1/f = 1/o + 1/i$$
$$1/(2 \text{ cm}) = 1/(1.5 \text{ cm}) + 1/i$$
$$i = -6 \text{ cm}$$

19. What is the power of the eyepiece of the telescope in Figure 1?

A. 2 diopters
B. 5 diopters
C. 20 diopters
D. 50 diopters

D The power of a lens in diopters is equal to the reciprocal of its focal length. Remember that focal length is measured in meters.

$$P = 1/f = 1/(0.02 \text{ m}) = 50 \text{ D}$$

20. If the eyepiece lens were replaced with a lens composed of a material with a refractive index greater than 1.5, which of the following would be expected to occur?

A. The magnification of the telescope would increase.
B. The magnification of the telescope would be unchanged.
C. The magnification of the telescope would decrease.
D. The effect on the magnification cannot be determined.

A Increasing the refractive index would decrease the focal length. Decreasing the focal length of the eyepiece lens causes the magnification of the telescope to increase since it is proportional to $1/f$.

21. A certain material has an index of refraction which depends strongly on the frequency of the incident light. Why would this material be a poor choice for use in telescope lenses?

A. The image would not be inverted.
B. Objects that emit multiple wavelengths of light would not be in focus.
C. No light would be transmitted through the telescope.
D. The magnification would not be large enough to be useful.

B For the telescope to be in focus, the focal lengths of the objective and eyepiece lenses must coincide at a point inside the telescope. If the index of refraction were not constant, then this could only happen for one wavelength of light at a time, thus leaving all other wavelengths out of focus to varying degrees.

Free-Standing Questions (22–27)

22. An object of mass m is sliding down a frictionless ramp that is elevated at an angle of 60°. What is the magnitude of the object's acceleration parallel to the ramp?

A. $g \cos 60°$
B. $g \sin 60°$
C. $mg \cos 60°$
D. $mg \sin 60°$

B The gravitational force parallel to the ramp is equal to $mg \sin 60°$, so
$$ma = mg \sin 60°$$
$$a = g \sin 60°$$

23. Which of the following electronic configurations belongs to a diamagnetic element in its ground state?

A. $1s^2 2s^1$
B. $1s^2 2s^2 2p^1$
C. $1s^2 2s^2 2p^4$
D. $1s^2 2s^2 2p^6$

D Diamagnetic elements have no unpaired electrons, and that's the situation reflected in choice D. Choices A and B show an odd number of electrons, meaning that some electrons are unpaired. Choice C is wrong even though it shows an even number of electrons. According to Hund's rule, electrons occupy orbitals singly until all orbitals within the relevant subshell are occupied by one electron. When the three orbitals of the p subshell carry four electrons, two are unpaired.

24. A constant current of 5 amperes is passing through a 10-ohm resistor. How much energy is dissipated in the resistor over the course of 10 seconds?

A. 250 J
B. 500 J
C. 1000 J
D. 2500 J

D Power is a measure of energy per unit of time. In electrical contexts, units are so defined as to allow for the expression of power as $P = I^2 R = (5)^2(10) = 250$ J/s. We ascertain the dissipated energy when we multiply 250 J/s by the applicable time, 10 seconds: $E = (250 \text{ J/s})(10\text{s}) = 2500$ J.

25. An object of mass 2 kg, moving horizontally at 10 m/s, collides with a smaller object, initially at rest, of mass 0.5 kg. After the collision, the smaller object moves with velocity 8 m/s at an angle of 30° above the horizontal. What is the vertical speed of the larger object after the collision?

A. 0.25 m/s
B. 0.5 m/s
C. 1 m/s
D. 2 m/s

C Momentum is conserved in the collision. Because momentum is a vector, the horizontal momentum and the vertical momentum must each be separately conserved. Since the system had zero vertical momentum before the collision, it must have zero vertical momentum after the collision, too. Let the masses of the larger and smaller objects be M and m, respectively. If the post-collision velocities of these objects are V and v, respectively, then $0 = MV_y + mv_y$, so

$$V_y = -\frac{m}{M} v_y = -\frac{0.5 \text{ kg}}{2 \text{ kg}} (8 \text{ m/s} \cdot \sin 30°) = -1 \text{ m/s}$$

Therefore, the vertical *speed* of the larger object after the collision is the magnitude of its vertical velocity, namely, 1 m/s.

26. The pressure of a gas at a temperature of 27°C is measured to be P. If the temperature is increased to 127°C while all other factors are kept constant, what will be the new pressure of the gas?

A. $1/5\ P$
B. $3/4\ P$
C. $4/3\ P$
D. $5P$

C Remember (1) that temperature and pressure are directly proportional, and (2) that you must convert temperature to the Kelvin scale.

$$P_2/P_1 = T_2/T_1$$

$$P_2 = \frac{400}{300}P_1$$

$$P_2 = \frac{4}{3}P_1$$

27. As an ideal fluid flowing in a cylindrical pipe through a constant pressure differential moves from a region of larger diameter to a region of smaller diameter, which of the following will occur?

A.   Flow rate will remain constant and fluid velocity will increase.
B.   Flow rate will remain constant and fluid velocity will remain constant.
C.   Flow rate will increase and fluid velocity will increase.
D.   Flow rate will increase and fluid velocity will remain constant.

A Flow rate expresses the volume of fluid that passes a given point in a given time period. It is measured in units of volume per unit of time. For fluid flowing within a single ideal system, flow rate is constant at all points, even though the cross-sectional area of the pipe might vary from place to place. By the equation of continuity, $Av =$ constant, where A is the cross-sectional area of the pipe and v is the flow speed, it follows that v increases as A decreases (which happens when the diameter of the pipe gets smaller).

Passage V (Questions 28–33)

28. The process of tooth decay is most likely to occur in saliva maintained at which of the following pOH values?

A.   8.0
B.   7.0
C.   6.0
D.   5.0

A Acidity increases with pOH, so A is the most acidic of the answer choices.

29. The oxidation state of calcium in the hydroxyapatite molecule is:

A.   −1
B.   0
C.   +1
D.   +2

D The oxidation states of all atoms within a neutral molecule must sum to zero. You should know that the oxidation state of PO_4 is (−3) and that of OH is (−1). $(5) \times$ (Oxidation state of Ca) $+ 3(-3) + 1(-1) = 0$. The oxidation state of Ca = +2. You would also have arrived at this answer by knowing that calcium has two valence electrons that it tends to lose in chemical bonding, or by looking at Reaction 1.

30. Fluorapatite is more resistant to tooth decay than hydroxyapatite because compared to hydroxide ion, the fluoride ion is:

   A. a stronger base that interacts less with hydrogen ions in saliva.
   B. a weaker base that interacts less with hydrogen ions in saliva.
   C. a stronger base that reacts more with hydrogen ions in saliva.
   D. a weaker base that reacts more with hydrogen ions in saliva.

   B Hydrofluoric acid (HF) is classified as a weak acid (pKa = 3.2). Therefore, its conjugate base, F^-, will have some basic activity in solution. However, F^- is not nearly as strong a base as OH^-. The more basic a compound, the higher is its tendency to react with a hydrogen ion. If an acid is introduced to saliva, it will react with both OH^- and F^-, driving the equilibrium of Reactions 1 and 2 to the right. The effect on Reaction 1 is much greater than on 2, because OH^- has a greater tendency to react with acid than F^-. Therefore, hydroxyapatite is more likely to dissociate in the presence of acid than fluorapatite is.

31. The presence of acid in saliva acts to promote tooth decay because acid in saliva will:

   A. increase the hydroxide concentration.
   B. increase the hydroxyapatite concentration.
   C. decrease the hydroxide concentration.
   D. decrease the calcium concentration.

   C Acid will tend to reduce the amount of hydroxide in solution, which will shift the equilibrium in Reaction 1 to the right, promoting tooth decay.

32. If observing Reaction 1 in a laboratory, adding which of the following would have the least effect on its equilibrium?

   A. 0.5 mol of sulfuric acid
   B. 1 mol of hydrochloric acid
   C. 0.33 mol of nitric acid
   D. 0.33 mol of phosphoric acid

   D Sulfuric acid, hydrochloric acid, and nitric acid are all strong acids that will completely dissociate into hydrogen ions and their respective conjugate bases in solution. Phosphoric acid is not a strong acid and does not completely dissociate in solution. Therefore, although all of these solutions will shift the equilibrium of Reaction 1 to the right, phosphoric acid will do this the least because it contributes the least amount of protons of all of the acids listed.

33. Reaction 2 is examined under controlled conditions in order to examine how changes in various factors will affect its equilibrium. An increase in the pressure in the vessel in which the reaction occurs would be expected to:

   A. have no effect on the equilibrium.
   B. shift the equilibrium to the right.
   C. shift the equilibrium to the left.
   D. prevent the reaction from occurring.

   A Ambient pressure affects only those reactions involving gases. For Reaction 2, all reactants and products are in aqueous solution. Surrounding pressure is insignificant to equilibrium.

Passage VI (Questions 34–39)

34. In the absence of air resistance, which of the following quantities remains constant throughout the flight of a projectile?

   I. Horizontal speed
   II. Momentum
   III. Acceleration

   A. I only
   B. II only
   C. I and II only
   D. I and III only

   D Item I is true because a projectile experiences no horizontal force—none to the right, and none to the left; its horizontal speed is constant throughout flight. Item II is not true because a projectile experiences a downward vertical acceleration due to gravity. Its vertical speed therefore changes during flight. It slows during ascent and speeds up during descent. Item III is true because the acceleration due to gravity is an unchanging 9.8 m/s^2 throughout flight.

35. In which trial of Experiment 1 did gravity do the greatest amount of work during the projectile's descent?

- **A.** Trial 1
- **B.** Trial 4
- **C.** Trial 5
- **D.** Trial 8

D Although the path of the projectile is curved (it's a parabola), the work done by gravity during the descent is equal to mgh, where h is the height from which the projectile descends. Since the projectile in Trial 8 reached the greatest height, the work done by gravity during descent will be greatest in this trial.

36. If a ninth trial of Experiment 1 had been performed, and the projectile had traveled a horizontal distance of 28 m, its initial angle of elevation could have been:

- **A.** 22°.
- **B.** 28°.
- **C.** 32°.
- **D.** 38°.

A As the initial angle of elevation increases from 0° to 45°, the horizontal distance the projectile will travel increases. A distance of 28 m is between the distances traveled by the projectiles in Trials 2 and 3, but is closer to the distance traveled in Trial 2. Therefore, the initial angle of elevation should be between 20° and 30°, and be closer to 20°. Choice A is best.

37. In Trial 3 of Experiment 1, what was the ratio of the projectile's kinetic energy at impact to its kinetic energy at launch?

- **A.** $1\sqrt{2}$
- **B.** 1
- **C.** $\sqrt{2}$
- **D.** 2

B The passage states that effects due to the air were negligible in Experiment 1, so total mechanical energy would be conserved. Since the potential energy is the same at launch as at impact, this means the kinetic energy is also the same at impact as at launch. Therefore, the desired ratio is 1.

38. What was the approximate speed of the projectile in Trial 3 of Experiment 2 as it impacted the ground?

- **A.** 30 m/s
- **B.** 44 m/s
- **C.** 53 m/s
- **D.** 62 m/s

B For the projectile in Trial 3, the horizontal speed v_x remains a constant 30 m/s during flight. Its vertical speed v_y increases from 0 to $at = gt = (10 \text{ m/s}^2)(3.2 \text{ s}) = 32$ m/s at impact. Therefore, the total speed of the projectile at impact is:

$$v = \sqrt{v_x^2 + v_y^2} = \sqrt{30^2 + 32^2}$$
$$\approx \sqrt{32^2 + 32^2}$$
$$= \sqrt{32^2 \cdot 2}$$
$$= 32\sqrt{2}$$
$$\approx 32(1.4)$$
$$\approx 45 \text{ m/s}$$

39. If Experiment 2 were performed a second time, with the initial height set at 125 m, what would be the expected flight time for the projectiles?

- **A.** 5 sec
- **B.** 6 sec
- **C.** 7 sec
- **D.** 8 sec

A Since the initial vertical velocity of each projectile is zero, the time t it takes to fall to the ground is given by the equation $y = (1/2)gt^2$, where y is the initial height. Solving this equation for t, we get $t = \sqrt{2y / g}$. So, if $y = 125$ m, we find that:

$$t = \sqrt{2(125 \text{ m})/(10 \text{ m/s}^2)} = 5 \text{ sec}$$

Passage VII (Questions 40–45)

40. Regarding the reaction taking place in Experiment 1, which of the following statements must be true?

  A. The free-energy change is positive.
  B. The free-energy change is negative.
  C. The free energy does not change.
  D. The free-energy change is equal to the voltage.

B The voltmeter registers a voltage for the reaction, which means that the reaction proceeds spontaneously; electrons are exchanged between the two compartments in the cell via the wire. For any spontaneous reaction, the free-energy change, ΔG, is negative.

Choice A is wrong because a positive free-energy change would indicate a nonspontaneous reaction, which would mean, in turn, that the voltmeter would fail to register a voltage. Choice C is wrong because, as explained, positive voltage indicates negative free energy. Choice D, too, is wrong. Voltage and free-energy change are related by the equation $\Delta G = -nFx$, where x is the cell potential or voltage.

41. If it is known that $Z(s)$ for Experiment 1 is solid magnesium, the student should determine that the identity for $Y(s)$ is:

  A. barium.
  B. beryllium.
  C. zinc.
  D. cadmium.

B For the reaction in Experiment 1, voltage is 0.5 V. For the oxidation of magnesium, voltage = 2.4 V, as shown in Table 1.

Recall that $E_{reaction} = E_{ox} + E_{red}$; $0.5\ V = 2.4\ V + E_{red}$; $E_{red} = -1.9\ V$. Examining Table 1 once again, you find that the reduction potential of -1.9 V corresponds to the reduction of Be^{2+} to form Be^0.

42. Which of the following could be the identities of $Y^{2+}(aq)$ and $Z(s)$ in Experiment 2?

  A. $Be^{2+}(aq)$ and $Mn(s)$
  B. $Mg^{2+}(aq)$ and $Ba(s)$
  C. $Cd^{2+}(aq)$ and $Zn(s)$
  D. $Zn^{2+}(aq)$ and $Be(s)$

A In Experiment 2, the reaction generates zero voltage, which means the reaction is nonspontaneous. The reaction potential for this cell must therefore be less than zero. Examining Table 1, together with the answer choices, you learn that:

(Choice A:) $Be^{2+} + Mn^0 \rightarrow Be^0 + Mn^{2+}$ $E = -0.7\ V$
(Choice B:) $Mg^{2+} + Ba^0 \rightarrow Mg^0 + Ba^{2+}$ $E = +0.5\ V$
(Choice C:) $Cd^{2+} + Zn^0 \rightarrow Cd^0 + Zn^{2+}$ $E = +0.4\ V$
(Choice D:) $Zn^{2+} + Be^0 \rightarrow Zn^0 + Be^{2+}$ $E = +1.1\ V$

Among those listed in the choices, only the reaction involving beryllium and manganese shows a reaction potential less than zero.

43. The student conducts a fourth experiment by connecting a voltmeter to the electrodes of another galvanic cell. If the voltmeter reads 0.6 V, what conclusion can the student draw?

  A. Neither half-reaction is present in Table 1.
  B. At least one of the half-reactions is not present in Table 1.
  C. At least one of the half-reactions is present in Table 1.
  D. Both half-reactions are present in Table 1.

B There is no difference of 0.6 V between any pair of half-reactions in Table 1, which means that one of them is not known. It could be that both are unknown, but this does not HAVE to be true.

44. Among the species listed in Table 1, which is the strongest reducing agent?

A. $Cd^{2+}(aq)$
B. $Cd(s)$
C. $Ba^{2+}(aq)$
D. $Ba(s)$

D A reducing agent is itself oxidized, and an oxidizing agent is itself reduced. The strongest reducing agent is that which most readily undergoes oxidation. Ba^{2+} and Cd^{2+} are positively charged and are not likely to undergo further oxidation; they will not "want" to lose additional electrons. The answer, therefore, is neutral Ba or neutral Cd.

For the two half-reactions involving Ba and Cd, ascertain the oxidation of the *reverse* half-reaction by taking the reduction potential and changing its sign (negative to positive, or positive to negative).

$$Ba^0 \rightarrow Ba^{2+} + 2e^- \quad E = +2.9 \text{ V}$$
$$Cd^0 \rightarrow Cd^{2+} + 2e^- \quad E = +0.4 \text{ V}$$

Barium shows a greater oxidation potential than does cadmium.

45. The positive electrode in Figure 1 is the:

A. anode, where reduction takes place.
B. anode, where oxidation takes place.
C. cathode, where reduction takes place.
D. cathode, where oxidation takes place.

C In a galvanic cell, the positive electrode is the cathode.
Recall the mnemonic AN OX and RED CAT:
OXidation occurs at the ANode.
REDuction occurs at the CAThode.

Passage VIII (Questions 46–50)

46. What is the frictional force on a sphere of glycerin of radius 1 cm falling at a speed of 1.6 m/s through water?

A. 3×10^{-5} N
B. 3×10^{-4} N
C. 2.5×10^{-3} N
D. 2.5×10^{-2} N

B Since Table 1 tells us that the viscosity of water is $\eta = 1 \times 10^{-3}$ N-s/m^2, the equation given in the passage for the frictional force yields:

$$
\begin{aligned}
F_f &= 6\pi\eta rv \\
&= 6\pi(1 \times 10^{-3} \text{ N-s/m}^2)(10^{-2} \text{ m})(1.6 \text{ m/s}) \\
&= 3 \times 10^{-4} \text{ N}
\end{aligned}
$$

47. For an object descending through fluid, which of the following best describes the change in frictional force as the object's speed increases?

A. Linear and increasing
B. Linear and decreasing
C. Constant
D. Quadratic and increasing

A $F_f = 6\pi\eta rv$, so it is linear and increases with increasing speed.

48. Two spherical drops with equal radii fall through the air. One is composed of glycerin and the other of ethyl alcohol. Which would be expected to reach the greater terminal velocity?

A. Ethyl alcohol, because it has the lower viscosity

B. Ethyl alcohol, because it has the lower density

C. Glycerin, because it has the higher viscosity

D. Glycerin, because it has the higher density

D The two drops are of equal volume and fall through the same medium. Table 1 shows that glycerin is more dense than ethyl alcohol. This means that the mass and weight of the glycerin drop are greater than that of the ethyl alcohol drop. Because the drops are of equal volume and fall through the same medium, they experience identical forces of buoyancy. [Buoyancy = F_b = (density of the displaced fluid)(volume of fluid displaced)(g).] At terminal velocity, the glycerin drop must experience greater *frictional* force than the ethyl alcohol drop in order for its greater weight to be compensated by greater frictional force. Examine the equation set forth in the passage. Frictional force is proportional to velocity, radius, and viscosity (of the air). For these two equal-size drops falling through the same medium, viscosity (of the air) and radius are equal. Differences in frictional force are attributable only to differences in velocity. Since, at terminal velocity, the frictional force for glycerin must exceed the frictional force for ethyl alcohol, the terminal velocity of the glycerin must exceed that of the ethyl alcohol.

Choices A and C are wrong because in the equation set forth in the passage, viscosity refers to the viscosity of the medium through which the spheres travel, not to the viscosity of the spheres themselves. Choice B is wrong because lower density will make not for a greater terminal velocity but rather for a lower one.

49. Which of the following will affect the buoyant force experienced by a solid object falling through a fluid?

A. Density of the object

B. Density of the fluid

C. Speed of the object

D. Viscosity of the fluid

B The buoyant force exerted on an object is given by the equation: F_b = (density of the displaced fluid)(volume of fluid displaced)(g). Among the listed factors, only density of the fluid affects buoyant force.

50. If an object is at rest inside a container of fluid (not at the top or bottom), then:

A. the object and fluid have equal densities.

B. the object and fluid have equal viscosities.

C. the frictional force exceeds the object's weight.

D. this situation is impossible.

A If the object is at rest, then frictional force is zero, so buoyant force equals weight. Since the object has the same volume as the fluid it is displacing, the object and fluid must have the same density.

Free-Standing Questions (51–55)

51. A chamber at constant temperature contains 10 moles of helium gas and 1 mole of neon gas. Which of the following is NOT true?

    A. The average speed of the helium atoms is greater than the average speed of the neon atoms.

    B. The partial pressure due to the helium atoms is greater than the partial pressure due to the neon atoms.

    C. The total mass of helium present in the chamber is greater than the total mass of neon present in the chamber.

    D. The average kinetic energy of the helium atoms is greater than the average kinetic energy of the neon atoms.

D You are searching for a false statement. For any gas, average kinetic energy is proportional to temperature. Choice D, therefore, represents a false statement.

Choice A is wrong because it represents a true statement. Since the two gases have equal kinetic energy, and kinetic energy $= 1/2 mv^2$, the gas molecules of lesser mass must have greater velocity. Choice B, too, represents a true statement. The partial pressure of any gas, g, within a mixture of gases is equal to the fraction:

$$\frac{\text{number of moles of gas, } g, \text{ present in mixture}}{\text{total number of moles of all gases present in mixture}}$$

In this sample, the number of helium atoms is greater than the number of neon atoms, and helium's partial pressure is therefore greater than neon's. Choice C is wrong because it, too, makes a true statement:

(10 moles He) × (4 g/mole) = 40 g;
(1 mole Ne) × (20 g/mole) = 20 g.

52. Which of the following subatomic particles would experience the greatest force when exposed to an electric field?

    A. An alpha particle

    B. A beta particle

    C. A proton

    D. A neutron

A A particle exposed to an electric field experiences a force proportional to the magnitude of its own charge. Recall the charge associated with each of the listed particles: alpha: +2, beta: –1, proton: +1, neutron: 0. The charge magnitude on the alpha particle is 2 and is greater than that on any of the other listed particles.

53. A student prepares a 1 molal aqueous solution of each of the following salts. Which solution will show the greatest boiling point elevation?

    A. NaCl (aq)

    B. $MgCl_2 (aq)$

    C. $NaNO_3 (aq)$

    D. $MgSO_4 (aq)$

B The degree of boiling point elevation (or freezing point depression) produced by any solute is proportional to the number of ions (or particles) into which its molecule dissociates when dissolved. On dissociation, the $MgCl_2$ molecule generates three separate ions: one Mg^+ ion and two Cl^- ions. All other listed salts generate two ions only.

54. An object of specific gravity 0.4 and volume 0.5 m^3 is floating in a fluid of specific gravity 2. What percentage of the object's volume lies above the surface of the fluid?

   A. 20%
   B. 40%
   C. 60%
   D. 80%

D If an object floats in a fluid, then the buoyant force must balance the object's weight. The weight of an object whose density is ρ_{obj} is given by $mg = \rho_{obj}Vg$. Archimedes' principle tells us that the buoyant force on the object is $\rho_{fluid}V_{sub}g$, where V_{sub} denotes the volume of the object that is submerged. Equating these two expressions, we find that

$$\rho_{obj}Vg = \rho_{fluid}V_{sub}g$$

$$\frac{V_{sub}}{V} = \frac{\rho_{obj}}{\rho_{fluid}}$$

Therefore, the fraction of the object's volume that is submerged in this case is $(0.4)/2 = 0.2$. This means that 0.8, or 80% of the object's volume is *above* the surface of the fluid.

55. Samples of which of the following molecules will exhibit the strongest intermolecular interactions?

   A. O_2
   B. N_2
   C. CO_2
   D. H_2O

D Water exhibits hydrogen bonding, which makes its intermolecular attractions stronger than those of the other three molecules listed. As a consequence, water is the only one of the four that is liquid at room temperature.

Passage IX (Questions 56–62)

56. Solar radiation with which of the following properties will make the most energy available in storage by the device?

   A. A long wavelength
   B. A high velocity
   C. A high frequency
   D. A long period of vibration

C For electromagnetic radiation, higher frequency is associated with greater energy.

Choice B is wrong because in a given medium, the speed of light is constant. In a vacuum, it is 3.0×10^8 m/s. Choice A refers to a long wavelength which, in turn, denotes low frequency, since (wavelength) × (frequency) = speed. The phrase "long period of vibration" indicates a cycle of relatively long endurance. That, too, denotes long wavelength and low frequency.

57. Reaction 1 occurs spontaneously at high temperatures. The most probable cause for this phenomenon is that at high temperatures:

   A. increasing entropy compensates for increasing enthalpy.
   B. increasing entropy compensates for decreasing enthalpy.
   C. decreasing entropy compensates for increasing enthalpy.
   D. decreasing entropy compensates for decreasing enthalpy.

A If a reaction is endothermic, its system absorbs heat from the surroundings, and the enthalpy of the reaction (ΔH) is positive. Positive enthalpy is disfavored, however, and an endothermic reaction will only proceed spontaneously if its entropy is sufficiently positive to generate, overall, a negative free energy. In Reaction 1, the number of moles of products exceeds the number of moles of reactants, which, in this case, indicates that entropy increases. The reaction is spontaneous because increased entropy compensates for increased enthalpy and generates, overall, negative free energy.

58. The heat of formation of $SO_3(g)$ is –396 kJ/mol. What is the heat of formation of $SO_2(g)$?

A. –396 kJ/mol
B. –297 kJ/mol
C. –198 kJ/mol
D. –495 kJ/mol

B You may work the problem by referring to Reaction 1 or Reaction 2. Recall that the heat of formation of an element in its standard state is zero. Selecting Reaction 1, remember that:

$$H_{f\,reaction} = H_{f\,products} - H_{f\,reactants}$$

$$198\ kJ = (2\ mol)(H) - (2\ mol)(-396\ kJ/mol)$$
$$H = -297\ kJ/mol$$

59. How many moles of sulfur dioxide would be needed to generate enough energy to power a 60 W light bulb for one week straight, assuming 100% efficiency?

A. 6.1 mol
B. 15.3 mol
C. 183 mol
D. 367 mol

D 2 mol/198,000 J × 60 J/s × 60 s/min × 60 min/hr × 24 hr/day × 7 day/week = 366.5 mol/week.

60. One of the advantages of the solar energy conversion device is that the energy can be stored indefinitely and released when desired. That is because:

A. all of the reactants and products are in the gas phase.
B. the endothermic reaction takes place only at high temperatures.
C. the exothermic reaction takes place only in the presence of a catalyst.
D. the exothermic reaction releases more energy than is stored by the endothermic reaction.

C Reaction 2 requires a catalyst. Until the catalyst is supplied, energy remains housed within the chemical bonds resulting from Reaction 1. When the catalyst is introduced, Reaction 2 occurs, and the energy is released as heat.

Choices A and B make true statements but do not answer the question. The gas phase and high temperature do not explain how the device stores energy until its release is sought. Choice D makes a false statement. The exothermic reaction can release no more energy than is absorbed during the exothermic reaction; *recall that energy is conserved.*

61. The formation of oxygen gas in Reaction 1 would be promoted by:

A. increasing the pressure of the reaction chamber.
B. decreasing the pressure of the reaction chamber.
C. increasing the concentration of sulfur dioxide in the reaction chamber.
D. decreasing the concentration of sulfur trioxide in the reaction chamber.

B The left side of Reaction 1 shows 2 moles of gas, and the right side shows 3. Pressure on the right is therefore greater than pressure on the left. In a limited sense, pressure is a "product" of the reaction. Applying LeChatelier's principle, you know that the removal of any product drives a reaction to the right. Alternatively you may think of pressure as a "stress." Alleviation of the stress allows the reaction to move more readily in the direction that regenerates the stress. Since reduction of pressure drives the reaction forward, and oxygen is generated in the forward reaction, reducing pressure promotes the formation of oxygen.

Choice A is wrong because increased pressure would drive the reaction to the left and reduce oxygen formation. Choice C is wrong as well. Sulfur dioxide appears on the right side of the reaction. Increasing its concentration will drive the reaction to the left and, once again, reduce oxygen formation. Choice D is wrong for analogous reasons. Sulfur trioxide is a reactant. Reducing the concentration of a reactant tends to drive a reaction to the left. That would mean, yet again, reducing the formation of oxygen.

62. If 1 mole of oxygen gas is consumed by Reaction 2 over the course of 1 hour, what is the power of the conversion device?

  A. 3 W
  B. 22 W
  C. 55 W
  D. 330 W

C For every mole of oxygen gas consumed, 198 kJ of energy are released. Power is measured in watts (W); 1 watt = 1 joule/second. Simple algebra reveals that:

$$\frac{198{,}000 \text{ J}}{1 \text{ hr}} \times \frac{1 \text{ hr}}{3600 \text{ sec}} = 55 \text{ J/sec} = 55 \text{ W}$$

Passage X (Questions 63–68)

63. Which of the following graphs best relates *E*, the total energy of the spring and mass system, to the initial displacement, *D*, from rest position?

A.

C.
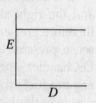

B.
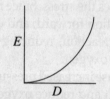

D.

B The total energy of the mass and spring system is equal to the total energy at any point during oscillation. In particular, it is equal to the total energy just before the mass is released from rest. At this point, the kinetic energy of the mass is zero, so the total energy is equal to the elastic potential energy of the spring, which is $(1/2)kX^2$. So, at $X = D$, the potential energy is $(1/2)kD^2$, and this will be the total energy of the spring and mass system at any point during oscillation. The slope of $E = (1/2)kD^2$ is best shown in graph B.

64. If the mass, while moving to the left at a distance *X* to the left of the rest position, collided elastically with a block and transferred all of its momentum to the block, how much kinetic energy would the block have?

  A. $1/2 \, kX^2$
  B. $kD^2 - kX^2$
  C. kX^2
  D. $1/2 \, kD^2 - 1/2 \, kX^2$

D Total energy originally in the mass–spring system was $1/2 \, kD^2$, and after the collision the total energy left is $1/2 \, kX^2$, so the block must have taken away the difference between the two.

65. Which of the following changes to the system would produce the greatest increase in the block's speed at a given displacement from the resting position?

  A. Increasing the mass of the block and the spring constant of the spring
  B. Decreasing the mass of the block and the spring constant of the spring
  C. Increasing the mass of the block and decreasing the spring constant of the spring
  D. Decreasing the mass of the block and increasing the spring constant of the spring

D Examine Equation 1 and note that speed, v, is directly proportional to the square root of k and inversely proportional to the square root of m. To increase the square root of any variable, the variable itself must be increased. To increase the value of a fraction, the numerator must be increased and/or the denominator decreased. Choice D indicates that the numerator is increased *and* the denominator decreased.

Choice A refers to increased denominator and numerator. Choice B refers to decreased denominator and numerator. Choice C refers to an increased denominator and a decreased numerator, which surely would decrease the block's velocity.

66. As the block moves through the point shown in Figure 2, the magnitude of its acceleration:

    A. increases.
    B. decreases.
    C. remains unchanged with a positive value.
    D. is equal to zero.

B Don't confuse velocity with acceleration. Acceleration follows from force. When the spring is fully compressed or fully expanded, it is "set" to deliver maximum force. As it then moves the block toward the resting position, the acceleration *declines* although velocity increases until, *at* the resting position, acceleration is zero and velocity reaches its maximum. As the block then moves past the center, toward either compression or extension, the spring subjects it to a negative acceleration ("deceleration"). The negative acceleration increases as the spring undergoes increased compression or expansion. Velocity decreases until negative acceleration reaches a maximum and velocity is zero.

Choice A would be correct if the question concerned not acceleration, but velocity. Choice C would be correct if the question concerned total energy of the system. Choice D would be correct if the question concerned (1) acceleration at the resting position or (2) velocity at the terminal positions.

67. Which of the following combinations would result in the total energy in the mass–spring system being doubled?

    A. m unchanged, k doubled, D halved
    B. m doubled, k doubled, D unchanged
    C. m halved, k doubled, D doubled
    D. m doubled, k unchanged, D doubled

B Total energy in the system is $1/2kD^2$, independent of m. Total energy is multiplied by a factor of .5 in A, 2 in B, 8 in C, and 4 in D, so B is correct.

68. The mass is now placed between two identical springs, each attached to a wall at the other end, such that the total energy of the system is 0 when the mass is midway between the walls. Now, if the mass were displaced a distance D from the rest position and released, by what factor would its maximum velocity from the original setup be multiplied?

    A. 1
    B. $\sqrt{2}$
    C. 2
    D. 4

B $v_{max} = \sqrt{2E/m}$ where E is the total energy in the system. Using two springs doubles the total energy in the system, which multiplies the maximum velocity obtained by the block by $\sqrt{2}$.

Passage XI (Questions 69–73)

69. What is the energy of an electron occupying the third quantum level ($n = 3$) of a hydrogen atom?

    A. -1.96×10^{-17} J
    B. -2.42×10^{-19} J
    C. -6.54×10^{-18} J
    D. -7.27×10^{-19} J

B Apply the equation set forth in the passage:

$$E_n = -E_g \left(\frac{1}{n^2} \right) = -(2.18 \times 10^{-18} \text{ J}) \times \left(\frac{1}{3^2} \right) =$$

$$-(2.18 \times 10^{-18} \text{ J}) \times 1/9 = -2.42 \times 10^{-19}$$

Having recognized that the relevant calculation was 2.18×10^{-18} J $\times 1/9$, you might have (1) divided E_g by 10 to arrive at 2.18×10^{-19} and (2) then looked among the answer choices for a slightly larger value.

70. Which of the lists below could represent the wavelengths of the electromagnetic radiation emitted by hydrogen atoms?

   A. 410 nm, 434 nm, 486 nm, 580 nm
   B. 410 nm, 434 nm, 486 nm, 656 nm
   C. 410 nm, 486 nm, 580 nm, 656 nm
   D. 410 nm, 486 nm, 628 nm, 656 nm

B The emitted wavelengths correspond to the energy levels that the electron is "permitted" to occupy, and they also correspond to the emission spectrum shown in Figure 1. Figure 1 shows three bands between 400 nm and 500 nm and one band between 600 nm and 700 nm. Among the choices, only choice B satisfies that condition. The values 410 nm, 434 nm, and 486 nm fall between 400 nm and 500 nm. The value 656 nm falls between 600 nm and 700 nm.

Choice A is incorrect because it presents a value that falls between 500 nm and 600 nm. Moreover, it fails to present a value between 600 nm and 700 nm. Choices C and D are erroneous for analogous reasons.

71. When an electron moves, within a hydrogen atom, from the third quantum level ($n = 3$) to the second quantum level ($n = 2$), which of the following is true?

   A. ΔE will be positive and a photon will be emitted.
   B. ΔE will be positive and a photon will be absorbed.
   C. ΔE will be negative and a photon will be emitted.
   D. ΔE will be negative and a photon will be absorbed.

C From the passage and your own review, you know that an electron falling from a higher energy state to a lower energy state emits energy and ΔE is negative.

72. A photon of which of the following wavelengths will have the highest energy?

   A. 400 nm
   B. 500 nm
   C. 600 nm
   D. 700 nm

A The energy of a photon of frequency f is given by $E = hf$ (a formula that is also included in the passage). Since $f = c/\lambda$, where c is the speed of light, the energy E can be written in terms of wavelength: $E = hc/\lambda$. This shows that the energy of a photon is inversely proportional to the wavelength, and therefore, the shorter the wavelength, the greater the photon's energy. Of the choices given, A is the shortest wavelength.

73. An increase in an electron's quantum number will produce:

   A. increased stability and increased energy.
   B. increased stability and decreased energy.
   C. decreased stability and decreased energy.
   D. decreased stability and increased energy.

D Higher quantum number means higher energy state. Recall from your review of thermodynamics and subatomic chemistry that lower energy is associated with greater stability. Higher energy is associated with lower stability.

Free-Standing Questions (74–77)

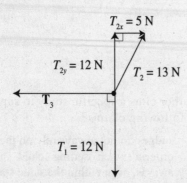

74. The figure above (not drawn to scale) shows three cables under tension, all connected to a common point and in static equilibrium. If $T_1 = 12$ N and $T_2 = 13$ N, what is the magnitude of $\mathbf{T}_3$?

    A. 1 N
    B. 5 N
    C. 12.5 N
    D. 25 N

B   In order for the system to be in static equilibrium, the vertical forces must balance and the horizontal forces must balance. Once we draw the vertical and horizontal components of $\mathbf{T}_2$, we see that $T_{2y} = 12$ N, because $\mathbf{T}_{2y}$ must balance $\mathbf{T}_1$. Now, since $\mathbf{T}_2$ has magnitude 13 N and a vertical component of 12 N, the Pythagorean theorem says that its horizontal component is $T_{2x} = \sqrt{13^2 - 12^2} = 5$ N. Since $\mathbf{T}_3$ must balance this horizontal component, we conclude that $T_3 = 5$ N.

75. Barium fluoride is a slightly soluble salt with $K_{sp} = 1.7 \times 10^{-6}$. If the concentration of barium ions in a saturated aqueous solution is equal to 4.3×10^{-3} M, what is the concentration of fluoride ions in the solution?

    A. 4.0×10^{-4} M
    B. 2.0×10^{-2} M
    C. 4.0×10^{-2} M
    D. 2.0×10^{-1} M

B   Your review of inorganic chemistry will remind you that for any soluble salt $A_bC_{d'}$ the solubility product, $K_{sp'}$ is equal to the product $[A]^b \times [C]^d$ with the concentrations of A and C measured at saturation. In this instance, the solubility product $= K_{sp} = [Ba^{2+}]^1[F^-]^2 = 1.7 \times 10^{-6} = (4.3 \times 10^{-3})(x^2); 4.0 \times 10^{-4} = x^2; x = 2.0 \times 10^{-2}$.

76. An object of mass m is tied to a string of length r. The object is whirled around and maintained in a circular path by the tension T in the string. Which of the following graphs best represents the change in v as the path's radius, r, is changed?

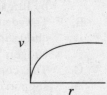

C   The tension in the string provides the necessary centripetal force: $T = mv^2/r$. Solving this equation for v, we get $v = \sqrt{(T/m)r}$. So, if T and m are constant, then v is proportional to $\sqrt{r}$. This is best shown by the graph in C.

77. In the circuit above, what is the current through the 6-ohm resistor?

    A.   1.5 A
    B.   1.75 A
    C.   2 A
    D.   2.5

A   The effective resistance of the parallel combination is 2 ohms, because if $1/3 + 1/(4 + 2) = 1/R$, then $R = 2$. Since this is in series with the 6-ohm resistor, the overall resistance of the entire circuit is $2 + 6 = 8$ ohms. Therefore, the current through the 6-ohm resistor is (12 volts)/(8 ohms) = 1.5 amps.

ANSWERS AND EXPLANATIONS

VERBAL REASONING

Questions 78–137

Passage I (Questions 78–83)

78. Which of the following statements is most supported by the passage?

A. The compliance gap measures the court costs of child support proceedings unpaid by litigants and covered by state budgets.

B. The adequacy gap measures the court costs of child support proceedings unfunded by state budgets and covered by federal assistance.

C. The compliance gap measures the child support dollar amount awarded in courts and unpaid by parents.

D. The adequacy gap measures the child support dollar amount awarded in courts and unpaid by parents.

C The question requires that you infer from your reading the meaning of the two phrases. "Adequacy gap" seems to refer to the difference between the "realistic...cost of child rearing" (line 17) and the amounts awarded. The "compliance gap" can only mean the difference between the amounts awarded and the amounts actually paid.

Choices A and B seek to mislead you with information about court costs, which is not directly relevant to the passage. Choice D confuses the concepts of adequacy and compliance.

79. The author cites a specific study to support which of the following claims?

    I. Judges do not always rely on the same criteria when setting child support awards, even within the same state.

    II. Fairness dictates that noncustodial spouses in comparable circumstances should be treated alike.

    III. The "compliance gap" is likely to increase.

A. I

B. I and II only

C. II and III only

D. I, II, and III

A Sentence 2 of paragraph 3 (lines 28–30) presents the meaning of Statement I in different words and sentence 4 (lines 33–37) refers to a Colorado study in support of the claim. The author asserts Statement II in lines 25–28 of that same paragraph as a given ethical precept, but does not support it by citing a study. Similarly, the author's forecast about the compliance gap (lines 21–24) is not buttressed by a specific study or finding. Census data is given to document the existing compliance gap, not to support the prediction of an increase in the future.

80. Which of the following is most analogous to the relationship between the flat rate and income shares models described in the passage?

    A. Local telephone charge at a monthly flat rate or a rate based on the amont of monthly usage.

    B. Long-distance telephone rates based on a flat rate per minute or based on mileage between the call origination phone and the call destination phone.

    C. Monthly loan interest at a fixed rate or at a variable rate

    D. An income tax system based on a single tax rate or on a graduated rate that escalates with income.

D The essential difference between the flat rate and income shares models is that the latter is calculated based on relative incomes. An analogous relationship exists between a flat rate tax system and a graduated system, where rate increases with income. Choice A presents a relationship that might be analogous if the income shares model based support contributions on the amount of time each parent spent with the children. Choice B might be analogous if the income shares model were based on the amount of time each parent had to travel to visit with the children. As for choice C, under a variable interest rate, although the rate itself would change over time, at any one point in time everyone would pay the same percentage in interest. Under the "income shares" model, different people would pay different percentages at the same point in time.

81. Which of the following conclusions can justifiably be drawn from the author's discussion of judges?

    A. Individual judges are inconsistent in the criteria they apply.

    B. Judges often set awards according to capricious standards.

    C. The amount of child support may be different depending on the judge who awards it.

    D. If each state were to establish set criteria for child support awards, noncustodial parents would be treated fairly by the courts.

C Lines 30–33 state that the award "will depend on the judge who sets the support award." Choices A and B are contradicted by lines 25–28, which state that individual judges are "fairly consistent" in the awards they apply. Also, if individual states were to set criteria, awards might be different from state to state and therefore not necessarily fair (choice D).

82. Which of the following statements, if true, would most strengthen the position of those who oppose leaving child support legislation up to the individual states?

    A. State governments should protect the "life, liberty, and pursuit of happiness" of the nation's children.

    B. Divorced individuals often do not live in the same part of the country as their former spouses.

    C. The federal government can best evaluate statistical variations in the cost of living index from state to state.

    D. The federal government has a constitutional obligation to ensure due process of law for all persons, including those involved in divorce proceedings.

B The final sentence of the passage mentions the author's concern that approaches that vary from state to state "will not bring about parity."

None of the other choices strengthen the claim that guidelines should not be left to the individual states, or that the federal government should intervene. Choice A still leaves the discretion to the states to decide how best to protect children's interests. Choice C does not indicate why policy should be made on a federal level. Finally, the issue of the passage is not due process under the law, but whether law on the state level can adequately protect children affected by divorce proceedings. Therefore, D does not strengthen the claim that child support legislation should not be left up to the states.

83. A recent theory suggests that children of divorced spouses whose custodial parent received regular and sufficient child support payments will score higher on scales measuring self-esteem and self-confidence than those whose parents do not comply with court-ordered support. Social workers who accept this theory would be LEAST likely to support which of the following?

A. Support groups at the local level that help parents who do not meet child support obligations deal with the resulting psychological issues

B. Support groups at the local level for custodial parents and their children who do not receive regular and sufficient child support

C. Federal regulations that make it more difficult for parents to avoid compliance with court-ordered support judgments

D. State laws requiring automatic deductions from payroll checks of parents convicted of failing to pay child support

A Given the sense of the question, social workers would less likely be concerned about the psychological needs of payment avoiders than about those who do not receive adequate support (choice B).

Choices C and D both present propositions designed to improve child support compliance, and social workers would be likely to support them.

Passage II (Questions 84–90)

84. The passage suggests that Africans' long-standing coexistence with elephants has caused them to regard elephants primarily with:

A. appreciation.
B. contempt.
C. fear.
D. reverence.

A According to lines 10–13, to Africans, "the elephant is known in fuller dimensions. It has been a source of food, materials, and riches; a fearsome rival for resources; and a highly visible, provocative neighbor." The choice that best characterizes the full range of an elephants' impact on Africans is A.

Although "fearsome" is mentioned in the description of the elephant's role in African people's lives, choice C can be ruled out because fear is, according to the passage, by no means the defining attitude of Africans toward elephants. Choices B and D are not supported by the passage because neither hate nor worship characterizes Africans' relationship to the elephant.

85. Suppose that the elephants in a particular region of Africa were to disappear. How would this new information affect the author's claims about the animal's impact on the artistic product of humans living in the area?

A. Owing to their scarcity, talismanic objects carved from elephant tusks would acquire considerable value as magical totems.

B. Communities would barter their local products for cultural works and artisan crafts from communities that remained physically close to elephants.

C. The dance and song of the local inhabitants would gradually lose all traces of elephant imagery.

D. Elephant imagery would continue to play an important role in the local culture.

D Lines 14–16 of paragraph 1 furnish the justification: "Even in areas where the elephant has now vanished, it persists as a symbol in expressive culture."

Neither choice A nor choice B is supported by the passage. Choice C is excluded because it directly contradicts the substance of lines 14–16.

86. Suppose it is discovered that muralists in a number of African communities portrayed jaguars as provisioners of food, material, and wealth; as dangerous competitors for resources; and as dramatically inspirational cohabitants. How would this information affect the author's claims about the interchangeability of symbolic function?

- **A.** It would support the claim that culture and circumstance help determine which qualities are ascribed to which animals.
- **B.** It would support the claim that some people believe the gap between animals and humans to be enormous.
- **C.** It would weaken the claim that Senegalese glass paintings are comparable in their imagery to Noah's ark.
- **D.** It would weaken the claim that the elephant may be viewed as a microcosm.

A Lines 11–13 explain that in African culture, the elephant is known as "a source of food, material, and riches; a fearsome rival for resources; and a highly visible, provocative neighbor." The question represents these same characteristics in different words and ascribes them to the jaguar, in effect making the elephant interchangeable with the jaguar in a different cultural milieu (see lines 27–30 for the author's observation of interchangeability). None of the statements presented by the other options would be affected by the new information.

87. The claim that elephant imagery in African culture reveals information about Africans' social lives is based mainly on:

- **A.** western European cultural analysis.
- **B.** African representations of the microcosm and macrocosm.
- **C.** Nigerian thorn carvings.
- **D.** Ethiopian popular art.

B The final two sentences of paragraph 3 contain the relevant information: "...African depictions of the elephant have as much to say about human society as about the animal itself...[and] historical events, social responsibilities, religious beliefs, and political relationships are the primary subjects of elephant imagery." The author makes this statement in the context of a discussion of the elephant as both microcosm and macrocosm.

Choice A might tempt you, but you don't know if the author writes from a European, African, Asian, Latin, or other perspective. Nigerian carvings (choice C) and Ethiopian art (choice D) show animals treated equally; this does not give us information specifically about the relevence of elephant imagery to Africans' social lives.

88. Levi-Strauss and Mary Midgley are cited in the passage in order to support the point that:

- **A.** African cultures tend to anthropomorphize to a much greater degree than European cultures.
- **B.** science scholars have systematically identified a number of human qualities in animals.
- **C.** the human capacity to liken human characteristics to animal traits is a complex and contradictory phenomenon.
- **D.** anthropological scholars have achieved a general consensus of opinion with regard to anthropomorphism.

C Paragraph 4 presents the contradictory points of view. On the one hand, "finding *human* traits in *animals* is...a fundamental activity of the human mind." At the same time, among nonscientists, "finding *animal* traits in *humans* tends to be seen...as pernicious and degrading." Nothing in the passage supports any of the other options; in fact, the paragraph just cited tends to contradict them.

89. According to the passage, a gap exists between all of the following EXCEPT:

   A. African and Western versions of elephant imagery.

   B. the size of an elephant and its symbolic import.

   C. actual elephants and elephant imagery.

   D. the perspective of the elephant as a microcosm and as a macrocosm.

B Remember that you are looking for a statement that is *not* correct. The passage begins with the phrase, "As the largest land animal on the planet, the elephant is a potent symbol..." In addition, lines 39–41 state, "By virtue of its sheer size and prominence the roles [the elephant] plays in art and historical processes are magnified." Therefore the size and symbolic import of the elephant are both large, and there is no gap.

The remainder of paragraph 1 emphasizes the discrepancy between the African and Western modes of elephant imagery, thus negating choice A. Choice C is ruled out by lines 16–18 and lines 47–51, which deal with the differences between the actuality of elephants and images of them. Choice D can be ruled out based on lines 38–44, where the author indicates a difference between the elephant as microcosm and as macrocosm.

90. In can be inferred from the passage that humans view their relationship to animals:

   A. in nearly universal symbols across different cultures.

   B. in varied ways that depend on each culture's symbolic forms.

   C. in superficial and simplistic terms.

   D. in more practical than symbolic terms.

B Lines 44–47 state the case unambiguously: "In Africa as elsewhere, people represent their relationship to animals in multiple ways, and their complex experience of it can be read in the symbolic language of their respective cultures."

Choices A and C contradict the above citation, and run counter to the general sense of the passage. Paragraphs 4 and 5 make choice D incorrect.

Passage III (Questions 91–96)

91. The passage suggests that the facet of artificial intelligence that particularly intrigued early computer scientists was the fact that:

   A. a mechanical apparatus could be taught to translate human languages.

   B. a computer could learn to accomplish thinking tasks completely independently of any live human being.

   C. a machine might be able to perform tasks that required intelligence without the immediate participation of humans.

   D. a machine could teach human beings artificial modes of mental activity.

C Paragraph 1 discusses the pioneer's fascination with the concept of machines performing tasks without the direct participation of human beings, as set forth in choice C. Choice A misrepresents the passage. The author describes language translation as an early project, but not as a fundamental reason why early computer scientists were intrigued by artificial intelligence. Choice B offers an absolute that is not contained in the passage, and choice D inverts the teaching relationship between humans and computers.

92. According to the passage, artificial intelligence programmers initially approached language translation by:

  A. providing computers with independent memory of diverse systems of semiotic linguistic representation.

  B. liberating computers from confinement in semantic-free meaning.

  C. eliminating from translation programs languages with similar vocabulary and parallel syntax.

  D. teaching computers to recognize a word-based message connected to a programmed syntax replacement.

D It rephrases the author's statement, made in the second paragraph, lines 8–11: "Rudimentary efforts to teach computers language translation relied solely on word equivalences programmed in the computer's dictionary and linked to automated syntax substitution." Choice A is incorrect; the author does not state that early programmers supplied computers with "diverse systems" with which to represent language. Choice B reverses the passage's description of disrupted translation: Words, not meaning, limited computer effectiveness. Choice C distorts the reference to languages with similar structures.

93. The author implies that in relation to playing games:

  A. computers will never be able to master the game of chess as well as humans.

  B. chess is the only game in which computers can effectively compete with humans.

  C. computer learning has been generally more effective in the area of game playing than in language translation.

  D. computers usually prevail over human opponents in chess, except against internationally elite linguists.

C It reflects a statement made in the third paragraph: "In the area of game strategy, computers have realized considerably more success than in language translation." Choices A and B are both too strong to be supported by the passage. Choice D distorts the reference in paragraph 3 to computers' vulnerability in chess to human masters: Elite masters of the chess game, not elite linguists, are the ones who can defeat computers.

94. According to passage information, computer defect analysis functions differently from simple data retrieval in that:

  A. it incorporates a program of guidelines to selectively retrieve stored data.

  B. it excludes reductive elimination as a retrieval tool.

  C. it requires detailed inputs as retrieval prompts.

  D. there is no essential difference between the two processes.

A It reflects a statement (lines 36–38) where the author reports that defect identification "include[s] a set of rules as well, which serve to direct the computer's search according to interactive inputs." Choice B inverts the author's meaning. Lines 41–47 explicitly describe reductive elimination as a tool in the service of defect analysis. Choice C misrepresents the author's text, which nowhere implies that detailed prompts are uncharacteristic of simple data retrieval. Choice D contradicts the passage, which explicitly describes the difference between the two processes.

95. Discussing the relation of analytical logic to artificial intelligence, the author states that:

A. coherent linkage of knowledge frames occurs independently of IF/THEN propositions.
B. syllogistic procedures define tuple-based information retrieval.
C. syllogistic principles provide the basis for connecting integral knowledge objects.
D. it is impossible to arrange tuples for medical diagnosis as logically correlated objects.

C Choice C paraphrases information set forth in paragraphs 6 and 7. Choice A misrepresents the relationship between coherent linkage and IF/THEN statements. Choice B distorts the reference to database retrieval at the end of paragraph 6. Choice D presents an absolute, and also reverses textual information (from paragraph 6).

96. For which of the following statements regarding neural networks does the passage offer the most support?

A. Established informational relationships are generally inadequate to bridge nodal synapses.
B. Established informational relationships are wholly unaffected by inputted information.
C. For computers to construct neural links between information nodes, human operators must provide programmed rules of relative probability.
D. Through empirical learning methods, computers can decide and apportion weighted linkage.

D The passage refers to a "computer with the ability to derive its own rules of linkage," and the capacity to determine "relative regulatory influence among contrasting and/or complementary rules" (lines 77–82). Choice D expresses that idea.

Choices A, B, and C make statements opposite to those made by the author (paragraph 8).

Passage IV (Questions 97–102)

97. The main idea of the passage is that:

A. artists serve as mediators between our daily reality and the world of the unconscious.
B. as human society has evolved and become more sophisticated, so has human artistic expression.
C. artistic expression reflects the psychological processes and makeup of its creator.
D. the essential appeal of art is its power to mystify.

C In lines 10–13, the author lists "the skills that go into adult art: coordination, intellect, personality, imagination, creativity, and aesthetic judgment." According to the passage, the making of an artist is "a process as fragile as growing up itself" (line 14). Lines 24–25 state that art is "a positive expression that integrates diverse aspects of personality." Furthermore, in lines 36–38, the author observes that "the imagination...acts in lawful, if unpredictable, ways that are determined by the psyche and the mind."

Although lines 32–33 say that the imagination is "the connector between the conscious and the subconscious"; and lines 55–59 add that artists were believed "able to enter the underworld of the subconscious... but, unlike ordinary mortals, they were then able to return to the realm of the living," this motif represents a subordinate theme and not the main idea of the passage; choice A is wrong. Paragraphs 1, 2, and 5 contain information that may lead you to choose B, but this idea is more implied than directly addressed in the passage. Lines 59–61 claim that "the artist remains a magician whose work can mystify and move us," but this notion, expressed in choice D, is too narrow to be the main idea of the passage.

98. In the context of the passage, the word "genius" (line 30) refers primarily to:

    A. the recognition and appreciation of an artist's ability by critics and the public at large.

    B. the psychological sensitivity to reality that an artist develops.

    C. the intellectual attainments of individual artists.

    D. the neurotic and psychotic manifestations of artistic perception.

B In lines 5–7, the passage states that the artist's imagination "is subject to the taste and outlook of the society that shapes his or her personality," that forms, that is, his or her sensibility. The word "genius" appears in the opening sentence of paragraph 3, in which the author asserts that a psychotic sensibility cannot make truly great art. Later in the same paragraph, imagination appears as "the very glue that holds our personality, intellect, and spirituality together," (lines 34–35). Lines 66–71 of the last paragraph add that "art has the power to penetrate to the core of our being," and "represents its creator's deepest understanding and highest aspirations...our shared beliefs and values," the outside reality an artist creates from, about, and to.

While the author does discuss the response of others to an artist's work (lines 7–9 and 65–71), the passage does not use the response of critics or others as a criterion for evaluating genius. Therefore, choice A is not the best answer in relation to this question. The word "genius" may refer, generally, to one's intellectual capability and/or achievements, but in this passage, it is not used in that sense. Choice C is incorrect. Paragraphs 2 and 3 directly contradict choice D, as explained above.

99. The passage implies that art relates to its audience:

    A. by delivering both a personal and a universal communication from artist to audience.

    B. less intensely today because, no longer associated with magic, its power to mystify and to move has dwindled.

    C. by providing insight into another's creativity only, while science and religion allow us to comprehend ourselves and the universe.

    D. irrespective of an audience's emotional and spiritual needs.

A Lines 38–40 note that "even the most private artistic statements can be understood on some level, even if only an intuitive one," implying a relationship between the intensely personal and the universal. Later, lines 68–71 emphasize that "art represents its creator's deepest understanding and highest aspirations; at the same time, the artist often plays an important role as the articulator of our shared beliefs and values."

Choice B is clearly contradicted by lines 59–62: "Even today, the artist remains a magician whose work can mystify and move us." Choice C claims that we can find no universal truth in art, a statement contradicted by the citations above. Choice D is ruled out by lines 59–62 and 68–71.

100. The passage suggests that the ability to create art:

A. evolved before the imagination evolved.

B. evolved primarily as a survival skill.

C. has been documented to exist as early as two million years ago, when humans first inhabited the Earth.

D. was the result of a long developmental process that occurred within stable societies.

D Lines 51–54 point the way: "[Prehistoric art]... was the culmination of a long development"; and "even the most 'primitive' ethnographic art represents a late stage of development within a stable society." Lines 41–46 state that "the imagination is important...in a way that has real survival value... The ability to make art, in contrast, must have been acquired relatively recently in the course of human evolution." Choices A and B contradict that text. Lines 49–50 establish that the oldest known prehistoric art is dated only 35,000 years ago, which excludes choice C.

101. According to the passage, why is art embarrassing to some people who pride themselves on their civilized rationality?

A. Art's essential mystery frustrates those who like to appear cultivated.

B. Art makes many social sophisticates feel ignorant.

C. Art's simultaneous universality and individual relevance seems paradoxical to some who pride themselves on their logical powers.

D. Art is able to access the most fundamental and private essence of the self.

D Lines 61–62 refer to "civilized people, who do not readily relinquish their veneer of rational control," and in lines 66–67, the author observes that "art has the power to penetrate to the core of our being." Taken together, these two assertions make D the best choice.

Choices A, B, and C may all reflect some element of truth, but they are truths not touched on in the passage.

102. The author's discussion of Sigmund Freud's view of art and artists most supports the claim that:

A. art represents an integrative psychological function rather than an uncontrolled psychic expression.

B. art, which sublimates psychological ambiguity, is superior to that which generates mystery.

C. successful psychotherapy would enable an artist to sublimate the need for artistic expression.

D. development of individual artistic consciousness retraces much of humans' evolutionary past.

A Lines 23–25 state that "art is not simply a negative force at the mercy of our neuroses but a positive expression that integrates diverse aspects of personality." This assertion immediately follows the allusion to Freud, and serves, generally, to negate Freud's hypothesis as presented.

Choice C does not follow logically from the passage; nowhere is it supported by the text. Choice B seeks to confuse you with a hodgepodge of tempting terminology. Paragraph 2 actually does reflect the assertion offered in option D, but it is not directly related to the discussion of Freud.

Passage V (Questions 103–112)

103. The author's claim that "structuralist" criticism represents an attempt to "uproot the critical enterprise" rests on the New Critics' belief that:

A. the complexities of theoretical disciplines should inform all literary commentary.

B. theoretical foundations are totally useless to the task of literary criticism.

C. the essential mission of literature unmasks disguises of similitude and dissimilitude.

D. literary criticism should focus primarily on the literary work.

D By paraphrase, it accurately describes the New Critics' beliefs, as discussed throughout the passage.

Choice A inverts the statement in the passage about the New Critics' appreciation of theoretical approaches. Choice B is an absolute, unsupported by the passage, and choice C distorts the information in the passage.

104. The author most likely believes that New Critics view their opponents as undermining and subjugating literature by:

A. placing a fundamental emphasis on humanistic interpretation.

B. utilizing external discourses as the basis for the critical endeavor.

C. negating the usurpation of literature's unique discourse.

D. rejecting interdisciplinary methodology as a basis for discourse.

B In lines 19–20, the author states that the structuralists subvert the New Criticism's "uniquely interpretive text with a multitude of diverse, alien, and/or tangential discourses," which is paraphrased in choice B as "utilizing external discourses as the basis for the critical endeavor."

Choice A inverts the passage's assertions regarding humanistic interpretation. Choice C distorts the concept of usurpation as described in the passage. Choice D reverses the passage's observations about the opponents of New Criticism and their use—not rejection—of interdisciplinary methodology.

105. According to the passage, empirical reasoning represents:

A. a diversion for traditionalist literary critics.

B. a threat to "structuralist" critics.

C. a rebuttal to feminist extrapolations of eighteenth-century novels.

D. a mode of analysis antithetical to traditional literary concerns.

D Choice D paraphrases lines 30–33. Choice A inverts the author's assertion to the effect that traditionalists feel the need "to defend" their discipline against systems of empirical inquiry. Choice B substitutes "structuralist" for "traditionalist." Choice C distorts the passage's reference to a feminist approach to Shakespeare in lines 40–44.

106. Based on information in the passage, students who are drawn to a humanistic interpretive approach:

A. ignore the metatextual domains of the literary universe.

B. reject the traditionalist school of literary criticism.

C. are excluded by the theoretical structuralists.

D. are animated by the nihilistic exclusivity of ideological analysis.

C The relevant information is found in lines 51–61. According to the author, the humanistic interpretive approach is consigned "to the margins." Those who take a humanist approach are, in other words, excluded by theoretical and ideological analysts. Choice A represents an absolute that is not supported in the passage. Choice B distorts the passage's discussion of the relationship between "the traditionalist school" and humanistic interpretation. Choice D is wrong because students interested in the humanistic approach would hardly be animated by ideologues who exclude them.

107. Based on information in the passage, "inclusivity" as conceived by theoretical advocates conforms with:

A. an identity politics unwittingly serving reactionary forces.

B. an identity politics serving to liberate its disciples from restriction and taboo.

C. a universalist humanism tending to embrace multicultural perspectives.

D. a universalist humanism working to defuse reactionary apartheidism.

A Choice A rewords information set forth in paragraph 5, where the author writes that such "inclusivity" "nicely conforms with the reactionary apartheidism espoused and embraced by the fashionable tenets of identity politics." Choice B reverses the role that identity politics play vis-à-vis restriction and taboo (lines 64–67). Choice C inverts information set forth in the passage. The passage states that humanism is consigned to the margins by theoretical inclusivity (lines 55–61). Choice D also distorts the author's meaning. The passage indicates that identity politics, not universalist humanism, collaborates with apartheidism.

108. The author implies that the underlying objectives of deconstruction inevitably distort literary expression because they:

A. can never effectively negate the humanistic principles of literary criticism.

B. infer a semiotic relationship to the mechanics of novelistic form.

C. impart meaning to a narrative's emotional content.

D. reject inherent meaning and motive as appropriate subjects for critical consideration.

D It accurately paraphrases the information found in lines 45–50 and 70–73 of the passage. Choice A is an absolute. Choice B distorts the passage's reference to "semiotics" (lines 70–73). Choice C inverts the author's statements relating deconstruction and emotional content, and stands in virtual opposition to choice D.

109. The author cites Wellek and Warren in order to support the claim that:

A. traditional criticism is not entirely exclusive.

B. authors should use their imaginative powers to serve textual exegesis.

C. structuralism's "inclusivity" violates humanism.

D. criticism should focus on the values explicitly described in the text itself.

A Choice A is a paraphrase of lines 25–26, which is the reason the author is citing Wellek and Warren. Choices B and C incorrectly quote irrelevant passage information. While choice D may be true, it's not the reason the author cited Wellek and Warren.

110. Of which of the following critical approaches would a traditionalist most likely approve?

A. A psychoanalytic analysis of T.S. Eliot as revealed by images used in "The Wasteland."

B. A study of racial and identity politics that influenced the writing of Richard Wright's *Native Son*.

C. An analysis of the structure and characterization within Steinbeck's *Of Mice and Men*.

D. A feminist scholar's focus on the oppressive conditions that led to the female images in Sylvia Plath's poetry.

C Traditional New Criticism focuses on what is expressed in the text itself (lines 20–24, 48–54, and 73–75), so a traditionalist would approve of choice C. All of the other choices use nontraditional discourses which focus on matters external to the work itself.

111. The author argues that structuralist analysis poses an anti-intellectual threat to literature's existence. Which of the following circumstances, if true, would LEAST strengthen the argument?

    A. A multidisciplinary committee urges that the Literature faculty be dispersed among other Humanities and Social Science departments.

    B. An associate dean of Academic Affairs proposes that Literature course offerings be cut in half.

    C. A feminist critic of Chaucer's poetry offers his course through the Women's Studies department.

    D. A Freudian critic of James Joyce's novels offers her course through the Literature department.

C The author's basic argument with the "structuralists" is that they take ideas from other disciplines and use those belief systems to teach literature. A person who believes that Chaucer can be used as a vehicle to teach feminist ideas, and who offers such a course in the Women's Studies department would not be pretending to teach Chaucer, only feminism, and so would not threaten literature's own identity. The author would view someone who wants to teach Freudian psychology as a course in the Literature department (choice D) as a person willing to substitute psychology for literature. That substitution would strengthen the author's argument. Choices A and B would strengthen the author's argument that literature's being is under attack.

112. Suppose a course description in a college bulletin promises "an in-depth literary examination of the novels of William Faulkner and Mark Twain." Students later find that the course focuses nearly exclusively on themes of cultural injustice. Based on your reading of the passage, this new information would probably lead the author to:

    A. support a student who accused the professor of false advertising.

    B. organize a boycott of the course the following semester.

    C. publish an article defending the professor's academic freedom.

    D. oppose a dean who suggested moving the course to the Political History department.

A A professor who ignored the richly varied themes of Faulkner and Twain to concentrate exclusively on questions of cultural injustice would not be teaching literature, in the view of the author of the passage. Thus, he or she might well support a student who accused such a professor of falsely describing the course in the catalogue. Although nothing in the passage indicates that the author would deny academic freedom to such a professor, it is unlikely, given the ideas in the passage, that he or she would go out of his or her way to defend that professor (choice C). The author would probably applaud, not oppose, a dean who felt that such a course belonged more appropriately to a Political History curriculum (choice D). Choice B is too strong to be supported by the passage.

Passage VI (Questions 113–118)

113. The author's claim that science educators must set "practical goal[s]" before aspiring to loftier objectives (lines 13–15) is supported by which of the following observations?

    A.   There is a relative lack of competition from other departments for the science majors' interest.
    B.   General students seek large numbers of science courses.
    C.   Science departments seek large numbers of science faculty.
    D.   Society has a compelling need to achieve widespread scientific literacy.

C The key phrase is found in lines 23–27, where the author points out that generally, a science department's primary "underlying motive is more to attract critical masses of faculty and adequate equipment budgets for research than to satisfy some compelling educational need of the general (nonscience) student." Choice A is disproven in lines 20–23 "science departments, whether in our schools or colleges, are no different from most other disciplines in seeking to increase the enrollment of nonmajors in their courses," and in lines 28–29. "The competition is keen in most faculties to be included in the distribution requirements for all students." This last citation, implying that most general students take science largely to fulfill distribution requirements, also rules against choice B. Lines 1–15, 23–27, and 52–57 indicate that the ideal of creating a scientifically literate society is less a genuine or practical goal of science educators than it is a "delusion" (lines 52–53). Thus, choice D is debunked.

114. The passage suggests that one of the main purposes of teaching general science to masses of students is to:

    A.   enable large numbers of citizens to participate intelligently in a scientifically oriented economy.
    B.   provide an understanding of empirical methodology to all students as an essential problem-solving skill.
    C.   familiarize nonscience majors with newly challenging ethical issues generated by scientific technology.
    D.   justify the maintenance of a large academic and research establishment in science.

D Choice D is supported by lines 19–27 and 33–40. While the passage does indicate that scientific literacy is useful to students and to society, the author mentions neither a "scientifically oriented economy" (choice A) nor "ethical issues generated by scientific technology" (choice C). Similarly, choice B is a perfectly sensible goal but is never discussed as such in the passage.

115. Given the information in the passage, most nonscience majors who study general science in either high school or college will most likely:

    A.   enroll in pseudo-scientific courses such as "Physics for Poets," etc.
    B.   do so to meet course distribution and "point credits" requirements.
    C.   subscribe to popular science periodicals after graduation.
    D.   retain little science knowledge after graduation.

D Lines 66–67 state, "We know that the staying power of science courses is very poor." The phenomenon of pseudo-science courses is mentioned in lines 43–45, but the author never claims that the majority of nonscience majors enroll in such courses. Lines 40–43 of that same paragraph mention "point credits" as the basis on which university departments must justify their positions and budgets, not a requirement with which students must comply. Thus choice B is wrong. According to choice C, nonscience majors subscribe to popular science magazines after graduation, but the passage makes no such statement.

116. Based on information in the passage, if science departments taught fewer "promotional course[s]" (line 43) to undergraduates, which of the following outcomes would likely occur?

- **A.** Colleges and universities would produce significantly higher numbers of scientifically literate graduates.
- **B.** All students would graduate with significantly greater scientific literacy.
- **C.** Science departments might risk decreased budgetary support from administrations.
- **D.** Nonscience departments might be overwhelmed by increasing student enrollments.

C According to lines 40–43, "Many university science departments survive only by virtue of the 'point credits' they earn through their introductory courses." In the context of the passage, the author clearly implies that in the absence of such gut courses, science departments might have a difficult time filling their rolls, and thus justifying high budgets. Neither choice A nor B is discussed in the passage. Choice D might be a by-product of a decrease in pseudo-science courses, but the passage does not directly suggest it. Choice C remains the better answer.

117. The author suggests that restricting high school science departments to only science majors would result in:

- **A.** the demise of many high school science departments.
- **B.** the proliferation of specialized state or national high schools.
- **C.** improved high school science curricula.
- **D.** better utilization of academic resources.

A The information you need to answer this question is found in lines 36–40: "Most science departments would collapse for lack of a critical mass of faculty...." That same sentence continues, "...the training of science professionals would have to be given over to a relatively few specialized state or national high schools and colleges." Choice B speaks of a "proliferation" of such specialty schools, not "few" of them. Choice C presents a dubious proposition that is not endorsed anywhere in the passage. Some might argue for the merits of choice D, but the author does not.

118. Suppose the majority of high school graduates were found to demonstrate an educated interest in science and science-related issues fifteen years post graduation. This new information would most *challenge* the claim that:

- **A.** schools are guided more by immediate feedback than by long-term results.
- **B.** most scientifically illiterate graduates believe themselves to be scientifically knowledgeable.
- **C.** having literate students who become scientifically illiterate adults does not do much for society.
- **D.** the staying power of science courses is very poor.

D This choice is the most directly affected by the new information. Choice A offers a tempting alternative, and while the assertion it presents arguably would be challenged by the new information, choice D is still the better choice. The new information would not affect the validity of the statements in choices B and C.

Passage VII (Questions 119–124)

119. The author suggests which of the following to be true of "Western Civilization values"?

- A. They are superior to the value systems of other cultural groups.
- B. They are entirely inappropriate as moral guidelines for other cultural groups.
- C. Their imposition on economically deprived communities is responsible for maladaptive behaviors among some adolescents.
- D. They contain many elements accepted across many cultures.

D Paragraphs 2, 3, and 4 provide information supporting this choice (see in particular lines 16–22, 26–31, and 39–44). Nothing in the passage is said about the relative superiority (choice A) of one system of cultural values vis-à-vis another. The rhetorical question, which opens paragraph 4, rules out choice B, which reverses the author's true opinion. Some readers may find an oblique reference to choice C in the passage's opening sentence, but the very next sentence—and the rest of the text—makes clear that the view choice C expresses does not coincide with the author's.

120. The author states that remarks of summit speakers who blamed "Western Civilization values" for antisocial behavior among today's youth:

- A. imply that "Western Civilization values" teach inequality and injustice.
- B. should have been censored.
- C. were probably imprecisely reported.
- D. have led to a general decline in moral civility.

C Choice C is directly supported in lines 11–15. Choice A distorts the reported comments' reference to the problems of immorality and violence among some economically deprived youth (lines 1–8). The author certainly expresses her disapproval in lines 8–11, but nowhere calls for censorship, so choice B is excluded. Her disapproval may imply that she feels a decline in civility due to the reported rhetoric (choice D), but she does not say so directly. For that reason, choice C is the better choice.

121. With which of the following statements would the author most likely agree?

- A. "Western Civilization" is a term more useful to sociology than to everyday reality.
- B. "Western Civilization" is useful only as a rhetorical term.
- C. "Western Civilization" refers to a distinct geographical group.
- D. "Western Civilization" refers to a distinct cultural group.

B Lines 45–50 make choice B the best answer to this question. That same sentence rules out choices C and D which invert the author's meaning. Choice A distorts the reference to "quasisociological" in an attempt to mislead you.

122. The author suggests that the true reason(s) for antisocial behavior among some adolescents is/are:

- I. the principle that respect is earned on the basis of character.
- II. the distortion of a humanistic value system.
- III. the negative influence of some more mature members of society.

- A. I only
- B. II only
- C. II and III only
- D. I, II, and III

C Paragraphs 4 and 5 support statement II. Lines 54–60 and 70–72 support statement III. Paragraph 3 mentions the relationship between character and respect (statement I), but nowhere is that relationship linked to antisocial behavior. To do so would be to completely invert the author's idea. Thus, only statements II and III are connected by the author to antisocial behavior.

123. Among the following, the author *most* likely believes that some of the responsibility for urban social maladies is due to:

   A.   "Western Civilization values."
   B.   non–"Western Civilization values."
   C.   ancient mercenaries of diverse backgrounds.
   D.   people who sell guns on the streets.

D Lines 53–65, make this choice the best of the choices offered. Choice A asserts the exact opposite of the author's main thesis. Choice B is essentially irrelevant to the passage and constitutes a distortion of the author's themes. The author does not discuss the influence of ancient mercenaries on modern society. Therefore choice C is incorrect.

124. The author argues that "Western Civilization values" are founded on true belief, personal bravery, and moral action. Which of the following findings, if true, would most *weaken* the author's contention?

   A.   Most Americans believe that violence is the most appropriate way to resolve personal disputes.
   B.   Many Americans learn moral commitment as a part of their religious training.
   C.   Most Americans believe that bravery is the most important of all values.
   D.   Most Americans believe that bravery, honesty, and commitment are the keys to a civilized society.

A If most Americans believed in violence as a way to resolve disputes, it would undermine the author's argument in paragraphs 4 and 5 that people who act in violent or antisocial ways are not representative of "Western civilization values." (See in particular lines 53–65.)

Choices B, C, and D would strengthen, not weaken, the author's argument.

Passage VIII (Questions 125–130)

125. What is the main idea of the passage?

   A.   African art serves as a barrier between the artist class and the community.
   B.   African art is essentially inaccessible to students of Western art.
   C.   African art participates in diverse functional ways in the community's daily life.
   D.   Western art is divorced from the community's daily functioning.

C Lines 26–27 state that Dan masks play "a significant role" in daily community life. Also, lines 56–61 of the passage emphasize the importance of African art in daily life. Lines 56–61 also rule out choice A, which is inconsistent with the passages's description of the artist's relationship to the communtiy. Choice B might tempt those who believe that differences between distinct cultures are unbridgeable, but the author would likely not have bothered to write the essay at all if choice B were his central idea. Although choice D offers an idea that some might infer from the author's words (lines 2–5 and 53–56), it represents an absolute statement not directly related to the passage's central theme.

126. To emphasize the idea that African art is unlike Western art, the author explicitly cites all of the following information EXCEPT:

A. structures housing African art are built according to ritual practices and laws.

B. once completed, some African sculptures are allowed to crumble and rot.

C. African sculptures often depict historical heroes.

D. African art includes common objects of daily household use.

C The correct answer will NOT represent a stated or implied difference between African and Western art. While the author mentions sculptures of "human figures of myth and history" in the mbari houses (lines 21–22), the passage does not state or imply that these include statues of heroes. Thus choice C is not supported, and is the correct answer. The other answers all refer to contrasts drawn by the author between African and Western or European art. The author introduces the passage with the statement that "We cannot understand [African Art] without first abandoning some conventional notions. African art goes beyond monuments and that which one might observe in a museum" (lines 1–5). Next comes discussion of the mbari house which is built according to ritual practice (lines 6–9) and which houses sculptures which are allowed to decay (lines 9–11). Thus we can infer that the author is contrasting the mbari house with Western museums in terms of how the structure itself is built and how the sculptures are or are not maintained. Therefore, choices A and B are supported by the passage, and should be eliminated. In the last paragraph, the author claims that "The African culture differs from the European in that artwork is not separate from utilitarian objects," and that African art includes eating utensils, etc. This eliminates choice D, which is supported by lines 53–58.

127. The term "literature" (line 52) is used in the sense of:

A. an unbound collected body of tribal writings.

B. a catalogue of religious sculptures and myths.

C. family stories passed down through generations of oral tradition.

D. cultural narratives based on tribal values and beliefs.

D We are told that "performances constitute literature." Combining that information with your own insight into the word, you should arrive at choice D. You might also select choice D by eliminating the other choices. The passage clearly states (lines 50–52) that the Gelade "performances constitute literature." That observation rules out both choices A and B, which refer to written work, not performances. Although it is possible that some Gelade performances draw, in part, on family stories and oral traditions (choice C), the author notes that social commentary is the masker's primary focus (lines 48–50). Narratives relevant to the Yoruba culture, observing foibles and failings of various familiar characters (lines 44–48) who fail—or surpass—in one way or another the community's shared values and beliefs, seem closer to what the author had in mind by social commentary.

128. Which of the following circumstances, if true, would most *challenge* the notion that the Dan poro masks serve to protect their wearers while executing official duties in the community?

 A. Members of the poro are selected through a democratic process rather than on the basis of clan affiliation.

 B. Community officers are chosen in tribal electoral campaigns instead of designated from within the poro.

 C. The poro's mask-making activities begin to consume twice the amount of time it had previously.

 D. The poro gradually evolves into a guild of craftspersons that institutes bylaws and secret oaths.

B According to the passage (lines 29–31), the masks hide the identities of Dan officials from the community, protecting those who must perform unpopular duties. Public electoral campaigns to choose officials would obviously prevent Dan officials from maintaining their anonymity. A democratic election to the poro, as offered in choice A, would not necessarily identify specific officials publicly. The passage does not indicate that the identities of the mask-making poro are unknown to the community, only that of a specific member performing a specific duty. Options C and D are not directly relevant to the question of Dan anonymity as discussed in the passage.

129. Based on the passage, it is reasonable to conclude that the masks of the Dan tribe differ from those of the Yoruba Gelade in that a Dan mask:

 A. might accurately describe the role of the person who wears it.

 B. is rarely designed by the person who wears it.

 C. is designed to mollify the cult of magic practitioners.

 D. has a special relationship to social function.

A The author describes the Dan and Yoruba masks in paragraphs 3 and 4. Among the Dan, a judge wears a judge's mask. Among the Yoruba, masks are used as performance costumes, and nothing more. In the Dan community, the mask represents the actual role of the person wearing it. In the Yoruba community, the role represented by the mask is make-believe. Choice B distorts the information (paragraph 3) about the poro mask-making activities and their relationship to the person who might wear a particular mask. Choice C inverts the author's meaning. Lines 39–41 state that the Yoruba Gelade, not the Dan poro, use masks to appease the forces of sorcery. Choice D also distorts information regarding the function of masks in each culture. As has been explained, although the function of the mask differs according to the culture, in both cultures—not just the Dan—the masks serve a "social function."

130. If a member of the Yoruba community were kidnapped and transported to a Dan village, one might reasonably expect that in participating in the daily activities of the Dan:

 A. the Yoruban might confuse ceremony with commentary.

 B. the Yoruban might confuse governance with utilitarianism.

 C. the Yoruban might confuse reality with the unconscious.

 D. the Yoruban might confuse reality with criticism.

D A member of the Yoruba would be accustomed to seeing masks representing different personages and characters in the course of performances providing social commentary (lines 48–50). We can assume that this commentary might include criticism. In the Dan village, masks are used to represent real offices and functions (lines 29–37); the author does not suggest that the Dan use masks to comment on or criticize how people carry out those functions.

Choice A mentions two ways in which Yorubans use masks (see paragraph 4). There is no reason why a Yoruban in a Dan village would confuse the two with each other. Choice B distorts the reference in the final paragraph to utilitarianism, which is a characteristic of African art common to each of the communities described by the author. Choice C brings in "the unconscious," which is never discussed in the passage.

Passage IX (Questions 131–137)

131. According to the passage, modern scientists believe that star formation involves all of the following EXCEPT:

A. processes that tend to form star pairs more often than single stars.

B. separation of protostellar material to yield protostars.

C. diminution in size facilitated by Gaussian rules.

D. the aggregation of molecular matter around a hyperdense core.

D Remember, this is an EXCEPT question. The answer is found in lines 23–28, where the author states the exact opposite of choice D: the "hyperdense core" was part of previous theories. Lines 48–54 contain information supporting the accuracy of choice A. Choice B is upheld in lines 37–49. Paragraph 3 confirms the truth of choice C.

132. The author refers to spectroscopic measurements in order to support the claim that:

A. quadruples occur more often than triples.

B. triples occur less often than singles.

C. singles occur more often than doubles.

D. doubles occur less often than triples.

B The fifth paragraph describes spectroscopic measurement, showing that singles occur about half as often as doubles. The same paragraph rules out options C and D, and also states that quadruples occur about one-thirtieth as often as doubles (rules out option A).

133. Compared to a star in the main sequence phase, a T-Tauri star is, according to the passage:

A. younger and larger.

B. younger and smaller.

C. older and larger.

D. older and smaller.

A Lines 7–8 identify our sun as a main sequence star, and lines 16–18 state that it contracted from its previous size as a T-Tauri star. Therefore, in its present main sequence phase, it is older and smaller than its T-Tauri ancestor. That means that the T-Tauri star is younger and larger than a main sequence star.

Choices B, C, and D contradict information in paragraph 2.

134. According to the passage, the "power law" of molecular distribution is challenged by the observation that:

A. our own sun is a G-dwarf class star.

B. many stars are formed as pairs.

C. protostars have centers of very high density.

D. astroradiometry may be employed in extremely small wavelengths.

B Lines 32–36 point out that "the absence of... a Gaussian distribution would make...'double' stars... virtually impossible." The recognition that paired stars do exist, therefore, requires the inference of a Gaussian molecular distribution of protostellar hydrogen clouds. The existence of a Gaussian distribution precludes the possibility of the "power law" defined in lines 24–26 as the coalescence of molecular material around "the hyperdense center." If one confused "dense hydrogen cloud collapse" with the "power law" theory of a hyperdense cloud center, one might choose A because lines 18–20 refer to "dense hydrogen cloud collapse" having formed our sun as a G-class star. Choice C inverts the sense of lines 37–49. Protostars are produced by "fragmentation," and are held together by gravity. The following sentence says protostellar clouds—not protostars—are "dense ... formations." Choice D attempts to distort the importance of small-wavelength astroradiometry as discussed in the passage (lines 28–29). While that technology led Ward-Thompson's team to discard the "power law" hypothesis, it was the findings of the experiment—not the mechanism of its technology (small waves)—which permitted them to do that.

135. Which of the following is evidence used by the author to support the claim that our own sun is probably not part of a star pair?

- **A.** The other star of the pair would have to exist outside our own galaxy.
- **B.** Comet showers are known to occur with a frequency greater than once every thirty million years.
- **C.** The other star of the pair would cause the extinction of most of Earth's animal species.
- **D.** Investigations reveal no star sufficiently close to the sun to exert significant gravitational force on it.

D This choice paraphrases lines 73–74. Choice A distorts the information regarding the enormous distance between our sun and its hypothetical pair. As for choice B, the author does state in the passage that if our sun was one-half of a binary system, this could cause comet showers every thirty million years (lines 71–72). However, the author never states that comet showers have occurred more frequently than that. Therefore B states something that does not appear in the passage. In that same paragraph, the author states that comet showers released by a partner star could cause planetary extinctions like that which led to the disappearance of the dinosaurs. However, the author does not argue that such extinctions would happen every thirty million years, or that they would eliminate most of Earth's species. As with choice B, this statement is not made in the passage. Therefore, choice C is incorrect.

136. According to the passage, the termination of the phase now occupied by our sun will cause some planets to:

- **A.** become red giants.
- **B.** enter their main sequence phase.
- **C.** shrink in diameter.
- **D.** disappear.

D The information is explicitly set forth in lines 7–10. Choice A inverts the reference to red giant stars. Planets will not become red giants, but when the sun becomes one, it will obliterate the inner planets. Choice B distorts the reference to a main sequence phase. Stars, like our sun, enter main sequence phases; planets do not (lines 4–8). Choice C is also about stars, while the question refers to planets.

137. The discovery that star formation is governed not by the "power law" but by Gaussian rules might best be analogized to the finding that:

- **A.** a given disease spreads not directly from one patient to another but by an insect bite, which explains why a person could contract the disease without exposure to an afflicted patient.
- **B.** left-handedness corresponds not to a longer life span but to a shorter life span, which explains the fact that left-handed persons tend to have a greater facility for artistic and verbal creativity.
- **C.** the first carts and wagons tended to break apart on encountering bumps, which led to the installation of springs and, later, shock absorbers.
- **D.** certain isolated societies have no concept of property or ownership, which explains why such peoples never developed weapons of mass destruction.

A The passage indicates that measuring molecular densities in protostellar clouds by using astroradiometry (lines 28–32) revealed a physical fact previously "invisible" to researchers: that densities at the center of hydrogen clouds were considerably lower than had been estimated. That which had been invisible became visible. Choice A describes a discovery of similar significance. Before its discovery, the insect bite was an invisible force affecting the spread of epidemic disease. Choice C is not as good as choice A because the bumps were not invisible. Choices B and D have no direct relationship to the author's contrast between the "power law" and Gaussian rules.

ANSWERS AND EXPLANATIONS
WRITING SAMPLE

Note: There is no single "correct" or "best" answer to any particular writing sample question. The essays provided in this section are possible responses; they display the characteristics of a top-scoring essay.

Part 1
Trial by jury ensures a fair verdict.

The right to be tried by a jury of one's peers stands at the center of our legal system. Underlying that right is the assumption that justice is more likely when a group of fellow citizens deliberates and decides on the case than when a single authority, who may be swayed by political or personal considerations, holds all of the power. In fact, trial by jury has its roots in English history when judicial power was taken away from the manorial courts, where a local lord decided the guilt or innocence of the people who lived on his land. By putting the power into the hands of citizens, we expect them to leave aside any personal emotions or interests, and to decide based only on the facts of the case. A "fair verdict" in this instance means that jurors do in fact abide by the rules, listening to all the evidence, obeying the instructions of the judge, and entering into deliberations with a reasonably open mind. Even a fair system can sometimes come to an unjust verdict, as we have seen in cases of people on death row who have been exonerated by only recently available DNA analysis. However, in most cases, trial by a jury is likely to lead to a fair verdict, meaning a verdict that can reasonably be reached on the basis of the available evidence.

However, there are also many cases in which it seems obvious that a fair verdict was not reached. One such example is the case of the 1992 trial of officers accused of beating the African American motorist Rodney King. It seems clear that the "not guilty" verdict was not only unjust but unfair, given in particular the videotape of the beating and the lack of any real evidence that King posed a danger to the officers. In this case, the jurors, who were drawn from the largely white and conservative Simi Valley area, did not appear to evaluate the evidence as they should have. One possible interpretation is that they allowed popular opinion in their own community, as well as the personal beliefs and biases they brought with them into the trial (including trust and sympathy for the police), to sway their verdict. Because of the social context in which the trial occurred, and because of the high stakes involved (the possibility of sending police officers to jail for quite some time), one could argue that trial by jury in this case was unlikely to lead to a fair outcome.

Jurors are human beings, and human beings find it difficult at times to hold out against public opinion. In a high profile case that involves serious charges and is widely reported in the media, trial by jury is less likely to result in a fair verdict. Jurors in these cases are likely to worry about answering to their friends and neighbors after the trial is over, being forced to defend a decision that is unpopular in their own community. On the other hand, if no one cares about the case except for the people who are directly involved, jurors are much more likely to play by the rules. People also tend to have great respect for the rules and tenets of our judicial system, and they want to do the right thing. If there is little or no personal cost involved, doing the right thing becomes much easier. Cases such as that of the hold-out juror in the trial of the Tyco executives (who were tried in 2004 on charges of corruption) are rare;

most people would fold under the intense scrutiny and criticism lavished upon the woman who stood alone against her 11 fellow jurors. Leaving the issue of guilt or innocence in that case aside, all of us, if falsely accused, would pray for someone on our jury willing to pay the cost for the strength of her own convictions.

Part 2
The greater the fear of failure, the lower the likelihood of success.

We as human beings like to think of ourselves as rational beings who make decisions on the basis of evidence and reason. However, we are not so divorced from our animal instincts as we like to think. In times of crisis, our "fight or flight" instinct often takes over in a counterproductive way. When we fear for our lives (or livelihood), we might take actions that only seem to protect us. In the late 1920's, for example, the economy was booming and stock prices hit an all-time peak. When the bubble burst and prices fell, it created a panic as individuals and institutions rushed like lemmings to sell their stock while they could still get something for it. Multiplying the effect of the crash in stock prices was the subsequent run on the banks, as people feared that their savings would disappear. The result of all of this was the Great Depression. A similar process occurred in the 1987 crash, made worse by computerized programs that caused huge blocks of stock to be sold off once they went below a certain price. The more stock that was traded, the more prices fell, feeding into the fear of financial failure and continuing the downward spiral. Therefore, people acting on their individual fears of financial ruin in fact caused that ruin to occur. In the late 20's and early 30's, it went so far as to cause the failure of the economy as a whole. Ironically, sometimes actions that protect the individual against failure in the short run, when combined with the self-interested decisions of all the other individuals, add up to a result that is counterproductive for everyone.

However, sometimes fear of failure is a great motivator, and can help us not only to survive but also to improve our condition, either individually or as a society. The "J Curve" theory says that revolutions tend to happen not when people have nothing to lose, but instead when they fear losing something of value. Thus rebellions often occur when things have been fairly good, but then there is a sudden downturn and the system suddenly seems to be failing. For example, the French Revolution occurred after a period of relative prosperity, and during the time of the Enlightenment, when liberal ideals of representation and fairness were spreading. However, an economic downturn, a subsequent increase in taxes on both the rich and the poor, and a reassertion of royal authority led people at all levels of society to fear losing what they had. Out of rebellion against royal authority came a representative body called the National Assembly, which replaced the elitist Estates General. While the revolution descended into violence and chaos, what eventually came out of it was a system of democratic representation, and a system in which the poor had greater rights and protections.

Franklin D. Roosevelt said, "We have nothing to fear but fear itself," meaning that if we are afraid, we are likely to fail. Why then, does this seem to be true in some cases and not in others? In the first example, people and institutions saw themselves, and acted as, individuals, thinking only about self-preservation. Furthermore, decisions had to be made quickly — the longer they waited, the more they would lose as the market continued to fall. And yet the sum of all these individual actions, motivated by fear, led to an outcome in which everyone was worse off. In the case of the French Revolution, people acted largely in groups, be they peasant leagues or political committees. They also had more time to think and plan, as the revolution unfolded over time. When people feel alone, and are afraid for their immediate physical or economic lives, they tend to flee rather than fight, with the result that no one is really looking out for the good of the whole. When people confronted with the possibility of failure feel like they are part of a group, they tend to take more positive, and so more well thought out and reasoned action, which is more likely to lead to a successful outcome.

ANSWERS AND EXPLANATIONS

BIOLOGICAL SCIENCE

Questions 138–214

Passage I (Questions 138–142)

138. An uncoupler of oxidative phosphorylation such as dinitrophenol allows the mitochondrial respiratory chain to proceed without subsequent ATP synthesis, by neutralizing the proton gradient. Specifically, this is done by transporting protons along their concentration gradient across the inner mitochondrial membrane. Which of the following is an uncoupler of ATP synthesis?

    A.   NADH-Q reductase
    B. $FADH_2$
    C.   Antimycin A
    D.   None of the above

    D   After electron transport, ATP synthetase uses the proton gradient generated by the mitochondrial respiratory chain to drive the formation of ATP from $ADP + P_i$. This proton gradient is formed by transporting protons AGAINST their concentration gradient, thereby increasing the gradient. The question reminds the reader that an uncoupler of oxidative phosphorylation acts specifically by transporting protons ALONG their concentration gradient, thereby neutralizing the proton gradient. By reviewing below, and using POE (Process of Elimination), it is clear to see why answer choice D is best.

    Choice A, NADH-Q reductase, is an enzyme complex (also called Complex I) that receives electrons from NADH and thereby transports protons AGAINST their concentration gradient, contributing to the formation of the proton gradient, NOT its neutralization. Choices B and C are not involved in proton transport, nor are they involved in the direct generation of ATP, as can be seen in Figure 1.

139. Substance X is known to noncompetitively inhibit NADH-Q reductase. A high cellular concentration of which of the following phosphorus-containing compounds would allow the cell to partially continue oxidative phosphorylation despite the addition of Substance X?

    A. $FADH_2$
    B.   NADPH
    C.   ADP
    D.   NADH

    A   The diagram indicates that $FADH_2$ bypasses inhibition of NADH-Q reductase. That's because $FADH_2$ enters the respiratory chain *beyond* the site of NADH-Q reductase inhibition. (A blocked bridge won't stop you from reaching your destination if your route *doesn't cross the bridge*.) Choice B should be eliminated because NADPH is not a component of the respiratory chain. Choice C is wrong because although ADP is needed for the generation of ATP, ATP synthetase uses the energy of the proton gradient to drive this reaction. Thus, the presence of ADP alone is not sufficient to drive ATP synthesis. Choice D is wrong because NADH enters the respiratory chain "upstream" of the site at which NADH-Q reductase inhibition occurs.

140. The heme-containing structure of cytochrome *b* in Figure 2 above possesses how many chiral centers?

    A. 3
    B. 2
    C. 1
    D. 0

D Close inspection of the heme-containing molecule in Figure 2 reveals that every atom within the aromatic structure of the heme group is involved in one double bond. The definition of chirality requires that an atom be bonded to four distinct and unique groups. The presence of such double bonds prevents any of these atoms within the aromatic rings from bonding to four different groups, thereby excluding these atoms from being considered chiral. Furthermore, each of the specific nitrogen atoms bonded to the central iron atom are themselves only bonded to a total of three atoms, thus falling short of the requirement that they be bonded to four distinct substituents. Thus choice D is correct.

141. To further characterize cytochrome *b*, the researchers reacted its sulfur-containing amino acids with performic acid and then broke apart the polypeptide into individual amino acid residues. The most probable means of performing this latter task is to:

    A. reduce cysteine residues.
    B. decarboxylate acidic residues.
    C. oxidize amide linkages.
    D. hydrolyze amide linkages.

D After reviewing the biochemistry of cells, you'll know that a "peptide bond" is an "amide bond." (It's the amide bond that holds amino acids together to make proteins.) If one hydrolyzes peptide bonds, one is hydrolyzing amide bonds.

Choice A should be eliminated. It's irrelevant. Choice B is also wrong. The process of breaking a polypeptide into its component amino acids does not involve decarboxylation. Choice C can be eliminated because the breakage of an amide linkage occurs through *hydrolysis*, not oxidation.

142. The heme portions of cytochrome molecules are able to transfer electrons among themselves because of:

    A. thioether linkages.
    B. pi-electron delocalization.
    C. enol-intermediate racemization.
    D. shortened bond length.

B The question is unrelated to the passage. It requires that you know that the heme portions of cytochromes are characterized by pi-electron delocalization, which stabilizes the structure.

Choice A is incorrect. Thioethers are thiol derivatives and are not associated with heme resonance structure. Choice C is also wrong. An enol-intermediate represents one of the forms that carbonyl molecules assume. It is *not* associated with heme resonance structure. Choice D is wild and irrelevant.

Passage II (Questions 143–147)

143. Which of the following best describes the appearance of *Lactobacillus experimentalis* when stained and then viewed with a light microscope?

    A. Spherical
    B. S-shaped
    C. Rodlike
    D. Asymmetrical

C The name *Lactobacillus* indicates that these bacteria belong to the bacterial group "bacilli." After reviewing microbiology, you'll recall that bacilli are rod shaped.

Choices A and B are wrong because spherical and S-shaped bacteria describe the appearance of cocci and spirilli, respectively. Choice D is wrong because symmetry of form has no bearing on the classification of bacteria.

144. The proliferation of *Lactobacillus* in milk samples indicates:

    A. high lactose concentration.
    B. a drop in the pH.
    C. predominance of spore-forming bacteria.
    D. the absence of *Streptococcus faecalis*.

B Paragraph 1 describes the environmental conditions that promote growth of lactobacilli. A reduced pH via production of lactic acid by *Streptococcus lactis*, for example, provides a receptive environment for lactobacilli.

Choice A should be eliminated because it contradicts paragraph 1, which tells you that lactose must be converted to lactic acid to spur *Lactobacillius* growth. Choices C and D are wrong because in relation to the growth of *Lactobacillus*, the passage does not mention spore-forming bacteria or *Streptococcus faecalis*.

145. If one of the raw milk samples were slowly heated to 100°C and then held at that temperature for fifteen minutes, which of the following graphs would best represent resulting spore-forming and non–spore-forming bacterial populations during this time period?

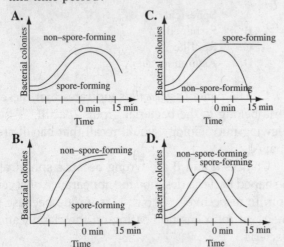

C The essential information is provided in paragraph 1, where you're told that pasteurization kills non–spore-forming bacteria. From this, you may infer that spore-forming bacteria are better able to resist the high temperatures of pasteurization.

Choice B should be eliminated because the graph it presents indicates high survival rates for the non–spore-forming bacteria. Paragraph 1 states that non–spore-forming bacteria do *not* survive pasteurization. Choices A and D are wrong because they indicate that pasteurization kills spore-forming bacteria.

146. The Gram-staining procedure used in the laboratory enables the inspector to:

    A. identify bacterial species present in the incubate.
    B. distinguish between aerobic and anaerobic organisms.
    C. differentiate pathogenic from nonpathogenic colonies.
    D. distinguish between bacteria whose peptidoglycan layer lies outside the cell membrane or within the periplasmic space.

D Recall that gram-positive bacteria have a thick peptidoglycan layer lying on the outside of the cell membrane. It is this outermost layer of peptidoglycan that takes up the Gram dye and gives a positive Gram-stain result. Gram-negative bacteria, on the other hand, have a considerably thinner layer of peptidoglycan, which is located within the periplasmic space and is isolated from the outside environment by an outer phospholipid membrane. Both of these factors decrease the net amount of Gram dye taken up by the peptidoglycan layer of these latter bacteria, thus making them "gram-negative." Choice A is incorrect as Gram-staining does not allow specific identification of bacterial species—it only narrows the options by specifying whether the bacteria are gram-positive or gram-negative. Choices B and C are wrong because Gram staining does not elucidate metabolic processes or pathogenicity.

147. Which of the following environmental factors will negatively impact the growth of *Streptococcus faecalis*?

    I. A decrease in the nutritional content of the milk
    II. The process of pasteurization
    III. A decrease in ambient oxygen concentration

A. I only
B. I and II only
C. II and III only
D. I, II, and III

A The relevant information is provided in paragraph 1. We're reminded that *Streptococcus faecalis* uses the sugar found in milk, lactose, for fermentation, thereby generating lactic acid. A quick review of glycolysis will remind the reader that bacterial anaerobic respiration often results in the production of lactic acid as well as of ATP; the latter is used by the organism for growth. Therefore, option I is correct. Option II is incorrect because *Streptococcus faecalis* is a spore-forming bacteria, and pasteurization kills only non–spore-forming bacteria. Option III is incorrect because *Streptococcus faecalis* is a facultative anaerobe, meaning that it does not require oxygen for growth.

Passage III (Questions 148–153)

148. When alkyl halides react with potassium hydroxide to yield alkene derivatives, the potassium hydroxide acts as:

A. an acid.
B. a base.
C. a proton donor.
D. a reductant.

B Choices A and C should be eliminated because OH^- is not an acid and cannot *donate* a proton. Choice D is wrong because the OH^- does not *reduce* the carbon.

149. If one were to substitute heavy water (D_2O) in the last steps of the Grignard reaction as shown above, the reaction would lead to the synthesis of:

A. R-R.
B. R-OD.
C. R-D.
D. R-H.

C Grignard reagents (RMgX) react with water to form $Mg(OD)_2$ and the alkane:

$$RMgX + D_2O \rightarrow RD + Mg(OD)_2$$

Choice A should be eliminated since individual alkyl groups will not react with one another. Choices B and D are wrong because no such products would result from the process in question. You should quickly eliminate choice D by remembering that heavy water (D_2O) contains deuterium instead of hydrogen.

150. Alkyl halides are not usually prepared by direct halogenation of alkanes because:

A. alkanes are not very reactive compounds.
B. alkanes have low boiling points.
C. alkanes are converted to alkenes by halogenation.
D. alkanes do not dissolve in polar solutions.

A After you study the alkanes and their reactions, you'll know that alkanes are *not* terribly reactive. Direct halogenation of an alkane occurs only under special conditions of extremely high temperatures or in the presence of certain light wavelengths.

Choice B makes a true statement, but it does not explain why direct halogenation is not generally used to prepare alkyl halides. Choice C is wrong because alkanes don't have double bonds. Choice D makes a true statement, but like choice B, it fails to answer the question.

151. The addition of a peroxy acid to the alkene product shown in Figure 1 would lead to the formation of:

A. a *cis*-diol product
B. an epoxide and a carboxylic acid
C. a dihaloalkane
D. an alcohol via acid-catalyzed hydration of the alkene

B The question has little to do with the passage and requires only knowledge of pertinent organic reactions. Review of organic reactions will remind the reader that the addition of a peroxy acid to an alkene results in the formation of an epoxide product and a carboxylic acid. It is important to note that further hydrolysis of the epoxide (although not mentioned in the question) would give enantiomeric *trans*-diols (NOT *cis*-diols), thereby eliminating choice A. Additionally, *cis*-diol formation is made from alkenes only upon oxidation of the alkene pi-bond with dilute $KMnO_4$ (potassium permanganate) or OsO_4 (osmium tetroxide), both of which require syn-addition of the two alcohol groups to yield the *cis*-diol. Choice C is wrong, as a dihaloalkane is only formed from an alkene upon reaction of the alkene with molecular halogen (X_2). Choice D is wrong because acid-catalyzed hydration of an alkene will yield an alcohol Markovnikov-addition.

152. Alkyl halides are often insoluble in water because:

A. they are hydrophilic.
B. they are ionic compounds.
C. they contain large aliphatic groups.
D. they contain electron-withdrawing groups.

C This question is unrelated to the passage. It requires that you know something about polarity and its relationship to water solubility. Solubility in water *requires* polarity. If alkyl halides could form hydrogen bonds, they would necessarily be polar and, hence, soluble in water.

Choice A is wrong because hydrophilic *means* water-soluble. Choice B is wrong because alkyl halide bonds are generally covalent. Choice D is true, but it is irrelevant and does not answer the question.

153. Distinction between alcohols may be accomplished using all of the following EXCEPT:

A. boiling point determination.
B. density determination.
C. observation of a strong and broad stretch from 3600–3200 cm^{-1} on IR spectroscopy.
D. melting point determination.

C A peak for the OH stretch is easily seen and therefore is indicative of any alcohol. Although alcohols differ as to their boiling points, densities, and melting points, IR spectroscopy identifies the presence of the OH group and consequently identifies alcohols in general.

Free-Standing Questions (154–158)

154. An *eclipsed* conformation of *n*-butane is illustrated below, in the figure on the left. Which of the circled positions in the figure on the right corresponds to the terminal methyl groups placed in the *anti* conformation?

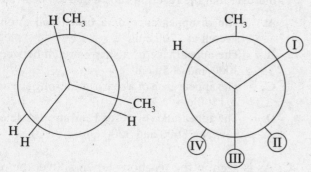

    A. I
    B. II
    C. III
    D. IV

C Butane has free rotation about the C_2-C_3 carbon–carbon single bond. The *eclipsed* conformation means that the methyl groups overlap. The *anti* conformation means the methyl groups are situated "across" from one another (as well as on the two different carbons), and in a staggered formation. With reference to the picture, the position that's directly across from the *n*-butane's methyl group is position III. That's why choice C is correct.

155. When lettuce is placed in deionized water, it remains crisp because:

    A. the cells lose H_2O.
    B. the cells swell with H_2O.
    C. the stomates close in response to excess water.
    D. the chloroplasts generate greater levels of ATP.

B A medium of pure water is hypotonic compared with a cell placed within it. Water will enter the cell in an "attempt" to balance the high solute concentration within the cell. Choice A is wrong for this reason: water would leave the cell only if the cell's solute concentration were *lower* than that of its surrounding medium. Choice C is wrong because stomata tend to *open* in the presence of water. Choice D is wrong because chloroplast activity is irrelevant to the question.

156. Which statement below most accurately describes the characteristic features of striated muscle cells?

    A. Striated muscle cells are stimulated by the autonomic nervous system and contain few mitochondria.
    B. Striated muscle cells are mononucleate and arranged in syncytial bundles.
    C. Striated muscle cells have alternating A-bands and I-bands arranged in a transverse pattern.
    D. Striated muscle cells are similar to smooth muscle cells except that they lack internal stores of calcium.

C Striated muscle cells contain "thick filaments" that correspond to the sarcomere's A-band and "thin filaments" that correspond to its I-band. Choice A is wrong because striated muscle cells are not stimulated by the *autonomic* nervous system. They're stimulated by the *somatic* nervous system. Choices B and D are wrong because striated muscle cells are multinucleate and are structurally dissimilar to smooth muscle cells (although both smooth and striated muscle cells store calcium).

157. Sickle-cell anemia is a blood disorder due to a point mutation in a single gene and is inherited as an autosomal recessive trait. If a woman who is heterozygous for this disorder and a man who is homozygous dominant have a son, then the son most likely has:

A. full-blown sickle-cell anemia.

B. sickle-cell trait, a carrier disease.

C. the same chance of inheriting the sickle-cell gene as his sister.

D. no signs of symptoms or the disease.

C This question tests understanding of the transmission of autosomal traits and requires knowledge of genetic nomenclature. The question states that sickle-cell anemia is inherited as an autosomal recessive trait, meaning that there is no gender preference in the transmission of this gene, as there would be if the gene were X-linked. Undoubtedly, the daughter of this couple (the son's sister) has as great a probability of inheriting this autosomal trait as the son does, making choice C the best answer.

The woman described in the question is heterozygous for sickle-cell anemia and has sickle-cell trait: she has certain adverse symptoms associated with sickled blood cells, but does not have full-blown sickle-cell anemia. Because the woman is a heterozygote, she has only a 50% chance of passing the mutated gene to her offspring. The father, on the other hand, is homozygous dominant, meaning that he does not carry the sickle-cell gene mutation. Thus, the father can only donate a normal, or wild-type, allele to his offspring and cannot contribute to their chance of getting the disease. Because the father does not have a mutant allele, choice A is incorrect as it is impossible for the son to inherit two autosomal recessive alleles (which is necessary for him to have full-blown sickle-cell anemia).

In short, the chance that the son will inherit a mutant gene from his mother is 50% (choice B). It is also important to note that the son has a 50% chance of inheriting a wild-type allele from his mother, and being unaffected (choice D). This eliminates both choices B and D, as the question asks which is *most* likely.

158. Consider the reaction below:

$$CH_3CH_2CH_2OH \xrightarrow[CH_2Cl_2]{PCC} CH_3CH_2CHO$$

Which of the following observations about the infrared spectrum of the reaction mixture would indicate that the reaction shown above occurred?

A. The disappearance of a broad and strong stretch at 1700 cm^{-1}

B. The appearance of a sharp stretch between 3000 and 2850 cm^{-1}

C. The appearance of a sharp and strong stretch at 1700 cm^{-1}

D. The appearance of a broad and strong stretch between 3600 and 3200 cm^{-1}

C As is seen in the reaction shown above, the reactant on the left is an alcohol, and the product on the right is an aldehyde. A review of IR spectroscopy reveals that the above reaction would result in the disappearance of a broad and strong stretch between 3600 and 3200 cm^{-1} (the alcohol stretch) and the appearance of a sharp and strong stretch at 1700 cm^{-1} (the carbonyl stretch). The aldehyde product contains a carbonyl group which should produce a very strong and *sharp* stretch at 1700 cm^{-1}, eliminating choice A, which indicates the appearance of a *broad* and strong stretch at 1700 cm^{-1}. The appearance of a sharp stretch between 3000 and 2850 cm^{-1} is indicative of a sp^3 C-H bond, which is neither created nor removed during the course of the reaction, eliminating choice B. Choice D is wrong, since the appearance of a broad and strong stretch between 3600 and 3200 cm^{-1} indicates the formation of an alcohol, which is clearly not being produced in the above reaction.

Passage IV (Questions 159–163)

159. On the basis of urinary excretion as shown in Table 1, which two subject test groups showed the greatest level of estrogen output?

   I.   Onset of menstruation
   II. Ovulation peak
   III. Pregnancy, 160 days
   IV. Pregnancy, term

   A. I and III
   B. I and IV
   C. II and III
   D. III and IV

D This question requires that you consider Table 1, keeping a particularly close watch over the relevant units. Look at the test groups labeled "pregnancy, 160 days" and "pregnancy, term." For these two groups, estrogen secretion is measured in mg. In all other test groups, estrogen level is measured in μg, a smaller unit. Once you're alerted to the units, you can see that the two named test groups show the highest levels of estrogen synthesis and secretion. That's why options III and IV are correct.

160. From Table 1, which variable would prove to be the best marker for the term stage of normal pregnancy, as indicated by the Kober test?

   A. The oxidation of estradiol
   B. The presence of estriol
   C. The presence of 16α-hydroxyestrone
   D. A positive Kober reaction

C The question calls for some common sense. Table 1 shows you that 16α-hydroxyestrone appears only for the test group labeled "pregnancy, term." Hence, it would *tell you* that a patient is in the term stage of pregnancy. That's another way of saying 16α-hydroxyestrone acts as an *indicator* for the term stage of pregnancy. Choice A should be eliminated. With reference to the term stage of pregnancy, the passage does not mention estradiol oxidation. Choice B is incorrect because estriol is present in *all* test groups. Choice D is also wrong. A positive Kober test indicates only that estrogen is present, and estrogen is present in *all* test groups.

161. All of the following are true of oogenesis EXCEPT:

   A. primary oocytes can be frozen in prophase I for decades.
   B. all gamete precursors (primary oocytes) are formed while a female is still an embryo in the womb.
   C. secondary oocytes do not finish meiosis II unless they are fertilized by a sperm.
   D. the egg and sperm nuclei fuse before the egg extrudes the second polar body.

D During oogenesis, the egg and sperm nuclei do not fuse until *after* the egg extrudes the second polar body and completes its maturation process to become an ovum. Thus, choice D is untrue and is the correct answer. Choices A, B, and C are wrong because they are all true statements.

162. According to the passage, what change in the ratio of estrone to estradiol is expected to occur as women enter postmenopause?

   A. The ratio increases, because estradiol levels decrease relatively more than estrone levels decrease.
   B. The ratio increases, because estradiol levels decrease while estrone levels are unaffected.
   C. The ratio is unchanged, because both estrogen hormone levels decrease in the postmenopausal period.
   D. The ratio decreases, because estrone levels decrease more than estradiol levels.

A Table 1 provides the relevant information. For premenopausal women, the ratio of estrone to estradiol levels is approximately 2:1. For postmenopausal women, it's about 4:1.

163. Researchers further studied estrogen levels in subjects at the luteal minimum of estrogen secretion and at the 210th day of pregnancy. Which findings would NOT indicate a trend similar to that found during the original procedures?

    A.   The levels of estriol are greater than the levels of estradiol in both pregnant and luteal minimum groups.

    B.   The levels of estradiol are lower than those of estrone in the pregnant group.

    C.   The estrone levels are elevated in the pregnant group compared with the luteal minimum group.

    D.   The ratio of 16-epiestriol levels between the pregnant and luteal minimum groups is 1:2.

D According to Table 1, 16-epiestriol appears *only* at the term stage of pregnancy and not during the luteal stage. The results listed in choice D would contradict the trend seen in the table. Choices A, B, and C are wrong because each of the named findings is consistent with the data set forth in Table 1.

Passage V (Questions 164–169)

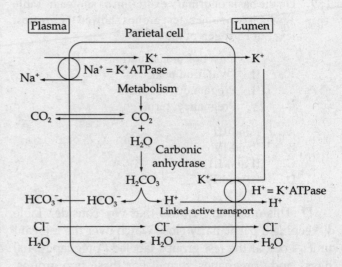

Figure 1 Acid secretion by parietal cells

164. All of the following statements regarding pepsinogen are true EXCEPT that:

    A.   it is an inactive zymogen.

    B.   gastric acid facilitates conversion of pepsinogen to the active enzyme pepsin.

    C.   it is secreted by gastric chief cells.

    D.   it initiates the digestion of lipids.

D An acid environment transforms the enzyme precursor pepsinogen to the active enzyme pepsin. Pepsin cleaves peptide bonds, which link the amino acid constituents of a protein. Pepsin therefore initiates the digestion not of lipid but of protein. Choice A makes a true statement. Pepsinogen is an inactive zymogen; it is an enzyme precursor that requires some further modification, or environmental stimulus, to facilitate its activity. Choice B also makes a true statement. The zymogen pepsinogen is rendered active by the stomach's acid environment. Choice C makes an accurate statement as well; pepsinogen is secreted by gastric chief cells.

165. According to Figure 1, which ion shows lower concentration in gastric secretions than in plasma?

A. Potassium
B. Chloride
C. Hydrogen
D. Sodium

D Figure 1 shows that potassium, hydrogen, and chloride are secreted from the luminal face of the parietal cell into the lumen of the stomach. The diagram also makes clear that the cell secretes none of these ions into the plasma. The concentration of all three ions must therefore be higher in the stomach than in the plasma. Sodium, on the other hand, is not secreted into the stomach but into the plasma by action of an ATPase (as shown at the upper left aspect of the diagram). Sodium concentration, therefore, is lower in gastric secretions than in the plasma.

166. Hydrogen and chloride ions in the stomach draw water into the lumen so that gastric secretions are isotonic to plasma. This form of movement is most appropriately termed:

A. active transport.
B. passive transport.
C. osmosis.
D. facilitated transport.

C Osmosis denotes the passive movement of water along its concentration gradient in response to osmotically active ions. Choice A refers to active transport, which involves energy-dependent movement of an electrolyte against its concentration or electrical gradient. Choice B refers to passive transport and refers to the movement of ions (not fluid) in accordance with their concentration or electrical gradient. Choice D refers to facilitated transport, a process in which lipid- insoluble matter crosses a lipid membrane by combining with a lipid soluble "carrier molecule." Like osmosis and passive transport, it is an energy-independent phenomenon.

167. Studying the gastric activities of a volunteer, a group of researchers monitor the stomach's venous blood and report a transitory period during which it is highly basic. With which of the following is the period of basicity most likely associated?

A. Active acid secretion
B. Reduced gastrin secretion
C. Active secretin secretion
D. Reduced pepsinogen secretion

A Both the passage text and Figure 1 indicate that for every hydrogen ion secreted into the stomach's lumen, one HCO_3^- ion moves into the plasma. A high concentration of HCO_3^- in the blood produces an alkaline pH (above 7.0). A high HCO_3^- concentration in the gastric venous blood likely follows recent gastric acid secretion, since each release of H^+ into the lumen engenders a concomitant release of HCO_3^- to the plasma. Choice B is wrong because reduced gastrin secretion would lead to reduced acid secretion. Choice C is wrong because, as the passage states, secretin inhibits acid secretion, so active secretion of secretin would lead to reduced acid secretion. Choice D is wrong because the secretion of acid accompanies the secretion of pepsinogen. Thus, if secretion of pepsinogen is reduced, acid secretion would also be reduced.

168. Carbonic acid that is produced by the parietal cell is formed from:

A. carbon dioxide and hydrogen ion with facilitation by carbonic anhydrase.
B. carbon dioxide and hydrogen ion with facilitation by ATPase.
C. carbon dioxide and water with facilitation by carbonic anhydrase.
D. carbon dioxide and water with facilitation by ATPase.

C Your review of biology should remind you that carbonic acid is produced by the reaction of carbon dioxide and water. Moreover, the diagram demonstrates that CO_2 and H_2O combine to produce H_2CO_3 with catalysis by carbonic anhydrase. Choice A is wrong. Hydrogen is not a substrate in the formation of carbonic acid. Choices B and D are wrong because, among other reasons, ATPases catalyze only those reactions in which ATP is hydrolyzed.

169. Which of the following pharmacological agents would most likely stimulate gastric motility?

- **A.** An agent that mimics the action of secretin
- **B.** An agent that acts as a terminal parasympathetic transmitter
- **C.** An agent that blocks parasympathetic transmission
- **D.** An agent that acts as a sympathetic transmitter

B The "terminal" parasympathetic transmitter is the one released onto the organ. If an agent mimics such a transmitter, it will likely have the same effect as parasympathetic stimulation would and "fool" the gastric muscle into contracting. Choice A is wrong because secretin is not a neurotransmitter but a hormone whose effects do not include the stimulation of gastric motility. Choice C is wrong because parasympathetic stimulation *promotes* gastric motility. Choice D is wrong as well. Sympathetic stimulation would likely oppose the effects of parasympathetic stimulation and therefore inhibit gastric motility.

Passage VI (Questions 170–175)

170. Serotonin is derived from:

- **A.** an amino acid.
- **B.** an enzyme.
- **C.** another neurotransmitter.
- **D.** a hormone.

A The third sentence of the first paragraph states that serotonin is a product of tryptophan metabolism. Recall that tryptophan is an essential amino acid.

171. Among the following, which graph best describes the degree of axonal degeneration as a function of MDMA dose?

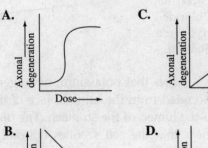

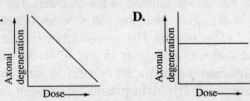

C The passage states that damage to serotonin-producing axons is most likely directly related to dosage. The graph depicted in choice C shows a linear relationship between the dose of the drug and the damage to axons. As dose increases, so does the damage. Choice A depicts a relationship in which dose produces increased damage at relatively high doses, but produces little damage at relatively low doses. Choice B depicts dose and damage as inversely proportional. Choice D indicates that dose has *no* effect on axonal health.

172. If MDMA is found to produce insomnia, the reason might be that:

- **A.** it inhibits serotonin synthesis in brain stem neurons.
- **B.** it destroys serotonin-containing axons in the brain stem.
- **C.** it competes for serotonin binding sites on serotonergic neurons.
- **D.** it causes degeneration of cell bodies of serotonin-producing neurons.

B If, as here, you must speculate, have your speculation conform to information supplied in the passage. The passage indicates that MDMA destroys axons that release serotonin. If an axon releases serotonin, it must first contain serotonin. Choices A, C, and D are not inherently wrong, but they find no justification in the passage.

173. The most likely explanation for the differences in axonal regeneration to the three connecting targets, as demonstrated by the squirrel monkey results on Table 1, is that:

   A. excessive axonal repair to the amygdala and hypothalamus inhibits reconnection to the cortex.

   B. dendrites of neurons in the cortex can compensate for axonal deficiencies.

   C. longer axonal projections regenerate more easily than do shorter ones.

   D. shorter axonal projections regenerate more easily than do longer ones.

D The passage states that MDMA "acts on serotonin pathways by destroying *axons* that release serotonin." Thus, the correct answer choice should discuss axonal repair, and B can be eliminated. Choices A, C, and D could all explain the differences, but the question asks for the *most likely* explanation. There is no reason to assume choice A, and it seems logical that shorter axons would regenerate more easily. Both the amygdala and the hypothalamus lie closer to the brain stem than the cortex, and this is the most likely reason for the repair pattern seen.

174. A drug that prevented the reuptake of serotonin would most likely:

   A. produce an action potential in the presynaptic neuron by binding to receptors on the axonal membrane.

   B. reduce the intensity of an action potential in the postsynaptic neuron.

   C. prevent the postsynaptic neuron from undergoing frequent action potentials.

   D. increase the amount of stimulation received by dendrites of the postsynaptic neuron.

D A drug that prevents the reuptake of serotonin from the synaptic cleft would cause serotonin to remain there, prolonging the amount of stimulation received at the postsynaptic dendrites. Choice A is wrong because although presynaptic neurons may have neurotransmitter-specific receptors (specific for serotonin, in this case) on their cell surface, neither anterograde nor retrograde action potentials are generated in the nervous system by this mechanism. Choice B is wrong because an action potential is an "all-or-none" phenomenon. When a stimulus reaches threshold, a neuron undergoes a full action potential whose intensity does not change as the action potential travels down the neuron. Choice C is wrong, too. It describes an effect opposite to that which should be expected.

175. All of the following statements correctly describe events associated with synaptic transmission of a nerve impulse EXCEPT:

   A. mitochondria supply the ATP needed for synthesis of neurotransmitter.

   B. neurotransmitters are released into the synaptic cleft in direct response to an action potential.

   C. calcium is actively sequestered in direct response to an action potential.

   D. neurotransmitters bind to receptors on the postsynaptic membrane and cause a change in permeability of the membrane.

C When an action potential reaches the terminal end of an axon, it causes not sequestration of calcium but the opening of voltage-gated calcium channels. The influx of calcium into the terminal end of the axon causes synaptic vesicles there to fuse with the axonal membrane. The vesicles exocytose (release) neurotransmitter into the cleft. The neurotransmitter then diffuses across the cleft, binds to receptors on the postsynaptic cell, and causes a change in permeability to one or more ions.

Free-Standing Questions (176–180)

176. Within the cell, protein turnover reflects a balance between the rates of protein synthesis and degradation. For a given eukaryotic protein, the rate of synthesis is most tightly regulated by which of the following factors?

A. The amount of heterochromatin available for transcription

B. The number of mRNA transcripts available for translation

C. The amount of RNA polymerase bound at the Pribnow box promoter site

D. The amount of RNA-dependent RNA polymerase available for transcription

B Regulation of protein synthesis lies at the level of mRNA. The number of copies of mRNA that are transcribed from a single DNA template governs cellular production of a given protein, as does the number of freely available ribosomes within the cell. Choice A is wrong because heterochromatin is the condensed, compact form of DNA in the cell and is not transcribed. Remember that it is "euchromatin" that is the unwound, actively transcribed form of DNA. Choice C is wrong since the Pribnow box is found only in prokaryotic organisms and the question refers specifically to eukaryotic transcription. While RNA polymerase does bind to the Pribnow box to promote transcription in prokaryotic organisms, the Pribnow box promoter sequence is not found in eukaryotic organisms. Choice D is wrong because eukaryotes do not possess RNA-dependent RNA polymerase, which is found only in RNA viruses. All RNA viruses, which contain a single-stranded RNA genome, use RNA-dependent RNA polymerase to replicate their genome once inside the host cell.

177. The likelihood of a given allele's sudden predominance within a small, isolated population independent of adaptive advantage is best attributed to:

A. the Hardy-Weinberg law.

B. genetic drift.

C. adaptive radiation.

D. survival of the fittest.

B Genetic drift occurs in small, isolated populations. It refers to the statistical possibility that deleterious alleles might nonetheless predominate. The limited gene pool associated with small populations contributes to random "genetic accidents of misfortune," and to the potential predominance of disadvantageous alleles. Choice A is incorrect because the Hardy-Weinberg law applies to very large populations and predicts stability of the gene pool. Choice C refers to the likelihood that a given species may "radiate" to produce new ones, as competing organisms "force" themselves to find environments and niches that reduce competition. Choice D is contrary to the phenomenon described in the question.

178. If 1-propanol is subjected to ^{1}H NMR, the protons on the methyl group will be split into a:

A. singlet.

B. doublet.

C. triplet.

D. quadruplet.

C Recognize that the signal attributable to the methyl group is split into a triplet by coupling with the neighboring CH_2 protons.

179. Which of the following represents an effect of antidiuretic hormone (ADH) on the renal nephron?

    A.   It increases water loss by reducing the permeability of the collecting duct to water.

    B.   It reduces water loss by increasing the permeability of the collecting duct to water.

    C.   It reduces water loss by increasing the permeability of the loop of Henle to water.

    D.   It increases water loss by reducing the permeability of the loop of Henle to water.

B ADH renders the collecting duct permeable to water. Because the fluid within the duct is less concentrated than the interstitial fluid, increased permeability causes water to move by osmosis from duct to interstitium. This, in turn, creates a relatively less voluminous and more concentrated urine. Choice A is opposite to fact. Choices C and D speak to effects at the loop of Henle. ADH does not operate at that site.

180. A man whose mother is a carrier for color-blindness and whose father was color-blind has a male child with a normal female. What are the chances that the male child will be color-blind?

    A.   0%

    B.   25%

    C.   50%

    D.   100%

A Color-blindness is a sex-linked (or "X-linked") trait. It is carried on the X chromosome only. Since a father delivers only a Y chromosome to a male child, he cannot pass the gene for color-blindness to a male, even if he himself carries it. Put more broadly, an X-linked trait cannot pass from a male to a male. In this case, the father himself has a 50% chance of being color-blind; from his own mother he might have received either the mutant or the normal gene. But even if he did receive the mutant gene, he cannot pass it to a male child (although he can pass it to a female child).

Passage VII (Questions 181–186)

181. Based on the passage, one could estimate a dicarboxylic acid's K_1 value by determining:

    A.   its concentration in a nonequilibrium mixture.

    B.   the stability of the anion form versus the stability of the acid form.

    C.   its tendency to undergo decarboxylation.

    D.   its crystallization structure.

B When you deal with chemical equilibria, you must remember: The more stable the products, the more likely it is that the reaction will proceed to completion. This means that K_1 is determined by the *relative stabilities* of a dicarboxylic acid's protonated and deprotonated forms. Choices A, C, and D are wrong because none of the named factors characterizes or influences equilibrium. Equilibrium is characterized by the *ratio of products to reactants*.

182. Glutaric acid is a dicarboxylic acid with the formula $HOOC(CH_2)_3COOH$. This acid is most likely to have a K_1 constant closest in value to which substance listed in the table?

    A.   Fumaric acid

    B.   Maleic acid

    C.   Succinic acid

    D.   Oxalic acid

C If you know that K_1 values tend to be similar for acids that are relatively similar in their bond type and in the length of their carbon chains, you'll realize that you should be looking for a compound whose structure is similar to that of glutaric acid. Among the choices, glutaric acid's molecular formula is most like that of succinic acid. (Glutaric acid has one more $[CH_2]$ group than succinic acid.)

183. If equal concentrations of succinic acid, malonic acid, and maleic acid were heated in a weakly basic solution, which of the following products would NOT be expected to be found at equilibrium?

    A. $HOOCCH_2COO^-$
    B. $HOOC(CH_2)_2COO^-$
    C. $HOOCCH=CHCOO^-$
    D. $HOOC-COOH$

D The question requires that you (a) examine the chemical formulas shown in Table 1 for the three acids named in the question, and (b) determine which of the species shown in choices A – D does *not* correspond to one of those three. Choices A, B, and C represent the anions that would follow from a single deprotonation of malonic acid, succinic acid, and maleic acid, respectively. Choice A reflects the single deprotonation of *malonic acid* (the second entry in Table 1):

$$HOOCCH_2COOH + H_2O \leftrightarrows HOOCCH_2COO^- + H_3O^+$$

Choice B reflects the single deprotonation of *succinic acid* (the third entry in Table 1):

$$HOOC(CH_2)_2COOH + H_2O \leftrightarrows HOOC(CH_2)_2COO^- + H_3O^+$$

Choice C reflects the single deprotonation of *maleic acid* (the fourth entry in Table 1):

$$HOOCCH=CHCOOH \leftrightarrows HOOCCH=CHCOO^- + H_3O^+$$

According to the question, all three of these acids were present in the original mixture. Consequently, all three corresponding anions *would* be present in the equilibrium to which the question refers. Choice D ($HOOC-COOH$) describes oxalic acid (the first entry in Table 1). Since oxalic acid was *not* present in the original mixture, it would not be present in the equilibrium described by the question.

184. Based on information in the passage, it would be difficult to estimate K_2 for a molecule with the formula $HOOCCH_2CHCOO^-$ because:

    NH_3^+

    A. a compound substituted with an amino group cannot be compared directly to succinic acid.
    B. it cannot exist in the deprotonated form.
    C. it must form an insoluble compound.
    D. it represents an unstable compound.

A The anion of the indicated compound is not directly comparable to any structure listed on Table 1 for the simple reason that *it contains an amine group*.

185. In an aqueous mixture known to contain only maleic and fumaric acids, the proportion of maleic to fumaric can best be determined by?

    A. Radioactive tagging of the corresponding alkene
    B. Bydration of the anion solution
    C. Acidification of the solution
    D. Nuclear magnetic resonance spectroscopy of the mixture

D After you study NMR spectroscopy, you'll know that it is well suited to differentiate between *cis* and *trans* configurations. Answer choices A, B, and C are wrong for the simple reason that none of the named processes distinguishes between *cis* and *trans* configurations.

186. The value of K_1 of the dicarboxylic compound glutamic acid is larger than the K_1 of glutaric acid because:

   A.   glutamate is readily convertible into a nonpolar zwitterion.

   B.   the deprotonated form of glutamic acid is less stable than the glutarate anion.

   C.   glutamate is an acidic amino acid.

   D.   glutamic acid is a stronger acid than glutaric acid.

D From the passage, you learn that a lower K_1 value indicates a relatively lower tendency to deprotonate and that the larger the K value, the stronger the acid. After you study equilibria phenomena and acid–base organic chemistry, you'll know that the tendency to deprotonate, in turn, is a function of anion stability. Glutamic acid has a K_1 larger than that of glutaric acid, which means that its anion is more stable than that of glutaric acid. There is another way to think about this phenomenon. A review of acid–base chemistry will also reveal that K_a is a form of K_{eq} which specifically deals with acids. Furthermore, the pK_a (also known as $-\log K_a$) is inversely indicative of the strength of the acid: The lower the value of the pK_a, the stronger is the acid. The pK_1 of glutamic acid is 2.10, while the pK_1 of glutaric acid is 4.34, indicating that glutamic acid is simply a stronger acid than is glutaric acid.

Choices A and C are wrong because the phenomena to which they refer are irrelevant to the question.

Passage VIII (Questions 187–191)

187. The substrate in the experiment is:

   A.   catalase.

   B.   potassium permanganate.

   C.   hydrogen peroxide.

   D.   water.

C Catalase is an enzyme that acts on hydrogen peroxide, reducing it to water and oxygen. In an enzymatic reaction, the substrate is that on which the enzyme acts. Choice A is clearly wrong; catalase is the enzyme. Choice B is wrong as well. Potassium permanganate serves in the titration but is not the substrate. Choice D refers to water, a product.

188. The primary function of lysosomes is to:

   A.   sequester degradative enzymes from the cytoplasm.

   B.   store water and other materials.

   C.   digest worn cells and organelles.

   D.   modify secretory enzymes before they are sent from the cell.

C Lysosomes digest worn cells and organelles using degradative enzymes contained within their membranes. Choice A speaks to sequestration. Lysosomes do sequester enzymes, but that is not their principal function. Choice B refers to the storage of water, a function served by vacuoles. Choice D describes not lysosomes, but the Golgi apparatus.

189. With reference to the experiment, which of the following did NOT occur during the three-minute period following the introduction of catalase?

- **A.** The substrate bound to the enzyme.
- **B.** A substrate-enzyme complex was formed.
- **C.** The reaction proceeded.
- **D.** A new enzyme was synthesized.

D Finding 2 indicates that much hydrogen peroxide disappeared from the reaction vessel *without* participation of potassium permanganate. The increased disappearance was attributable to the presence of catalase and represents an enzyme-catalyzed reaction. An enzyme molecule is characteristically regenerated at the conclusion of the reaction it catalyzes only to "reenlist in the service" and catalyze its reaction over and over again. Nothing in the experimental procedure or findings indicates that a *new* enzyme was synthesized. The events described in choices A and B are characteristic of catalysis. Choice C, of course, makes a true statement, since it is clear that the catalyzed decomposition of hydrogen peroxide did occur.

190. Reduction of temperature would have which of the following effects on the second trial?

- **A.** It would impair catalase activity.
- **B.** It would enhance catalase activity.
- **C.** It would prevent regeneration of the catalase at the conclusion of the reaction.
- **D.** It would convert the catalase to an inorganic catalyst.

A Enzyme activity normally increases with increased temperature and decreases with decreased temperature. Choice B contravenes scientific observation. Choice C is wrong because it is inherent in the nature of a catalyst, however impaired its activity, that it is regenerated at the conclusion of catalysis. Choice D is implausible. There is no basis on which to suppose that reducing the temperature of a protein will convert its chemical structure.

191. Extreme high temperature would have which of the following effects on the second trial?

- **A.** It would increase the required amount of potassium permanganate to approximately 18 mL.
- **B.** It would increase the required amount of potassium permanganate to approximately 28 mL.
- **C.** It would maintain the required amount of potassium permanganate at approximately 9 mL.
- **D.** It would reduce the required amount of potassium permanganate to approximately 1 mL.

B Although enzyme activity normally increases with increasing temperature, *extreme* high temperature denatures the enzyme and renders it inactive. Twenty-eight milliliters of potassium permanganate were required to titrate the hydrogen peroxide in the absence of enzyme (Finding 1). With catalase rendered inactive by extreme high temperature, the reaction vessel would be functionally devoid of enzyme. As in the first trial, 28 mL of potassium permanganate solution would be required to titrate the hydrogen peroxide.

Passage IX (Questions 192–197)

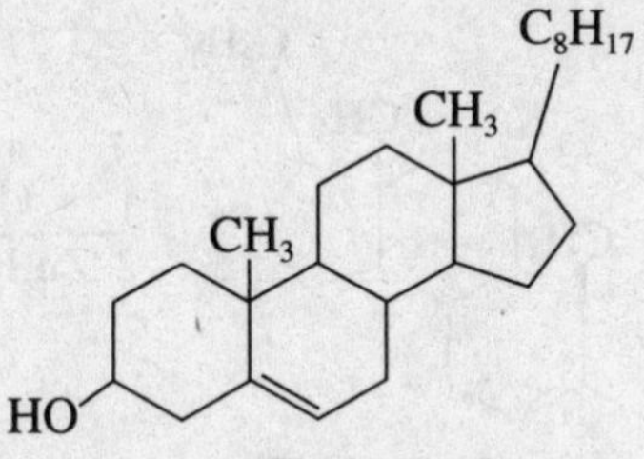

Cholesterol

192. How many chiral centers does the above cholesterol molecule feature?

- **A.** 7
- **B.** 6
- **C.** 5
- **D.** 4

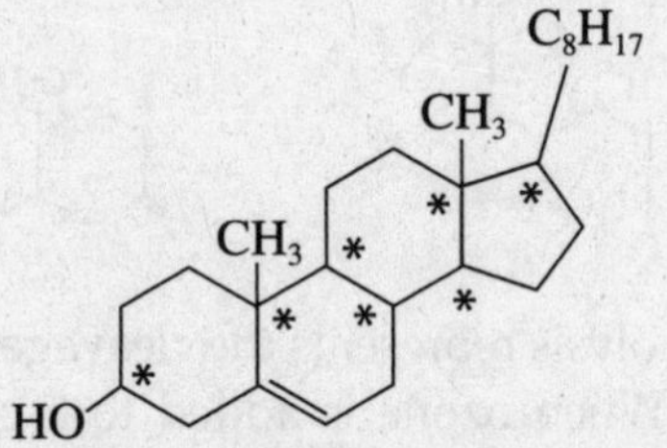

Cholesterol

A The definition of chirality requires that a tetrahedral central atom be connected to four different atoms. Thus, any atom that is involved in a double bond or is bonded to less than four different atoms or groups cannot be considered chiral. A careful examination of the structure of cholesterol, as it is depicted in Figure 1, will reveal that it has seven chiral carbon atoms.

193. What is the product of the reaction shown below?

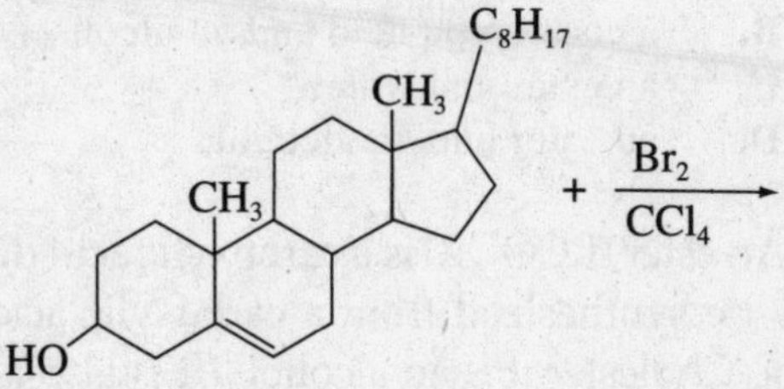

A.

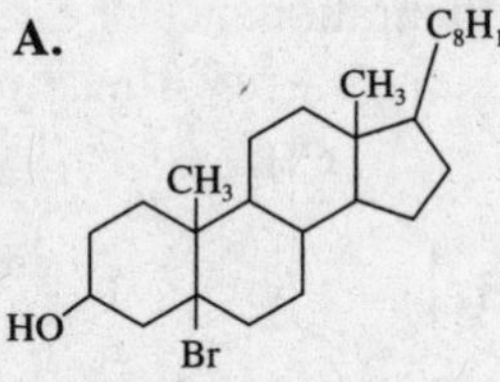

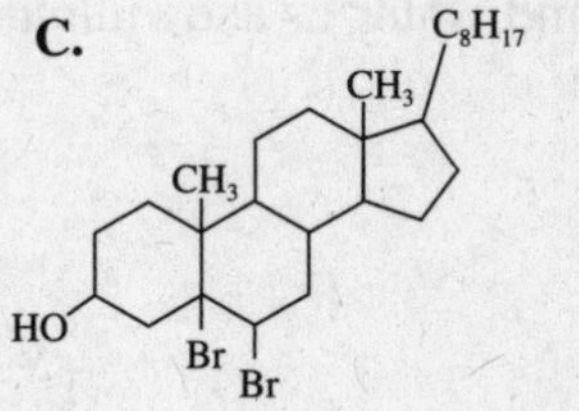

B.

C.

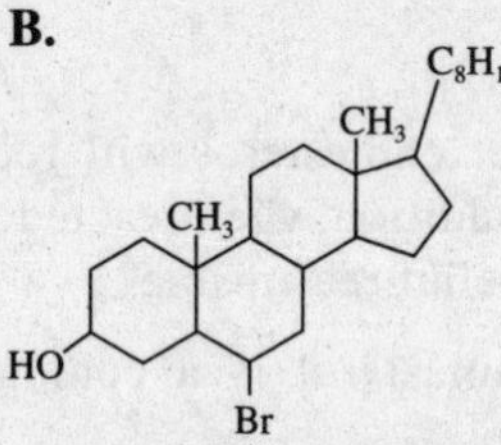

D.

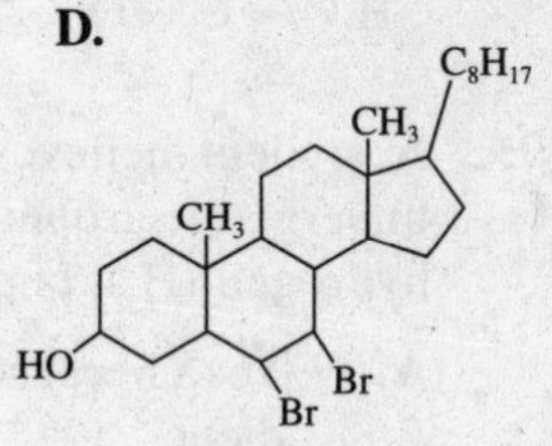

C Halogen molecules undergo electrophilic addition reactions with alkenes. In this case, the bromine molecule adds to the carbon-carbon double bond. As Br_2 approaches the double bond, the Br–Br bond is polarized and ultimately breaks. Choice A is wrong because it shows not two but one bromine atom bonded to the product. Choice B is wrong for the same reason. Choice D is wrong as well. It shows the bromine atoms incorrectly positioned; they should be positioned on either side of the preexisting double bond.

194. When cholesterol reacts with CH_3COOH, it forms:

    A. a carboxylic acid and water.
    B. a carboxylic acid and an alcohol.
    C. an ester and water.
    D. an ester and an alcohol.

C An ester (RCOOR) is a carboxylic acid derivative. It may be synthesized from a carboxylic acid and an alcohol. Cholesterol *is* an alcohol. (It is also a steroid.) When it reacts with a carboxylic acid, it forms an ester and water, as shown in this illustration:

195. A student believes that cholesterol will readily undergo electrophilic addition when reacted with hydrogen (H_2). Is the belief reasonable?

    A. Yes, because cholesterol is a conjugated diene.
    B. Yes, because cholesterol may undergo a hydrogenation reaction.
    C. No, because cholesterol is not aromatic.
    D. No, because electrophilic addition of H_2 requires catalysis.

D Recall that in the presence of H_2 and a metal catalyst such as nickel, palladium, or platinum, an alkene will undergo electrophilic addition of hydrogen across the alkene double bond. As is seen in the figure of cholesterol above, one of the functional groups within the cholesterol molecule is a double bond, enabling cholesterol to undergo hydrogenation via an electrophilic addition reaction but only in the presence of a metal catalyst, which the question does *not* mention. Choice A is wrong because a conjugated diene features single and double bonds in alternating series. Cholesterol does not. Choice B is true, but not under the conditions provided in the question. Choice C has no bearing on the issue raised in the question.

196. Which of the following is the most probable product when cholesterol undergoes ozonolysis?

$$\begin{array}{c} 1. \quad O_3 \\ \hline 2. \ Zn_2H_3O^+ \end{array}$$

C Ozonolysis represents the cleavage of a molecule by ozone. When ozone is added to a carbon–carbon double bond in the pictured reaction, two carbonyl entities result, as shown in choice C.

197. Suppose an investigator attempts to produce 5-cholestene-3-one from cholesterol. Which of the following infrared spectroscopic findings would inform the investigator that the reaction has occurred?

Cholesterol →(Jones' reagent)→ 5-Cholestene-3-one

A. The disappearance of OH absorption from the reactant
B. The disappearance of the carbonyl group in the product
C. The disappearance of a double bond from the reactant
D. The disappearance of a methyl group from the reactant

A Infrared spectroscopy identifies a molecule's functional groups. Examine the illustration that depicts the reaction. The reactant features a hydroxyl group. The product shows a carbonyl group but no OH group. The investigator will know the reaction has occurred if IR spectroscopy shows the disappearance of an OH group. Choice B refers to the disappearance of a carbonyl group in the product. Since the product features a carbonyl group, such a finding is incorrect. Choice C refers to the disappearance of an alkene group from the reactant. Again, both reactant and product feature alkene groups; the alkene group does not disappear. Choice D refers to the disappearance of the methyl group in the reactant, an event that does not arise with this reaction.

Passage X (Questions 198–203)

198. Which of the following does NOT occur at the same time that the mitotic spindle assembles in the dividing cell?

A. Chromosomes condense and become visible when viewed with a microscope.
B. The nuclear membrane begins to disintegrate.
C. Chromosomes line up along the cell's equator.
D. Centrioles divide and each one moves to an opposite pole of the cell.

C Review the stages of mitosis and recall that the spindle apparatus begins to appear in prophase and the chromosomes begin to align themselves along its fibers late in early metaphase. Choices A, B, and D describe events that occur during prophase. In prophase, centrioles move to opposite sides of the cell, microtubules assemble to form the spindle apparatus, and the nuclear membrane begins to degenerate. Chromosomes align on the cell equator during metaphase.

199. The mating shown below would create offspring that exhibit which of the following shell-coiling patterns?

DD (male) × dd (female) → Dd (offspring)

A. All right-coiling
B. All left-coiling
C. 50% right-coiling and 50% left-coiling
D. Cannot be determined from the information provided

B Although D (right-coiling) is the dominant allele, the passage states that direction of coiling in the offspring is governed not by the genotype of the offspring itself, but by that of its mother. In this case, the offspring's mother has a genotype that codes for left-handed coiling (dd). That is what the offspring will exhibit.

200. In mammals, oogenesis involves:

    A. two divisions that ultimately produce one haploid ovum.

    B. two divisions that ultimately produce four haploid ova.

    C. one division that ultimately produces one haploid ovum.

    D. one division that ultimately produces two haploid ova.

A Oogenesis is the meiotic process that produces the haploid female gamete, the ovum. Theoretically, the first and second meiotic divisions should yield four haploid progeny. In mammalian oogenesis, however, the overwhelming mass of cytoplasm belonging to the progenitor cell is delivered to only one of its four progeny. The remaining three are dwarfed by comparison. They are termed "polar bodies" and degenerate. (In mammalian spermatogenesis, a single diploid progenitor does produce four haploid spermatozoa.)

201. When scientists injected a low-molecular-weight yellow dye into a single cell of a sixteen-cell mollusk embryo, they discovered that the dye was confined to that cell and its progeny. When they injected the dye into a single cell of a thirty-two–cell embryo, they located the dye in that cell as well as in adjacent cells. Based on these findings, it is most reasonable to conclude that communication between cells of a developing mollusk embryo develops at the:

    A. zygote stage.
    B. neurula stage.
    C. gastrula stage.
    D. blastula stage.

D The blastula is a fluid-filled ball of cells that arises after cleavage and contains at least 32 cells. Recall that a morula is a solid ball of cells and contains up to 16 cells. Choice A can be ruled out because the zygote is a single cell. Choices B and C can be ruled out because these constitute later developmental stages that involve many more cells than the thirty-two-cell embryo examined in the experiment.

202. Members of a given species:

    A. have identical genotypes.
    B. have identical phenotypes.
    C. are unable to breed with one another to produce viable offspring.
    D. are unable to produce fertile offspring with members of another species.

D By definition two individuals belong to the same species if they can produce fertile offspring. And, if two individuals belong to different species, they cannot produce fertile offspring. (Note that the dogma just described allows for breeding between individuals of two different species. The horse and the donkey, for example, belong to different species but might mate to produce a mule. The mule, however, is sterile.)

203. If, with regard to a particular population of *Lymnaea peregra*, all conditions for operation of the Hardy-Weinberg Law are fully satisfied, then, over time, the prevalence in the population of the left-handed (d) allele would most likely:

    A. increase significantly.
    B. decrease significantly.
    C. increase significantly and then decrease significantly.
    D. remain relatively constant.

D According to the Hardy-Weinberg Law, the occurrence of dominant and recessive alleles within a population remains *constant* over time so long as (1) population size is very large, (2) mating is random, (3) mutation does not occur, (4) the population takes in no genes from other populations, and (5) selection does not occur. These are the five conditions to which the question refers. So long as they are satisfied, the occurrence of the recessive (d) allele will remain relatively constant.

Passage XI (Questions 204–208)

204. In the preparation of isopropyl alcohol, what is the role of sulfuric acid?

    A. It acts as a catalyst.
    B. It increases the pH of the solution.
    C. It ionizes the alkene.
    D. It causes a reduction of the alkene.

A Examine the two steps set forth in the passage and note that sulfuric acid is present at the beginning of the first (in dissociated form, as H^+ and HSO_4^-) and at the end of the reaction as well. That a substance should be necessary to a reaction and regenerated at its conclusion is strong evidence that it serves as a catalyst. Choice B is wrong because sulfuric acid is a strong acid and decreases ambient pH. Choice C is a true statement, but A is a more complete answer for the role of the acid. Choice D is wrong because there is no basis to conclude that sulfuric acid reduces the alkene.

205. How many chiral centers are featured within the isopropyl alcohol molecule?

    A. 0
    B. 1
    C. 2
    D. 3

A A chiral center is a carbon atom bonded to four substituents, none of which is identical to any other. The isopropyl alcohol molecule features three carbons. The central carbon is bound to two CH_3 moieties and cannot be chiral. The other two carbons are those of the CH_3 moieties themselves, and each, quite obviously, is bound to three hydrogen atoms. None of the carbon atoms can "boast" four dissimilar substituents.

206. What property of isopropyl alcohol makes it most useful as a skin-cooling agent?

    A. It forms hydrogen bonds.
    B. It is weakly acidic.
    C. It is relatively volatile.
    D. It acts as a proton acceptor.

C "Rubbing alcohol" is designed to cool the skin. A volatile liquid—one that tends rapidly to vaporize—will cool the skin by drawing heat away from it as it moves from the liquid to the gaseous phase. Choices A, B, and D all represent isopropyl alcohol's properties, but they do not explain the cooling of skin.

207. Between isopropyl alcohol and *n*-propanol, which compound likely has the higher boiling point?

    A. *N*-propanol, because it has the higher molecular weight
    B. *N*-propanol, because it is a straight chain alcohol
    C. Isopropyl alcohol, because its density is higher than that of *n*-propanol
    D. Isopropyl alcohol, because its carbon chain branches

B Recognize that because *n*-propanol is a straight-chain alcohol, its molecules experience increased van der Waals attractions. Choices A and C are true, but have no bearing on the question; they're irrelevant. Choice D is wrong because branching tends to *reduce* boiling point.

208. All of the following are isomers of isobutyl alcohol EXCEPT:

    A. $(CH_3)_3COH$.
    B. $CH_3CH_2COCH_3$.
    C. $CH_3CH_2CH_2OH$.
    D. $CH_3CHOHCH_2CH_3$.

B The term "isomer" refers to two compounds whose molecular formulas are identical but differ in the arrangement of their composite atoms. The isobutyl alcohol molecule is composed of four carbon atoms, one oxygen atom, and ten hydrogen atoms. Examine the four molecules shown in the answer choices. Note that all have four carbon atoms, all have one oxygen atom, and all *except* choice B have ten hydrogen atoms. The molecule shown in choice B has only eight hydrogen atoms.

Free-Standing Questions (209–214)

209. On a single human gene, a researcher discovers a point mutation in which one nucleotide residue has been substituted for another. She further discovers that transcription of the affected gene alters the resulting messenger RNA codon, but that the altered codon does not affect the polypeptide produced when the messenger RNA undergoes translation. Among the following, the most likely explanation for the unchanged polypeptide is that:

   A. the point mutation did not impair the efficacy of DNA polymerases.
   B. the point mutation did not impair the efficacy of RNA polymerases.
   C. the point mutation caused a shift in the ribosomal reading frame.
   D. the genetic code is degenerate.

D To say that the genetic code is "degenerate" is to say that two different mRNA codons might, during translation (polypeptide synthesis), code for the same amino acid (although no single mRNA codon codes for more than one amino acid). A point mutation that substitutes one nucleotide residue for another might simply convert the codon to another codon that specified the same amino acid as was associated with the original codon. Choices A and B refer to the enzymes necessary to the processes of DNA replication and RNA synthesis, respectively. The fact that these enzymes remain undamaged does not explain the failure of the point mutation to alter the genetic polypeptide product. Choice C apparently refers to frameshift mutations, which do not result from the substitution on a DNA molecule of one nucleotide residue for another.

210. All of the following statements about RNA polymerase and DNA polymerase are true EXCEPT:

   A. RNA polymerase normally catalyzes the addition of a thymine subunit to a nascent RNA strand.
   B. RNA polymerase normally catalyzes the elongation of a nascent polymer in the 5' to 3' direction.
   C. DNA polymerase is not affected by the presence of upstream regulatory elements.
   D. DNA polymerase normally catalyzes the elongation of a nascent polymer in the 5' to 3' direction.

A The two enzymes mentioned in the question catalyze the synthesis of RNA and DNA, respectively. The correct answer lies within this simple truth: RNA does not contain the pyrimidine thymine; it contains uracil instead. Naturally, therefore, the enzyme that catalyzes RNA synthesis does not add a thymine residue to a growing chain. Choices B, C, and D all make correct statements regarding the two polymerase enzymes. Both RNA and DNA polymerase catalyze polymerization in the 5' to 3' direction (choices B and D). Regarding choice C, DNA polymerase is not affected by upstream regulatory elements; this is true of RNA polymerase, which is influenced by upstream regulatory sequences and promoter regions.

211. A virus that employs reverse transcriptase to carry out its infective cycle within a host cell has as its nucleic acid core:

   A. RNA.
   B. DNA.
   C. either RNA or DNA.
   D. neither RNA nor DNA.

A Reverse transcriptase is an enzyme capable of producing DNA from an RNA template. Therefore, the virus in question contains RNA as its nucleic acid core. Choices B and C are wrong because they refer to virons that contain DNA. Viruses that have DNA as their nucleic acid have no call for reverse transcriptase. Choice D is wrong because a viral genome must be composed of some nucleic acid.

212. Formation of ATP from ADP and inorganic phosphate occurs via:

- **A.** hydrolysis, which involves the removal of a molecule of water.
- **B.** hydrolysis, which involves the addition of a molecule of water.
- **C.** dehydration synthesis, which involves the removal of a molecule of water.
- **D.** dehydration synthesis, which involves the addition of a molecule of water.

C ATP (adenosine triphosphate), commonly called the cell's "energy currency" is formed from ADP (adenosine diphosphate) by dehydration synthesis in which a molecule of water is removed. The bond that bears the third phosphate residue is ordinarily a "high energy" bond, the energy constituting the ultimate source of energy that drives cellular function. The ultimate significance of glycolysis, the Krebs cycle, and oxidative phosphorylation is that through a variety of intermediates and co-factors they produce ATP from ADP and inorganic phosphate, "relocating" the energy originally housed within glucose to create ATP.

213. Which of the following ovarian cell organelles will show the greatest levels of activity during the secretion of estrogen?

- **A.** Lysosomes
- **B.** Smooth ER
- **C.** Golgi apparatus
- **D.** Ribosomes

B Recall that the smooth ER synthesizes and packages steroids (and other lipid-based substances) destined for secretion. In an actively secreting, steroid-producing cell, the smooth ER is highly active. Choice A is incorrect because lysosomes contain and degrade "old" and "worn out" cell structures. Choice C is wrong because the Golgi apparatus is involved in protein secretion, and steroids are lipid-based (derived from cholesterol). Choice D can be eliminated because ribosomes are active in protein synthesis.

214. During the replication of a human chromosome, the lagging strand:

- **A.** acts as a template for the leading strand.
- **B.** must undergo semidiscontinuous synthesis due to antiparallel orientation of the DNA double helix.
- **C.** undergoes frequent mutations because base-pairing tends to lag behind base-pairing on the leading strand.
- **D.** undergoes nucleotide addition by DNA polymerase at the 5' end of the growing chain.

B The two strands of a DNA molecule are in antiparallel orientation. That means that during DNA replication one of the nascent daughter strands presents its 3' end to the proximal (open) end of the replication fork. That strand is the lagging strand. The other newly forming daughter strand, called the leading strand, presents its 5' end to the proximal aspect of the replication fork. DNA polymerase will add nucleotide subunits only to the 3' end of a growing chain. For that reason, the lagging strand must undergo "semidiscontinuous synthesis," mediated by Ozaki fragments. Choice A makes a false statement. During DNA replication, each parent strand acts as template for a newly forming daughter strand. The leading and lagging strands are both *daughter* strands. Choice C is biological double-talk but might appeal to the student who fixes on the word "lag." There is no reason to assume that mutations occur more frequently simply because the rates of replication differ. Choice D states a falsehood; DNA polymerase does not add nucleotide subunits to the 5' end of a growing chain—not on the leading strand and not on the lagging strand.

ABOUT THE AUTHOR

Theodore Silver holds a medical degree from the Yale University School of Medicine, a bachelor's degree from Yale University and, in addition, a law degree from the University of Connecticut. He has been intensely involved in the field of education, testing, and test preparation since 1976 and has written several books and computer tutorials pertaining to those fields.

Dr. Silver is Associate Professor of Law at Touro College Jacob D. Fuchsberg Law Center, where he teaches the law of medical practice and malpractice, contracts, and federal income taxation.

NOTES

NOTES

NOTES

NOTES

NOTES

NOTES

NOTES

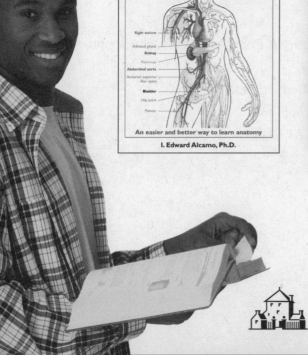

Need More?

If you want to learn more about raising your MCAT score, you're in the right place. Our expertise extends far beyond full-length practice tests, and we have helped countless students get into their top-choice med schools.

One way to increase the number of acceptance letters you get is to raise your test scores. So if you're experiencing some trepidation, consider all your options.

We consistently improve prospective med school students' scores through our books, classroom courses, and private tutoring. Call 800-2Review or visit *PrincetonReview.com* for details.

If you like our *Full-Length Practice MCATs*, check out:
- *Cracking the MCAT*
- *Complete Book of Medical Schools*
- *Best 83 Medical Schools*
- *Hyperlearning* MCAT Classroom Courses
- MCAT Private Tutoring

Contents

Contents

Preface

Passing the Georgia Mathematics II End-of-Course Test will help you review and learn important concepts and skills related to algebra, geometry, and data analysis. First, take the Diagnostic Test beginning on page 1 of the book. Next, complete the evaluation chart with your instructor in order to help you identify the chapters which require your careful attention. When you have finished your review of all of the material your teacher assigns, take the practice tests to evaluate your understanding of the material presented in this book. **The materials in this book are based on the Georgia Performance Standards that are published by the Georgia Department of Education. The complete list of standards is located in the Answer Key. Each question in the Diagnostic and Practice Tests is referenced to the standard, as is the beginning of each chapter.**

This book contains several sections. These sections are as follows: 1) A Diagnostic Test; 2) Chapters that teach the concepts and skills for *Passing the Georgia Mathematics II End-of-Course Test*; and 3) Two Practice Tests. Answers to the tests and exercises are in a separate manual.

ABOUT THE AUTHORS

Erica Day has a Bachelor of Science Degree in Mathematics and is working on a Master of Science Degree in Mathematics. She graduated with high honors from Kennesaw State University in Kennesaw, Georgia. She has also tutored all levels of mathematics, ranging from high school algebra and geometry to university-level statistics, calculus, and linear algebra. She is currently writing and editing mathematics books for American Book Company, where she has coauthored numerous books, such as *Passing the Georgia Algebra I End of Course*, *Passing the Georgia High School Graduation Test in Mathematics*, *Passing the Arizona AIMS in Mathematics*, and *Passing the New Jersey HSPA in Mathematics*, to help students pass graduation and end of course exams.

Colleen Pintozzi has taught mathematics at the middle school, junior high, senior high, and adult level for 22 years. She holds a B.S. degree from Wright State University in Dayton, Ohio and has done graduate work at Wright State University, Duke University, and the University of North Carolina at Chapel Hill. She is the author of many mathematics books including such best-sellers as *Basics Made Easy: Mathematics Review*, *Passing the New Alabama Graduation Exam in Mathematics*, *Passing the Louisiana LEAP 21 GEE*, *Passing the Indiana ISTEP+ GQE in Mathematics*, *Passing the Minnesota Basic Standards Test in Mathematics*, and *Passing the Nevada High School Proficiency Exam in Mathematics*.

Timothy Trowbridge graduated with summa cum laude honors from Hawaii Loa College with a Bachelor of Arts Degree in Mathematics. He taught in Japan as a participant in the Japan Exchange and Teaching (JET) Program, and he has written and edited parts of various mathematics textbooks for several major educational publishers.

Mathematics II Formula Sheet

Below are the formulas you may find useful as you work the problems. However, some of the formulas may not be used. You may refer to this page as you take the test.

Area

Rectangle / Parallelogram $A = bh$
Triangle $A = \frac{1}{2}bh$
Circle $A = \pi r^2$

Circumference

$C = \pi d$ $\pi \approx 3.14$

Volume

Rectangular Prism $V = Bh$

Pyramid/Cone $V = \frac{1}{3}Bh$

Sphere $V = \frac{4}{3}\pi r^3$

Surface Area

Rectangular Prism $SA = 2lw + 2wh + 2lh$

Cylinder $SA = 2\pi r^2 + 2\pi rh$

Sphere $SA = 4\pi r^2$

Trigonometric Relationships

$\sin(\theta) = \dfrac{\text{opp}}{\text{hyp}}$; $\cos(\theta) = \dfrac{\text{adj}}{\text{hyp}}$; $\tan(\theta) = \dfrac{\text{opp}}{\text{adj}}$

Quadratic Formula

$$x = \frac{-b \pm \sqrt{b^2 - 4ac}}{2a}$$

Standard Form $ax^2 + bx + c = y$

Vertex Form $a(x - h)^2 + k = y$

Mean Absolute Deviation

$$\frac{\sum_{i=1}^{N} \left| x_i - \overline{x} \right|}{N}$$

the average of the absolute deviations from the mean for a set of data

Population Standard Deviation

$$\sigma = \sqrt{\frac{\sum_{i=1}^{N}(x_i - \overline{x})^2}{N}}$$

Sample Standard Deviation

$$S = \sqrt{\frac{\sum_{i=1}^{N}(x_i - \overline{x})^2}{N - 1}}$$

Special Right Triangles

45° - 45° - 90° Triangle   **30° - 60° - 90° Triangle**

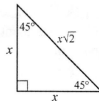

Diagnostic Test

Part 1

1. Jeff's Wholesale Auto Dealership holds an auction once a month. What is the average number of cars sold at the auction for the past 6 months?

   Month 1: 288 Cars   Month 4: 558 Cars
   Month 2: 432 Cars   Month 5: 366 Cars
   Month 3: 330 Cars   Month 6: 258 Cars

   A. 318.9 cars
   B. 350 cars
   C. 446.6 cars
   D. 372 cars

   MM2D1b

2. Find the value of each variable.

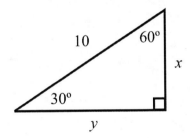

   A. $x = 5$, $y = 5\sqrt{3}$
   B. $x = 5\sqrt{3}$, $y = 5$
   C. $x = 5$, $y = 10\sqrt{3}$
   D. $x = 5$, $y = 2\sqrt{3}$

   MM2G1a

3. What is the y-intercept of the equation $6x^2 + y = 18$?

   A. $(0, 18)$
   B. $(0, 3)$
   C. $(18, 0)$
   D. $(3, 0)$

   MM2A3c

4. Sue has decided to investigate which local pizza place has a faster delivery time. Over the course of 6 months she had pizza delivered to her house ten times from each restaurant. How would Sue come to a conclusion about the two pizza restaurants?

   A. Find the average of all the delivery times and divide it by 6.
   B. Compare the range of the delivery time from each restaurant.
   C. Compare the fastest delivery time from each restaurant.
   D. Find the average of each restaurant's delivery time and compare the two.

   MM2D1a

5. If $\overline{CA}$ is 7, what is the length of AB?

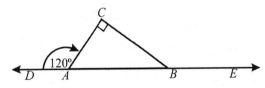

   A. 10
   B. 12
   C. 14
   D. 16

   MM2G1a

6. Which of the following quadratic equations in standard form has a vertex of $(1, -1)$?

   A. $f(x) = -2x^2 - 4x + 1$
   B. $f(x) = 2x^2 - 4x + 1$
   C. $f(x) = -2x^2 + 4x + 1$
   D. $f(x) = 2x^2 + 4x - 1$

   MM2A3c

7. Nina wants to see whether doctors or nurses work more hours in a five day work week. She interviewed a random group of 5 nurses and asked them how many hours they worked in the last week. She then interviewed a random group of 5 doctors and asked them the same question.

Nurses	48	50	49	47	51
Doctors	53	54	53	51	52

Looking at the chart above, which data set has the lower mean?

A. Doctors
B. The mean cannot be determined.
C. Nurses
D. They have the same mean.

MM2D1c

8. What is the value of y?

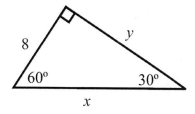

A. 16
B. 12
C. $3\sqrt{8}$
D. $8\sqrt{3}$

MM2G1a

9. The graph of the function $f(x) = x^2$ has been translated so that its new vertex is the point $(2, 1)$. What is the equation of the function with this vertex in standard form?

A. $f(x) = x^2 - 4x + 5$
B. $f(x) = x^2 + 4x + 1$
C. $f(x) = x^2 - 2x + 1$
D. $f(x) = x^2 + 2x - 1$

MM2A3a

10. Which of the following arithmetic series has a sum of 100?

A. $\sum_{n=1}^{5} 5 + 3(n+2)$

B. $\sum_{n=1}^{5} 4 + 2(n+3)$

C. $\sum_{n=1}^{4} 6 + 3(n+3)$

D. $\sum_{n=1}^{5} 5 + 3(n-1)$

MM2A3d

11. What is the length of the line segment b in the figure below?

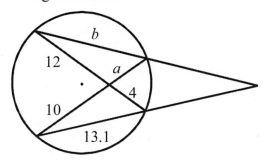

A. 9.16
B. 10.92
C. 15.72
D. 14.5

MM2G3a

12. Which of the following is the solution to $|2x - 3| \leq 7$?

A. $-2 \leq x \leq 10$
B. $x \geq -2$
C. $x \leq 5$
D. $-2 \leq x \leq 5$

MM2A1c

13. Anna plays basketball for her high school team. During the 10 game season she scored:

Game 1: 12 points   Game 6: 18 points
Game 2: 7 points   Game 7: 11 points
Game 3: 11 points   Game 8: 15 points
Game 4: 10 points   Game 9: 9 points
Game 5: 14 points   Game 10: 15 points

What is the approximate standard deviation of this set of data?

A. 7 points
B. 5 points
C. 3 points
D. 2 points

MM2D1b

14. If $\angle A = 60°$, what is measure of arc BC?

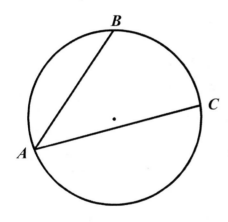

A. 60
B. 90
C. 120
D. 140

MM2G3b

15. Which of the following is the inverse of $f(x) = x^2$?

A. $x = \pm\sqrt{y}$
B. $y = x^2$
C. $x^2 = y$
D. $y = \pm\sqrt{x}$

MM2A5b

16. To find the average number of purses owned by women, the number of purses owned by each woman in a large random sample of 2,000 women was determined. The mean number of purses owned by women in this population is 17 purses, and the standard deviation of the number of purses is 8 purses. A smaller data sample was observed also. This smaller set consisted of 443 women. The mean for this sample was 28 purses, and the standard deviation was 7 purses. What can you conclude from this data?

A. The population distribution of the larger sample and the distribution of the smaller sample are the same.

B. The population distribution of the larger sample has more variability than the distribution of the smaller sample.

C. The population distribution of the smaller sample has more variability than the distribution of the larger sample.

D. The mean of the larger sample is higher than the mean of the smaller sample.

MM2D1d

17. Which of the following is the function $f(x) = |4x + 1| - 2$ written as a piecewise function?

A. $f(x) = \begin{cases} 4x - 1 & \text{if } x \geq 0 \\ -4x - 1 & \text{if } x < 0 \end{cases}$

B. $f(x) = \begin{cases} 4x - 1 & \text{if } x \geq -\frac{1}{4} \\ -4x - 1 & \text{if } x < -\frac{1}{4} \end{cases}$

C. $f(x) = \begin{cases} 4x + 1 & \text{if } x < -2 \\ 4x - 1 & \text{if } x \geq -2 \end{cases}$

D. $f(x) = \begin{cases} 4x + 1 & \text{if } x > -\frac{1}{4} \\ 4x - 3 & \text{if } x \geq -\frac{1}{4} \end{cases}$

MM2A1a

18. Five Flags is building a new roller coaster. The last section will have 987 feet of track running at a 75° angle from the ground. What is the highest point of the track?

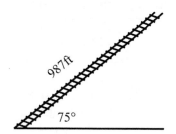

A. 953 ft
B. 698 ft
C. 913 ft
D. 754 ft

MM2G2c

19. What is the surface area of the sphere?

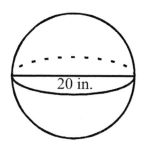

20 in.

A. 125.6 in²
B. 502.4 in²
C. 1256 in²
D. 5024 in²

MM2G4a

20. What is the domain of the inverse of $y = x^3 - 7$?

A. $-7 \le x < \infty$
B. $-\infty < x < \infty$
C. $-\infty < y \le -7$
D. $-7 \le y < \infty$

MM2A5a

21. Find the standard deviation of the following set of data: 48 pounds; 73 pounds; 105 pounds; 57 pounds; 42 pounds; 69 pounds

A. 22.62 pounds
B. 33.84 pounds
C. 23.47 pounds
D. 18.73 pounds

MM2D1b

22. Which angle has a cosine ratio equal to $\frac{3}{5}$?

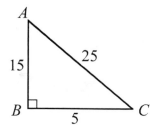

A. $\angle A$
B. $\angle B$
C. $\angle C$
D. None of the angles.

MM2G2c

23. Use the formula for volume of a sphere to determine the volume of the hemisphere below. Volume of a sphere $= \frac{4}{3}\pi r^3$.

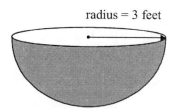

radius = 3 feet

A. 4π
B. 12π
C. 18π
D. 36π

MM2G4a

24. Which of the following arithmetic series has a sum of 60?

A. $\sum\limits_{n=1}^{4} 10 - (2 + n)$

B. $\sum\limits_{n=1}^{5} 12 - (3 - n)$

C. $\sum\limits_{n=1}^{4} 11 + (4 - n)$

D. $\sum\limits_{n=1}^{5} 9 + (3 + n)$

25. Beth is blowing up balloons for her daughter's birthday surprise. The balloons inside the house have a diameter of 1 ft, but the balloons she plans on putting in the backyard will have a diameter twice as big as the balloons inside. What is the change in surface area of the inside balloons to the outside balloons?

A. the surface area will be 2 times smaller
B. the surface area will be 2 times larger
C. the surface area will be 3 times larger
D. the surface area will be 4 times larger

26. Consider the quadratic equation $x^2 - 4x + 7 = 0$. Find the discriminant and give the numbers and type of solutions of the equation.

A. $(7)^2 - (4)(1)(4) = 33$; two real solutions
B. $(4)^2 - (4)(1)(7) = -12$; two real solutions
C. $(-4)^2 - (4)(1)(7) = -12$; two imaginary solutions
D. $(-4)^2 - (7)^2(4) = -180$; two imaginary solutions

27. What is the value of x?

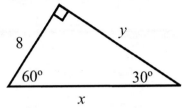

A. 12
B. 16
C. $8\sqrt{3}$
D. $8\sqrt{2}$

28. How is the graph of $f(x) = -x^2$ different from the graph of $f(x) = x^2$?

A. The graph of $f(x) = -x^2$ is shifted down one unit.
B. The graph of $f(x) = -x^2$ is reflected over the x-axis from the graph of $f(x) = x^2$ and opens downward.
C. The graph of $f(x) = -x^2$ is reflected over the x-axis from the graph of $f(x) = x^2$ and opens upward.
D. The graph of $f(x) = -x^2$ is shifted left one unit from the graph of $f(x) = x^2$.

29. What is the approximate measure of $\angle D$ in $\triangle ADE$?

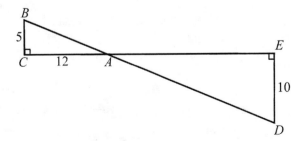

A. 23°
B. 25°
C. 65°
D. 67°

30. If $11x^2 + 31x - 6 > 0$, which of the following solutions for x is correct?

   A. $x > -3$

   B. $x < \frac{2}{11}$

   C. $x < -3$ and $x > \frac{2}{11}$

   D. $x < -\frac{2}{11}$ and $x > 3$

MM2A4d

31. Find the length of $\overline{AB}$.

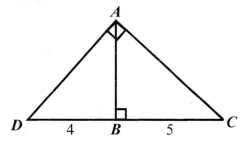

   A. $5\sqrt{2}$

   B. $2\sqrt{5}$

   C. $3\sqrt{5}$

   D. $5\sqrt{3}$

MM2G2b

32. Joe has experienced a slight loss of hearing since he got his new stereo. Which of the following would imply causation?

   A. number of hours listening to the stereo

   B. high volume level while listening to the stereo

   C. type of music listened to

   D. brand of stereo

MM2D2d

33. Which of the following functions is represented by the graph?

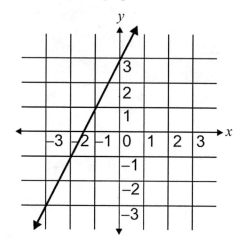

   A. $f(x) = -3x + 3$

   B. $f(x) = -\frac{1}{3}x + 3$

   C. $f(x) = 3x - 3$

   D. $f(x) = 2x + 3$

MM2D2a

34. Look at the table below.

x	f(x)
-4	-7
0	1
1	3
6	13

Which of these equations is the line that generalizes the pattern of the data in the table?

   A. $f(x) = -4x - 7$

   B. $f(x) = x + 2$

   C. $f(x) = 2x + 1$

   D. $f(x) = -7x - 4$

MM2D2a

35. Professor Bonheur tested her 23 students for their French comprehension. The graph below shows her students' comprehension plotted against the number of times they had gone over the material (not including initially hearing it in class). A curve of best fit is drawn.

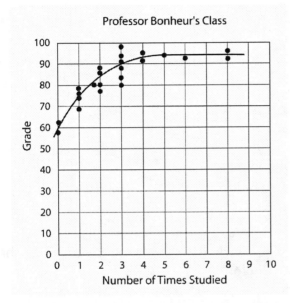

Professor Bonheur's Class

Based on the curve of best fit, how many times would a student need to go over the material to score a 90%?

A. 2 times
B. 3 times
C. 4 times
D. 5 times

MM2D2b

36. This graph shows the number of miles per hour family drove during their vacation.

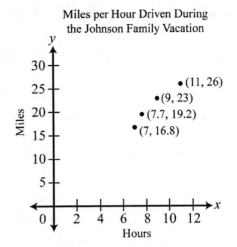

Miles per Hour Driven During the Johnson Family Vacation

Which linear regression model represents these data?

A. $y = -2.3x - 1.5$
B. $y = -2.3x + 1.5$
C. $y = 2.3x - 1.5$
D. $y = 2.3x + 1.5$

MM2D2c

37. The shortest leg of a $30° - 60° - 90°$ triangle has length $\sqrt{5}$. What are the lengths of the other two sides?

   A. $10, \sqrt{15}$
   B. $3\sqrt{5}, \sqrt{15}$
   C. $\sqrt{15}, 2\sqrt{5}$
   D. $\sqrt{10}, 3\sqrt{5}$

   MM2G1a

38. Andrea began an exercise program on Monday. The first day she did 10 sit-ups. Each day she added 5 more sit-ups to her total from the day before. How many sit-ups will she have done by the end of the first Saturday of her program?

   A. 35
   B. 100
   C. 135
   D. 155

   MM2A3d

39. Using the information from question 38, which summation notation will show Andrea how many sit-ups she will have done after 10 days?

   A. $\sum_{n=0}^{10} 10 + 5n$

   B. $\sum_{n=1}^{10} 10 + 5n$

   C. $\sum_{n=0}^{9} 10 + 5n$

   D. $\sum_{n=1}^{9} 10 + 5n$

   MM2A3d

40. What is the measure of the diagonal of the square?

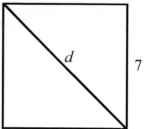

   A. $2\sqrt{7}$
   B. $7\sqrt{2}$
   C. 14
   D. 49

   MM2G1b

41. Which of the following $\sqrt{-16}$ in imaginary form?

   A. $4\sqrt{-1}$
   B. $4i$
   C. $16i$
   D. -4

   MM2N1a

42. Sample: mean $= 23$ pints; standard deviation $= 2$ pints; Population size: $7,500$; Range: 21 pints to 25 pints. What is the number of data values in the population that fall within the given range?

   A. $1,125$
   B. $7,500$
   C. $2,250$
   D. $5,250$

   MM2D1d

43. If the measure of $\angle A$ is 30°, find the measure of length x.

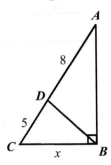

A. 6.5
B. $6\sqrt{3}$
C. 13
D. 26

MM2G2b

44. Consider the equation $y = 4^{x-1}$. What is the domain and range?

A. domain: all real numbers; range: $y \leq 0$
B. domain: $x > 0$; range: $y < 1$
C. domain: all real numbers; range: all positive real numbers
D. domain: all positive integers; range: $y > \frac{1}{4}$

MM2A2b

45. Joe has decided to investigate whether high school girls or high school boys have higher SAT scores. To do this he took a random sample of high school girls' SAT scores and a random sample of high school boys' SAT scores. To come to his conclusion Joe determined the average test score for each group and compared the two. What are the samples being compared?

A. male and female SAT scores
B. The average SAT score of a High school boy
C. The average SAT score of a high school girl
D. the SAT scores of high school girls and boys

MM2D1a

46. If $a = 6$, $c = 5.2$, and $d = 8.4$, what is the measure of b?

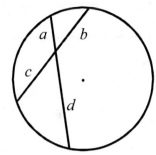

A. 3.7
B. 5.2
C. 7.28
D. 9.69

MM2G3a

47. Simplify: 2^{-3}

A. $\frac{1}{8}$
B. -8
C. -6
D. $-\frac{1}{8}$

MM2A2a

48. Find the value of the variable in the diagram below.

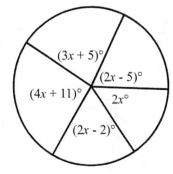

A. $x = 23$
B. $x = 27$
C. $x = 29$
D. $x = 31$

MM2G3d

49. Which of the following is the function $f(x) = |x - 3| + 2$?

A. $f(x) = \begin{cases} x - 3 & \text{if } x \geq 3 \\ -x + 3 & \text{if } x < 3 \end{cases}$

B. $f(x) = \begin{cases} x - 5 & \text{if } x \geq 3 \\ x - 1 & \text{if } x < 3 \end{cases}$

C. $f(x) = \begin{cases} x - 1 & \text{if } x \geq 3 \\ -x + 5 & \text{if } x < 3 \end{cases}$

D. $f(x) = \begin{cases} x + 5 & \text{if } x > 3 \\ x + 1 & \text{if } x \leq 3 \end{cases}$

MM2A1a

50. The Georgia Department of Transportation is building a new road climbing up a mountain. The road reaches a height of 800 feet and is 1200 feet long. What is the angle of the road with the horizon?

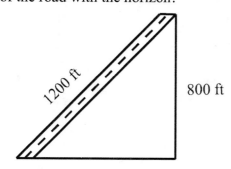

800 ft

A. $90°$
B. $48.2°$
C. $41.8°$
D. $43.6°$

MM2G2c

51. What is the domain of the inverse of the following function?

$y = x^3$

A. $0 \leq x < \infty$
B. $3 \leq x < \infty$
C. $-\infty < x < \infty$
D. $0 < x < \infty$

MM2A5a

52. Find the standard deviation of the following set of data: 20 hours; 27 hours; 46 hours; 23 hours; 34 hours; 41 hours; 38 hours

A. 11.07 hours
B. 8.54 hours
C. 9.69 hours
D. 10.38 hours

MM2D1b

53. Find the value of x.

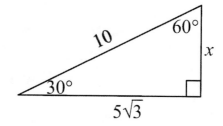

A. 10

B. $\dfrac{5\sqrt{3}}{2}$

C. 5

D. 15

MM2G1a

54. Consider the quadratic equation $x^2 + 6x + 9 = 0$. Find the discriminant and give the numbers and type of solutions of the equation.

A. $(6)^2 + (-4)(1)(-9) = 72$; two real solutions

B. $(6)^2 - (4)(1)(9) = 0$; one real solution

C. $(9)^2 - (4)(1)(4) = 65$; two real solutions

D. $(-6)^2 + (4)(1)(9) = 72$; two imaginary solutions

MM2A4c

55. What is the length of x?

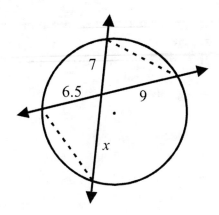

A. 5.05
B. 8.36
C. 9.69
D. 9.82

MM2G3a

56. Simplify and put in standard form: $\dfrac{7i - 2}{4}$

A. $\dfrac{7}{4}i - \dfrac{1}{2}$

B. $\dfrac{7}{4}i - \dfrac{2}{4}$

C. $\dfrac{7}{4}i - 2$

D. $-\dfrac{1}{2} + \dfrac{7}{4}i$

MM2N1d

57. Simplify the expression $3i\,(-4 + i)$ and express as a complex number in standard form.

A. $-3 - 12i$

B. $-3 - 21i$

C. $-12i + 3i^2$

D. $i\,(-12 + 3i)$

MM2N1c

58. Caliyaah wants to see which high school basketball team scores the most points per game, Etowah High School or Woodstock High School. To do so, she went to six games at Etowah and six games at Woodstock. She recorded the final scores for each game in the chart below.

EHS	56	64	59	75	61	89
WHS	41	29	67	55	65	60

What can you conclude from the chart?

A. WHS has a higher mean than EHS.

B. EHS has a higher standard deviation than WHS.

C. WHS has a higher standard deviation than EHS.

D. EHS and WHS have the same standard deviation.

MM2D1c

59. The diameter of the circle below is 8 cm. What is the area of the sector AOB?

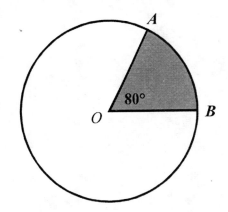

A. 5.58 cm^2

B. 11.16 cm^2

C. 2.79 cm^2

D. 44.66 cm^2

MM2G3c

60. Chris walked east from his house to the gas station, which was 1.2 miles away. Then, he walked south from the gas station to his piano teacher's house. His piano teacher lives 0.4 miles from the gas station. Using a trigonometric ratio, find the angle measure between the direct path from Chris's house to the gas station and the direct path from Chris's house to his piano teacher's house. (Round your answer to the nearest tenth.)

A. $72.5°$
B. $18.4°$
C. $19.5°$
D. $71.6°$

MM2G2c

61. Simplify the expression $(5 + 2i)(5 - 2i)$ and express as a complex number in standard form.

A. $25 - 4i^2$
B. $25 - (2i)^2$
C. 29
D. $25 + 4i$

MM2N1c

62. The volume of a sphere is 24000π cm^3. What is its surface area?

A. 2747.31π cm^2
B. 72000π cm^2
C. 915.77π cm^2
D. 13500π cm^2

MM2G4a

63. For the equation $y = 3^x$, what is the y-intercept and the asymptote of the graph of the function?

A. $(0,0)$; the y-axis
B. $(0,1)$; the x-axis
C. $(0,0)$; the x-axis
D. $(0,-1)$; the x-axis

MM2A2b

64. Mr. Stewart's science class is studying aerodynamics. Mr. Stewart has split the class into 6 groups and told each group to build their own paper airplane. Each group then launched their airplane from the same device to see how far they would fly. The results were as follows:

Group 1: 2 feet   Group 4: 16 feet
Group 2: 10 feet   Group 5: 6 feet
Group 3: 8 feet   Group 6: 18 feet

What is the average number of feet that each group's paper airplane flew?

A. 8 feet
B. 10 feet
C. 60 feet
D. 12 feet

MM2D1b

65. Jack is going to paint the ceiling and four walls of a room that is 10 feet wide, 12 feet long, and 10 feet from floor to ceiling. How many square feet will he paint?

A. 120 square feet
B. 560 square feet
C. 680 square feet
D. $1,200$ square feet

MM2G2c

66. In comparing the graphs of $y = |x|$ and $y = 4|x|$, the graph of $4|x|$

A. opens down, is narrower
B. opens up, is wider
C. opens up, is narrower
D. opens down, is the same width

MM2A1b

67. Patrick recently pulled a muscle in his leg while at the gym. Which of the following is a correlation variable?

A. Number of hours spent at the gym
B. Water intake
C. Type of exercise
D. All of the above

MM2D2d

68. Using the data points below, what is the equation of the linear function that can be used to model the situation?

(2 months, 3 books), (6 months, 11 books)

A. $y = 0.5x - 4$

B. $y = 2x - 4$

C. $y = 6x + 2$

D. $y = 0.2x + 2$

MM2D2a

69. Which of these tables of values below represents the function $y = 2x - 3$?

A.

x	y
0	−3
1	−1
2	1

B.

x	y
−1	5
−2	0
1	3

C.

x	y
0	2
−1	0
−2	−1

D.

x	y
2	3
5	7
8	9

MM2D2a

70. Susie wants to rent a bike while she is at the beach the graph below shows the total cost she has paid for the number of days she has rented the bike.

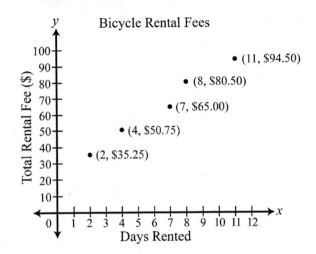

The linear regression model for these data $y = 6.6x + 22.8$. Based on this model, how much is Susie paying, on average, per day?

A. $35.25

B. $16.20

C. $29.40

D. $17.63

MM2D2c

71. The Harry's car dealership charges $599 document fee every time a car is sold. The dealership also charges 8% tax on each vehicle before the document fee. Which equation best fits this situation?

p is the advertised price

f is the final cost of car to a customer

A. $f = 1.08 \cdot p + 599$

B. $f = (p + 599) \cdot 1.08$

C. $f = p + 599 \cdot 8$

D. $f = 1.08p - 599$

MM2D2a

72. Cameron has noticed that when driving around town, the number of stoplights she goes through is the best indicator of her travel time. She made the graph below based on different trips she made, how many stoplights she went through, and how long they took.

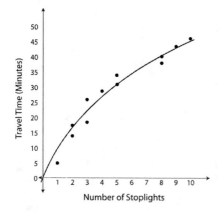

Based on the curve of best fit, how long should it take her to make a trip passing through 6 stoplights?

A. 20 min
B. 35 min
C. 25 min
D. 40 min

MM2D2b

Evaluation Chart for the Diagnostic Mathematics Test

Directions: On the following chart, circle the question numbers that you answered incorrectly. Then turn to the appropriate topics (listed by chapters), read the explanations, and complete the exercises. Review the other chapters as needed. Finally, complete the *Passing the Georgia Mathematics II End-of-Course Test* Practice Tests to further review.

		Questions Part 1	Questions Part 2	Pages
Chapter 1:	Complex Numbers		41, 56, 57, 61	16–23
Chapter 2:	Solving Quadratic Equations and Inequalities	3, 26, 30	54	24–40
Chapter 3:	Quadratic Functions	4, 9, 10, 24, 28	38, 39	41–58
Chapter 4:	Inverse Functions	15, 20	51	59–76
Chapter 5:	Triangles	2, 4, 8, 18, 22, 27, 29, 31	37, 40, 43, 50, 53, 60, 65	77–94
Chapter 6:	Circles and Spheres	11, 14, 19, 23, 25	46, 48, 55, 59, 62	95–108
Chapter 7:	Data Analysis	1, 4, 7, 13, 16, 21	42, 45, 52, 58, 64	109–124
Chapter 8:	Step and Piecewise Functions	12, 17	49	125–142
Chapter 9:	Exponents		47	143–147
Chapter 10:	Exponential Functions		44, 63, 66	148–165
Chapter 11:	Using Algebra for Data Analysis	32, 33, 34, 35, 36	67, 68, 69, 70, 71, 72	166–202

Chapter 1
Complex Numbers

This chapter covers the following Georgia Performance Standards:

MM2N	Number and Operations	MM2N1a
		MM2N1b
		MM2N1c
		MM2N1d

Complex numbers are usually written in the form $a + bi$, where a and b are real numbers and i is defined as $\sqrt{-1}$. Because $\sqrt{-1}$ does not exist in the set of real numbers, i is referred to as the imaginary unit.

When talking about a complex number, $a + bi$, the real number a is called the real part, and the real number b is called the imaginary part.

If the real part, a, is zero, then the complex number $a + bi$ is just bi, so it is imaginary.

If the real part, b, is zero, then the complex number $a + bi$ is just a, so it is real.

Example 1: What is the real part of the complex number $9 + 16i$?

Solution: The complex number $9 + 16i$ is written in the form $a + bi$. Here $a = 9$ and $b = 16$. The real part of the complex number $9 + 16i$ is 9.

Example 2: What is the imaginary part of the complex number $23 - 6i$?

Solution: The complex number $23 - 6i$ is written in the form $a + bi$. Here $a = 23$ and $b = -6$. The imaginary part of the complex number $a + bi$ is b. The imaginary part of the complex number $23 - 6i$ is -6.

Name the real part of each of the following complex numbers.

1. $-\frac{4}{5} - 3i$

2. $7 + 2i$

3. $20 - 11i$

4. $\frac{2}{9}$

5. $15i$

6. $-13 + \frac{i}{4}$

7. $12 + 5i$

8. $\frac{-9 + 2i}{25}$

Name the imaginary part of each of the following complex numbers.

9. $4 - i$

10. $\frac{6i}{5}$

11. $5 + \frac{2}{3}i$

12. $-9 + 8i$

13. 18

14. $\frac{1 - 3i}{2}$

15. $51 - 2i$

16. $14 + i$

1.1 Imaginary Numbers

The square root of a negative number is an imaginary number. You know that $\sqrt{-1} = i$. Therefore, $i^2 = -1$.

Where n is some natural number $(1, 2, 3...)$, then $\sqrt{-n} = \sqrt{(-1) \times n} = \sqrt{-1} \times \sqrt{n} = i\sqrt{n}$. To remove the negative number from under the radical, just take i out. Remember $\sqrt{-n} = i\sqrt{n}$.

Example 3: Simplify: $\sqrt{-450}$

    Step 1: Factor -450 and rewrite: $\sqrt{-450} = \sqrt{225 \times 2 \times (-1)}$.

    Step 2: By root laws, $\sqrt{225 \times 2 \times (-1)} = \sqrt{225} \times \sqrt{2} \times \sqrt{-1}$.

    Step 3: Since $\sqrt{225} = 15$ and $\sqrt{-1} = i$, we have $\sqrt{225} \times \sqrt{2} \times \sqrt{-1} = 15 \times \sqrt{2} \times i$.

    Step 4: Write in standard form as $15i\sqrt{2}$.

Example 4: Multiply: $5i \times 2i$

    Step 1: Using the basic rules of multiplication, we know $5i \times 2i = 5 \times i \times 2 \times i$.

    Step 2: Use the commutative property of multiplication, $5 \times i \times 2 \times i = 5 \times 2 \times i \times i$.

    Step 3: Simplify: $5 \times 2 \times i \times i = 10 \times i^2$.

    Step 4: Since $i^2 = -1$, then $10 \times i^2$ can be simplified to $10 \times -1 = -10$.

Find the square root of each of the following numbers.

1. -8 3. -441 5. -44 7. -144

2. $-\dfrac{4}{49}$ 4. $-\dfrac{81}{16}$ 6. -0.0121 8. -64

Use what you know about the imaginary number i to solve the following problems.

9. $-3i + \sqrt{-3}$ 11. $\sqrt{-4} \times \sqrt{-9}$ 13. $\left(\sqrt{-16}\right) \div (2i)$ 15. $\sqrt{-25} - 3i$

10. $7i - 8i$ 12. $2i \times (-4i)$ 14. $14i + i$ 16. $(12i) \div (3i)$

1.2   Adding and Subtracting Complex Numbers

Complex numbers, written as $a + bi$ or $c + di$ may be added and subtracted. The real parts are added or subtracted together and the imaginary parts are added or subtracted together. So, where a, c are the real parts of two complex numbers and b, d are the corresponding imaginary parts.

$$(a + bi) + (c + di) = (a + c) + (b + d)\,i$$

Example 5:   What is $(6 + i) - (5 - 7i)$?

Solution: Collect the real parts and the imaginary parts and do the arithmetic.
$$(6 + i) - (5 - 7i) = 6 + i - 5 + 7i = (6 - 5) + (i + 7i) = 1 + 8i$$

Example 6:   What is $(10 + 3i) + (-7 - 6i) + (18 - 5i)$?

Step 1:   Group the real and imaginary parts.
$$(10 + 3i) + (-7 - 6i) + (18 - 5i) = (10 - 7 + 18) + (3 - 6 - 5)\,i$$

Step 2:   Add or subtract the real and imaginary parts separately.
$$(10 - 7 + 18) + (3 - 6 - 5)\,i = 21 - 8i$$

Example 7: z and v are complex numbers. $z = -2 + 3i$ and $v = 3 - 2i$. Compute $z - v$.

Solution: $z - v = (-2 + 3i) - (3 - 2i) = (-2 - 3) + (3i + 2i) = -5 + 5i$

Add.

1. $(5 + 2i) + (-3 - 11i)$
2. $(1 - 5i) + \left(4 + \frac{4i}{3}\right) + (20 - 7i)$
3. $(12 + 2i) + \left(\frac{4}{5} - i\right)$
4. $(3 + 8i) + (4 + 9i) + (2 - 3i)$
5. $(-13 + 4i) + \left(9 - \frac{i}{5}\right)$
6. $22 + (3 - 7i) + (-1 + 20i)$
7. $(16 - 10i) + (-3 - 4i) + 19i$
8. $(2 - 6i) + \left(5 + \frac{9i}{2}\right)$
9. $(30 + 7i) + (-23 - 15i) + (8 + 6i)$
10. $(-4 + i) + (21 - 18i) + 10$
11. $\left(\frac{9}{10} - 17i\right) + (9 + 13i)$
12. $(12 + 2i) + (2 - 12i) + 23i$

Subtract.

13. $(17 + 10i) - (6 + 12i)$
14. $(11 - i) - \left(2 + \frac{2}{11}i\right)$
15. $(3 - 2i) - (-4 + 5i) - (2 - 16i)$
16. $\left(9 + \frac{i}{8}\right) - (20 - 22i)$
17. $(40 + 4i) - (2 + 13i) - i$
18. $(5 - 4i) - (4 + 3i) - (18 + 3i)$
19. $(7 - i) - (10 + 35i) - 8$
20. $(12 + 8i) - (5 - 8i) - (1 + i)$
21. $(6 + 3i) - (5 + 4i) - (11 - i)$
22. $\left(13 - \frac{7i}{6}\right) - \left(31 + \frac{6i}{7}\right)$
23. $(2 + 20i) - (-1 + 6i) - (3 + 14i)$
24. $(-11 - 5i) - (5 - 11i) - 11i$

1.3   Multiplying Complex Numbers

Multiplying two complex numbers, $a + bi$ and $c + di$, should remind you of the FOIL (First Outside Inside Last) method for multiplying two binomials like $(x + 2)(x + 3) = x^2 + 2x + 3x + 6 = x^2 + 5x + 6$. Generally, multiplying two complex numbers is the same:

$$(a + bi)(c + di) = ac + adi + bci + bdi^2$$

Simplify:

Remember that $i^2 = \left(\sqrt{-1}\right)^2 = -1$, so $ac + adi + bci + bdi^2 = ac + (ad + bc)i - bd$

Example 8:   Multiply $1 + 2i$ and $-4 + 3i$.

Step 1:   Use the FOIL method to multiply:
$(1 + 2i)(-4 + 3i) = (1)(-4) + (1)(3i) + (2i)(-4) + (2i)(3i)$

Step 2:   Simplify:
$(1)(-4) + (1)(3i) + (2i)(-4) + (2i)(3i) = -4 + 3i - 8i + 6i^2 =$
$-4 - 5i + 6i^2 = -4 - 5i + 6(-1)$

Step 3:   Combine like terms:
$-4 - 5i + 6(-1) = -10 - 5i$

Example 9:   What is $-7i \times -4i$?

Solution: $-7i \times -4i = 28i^2 = -28$

Example 10:   Compute $(4 - 8i)(6 + 2i)$.

Solution: Use the FOIL method and add the results.
$(4 - 8i)(6 + 2i) = 24 + 8i - 48i - 16i^2 = 40 - 40i$

Multiply.

1. $(4 + 7i) \times (1 - i)$

2. $(5 - 2i) \times (6 + 3i) \times 2$

3. $(8 + 4i) \times (2 + 5i) \times (4 + i)$

4. $(10 - i) \times (2 - 3i) \times 12i$

5. $(25 + 7i) \times (25 - 7i)$

6. $(3 - i)^3$

7. $\left(\frac{1}{4} + 4i\right) \times (4 - 8i)$

8. $(7 + 5i) \times (7 + 5i)$

9. $(1 - 8i) \times (1 - 8i) \times (1 + 8i)$

10. $(6 - i) \times (7 - i) \times i$

11. $(11 - 9i) \times (11 + 9i)$

12. $(3 + 4i) \times (1 + 10i) \times 3$

1.4   Dividing Complex Numbers

There are three steps to remember when dividing complex numbers.

1. Write the complex number as a fraction.

2. Multiply the numerator and denominator of the fraction by the complex conjugate of the denominator. The **complex conjugate** of $a + bi$ is $a - bi$.

3. Simplify.

Example 11:   What is $(6 + 3i) \div (2 + i)$?

Step 1:   Write the expression as a fraction:
$$\frac{6 + 3i}{2 + i}$$

Step 2:   Multiply the top (numerator) and the bottom (denominator) by $2 - i$, the complex conjugate of the denominator.
$$\frac{6 + 3i}{2 + i} \times \frac{2 - i}{2 - i}$$

Step 3:   Simplify.
$$\frac{6 + 3i}{2 + i} \times \frac{2 - i}{2 - i} = \frac{12 - 6i + 6i - 3i^2}{4 - 2i + 2i - i^2} = \frac{12 - 3(-1)}{4 - (-1)} = \frac{15}{5} = 3$$

Example 12:   What is $(5 - 4i) \div (7 - 8i)$?

Step 1:   Write the expression as a fraction, $\dfrac{5 - 4i}{7 - 8i}$.

Step 2:   Multiply by $\dfrac{7 + 8i}{7 + 8i}$.

Step 3:   Simplify:
$$\frac{5 - 4i}{7 - 8i} \times \frac{7 + 8i}{7 + 8i} = \frac{35 + 40i - 28i - 32i^2}{49 + 56i - 56i - 64i^2} = \frac{35 + 12i - 32(-1)}{49 - 64(-1)}$$
$$= \frac{67 + 12i}{113} = \frac{67}{113} + \frac{12}{113}i.$$

Divide.

1. $(7 + i) \div (4 - 3i)$

2. $25 \div (-1 + 5i)$

3. $(10 - 2i) \div (3 + 6i)$

4. $(-9 - 4i) \div (9 - 4i)$

5. $(5 + 3i) \div (-2 + i)$

6. $(8 - 7i) \div (1 - 8i)$

7. $(-11 - i) \div (7 + 3i)$

8. $(20 + i) \div 9i$

9. $(3 - 8i) \div (-8 + 3i)$

10. $(6 + 2i) \div (10 + i)$

11. $(-1 + 5i) \div (1 - 5i)$

12. $(15 + 2i) \div (3 - 7i)$

1.5   Simplify Complex Numbers

The order of operations for expressions with complex numbers is the same as the order of operations for real number expressions.

The **absolute value** of $a + bi$ is $\sqrt{a^2 + b^2}$.

Example 13:   Simplify the expression $12 \times [(-1 + 4i)^2 + (2 - 3i)] \div i$.

Step 1:   First, $-1 + 4i$ is squared.

$(-1 + 4i)^2 = (-1 + 4i)(-1 + 4i) = 1 - 4i - 4i + 16i^2 = 1 - 8i + 16\,(-1) = -15 - 8i$

Step 2:   Plug the result into the original expression.

$12 \times [(-15 - 8i) + (2 - 3i)] \div i$

Step 3:   Add $-15 - 8i$ and $2 - 3i$:

$(-15 - 8i) + (2 - 3i) = -15 - 8i + 2 - 3i = (-15 + 2) + (-8 - 3)\,i = -13 - 11i$

Step 4:   Plug the result from step 3 into equation in step 2:

$12 \times (-13 - 11i) \div i$.

Step 5:   Multiply first:

$12 \times (-13 - 11i) = (12)(-13) + (12)(-11i) = -156 - 132i$

The equation in step 4 can now be written as $\dfrac{-156 - 132i}{i}$.

Step 6:   Finally, $-156 - 132i$ is divided by i as follows:

$$\frac{-156 - 132i}{i} = \frac{(-156 - 132i)(-i)}{(i)(-i)} = \frac{(-156)(-i) + (-132i)(-i)}{(i)(-i)}$$

$$= \frac{156i + 132i^2}{-i^2} = \frac{156i + 132(-1)}{-(-1)} = \frac{156i - 132}{1} = -132 + 156i$$

Simplify each of the following expressions.

1. $(-10 + i) + (5 - 4i) \times (1 + 13i)$

2. $(4 - 5i) - (7 + 2i) \div (2 - i)^2$

3. $((9 - 3i) + (3 + 9i)) \times (6i + (3 + i))$

4. $((17 - 2i) + (-15 + 4i))^2$

5. $((8 + 5i)^2 - (33 + 75i))^2$

6. $(2 + 11i) \div ((1 - 7i) - (8 - 8i))$

7. $\dfrac{3 + i}{3 - i} + \dfrac{2 + i}{4 + 3i}$

8. $((39 - 36i) - (4 - 5i)^2)^2$

9. What is the absolute value of $5 - 2i$?

10. What is the absolute value of $-3 + 9i$?

Chapter 1 Review

Name the real part of each of the following complex numbers.

1. $-38 + 17i$

2. $\dfrac{8}{5} - \dfrac{13}{5}i$

Name the imaginary part of each of the following complex numbers.

3. $11 - 16i$

4. $225 + 725i$

Use what you know about the imaginary number i to solve the following problems.

5. $-5i + 18i$

6. $\sqrt{-12} \times \sqrt{3}$

Find the square root of each of the following numbers.

7. -64

8. -361

Add.

9. $(-14 - 3i) + (7 + 9i)$

10. $\left(\dfrac{3}{10} - 20i\right) + \left(-8 + \dfrac{1}{5}i\right)$

11. $(4 - 15i) + (12 + 19i)$

12. $(-21 + 20i) + (32 - 5i)$

Subtract.

13. $(10 - 4i) - (42 + 7i)$

14. $(-13 + 23i) - (18 - 6i)$

15. $(76 - 52i) - (43 + 27i)$

16. $\left(26 + \dfrac{4}{9}i\right) - \left(31 - \dfrac{2}{3}i\right)$

Multiply.

17. $(1 - 6i) \times (5 + 5i)$

18. $(4 + 2i) \times (10 - 15i)$

19. $(8 + i) \times (-4 - 3i)$

20. $(13 - 4i) \times (13 + 4i)$

Divide.

21. $(5 + 4i) \div (-3 - 2i)$

22. $(14 - 7i) \div (7 + i)$

23. $(6 + 3i) \div (-8 - 4i)$

24. $(-2 + 8i) \div (-10 + 2i)$

25. $104 \div (10 - 2i)$

26. $89 \div (-5 + 8i)$

Chapter 1 Test

1. What is $\dfrac{-9-2i}{3-i}+\dfrac{2+7i}{1-4i}$?

   A. $-\dfrac{137}{34}-\dfrac{21}{34}i$

   B. $-\dfrac{137}{34}+\dfrac{21}{34}i$

   C. $\dfrac{137}{34}-\dfrac{21}{34}i$

   D. $\dfrac{137}{34}+\dfrac{21}{34}i$

2. Which of the following statements is true?

   A. Every real number is a complex number with an imaginary part of -1.
   B. Every real number is a complex number with an imaginary part of 0.
   C. Every real number is a complex number with an imaginary part of 1.
   D. Every complex number is a real number with an imaginary part of 1.

3. What is the complex conjugate of $\frac{1}{10}-\frac{3}{10}i$?

   A. $-\frac{1}{10}-\frac{3}{10}i$
   B. $-\frac{1}{10}+\frac{3}{10}i$
   C. $\frac{1}{10}-\frac{3}{10}i$
   D. $\frac{1}{10}+\frac{3}{10}i$

4. What is $(8-18i)-(-3-13i)$?

   A. $5-31i$
   B. $5-5i$
   C. $11-31i$
   D. $11-5i$

5. What is $(4-i)-\left(8+\frac{1}{2}i\right)\times(2+6i)^2$?

   A. $-272-177i$
   B. $-264-175i$
   C. $272-177i$
   D. $264-175i$

6. What is $(2-9i)\div(-4+6i)$?

   A. $-\dfrac{31}{26}-\dfrac{6}{13}i$

   B. $-\dfrac{31}{26}+\dfrac{6}{13}i$

   C. $\dfrac{31}{26}-\dfrac{6}{13}i$

   D. $\dfrac{31}{26}+\dfrac{6}{13}i$

7. What is $\left(-\frac{5}{6}-\frac{1}{3}i\right)+\left(\frac{1}{2}+\frac{1}{6}i\right)$?

   A. $-\frac{1}{3}-\frac{1}{6}i$
   B. $-\frac{1}{3}+\frac{1}{6}i$
   C. $\frac{1}{3}-\frac{1}{6}i$
   D. $\frac{1}{3}+\frac{1}{6}i$

8. What is the imaginary part of the complex number $\dfrac{76}{3}-\dfrac{32}{3}i$?

   A. i

   B. $-\dfrac{32}{3}$

   C. $\dfrac{32}{3}$

   D. $\dfrac{76}{3}$

9. When multiplying two complex numbers that both have a real part and an imaginary part not equal to 0, which of the following statements is true regarding the result?

   A. It will always have a real part equal to 0.
   B. It will always have an imaginary part equal to 0.
   C. It will sometimes have an imaginary part equal to 0.
   D. It will never have an imaginary part equal to 0.

Chapter 2
Solving Quadratic Equations and Inequalities

This chapter covers the following Georgia Performance Standards:

MM2A	Algebra	MM2A3c
		MM2A4a
		MM2A4b
		MM2A4c
		MM2A4d

You can factor polynomials such as $y^2 - 4y - 5$ into two factors:

$$y^2 - 4y - 5 = (y + 1)(y - 5)$$

In this chapter, we learn that any equation that can be put in the form $ax^2 + bx + c = 0$ is a quadratic equation if a, b, and c are real numbers and $a \neq 0$. $ax^2 + bx + c = 0$ is the standard form of a quadratic equation. To solve these equations, follow the steps below.

Example 1: Solve $y^2 - 4y - 5 = 0$

Step 1: Factor the left side of the equation.

$$y^2 - 4y - 5 = 0$$
$$(y + 1)(y - 5) = 0$$

Step 2: If the product of these two factors equals zero, then the two factors individually must be equal to zero. Therefore, to solve, we set each factor equal to zero.

$$
\begin{array}{r}
(y + 1) = 0 \\
\underline{-1 \quad -1} \\
y = -1
\end{array}
\qquad
\begin{array}{r}
(y - 5) = 0 \\
\underline{+5 \quad +5} \\
y = 5
\end{array}
$$

The equation has two solutions: $y = -1$ and $y = 5$

Check: To check, substitute each solution into the original equation.

When $y = -1$, the equation becomes: When $y = 5$, the equation becomes:
$$
\begin{aligned}
(-1)^2 - (4)(-1) - 5 &= 0 \\
1 + 4 - 5 &= 0 \\
0 &= 0
\end{aligned}
\qquad
\begin{aligned}
5^2 - (4)(5) - 5 &= 0 \\
25 - 20 - 5 &= 0 \\
0 &= 0
\end{aligned}
$$

Both solutions produce true statements.
The solution set for the equation is $\{-1, -5\}$.

Solve each of the following quadratic equations by factoring and setting each factor equal to zero. Check by substituting answers back in the original equation.

1. $x^2 + x - 6 = 0$

2. $y^2 - 2y - 8 = 0$

3. $a^2 + 2a - 15 = 0$

4. $y^2 - 5y + 4 = 0$

5. $b^2 - 9b + 14 = 0$

6. $x^2 - 3x - 4 = 0$

7. $y^2 + y - 20 = 0$

8. $d^2 + 6d + 8 = 0$

9. $y^2 - 7y + 12 = 0$

10. $x^2 - 3x - 28 = 0$

11. $a^2 - 5a + 6 = 0$

12. $b^2 + 3b - 10 = 0$

13. $a^2 + 7a - 8 = 0$

14. $x^2 + 3x + 2 = 0$

15. $x^2 - x - 42 = 0$

16. $a^2 + a - 6 = 0$

17. $b^2 + 7b + 12 = 0$

18. $y^2 + 2y - 15 = 0$

19. $a^2 - 3a - 10 = 0$

20. $d^2 + 10d + 16 = 0$

21. $x^2 - 4x - 12 = 0$

Quadratic equations that have a whole number and a variable in the first term are solved the same way as the previous page. Factor the trinomial, and set each factor equal to zero to find the solution set.

Example 2:   Solve $2x^2 + 3x - 2 = 0$
$(2x - 1)(x + 2) = 0$
Set each factor equal to zero and solve:

$$
\begin{array}{cc}
2x - 1 = 0 \\
\underline{+1 \quad +1} \\
\dfrac{2x}{2} = \dfrac{1}{2} \\
x = \dfrac{1}{2}
\end{array}
\qquad
\begin{array}{cc}
x + 2 = 0 \\
\underline{-2 \quad -2} \\
x = -2
\end{array}
$$

The solution set is $\left\{ \dfrac{1}{2}, -2 \right\}$.

Solve the following quadratic equations.

22. $3y^2 + 4y - 32 = 0$

23. $5c^2 - 2c - 16 = 0$

24. $7d^2 + 18d + 8 = 0$

25. $3a^2 - 10a - 8 = 0$

26. $11x^2 - 31x - 6 = 0$

27. $5b^2 + 17b + 6 = 0$

28. $3x^2 - 11x - 20 = 0$

29. $5a^2 + 47a - 30 = 0$

30. $2c^2 - 5c - 25 = 0$

31. $2y^2 + 11y - 21 = 0$

32. $5a^2 + 23a - 42 = 0$

33. $3d^2 + 11d - 20 = 0$

34. $3x^2 - 10x + 8 = 0$

35. $7b^2 + 23b - 20 = 0$

36. $9a^2 - 58a + 24 = 0$

37. $4c^2 - 25c - 21 = 0$

38. $8d^2 + 53d + 30 = 0$

39. $4y^2 + 37y - 30 = 0$

40. $8a^2 + 37a - 15 = 0$

41. $3x^2 - 41x + 26 = 0$

42. $8b^2 + 2b - 3 = 0$

2.1   Using the Quadratic Formula

You may be asked to use the quadratic formula to solve an algebra problem known as a **quadratic equation**. The equation should be in the form $ax^2 + bx + c = 0$.

Example 3:   Using the quadratic formula, find x in the following equation: $x^2 - 8x = -7$.

Step 1:   Make sure the equation is set equal to 0.

$$x^2 - 8x + 7 = -7 + 7$$
$$x^2 - 8x + 7 = 0$$

The quadratic formula, $\dfrac{-b \pm \sqrt{b^2 - 4ac}}{2a}$, will be given to you on your formula sheet with your test.

Step 2:   In the formula, a is the number x^2 is multiplied by, b is the number x is multiplied by and c is the last term of the equation. For the equation in the example, $x^2 - 8x + 7$, $a = 1$, $b = -8$, and $c = 7$. When we look at the formula we notice a $\pm$ sign. This means that there will be two solutions to the equation, one when we use the plus sign and one when we use the minus sign. Substituting the numbers from the problem into the formula, we have:

$$\frac{8 + \sqrt{8^2 - (4)(1)(7)}}{2(1)} = 7 \qquad \text{or} \qquad \frac{8 - \sqrt{8^2 - (4)(1)(7)}}{2(1)} = 1$$

The solutions are $\{7, 1\}$.

For each of the following equations, use the quadratic formula to find two solutions.

1. $x^2 + x - 6 = 0$

2. $y^2 - 2y - 8 = 0$

3. $a^2 + 2a - 15 = 0$

4. $y^2 - 5y + 4 = 0$

5. $b^2 - 9b + 14 = 0$

6. $x^2 - 3x - 4 = 0$

7. $y^2 + y - 20 = 0$

8. $d^2 + 6d + 8 = 0$

9. $y^2 - 7y + 12 = 0$

10. $x^2 - 3x - 28 = 0$

11. $a^2 - 5a + 6 = 0$

12. $b^2 + 3b - 10 = 0$

13. $a^2 + 7a - 8 = 0$

14. $c^2 + 3c + 2 = 0$

15. $x^2 - x - 42 = 0$

16. $a^2 + 5a - 6 = 0$

17. $b^2 + 7b + 12 = 0$

18. $y^2 + y - 12 = 0$

19. $a^2 - 3a - 10 = 0$

20. $d^2 + 10d + 16 = 0$

21. $x^2 - 4x - 12 = 0$

2.2 Solving Quadratic Equations with Complex Roots

Some quadratic equations do not have real number solutions. In this section, we will find complex solutions to each equation.

Example 4: Find the roots of the quadratic equation $7x^2 - 8x + 3 = 0$.

Step 1: The quadratic equation cannot be factored, so the quadratic formula must be used.

$$x = \frac{-b \pm \sqrt{b^2 - 4ac}}{2a} = \frac{-(-8) \pm \sqrt{(-8)^2 - 4(7)(3)}}{2(7)} = \frac{8 \pm \sqrt{-20}}{14}$$

Step 2: As stated earlier, i is defined as $\sqrt{-1}$, so if $\dfrac{8 \pm \sqrt{-20}}{14}$ is rewritten as

$\dfrac{8 \pm \sqrt{20 \times (-1)}}{14}$, and it can be simplified to $\dfrac{8 \pm i\sqrt{20}}{14}$.

This can be simplified as follows:

$$\frac{8 \pm i\sqrt{20}}{14} = \frac{8 \pm i\sqrt{4 \times 5}}{14} = \frac{8 \pm 2i\sqrt{5}}{14} = \frac{4 \pm i\sqrt{5}}{7} = \frac{4}{7} \pm \frac{\sqrt{5}}{7}i.$$

Therefore, the roots of the equation are $x = \dfrac{4}{7} + \dfrac{\sqrt{5}}{7}i$ or $\dfrac{4}{7} - \dfrac{\sqrt{5}}{7}i$.

Example 5: Find the roots of the quadratic equation $3x^2 - x + 5 = 0$.

Step 1: Plug the values for this equation into the quadratic formula: $a = 3$, $b = -1$, $c = 5$.

Step 2: Solve for x.

$$x = \frac{-(-1) \pm \sqrt{(-1)2 - 4(3)(5)}}{2(3)} = \frac{1 \pm \sqrt{1 - 60}}{6} = \frac{1}{6} \pm \frac{\sqrt{-59}}{6}$$

Step 3: Apply the definition of i. $x = \dfrac{1}{6} \pm \dfrac{\sqrt{-59}}{6} = \dfrac{1}{6} \pm \dfrac{\sqrt{59}}{6}i.$

Find the roots of each of the following quadratic equations.

1. $9x^2 - 6x + 3 = 0$

2. $\frac{3}{4}x^2 - x + 12 = 0$

3. $-11x^2 + 10x - 3 = 0$

4. $14x^2 - 3x + \frac{1}{2} = 0$

5. $-x^2 - 3x - 16 = 0$

6. $8x^2 + 9x + 10 = 0$

7. $x(19x - 2) = -1$

8. $x(1 - 5x) = 5$

9. $-10x^2 + \frac{x}{2} - 7 = 0$

10. $8x^2 + 3x + 10 = 0$

11. $-6x^2 - 5x - 11 = 0$

12. $13x^2 + 12x + 7 = 0$

13. $4x^2 - 10x + 11 = 0$

14. $-5x^2 - x - 3 = 0$

15. $18x^2 - 5x + 1 = 0$

2.3   Solving the Difference of Two Squares

To solve the difference of two squares, first factor. Then set each factor equal to zero.

Example 6: $25x^2 - 36 = 0$

Step 1:   Factor the left hand side of the equation.

$$25x^2 - 36 = 0$$
$$(5x + 6)(5x - 6) = 0$$

Step 2:   Set each factor equal to zero and solve.

$$
\begin{array}{cc}
5x + 6 = 0 & 5x - 6 = 0 \\
\underline{-6 \quad -6} & \underline{+6 \quad +6} \\
\dfrac{5x}{5} = \dfrac{6}{5} & \dfrac{5x}{5} = \dfrac{6}{5} \\
x = -\dfrac{6}{5} & x = \dfrac{6}{5}
\end{array}
$$

Check: Substitute each solution in the equation to check.

for $x = -\dfrac{6}{5}$:

$$25x^2 - 36 = 0$$

$$25\left(-\frac{6}{5}\right)\left(-\frac{6}{5}\right) - 36 = 0 \longleftarrow \text{Substitute } -\frac{6}{5} \text{ for } x.$$

$$25\left(\frac{36}{25}\right) - 36 = 0 \longleftarrow \text{Cancel the 25's.}$$

$$36 - 36 = 0 \longleftarrow \text{A true statement. } x = -\frac{6}{5} \text{ is a solution.}$$

for $x = \dfrac{6}{5}$:

$$25x^2 - 36 = 0$$

$$25\left(\frac{6}{5}\right)\left(\frac{6}{5}\right) - 36 = 0 \longleftarrow \text{Substitute } \frac{6}{5} \text{ for } x.$$

$$25\left(\frac{36}{25}\right) - 36 = 0 \longleftarrow \text{Cancel the 25's.}$$

$$36 - 36 = 0 \longleftarrow \text{A true statement. } x = \frac{6}{5} \text{ is a solution.}$$

The solution set is $\left\{\dfrac{-6}{5}, \dfrac{6}{5}\right\}$.

Find the solution sets for the following.

1. $25a^2 - 16 = 0$

2. $c^2 - 36 = 0$

3. $9x^2 - 64 = 0$

4. $100y^2 - 49 - 0$

5. $4b^2 - 81 = 0$

6. $d^2 - 25 = 0$

7. $9x^2 - 1 = 0$

8. $16a^2 - 9 = 0$

9. $36y^2 - 1 = 0$

10. $36y^2 - 25 = 0$

11. $d^2 - 16 = 0$

12. $64b^2 - 9 = 0$

13. $81a^2 - 4 = 0$

14. $64y^2 - 25 = 0$

15. $4c^2 - 49 = 0$

16. $x^2 - 81 = 0$

17. $49b^2 - 9 = 0$

18. $a^2 - 64 = 0$

19. $x^2 - 1 = 0$

20. $4y^2 - 9 = 0$

21. $t^2 - 100 = 0$

22. $16k^2 - 81 = 0$

23. $a^2 - 4 = 0$

24. $36b^2 - 16 = 0$

2.4   Solving Perfect Squares

When the square root of a constant, variable, or polynomial results in a constant, variable, or polynomial without irrational numbers, the expression is a **perfect square**. Some examples are 49, x^2, and $(x-2)^2$.

Example 7:   Solve the perfect square for x. $(x-5)^2 = 0$

Step 1:   Take the square root of both sides.
$$\sqrt{(x-5)^2} = \sqrt{0}$$
$$(x-5) = 0$$

Step 2:   Solve the equation.
$$(x-5) = 0$$
$$x-5+5 = 0+5$$
$$x = 5$$

Example 8:   Solve the perfect square for x. $(x-5)^2 = 64$

Step 1:   Take the square root of both sides.
$$\sqrt{(x-5)^2} = \sqrt{64}$$
$$(x-5) = \pm 8$$
$$(x-5) = 8 \text{ and } (x-5) = -8$$

Step 2:   Solve the two equations.
$$(x-5) = 8 \qquad \text{and} \quad (x-5) = -8$$
$$x-5+5 = 8+5 \quad \text{and} \quad x-5+5 = -8+5$$
$$x = 13 \qquad\quad \text{and} \quad x = -3$$

Solve the perfect square for x.

1. $(x-2)^2 = 0$

2. $(x+1)^2 = 0$

3. $(x+11)^2 = 0$

4. $(x-4)^2 = 0$

5. $(x-1)^2 = 0$

6. $(x+8)^2 = 0$

7. $(x+3)^2 = 4$

8. $(x-5)^2 = 16$

9. $(x-10)^2 = 100$

10. $(x+9)^2 = 9$

11. $(x-4.5)^2 = 25$

12. $(x+7)^2 = 36$

13. $(x+2)^2 = 49$

14. $(x-1)^2 = 4$

15. $(x+8.9)^2 = 49$

16. $(x-6)^2 = 81$

17. $(x-12)^2 = 121$

18. $(x+2.5)^2 = 64$

2.5 Completing the Square

"Completing the Square" is another way of factoring a quadratic equation. To complete the square, convert the equation into a perfect square.

Example 9: Solve $x^2 - 10x + 9 = 0$ by completing the square.

Completing the square:

Step 1: The first step is to get the constant on the other side of the equation. Subtract 9 from both sides:
$x^2 - 10x + 9 - 9 = -9$
$x^2 - 10x = -9$

Step 2: Determine the coefficient of the x. The coefficient in this example is -10. Divide the coefficient by 2 and square the result.
$(-10 \div 2)^2 = (-5)^2 = 25$

Step 3: Add the resulting value, 25, to both sides:
$x^2 - 10x + 25 = -9 + 25$
$x^2 - 10x + 25 = 16$

Step 4: Now factor the $x^2 - 10x + 25$ into a perfect square:
$(x - 5)^2 = 16$

Solving the perfect square:

Step 5: Take the square root of both sides.
$\sqrt{(x - 5)^2} = \sqrt{16}$
$(x - 5) = \pm 4$
$(x - 5) = 4$ and $(x - 5) = -4$

Step 6: Solve the two equations.
$(x - 5) = 4$ and $(x - 5) = -4$
$x - 5 + 5 = 4 + 5$ and $x - 5 + 5 = -4 + 5$
$x = 9$ and $x = 1$

Solve for x by completing the square.

1. $x^2 + 2x - 3 = 0$
2. $x^2 - 8x + 7 = 0$
3. $x^2 + 6x - 7 = 0$
4. $x^2 - 16x - 36 = 0$
5. $x^2 - 14x + 49 = 0$

6. $x^2 - 4x = 0$
7. $x^2 + 12x + 27 = 0$
8. $x^2 + 2x - 24 = 0$
9. $x^2 + 12x - 85 = 0$
10. $x^2 - 8x + 15 = 0$

11. $x^2 - 16x + 60 = 0$
12. $x^2 - 8x - 48 = 0$
13. $x^2 + 24x + 44 = 0$
14. $x^2 + 6x + 5 = 0$
15. $x^2 - 11x + 5.25 = 0$

2.6   Discriminant

The **discriminant**, D, is determined from the coefficients of the quadratic equation $ax^2 + bx + c = 0$. The formula for the discriminant is shown below.

$$D = b^2 - 4ac$$

The discriminant illustrates how many real roots the quadratic equation has. Look at the table below:

Discriminant	Roots
$D < 0$	no real roots (only complex roots)
$D = 0$	one real roots
$D > 0$	two real roots

Example 10:   Find the discriminant, D, of the equation $x^2 + 7x + 12 = 0$.

Step 1:   Determine what a, b, and c are in the quadratic equation $x^2 + 7x + 12 = 0$. $a = 1, b = 7, c = 12$

Step 2:   Plus the values for a, b, and c into the formula for the discriminant. $D = b^2 - 4ac = 7^2 - 4(1)(12) = 49 - 48 = 1$

Step 3:   The discriminant is 1. Looking at the chart above, we see that $1 > 0$, so there are two real roots of the quadratic equation $x^2 + 7x + 12 = 0$.

NOTE: $x^2 + 7x + 12 = 0$ factors to $(x + 3)(x + 4) = 0$

Solve for x:
$$\begin{array}{cccccc} x + 3 & = & 0 & \quad x + 4 & = & 0 \\ x & = & -3 & \quad x & = & -4 \end{array}$$

We see that the roots are -4 and -3. Therefore, there are two real roots for the quadratic equation $x^2 + 7x + 12 = 0$.

Find the discriminant of the quadratic equations.

1. $x^2 + 4x + 4 = 0$
2. $x^2 + 8x - 33 = 0$
3. $x^2 - 9 = 0$
4. $2x^2 + 3x - 14 = 0$

5. $x^2 - 11x + 30 = 0$
6. $2x^2 + 5x - 6 = 0$
7. $x^2 - 4x + 2 = 0$
8. $5x^2 - 6x + 21 = 0$

9. $x^2 + 9x + 14 = 0$
10. $x^2 - 3x + 15 = 0$
11. $x^2 - 6x + 9 = 0$
12. $3x^2 + x + 6 = 0$

First, find the discriminant. Then, look at the chart above to determine how many roots the equations have.

13. $x^2 + 8x + 16 = 0$
14. $3x^2 - x + 2 = 0$
15. $x^2 - 7x + 12 = 0$

16. $x^2 + 8x + 15 = 0$
17. $2x^2 - 20x + 50 = 0$
18. $x^2 - 10x + 24 = 0$

2.7 Graphing Quadratic Equations

Equations that you may encounter on the GA Math II EOC test will possibly involve variables which are squared (raised to the second power). The best way to find values for the x and y variables in an equation is to plug one number into x, and then find the corresponding value for y. Then, plot the points and draw a line through the points.

Example 11: Graph $y = x^2$.

Step 1: Make a table and find several values for x and y.

x	y
-2	4
-1	1
0	0
1	1
2	4

Step 2: Plot the points, and draw a curve through the points. Notice the shape of the curve. This type of curve is called a **parabola**. Equations with one squared term will be parabolas.

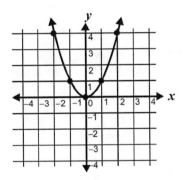

Note: In the equation $y = ax^2 + c$, changing the value of a will widen or narrow the parabola around the y-axis. If the value of a is a negative number, the parabola will be reflected across the x-axis (the vertex will be at the top of the parabola instead of at the bottom.) If $a = 0$, the graph will be a straight line, not a parabola. Changing the value of c will move the vertex of the parabola from the origin to a different point on the y-axis.

Graph the equations below on a Cartesian plane.

1. $y = 2x^2$
2. $y = 3 - x^2$
3. $y = x^2 - 2$
4. $y = -2x^2$
5. $y = x^2 + 3$
6. $y = -3x^2 + 2$
7. $y = 3x^2 - 5$
8. $y = x^2 + 1$
9. $y = -x^2 - 6$
10. $y = -x^2$
11. $y = 2x^2 - 1$
12. $y = 2 - 2x^2$

2.8   Finding the Intercepts of a Quadratic Equation

A **quadratic equation** is an equation where either the y or x variable is squared. Finding the intercepts of a quadratic equation is similar to finding the intercepts of a line. In most cases, the variable x is squared, which means there could be two x-intercepts. There could be one, two, or zero x-intercepts. The x-intercepts of a quadratic equation are called the **zeros** or **solutions** of a quadratic equation.

Example 12:   Find the x-intercept(s) of the quadratic equation, $y = x^2 - 4$.

Step 1:   Find the x-intercept(s). The x-intercept is the point, or points in this case, where the graph crosses the x-axis. In this case, we plug 0 in for y because y is always zero along the x-axis. Solve for x.

$$y = x^2 - 4$$
$$0 = x^2 - 4$$
$$0 + 4 = x^2 - 4 + 4$$
$$4 = x^2$$
$$\sqrt{4} = \sqrt{x^2}$$
$$\sqrt{4} = x$$

Thus, $x = \sqrt{4}$ and $\sqrt{4} = -2$ or 2, so $x = -2$ or $x = 2$.
The x-intercepts are $(-2, 0)$ and $(2, 0)$.

Step 2:   To verify that the intercepts are correct, graph the equation on the coordinate plane.

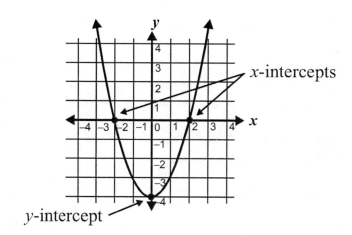

Example 13:   Find the x-intercept(s) of the quadratic equation, $y = x^2 + 2$.

Step 1:   Find the x-intercept. Plug 0 in for y and solve for x.
$$y = x^2 + 2$$
$$0 = x^2 + 2$$
$$0 - 2 = x^2 + 2 - 2$$
$$-2 = x^2$$
$$\sqrt{-2} = \sqrt{x^2}$$
$$\sqrt{-2} = x$$
You cannot take the square root of a negative number and get a real number as the answer, so there is no x-intercept for this quadratic equation.

Step 3:   To verify that the intercepts are correct, graph the equation on the coordinate plane. As you can see from the graph, the tails of the parabola are increasing in the positive y direction, so they will never come back down, which means they will never cross the x-axis.

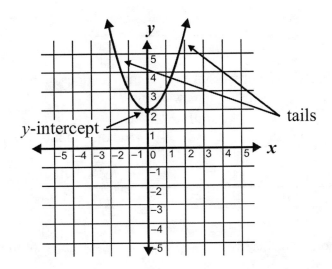

Find the x-intercept(s) of the following quadratic equations.

1. $y = x^2$

2. $y = 2x^2 - 4$

3. $y = -x^2 + 2$

4. $y = x^2 + 6$

5. $y = -x^2 - 1$

6. $y = x^2 - 5$

7. $y = 4x^2 + 8$

8. $y = x^2 + 2x + 1$

9. $y = x^2 - 7x + 12$

2.9   Solving Quadratic Inequalities

A **quadratic inequality** is a polynomial inequality of degree 2. The standard form of a quadratic inequality is similar to that of a quadratic equation, which has the standard form $ax^2 + bx + c = 0$, where $a \neq 0$. The only difference in the standard form of a quadratic inequality is that the equal sign in the standard form of a quadratic equation is replaced by either $>$, $\geq$, $<$, or $\leq$.

Example 14:   Solve the inequality $-x(x - 2) < -3$.

Step 1:   First put all of the terms in the quadratic inequality on one side of the inequality sign.
$$-x(x - 2) < -3 \rightarrow -x^2 + 2x + 3 < 0$$

Step 2:   Now find the root(s) of the corresponding quadratic equation.
$$(x - 3)(-x - 1) = 0$$
$$\begin{array}{lll} x - 3 = 0 & -x - 1 = 0 & \text{Set each factor equal to zero.} \\ x = 3 & x = -1 \end{array}$$

Step 3:   Graphing the two points -1 and 3 on a number line determines the three regions that could satisfy the inequality.

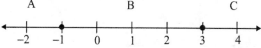

Step 4:   Now, pick a number from each of three regions in the graph above to determine which region satisfies the inequality.

Region	Number Chosen	Substitute into Equation	Satisfy Inequality?
A $(x < -1)$	-2	$-(-2)^2 + 2(-2) + 3 = -5 < 0$	Yes
B $(-1 < x < 3)$	0	$-(0)^2 + 2(0) + 3 = 3 > 0$	No
C $(x > 3)$	4	$-(4)^2 + 2(4) + 3 = -5 < 0$	Yes

Step 5:   The numbers from region A and C satisfy the inequality. The solution to the quadratic inequality is $x < -1$ or $x > 3$. A graph of this solution is shown below.

Solve each of the following quadratic inequalities.

1. $x^2 + 2x - 8 > 0$

2. $x(x + 7) \geq -12$

3. $-x^2 - 5x + 14 < 0$

4. $5x^2 + 34x - 7 \leq 0$

5. $x^2 - 14x + 24 \geq 0$

6. $x(x + 8) \leq 9$

7. $x^2 - 11x + 30 > 0$

8. $3x^2 + 8x < 16$

9. $-x^2 + x + 56 > 0$

10. $-x^2 + 4x - 9 \leq 0$

11. $x^2 - x + 7 < 0$

12. $x(x - 4) > -5$

13. $4x^2 - x + 1 \geq 0$

14. $(x - 3)^2 < 0$

15. $x^2 + 2x + 6 \leq 0$

16. $5x(x - 1) > -2$

17. $8x^2 - 7x + 2 \geq 0$

18. $-x^2 + 3x - 11 > 0$

2.10   Graphing Quadratic Inequalities

A **quadratic inequality** can also be solved by graphing the inequality on a coordinate plane.

Example 15:   Graph the quadratic inequality $y < -2x^2 + 4$, then find the solution.

Step 1:   Change the inequality to an equality: $y = -2x^2 + 4$. Graph the quadratic equation as you did on page 33.

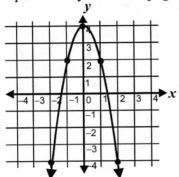

Step 2:   Change the equality back to an inequality: $y < -2x^2 + 4$. This inequality is less than, so it will have a dotted line instead of a solid line. Also, the less than sign implies that there will be shading below the graph instead of above it.

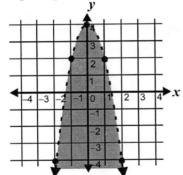

Step 3:   To find the solution for the quadratic inequality, find the x-intercepts first. The x-intercepts are $(\pm\sqrt{2}, 0)$. Then looking at the graph, we see the shaded portion of the graph is between the two intercepts.
Therefore, the solution of the inequality is $-\sqrt{2} < x < \sqrt{2}$.

Graph the inequalities below on a Cartesian plane, then find the solution(s).

1. $y \leq 2x^2$

2. $y > 3 - x^2$

3. $y \geq x^2 + 2x - 2$

4. $y \leq -3x^2 + 2$

5. $y > x^2 + 1$

6. $y > x^2$

7. $y \geq x^2 + 6x + 1$

8. $y \leq x^2 - 2x + 3$

Chapter 2 Review

Factor and solve each of the following quadratic equations.

1. $16b^2 - 25 = 0$

2. $a^2 - a - 30 = 0$

3. $x^2 - x = 6$

4. $100x^2 - 49 = 0$

5. $81y^2 = 9$

6. $y^2 = 21 - 4y$

7. $y^2 - 7y + 8 = 16$

8. $6x^2 + x - 2 = 0$

9. $3y^2 + y - 2 = 0$

10. $b^2 + 2b - 8 = 0$

11. $4x^2 + 19x - 5 = 0$

12. $8x^2 = 6x + 2$

13. $2y^2 - 6y - 20 = 0$

14. $-6x^2 + 7x - 2 = 0$

15. $y^2 + 3y - 18 = 0$

Using the quadratic formula, find both solutions for the variable.

16. $x^2 + 10x - 11 = 0$

17. $y^2 - 14y + 40 = 0$

18. $b^2 + 9b + 18 = 0$

19. $y^2 - 12y - 13 = 0$

20. $a^2 - 8a - 48 = 0$

21. $x^2 + 2x - 63 = 0$

22. $-3x^2 - 2x - 2 = 0$

23. $4x^2 + x + 5 = 0$

24. $2x^2 - 8x + 9 = 0$

Solve each of the following quadratic inequalities.

25. $2x^2 + x - 15 \geq 0$

26. $-2x^2 + 21x + 11 < 0$

27. $x(3x + 1) \leq 24$

28. $-5x^2 - 9x - 12 > 0$

29. $x^2 + 8x + 30 \geq 0$

30. $6x^2 - 7x + 8 \leq 0$

Find the x-intercept(s) of the following quadratic equations.

31. $y = 2x^2 - 8$

32. $y = -x^2 - 9$

33. $y = 5x^2 + 1$

34. $y = x^2 - 6$

Graph the equations below on a Cartesian plane.

35. $y = -x^2 + 4$

36. $y = 3x^2 - 1$

37. $y = 4 - x^2$

38. $y = 3x^2 + 6$

Graph the inequalities below on a Cartesian plane, then find the solution(s).

39. $y < -x^2 - 6$

40. $y < x^2 + 4x - 1$

41. $y > x^2 + 2$

42. $y > 3x^2 + 4$

Chapter 2 Test

1. Solve: $4y^2 - 9y = -5$

   A. $\left\{1, \dfrac{5}{4}\right\}$

   B. $\left\{-\dfrac{3}{4}, -1\right\}$

   C. $\left\{-1, \dfrac{4}{5}\right\}$

   D. $\left\{\dfrac{5}{16}, 1\right\}$

2. Solve for y: $2y^2 + 13y + 15 = 0$

   A. $\left\{\dfrac{3}{2}, \dfrac{5}{2}\right\}$

   B. $\left\{\dfrac{2}{3}, \dfrac{2}{5}\right\}$

   C. $\left\{-5, -\dfrac{3}{2}\right\}$

   D. $\left\{5, -\dfrac{3}{2}\right\}$

3. Solve for x.

   $x^2 - 3x - 18 = 0$

   A. $\{-6, 3\}$
   B. $\{6, -3\}$
   C. $\{-9, 2\}$
   D. $\{9, -2\}$

4. What are the values of x in the quadratic equation?

   $x^2 + 2x - 15 = x - 3$

   A. $\{-4, 3\}$
   B. $\{-3, 4\}$
   C. $\{-3, 5\}$
   D. Cannot be determined

5. Solve the equation $(x + 9)^2 = 49$

   A. $x = -9, 9$
   B. $x = -9, 7$
   C. $x = -16, -2$
   D. $x = -7, 7$

6. Solve the equation $c^2 + 8c - 9 = 0$ by completing the square.

   A. $c = \{1, -9\}$
   B. $c = \{-1, 9\}$
   C. $c = \{3, 3\}$
   D. $c = \{-3, -3\}$

7. Using the quadratic formula, solve the following equation:

   $3x^2 = 9x$

   A. $x = \{0, 1\}$
   B. $x = \{3, 1\}$
   C. $x = \{0, 3\}$
   D. $x = \{3, -3\}$

8. Solve $6a^2 + 11a - 10 = 0$, using the quadratic formula.

   A. $\left\{-\frac{2}{5}, \frac{3}{2}\right\}$

   B. $\left\{\frac{2}{5}, \frac{2}{3}\right\}$

   C. $\left\{-\frac{5}{2}, \frac{2}{3}\right\}$

   D. $\left\{\frac{5}{2}, \frac{2}{3}\right\}$

9. Which of the following quadratic inequalities has no real solution?

   A. $3x^2 - 17x - 6 < 0$

   B. $-4x^2 - 11x + 3 > 0$

   C. $5x^2 - 7x - 6 \le 0$

   D. $-6x^2 - 3x - 8 \ge 0$

10. Which of the following solutions is correct for the quadratic inequality $6x^2 - 41x - 7 \leq 0$?

   A. $x \leq -6$ or $x \geq 7$

   B. $x \leq -\frac{1}{6}$ or $x \geq 7$

   C. $-6 \leq x \leq 7$

   D. $-\frac{1}{6} \leq x \leq 7$

11. Which of the following graphs represents $y = 2x^2$?

   A.

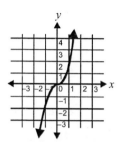

   B.

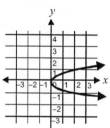

   C.

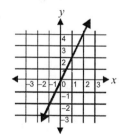

   D.

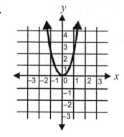

12. Which of the following expressions is a root of the quadratic equation $-7x^2 - x - 3 = 0$?

   A. $-\dfrac{1}{14} - \dfrac{\sqrt{83}}{14}$

   B. $1 + \sqrt{83}i$

   C. $-\dfrac{1}{14} - \dfrac{\sqrt{83}}{14}i$

   D. $1 - \sqrt{83}i$

13. What are the x-intercept(s) of the equation $y = -2x^2 + 8$?

   A. $(-2, 0)$ and $(2, 0)$
   B. $(-4, 0)$ and $(4, 0)$
   C. $(8, 0)$
   D. There are no x-intercepts.

14. What are the x-intercept(s) of the equation $y = x^2 + 9$

   A. $(9, 0)$
   B. $(-3, 0)$ and $(3, 0)$
   C. $(-9, 0)$ and $(9, 0)$
   D. There are no x-intercepts.

15. Looking at the graph below, what is the solution to the inequality $y \leq x^2 - 10x + 19$?

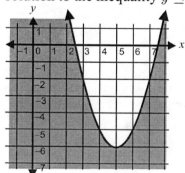

   A. $x = 5 \pm \sqrt{6}$
   B. $x < 5 - \sqrt{6}$ or $x > 5 + \sqrt{6}$
   C. $5 - \sqrt{6} \leq x \leq 5 + \sqrt{6}$
   D. $x \leq 5 - \sqrt{6}$ or $x \geq 5 + \sqrt{6}$

Chapter 3
Quadratic Functions

This chapter covers the following Georgia Performance Standards:

MM2A	Algebra	MM2A3a
		MM2A3b
		MM2A3c
		MM2A3d
		MM2A3e

3.1   Converting Quadratic Functions Between Standard and Vertex Form

The **standard form** of a quadratic function is $f(x) = ax^2 + bx + c$, where a, b, and c are constants, and $a \neq 0$.

The **vertex form** of a quadratic function is $f(x) = a(x - h)^2 + k$, where a, h, and k are constants, and $a \neq 0$. The reason why $f(x) = a(x - h)^2 + k$ is referred to as vertex form is because the point (h, k) is the vertex of the graph of the quadratic function.

Example 1:   Convert the quadratic function $f(x) = 5(x + 2)^2 - 9$ from vertex form to standard form.

Step 1:   To convert the function to standard form, simplify the function using order of operations.
$$f(x) = 5(x + 2)^2 - 9$$
$$f(x) = 5(x + 2)(x + 2) - 9$$
$$f(x) = 5(x^2 + 4x + 4) - 9$$
$$f(x) = 5x^2 + 20x + 20 - 9$$

Step 2:   Now, combine like terms.
$$f(x) = 5x^2 + 20x + 20 - 9 = 5x^2 + 20x + 11$$

The standard form of the function $f(x) = 5(x + 2)^2 - 9$ is
$$f(x) = 5x^2 + 20x + 11$$

Convert each of the following quadratic functions from vertex form to standard form.

1. $f(x) = -3(x - 4)^2 + 7$

2. $f(x) = \frac{2}{3}(x + 1)^2 - 8$

3. $f(x) = 6(x + 10)^2 - 2$

4. $f(x) = 4(x - 7)^2 + 11$

5. $f(x) = -(x + 4)^2 - 3$

6. $f(x) = 7(x - 9)^2 + 1$

7. $f(x) = 5(x + 3)^2 - 4$

8. $f(x) = 2(x - 5)^2 + 9$

9. $f(x) = 9(x + 2)^2 - 5$

Example 2:   Convert the quadratic function $f(x) = 5x^2 - 40x + 67$ from standard form to vertex form.

Step 1:   To convert the function to vertex form, the completing the square technique must be used. The first step is to subtract the constant from both sides of the equation:
$$f(x) = 5x^2 - 40x + 67$$
$$f(x) - 67 = 5x^2 - 40x + 67 - 67$$
$$f(x) - 67 = 5x^2 - 40x$$

Step 2:   Next, 5 should be factored from the right side of the equation:
$$f(x) - 67 = 5x^2 - 40x = 5(x^2 - 8x)$$

Step 3:   Next, the square should be completed on the right side of the equation. To review completing, refer to page 31. Divide the coefficient of x by 2, then square the result. $(-8) \div 2 = -4$. $(-4)^2 = 16$. Add 16 to the binomial in the parenthesis.
$$f(x) - 67 = 5(x^2 - 8x)$$
$$f(x) - 67 = 5(x^2 - 8x + 16)$$

Step 4:   Since 16 is added to the right side of the function within the parentheses, it is multiplied by 5. This means that we added $5(16) = 80$ to the right side of the function, not just 16. So we must add 80 to the left side of the function in order for the function to be balanced.
$$f(x) - 67 + 80 = 5(x^2 - 8x + 16)$$

Step 5:   Next, simplify the function by factoring the trinomial on the right and combining like terms on the left.
$$f(x) - 67 + 80 = 5(x^2 - 8x + 16)$$
$$f(x) + 13 = 5(x - 4)^2$$

Step 6:   Finally, 13 should be subtracted from both sides of the equation so that the function is in vertex form.
$$f(x) + 13 = 5(x - 4)^2$$
$$f(x) + 13 - 13 = 5(x - 4)^2 - 13$$
$$f(x) = 5(x - 4)^2 - 13 \text{ is the vertex form of the function.}$$

Convert each of the following quadratic functions from standard form to vertex form.

1. $f(x) = 8x^2 - 16x + 27$

2. $f(x) = -2x^2 - 24x - 75$

3. $f(x) = 3x^2 + 42x + 121$

4. $f(x) = 5x^2 - 10x + 37$

5. $f(x) = 6x^2 + 72x + 228$

6. $f(x) = -4x^2 + 64x - 270$

7. $f(x) = 7x^2 + 28x + 19$

8. $f(x) = -3x^2 - 24x - 154$

9. $f(x) = 9x^2 - 54x - 10$

3.2 Graphing Transformations of the Quadratic Parent Function

The quadratic parent function is $f(x) = x^2$. All quadratic functions can be graphed as a transformation of the parent function. The function must first be put into vertex form, $g(x) = a(x-h)^2 + k$. This allows us to see the transformations more clearly. Four types of transformations can occur:

1. If $a \neq 1$, then horizontal stretching/shrinking of the graph of x^2 occurs. It becomes wider when $0 < a < 1$ or thinner if $a > 1$.

2. If $h \neq 0$, then a translation left or right will occur. Move the graph h units horizontally.

3. If $k \neq 0$, then a translation up or down will occur. Move the graph k units vertically.

4. If a is negative, reflect the graph over the x-axis.

Note: It does not matter which type of transformation happens first.

Example 3: Graph the quadratic function $f(x) = \frac{1}{3}(x+4)^2 - 10$ as a transformation of the function $f(x) = x^2$.

The graph of $f(x) = x^2$ is graphed below.

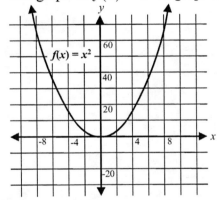

Step 1: To transform the graph of the function $f(x) = x^2$ into the graph of the function $f(x) = \frac{1}{3}(x+4)^2 - 10$, we will start with horizontal stretching. Since $a = \frac{1}{3} < 1$, we know that the parent function will become wider. When this is done, the function becomes $f(x) = \frac{1}{3}x^2$.

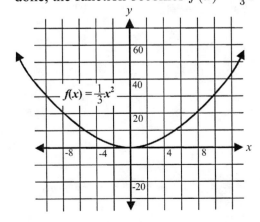

Step 2:   Next, a translation of 10 units down will be applied, $k = -10$. When this is done, the function becomes $f(x) = \frac{1}{3}x^2 - 10$.

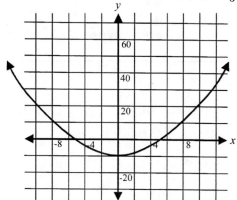

Step 3:   Finally, a translation of 4 units left will be applied, $h = -4$. When this is done, the function becomes $f(x) = \frac{1}{3}(x + 4)^2 - 10$.

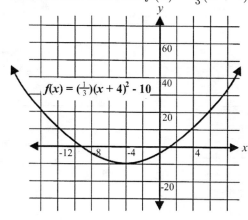

Graph each of the following quadratic functions as transformations of the parent function.

1. $f(x) = 3(x + 2)^2 - 4$

2. $f(x) = \frac{1}{4}(x - 6)^2 - 8$

3. $f(x) = 2(x + 5)^2 + 9$

4. $f(x) = 5(x - 1)^2 + 7$

5. $f(x) = \frac{2}{5}(x + 3)^2 - 1$

6. $f(x) = 4(x - 9)^2 - 3$

7. $f(x) = 7(x + 1)^2 + 5$

8. $f(x) = \frac{2}{3}(x - 2)^2 + 10$

9. $f(x) = 6(x + 4)^2 - 6$

10. $f(x) = 7x^2 + 28x + 18$

11. $f(x) = \frac{1}{2}x^2 - 8x + 44$

12. $f(x) = 5x^2 + 30x + 38$

13. $f(x) = -3x^2 + 12x - 34$

14. $f(x) = 4x^2 + 72x + 307$

15. $f(x) = \frac{1}{3}x^2 - 6x + 33$

16. $f(x) = -6x^2 - 12x + 23$

17. $f(x) = 15x^2 + 2x + 3$

18. $f(x) = 8x^2 - 48x + 57$

19. Explain why the graph of $f(x) = (-(x + 4))^2$ is not the graph of $f(x) = (x + 4)^2$ reflected in the y-axis.

3.3 Characteristics of Quadratic Functions

Every quadratic function has various characteristics.

The **domain** of the quadratic function $f(x)$ is all possible values of x for the function, the **range** is all possible values of $f(x)$.

The **zeros** or **roots** are the values of x that produce a value of 0 for $f(x)$, and the **extrema** is the maximum or minimum value of $f(x)$.

The graph of every quadratic function, which is a parabola, has certain properties as well.

The **axis of symmetry** of the graph of the function $f(x)$ is a line down the middle of the graph that passes through the vertex and divides the parabola into two equal parts.

The **vertex** of the graph is the point of intersection between the axis of symmetry and the parabola. It is the highest or lowest point in the center of a parabola.

The **intercepts** of the graph are the points where the parabola crosses the x- and y-axes.

The **intervals of increase and decrease** of the graph of the function $f(x)$ are the regions in which the parabola is going up or going down.

Example 4: The graph of the function $f(x) = 3(x + 4)^2 + 6$ is shown. List the function's domain, range, zeros, and extrema, and the graph's axis of symmetry, vertex, intercepts, and intervals of increase/decrease.

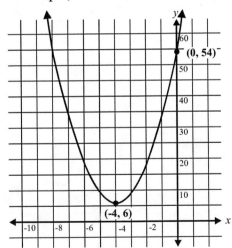

Domain: all real numbers

Range: $f(x) \geq 6$. The range of the function is $6 \leq y \leq \infty$.

Zeros: The function does not cross x-axis, so $f(x)$ never equals zero and the function has no zeros.

Extrema: The function has a minimum at 6.

Symmetry: Since the graph of the function can be reflected over the line $x = -4$ and produce the same graph, its axis of symmetry is $x = -4$.

Vertex: The graph's vertex is $(-4, 6)$. This can be found from the vertex form.

Intercepts: The graph does not have any x-intercepts. The function has a y-intercept at $(0, 54)$.

Intervals: The graph has an interval of decrease of $(-\infty, -4]$ and an interval increase of $[-4, \infty)$.

Example 5:   The graph of the function $f(x) = -5(x - 4)^2 + 2$ is shown. List the function's domain, range, zeros, and extrema, and the graph's axis of symmetry, vertex, intercepts, and intervals of increase/decrease.

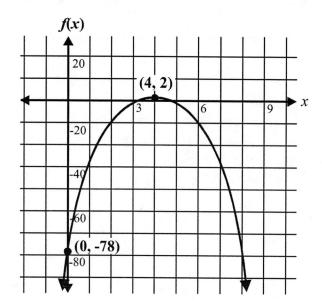

Domain: all real numbers

Range: The range of the function is all values less than or equal to 2.

Zeros: The zeros of the function can be determined by plugging 0 in for $f(x)$ and solving for x.

Extrema: Where $x = 4$, $f(x) = 2$. For all other values of x, $f(x) < 2$. Therefore, the function has a maximum value of 2, the extrema.

Symmetry: The graph of the function can be reflected on the line $x = 4$ and produce the same graph, its axis of symmetry is $x = 4$.

Vertex: The axis of symmetry intersects the parabola at the point $(4, 2)$, the graph's vertex is $(4, 2)$.

Intercepts: The zeros of the function are $x = 4 \pm \frac{\sqrt{10}}{5}$, the graph has x-intercepts at $x = 4 - \frac{\sqrt{10}}{5}$ and $x = 4 + \frac{\sqrt{10}}{5}$. Plugging in zero for x and solving for $f(x)$ shows that the function has a y-intercept at $f(x) = -78$.

Intervals: The graph has an interval of decrease of $[4, \infty)$ and an interval increase of $(-\infty, 4]$.

For each of the following quadratic functions, list the function's domain, range, zeros, and extrema, and for the graph of the function list the axis of symmetry, vertex, intercepts, and intervals of increase and decrease.

1. $f(x) = 2(x-5)^2 + 18$

2. $f(x) = \frac{1}{4}(x+9)^2 + 1$

3. $f(x) = 8(x-2)^2 + 3$

4. $f(x) = 9(x-1)^2 + 10$

5. $f(x) = 5(x+6)^2 + 14$

6. $f(x) = \frac{4}{5}(x+3)^2 + 2$

7. $f(x) = -2(x+8)^2 + 5$

8. $f(x) = 5(x-3)^2 - 11$

9. $f(x) = -\frac{5}{6}(x+1)^2 + 2$

10. $f(x) = \frac{7}{2}(x-2)^2 - 14$

11. $f(x) = 4(x-4)^2 - 5$

12. $f(x) = -3(x+5)^2 + 9$

Example 6: Determine the equation of the quadratic function whose graph has a vertex of $(5, 8)$ and a y-intercept of $(0, -67)$.

Step 1: Since the quadratic function has a graph whose vertex is $(5, 8)$, the equation of the function must be $f(x) = a(x-5)^2 + 8$, where a is a constant. Also, since the y-intercept of the graph is $f(x) = -67$, when 0 is plugged in for x, the value of $f(x)$ must equal -67. For this reason, a can be solved for as follows:

$-67 = a(0-5)^2 + 8$

$-67 = a(5)^2 + 8$

$-67 = 25a + 8$

$-67 - 8 = 25a + 8 - 8$

$-75 = 25a$

$a = -3$

Step 2: Therefore, the equation of the quadratic function must be $f(x) = -3(x-5)^2 + 8$.

Determine the equation of the quadratic function that has each of the following vertices and y-intercepts.

13. Vertex: $(-1, 7)$; y-intercept:$(0, 12)$

14. Vertex: $(6, -8)$; y-intercept: $(0, 64)$

15. Vertex: $(5, 2)$; y-intercept: $(0, 152)$

16. Vertex: $(-4, -11)$; y-int.: $f(x) = (0, -9)$

3.4   Determining the Rate of Change of Quadratic Functions

The average rate of change for a function is the change in $f(x)$ divided by the change in x. In linear equations, the rate of change (slope) is constant. In quadratic functions, the rate of change is not constant. For any point on a parabola, the rate of change is different. The average rate of change for $f(x)$ from one value of x, x_1, to another, x_2, can be calculated:

$$\frac{f(x_1) - f(x_2)}{x_1 - x_2}$$

By choosing a value of x_2 that is close to x_1 we can approximate the rate of change of f at x_1. Remember, you must keep the order of the terms in the numerator and the denominator consistent. A positive rate of change will have a graph that "goes up." A negative rate of change will have a graph that "goes down." A rate of change of 0 indicates a horizontal line. A very large rate of change indicates a nearly vertical line.

Example 7:   What is the average rate of change for $f(x) = -2(x+2)^2 + 2$ from $x = -2$ to $x = 2$?

Step 1:   Find $f(-2)$ and $f(2)$ by plugging in $x = -2$ and $x = 2$ into the equation.

$f(-2) = -2(-2+2)^2 + 2 = 2$

$f(2) = -2(2+2)^2 + 2 = -30$

Step 2:   Find the difference between $f(2)$ and $f(-2)$. Plug in the values for x.
$f(2) - f(-2) = -30 - 2 = -32$.

Step 3:   Find the difference between 2 and -2. $2 - (-2) = 4$

Step 4:   Divide the change in $f(x)$ by the change in x. $-32 \div 4 = -8$

The average rate of change of the function from $x = -2$ to $x = 2$ is -8.

Find average rate of change of each of the following quadratic functions from $x = 2$ to $x = 5$.

1. $f(x) = 7(x-1)^2 - 3$

2. $f(x) = x^2 - 6x + 19$

3. $f(x) = 9(x-8)^2 - 5$

4. $f(x) = 4x^2 - 7x - 2$

5. $f(x) = -2(x+9)^2 + 4$

6. $f(x) = x^2 + 4x - 21$

7. $f(x) = 5(x-7)^2 + 9$

8. $f(x) = 3x^2 + 36x + 107$

9. $f(x) = -6(x+1)^2 + 12$

10. $f(x) = x^2 - 3x - 18$

11. $f(x) = 10(x+2)^2 - 4$

12. $f(x) = -2x^2 - 8x - 21$

3.5 Using the $\sum$ Symbol

The Σ is used to write the sum of a series.

Series A $1 + 2 + 3 + \ldots + n + \ldots$

Series A starts with 1, +2, +3. Obviously the next item in the series would be 4.

Series B $1 + 4 + 7 + \ldots + (3n - 2) + \ldots$

Series B starts with 1, +4, +7 ...$(3n - 2)$. The expression in parenthesis shows how the pattern continues. The "n" in the expression is the item we're trying to find. We have 3 items: 1, 4, and 7. We are looking for the 4th item in the series so "n" = 4. $3n - 2$ where "n" = 4 is $3(4) - 2 = 10$. The next item in the series is 10.

Series B continues $1 + 4 + 7 + 10 + \ldots + (3n - 2) + \ldots$ to ∞ (infinity).

Series C $1 + 4 + 9 + \ldots + (n^2) + \ldots$

Replacing "n" with 4 in series C to find the 4th item in the series we have $4^2 = 16$. So now the series is $1 + 4 + 9 + 16 + \ldots + (n^2) + \ldots$

The sum of the first "n" terms of a series is called the **partial sum**, S_n. For example, in the series $3 + 6 + 9 + \ldots + 3n \ldots$

$$S_1 = 3 \qquad S_2 = 3 + 6 = 9 \qquad S_3 = 3 + 6 + 9 = 18$$

The Greek letter Σ, sigma, can be used to represent a sum. For example the third partial sum, S_3 of the series above can also be written as:

$$\sum_{k=1}^{3} 3k$$

So the series starts at $k = 1$ and ends at $k = 3$ and formula for the pattern is $3k$.

First $k = 1$ then 2, then 3. In expanded form we have: $3 + 6 + 9 = 18$. (We found the partial sum of the series.)

For each of the following write the Σ notation for each statement.

1. The sum of the series with the general term $k + 2$ from $k = 1$ to $k = 8$.

2. The sum of the series with the general term k^2 from $k = 1$ to $k = 5$.

3. The sum of the series with the general term $2k + 3$ from $k = 1$ to $k = 10$.

4. The sum of the series with the general term $2k - 6$ from $k = 3$ to $k = 8$.

5. The sum of the series with the general term $2m - 6$ from $m = 0$ to $m = 4$.

6. The sum of the series with the general term $2g^2$ from $g = 2$ to $g = 5$.

7. The sum of the series with the general term $g^2 + 2$ from $g = 3$ to $g = 7$.

8. The sum of the series with the general term $3h - 4$ from $h = 0$ to $h = 6$.

Example 8:   Write $\displaystyle\sum_{n=2}^{5} 3n$ in expanded form, then solve.

Step 1:   In this problem, $n = 2, 3, 4,$ and 5. Plug the values for n into the expression $3n$. We have $3 \cdot 2 + 3 \cdot 3 + 3 \cdot 4 + 3 \cdot 5$.

Step 2:   Simplify the expanded form and solve.
$3 \cdot 2 + 3 \cdot 3 + 3 \cdot 4 + 3 \cdot 5 = 6 + 9 + 12 + 15 = 42.$

Write each of the following in expanded form and find the sums.

1. $\displaystyle\sum_{n=3}^{5} 2n$

2. $\displaystyle\sum_{n=0}^{4} n^2$

3. $\displaystyle\sum_{n=0}^{4} 2n$

4. $\displaystyle\sum_{n=1}^{5} (2n - 1)$

5. $\displaystyle\sum_{n=0}^{3} (3n + 1)$

6. $\displaystyle\sum_{n=3}^{6} (3^n + 1)$

7. $\displaystyle\sum_{n=0}^{5} (2n + 1)$

8. $\displaystyle\sum_{n=1}^{4} (n - 6)$

9. $\displaystyle\sum_{n=4}^{6} (3n - 2)$

10. $\displaystyle\sum_{n=2}^{5} (6n - 4)$

3.6 Arithmetic Series

An **arithmetic sequence** is an ordered list of numbers where the difference between each successive number is constant. The sequence $\{1, 2, 3, 4, ...\}$ is an arithmetic sequence because the difference between one member and the next is 1. An **arithmetic series** is the sum of an arithmetic sequence of numbers.

To find any term of an arithmetic series, the formula $a_n = a_1 + d(n - 1)$ can be used, where a_1 is the first term, d is the common difference, and n is the number of the term to find.

To calculate the sum of the first n terms of an arithmetic series, use the formula $S_n = \dfrac{n(a_1 + a_n)}{2}$, where a_1 is the first term in the series and a_n is the nth term in the series. This formula will not be provided on your formula sheet.

Example 9:	Find the sum of the first 30 terms of the arithmetic series: $3 + 4 + 5 + 6 + 7 + \ldots$
Step 1:	First, find the pattern of the series. The pattern of this series is $n + 2$.
Step 2:	Next find all the variables for the summing equation, $S_n = \dfrac{n(a_1 + a_n)}{2}$. $a_1 = 3$ $n = 30$ (how many terms we will find the sum of) $a_n = a_{30} = 30 + 2 = 32$
Step 3:	Plug all the values into the equation. $S_{30} = \dfrac{30(3 + 32)}{2} = 525$. The sum of the arithmetic series is 525.

Example 10:	Calculate the sum of the first 10 natural numbers.
Method 1:	We can manually write out and compute the sum:. $1 + 2 + 3 + 4 + 5 + 6 + 7 + 8 + 9 + 10 = 55$
Method 2:	We can use the formula to find S_{10}, where $n = 10$, $a_1 = 1$, and $a_{10} = 10$. $S_{10} = \dfrac{n(a_1 + a_{10})}{2} = \dfrac{10(1 + 10)}{2} = 55$

Example 11:	What is the sum of the arithmetic series $\sum\limits_{n=1}^{6} [2 + 5(n - 1)]$?
Step 1:	Write out the numbers in the arithmetic series. The first number in the arithmetic series is $2 + 5(1 - 1) = 2 + 5(0) = 2 + 0 = 2$, while the second number in the arithmetic series is $2 + 5(2 - 1) = 2 + 5(1) = 2 + 5 = 7$. For this reason, the common difference of the arithmetic series must be $7 - 2$, or 5, and since there are 6 terms in the arithmetic series, it must be $2 + 7 + 12 + 17 + 22 + 27$.
Step 2:	Add the numbers in the arithmetic series together. $2 + 7 + 12 + 17 + 22 + 27 = 87$

Find the sum of the first 20 terms in the finite arithmetic series.

1. $5 + 6 + 7 + 8 + 9 + \ldots$

4. $4 + 6 + 8 + 10 + 12 + \ldots$

2. $-3 + -6 + -9 + -12 + -15 + \ldots$

5. $-1 + 0 + 1 + 2 + 3 + \ldots$

3. $0 + -1 + -2 + -3 + -4 + \ldots$

6. $-2 + -1 + 0 + 1 + 2 + \ldots$

Calculate the sum of the arithmetic series with each of the following descriptions.

7. $a_1 = 12$, $a_{16} = 117$, $n = 16$

10. $a_1 = 150$, $a_{25} = -354$, $n = 25$

8. $a_1 = -13$, $a_{22} = 92$; $n = 22$

11. $a_1 = -11$, $a_{31} = 259$, $n = 31$

9. $a_1 = 4$, $a_{19} = 202$, $n = 19$

12. $a_1 = 7$, $a_{51} = -293$, $n = 51$

Calculate the sum of each of the following groups of numbers.

13. the first 23 positive even integers

16. the first 31 multiples of 5

14. the first 18 multiples of 3

17. the first 100 positive even integers

15. the first 44 positive odd integers

18. the first 29 multiples of 4

Calculate the sum of each of the following arithmetic series.

19. $\sum_{n=1}^{5} [-3 + 4(n-1)]$

22. $\sum_{n=1}^{5} [-11 + 5(n-1)]$

20. $\sum_{n=1}^{6} [6 - 2(n-1)]$

23. $\sum_{n=1}^{6} [13 - 3(n-1)]$

21. $\sum_{n=1}^{4} [25 - 7(n-1)]$

24. $\sum_{n=1}^{4} [-8 + 2(n-1)]$

3.7 Exploring Sequences in an Arithmetic Series

If you list the partial sums of an arithmetic series repeatedly, you will get a sequence. This sequence can often be described using quadratic functions.

The rate of change of a quadratic function changes at a constant rate. For example, four points on the graph of the function $f(x) = x^2$ are $(1, 1), (2, 4), (3, 9)$, and $(4, 16)$.

Taking the differences between each $f(x)$ value and the previous $f(x)$ value, we get $4 - 1 = 3$, $9 - 4 = 5$, and $16 - 9 = 7$.

The first change in $f(x)$ is 3 units, the second change is 5 units, and the third change is 7 units. For this reason, for every change of 1 unit of x, the change in $f(x)$ is increasing by 2 units each time.

The sequences of partial sums of arithmetic series work in the same way, and are therefore examples of quadratic functions.

Example 12:   Calculate the first differences and the second differences of the sequence of partial sums of the arithmetic series $3 + 8 + 13 + 18 + 23 + 28 + 33$.

Step 1:   Determine the sequence of partial sums of the arithmetic series.

The partial sums of the arithmetic series are as follows:

$S_1 = 3$

$S_2 = 3 + 8 = 11$

$S_3 = 3 + 8 + 13 = 24$

$S_4 = 3 + 8 + 13 + 18 = 42$

$S_5 = 3 + 8 + 13 + 18 + 23 = 65$

$S_6 = 3 + 8 + 13 + 18 + 23 + 28 = 93$

$S_7 = 3 + 8 + 13 + 18 + 23 + 28 + 33 = 126$

Step 2:   Calculate the first differences of the sequence of partial sums of the arithmetic series.

The sequence of partial sums of the arithmetic series is 3, 11, 24, 42, 65, 93, 126. The first differences of the sequence can be calculated by subtracting each partial sum from the partial sum that follows it.
$11 - 3 = 8$
$24 - 11 = 13$
$42 - 24 = 18$
$65 - 42 = 23$
$93 - 65 = 28$
$126 - 93 = 33$

Step 3: Calculate the second differences of the sequence of partial sums of the arithmetic series.

The sequence of first differences of the partial sums of the arithmetic series is 8, 13, 18, 23, 28, 33. The second differences of the sequence can be calculated by subtracting each first difference from the first difference that follows it.

$$13 - 8 = 5 \qquad 28 - 23 = 5$$
$$18 - 13 = 5 \qquad 33 - 28 = 5$$
$$23 - 18 = 5$$

The second differences are all 5. When the second differences are all the same, it tells us that the polynomial for this sequence of the partial sums of an arithmetic series of values is a quadratic function.

Calculate the first differences and the second differences of the sequence of partial sums of each of the following arithmetic series.

1. $6 + 9 + 12 + 15 + 18$
2. $5 + 11 + 17 + 23 + 29$
3. $4 + 8 + 12 + 16 + 20$

4. $-8 + 0 + 8 + 16 + 24$
5. $9 + 7 + 5 + 3 + 1$
6. $54 + 42 + 30 + 18 + 6$

7. $7 + 12 + 17 + 22 + 27$
8. $13 + 10 + 7 + 4 + 1$
9. $1 + 10 + 19 + 28 + 37$

Example 13: The sequence of first differences of the partial sums of a series is 2, 4, 8, 16, 32. Determine if the series is arithmetic.

Step 1: Calculate the second differences of the sequence of partial sums of the series.

The second differences of the sequence can be calculated by subtracting each first difference from the first difference that follows it. Therefore, the second differences of the sequence are as follows:

$$4 - 2 = 2 \qquad 16 - 8 = 8$$
$$8 - 4 = 4 \qquad 32 - 16 = 16$$

Step 2: Determine if the second differences are all the same. If so, the series is arithmetic. If not, the series is not arithmetic.

The second differences are not all the same. Therefore, the series is not arithmetic.

Determine if the series with each of the following sequences of first differences of partial sums is arithmetic.

10. $11, 19, 27, 35, 43$
11. $3, 9, 27, 81, 243$

12. $1, 2, 3, 5, 8$
13. $5, 12, 19, 26, 33$

14. $2, 10, 50, 250, 1250$
15. $9, 14, 19, 24, 29$

Chapter 3 Review

Convert each of the following quadratic functions from vertex form to standard form.

1. $f(x) = 16(x - 1)^2 + 2$

2. $f(x) = \frac{4}{5}(x + 5)^2 - 9$

Convert each of the following quadratic functions from standard form to vertex form.

3. $f(x) = 6x^2 - 60x + 157$

4. $f(x) = \frac{1}{2}x^2 + 9x + \frac{61}{2}$

5. $f(x) = -3x^2 + 48x - 222$

6. $f(x) = 4x^2 - 24x + 87$

Graph each of the following quadratic functions as transformations of $f(x) = x^2$.

7. $f(x) = -5(x + 3)^2 - 7$

8. $f(x) = 8(x - 10)^2 - 1$

9. $f(x) = \frac{1}{4}(x + 6)^2 + 9$

10. $f(x) = 6x^2 - 24x + 1$

11. $f(x) = 2x^2 + 32x + 123$

12. $f(x) = -\frac{1}{2}x^2 + 7x - \frac{75}{2}$

For each of the following quadratic functions, list the function's domain, range, zeros, and extrema, and for the graph of the function list the axis of symmetry, vertex, intercepts, and intervals of increase and decrease.

13. $f(x) = 4(x - 28)^2 + 19$

14. $f(x) = \frac{1}{8}(x + 11)^2 + 9$

15. $f(x) = 14(x - 3)^2 + 1$

16. $f(x) = -8(x + 5)^2 + 28$

17. $f(x) = \frac{9}{2}(x - 10)^2 - 12$

18. $f(x) = 15(x + 7)^2 - 6$

Find the average rate of change of each of the following quadratic functions from $x = 1$ to $x = 5$.

19. $f(x) = 5(x - 12)^2 - 2$

20. $f(x) = -4(x + 9)^2 + 6$

21. $f(x) = 3x^2 + 12x - 9$

22. $f(x) = \frac{1}{5}x^2 - 4x + 13$

Calculate the sum of each of the following arithmetic series.

23. $\sum_{n=1}^{8} [10 - 3(n - 1)]$

24. $\sum_{n=1}^{7} [14 + 4(n - 1)]$

Find the sum of the finite series when $n = 10$.

25. $0 + 1 + 2 + 3 + 4 + \ldots$

26. $3 + 6 + 9 + 12 + 15 + \ldots$

27. $0 + -1 + -2 + -3 + -4 + \ldots$

28. $2 + 5 + 8 + 11 + 14 + \ldots$

Calculate the sum of the arithmetic series with each of the following descriptions. Use the formula $S_n = \dfrac{n(a_1 + a_n)}{2}$.

29. $a_1 = 5,\ a_{20} = 81;\ n = 20$

30. $a_1 = \frac{3}{2},\ a_{15} = \frac{45}{2};\ n = 15$

Calculate the sum of each of the following groups of numbers.

31. the first 75 positive odd integers

32. the first 59 multiples of 6

Calculate the first differences and the second differences of the sequence of partial sums of each of the following arithmetic series.

33. $29 + 26 + 23 + 20 + 17$

34. $2 + 11 + 20 + 29 + 38$

35. $-52 + 12 + 72 + 132 + 192$

36. $21 + 17 + 13 + 9 + 5$

Determine if the series with each of the following sequences of first differences of partial sums is arithmetic.

37. $4, 16, 64, 256, 1024$

38. $13, 20, 27, 34, 41$

Chapter 3 Test

1. Which of the following arithmetic series has a sum of 105?

   A. $\sum_{n=1}^{7} [5 + 2(n-1)]$

   B. $\sum_{n=1}^{7} [7 + 2(n-1)]$

   C. $\sum_{n=1}^{7} [9 + 2(n-1)]$

   D. $\sum_{n=1}^{7} [11 + 2(n-1)]$

2. Which of the following quadratic functions has a maximum?

   A. $f(x) = -(x+8)^2 + 9$

   B. $f(x) = \frac{3}{7}(x-7)^2 + 3$

   C. $f(x) = (x+8)^2 + 9$

   D. $f(x) = \frac{7}{3}(x+7)^2 - 3$

3. Which transformation can be applied to the graph of the quadratic function $f(x) = x^2$ to produce the graph of the function $f(x) = (x+9)^2$?

   A. A horizontal translation of 9 units left.
   B. A horizontal translation of 9 units right.
   C. A vertical translation of 9 units down.
   D. A vertical translation of 9 units up.

4. Today Mickey began collecting baseball cards by purchasing 1 pack of 20 cards. For each of the next 6 days, he plans on purchasing 3 more packs than he purchased the day before. How many baseball cards will Mickey have after the next 6 days?

   A. 700
   B. 1400
   C. 2100
   D. 2800

5. Which of the following quadratic equations can be solved with the graph shown?

   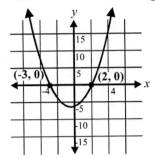

   A. $x^2 - x - 6 = 0$
   B. $x^2 - x + 6 = 0$
   C. $x^2 + x - 6 = 0$
   D. $x^2 + x + 6 = 0$

6. The table below shows the partial sums of a series, with n being the numbers of terms and S_n being the partial sums. Is the series arithmetic?

n	S_n
1	4
2	16
3	36
4	64

   A. Yes, because the second differences of the partial sums are each 4.
   B. Yes, because the second differences of the partial sums are each 6.
   C. Yes, because the second differences of the partial sums are each 8.
   D. No, because the second differences of the partial sums are not constant.

7. What is $f(x) = 8x^2 - 48x + 58$ in vertex form?

   A. $f(x) = 8(x-3)^2 - 14$
   B. $f(x) = 8(x-3)^2 + 14$
   C. $f(x) = 8(x+3)^2 - 14$
   D. $f(x) = 8(x+3)^2 + 14$

8. What is the average rate of change of the quadratic function $f(x) = 5(x + 4)^2 - 16$ from $x = 1$ to $x = 3$?

A. 30

B. 40

C. 50

D. 60

9. What is the y-intercept of the quadratic function $f(x) = \frac{5}{9}(x - 7)^2 + 4$?

A. $\left(0, \dfrac{245}{9}\right)$

B. $\left(0, \dfrac{281}{9}\right)$

C. $(0, 245)$

D. $(0, 281)$

10. Which transformation can be applied to the graph of the quadratic function $f(x) = x^2$ to produce the graph of the function $f(x) = 12x^2$?

A. A horizontal compression by a factor of $\frac{1}{12}$.

B. A horizontal stretch by a factor of 12.

C. A vertical compression by a factor of $\frac{1}{12}$.

D. A vertical stretch by a factor of 12.

11. The partial sums of an arithmetic series are plotted on a coordinate grid, with the x-coordinate of each point being the number of terms and the y-coordinate of each point being the partial sum. If the points are connected, which of the following is formed?

A. part of a circle

B. part of an ellipse

C. part of a hyperbola

D. part of a parabola

12. The graph of the quadratic function $f(x) = x^2 + 4x + 7$ is shown. Based on this information, how many solutions does the quadratic equation $x^2 + 4x = -7$ have?

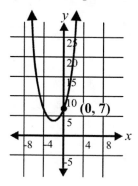

(0, 7)

A. 0

B. 1

C. 2

D. It cannot be determined.

13. The graph of the function $f(x) = x^2$ has been horizontally and vertically translated so that its new vertex is the point $(-5, -11)$. What is the equation of the function with the resulting graph in standard form?

A. $f(x) = x^2 - 10x + 14$

B. $f(x) = x^2 - 10x + 36$

C. $f(x) = x^2 + 10x + 14$

D. $f(x) = x^2 + 10x + 36$

Chapter 4
Inverse Functions

This chapter covers the following Georgia Performance Standards:

MM2A	Algebra	MM2A5a
		MM2A5b
		MM2A5c
		MM2A5d

4.1   Characteristics of Functions and Their Inverses

A function's domain is its inverse's range, and a function's range is its inverse's domain.

The domain and the range of a function are switched to produce the domain and the range of the function's inverse.

	Function	Function's Inverse
x	original domain	original range
y	original range	original domain

Example 1:   What are the domain and the range of the inverse of the function $f = \{(-7, 3), (-4, 1), (-3, 5), (0, 7), (3, 8), (8, 10)\}$?

Step 1:   Find the inverse of the function.

The inverse of the function f can be found by switching the x- and y-coordinates of each of the points. Therefore, the inverse of the function f (written f^{-1}) is
$f^{-1} = \{(3, -7), (1, -4), (5, -3), (7, 0), (8, 3), (10, 8)\}$.

Step 2:   Find the domain of f^{-1}.

The domain of f^{-1} is all possible values of x. Therefore, the domain of f^{-1} is $\{3, 1, 5, 7, 8, 10\}$.

Step 3:   Find the range of f^{-1}.

The range of f^{-1} is all possible values of y. Therefore, the range of f^{-1} is $\{-7, -4, -3, 0, 3, 8\}$.

Find the domain and the range of the inverse of each of the following functions.

1. $f = \{(-6, 7), (-1, -8), (1, -3), (5, 5), (6, -1), (10, 2)\}$

2. $g = \{(-8, -9), (0, 11), (2, -5), (3, 2), (7, 9), (12, -7)\}$

3. $f = \{(-10, 1), (-9, -4), (4, 0), (5, -5), (6, 0), (10, 1)\}$

4. $g = \{(-2, -3), (0, 14), (3, -2), (4, 12), (8, -1), (9, -2)\}$

5. $f = \{(-12, 0), (-6, -6), (0, -12), (3, 5), (7, 1), (11, -1)\}$

6. $g = \{(-1, 20), (1, 1), (2, -11), (5, 1), (6, 13), (19, -2)\}$

Example 2:   Determine whether or not the inverse of the function $f = \{(-10, 7), (-2, 8), (2, -4), (5, -1), (9, 7), (11, -6)\}$ is also a function.

   Step 1:   Find the inverse of the function.

   Using the information given in example 1, the inverse of the function f is $f^{-1} = \{(-6, 11), (-4, 2), (-1, 5), (7, -10), (7, 9), (8, -2)\}$.

   Step 2:   For f^{-1}, check to see if each value of x produces only one value of y. If so, f^{-1} is a function. If not, f^{-1} is not a function.

   Two of the points are $(7, -10)$ and $(7, 9)$, so the value of 7 for x produces two values of y. Therefore, f^{-1} is not a function.

Determine whether or not the inverse of each of the following functions is also a function.

7. $f = \{(-15, 0), (-3, -3), (1, 9), (4, -2), (5, -17), (6, 6)\}$

8. $g = \{(-6, 4), (-2, 1), (0, 5), (2, -11), (3, 4), (9, -10)\}$

9. $f = \{(-7, 0), (-1, 8), (6, 16), (7, 7), (9, -9), (18, 1)\}$

10. $g = \{(-22, 2), (-4, 10), (0, 0), (4, -10), (5, 6), (22, -2)\}$

11. $f = \{(-10, 8), (-5, -1), (2, 0), (3, -1), (7, -4), (17, 18)\}$

12. $g = \{(-11, -3), (-8, 22), (8, -22), (11, -3), (12, 5), (14, -6)\}$

4.2   Determining Inverses of Linear Functions

To determine the inverse of the linear function $f(x) = mx + b$, think of the function as $y = mx + b$, and then switch x and y so that the equation becomes $x = my + b$. Finally, solve for y.

The inverse of a linear function is also a function.

Example 3:   Find the inverse of the linear function $f(x) = \frac{1}{4}x - 9$.

   Step 1:   Rewrite the function $f(x) = mx + b$ in the form $y = mx + b$.

   The function $f(x) = \frac{1}{4}x - 9$ is the same as $y = \frac{1}{4}x - 9$.

   Step 2:   Now switch the x and y variables.

   When x and y are switched, the function $y = \frac{1}{4}x - 9$ becomes $x = \frac{1}{4}y - 9$.

   Step 3:   Solve $x = \frac{1}{4}y - 9$ for y.

   First add 9 to both sides of the equation:

   $x = \frac{1}{4}y - 9$

   $x + 9 = \frac{1}{4}y - 9 + 9$

   $x + 9 = \frac{1}{4}y$

   Next, multiply both sides of the equation by 4:

   $(4)(x + 9) = (4)\left(\frac{1}{4}y\right)$

   $(4)(x) + (4)(9) = (4)\left(\frac{1}{4}y\right)$

   $4x + 36 = y$

   Therefore, the inverse of the linear function $f(x) = \frac{1}{4}x - 9$ is $y = 4x + 36$, or $f^{-1}(x) = 4x + 36$.

Find the inverse of each of the following linear functions.

1. $f(x) = 2x + 7$

2. $g(x) = \frac{1}{10}x - 6$

3. $f(x) = -3x + 8$

4. $g(x) = -8x - 1$

5. $f(x) = \frac{4}{5}x + \frac{1}{5}$

6. $g(x) = 7x - 13$

7. $f(x) = 5x + 11$

8. $g(x) = -\frac{3}{8}x - \frac{1}{16}$

9. $f(x) = -12x - 5$

10. $f(x) = 4x + 3$

The inverse of the inverse of a function is the function itself. For this reason, in order to solve the following problems, the inverse of $f^{-1}(x)$ should be found, which will be the original function.

Example 4:   The inverse of the linear function $f(x)$ is $f^{-1}(x) = \frac{1}{9}x - \frac{7}{9}$. What is $f(x)$?

Step 1:   Rewrite the function $f^{-1}(x) = mx + b$ in the form $y = mx + b$.

The function $f^{-1}(x) = \frac{1}{9}x - \frac{7}{9}$ is the same as $y = \frac{1}{9}x - \frac{7}{9}$.

Step 2:   Now switch the x and y variables.

When x and y are switched, the function $y = \frac{1}{9}x - \frac{7}{9}$ becomes $x = \frac{1}{9}y - \frac{7}{9}$.

Step 3:   Solve $x = \frac{1}{9}y - \frac{7}{9}$ for y.

First add $\frac{7}{9}$ to both sides of the equation:

$x = \frac{1}{9}y - \frac{7}{9}$

$x + \frac{7}{9} = \frac{1}{9}y - \frac{7}{9} + \frac{7}{9}$

$x + \frac{7}{9} = \frac{1}{9}y$

Next, multiply both sides of the equation by 9:

$(9)\left(x + \frac{7}{9}\right) = (9)\left(\frac{1}{9}y\right)$

$(9)(x) + (9)\left(\frac{7}{9}\right) = (9)\left(\frac{1}{9}y\right)$

$9x + 7 = y$

Therefore, the linear function with an inverse of $f^{-1}(x) = \frac{1}{9}x - \frac{7}{9}$ is $y = 9x + 7$, or $f(x) = 9x + 7$.

For each of the following inverses, determine the linear function.

1. $g^{-1}(x) = -16x - 7$

2. $f^{-1}(x) = \frac{3}{4}x - \frac{9}{4}$

3. $g^{-1}(x) = -\frac{9}{10}x + 12$

4. $f^{-1}(x) = 11x - 2$

5. $g^{-1}(x) = \frac{2}{5}x + 10$

6. $f^{-1}(x) = -\frac{1}{6}x - 3$

7. $g^{-1}(x) = \frac{5}{2}x - 18$

8. $f^{-1}(x) = -4x + 21$

9. $f^{-1}(x) = \frac{1}{5}x + \frac{3}{5}$

10. $f^{-1}(x) = 2x - 6$

4.3   Determining Inverses of Quadratic Functions

The inverse of the quadratic function $f(x) = a(x - h)^2 + k$ is like finding the inverse of a linear function. However, the inverse of a quadratic function is not a function.

Example 5:   Determine the inverse of the quadratic function $f(x) = 2x^2 - 8x + 60$.

Step 1:   Convert the quadratic function into the vertex form $f(x) = a(x - h)^2 + k$. (This is covered is the beginning of chapter 3.)

First subtract 60 from both sides of the equation:

$$f(x) = 2x^2 - 8x + 60 \longrightarrow f(x) - 60 = 2x^2 - 8x$$

Next, factor 2 from the right side of the equation:

$$f(x) - 60 = 2(x^2 - 4x)$$

Next, complete the square inside the parentheses on the right side of the equation:

$$f(x) - 60 + 8 = 2(x^2 - 4x + 4) \longrightarrow f(x) - 52 = 2(x - 2)^2$$

Finally, add 52 to both sides of the equation:

$$f(x) - 52 + 52 = 2(x - 2)^2 + 52 \longrightarrow f(x) = 2(x - 2)^2 + 52$$

Step 2:   Rewrite the function $f(x) = a(x - h)^2 + k$ in the form of $y = a(x - h)^2 + k$.

The function $f(x) = 2(x - 2)^2 + 52$ is the same as $y = 2(x - 2)^2 + 52$.

Step 3:   Now switch the x and y variables.

When x and y are switched, the function $y = 2(x - 2)^2 + 52$ becomes $x = 2(y - 2)^2 + 52$.

Step 4:   Solve $x = 2(y - 2)^2 + 52$ for y.

First subtract 52 from both sides of the equation:

$$x = 2(y - 2)^2 + 52 \longrightarrow x - 52 = 2(y - 2)^2$$

Next, divide both sides of the equation by 2:

$$\frac{(x - 52)}{2} = \frac{2(y - 2)^2}{2} \longrightarrow \tfrac{1}{2}x - 26 = (y - 2)^2$$

Next, take the square root of both sides of the equation:

$$\pm\sqrt{\tfrac{1}{2}x - 26} = \sqrt{(y - 2)^2} \longrightarrow \pm\sqrt{\tfrac{1}{2}x - 26} = y - 2$$

Finally, add 2 to both sides of the equation:

$$\pm\sqrt{\tfrac{1}{2}x - 26} + 2 = y - 2 + 2 \longrightarrow y = 2 \pm \sqrt{\tfrac{1}{2}x - 26}$$

Therefore, the inverse of the quadratic function $f(x) = 2x^2 - 8x + 60$ is $y = 2 \pm \sqrt{\tfrac{1}{2}x - 26}$.

Determine the inverse of each of the following quadratic functions.

1. $f(x) = 5(x - 7)^2 + 3$

2. $g(x) = 3x^2 + 24x + 36$

3. $f(x) = -2(x + 8)^2 - 1$

4. $g(x) = 7x^2 - 14x - 7$

5. $f(x) = 6(x - 10)^2 + 11$

6. $g(x) = 9x^2 + 36x + 28$

7. $f(x) = -4(x + 3)^2 - 17$

8. $g(x) = 8x^2 - 48x + 47$

9. $f(x) = 12(x + 1)^2 + 5$

Example 6:   The inverse of the quadratic function $f(x)$ is $y = -4 \pm \sqrt{6x + 72}$. What is $f(x)$?

The inverse of the inverse of a function is the function itself. For this reason, in order to solve the problem, the inverse of $y = -4 \pm \sqrt{6x + 72}$ should be found.

Step 1:   Switch the x and y variables.

When x and y are switched, the relation $y = -4 \pm \sqrt{6x + 72}$ becomes $x = -4 \pm \sqrt{6y + 72}$.

Step 2:   Solve $x = -4 \pm \sqrt{6y + 72}$ for y.

First, add 4 to both sides of the equation:

$$x = -4 \pm \sqrt{6y + 72} \longrightarrow x + 4 = \pm\sqrt{6y + 72}$$

Next, square both sides of the equation:

$$(x + 4)^2 = \left(\pm\sqrt{6y + 72}\right)^2 \longrightarrow (x + 4)^2 = 6y + 72$$

Next, divide both sides of the equation by 6:

$$\frac{(x + 4)^2}{6} = \frac{6y + 72}{6} \longrightarrow \left(\tfrac{1}{6}\right)(x + 4)^2 = y + 12$$

Finally, subtract 12 from both sides of the equation:

$$\left(\tfrac{1}{6}\right)(x + 4)^2 - 12 = y + 12 - 12 \longrightarrow y = \tfrac{1}{6}(x + 4)^2 - 12$$

Therefore, the quadratic function with an inverse of $f^{-1}(x) = -4 \pm \sqrt{6x + 72}$ is $y = \tfrac{1}{6}(x + 4)^2 - 12$, or $f(x) = \tfrac{1}{6}(x + 4)^2 - 12$.

For each of the following inverses, determine the quadratic function $f(x)$.

10. $y = 15 \pm \sqrt{-5x - 55}$

11. $y = -11 \pm \sqrt{7x - 30}$

12. $y = 2 \pm \sqrt{9x + 85}$

13. $y = -6 \pm \sqrt{-8x - 72}$

14. $y = 8 \pm \sqrt{-4x + 18}$

15. $y = -17 \pm \sqrt{2x - 21}$

16. $y = 5 \pm \sqrt{4x + 102}$

17. $y = -19 \pm \sqrt{6x - 48}$

18. $y = 9 \pm \sqrt{20x + 1}$

4.4   Determining Inverses of Power Functions

The inverse of the power function $f(x) = kx^p$ is found similarly to the inverse of a linear function. The inverse of a power function may or may not be a function. If p is a positive odd integer, the inverse of the power function $f(x) = kx^p$ is a function, but if p is a positive even integer, the inverse is not a function.

Example 7:   Determine the inverse of the power function $f(x) = \frac{1}{8}x^5$.

Step 1:   Rewrite the function $f(x) = kx^p$ in the form $y = kx^p$.

The function $f(x) = \frac{1}{8}x^5$ is the same as $y = \frac{1}{8}x^5$.

Step 2:   Now switch the x and y variables.

When x and y are switched, the function $y = \frac{1}{8}x^5$ becomes $x = \frac{1}{8}y^5$.

Step 3:   Solve $x = \frac{1}{8}y^5$ for y.

First, multiply both sides of the equation by 8.

$$x = \frac{1}{8}y^5$$

$$(8)(x) = (8)\left(\frac{1}{8}y^5\right)$$

$$8x = y^5$$

Next, take the fifth root of each side of the equation.

$$\sqrt[5]{8x} = \sqrt[5]{y^5}$$

$$y = \sqrt[5]{8x}$$

Therefore, the inverse of the power function $f(x) = \frac{1}{8}x^5$ is $y = \sqrt[5]{8x}$, or $f^{-1}(x) = \sqrt[5]{8x}$.

Determine the inverse of each of the following power functions.

1. $f(x) = 2x^6$

2. $g(x) = 9x^5$

3. $f(x) = \frac{5}{6}x^4$

4. $g(x) = 82x^9$

5. $f(x) = \frac{1}{14}x^3$

6. $g(x) = -5x^7$

7. $f(x) = 4x^{10}$

8. $g(x) = 23x^8$

9. $f(x) = -3x^{13}$

Example 8:   The inverse of the power function $f(x)$ is $f^{-1}(x) = \pm\sqrt[6]{\frac{1}{35}x}$. What is $f(x)$?

The inverse of the inverse of a function is the function itself. For this reason, in order to solve the problem, the inverse of $y = \pm\sqrt[6]{\frac{1}{35}x}$ should be found.

Step 1:   Switch the x and y variables.

When x and y are switched, the relation $y = \pm\sqrt[6]{\frac{1}{35}x}$ becomes $x = \pm\sqrt[6]{\frac{1}{35}y}$.

Step 2:   Solve $x = \pm\sqrt[6]{\frac{1}{35}y}$ for y.

First, raise both sides of the equation to the sixth power.

$$x = \pm\sqrt[6]{\frac{1}{35}y}$$

$$x^6 = \left(\pm\sqrt[6]{\frac{1}{35}y}\right)^6$$

$$x^6 = \frac{1}{35}y$$

Next, multiply both sides of the equation by 35.

$$(35)(x^6) = (35)\left(\frac{1}{35}y\right)$$

$$y = 35x^6$$

Therefore, the power function with an inverse of $y = \pm\sqrt[6]{\frac{1}{35}x}$ is $y = 35x^6$, or $f(x) = 35x^6$.

For each of the following inverses, determine the power function $f(x)$.

1. $f^{-1}(x) = \sqrt[17]{\frac{1}{18}x}$

2. $y = \pm\sqrt[4]{\frac{8}{9}x}$

3. $f^{-1}(x) = \sqrt[9]{-\frac{1}{64}x}$

4. $y = \pm\sqrt[22]{\frac{11}{10}x}$

5. $f^{-1}(x) = \sqrt[11]{\frac{1}{30}x}$

6. $y = \pm\sqrt[8]{50x}$

7. $f^{-1}(x) = \sqrt[7]{-\frac{4}{3}x}$

8. $y = \pm\sqrt[12]{\frac{1}{45}x}$

9. $f^{-1}(x) = \sqrt[19]{\frac{5}{12}x}$

4.5   Determining Inverses of Functions of the Form $f(x) = \dfrac{a}{x}$

Finding the inverse of a function in the form $f(x) = \dfrac{a}{x}$ is similar to finding the inverse of a linear function. This is a special case where the inverse of a function in the form $f(x) = \dfrac{a}{x}$ is the function itself, so the inverse of a function in this form is also a function.

Example 9:   Determine the inverse of the function $f(x) = \dfrac{22}{x}$.

Step 1:   Rewrite the function $f(x) = \dfrac{a}{x}$ in the form $y = \dfrac{a}{x}$.

The function $f(x) = \dfrac{22}{x}$ is the same as $y = \dfrac{22}{x}$.

Step 2:   Now switch the x and y variables.

When x and y are switched, the function $y = \dfrac{22}{x}$ becomes $x = \dfrac{22}{y}$.

Step 3:   Solve for y.

First think of the equation as $\dfrac{x}{1} = \dfrac{22}{y}$ and cross-multiply.

$(x)(y) = (22)(1)$

$xy = 22$

Next, divide both sides of the equation by x.

$\dfrac{xy}{x} = \dfrac{22}{x}$

$y = \dfrac{22}{x}$

Therefore, the inverse of the function $f(x) = \dfrac{22}{x}$ is $y = \dfrac{22}{x}$, or $f^{-1}(x) = \dfrac{22}{x}$.
In other words, the inverse of the function is the function itself.

Determine the inverse of each of the following functions.

1. $f(x) = \dfrac{7}{x}$

2. $g(x) = \dfrac{15}{x}$

3. $f(x) = -\dfrac{6}{x}$

4. $g(x) = \dfrac{31}{x}$

5. $f(x) = \dfrac{2}{x}$

6. $g(x) = \dfrac{26}{x}$

7. $f(x) = -\dfrac{9}{x}$

8. $g(x) = \dfrac{72}{x}$

9. $f(x) = \dfrac{11}{x}$

Example 10:   The inverse of the function $f(x)$ is $f^{-1}(x) = \dfrac{38}{x}$. What is $f(x)$?

The inverse of the inverse of a function is the function itself. For this reason, in order to solve the problem, the inverse of $f^{-1}(x)$ should be found.

Step 1:   Rewrite the function $f^{-1}(x) = \dfrac{a}{x}$ in the form $y = \dfrac{a}{x}$.

The function $f^{-1}(x) = \dfrac{38}{x}$ is the same as $y = \dfrac{38}{x}$.

Step 2:   Now switch the x and y variables.

When x and y are switched, the function $y = \dfrac{38}{x}$ becomes $x = \dfrac{38}{y}$.

Step 3:   Solve for y.

First think of the equation as $\dfrac{x}{1} = \dfrac{38}{y}$ and cross-multiply.

$(x)(y) = (38)(1)$

$xy = 38$

Next, divide both sides of the equation by x.

$\dfrac{xy}{x} = \dfrac{38}{x}$

$y = \dfrac{38}{x}$

Therefore, the function with an inverse of $f^{-1}(x) = \dfrac{38}{y}$ is $y = \dfrac{38}{y}$, or $f(x) = \dfrac{38}{y}$. In other words, the inverse of the function is the function itself.

For each of the following inverses, determine the function $f(x)$.

1. $f^{-1}(x) = \dfrac{10}{x}$

2. $f^{-1}(x) = \dfrac{29}{x}$

3. $f^{-1}(x) = -\dfrac{35}{x}$

4. $f^{-1}(x) = \dfrac{4}{x}$

5. $f^{-1}(x) = \dfrac{8}{x}$

6. $f^{-1}(x) = -\dfrac{42}{x}$

4.6   Exploring Graphs of Functions and Their Inverses

The graph of the inverse of a function is a reflection of the graph of the function over the line $y = x$. Using the vertical line test, you can determine whether or not the function's inverse is a function.

Example 11:   Sketch the graph of the inverse of the exponential function $f(x) = 2^x$.

Step 1:   Create a table of values for $f(x)$.

x	-4	-3	-2	-1	0	1	2	3	4
$f(x) = 2^x$	$\frac{1}{16}$	$\frac{1}{8}$	$\frac{1}{4}$	$\frac{1}{2}$	1	2	4	8	16

Step 2:   Switch the x- and y-coordinates of the points.

x	$\frac{1}{16}$	$\frac{1}{8}$	$\frac{1}{4}$	$\frac{1}{2}$	1	2	4	8	16
$f^{-1}(x)$	-4	-3	-2	-1	0	1	2	3	4

Step 3:   Plot the new points, and draw a curve through the newly-plotted points.

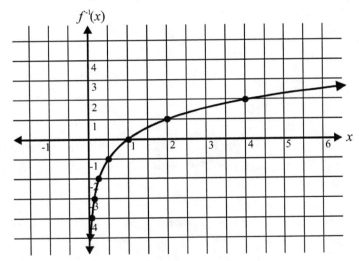

Since the maximum number of points at which a vertical line could intersect the graph of $f^{-1}(x)$ is 1, the inverse of the exponential function $f(x) = 2^x$ is also a function.

Sketch a graph of the inverse of each of the following exponential functions.

1. $f(x) = 3^x$

2. $f(x) = \left(\frac{1}{2}\right)^x$

3. $f(x) = 5^x$

4. $f(x) = 4^x$

5. $f(x) = (5)(2^x)$

6. $f(x) = \left(\frac{1}{4}\right)^x$

7. $f(x) = \left(\frac{1}{3}\right)^x$

8. $f(x) = (4)(3^x)$

9. $f(x) = (2)(4^x)$

Example 12:   Sketch the graph of the inverse of the absolute value function $f(x) = |x|$.

Step 1:   Create a table of values for $f(x)$.

x	-4	-3	-2	-1	0	1	2	3	4
$f(x)$	4	3	2	1	0	1	2	3	4

Step 2:   Switch the x- and y-coordinates of the points.

x	4	3	2	1	0	1	2	3	4
$f^{-1}(x)$	-4	-3	-2	-1	0	1	2	3	4

Step 3:   Plot the new points, and draw a curve through the newly-plotted points.

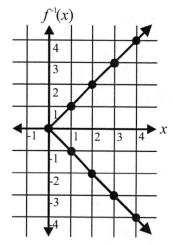

Since the maximum number of points at which a vertical line could intersect the graph of $f^{-1}(x)$ is 2, the inverse of the absolute value function $f(x) = |x|$ is not a function.

Sketch a graph of the inverse of each of the following absolute value functions.

1. $f(x) = |x + 1|$

2. $f(x) = |3x|$

3. $f(x) = |x - 2|$

4. $f(x) = |2x|$

5. $f(x) = |x + 3|$

6. $f(x) = |2(x - 1)|$

7. $f(x) = |x - 5|$

8. $f(x) = |6(x + 2)|$

9. $f(x) = |4x|$

10. Sketch the graph of a function in the form $f(x) = \dfrac{a}{x}$, and also draw the graph of the line $y = x$ on the same coordinate grid. Why does this graph show that the inverse of a function in the form $f(x) = \dfrac{a}{x}$ is the function itself?

11. Give an example of a function not in the form $f(x) = \dfrac{a}{x}$ whose inverse is the function itself.

4.7   Using Composition to Verify That Functions are Inverses of Each Other

The composition of the function $f(x)$ with the function $g(x)$ is written $(f \circ g)(x)$, or $f(g(x))$, and represents inputting $g(x)$ into the function $f(x)$. Likewise $(g \circ f)(x)$, or $g(f(x))$, represents inputting $f(x)$ into the function $g(x)$. $(f \circ g)$ is read "f composed with g" or "f of g."

When $f(x)$ and $g(x)$ are inverses of each other, $(f \circ g)(x) = x$ and $(g \circ f)(x) = x$.

Example 13:   Determine the inverse of the function $f(x) = \dfrac{7}{x^3}$ and verify that $f(x)$ and $f^{-1}(x)$ are inverses of each other using composition.

Step 1:   Rewrite the function $f(x) = \dfrac{k}{x^p}$ in the form $y = \dfrac{k}{x^p}$.

The function $f(x) = \dfrac{7}{x^3}$ is the same as $y = \dfrac{7}{x^3}$.

Step 2:   Now switch the x and y variables.

When x and y are switched, the function $y = \dfrac{7}{x^3}$ becomes $x = \dfrac{7}{y^3}$.

Step 3:   Solve $x = \dfrac{7}{y^3}$ for y.

First think of the equation as $\dfrac{x}{1} = \dfrac{7}{y^3}$ and cross-multiply.

$$(x)(y^3) = (7)(1) \longrightarrow xy^3 = 7$$

Next, divide both sides of the equation by x.

$$\frac{xy^3}{x} = \frac{7}{x} \longrightarrow y^3 = \frac{7}{x}$$

Next, take the cubed root of each side of the equation.

$$\sqrt[3]{y^3} = \sqrt[3]{\frac{7}{x}} \longrightarrow y = \sqrt[3]{\frac{7}{x}}$$

Therefore, the inverse of the function $f(x) = \dfrac{7}{x^3}$ is $y = \sqrt[3]{\dfrac{7}{x}}$, or $f^{-1}(x) = \sqrt[3]{\dfrac{7}{x}}$.

Step 4:   To verify the two functions really are inverses of each, use composition.

Let $f(x) = \dfrac{7}{x^3}$ and $g(x) = f^{-1}(x) = \sqrt[3]{\dfrac{7}{x}}$.

Solve $(f \circ g)(x) = f(g(x))$ by substituting $g(x)$ into $f(x)$ for x.

$$f(g(x)) = \frac{7}{\left(\sqrt[3]{\dfrac{7}{x}}\right)^3} = \frac{7}{\dfrac{7}{x}} = x$$

Since the composition of the two functions equals x, the two functions are inverses of each other.

Use composition to determine whether or not each of the following pairs of functions are inverses of each other.

1. $f(x) = \dfrac{2}{x^5}; \ g(x) = \sqrt[5]{\dfrac{2}{x}}$

2. $f(x) = \dfrac{1}{2}x - 9; \ g(x) = 2x - 18$

3. $f(x) = \sqrt[11]{\dfrac{x}{25}}; \ g(x) = 25x^{11}$

4. $f(x) = \dfrac{18}{x}; \ g(x) = \dfrac{x}{18}$

5. $f(x) = \dfrac{x - 7}{12}; \ g(x) = -12x + 7$

6. $f(x) = \sqrt[7]{\dfrac{13}{x}}; \ g(x) = \dfrac{7}{x^{13}}$

7. $f(x) = \dfrac{4343}{x}; \ g(x) = \dfrac{4343}{x}$

8. $f(x) = \dfrac{1}{50}x^9; \ g(x) = \sqrt[9]{50x}$

Example 14: Using composition, give a counterexample to prove that the functions $f(x) = \dfrac{3}{10}x + \dfrac{1}{10}$ and $f^{-1}(x) = 10x - 3$ are not inverses of each other.

Step 1: Choose a value for x and find $f^{-1}(x)$.

If $x = 1$, $f^{-1}(x) = 10(1) - 3 = 10 - 3 = 7$.

Step 2: Plug the value of $f^{-1}(x)$ that was found in the previous step into $f(x)$ and see if $f(x)$ equals the value of x that was chosen. If not, then this is a counterexample that proves that $f(x)$ and $f^{-1}(x)$ are not inverses of each other.

Since $f^{-1}(x) = 7$, $f(7) = \dfrac{3}{10}(7) + \dfrac{1}{10} = \dfrac{21}{10} + \dfrac{1}{10} = \dfrac{22}{10} = \dfrac{11}{5}$. Since $\dfrac{11}{5} \neq 1$, this is a counterexample that proves that $f(x) = \dfrac{3}{10}x + \dfrac{1}{10}$ and $f^{-1}(x) = 10x - 3$ are not inverses of each other.

Using composition, give a counterexample to prove that each of the following pairs of functions are not inverses of each other.

9. $f(x) = -5x + 8; \ f^{-1}(x) = \dfrac{1}{5}x - \dfrac{8}{5}$

10. $f(x) = \dfrac{12}{x}; \ f^{-1}(x) = 12x$

11. $f(x) = 5x^3; \ f^{-1}(x) = \sqrt[5]{\dfrac{x}{3}}$

12. $f(x) = \dfrac{4}{x^7}; \ f^{-1}(x) = 4x^7$

13. $f(x) = \sqrt[3]{\dfrac{x}{4}}; \ f^{-1}(x) = 3x^4$

14. $f(x) = \dfrac{5}{6}x - 8; \ f^{-1}(x) = \dfrac{6}{5}x - \dfrac{48}{5}$

15. $f(x) = x - 9; \ f^{-1}(x) = \dfrac{9}{x}$

16. $f(x) = \dfrac{1}{x^3}; \ f^{-1}(x) = \dfrac{1}{x^3}$

Chapter 4 Review

Find the domain and the range of the inverse of each of the following functions.

1. $f = \{(-13, 8), (-2, -14), (3, -9), (4, 12), (7, -11), (19, 1)\}$

2. $g = \{(-14, -1), (5, 2), (6, -16), (8, 20), (9, 19), (13, -21)\}$

3. $f = \{(-3, 23), (-1, -3), (2, 9), (10, -2), (12, 15), (14, 0)\}$

4. $g = \{(-32, -4), (1, 18), (5, -4), (9, 9), (16, -9), (21, -18)\}$

Determine whether or not the inverse of each of the following functions is also a function.

5. $f = \{(-17, 5), (-16, -5), (3, 3), (5, -17), (7, -7), (16, 5)\}$

6. $g = \{(-3, 11), (-1, 15), (1, 2), (8, -4), (12, -11), (13, -6)\}$

Determine the inverse of each of the following linear functions.

7. $f(x) = \frac{7}{9}x - 8$

8. $g(x) = -22x + 1$

9. $f(x) = -5x - \frac{4}{5}$

10. $g(x) = 11x - 4$

For each of the following inverses, determine the linear function.

11. $f^{-1}(x) = -\frac{8}{9}x + \frac{2}{9}$

12. $g^{-1}(x) = \frac{4}{3}x - \frac{1}{3}$

Determine the inverse of each of the following quadratic functions.

13. $f(x) = 9(x + 8)^2 - 40$

14. $g(x) = -2x^2 + 48x - 278$

15. $f(x) = -5(x - 1)^2 + 16$

16. $g(x) = 3x^2 + 60x + 277$

For each of the following inverses, determine the quadratic function $f(x)$.

17. $y = 2 \pm \sqrt{\dfrac{x + 99}{12}}$

18. $y = -4 \pm \sqrt{\dfrac{17 - x}{6}}$

Determine the inverse of each of the following power functions.

19. $f(x) = 28x^6$

20. $g(x) = \frac{1}{25}x^5$

21. $f(x) = 11x^8$

22. $g(x) = -76x^7$

For each of the following inverses, determine the power function $f(x)$.

23. $y = \pm \sqrt[8]{\dfrac{6}{7}x}$

24. $f^{-1}(x) = \pm \sqrt[11]{\dfrac{2}{9}x}$

Determine the inverse of each of the following functions.

25. $f(x) = -\dfrac{13}{x}$

27. $f(x) = \dfrac{34}{x}$

26. $g(x) = \dfrac{105}{x}$

28. $g(x) = \dfrac{21}{x}$

For each of the following inverses, determine the function $f(x)$.

29. $f^{-1}(x) = \dfrac{56}{x}$

30. $f^{-1}(x) = -\dfrac{38}{x}$

Sketch a graph of the inverse of each of the following functions.

31. $f(x) = \left(\dfrac{1}{5}\right)^x$

33. $f(x) = 6^x$

35. $f(x) = \left|\dfrac{1}{2}(x+4)\right|$

32. $f(x) = (2)(3^x)$

34. $f(x) = |5x|$

36. $f(x) = |x - 6|$

Use composition to determine whether or not each of the following pairs of functions are inverses of each other.

37. $f(x) = 5x - 17;\ g(x) = \dfrac{1}{5}x + \dfrac{17}{5}$

39. $f(x) = \dfrac{253}{x};\ g(x) = 253x$

38. $f(x) = \sqrt[7]{\dfrac{14}{x}};\ g(x) = \dfrac{7}{x^{14}}$

40. $f(x) = -9x^{15};\ g(x) = \sqrt[15]{\dfrac{1}{9}x}$

Using composition, give a counterexample to prove that each of the following pairs of functions are not inverses of each other.

41. $f(x) = 3x + 8;\ f^{-1}(x) = \dfrac{1}{3}x + \dfrac{8}{3}$

42. $f(x) = \dfrac{x}{312};\ f^{-1}(x) = \dfrac{312}{x}$

Chapter 4 Test

1. The inverse of which of the following power functions is not a function?

   A. $f(x) = \frac{1}{27}x^{27}$

   B. $f(x) = -29x^{29}$

   C. $f(x) = 30x^{30}$

   D. $f(x) = -\frac{1}{31}x^{31}$

2. The graph of the function $f(x)$ is shown. What can be determined about the function's inverse?

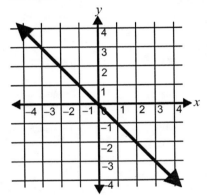

   A. It is not a function.
   B. It is a linear function with a slope of 1.
   C. It is the same as the function itself.
   D. Nothing can be determined.

3. If $f(8) = 26$, which of the following statements is true?

   A. If $f(x)$ and $g(x)$ are inverses of each other, then $g(-26)$ must equal 8.

   B. If $f(x)$ and $g(x)$ are inverses of each other, then $g(-8)$ must equal 26.

   C. If $f(x)$ and $g(x)$ are inverses of each other, then $g(8)$ must equal 26.

   D. If $f(x)$ and $g(x)$ are inverses of each other, then $g(26)$ must equal 8.

4. The function $f(x)$ has the inverse $f^{-1}(x) = \frac{11}{2}x - \frac{1}{4}$. Which of the following functions is $f(x)$?

   A. $f(x) = -\frac{2}{11}x - \frac{1}{22}$

   B. $f(x) = -\frac{2}{11}x + \frac{1}{22}$

   C. $f(x) = \frac{2}{11}x - \frac{1}{22}$

   D. $f(x) = \frac{2}{11}x + \frac{1}{22}$

5. Which of the following statements is true regarding a quadratic function in the form $f(x) = a(x - h)^2 + k$, where $a \neq 0$?

   A. Its inverse is always a function.

   B. Its inverse is a function only if $h = 0$.

   C. Its inverse is a function only if $k = 0$.

   D. Its inverse is never a function.

6. What is the inverse of the function $f(x) = \dfrac{198}{x}$?

   A. $f^{-1}(x) = -\dfrac{x}{198}$

   B. $f^{-1}(x) = -\dfrac{198}{x}$

   C. $f^{-1}(x) = \dfrac{x}{198}$

   D. $f^{-1}(x) = \dfrac{198}{x}$

7. If the inverse of the function $f = \{(1, 2), (3, 4), (5, y)\}$ is also a function, which of the following cannot be the value of y?

   A. 1 or 2
   B. 2 or 4
   C. 3 or 4
   D. 5

8. Which of the following pairs of functions are not inverses of each other?

A. $f(x) = \dfrac{1}{13}x^{21}$; $g(x) = \sqrt[21]{\dfrac{1}{13}x}$

B. $f(x) = 7x - 1$; $g(x) = \dfrac{1}{7}x + \dfrac{1}{7}$

C. $f(x) = -\dfrac{301}{x}$; $g(x) = -\dfrac{301}{x}$

D. $f(x) = \sqrt[25]{\dfrac{19}{x}}$; $g(x) = \dfrac{19}{x^{25}}$

9. The point (a, b) lies on the graph of the function $f(x) = \dfrac{67}{x}$. Which of the following points must also lie on the graph of the function $f(x) = \dfrac{67}{x}$?

A. $(-a, b)$

B. $(-b, a)$

C. $(a, -b)$

D. (b, a)

10. What is the inverse of the function

$f(x) = \dfrac{2}{35}x^{17}$?

A. $f^{-1}(x) = \sqrt[17]{-\dfrac{35}{2}x}$

B. $f^{-1}(x) = \sqrt[17]{-\dfrac{2}{35}x}$

C. $f^{-1}(x) = \sqrt[17]{\dfrac{2}{35}x}$

D. $f^{-1}(x) = \sqrt[17]{\dfrac{35}{2}x}$

11. What is the y-intercept of the inverse of the linear function $f(x) = -9x - 36$?

A. -9

B. -4

C. 4

D. 9

12. The graph of the function $f(x)$ that is shown has the x-axis as an asymptote. What is the asymptote of $f^{-1}(x)$?

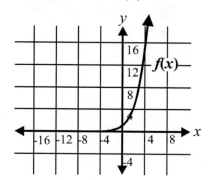

A. the x-axis

B. the y-axis

C. the line $y = x$

D. The function $f^{-1}(x)$ does not have an asymptote.

13. What is the inverse of the function

$f(x) = 8x^2 + 96x + 243$?

A. $y = -6 \pm \sqrt{\dfrac{x + 45}{8}}$

B. $y = -6 \pm \sqrt{8x + 360}$

C. $y = 6 \pm \sqrt{\dfrac{x + 45}{8}}$

D. $y = 6 \pm \sqrt{8x + 360}$

14. If $f(x)$ equals the values below, what is $f^{-1}\left(\frac{1}{5}\right)$?

$\left\{\left(-\frac{1}{5}, -\frac{6}{5}\right), \left(\frac{1}{5}, \frac{6}{5}\right), \left(4, -\frac{1}{5}\right), (5, 6), (6, 5)\right\}$

A. $-\dfrac{6}{5}$

B. $\dfrac{6}{5}$

C. 4

D. Undefined

Chapter 5
Triangles

This chapter covers the following Georgia Performance Standards:

MM2G	Geometry	MM2G1a
		MM2G1b
		MM2G2a
		MM2G2b
		MM2G2c

5.1   Types of Triangles

A triangle is an **equilateral triangle** if all of its sides and angles are equal. A triangle is an **isosceles triangle** if two of its sides and the angles opposite those sides are equal. A triangle is a **right triangle** if one of its angles equals 90°.

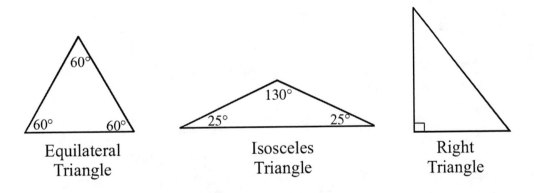

| Equilateral Triangle | Isosceles Triangle | Right Triangle |

5.2   Special Right Triangles

Two right triangles are **special right triangles** if they have fixed ratios among their sides.

45-45-90 Triangles

In a 45-45-90 triangle, the two sides opposite the 45° angles will always be equal. The length of the hypotenuse is $\sqrt{2}$ times the length of one of the sides opposite a 45° angle.

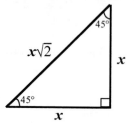

Example 1:   What are the lengths of sides a and b?

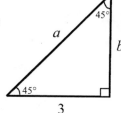

Step 1:   The two sides opposite the 45° angles are equal. Therefore, side $b = 3$.

Step 2:   The hypotenuse is $\sqrt{2}$ times the length of a side opposite a 45° angle. Therefore, $a = 3 \times \sqrt{2}$
Simplify: $a = 3\sqrt{2}$

30-60-90 Triangles

In a 30-60-90 triangle, the side opposite the 30° angle is the shortest leg. The side opposite the 60° angle is $\sqrt{3}$ times as long as the shortest leg, and the hypotenuse is twice as long as the shortest leg.

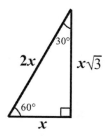

Example 2:   What are the lengths of sides a and b?

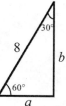

Step 1:   The hypotenuse is 2 times the side opposite the 30° angle.
Write the above statement using algebra and then solve.
$8 = 2a$
$\dfrac{8}{2} = \dfrac{2a}{2}$
$4 = a$

Step 2:   Now that it is known that the shortest leg has a length of 4, the side opposite the 60° angle can be calculated.
$b = a \times \sqrt{3} = 4 \times \sqrt{3}$
$b = 4\sqrt{3}$

Find the missing leg of each of the special right triangles. Simplify your answers.

1.

3.
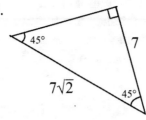

5.
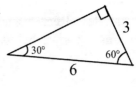

2.
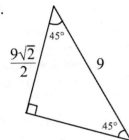

4.
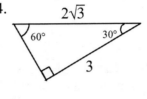

6.
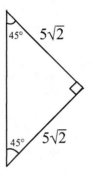

Find the lengths of sides *a* and *b* in each of the special right triangles.

7.
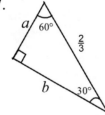

9.
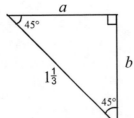

11.
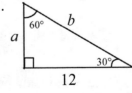

8.
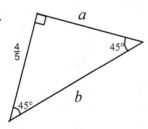

10.
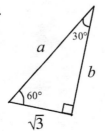

12.
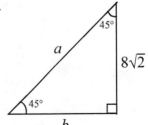

5.3   Introduction to Trigonometric Ratios

Trigonometry is a mathematical topic that applies the relationships between sides and angles in right triangles. Recall that a right triangle has one 90° angle and two acute angles. Consider the right triangle shown below. Note that the angles are labeled with capital letters. The sides are labeled with lowercase letters that correspond to the angles opposite them.

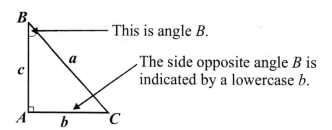

This is angle B.

The side opposite angle B is indicated by a lowercase b.

Trigonometric ratios are ratios of the measures of two sides of a right triangle and are related to the acute angles of a right triangle, not the right angle. The value of a trigonometric ratio is dependent on the size of the acute angle and the ratio of the lengths of the sides of the triangle.

We will consider the three basic trigonometric ratios in this section: **sine, cosine, and tangent**.

Definitions and descriptions of the sine, cosine, and tangent functions are presented below.

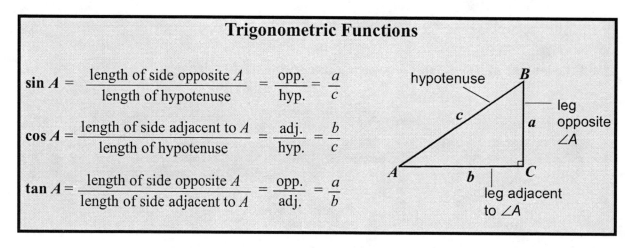

Trigonometric Functions

$$\sin A = \frac{\text{length of side opposite } A}{\text{length of hypotenuse}} = \frac{\text{opp.}}{\text{hyp.}} = \frac{a}{c}$$

$$\cos A = \frac{\text{length of side adjacent to } A}{\text{length of hypotenuse}} = \frac{\text{adj.}}{\text{hyp.}} = \frac{b}{c}$$

$$\tan A = \frac{\text{length of side opposite } A}{\text{length of side adjacent to } A} = \frac{\text{opp.}}{\text{adj.}} = \frac{a}{b}$$

Example 3:   For right triangle ABC, find $\sin A$, $\cos A$, $\tan A$, $\sin C$, $\cos C$, and $\tan C$.

$$\sin A = \frac{\text{opp.}}{\text{hyp.}} = \frac{3}{5} = 0.6 \qquad \sin C = \frac{\text{opp.}}{\text{hyp.}} = \frac{4}{5} = 0.8$$

$$\cos A = \frac{\text{adj.}}{\text{hyp.}} = \frac{4}{5} = 0.8 \qquad \cos C = \frac{\text{adj.}}{\text{hyp.}} = \frac{3}{5} = 0.6$$

$$\tan A = \frac{\text{opp.}}{\text{adj.}} = \frac{3}{4} = 0.75 \qquad \tan C = \frac{\text{opp.}}{\text{adj.}} = \frac{4}{3} = 1.\overline{3}$$

Find $\sin A$, $\cos A$, $\tan A$, $\sin B$, $\cos B$, and $\tan B$ in each of the following right triangles. Express answers as fractions and as decimals rounded to three decimal places.

1.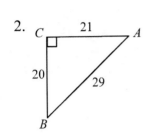

3.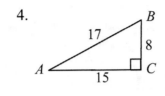

5.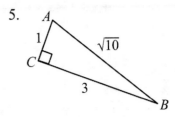

2.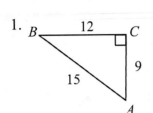

4.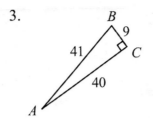

6.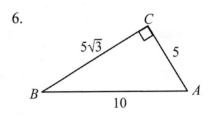

Once the values of the trigonometric ratios are found, then the measures of the angles within the triangle can be found using the arcsine and arccosine. The arcsine and arccosine can also be written as $\sin^{-1}$ and $\cos^{-1}$. The arc functions' identities can be defined as:

$$\arcsin\left(\sin\left(A\right)\right) = A$$
$$\arccos\left(\cos\left(A\right)\right) = A$$
$$\arctan\left(\tan\left(A\right)\right) = A$$

Example 4: For right triangle ABC, where $\sin A = 0.6$, find the measures of angles A and C. Round to the nearest whole number.

Step 1: Using your calculator, arcsine is $\sin^{-1}$.**
$\sin A = 0.6$
$\sin^{-1}\left(\sin A\right) = \sin^{-1}\left(0.6\right)$ Take the arcsine of both sides.
$A = 37°$

Step 2: Since all the angles in a triangle add up to $180°$, and $A = 37°$ and $B = 90°$, then
$A + B + C = 180°$.
$37° + 90° + C = 180°$
$C = 180° - 37° - 90° = 53°$
Therefore, $A = 37°$, $B = 90°$, and $C = 53°$

** To find the arcsine, arccosine, or arctangent using a scientific calculator, first enter the trig ratio without rounding, such as $\frac{3}{5}$ from the example above. Then, type 2nd SIN, 2nd COS, or 2nd TAN. If there isn't a 2nd button, you will have to press the inverse button and then the SIN, COS, or TAN button. The inverse button is usually abbreviated INV. When finding an angle using a scientific calculator, you must always remember to be in degree mode. To check this, look at the top of the screen, and it will show DEG in small print. If DEG is not shown, then press DRG or the degree button until DEG shows on the top of the screen.

Find the measures of the angles given the trigonometric function. Round your answers to the nearest degree.

1. $\sin A = 0.4$

2. $\tan x = 1$

3. $\sin b = 0.7$

4. $\cos C = \frac{\sqrt{2}}{2}$

5. $\tan A = -1.5$

6. $\cos y = -1$

7. $\sin B = -0.6$

8. $\cos A = 0$

9. $\tan z = 2.6$

10. $\tan c = 50$

11. $\sin x = \frac{\sqrt{2}}{2}$

12. $\cos x = 0.1$

13. $\tan y = 0$

14. $\cos a = -0.4$

15. $\sin C = 1$

Example 5:   Find the values of the sine, cosine, and tangent functions of both acute angles in the right triangle ABC shown below.

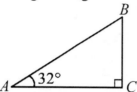

Step 1:   Find the third angle.
$$A + B + C = 180°$$
$$32° + B + 90° = 180°$$
$$B + 90° = 180° - 32° - 90° = 58°$$

Step 2:   Plug the angle values into $\sin A$, $\cos A$, $\tan A$, $\sin B$, $\cos B$, and $\tan B$.

$\sin A = \sin 32° = 0.5299$ $\sin B = \sin 58° = 0.8480$

$\cos A = \cos 32° = 0.8480$ $\cos B = \cos 58° = 0.5299$

$\tan A = \tan 32° = 0.6249$ $\tan B = \tan 58° = 1.600$

Find $\sin A$, $\cos A$, $\tan A$, $\sin B$, $\cos B$, and $\tan B$ in each of the following right triangles. Express answers as decimals rounded to three decimal places.

1.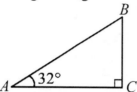

3.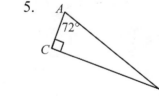

5.

2.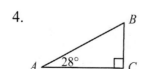

4.

6.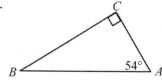

When given one acute angle and one side of a right triangle, the other angle and two sides can be found using trigonometric functions.

Example 6:   Find the third angle and the other two sides of the triangle.

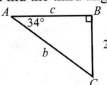

Step 1:   Find the third angle. Since all the angles in a triangle add up to 180°, and $A = 34°$ and $B = 90°$, then
$$A + B + C = 180°$$
$$34° + 90° + C = 180°$$
$$C = 180° - 34° - 90° = 56°$$

Step 2:   Find the missing sides. This can be done several different ways using sine, cosine, or tangent. We are going to use sine to find b and tangent to find c.

$$\sin A = \frac{\text{opp.}}{\text{hyp.}} \qquad\qquad \tan A = \frac{\text{opp.}}{\text{adj.}}$$

$$\sin 34° = \tfrac{2}{b} \qquad\qquad\qquad \tan 34° = \tfrac{2}{c}$$

$$0.5592 = \tfrac{2}{b} \qquad\qquad\qquad 0.6745 = \tfrac{2}{c}$$

$$0.5592b = 2 \qquad\qquad\qquad 0.6745c = 2$$

$$\frac{0.5592b}{0.5592} = \frac{2}{0.5592} \qquad\qquad \frac{0.6745c}{0.6745} = \frac{2}{0.6745}$$

$$b = 3.58 \qquad\qquad\qquad\qquad c = 2.97$$

$$C = 56°, b = 3.58, \text{ and } c = 2.97$$

Note: After you have calculated the second side using one of the trigonometric ratios, you can use the Pythagorean Theorem to find the third side.

$$3.58^2 = 2^2 + c^2 \longrightarrow c^2 = 3.58^2 - 2^2 \longrightarrow c^2 = 8.8164 \longrightarrow c = 2.97$$

Find the missing sides and angles using the information given.

1.

3.

5.

2.

4.

6.

Use the pictures to help solve the problems.

1. An F-22 is flying over two control towers. There is a point above the two towers where the fighter pilot can get a clean signal to both the towers. If he is 120 feet from tower one and is making a 59° angle with the two towers, find the distance, x, the F-22 is from the second tower and find the distance, y, between the two towers.

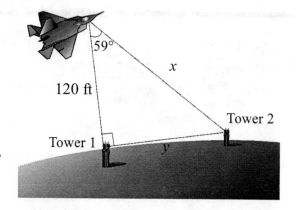

2. Sandra is trying to use her old cell phone to call her best friend. She can be no more than 3 miles from a tower in order to get a signal for her phone. If the telephone tower is 252 feet tall, find the angle of elevation, m, when Sandra's phone is the maximum 3 miles from the tower.
   HINT: Convert 3 miles to feet first.
       1 mile = 5280 feet

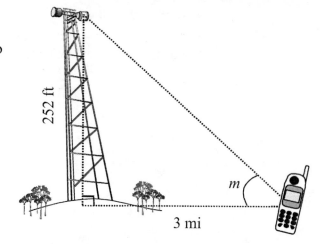

3. Sir Stephen is returning from fighting a war. His first concern on his homecoming journey is to see if his family's banner still flies above their castle. If the flag rises 95 feet above his head, and he emerges from the forest 185 feet from the tower, at what angle, m, is his line of sight to the banner?

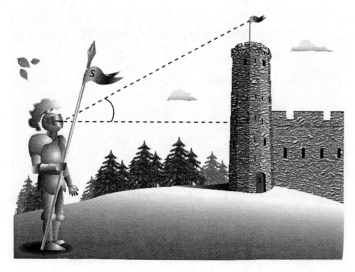

5.4 Similar Triangles

Two triangles are similar if the measurements of the three angles in both triangles are the same. If the three angles are the same, then their corresponding sides are proportional.

Corresponding Sides - The triangles below are similar. Therefore, the two shortest sides from each triangle, c and f, are corresponding. The two longest sides from each triangle, a and d, are corresponding. The two medium length sides, b and e, are corresponding.

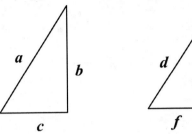

Proportional - The corresponding sides of similar triangles are proportional to each other. This means if we know all the measurements of one triangle, and we know only one measurement of the other triangle, we can figure out the measurements of the two other sides with proportion problems. The two triangles below are similar.

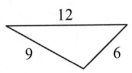 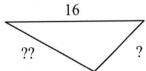

Note: To set up the proportion correctly, it is important to keep the measurements of each triangle on opposite sides of the equal sign.

To find the short side:	To find the medium length side:
Step 1: Set up the proportion	**Step 1:** Set up the proportion

$$\frac{\text{long side}}{\text{short side}} \quad \frac{12}{6} = \frac{16}{?}$$

$$\frac{\text{long side}}{\text{medium}} \quad \frac{12}{9} = \frac{16}{??}$$

Step 2: Solve the proportion. Multiply the two numbers diagonal to each other and then divide by the other number.

$$16 \times 6 = 96$$
$$96 \div 12 = 8$$

Step 2: Solve the proportion. Multiply the two numbers diagonal to each other and then divide by the other number.

$$16 \times 9 = 144$$
$$144 \div 12 = 12$$

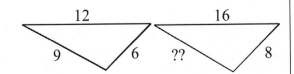 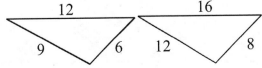

To find the scale factor in the problem on the previous page, we must divide a value from the second triangle by the corresponding value from the first triangle. The value 16 is from the second triangle, and the corresponding value from the first triangle is 12. $k = \dfrac{16}{12} = \dfrac{4}{3}$

The scale factor in this problem is $\frac{4}{3}$.

To check this answer multiply every term in the first triangle by the scale factor, and you will get every term in the second triangle.

$$12 \times \frac{4}{3} = 16 \qquad 9 \times \frac{4}{3} = 12 \qquad 6 \times \frac{4}{3} = 8$$

Find the missing side from the following similar triangles.

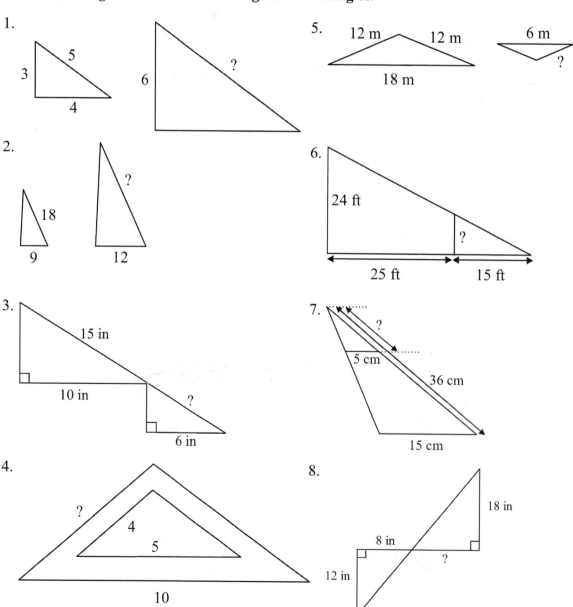

1.

2.

3.

4.

5.

6.

7.

8.

Trigonometric ratios can be useful when finding missing information in similar triangles.

Example 7: $\triangle ABC$ is similar to $\triangle DEF$. Use trig ratios to find the measure of $\angle F$.

Step 1: Since $\triangle ABC \sim \triangle DEF$, we know that the measures of the angles in $\triangle ABC$ are equal to the measure of the angles in $\triangle DEF$. Therefore, $\angle A \approx \angle D$, $\angle B \approx \angle E$, and $\angle C \approx \angle F$. In order to find the measure of $\angle F$, we can just find the measure of $\angle C$.

Step 2: To find the measure of $\angle C$, use a trig ratio. We will find sine of $\angle C$.

$$\sin C = \frac{\text{opp.}}{\text{hyp.}} = \frac{21}{29}$$

Step 3: Take the arcsine of both sides to find C. (Make sure your calculator is in DEGREE mode.)

$$\sin^{-1}(\sin C) = \sin^{-1}\left(\frac{21}{29}\right)$$

$C \approx 46.4°$ Since $\angle C \approx \angle F$, the measure of $\angle F \approx 46.4°$.

Use trigonometric ratios to solve the similar triangle problems.

1. $\triangle ABC \sim \triangle DEF$. Find the measures of $\angle E$ and $\angle D$.

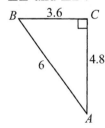
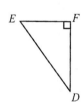

2. $\triangle ABC \sim \triangle ECD$. Find the measure of $\overline{CD}$.

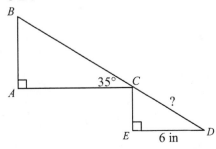

3. $\triangle ABC \sim \triangle DEF$. Find the measures of $\overline{FD}$ and $\overline{EF}$.

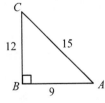

4. $\triangle ABC \sim \triangle ADE$. Find the measure of $\angle E$.

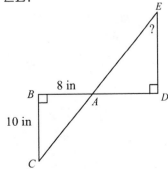

5.5   More Trigonometric Ratios

Two angles are **complementary** if the sum of the measures of the angles is 90°.

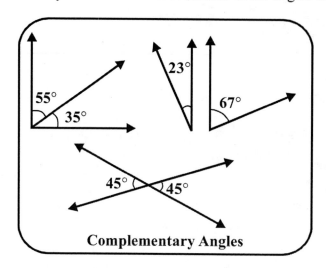

Complementary Angles

In a right triangle, one angle equals 90°. The other two angles add together to equal 90°. These two angles in the right triangle are complementary angles. In the triangle below, angle B and angle C are complementary angles. $\angle B + \angle C = 90°$. This can also be applied to trigonometric ratios.

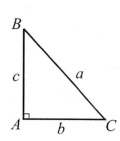

$$\sin B = \frac{b}{a} \qquad \sin C = \frac{c}{a} = \cos B$$

$$\cos B = \frac{c}{a} \qquad \cos C = \frac{b}{a} = \sin B$$

$$\tan B = \frac{b}{c} \qquad \tan C = \frac{c}{b} = \frac{1}{\tan B}$$

Example 8:   Find the measure of $\angle C$.

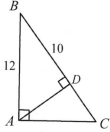

Step 1: $\triangle DAB$ is a right triangle. Using a trig ratio, we can find the measure of $\angle B$.

$$\cos B = \frac{\text{adjacent}}{\text{hypotenuse}} = \frac{10}{12}$$

$$\cos^{-1}(\cos B) = \cos^{-1}\left(\frac{10}{12}\right)$$

$$B = 33.6°$$

Step 2: $\triangle ABC$ is a also right triangle. Since $\angle A = 90°$, $\angle B + \angle C = 90°$.

$\angle B + \angle C = 90°$ Substitute the measure of $\angle B$ into the equation.
$33.6° + \angle C = 90°$ Solve for $\angle C$.
$\angle C = 90° - 33.6°$
$\angle C = 56.4°$

The measure of $\angle C$ is $56.4°$.

Use trigonometric ratios to solve the triangle problems.

1. Find the measure of $\angle B$.

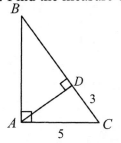

2. Find the measure of $\angle B$.

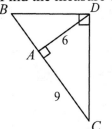

3. If $\sin C = \frac{4}{5}$, what is $\cos B$?

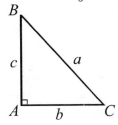

4. Find the measure of $\angle A$.

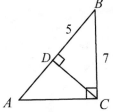

5. Find the measure of $\angle ADB$.

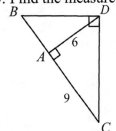

6. Find the measure of $\angle DAB$.

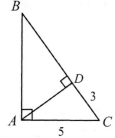

7. If $\cos C = \frac{10}{17}$, what is $\sin B$?

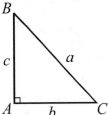

8. Find the measure of $\angle ACD$.

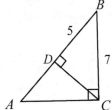

5.6   Trigonometric Ratios Applied to Other Shapes

Example 9:   Find the area of the trapezoid.

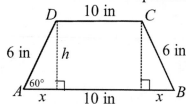

Step 1:   Define the area of a trapezoid. $A = \frac{1}{2}h(b_1 + b_2)$

We need to find the h and the value of x to find b_2 to solve for the area.

Step 2:   Find the height. We are given the hypotenuse and measurement $\angle A$.

$$\sin(x) = \frac{\text{opp}}{\text{hyp}} \qquad \cos(x) = \frac{\text{adj}}{\text{hyp}} \qquad \tan(x) = \frac{\text{opp}}{\text{adj}}$$

We have the measures of the opposite leg and the hypotenuse, so we'll use the sine ratio to find h.

$$\sin(60) = \frac{h}{6} \rightarrow 0.866 = \frac{h}{6} \rightarrow 5.186 = h$$

Step 3:   Find the value of x to determine b_2.

$$\cos(60) = \frac{x}{6} \rightarrow 0.5 = \frac{x}{6} \rightarrow 3 = x$$

$$b_2 = x + 10 + x = 3 + 10 + 3 = 16$$

Step 4:   Now that we have solved for all of the unknowns, plug the known variables into the equation and solve.

$$A = \frac{1}{2}h(b_1 + b_2) = \frac{1}{2} \times 5.196 (10 + 16) = 67.55 \text{ in}^2$$

Find the area. (Figures are not drawn to scale.)

1.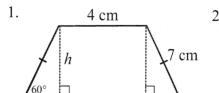

2.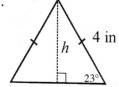

3.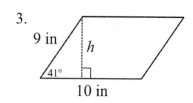

Copyright © American Book Company

Chapter 5 Review

Find the length of a and b in each of the special right triangles. Simplify your answers.

1.
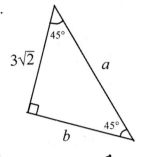

2.
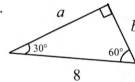

3.
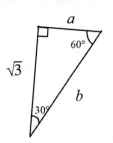

4.
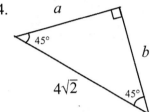

For both of the right triangles shown in questions 5 and 6, find the three trigonometric ratios for $\angle A$. (Hint: $\angle C = 90°$)

5.
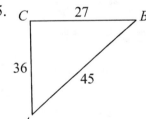

6.
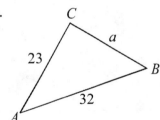

For questions 7 and 8, find the value of x.

7. $\sin x = 0.5$

8. $\tan x = -1$

For questions 9 and 10, find the missing angle and sides.

9.
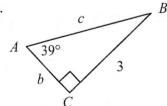

10.
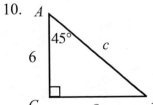

11. If the ratio of the lengths of the legs of a right triangle is 7 : 13, what is the sine of the angle formed by the shorter leg and the hypotenuse?

12. The length of one leg of a right triangle is 9 times the length of the other leg. What is the measurement to the nearest degree of the angle formed by the longer leg and the hypotenuse?

13. If the length of a leg of a right triangle it 55 percent of the length of the hypotenuse, what is the measurement to the nearest degree of the angle formed by the leg and the hypotenuse?

Solve the following problems.

14. What is the length of line segment $\overline{WY}$?

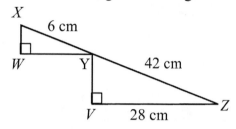

18. Find the measure of $\angle A$.

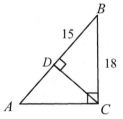

15. Find the height of the parallelogram.

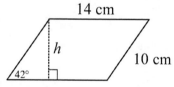

19. If $\tan C = \frac{9}{11}$, what is $\tan B$?

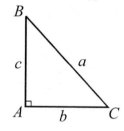

16. Find the missing side of the triangle below.

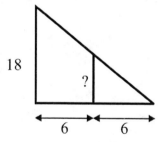

20. $\triangle ABC \sim \triangle DEF$. Find the measures of $\angle F$ and $\angle D$.

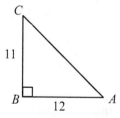
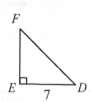

17. $\triangle ABC \sim \triangle DEF$. Find the measures of $\overline{FD}$ and $\overline{EF}$.

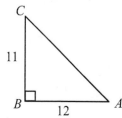
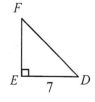

21. Find the measure of $\angle ACD$.

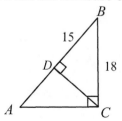

Chapter 5 Test

1. Solve for x. Round your answer to the nearest degree.

$\tan x = 0.5$

A. 27°

B. 30°

C. 60°

D. 0°

2.

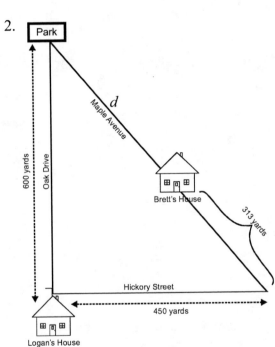

Logan enjoys taking his dog to the park. He walks down Hickory St., turns onto Maple Ave. to meet his friend, Brett, and then continues on Maple Ave. to the park. What is the approximate distance (d) from Brett's house to the park?

A. 350 yards

B. 437 yards

C. 687 yards

D. 532 yards

3. What is the measure of $\overline{AB}$?

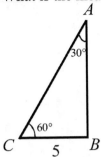

A. $5\sqrt{3}$

B. 10

C. 5

D. 2.5

4. Solve for x. Round your answer to the nearest degree.

$\sin x = 0.5$

A. 27°

B. 30°

C. 60°

D. 0°

5. What is the approximate measure of $\angle D$ in $\triangle ADE$?

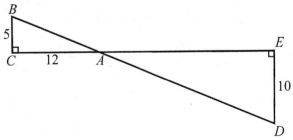

A. 23°

B. 25°

C. 65°

D. 67°

6. Harrison steps outside his house to see the hot air balloon pass by. He raises his eyes at a 35° angle to view the balloon. If the balloon is 5,000 feet above the ground, about how far is it from Harrison?

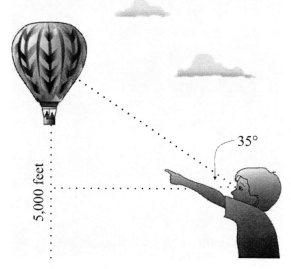

HINT: Harrison's eye level is 5.2 feet from the ground. $\sin(35°) \approx 0.57$ and $\cos(35°) \approx 0.82$

A. 6, 100 feet

B. 8, 700 feet

C. 7, 100 feet

D. 2, 900 feet

7. What is the measure of $\angle Z$?

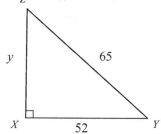

A. 0.014°
B. 36.87°
C. 51.34°
D. 53.13°

8. What is the measurement of $\angle Z$ to the nearest degree?

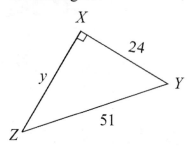

A. 25°
B. 28°
C. 30°
D. 62°

9. If $\cos C = \frac{4}{7}$, what is $\sin B$?

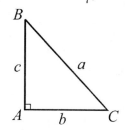

A. $\frac{4}{7}$

B. $\frac{7}{4}$

C. $\frac{6}{7}$

D. Cannot be determined with the information given.

10. What is the measure of $\angle F$ if $\triangle ABC \sim \triangle DEF$?

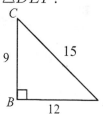

A. 53.1°
B. 36.9°
C. 45°
D. 29.4°

Chapter 6
Circles and Spheres

This chapter covers the following Georgia Performance Standards:

MM2G	Geometry	MM2G3a
		MM2G3b
		MM2G3c
		MM2G3d
		MM2G4a
		MM2G4b

6.1   Parts of a Circle

A **circle** is defined as all points in a plane that are an equal distance from a point called the **center**. The circle is named by the center point.

A **chord** is a segment that has its endpoints on the circle.

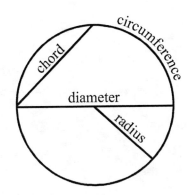 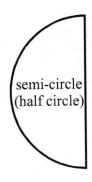 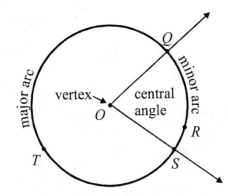

A **central angle** of a circle has the center of the circle as its vertex. The rays of a central angle each contain a radius of the circle. $\angle QOS$ is a central angle.

The points Q and S separate the circle into **arcs**. The arc lies on the circle itself. It does not include any points inside or outside the circle. $\overset{\frown}{QRS}$ or $\overset{\frown}{QS}$ is a **minor arc** because it is less than a semicircle. A minor arc can be named by 2 or 3 points. $\overset{\frown}{QTS}$ is a **major arc** because it is more than a semicircle. A major arc must be named by 3 points.

An **inscribed angle** is an angle whose vertex lies on the circle and whose sides contain **chords** of the circle. $\angle ABC$ in Figure 1 is an inscribed angle.

A line is **tangent** to a circle if it only touches the circle at one point, which is called the point of tangency. See Figure 2 for an example.

A **secant**, shown in Figure 3, is a line that intersects with a circle at two points. Every secant forms a chord. In Figure 3, secant $\overleftrightarrow{AB}$ forms chord $\overline{AB}$.

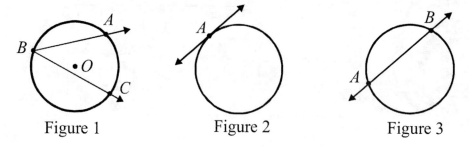

Figure 1   Figure 2   Figure 3

Refer to the figure below, and answer the following questions.

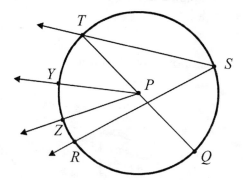

1. Identify the 2 line segments that are chords of the circle but not diameters.

2. Identify the largest major arc of the circle that contains point S.

3. Identify the center of the circle.

4. Identify the inscribed angle(s).

5. Identify the central angle(s).

6. Identify the diameters(s).

7. Identify the secant(s).

8. Name one major arc that has T as one of its ends.

6.2   Arc Lengths

The measure of a minor arc is the measure of its central angle.

In the circle at right, $\angle AOC$ measures $80°$.

Therefore, $m\overset{\frown}{AC} = 80$.

A complete rotation about the center point of a circle is $360°$.

The measure of a major arc is 360 minus the measure of its central angle.

In the circle at right, $m\overset{\frown}{ADC} = 360 - 80 = 280$.

The measure of a semicircle is 180°.

In the circle at right, $\overline{AD}$ is a diameter of the circle.

Therefore, $\overset{\frown}{ACD}$ is a semicircle and $m\overset{\frown}{ACD} = 180$.

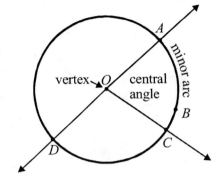

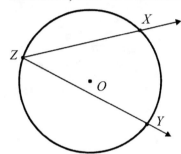

If an angle is inscribed in a circle, then the measure of the minor arc is two times the measure of the inscribed angle.

In the circle at left, $\angle XZY$ measures $45°$.

Therefore, $m\overset{\frown}{XY} = 2 \times 45$.

Simplified, $m\overset{\frown}{XY} = 90$.

In the circle below, $m\angle KOJ = 26°$, $m\angle MON = 37°$, and $\overline{KM}$ and $\overline{JL}$ are diameters. Find each measure.

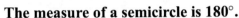

1. $m\overset{\frown}{NM} = \underline{\hspace{1cm}}$ 5. $m\overset{\frown}{LKJ} = \underline{\hspace{1cm}}$

2. $m\overset{\frown}{KJ} = \underline{\hspace{1cm}}$ 6. $m\overset{\frown}{LKN} = \underline{\hspace{1cm}}$

3. $m\overset{\frown}{LM} = \underline{\hspace{1cm}}$ 7. $m\overset{\frown}{MJK} = \underline{\hspace{1cm}}$

4. $m\overset{\frown}{JN} = \underline{\hspace{1cm}}$ 8. $m\overset{\frown}{MNJ} = \underline{\hspace{1cm}}$

In the circle below, $\overline{AC}$ is a diameter. $\angle DAC = 45°$, $\angle BCD = 110°$, $m\overset{\frown}{AD} = 90$, and $m\overset{\frown}{BC} = 50$. Find each measure.

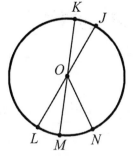

9. $\angle ACD = \underline{\hspace{1cm}}$ 13. $m\overset{\frown}{ABC} = \underline{\hspace{1cm}}$

10. $\angle BAC = \underline{\hspace{1cm}}$ 14. $\angle CDA = \underline{\hspace{1cm}}$

11. $\angle BCA = \underline{\hspace{1cm}}$ 15. $m\overset{\frown}{CD} = \underline{\hspace{1cm}}$

12. $\angle ABC = \underline{\hspace{1cm}}$ 16. $m\overset{\frown}{BCD} = \underline{\hspace{1cm}}$

6.3   More Circle Properties

An angle created by two secants or by a secant and a tangent has a measure equal to half the difference of the corresponding arc measures.

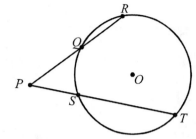

$$m\angle RPT = \frac{1}{2}\left(m\widehat{RT} - m\widehat{QS}\right)$$

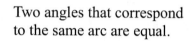

$$m\angle RPT = \frac{1}{2}\left(m\widehat{RT} - m\widehat{RS}\right)$$

If two chords intersect, the angles created have a measure equal to the average of the corresponding arc measures.

Two angles that correspond to the same arc are equal.

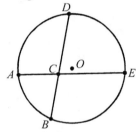

$$m\angle ACB = m\angle DCE = \frac{1}{2}\left(m\widehat{AB} + m\widehat{DE}\right)$$

$$m\angle ACD = m\angle BCE = \frac{1}{2}\left(m\widehat{AD} + m\widehat{BE}\right)$$

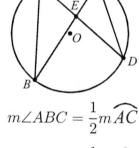

$$m\angle ABC = \frac{1}{2}m\widehat{AC}$$

$$m\angle ADC = \frac{1}{2}m\widehat{AC}$$

Use the circles to find the measures of the angles and arcs.

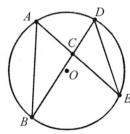

$m\angle BDE = 50°$
$m\angle ABD = 25°$
$m\widehat{AB} = 120$

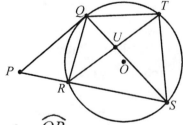

$m\angle QTR = 20°$
$m\angle TSQ = 25°$
$m\angle TRS = 60°$

1. $m\widehat{AD}$
2. $m\angle ACD$
3. $m\angle AED$
4. $m\angle ACB$
5. $m\widehat{DE}$

6. $m\widehat{QR}$
7. $m\angle TUS$
8. $m\angle QPS$
9. $m\widehat{QT}$
10. $m\angle RUS$

6.4   Comparing Diameter, Radius, and Circumference in a Circle

Circumference, C, is the distance around the outside of a circle. ($C = 2\pi r$ or $C = \pi d$)

Diameter, d, is a line segment passing through the center of a circle from one side to the other.

Radius, r, is a line segment from the center of a circle to the edge of the circle.

Pi, π, is the ratio of the circumference of a circle to its diameter. $\left(\pi \approx 3.14 \text{ or } \frac{22}{7} \right)$

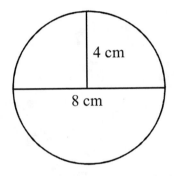

Answer the following questions about the circle above.

1. What is radius of the circle?

2. What is the diameter of the circle?

3. Pi is the ratio of which two parts of a circle?

4. What is the circumference of the circle?

5. What is the symbol for Pi?

6. How many different ways can you draw the radius of the circle?

7. Does the diameter have to pass through the center of the circle?

8. Pi can be written as 3.14. How else can it be written?

6.5   Circumference

Circumference, C - the distance around the outside of a circle

Diameter, d - a line segment passing through the center of a circle from one side to the other

Radius, r - a line segment from the center of a circle to the edge of a circle

Pi, π- the ratio of a circumference of a circle to its diameter $\pi \approx 3.14$ or $\pi \approx \frac{22}{7}$

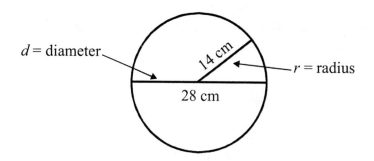

The formula for the circumference of a circle is $C = 2\pi r$ or $C = \pi d$. (The formulas are equal because the diameter is equal to twice the radius, $d = 2r$.)

Example 1:   Find the approximate circumference of the circle above.

$$C = \pi d \quad \text{Use } \pi \approx 3.14 \qquad \qquad C = 2\pi r$$
$$C \approx 3.14 \times 28 \qquad \qquad \qquad \quad C \approx 2 \times 3.14 \times 14$$
$$C \approx 87.92 \, \text{cm} \qquad \qquad \qquad \quad \; C \approx 87.92 \, \text{cm}$$

Use the formulas given above to find the approximate circumferences of the following circles. Use $\pi \approx 3.14$.

1. 8 in $C =$ _____

2. 14 ft $C =$ _____

3. 2 cm $C =$ _____

4. 6 m $C =$ _____

5. 8 ft $C =$ _____

Use the formulas given above to find the approximate circumferences of the following circles. Use $\pi \approx \frac{22}{7}$.

6. 3 ft $C =$ _____

7. 12 in $C =$ _____

8. 6 m $C =$ _____

9. 5 cm $C =$ _____

10. 16 in $C =$ _____

6.6   Area of a Circle

The formula for the area of a circle is $A = \pi r^2$. The area is how many square units of measure would fit inside a circle.

Example 2:   Find the approximate area of the circle, using both values for π.

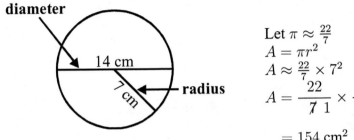

diameter

14 cm

7 cm — radius

$$\text{Let } \pi \approx \frac{22}{7}$$
$$A = \pi r^2$$
$$A \approx \frac{22}{7} \times 7^2$$
$$A = \frac{22}{7} \times \frac{\cancel{49}\,7}{1}$$
$$= 154 \text{ cm}^2$$

$$\text{Let } \pi \approx 3.14$$
$$A = \pi r^2$$
$$A \approx 3.14 \times 7^2$$
$$A = 3.14 \times 49$$
$$= 153.86 \text{ cm}^2$$

Find the approximate area of the following circles. Remember to include units.

Fill in the chart below. Include appropriate units.

	$\pi \approx 3.14$	$\pi \approx \frac{22}{7}$
1. 5 in	$A = \underline{\hspace{1cm}}$	$A = \underline{\hspace{1cm}}$
2. 16 ft	$A = \underline{\hspace{1cm}}$	$A = \underline{\hspace{1cm}}$
3. 8 cm	$A = \underline{\hspace{1cm}}$	$A = \underline{\hspace{1cm}}$
4. 3 m	$A = \underline{\hspace{1cm}}$	$A = \underline{\hspace{1cm}}$

		Area		
	Radius	Diameter	$\pi \approx 3.14$	$\pi \approx \frac{22}{7}$
5.	9 ft			
6.		4 in		
7.	8 cm			
8.		20 ft		
9.	14 m			
10.		18 cm		
11.	12 ft			
12.		6 in		

6.7   Area of a Sector

A sector of a circle is a region bounded by a central angle and its intercepted arc. In the circle below $\angle AOB$ is a central angle measuring $80°$. Therefore, $\overset{\frown}{AB}$ is $80°$. $\angle AOB$ and $\overset{\frown}{AB}$ form a sector of the circle.

Example 3:   Find the approximate area of the sector formed by $\angle AOB$ and $\overset{\frown}{AB}$.

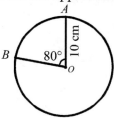

Step 1:   The area of a sector is a fraction of the area of the circle. So we must find the approximate area of the circle.
$A = \pi r^2$
$A \approx 3.14 \times 10^2 = 3.14 \times 100 \approx 314 \text{ cm}^2$

Step 2:   Now we need to find the fraction of the circle that the sector occupies. Remember that the sum of the measures of the central angles of a circle is 360. The fraction that the sector occupies is the measure of the central angle, denoted by the letter N, divided by 360.
Fraction that sector occupies $= \dfrac{N}{360} = \dfrac{80}{360} = \dfrac{2}{9}$

Step 3:   Now we can calculate the approximate area of the sector.
$A = \dfrac{N}{360}\pi r^2 \approx \dfrac{2}{9} \times 3.14 \text{ cm}^2 \times 10^2 \approx \dfrac{628}{9} \text{ cm}^2$
Simplified, $A \approx 69\frac{7}{9} \text{ cm}^2$

Each of the following is a measurement for a central angle. Calculate the fraction of a circle that the central angle occupies. Simplify your answers.

1. 30°	3. 16°	5. 45°	7. 120°	9. 15°	11. 60°
2. 2°	4. 52°	6. 72°	8. 270°	10. 108°	12. 90°

Find the approximate area of the sector bounded by $\angle XYZ$ and $\overset{\frown}{XZ}$ in each of the following circles. Use $\pi \approx 3.14$.

13.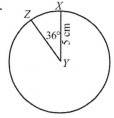

14.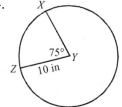

15.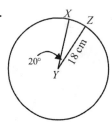

16.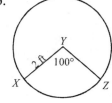

6.8   Volume of a Sphere

To find the volume of a solid, insert the measurements given for the solid into the correct formula and solve. Remember, volumes are expressed in cubic units such as in^3, ft^3, m^3, cm^3, or mm^3. The formula for the volume of a sphere is $V = \frac{4}{3}\pi r^3$.

Example 4:   Find the approximate volume of the sphere below. Use $\pi \approx 3.14$.

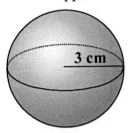

Step 1:   Substitute all known values into the equation $V = \frac{4}{3}\pi r^3$.

$r = 3$ $\pi \approx 3.14$

$V = \frac{4}{3}\pi r^3 \approx \frac{4}{3}(3.14)(3)^3$

Step 2:   Solve the equation.

$V \approx \frac{4}{3}(3.14)(3)^3 \approx \frac{4}{3} \times 3.14 \times 27 \approx 113.04 \text{ cm}^3$

Find the approximate volume of the following shapes. Use $\pi \approx 3.14$.

1.
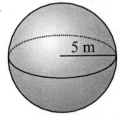
5 m

3.
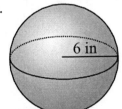
6 in

5.
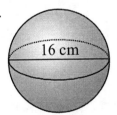
16 cm

2.
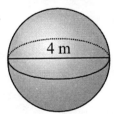
4 m

4.
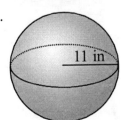
11 in

6.
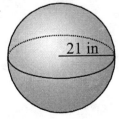
21 in

7. If a basketball measures 24 centimeters in diameter, about what volume of air will it hold? Use $\pi \approx 3.14$.

8. If a vinyl ball measures 5 inches in diameter, about what volume of air will it hold? Use $\pi \approx 3.14$.

9. A spherical dog toy has a radius of 6 cm. If this toy is stuffed with dog treats, about what volume of treats will it hold? Use $\pi \approx 3.14$.

6.9   Surface Area of a Sphere

The formula for the surface area of a sphere is $SA = 4\pi r^2$.

Example 5:   Find the approximate surface area of the sphere below. Use $\pi \approx 3.14$.

4 cm

Step 1:   Substitute all known values into the equation $SA = 4\pi r^2$.

$r = 4 \quad \pi \approx 3.14$

$SA = 4\pi r^2 \approx 4\,(3.14)\,(4)^2$

Step 2:   Solve the equation.

$SA \approx 4\,(3.14)\,(4)^2 \approx 4 \times 3.14 \times 16 \approx 200.96 \text{ cm}^2$

Find the approximate surface area of a sphere given the following measurements where $r =$ radius and $d =$ diameter. Use $\pi \approx 3.14$.

1. $r = 2$ in $SA \approx$ _____

2. $r = 6$ m $SA \approx$ _____

3. $r = \frac{3}{4}$ yd $SA \approx$ _____

4. $d = 8$ cm $SA \approx$ _____

5. $d = 50$ mm $SA \approx$ _____

6. $r = \frac{1}{4}$ ft $SA \approx$ _____

7. $d = 14$ cm $SA \approx$ _____

8. $r = \frac{1}{5}$ km $SA \approx$ _____

9. $d = 3$ in $SA \approx$ _____

10. $d = \frac{2}{3}$ ft $SA \approx$ _____

11. $r = 10$ mm $SA \approx$ _____

12. $d = 5$ yd $SA \approx$ _____

6.10   Geometric Relationships of Circles and Spheres

This section illustrates what happens to the area or volume of a figure when one or more of the dimensions changes.

Example 6:   How would doubling the radius of a sphere affect the volume?

The volume of a sphere is $V = \frac{4}{3}\pi r^3$. Just by looking at the formula, can you see that by doubling the radius, the volume would increase 8 times the original volume? So, a sphere with a radius of 2 would have a volume 8 times greater than a sphere with a radius of 1.

Example 7:   Sonya drew a circle which had a radius of 3 inches for a school project. She also needed to make a larger circle which had a radius of 9 inches. When Sonya drew the bigger circle, what was the difference in area?

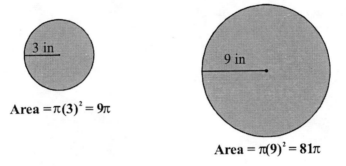

The area of the second circle is 9 times larger than the first.

Carefully read each problem below and solve.

1. Ken draws a circle with a radius of 5 cm. He then draws a circle with a radius of 10 cm. How many times larger is the area of the second circle?

2. The area of circle B is 9 times larger than the area of circle A. If the radius of circle A is represented by x, how would you represent the radius of circle B?

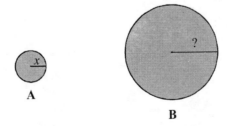

3. A sphere has a radius of 1. If the radius is increased to 3, how many times greater will the volume be?

4. In a sphere, how many times greater is the volume if you double the diameter?

5. In a sphere, how many times greater is the surface area if you double the radius?

Chapter 6 Review

1. In the circle below, $\overline{AE}$ is a diameter, $\angle DAE$ measures 30° and $m\overset{\frown}{BC} = 45$. What is the measure of $\overset{\frown}{DE}$ and $\angle BOC$?

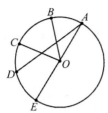

2. Find the area of the shaded part of the image below. Round your answer to the nearest whole number.

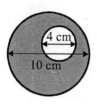

4 cm
10 cm

3. Calculate the approximate circumference and the area of the following circle. Use $\pi \approx \frac{22}{7}$.

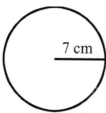

7 cm

4. Calculate the approximate circumference and the area of the following circle. Use $\pi \approx 3.14$.

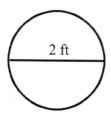

2 ft

5. Which line represents a tangent of the circle?

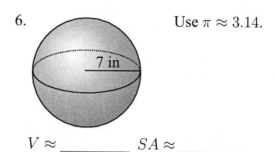

6.

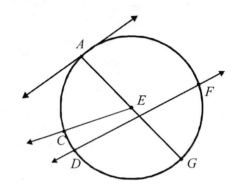

Use $\pi \approx 3.14$.

7 in

$V \approx$ _____ $SA \approx$ _____

7. If a ball is 4 inches in diameter, what is its approximate surface area? Use $\pi \approx 3.14$.

8. A gigantic bronze sphere is being added to the top of a tall building downtown. The sphere will be 24 ft in diameter. What will be the approximate surface area of the globe?

9. If a basketball measures 15 inches in diameter, about what volume of air will it hold? Use $\pi \approx 3.14$.

10. In a sphere, how many times greater is the volume if you quadruple the diameter?

Chapter 6 Test

1. What is the area of a circle with a radius of 7 cm? (Round to the nearest whole number)

   A. 154 square cm
   B. 196 square cm
   C. 347 square cm
   D. 616 square cm

2. Find the approximate circumference. Use $\pi \approx 3.14$.

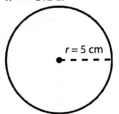

   A. 15.7 cm
   B. 62.8 cm
   C. 31.4 cm
   D. 0.314 cm

3. Find the approximate area. Use $\pi \approx 3.14$.

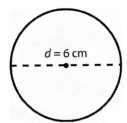

   A. 113.04 cm^2
   B. 28.26 cm^2
   C. 18.84 cm^2
   D. 188.4 cm^2

4. Which is an angle whose vertex lies on a circle and whose sides contain chords of the circle?

   A. central angle
   B. tangent
   C. inscribed angle
   D. secant

5. A line that touches a circle only at one point is called a

   A. tangent.
   B. chord.
   C. secant.
   D. inscribed line.

6. What does the measure of $\overset{\frown}{ABC}$ equal?

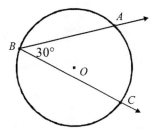

   A. 60
   B. 330
   C. 300
   D. 210

7. What is the approximate circumference of a circle that has a diameter of 10 cm?

   A. 15.7 cm
   B. 31.4 cm
   C. 78.5 cm
   D. 310 cm

8. If you decide to divide a pie that has a diameter of 8 in into 6 equal slices, what is the area of each slice?

   A. 8.37 in^2
   B. 4.19 in^2
   C. 33.49 in^2
   D. 50.24 in^2

9. If a sphere with a 6 m radius is cut out of a cube like the one shown below, about what would the new volume be? Use $\pi \approx 3.14$.

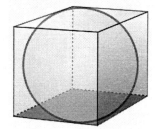

A. 823.68 m³
B. 1728 m³
C. 904.78 m³
D. 1441 m³

10. If the radius of a sphere is tripled, how much larger will the volume be?

A. 81 times larger
B. 9 times larger
C. 3 times larger
D. 27 times larger

11. What is the approximate surface area of a sphere that has a radius that measures 3 feet? Use $\pi \approx 3.14$.

A. 113.04 ft²
B. 84.82 ft²
C. 150.80 ft²
D. 201.06 ft²

12. Find the area of the shaded region.

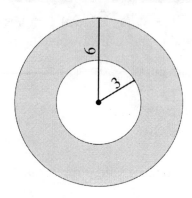

A. 24π
B. 3π
C. 27π
D. 15π

13. What is the approximate surface area of a sphere whose radius measures 8 cm?

A. 512 cm²
B. 804 cm²
C. 384 cm²
D. 268 cm²

14. If you double the diameter of a sphere, how does this effect the surface area.

A. The surface area becomes four times bigger.
B. The surface area becomes four times smaller.
C. The surface area becomes two times bigger.
D. The surface area becomes two times smaller.

Chapter 7
Data Analysis

This chapter covers the following Georgia Performance Standards:

MM2D	Data Analysis and Probability	MM2D1a
		MM2D1b
		MM2D1c
		MM2D1d

7.1   Collecting Samples from Two Different Populations

Sometimes samples from two different populations are collected. By comparing a sample of one population with a sample of the other, conclusions may be able to be drawn about one or more characteristics of the two populations.

Example 1: Kate has decided to investigate the old saying, "An apple a day keeps the doctor away." To do so she interviewed a random group of people who eat at least one apple every day and asked each of them how many times they had visited the doctor in the last year. She then interviewed a random group of people who do not eat at least one apple every day and asked them the same question. Finally, she came to a conclusion by determining the average number of doctor visits during the last year for a member of each group and comparing the two. What are the two populations being investigated? What is the difference between the two populations? Identify the two samples being compared. Finally, which statistic is being compared?

Step 1: Identify the two populations being investigated.

The first population being investigated is all the people who eat at least one apple every day, and the second population being investigated is all the people who do not eat at least one apple every day.

Step 2: Determine the difference between the two populations.

The difference between the two populations is the number of apples eaten by a member of each population every day.

Step 3: Identify the two samples being compared.

The first sample being compared is the random group of people who eat at least one apple every day, and the second sample being compared is the random group of people who do not eat at least one apple every day.

Step 4: Determine the statistic that is being compared.

The statistic that is being compared is the average number of doctor visits during the last year for a member of each sample.

Example 2:   Larry has decided to investigate whether single people or married people read more books. To do so he intends to interview a random group of single people and ask each of them how many books they have read in the last year. He then intends to interview a random group of married people and ask them the same question. To form his random groups, Larry is trying to decide between randomly selecting people he knows and putting them in the appropriate group or randomly calling people in the telephone book, asking them their marital status, and putting them in the appropriate group. Which is the better way to form the random groups?

Step 1:   Evaluate the effectiveness of the first choice.

The people whom Larry knows may all have certain characteristics in common. For example, Larry may be a college English professor, so the people he knows may all read a lot of books. Therefore, for Larry to randomly select people he knows may not be a very good choice.

Step 2:   Evaluate the effectiveness of the second choice.

People randomly selected from the telephone book will almost certainly have less in common than the people Larry knows. Therefore, this is the better way to form the random groups.

Use the following situation to answer questions 1–4.

Pedro has decided to investigate whether left-handed workers or right-handed workers have higher incomes. To do so he interviewed a random group of left-handed workers and asked them what their incomes were last year. He then interviewed a random group of right-handed workers and asked them the same question. Finally, he came to a conclusion by determining the average income of a member of each group and comparing the two.

1. What are the two populations being investigated?

2. What is the difference between the two populations?

3. Identify the two samples being compared.

4. What statistic is being compared?

Use the following situation to answer questions 5–8.

Kristen has decided to investigate whether adult men or adult women are better at spelling. To do so she had a random group of adult men take a spelling test. She then had a random group of adult women take the same test. Finally, she came to a conclusion by determining the average score on the test for a member of each group and comparing the two.

5. What are the two populations being investigated?

6. What is the difference between the two populations?

7. Identify the two samples being compared.

8. What statistic is being compared?

For each of the following pairs of choices, determine which choice is the better way to form a random group.

9. Which would you choose to determine the physical fitness of adult men?

  (A) Randomly selecting a group of adult men who work at a certain company

  (B) Randomly selecting a group of adult men from the voter polls

10. Which would you choose to determine the height of 12th grade girls?

  (A) Randomly selecting a group of 12th grade girls form the National Honor Society

  (B) Randomly selecting a group of 12th grade girls from a sports league

11. Which would you choose to determine the gas mileage of cars?

  (A) Randomly selecting a group of cars from a certain car dealership

  (B) Randomly a group of cars as they come through a toll booth

7.2   Mean

In statistics, the arithmetic mean is the same as the average. To find the arithmetic mean of a list of numbers, first add together all of the numbers in the list, and then divide by the number of items in the list.

Example 3:   Find the mean of 38, 72, 110, 548.

Step 1:   First add: $38 + 72 + 110 + 548 = 768$

Step 2:   There are 4 numbers in the list so divide the total by 4. $768 \div 4 = 192$
The mean is 192.

Practice finding the mean (average). Round to the nearest tenth if necessary.

1. Dinners served:
    489 561 522 450

2. Prices paid for shirts:
    $4.89 $9.97 $5.90 $8.64

3. Piglets born:
    23 19 15 21 22

4. Student absences:
    6 5 13 8 9 12 7

5. Paychecks:
    $89.56 $99.99 $56.54

6. Choir attendance:
    56 45 97 66 70

7. Long distance calls:
    33 14 24 21 19

8. Train boxcars:
    56 55 48 61 51

9. Cookies eaten:
    5 6 8 9 2 4 3

Find the mean (average) of the following word problems.

10. Val's science grades are 95, 87, 65, 94, 78, and 97. What is her average?

11. Ann runs a business from her home. The number of orders for the last 7 business days are 17, 24, 13, 8, 11, 15, and 9. What is the average number of orders per day?

12. Melissa tracks the number of phone calls she has per day: 8, 2, 5, 4, 7, 3, 6, 1. What is the average number of calls she receives?

13. The Cheese Shop tracks the number of lunches they serve this week: 42, 55, 36, 41, 38, 33, and 46. What is the average number of lunches served?

14. Leah drives 364 miles in 7 hours. What is her average miles per hour?

15. Tim saves $680 in 8 months. How much does his savings average each month?

16. Ken makes 117 passes in 13 games. How many passes does he average per game?

7.3   Finding Data Missing From the Mean

Example 4:   Mara knew she had an 88 average in her biology class, but she lost one of her papers. The three papers she could find had scores of 98%, 84%, and 90%. What was the score on her fourth paper?

Step 1:   Calculate the total score on four papers with an 88% average. $0.88 \times 4 = 3.52$

Step 2:   Add together the scores from the three papers you have. $0.98 + 0.84 + 0.9 = 2.72$

Step 3:   Subtract the scores you know from the total score. $3.52 - 2.72 = 0.80$. She had 80% on her fourth paper.

Find the data missing from the following problems.

1. Gabriel earns 87% on his first geography test. He wants to keep a 92% average. What does he need to get on his next test to bring his average up?

2. Rian earned $68.00 on Monday. How much money must she earn on Tuesday to have an average of $80 earned for the two days?

3. Haley, Chuck, Dana, and Chris enter a contest to see who could bake the most chocolate chip cookies in an hour. They bake an average of 75 cookies. Haley bakes 55, Chuck bakes 70, and Dana bakes 90. How many does Chris bake?

4. Four wrestlers make a pact to lose some weight before the competition. They lose an average of 7 pounds each over the course of 3 weeks. Carlos loses 6 pounds, Steve loses 5 pounds, and Greg loses 9 pounds. How many pounds does Wes lose?

5. Three boxes are ready for shipment. The boxes average 26 pounds each. The first box weighs 30 pounds; the second box weighs 25 pounds. How much does the third box weigh?

6. The five jockeys running in the next race average 92 pounds each. Nicole weighs 89 pounds. Jon weighs 95 pounds. Jenny and Kasey weigh 90 pounds each. How much does Jordan weigh?

7. Jessica makes three loaves of bread that weigh a total of 45 ounces. What is the average weight of each loaf?

8. Celeste makes scented candles to give away to friends. She has 2 pounds of candle wax which she melted, scented, and poured into 8 molds. What is the average weight of each candle?

9. Each basketball player has to average a minimum of 5 points a game for the next three games to stay on the team. Ben is feeling the pressure. He scored 3 points the first game and 2 points the second game. How many points does he need to score in the third game to stay on the team?

7.4   Standard Deviation

Standard deviation is the measure of the variability (or spread) of the values in a data set. It can be applied to a population or a smaller, sample data set. The formulas for standard deviation for a set $\{x_1, x_2, ..., x_n\}$ is

Sample Standard Deviation

$$S = \sqrt{\frac{1}{N-1}\left(\sum_{i=1}^{N}(x_i - \overline{x})^2\right)}$$

Population Standard Deviation

$$\sigma = \sqrt{\frac{1}{N}\left(\sum_{i=1}^{N}(x_i - \overline{x})^2\right)}$$

where x_i are the elements in the set $\{x_1, x_2, ..., x_n\}$ and $\overline{x}$ is the mean of the data set.

Example 5:   A randomly-selected group of 6 automobiles was formed, and the odometer reading was taken for each car. The number of miles on each was as follows:

Car 1: $23,000$ miles   Car 3: $120,000$ miles   Car 5: $27,000$ miles
Car 2: $44,000$ miles   Car 4: $31,000$ miles   Car 6: $19,000$ miles

What is the standard deviation of this data sample?

Step 1:   Calculate the mean $\overline{x}$ of the data set.

$$\overline{x} = \frac{23,000 + 44,000 + 120,000 + 31,000 + 27,000 + 19,000}{6} = 44,000$$
miles

Step 2:   Subtract the mean from each data value. The difference is called a **deviation**.

$x_1 - \overline{x} = 23,000 \text{ miles} - 44,000 \text{ miles} = -21,000 \text{ miles}$
$x_2 - \overline{x} = 44,000 \text{ miles} - 44,000 \text{ miles} = 0 \text{ miles}$
$x_3 - \overline{x} = 120,000 \text{ miles} - 44,000 \text{ miles} = 76,000 \text{ miles}$
$x_4 - \overline{x} = 31,000 \text{ miles} - 44,000 \text{ miles} = -13,000 \text{ miles}$
$x_5 - \overline{x} = 27,000 \text{ miles} - 44,000 \text{ miles} = -17,000 \text{ miles}$
$x_6 - \overline{x} = 19,000 \text{ miles} - 44,000 \text{ miles} = -25,000 \text{ miles}$

Step 3:   Now, plug the values into the equation $S = \sqrt{\frac{1}{N-1}\left(\sum_{i=1}^{N}(x_i - \overline{x})^2\right)}$.

$$S = \sqrt{\frac{(x_1 - \overline{x})^2 + (x_2 - \overline{x})^2 + (x_3 - \overline{x})^2 + (x_4 - \overline{x})^2 + (x_5 - \overline{x})^2 + (x_6 - \overline{x})^2}{N-1}}$$

$$= \sqrt{\frac{(-21,000)^2 + (0)^2 + (76,000)^2 + (-13,000)^2 + (-17,000)^2 + (-25,000)^2}{5}}$$

$$= \sqrt{\frac{7,300,000,000}{5}} = \sqrt{1,460,000,000} \approx 38,209.95 \text{ miles}$$

The standard deviation of the data set is $38,209.95$ miles.

Example 6: During his short football career, a running back had 7 rushes of 6 yards, 14 yards, 11 yards, 20 yards, 22 yards, 1 yard, and 3 yards, respectively. What is the standard deviation of this set of data?

Hint: This set of data represents the entire population of rushes that the running back had during his career.

Step 1: Calculate the mean of the set of data.

$$\overline{x} = \frac{6 + 14 + 11 + 20 + 22 + 1 + 3}{7} = \frac{77}{7} = 11 \text{ yards}$$

Step 2: Subtract the mean from each data value.

$$x_1 - \overline{x} = 6 - 11 = -5$$
$$x_2 - \overline{x} = 14 - 11 = 3$$
$$x_3 - \overline{x} = 11 - 11 = 0$$
$$x_4 - \overline{x} = 20 - 11 = 9$$
$$x_5 - \overline{x} = 22 - 11 = 11$$
$$x_6 - \overline{x} = 1 - 11 = -10$$
$$x_7 - \overline{x} = 3 - 11 = -8$$

Step 3: Now, plug the values into the population equation $\sigma = \sqrt{\frac{1}{N}\left(\sum_{i=1}^{N}(x_i - \overline{x})^2\right)}$.

$$\sigma = \sqrt{\frac{(-5)^2 + (3)^2 + (0)^2 + (9)^2 + (11)^2 + (-10)^2 + (-8)^2}{7}}$$

$$= \sqrt{\frac{400}{7}} \approx 7.56$$

The standard deviation of the population set is 7.56 yards.

** Remember to use the correct formula for standard deviation. The population standard deviation and sample standard deviation are different from each other. In this case, the population standard deviation is 7.56 yards, but the sample standard deviation is 8.16 yards.

Calculate the standard deviation of each of the following data samples. Use the appropriate unit of measurement in each answer.

1. 200 pounds, 60 pounds, 150 pounds, 160 pounds, 110 pounds, 90 pounds
2. 7 days, 12 days, 13 days, 2 days, 22 days, 20 days, 15 days, 21 days
3. 33 millimeters, 6 millimeters, 4 millimeters, 5 millimeters, 7 millimeters
4. $32,000, $19,000, $17,000, $29,000, $31,000, $27,000, $25,000
5. 4.5 radians, 1.8 radians, 2.6 radians, 0.9 radians, 3.9 radians, 4.1 radians
6. 6 pints; 9 pints, 7 pints, 8 pints, 6 pints, 5 pints, 8 pints, 4 pints, 6 pints, 5 pints
7. 1900 people, 1400 people, 2100 people, 2300 people, 3300 people, 3000 people
8. 3 goals, 2 goals, 4 goals, 3 goals, 5 goals, 4 goals, 5 goals, 1 goal, 2 goals
9. 44 watts, 29 watts, 51 watts, 49 watts, 33 watts, 22 watts, 53 watts, 57 watts

Calculate the standard deviation of each of the following population sets.

10. 314, 306, 299, 351, 301, 308, 349

11. 7, 6, 8, 7, 8, 5, 6, 9

12. 89, 76, 82, 83, 93, 74, 79

13. 45, 48, 30, 39, 58, 103

14. 17, 3, 5, 21, 16, 18, 1, 2

15. 43, 34, 54, 49, 66

7.5   Comparing Data Sets

The best way to compare statistics is to use summary statistics. To compare, you could use the mean or standard deviations.

Example 7: Compare Zack and Cody's test scores using the mean and standard deviation.

Zack	81	72	91	88	71	73	82	100	81	91
Cody	86	80	86	84	72	80	90	85	89	92

Compare the **mean** of Zack and Cody's test scores. Whose average is higher?

Zack: $\dfrac{81 + 72 + 91 + 88 + 71 + 73 + 82 + 100 + 81 + 91}{10} = \dfrac{825}{10} = 83$

Cody: $\dfrac{86 + 80 + 86 + 84 + 72 + 80 + 90 + 85 + 89 + 92}{10} = \dfrac{844}{10} = 84.4$

Cody's test average is higher.

Now compare their test scores using the **standard deviation**.

The formula for standard deviation is $S = \sqrt{\dfrac{1}{N-1}\left(\sum_{i=1}^{N}(x_i - \overline{x})^2\right)}$

Zack's standard deviation $= \sqrt{\dfrac{1}{N-1}\left(\sum_{i=1}^{N}(x_i - \overline{x})^2\right)}$

$= \sqrt{\dfrac{(-2)^2 + (-11)^2 + (8)^2 + (5)^2 + (-12)^2 + (-10)^2 + (-1)^2 + (17)^2 + (-2)^2 + (8)^2}{10 - 1}}$

$= 9.52$

Cody's standard deviation $= \sqrt{\dfrac{1}{N-1}\left(\sum_{i=1}^{N}(x_i - \overline{x})^2\right)}$

$= \sqrt{\dfrac{(1.6)^2 + (-4.4)^2 + (1.6)^2 + (-0.4)^2 + (-12.4)^2 + (-4.4)^2 + (-5.6)^2 + (0.6)^2 + (4.6)^2 + (7.6)^2}{10 - 1}}$

$= 5.85$

Cody's standard deviation is lower. This means that most of Cody's scores are closer to his mean, then Zack's scores are to his own mean.

Use the chart below for problems 1–3.

Sample A	60	71	73	69	80	82
Sample B	71	74	73	79	81	80

1. Find the means.

2. Find the standard deviations.

3. Use what you know from questions 1 and 2 to compare the data sets.

Use the bar graph below for problems 4–6.

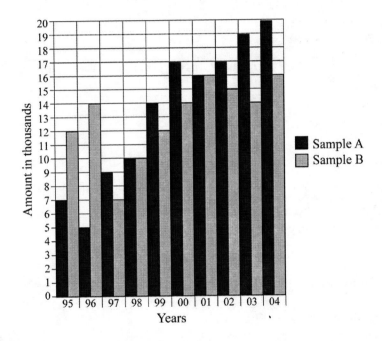

4. Find the means.

5. Find the standard deviations.

6. Use what you know from questions 4 and 5 to compare the data sets.

7. Kristen has decided to investigate whether coffee drinkers or tea drinkers consume more cups of their preferred beverage. To do so she interviewed a random group of 6 coffee drinkers and asked them how many cups of coffee they drank in the last week. She then interviewed a random group of 6 tea drinkers and asked them the same question. The mean amount of cups of coffee that a coffee drinker drank in the last week was 26, and the standard deviation of the coffee drinkers' responses was 4 cups. Also, the mean amount of cups of tea that a tea drinker drank in the last week was 22, and the standard deviation of the tea drinkers' responses was 3 cups. Which data set has the higher mean? Which data set has the higher standard deviation? What can you conclude?

7.6   Comparing Simple Data Sets to Corresponding Population Parameters

Statistics can also be used to compare a small group of data to a large group of data.

The mean (average) is the only value that is sensitive to extreme values. The process of comparing averages is used for samples that are very large. In cases where the sample is very large, we call the estimate of that data a **parameter**. In cases where we take the time to measure the entire population, the parameter becomes known as the **population parameter**.

Example 8:   Stephen is a student at North Cobb High School. Look at the following chart. The chart displays the average amount of money earned each week by each student (rounded to the nearest one) in Stephen's English class and the average amount of money earned each week by each of the students (rounded to the nearest one) in the ninth-grade class at his school. The chart also displays the standard deviation for each data set.

	Stephen's English Class	North Cobb High School's Ninth Grade
Mean	$21	$23
Standard Deviation	$2	$4

Compare the **means**. Whose average is higher?

The ninth grade class's average is higher.

Now compare the amount of money earned using the **standard deviation**.

The ninth grade class as a whole has a higher standard deviation. This means that the population distribution has more variability than the distribution of the smaller data set of Stephen's English class.

NOTE: The distribution of sample means has less variability than the population distribution.

Answer the questions about each situation.

1. To find the average number of calories consumed per day by 21- to 30-year-olds, the number of daily calories consumed by each member of a large random sample of people in this age group was determined. The mean number of calories consumed per day by members of the sample was 3500 calories, and the standard deviation of daily calories consumed was 250 calories. A smaller data sample was observed also. This smaller set consisted of 35 21- to 30-year-olds. The mean for this sample was 2800 calories, and the standard deviation was 165 calories. Which data set has the higher mean? Which data set has the higher standard deviation? What can you conclude?

2. To find the average number of ties owned by men, the number of ties owned by each man in a large random sample of 1600 men was determined. The mean number of ties owned by men in this population is 13 ties, and the standard deviation of the number of ties is 4 ties. A smaller data sample was observed also. This smaller set consisted of 43 men. The mean for this sample was 15 ties, and the standard deviation was 2 ties. Which data set has the higher mean? Which data set has the higher standard deviation? What can you conclude?

7.7   More Comparing Samples with Corresponding Population Parameters

Oftentimes, the data values in a population follow a normal distribution. In a normal distribution, the mean of the data is the center of the curve, where the probability of the event is 50%. If this curve below measured the wait in minutes for a table at a restaurant instead of percent, then you can see that a few people waited 2.15 minutes or less, a few people waited 97.7 minutes or more, but most of the people waited about 50 minutes.

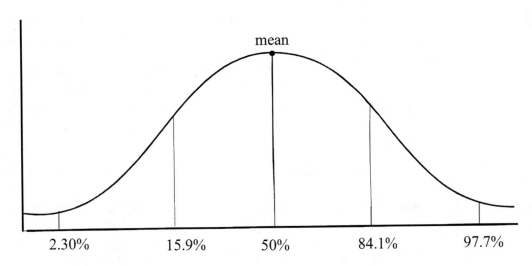

When a large random sample is drawn from a population, the mean and the standard deviation of the sample's data values approximate the mean and the standard deviation of the data values of the entire population, and if the data values of the population follow a normal distribution, the data values of the sample will also follow a normal distribution. The majority of people fall into the 15.9–84.1% range. This includes the range of people within one standard deviation from the mean.

Example 9:   To find the average age of the citizens of a country of $50,000,000$ people, the age of each citizen in a large random sample of citizens of the country was determined. The mean age of the citizens in the sample was 37 years, and the standard deviation of the ages of the citizens in the sample was 12 years. If the ages of the citizens of the country follow a normal distribution, how many citizens of the country are from 13 years old to 61 years old?

Step 1:   Determine how many standard deviations from the mean the range in question covers.

The range in question is from 13 years old to 61 years old. Since the mean age of the citizens in the sample was 37 years, and since the standard deviation of the ages was 12 years, the range in question covers ± 2 standard deviations from the mean. This is because $37 - (2)(12) = 37 - 24 = 13$ years old, and $37 + (2)(12) = 37 + 24 = 61$ years old.

Step 2:   Determine what percent of the population falls within the range in question.

Since the range from 13 years old to 61 years old covers ± 2 standard deviations from the mean, and since the ages of the citizens of the country follow a normal distribution, approximately 2.30–97.7% of the citizens of the country are from 13 years old to 61 years old, which is $97.7 - 2.30 = 95.4\%$ of the total population.

Step 3:   Determine how many data values of the population fall within the range in question.

Since 95.4% of the citizens of the country are from 13 years old to 61 years old, and since there are $50,000,000$ people in the country, the number of citizens of the country who are from 13 years old to 61 years old is $(0.954)(50,000,000)$, or $47,700,000$.

For each of the following questions, a large random sample was taken from a normally distributed population, and the sample mean, sample standard deviation, and population size are given. Determine the number of data values in the population that fall within the range in question.

1. Sample: mean $= 28$ weeks; standard deviation $= 3$ weeks; Population size: $30,000$;
   Range: 25 weeks to 31 weeks

2. Sample: mean $= \$40,000$; standard deviation $= \$1,000$; Population size: $125,000$;
   Range: $38,000 to $42,000

3. Sample: mean $= 55$ miles; standard deviation $= 6$ miles; Population size: $65,000$;
   Range: 49 miles to 61 miles

4. Sample: mean $= 195$ pounds; standard deviation $= 15$ pounds; Population size: $220,000$;
   Range: 165 pounds to 225 pounds

5. Sample: mean $= 79$ degrees; standard deviation $= 7$ degrees; Population size: $410,000$;
   Range: 65 degrees to 93 degrees

6. Sample: mean $= 42$ watts; standard deviation $= 5$ watts; Population size: $95,000$;
   Range: 37 watts to 47 watts

7. Sample: mean $= 82$ meters; standard deviation $= 9$ meters; Population size: $55,000$;
   Range: 64 meters to 100 meters

8. Sample: mean $= 75$ decibels; standard deviation $= 8$ decibels; Population size: $900,000$;
   Range: 67 decibels to 83 decibels

Chapter 7 Review

Use the following situation to answer questions 1–4.

Jay has decided to investigate whether runners or non-runners in the same age group have higher resting heart rates. To do so he took the resting heart rate of a random group of runners aged 35 to 40 years. He then did the same with a random group of non-runners aged 35 to 40 years. Finally, he came to a conclusion by determining the average resting heart rate for a member of each group and comparing the two.

1. What are the two populations being investigated?

2. What is the difference between the two populations?

3. Determine the two samples being compared.

4. What statistic is being compared?

Calculate the mean of each of the following sets of data. Use the appropriate unit of measurement in each answer.

5. 16 AU, 14 AU, 23 AU, 45 AU, 31 AU, 10 AU, 18 AU, 20 AU, 42 AU, 41 AU

6. 24 weeks, 25 weeks, 3 weeks, 5 weeks, 11 weeks, 15 weeks, 30 weeks, 7 weeks

7. 76 ounces, 68 ounces, 82 ounces, 59 ounces, 63 ounces, 73 ounces, 62 ounces

8. 3 decameters, 5 decameters, 8 decameters, 1 decameter, 2 decameters, 5 decameters

9. 43 minutes, 44 minutes, 39 minutes, 29 minutes, 40 minutes, 48 minutes, 44 minutes

10. 7 ohms, 6 ohms, 9 ohms, 5 ohms, 6 ohms, 7 ohms, 4 ohms, 7 ohms, 9 ohms, 10 ohms

Calculate the standard deviation of each of the following data samples. Use the appropriate unit of measurement in each answer.

11. 13 light years, 9 light years, 19 light years, 8 light years, 13 light years, 4 light years

12. 811 hertz, 799 hertz, 803 hertz, 804 hertz, 800 hertz, 802 hertz, 810 hertz, 809 hertz

13. 48 milligrams, 57 milligrams, 51 milligrams, 50 milligrams, 60 milligrams

14. 29 bushels, 39 bushels, 38 bushels, 31 bushels, 28 bushels, 37 bushels, 67 bushels

Calculate the standard deviation of each of the following sets of data. Assume that each set of data represents an entire population, and use the appropriate unit of measurement in each answer.

15. 105 kilowatts, 108 kilowatts, 120 kilowatts, 102 kilowatts, 116 kilowatts, 99 kilowatts

16. 310 Pa, 303 Pa, 321 Pa, 297 Pa, 307 Pa, 308 Pa, 311 Pa, 300 Pa, 301 Pa, 332 Pa

17. Bob has decided to investigate whether dog owners or cat owners spend more money on their pets. To do so he interviewed a random group of 5 dog owners and asked them how much money they spent on their dogs in the last year. He then interviewed a random group of 5 cat owners and asked them the same question. The mean amount of money that a dog owner spent on his pet in the last year was $5000, and the standard deviation of the dog owners' responses was $400. Also, the mean amount of money that a cat owner spent on his pet in the last year was $4900, and the standard deviation of the cat owners' responses was $300. Which data set has the higher mean? Which data set has the higher standard deviation? What can you conclude?

18. To find the average height in centimeters of the citizens of a country, the height of each citizen in a random sample of 1000 citizens of the country was determined. The mean height of the citizens in the sample was then calculated to be 165 centimeters. The standard deviation of the heights of the citizens in the country is 8 centimeters. A smaller data sample was observed also. This smaller set consisted of 50 citizens. The mean for this sample was 162 centimeters, and the standard deviation was 4.5 centimeters. Which data set has the higher mean? Which data set has the higher standard deviation? What can you conclude?

For each of the following questions, a large random sample was taken from a normally distributed population, and the sample mean, sample standard deviation, and population size are given. Determine the number of data values in the population that fall within the range in question.

19. Sample: mean = 9 inches; standard deviation = 2 inches; Population size: 180,000; Range: 5 inches to 13 inches

20. Sample: mean = 43 nanoseconds; standard deviation = 6 nanoseconds; Population size: 60,000; Range: 37 nanoseconds to 49 nanoseconds

21. Sample: mean = 126 people; standard deviation = 13 people; Population size: 990,000; Range: 100 people to 152 people

22. Sample: mean = 88 milliliters; standard deviation = 9 milliliters; Population size: 280,000; Range: 70 milliliters to 106 milliliters

23. Sample: mean = 22 yards; standard deviation = 3 yards; Population size: 40,000; Range: less than 19 yards

24. Sample: mean = 4.2 centuries; standard deviation = 0.4 centuries; Population size: 70,000; Range: more than 5 centuries

Chapter 7 Test

1. Erin has decided to investigate whether nurses or doctors work more hours. To do so she interviewed a random group of nurses and asked them how many hours per week they worked. She then interviewed a random group of doctors and asked them the same question. Which of the following is one of the populations being investigated?

   A. The random group of nurses
   B. The random group of doctors
   C. All doctors and nurses
   D. Erin

2. What is the mean of the following set of data: 2 days, 7 days, 3 day, 4 days?

   A. 4 days
   B. 4.5 days
   C. 5 days
   D. 5.5 days

3. A random sample of 7 students had the following scores on a quiz: 8 points; 9 points; 8 points; 6 points; 7 points; 6 points; 2 points. Which of the following is the best approximation of the standard deviation of the sample of quiz scores?

   A. 1.30 points
   B. 2.13 points
   C. 2.30 points
   D. 3.13 points

4. A large random sample was taken from a normally distributed population. The sample mean is 3 feet, the sample standard deviation is 0.5 feet, and population size is 850,000. Determine the number of data values in the population that are greater than 4 feet.

   A. 9,690
   B. 21,250
   C. 38,760
   D. 77,520

5. To determine the blood pressure of women over 60 years of age, a random group of women who are over 60 years old is to be formed. Which of the following is the best way to form the random group?

   A. Randomly choose women who are over 60 years old who shop at a certain store.
   B. Randomly choose women who are over 60 years old who go to a certain gym.
   C. Randomly choose women who are over 60 years old who take a certain medication.
   D. Randomly choose women who are over 60 years old who go to a certain library.

6. A data set consists of 8 values and has a mean of 227.5 gallons. 7 of the data values are as follows: 120 gallons; 280 gallons; 215 gallons; 325 gallons; 200 gallons; 135 gallons; 305 gallons. What is the 8th data value in the set?

   A. 220 gallons
   B. 230 gallons
   C. 240 gallons
   D. 250 gallons

7. The mean of a data sample was calculated, and it was then subtracted from each data value in the sample. Each difference was then squared, and the squared differences were then added together. Finally, the sum of the squared differences was divided by 1 less than the number of data values. What is the term used to describe the result?

   A. Deviation
   B. Mean
   C. Sample Standard Deviation
   D. Population Standard Deviation

8. To find the average value of a house in a state, the value of each house in a random sample of 3000 houses in the state was determined. The mean value of a house in the sample was then calculated, and the process was repeated many more times, with a new sample of 3000 houses used each time. Which of the following statements is true?

A. The variability of the sample means will be greater than the variability of the values of all the houses in the state.

B. The variability of the sample means will be less than the variability of the values of all the houses in the state.

C. The variability of the sample means will be the same as the variability of the values of all the houses in the state.

D. Nothing can be determined about the variability of the sample means.

9. If the data values in a population follow a normal distribution, about what percentage of the values will fall within ± 1 standard deviation of the mean?

A. 70%
B. 78%
C. 95%
D. 99.5%

Chapter 8
Step and Piecewise Functions

This chapter covers the following Georgia Performance Standards:

MM2A	Algebra	MM2A1a
		MM2A1b
		MM2A1c

8.1   Graphs of Step and Piecewise Functions

There are a number of types of graphs that you may see on the GA Math II which are not linear or quadratic.

A **piecewise** function is a function consisting of 2 or more formulas over a sequence of intervals. These intervals are defined by the possible values of x, also known as the domain of the function. The graph of a piecewise function consists of the graphs of each interval formula.

Example 1: $f(x) = \begin{cases} x & \text{where } x < -2 \\ 2x + 1 & \text{where } x \geq -2 \end{cases}$

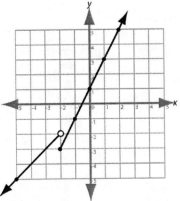

Notice that there is a break in the graph at $x = -2$. Whenever you would have to pick up your pencil in order to draw the graph from left to right, the function is **discontinuous**. At every other point in a function, the function is **continuous**.

A particular type of piecewise defined function is the **absolute value** function. The absolute value of a number is its distance from 0. The absolute value of x is written $|x|$.

Example 2: $f(x) = |x| = \begin{cases} -x & \text{where} \quad x < 0 \\ x & \text{where} \quad x \geq 0 \end{cases}$

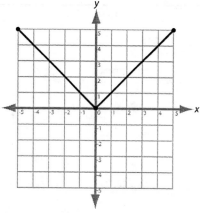

The absolute value function always gives a positive number, but it is **not** discontinuous at $x = 0$, because you do not have to pick up your pencil to draw it.

Another common type of piecewise defined function is a **step** function. Instead of a continuous increase or decrease of y from left to right, the y value stays the same for certain interval of x, then jumps to a higher or lower level. It therefore looks like a set of steps going up or down.

Example 3: $f(x) = \begin{cases} 0 & \text{where} \quad 0 \leq x < 1 \\ 1 & \text{where} \quad 1 \leq x < 2 \\ 2 & \text{where} \quad 2 \leq x < 3 \\ 3 & \text{where} \quad 3 \leq x < 4 \\ 4 & \text{where} \quad 4 \leq x \leq 5 \end{cases}$

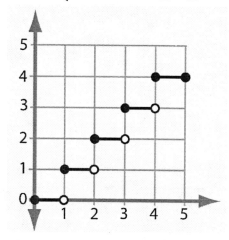

The graph is discontinuous at every "step," in this case $x = 1$, $x = 2$, $x = 3$, and $x = 4$.

8.2   Characteristics of Piecewise Functions

In addition to continuity, there are a number of features that you can identify from the graph of a piecewise function.

Zeros are the points where $y = 0$. The zeros are the function's x-intercepts.

The **maximum** (plural: maxima) is the highest y value that a function reaches.

The **minimum** (plural: minima) is the lowest y value that a function reaches.

The **range** is all of the y values that are defined by the function.

Similarly, the **domain** is all of the x values defined by the function.

Finally, you can determine the **rate of increase or decrease** between two points by finding the rise over the run (slope).

Example 4:   What are the zeroes, maximum, minimum, range, and domain of the function below? At what point is the function discontinuous? Also, what is the rate of increase between $x = 0$ and $x = 2$.

$$y = \begin{cases} 2x & \text{where} \quad 0 \leq x \leq 2 \\ \frac{x}{2} & \text{where} \quad 2 < x \leq 4 \end{cases}$$

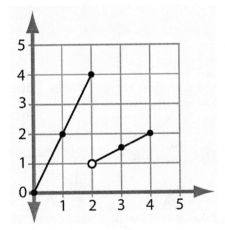

Zeros: Where does $y = 0$? Where does the graph intersect the x-intercept? Only at $x = 0$.

Maximum: Highest point is $(2, 4)$. Since the maximum point of the graph is always the largest y value that the graph reaches, 4 is the maximum.

Minimum: Lowest point is $(0, 0)$. Since the minimum point of the graph is always the smallest y value that the graph reaches, 0 is the minimum.

Range: Maximum $-$ Minimum $= 4 - 0 = 4$

Domain: Highest x $-$ Lowest $x = 4 - 0 = 4$

The function is discontinuous at $x = 2$.

Rate of increase between $x = 0$ and $x = 2$: At $x = 0$, $y = 0$. At $x = 2$, $y = 4$. Therefore, the rise is $4 - 0 = 4$, and the run is $2 - 0 = 2$.

Slope = rise over run $= \frac{4}{2} = 2$.

Use the following graph of the absolute value function $y = |x - 2|$ for questions 1 and 2.

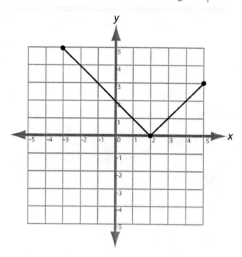

1. According to the graph, what is the minimum value of the function?

   A. -3
   B. 0
   C. 2
   D. 5

2. At what point is this graph discontinuous?

   A. $(-3, 5)$
   B. $(0, 2)$
   C. $(2, 0)$
   D. None of the above. The graph is continuous.

Use the following graph of a piecewise defined function for questions 3 and 4.

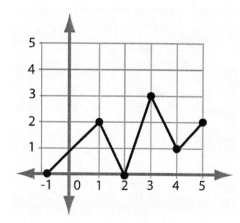

3. How many zeros does this function have?

   A. -1
   B. 0
   C. 1
   D. 2

4. What are the range and domain of the function?

   A. range: $0 \leq y \leq 3$, domain: $-3 \leq x \leq 5$
   B. range: $-3 \leq x \leq 3$, domain: $0 \leq y \leq 5$
   C. range: $-1 \leq x \leq 5$, domain: $0 \leq y \leq 3$
   D. range: $0 \leq y \leq 3$, domain: $-1 \leq x \leq 5$

Use the following graph of a step function for questions 5 and 6.

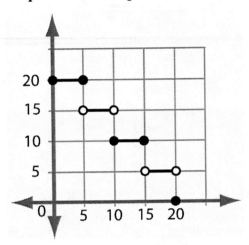

5. At how many points is this graph discontinuous?

   A. 4
   B. 8
   C. 6
   D. 2

6. What is the rate of increase of the function between 10 and 15?

   A. -5
   B. 0
   C. 1
   D. 5

Use the following graph of a step function for questions 7 and 8.

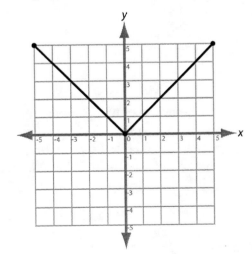

7. What is the vertex of this graph?

   A. $(0,0)$
   B. $(-5,5)$
   C. $(5,5)$
   D. $(0,5)$

8. What is the domain of this function?

   A. $-5 \leq x < 5$
   B. $0 \leq y < \infty$
   C. $0 \leq x < \infty$
   D. all real numbers

8.3   More Piecewise Functions

A **piecewise function** is a function consisting of 2 or more formulas over a sequence of intervals. These **intervals** are defined by the possible values of x, also known as the domain of the function. The graph of a piecewise function consists of the graphs of each interval formula.

Example 5: $f(x) = \begin{cases} 3 & \text{if } 0 \leq x < 1 \\ 2 & \text{if } 1 \leq x < 2 \\ 1 & \text{if } 2 \leq x < 3 \end{cases}$

Graph $f(x)$.

Step 1: Graph each formula over the given interval.

For example, $f(x) = 3$ when the domain is $0 \leq x < 1$. This means that you would draw the graph $y = 3$ first. (Recall that this is a horizontal line segment that passes through the point $(0, 3)$.) After this, you would only draw $y = 3$ between the points $(0, 3)$ and $(1, 3)$ because of the domain. The graph cannot go outside of those points.

When $f(x) = 2$ and the domain is $1 \leq x < 2$, draw the graph $y = 2$ between the points $(1, 2)$ and $(2, 2)$.

When $f(x) = 1$ and the domain is $2 \leq x < 3$, draw the graph $y = 1$ between the points $(2, 1)$ and $(3, 1)$.

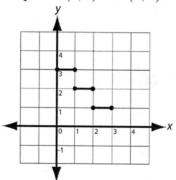

Step 2: Since the function cannot have two y values for an x value (otherwise, it would not be a function), you must look at the inequalities in the domain. When the inequality is less than or equal to ($\leq$), you must draw the endpoint as a filled in circle. This shows that the function includes that point. For the strict inequalities ($<$), you must draw an endpoint with an open (not filled in) circle.

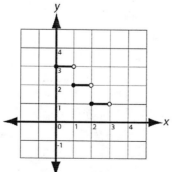

Example 6: $f(x) = \begin{cases} x^2 & \text{if } x \geq 2 \\ 3 - x & \text{if } x < 2 \end{cases}$

Find (A) $f(1)$, (B) $f(3)$, and (C) $f(2)$.

Step 1:   Determine which interval of the domain includes the value of x.
(A) For $f(1)$, $x = 1$. Since 1 is less than 2, you would plug $x = 1$ into $3 - x$.
(B) For $f(3)$, $x = 3$. Since 3 is greater than 2, you would plug $x = 3$ into x^2.
(C) For $f(2)$, $x = 2$. Since 2 is equal to 2, you would plug $x = 2$ into x^2.

Step 2:   Plug the value of x into the appropriate formula to solve for the value of $f(x)$.
(A) $f(x) = 3 - x$, so $f(1) = 3 - 1 = 2$
(B) $f(x) = x^2$, so $f(3) = (3)^2 = 9$
(C) $f(x) = x^2$, so $f(2) = (2)^2 = 4$

Graph each of the following functions.

1. $f(x) = \begin{cases} x & \text{if } x \geq 0 \\ -x & \text{if } x < 0 \end{cases}$

2. $f(x) = \begin{cases} 1 & \text{if } x < 1 \\ x^2 & \text{if } x \geq 1 \end{cases}$

3. $f(x) = \begin{cases} \sqrt{x} & \text{if } x \geq 2 \\ x^2 & \text{if } x < 2 \end{cases}$

4. $f(x) = \begin{cases} 2x + 3 & \text{if } x < 0 \\ 2x - 3 & \text{if } x \geq 0 \end{cases}$

5. $f(x) = \begin{cases} x^2 & \text{if } x < -1 \\ x & \text{if } -1 \leq x \leq 1 \\ -(x^2) & \text{if } x > 1 \end{cases}$

6. Phil's long distance phone service charges him 50 cents for the first 10 minutes and 10 cents for each minute afterwards. Graph the function that represents Phil's long distance phone service and find how much he would pay for

(A) a 5 minute call.
(B) a 10 minute call.
(C) a 15 minute call.

7. The tuition at State University is determined by the number of class hours a student takes. Tuition is $100 for the first three hours and doubles every 3 hours up to 12 hours. After 12 hours, tuition does not change. Graph the function that represents the tuition at State University and find the tuition for a student taking

(A) 6 class hours.
(B) 12 class hours.
(C) 15 class hours.

8.4   Solving Equations and Inequalities with Absolute Values

When solving equations and inequalities which involve variables placed in absolute values, remember that there will be two or more numbers that will work as correct answers. This is because the absolute value variable will signify both positive and negative numbers as answers.

Example 7: $5 + 3\,|k| = 8$ Solve as you would any equation.

   Step 1: $3\,|k| = 3$ Subtract 5 from each side.

   Step 2: $|k| = 1$ Divide by 3 on each side.

   Step 3: $k = 1$ or $k = -1$ Because k is an absolute value, the answer can be 1 or -1.

Example 8: $2\,|x| - 3 < 7$ Solve as you normally would an inequality.

   Step 1: $2\,|x| < 10$ Add 3 to both sides.

   Step 2: $|x| < 5$ Divide by 2 on each side.

   Step 3: $x < 5$ or $x > -5$ Because x is an absolute value, the answer is a set of both
   or $-5 < x < 5$ positive and negative numbers.

Read each problem, and write the number or set of numbers which solves each equation or inequality.

1. $7 + 2\,|y| = 15$

2. $4\,|x| - 9 < 3$

3. $6\,|k| + 2 = 14$

4. $10 - 4\,|n| > -14$

5. $-3 = 5\,|z| + 12$

6. $-4 + 7\,|m| < 10$

7. $5\,|x| - 12 > 13$

8. $21\,|g| + 7 = 49$

9. $-9 + 6\,|x| = 15$

10. $12 - 6\,|w| > -12$

11. $31 > 13 + 9\,|r|$

12. $-30 = 21 - 3\,|t|$

13. $9\,|x| - 19 < 35$

14. $-13\,|c| + 21 \geq -31$

15. $5 - 11\,|k| < -17$

16. $-42 + 14\,|p| = 14$

17. $15 < 3\,|b| + 6$

18. $9 + 5\,|q| = 29$

19. $-14\,|y| - 38 < -45$

20. $36 = 4\,|s| + 20$

21. $20 \leq -60 + 8\,|e|$

8.5   More Solving Equations and Inequalities with Absolute Values

Now, look at the following examples in which numbers and variables are added or subtracted within the absolute value symbols ($||$).

Example 9: $|3x - 5| = 10$ Remember an equation with absolute value symbols has two solutions.

Step 1: $3x - 5 = 10$ To find the first solution, remove the absolute value
$3x - 5 + 5 = 10 + 5$ symbol and solve the equation.
$\dfrac{\cancel{3}x}{\cancel{3}} = \dfrac{15}{3}$
$x = 5$

Step 2: $-(3x - 5) = 10$ To find the second solution, solve the equation for the
$-3x + 5 = 10$ negative of the expression in absolute value symbols.
$-3x + 5 - 5 = 10 - 5$
$-3x = 5$
$x = -\frac{5}{3}$

Solutions: $x = \left\{5, -\frac{5}{3}\right\}$

Example 10: $|5z - 10| < 20$ Remove the absolute value symbols and solve the inequality.

Step 1: $5z - 10 < 20$
$5z - 10 + 10 < 20 + 10$
$\dfrac{\cancel{5}z}{\cancel{5}} < \dfrac{30}{5}$
$z < 6$

Step 2: $-(5z - 10) < 20$ Next, solve the equation for the negative of the
$-5z + 10 < 20$ expression in the absolute value symbols.
$-5z + 10 - 10 < 20 - 10$

$\dfrac{-\cancel{5}z}{\cancel{5}} < \dfrac{10}{5}$
$-z < 2$
$z > -2$

Solution: $-2 < z < 6$

Example 11: $|4y + 7| - 5 > 18$

Step 1: $4y + 7 - 5 + 5 > 18 + 5$ Remove the absolute value symbols and solve the
$4y + 7 > 23$ inequality.
$4y + 7 - 7 > 23 - 7$
$4y > 16$
$y > 4$

Step 2: $-(4y + 7) - 5 > 18$ Solve the inequality for the negative of the
$-4y - 7 - 5 + 5 > 18 + 5$ expression in the absolute value symbols.
$-4y - 7 + 7 > 23 + 7$
$-4y > 30$
$y < -7\frac{1}{2}$

Solutions: $y > 4$ or $y < -7\frac{1}{2}$

Solve the following equations and inequalities below.

1. $-4 + |2x + 4| = 14$

2. $|4b - 7| + 3 > 12$

3. $6 + |12e + 3| < 39$

4. $-15 + |8f - 14| > 35$

5. $|-9b + 13| - 12 = 10$

6. $-25 + |7b + 11| < 35$

7. $|7w + 2| - 60 > 30$

8. $63 + |3d - 12| = 21$

9. $|-23 + 8x| - 12 > +37$

10. $|61 + 20x| + 32 > 51$

11. $|4a + 13| + 31 = 50$

12. $4 + |4k - 32| < 51$

13. $8 + |4x + 3| = 21$

14. $|28 + 7v| - 28 < 77$

15. $|62p + 31| + 43 = 136$

16. $18 - |6v + 22| < 22$

17. $12 = 4 + |42 + 10m|$

18. $53 < 18 + |12e + 31|$

19. $38 > -39 + |7j + 14|$

20. $9 = |14 + 15u| + 7$

21. $11 - |2j + 50| > 45$

22. $|35 + 6i| - 3 = 14$

23. $|26 - 8r| - 9 > 41$

24. $|25 + 6z| - 21 = 28$

25. $12 < |2t + 6| - 14$

26. $50 > |9q - 10| + 6$

27. $12 + |8v - 18| > 26$

28. $-38 + |16i - 33| = 41$

29. $|-14 + 6p| - 9 < 7$

30. $28 > |25 - 5f| - 12$

8.6 Solving Absolute Value Equations Graphically

To solve an absolute value equation graphically, consider one side of the equation as one function and the other side of the equation as another function. Then graph the two functions and see where they intersect.

Example 12: Solve the absolute value equation $|x - 8| = 6$ graphically.

Step 1: First, rewrite the absolute value part of the function as $f(x) = |x - 8|$. Graph the function.

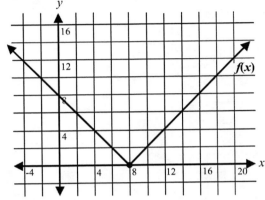

Step 2: Now, rewrite the other side of the equation as $g(x) = 6$. Graph the function on the same graph.

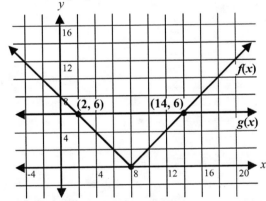

The solutions are the x-values when the y-value is 6. Looking at the graph, we can see that the two functions intersect at the points $(2, 6)$ and $(14, 6)$, so the solutions to the equation are $x = 2$ or $x = 14$.

Graph each of the following absolute value equations to find the solution, then check your answer analytically.

1. $|x + 4| = 11$

2. $|x - 3| = 8$

3. $|x - 5| = -1$

4. $|x + 10| = 2$

5. $|x - 7| = 0$

6. $|x + 6| = 13$

Example 13:   Solve the absolute value equation $-5\,|x+9| + 2 = -13$ graphically.

Step 1:   First, get the absolute value part of the equation to one side of the equation by itself.
Subtract 2 from both sides of the equation so that it becomes $-5\,|x+9| = -15$, and then divide both sides of the equation by -5 so that it becomes $|x+9| = 3$.

Step 2:   Now, rewrite the absolute value part of the function as $f(x) = |x+9|$. Graph the function.

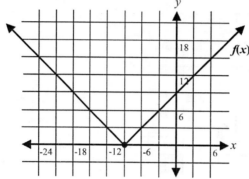

Step 3:   Now, rewrite the other side of the equation as $g(x) = 3$. Graph the function on the same graph.

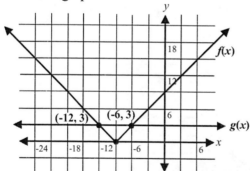

The solutions are the x-values when the y-value is 3. Looking at the graph, we can see that the two functions intersect at the points $(-12, 3)$ and $(-6, 3)$, so the solutions to the equation are $x = -12$ or $x = -6$.

Graph each of the following absolute value equations to find the solution, then check your answer analytically.

1. $6\,|x+2| - 1 = 11$

2. $-3\,|x-8| + 4 = -17$

3. $\frac{3}{5}\,|x+10| = 24$

4. $7\,|x-1| - 5 = 9$

5. $-2\,|x| + 17 = -19$

6. $8\,|x+7| - 2 = 46$

8.7 Solving Absolute Value Inequalities Graphically

To solve an absolute value inequality graphically, consider one side of the inequality as one function and the other side of the inequality as another function. Then graph the two functions and see where they meet the conditions of the inequality.

Example 14: Solve the absolute value inequality $|x + 5| < 2$ graphically.

Step 1: First, rewrite the absolute value part of the function as $f(x) = |x + 5|$. Graph the function.

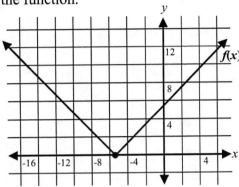

Step 2: Now, rewrite the other side of the inequality as $g(x) = 2$. Graph the function on the same graph.

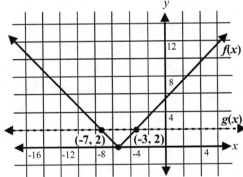

A dotted line is graphed at $g(x) = 2$. All of the x-values on the graph $f(x) = |x + 5|$ that are below (or less than) the graph of $g(x) = 2$ are solutions. The solution to the inequality is $-7 < x < -3$.

Graph each of the following absolute value inequalities to find the solution, then check your answer analytically.

1. $|x - 7| < 8$

2. $|x + 11| \leq 3$

3. $|x + 9| < 16$

4. $|x - 2| < 21$

5. $|x - 12| \leq 1$

6. $|x + 4| < 17$

Example 15:   Solve the absolute value inequality $7\,|x-2|-8 \geq 6$ graphically.

Step 1:   First, get the absolute value part of the inequality to one side of the equation by itself.
First add 8 to both sides of the inequality $7\,|x-2|-8 \geq 6$ so that it becomes $7\,|x-2| \geq 14$, and then to divide both sides of the inequality by 7 so that it becomes $|x-2| \geq 2$.

Step 2:   Now, rewrite the absolute value part of the function as $f(x) = |x-2|$. Graph the function.

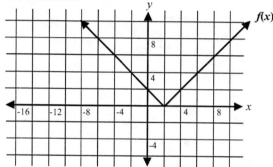

Step 3:   Now, rewrite the other side of the inequality as $g(x) = 2$. Graph the function on the same graph.

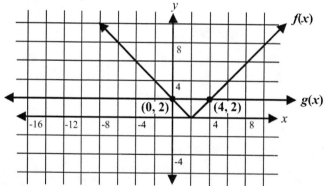

All of the x-values on the graph $f(x) = |x-2|$ that are above or on (greater than or equal to) the graph of $g(x) = 2$ are solutions. The solution to the inequality is $x \leq 0$ or $x \geq 4$.

Graph each of the following absolute value inequalities to find the solution, then check your answer analytically.

1. $3\,|x+9| > 24$

2. $-4\,|x-10|+5 \geq -11$

3. $2\,|x-6|-13 > 1$

4. $8\,|x+5|+4 \geq 36$

5. $9\,|x+1|-2 \geq 43$

6. $5\,|x-18|-6 > 9$

Chapter 8 Review

Solve the following equations and inequalities below.

1. $-11 |k| < -22$

2. $18 - 3 |w| > -18$

3. $2 |2(6x + 1)| = 6$

4. $21 = -4 + |5x + 5|$

5. $\left| x + \frac{7}{10} \right| = 1$

6. $\left| \frac{7x}{2} + 7 \right| = 4$

7. $|3x + 2| - 4 \geq -2$

8. $|10x + 4| < 7$

9. $|-3x - 7| \geq 11$

10. $4 |-6x + 8| > 12$

11. $|5(3x - 1)| = 20$

12. $\left| \frac{x}{6} - 16 \right| \leq 5$

13. $|6x + 1| = 11$

14. $7 |4x + 5| \geq 35$

15. $|15x - 2| > \frac{3}{4}$

16. $|4x - 3| = 10$

17. $|-2x + 9| = 13$

18. $\left| \frac{2x}{5} - 8 \right| = 9$

Solve each of the following absolute value equations graphically.

19. $|x + 16| = 2$

20. $|x - 9| = 5$

21. $4 |x - 3| = 52$

22. $-7 |x + 5| + 2 = -12$

23. $\frac{1}{18} |3(x + 5)| + 6 = 9$

24. $8 |2(x - 1)| - 1 = 15$

Solve each of the following absolute value inequalities graphically.

25. $|x - 9| \leq 22$

26. $|x + 17| > 31$

27. $3 |x - 7| - 19 < 5$

28. $4 |x + 13| - 24 > 8$

29. $8 |5(x - 7)| - 29 < 11$

30. $7 |2(x + 8)| + 3 > 59$

Answer the following questions about the nonlinear graphs.

Notre Pere College Preparatory Academy uses a 4.0 scale for its grades, to emphasize its college preparatory curriculum. Mr. Beau teaches the senior economics class, and he uses the grading scale graphed below.

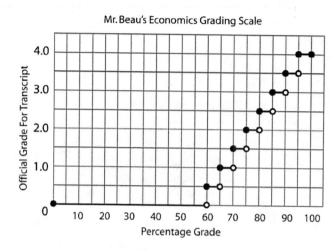

31. MaryLee scored an average of 83% in the course. What was her official 4.0 scale grade?

32. What the domain and range of this function?

Answer questions 33–34 about the graph.

The graph of function $y = \begin{cases} -x & \text{where } x < 0 \\ x^2 - 4 & \text{where } x \geq 0 \end{cases}$ is shown below.

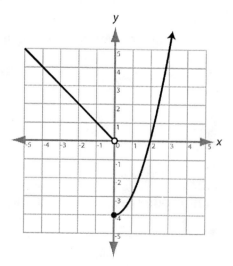

33. Where is the graph discontinuous?

34. What is (are) the zero(s) of this graph?

Chapter 8 Test

1. Which of the following absolute value equations can be solved with the graph shown?

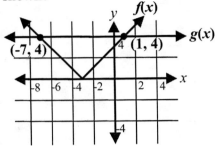

   A. $|x - 4| = 3$
   B. $|x - 3| = 4$
   C. $|x + 3| = 4$
   D. $|x + 4| = 3$

2. What is the solution to the absolute value inequality $|3(5x + 8)| < 42$?

   A. $x < -\frac{22}{5}$ or $x > \frac{6}{5}$

   B. $-\frac{22}{5} < x < \frac{6}{5}$

   C. $x < \frac{6}{5}$ or $x > \frac{22}{5}$

   D. $\frac{6}{5} < x < \frac{22}{5}$

3. If $3|x - 5| + 7 > 49$, and if $f(x) = |x - 5|$ and $g(x) = 14$, for what values of x is the graph of $f(x)$ above the graph of $g(x)$?

   A. $x < -19$ or $x > 9$
   B. $-19 < x < 9$
   C. $x < -9$ or $x > 19$
   D. $-9 < x < 19$

4. Which of the following absolute value inequalities has the solution $-14 \le x \le 10$?

   A. $-6|x - 2| \le -72$
   B. $-6|x - 2| \ge -72$
   C. $-6|x + 2| \le -72$
   D. $-6|x + 2| \ge -72$

5. The graph of the function $f(x) = \left|x + \frac{1}{5}\right|$ intersects the graph of the function $g(x) = a$ at one point. If $\left|x + \frac{1}{5}\right| \le a$, what is the value of a?

   A. $-\frac{1}{5}$

   B. 0

   C. $\frac{1}{5}$

   D. 5

6. Solve: $39 + |10x - 8| > 41$

   A. $x = 1$
   B. $x > 1$ or $x < \frac{3}{5}$
   C. $x > \frac{3}{5}$
   D. $x > 1$ or $x < -1$

7. Solve: $|4x + 13| = 5$

   A. $x = -2$
   B. $x = 2$ or $x = 4.5$
   C. $x = -4.5$
   D. $x = -4.5$ or $x = -2$

8. Solve: $4|7x - 6| \ge 60$

   A. $x \le -\frac{9}{7}$

   B. $x \le -\frac{9}{7}$ or $x \ge 3$

   C. $x \le 3$

   D. $-\frac{9}{7} \le x \le 3$

9. Solve: $|6(3x + 1)| = 42$

   A. $x = -\frac{8}{3}$ or $x = 2$

   B. $x = \frac{8}{3}$ or $x = -2$

   C. $x = 2$

   D. $x = -\frac{8}{3}$

Holly's family goes to the BWI airport to pick up her Grandma Jean, who is flying in today. They park in the Hourly parking garage, only to find out that Grandma Jean's flight is delayed. The graph below shows the cost of parking in the Hourly parking lot.

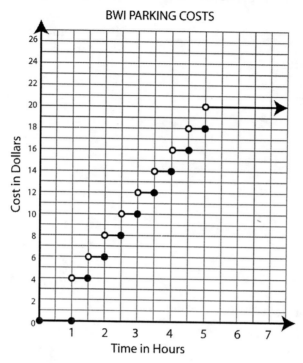

BWI PARKING COSTS

10. According to the graph, if Holly's family is parked for a total of 3 hours and 15 minutes, how much will they pay for parking?

   A. $12
   B. $13
   C. $14
   D. $16

11. What is the maximum amount Holly's family could pay for parking today in the Hourly parking lot?

   A. $0
   B. $20
   C. $80
   D. $108

Chapter 9
Exponents

This chapter covers the following Georgia Performance Standards:

| MM2A | Algebra | MM2A2a |

9.1 Understanding Exponents

Sometimes it is necessary to multiply a number by itself one or more times. For example, a math problem may need to multiply 3×3 or $5 \times 5 \times 5 \times 5$. In these situations, mathematicians have come up with a shorter way of writing out this kind of multiplication. Instead of writing 3×3, you can write 3^2, or instead of writing $5 \times 5 \times 5 \times 5$, 5^4 means the same thing. The first number is the **base**. The small, raised number is called the **exponent** or **power**. The exponent tells how many times the base should be multiplied by itself.

Example 1: 6^3 ← **exponent (or power)**   This means multiply by 6 three times: $6 \times 6 \times 6$
              ← **base**

Example 2:   **Negative numbers can be raised to exponents also.**
An **even** exponent will give a **positive** answer: $(-2)^2 = (-2) \times (-2) = 4$
An **odd** exponent will give a **negative** answer: $(-2)^3 = -2 \times -2 \times -2 = -8$

You also need to know two special properties of exponents:

> 1. **Any base number raised to the exponent of 1 equals the base number.**
> 2. **Any base number raised to the exponent of 0 equals 1.**

Example 3: $4^1 = 4$ $10^1 = 10$ $25^1 = 25$ $4^0 = 1$ $10^0 = 1$ $25^0 = 1$

Rewrite the following problems using exponents.

Example 4: $2 \times 2 \times 2 = 2^3$

1. $7 \times 7 \times 7 \times 7$ 2. 10×10 3. $12 \times 12 \times 12$ 4. $4 \times 4 \times 4 \times 4$

Use your calculator to figure what product each number with an exponent represents.

Example 5: $2^3 = 2 \times 2 \times 2 = 8$

5. $(-8)^3$ 6. 12^2 7. 20^1 8. 5^4

Express each of the following numbers as a base with an exponent.

Example 6: $4 = 2 \times 2 = 2^2$

9. 9   10. 16   11. 27   12. 36

9.2   Multiplication with Exponents

Rule 1:   To multiply two expressions with the same base, add the exponents together and keep the base the same.

Example 7: $2^3 \times 2^5 = 2^{3+5} = 2^8$

Rule 2:   If a power is raised to another power, multiply the exponents together and keep the base the same.

Example 8: $\left(2^3\right)^2 = 2^{3 \times 2} = 2^6$

Rule 3:   If a product in parenthesis is raised to a power, then each factor is raised to the power when parenthesis are eliminated.

Example 9: $(2 \times 4)^2 = 2^2 \times 4^2 = 4 \times 16 = 64$

Example 10: $(3a)^3 = 3^3 \times a^3 = 27a^3$

Example 11: $\left(7b^5\right)^2 = 7^2 b^{10} = 49b^{10}$

Simplify each of the expressions below.

1. $\left(5^3\right)^2$

2. $6^3 \times 6^5$

3. $4^3 \times 4^3$

4. $\left(7^5\right)^2$

5. $\left(6^2\right)^5$

6. $2^5 \times 2^3$

7. $(4 \times 5)^2$

8. $\left(3^4\right)^0$

9. $\left(3^3\right)^2$

10. $2^5 \times 2^5$

11. $(3 \times 3)^2$

12. $(2a)^4$

13. $\left(3^2\right)^4$

14. $4^5 \times 4^3$

15. $(3 \times 2)^4$

16. $\left(5^2\right)^2$

17. $(6 \times 4)^2$

18. $\left(9a^5\right)^3$

19. $4^3 \times 4^4$

20. $\left(6b^5\right)^2$

21. $\left(5^2\right)^3$

22. $3^7 \times 3^3$

23. $(3a)^2$

24. $\left(3^4\right)^2$

25. $\left(4^4\right)^2$

26. $\left(2b^3\right)^4$

27. $\left(5a^2\right)^5$

28. $\left(8a^3\right)^2$

29. $\left(9^2\right)^2$

30. $10^5 \times 10^4$

31. $(3 \times 5)^2$

32. $\left(7^3\right)^2$

9.3   Division with Exponents

Rule 1:   Expressions can also have negative exponents. Negative exponents do not indicate negative numbers. They indicate reciprocals, which is 1 over the original number.

Example 12: $2^{-3} = \dfrac{1}{2^3} = \dfrac{1}{8}$

Example 13: $3a^{-5} = 3 \times \dfrac{1}{a^5} = \dfrac{3}{a^5}$

Rule 2:   When dividing expressions with exponents that have the same base, subtract the exponents. Expressions in simplified form only have positive exponents.

Example 14: $\dfrac{3^5}{3^3} = 3^{5-3} = 3^2 = 9$

Example 15: $\dfrac{3^5}{3^8} = 3^{5-8} = 3^{-3} = \dfrac{1}{3^3} = \dfrac{1}{27}$

Rule 3:   If a fraction is raised to a power, then both the numerator and the denominator are raised to the same power.

Example 16: $\left(\dfrac{3}{4}\right)^3 = \dfrac{3^3}{4^3} = \dfrac{27}{64}$

Example 17: $(2x)^{-2} = \dfrac{1}{(2x)^2} = \dfrac{1}{4x^2}$

Reduce the following expressions to their simplest form. All exponents should be positive.

1. $5x^{-4}$

2. $\dfrac{2^2}{2^4}$

3. $\left(\dfrac{2}{3}\right)^2$

4. $6a^{-2}$

5. $\dfrac{3^6}{3^3}$

6. $(5a)^{-2}$

7. $\dfrac{3^4}{3^3}$

8. $\left(\dfrac{7}{8}\right)^3$

9. $(6a)^{-2}$

10. $\dfrac{(x^2)^3}{x^4}$

11. $\dfrac{(3y)^3}{3^2 y}$

12. $\dfrac{(3a^2)^3}{a^4}$

13. $(2x^2)^{-5}$

14. $2x^{-2}$

15. $(a^3)^{-2}$

16. $(2^{-2})^3$

17. $\left(\dfrac{1}{2}\right)^2$

18. $\dfrac{1}{3^{-2}}$

19. $(4y)^{-5}$

20. $4y^{-5}$

Chapter 9 Review

Simplify the following problems.

1. 15^0

2. $(-3)^3$

3. $5^2 \times 5^3$

4. $(4^4)^3$

5. $(3a^2)^{-2}$

6. $6x^{-3}$

7. $\dfrac{4^6}{4^4}$

8. $\left(\dfrac{3}{5}\right)^2$

9. $\dfrac{(3a^2)^3}{a^3}$

10. $\dfrac{6x^{-2}}{x^{-3}}$

11. $(4^4)^5$

12. $(4y^3)^3$

13. $x^3 \cdot x^{-7}$

14. $(2x)^{-4}$

15. $3^3 \times 3^2$

16. $(2^4)^2$

17. $5^7 \times 5^{-4}$

18. $(4^2)^{-2}$

19. $(5^{-9} \times 5^7)^{-2}$

20. $\dfrac{(2^3)^2}{2^4}$

21. $\dfrac{y^{-2}}{3y^4}$

22. $(4d^5)^{-3}$

Write as exponents.

23. $3 \times 3 \times 3 \times 3$

24. $6 \times 6 \times 6 \times 6 \times 6 \times 6$

25. $11 \times 11 \times 11$

26. $2 \times 2 \times 2 \times 2 \times 2 \times 2 \times 2 \times 2$

Simplify using laws of exponents.

27. If $y = z$, then $z^7 = ?$

28. If $m^5 = n^{15}$, then $m = ?$

29. If $d = f^3$, then $f^6 = ?$

30. If $g^2 = j^{16}$, then $g = ?$

Chapter 9 Test

1. What is $\dfrac{x^5}{x^3}$ in simplest terms?

   A. $x^{\frac{5}{3}}$

   B. x^8

   C. $x^5 x^{-3}$

   D. x^2

2. What is $\left(x^4\right)^3$ in simplest terms?

   A. x^{12}

   B. x^7

   C. x

   D. $\left(x^4\right)^3$

3. If $x = n^6$, then $n^{12} = ?$

   A. x^{12}

   B. $x^{\frac{1}{2}}$

   C. x^2

   D. x

4. What is $\left(x^7\right)^2$ in simplest terms?

   A. $\dfrac{1}{x^{14}}$

   B. x^5

   C. x^{-5}

   D. x^{14}

5. Simplify the expression shown below:
$$\frac{8x^4}{2x^2}$$

   A. $2x^4$

   B. $4x^2$

   C. $\dfrac{1}{4x^2}$

   D. $\dfrac{4x^2}{x}$

6. What is $a^4 \times a^7$ in simplest terms?

   A. a^{-3}

   B. a^{28}

   C. a^{11}

   D. a^3

7. If $x = n^2$, then $n^{10} = ?$

   A. n^{10}

   B. x^5

   C. n^2

   D. $x^{\frac{1}{5}}$

8. Simplify the following:
$$5 \cdot x^4 \cdot y^5 \cdot z^{-3}$$

   A. $\dfrac{5x^4 y^5}{z^3}$

   B. $\left(5xyz\right)^6$

   C. $\dfrac{625 x^4 y^5}{z^3}$

   D. $x^{20} y^{25} z^{-15}$

9. $x^2 \cdot x^4 =$

   A. x^8

   B. $8x$

   C. x^6

   D. $6x$

10. Write using exponents: $4a \times 4a \times 4a$

   A. $4a^3$

   B. $64a^3$

   C. $3\left(4a\right)$

   D. $\left(4 + a\right)^3$

Chapter 10
Exponential Functions

This chapter covers the following Georgia Performance Standards:

MM2A	Algebra	MM2A2b
		MM2A2c
		MM2A2d
		MM2A2e
		MM2A2f
		MM2A2g

10.1   Characteristics of Exponential Functions

An **exponential function** is a function in the form $f(x) = a^x$, where a is a constant. Every exponential function has various characteristics, such as its domain, range, and zeros, and the graph of every exponential function has certain properties as well, such as the graph's asymptotes, intercepts, intervals of increase/decrease, and end behavior.

The **domain** of the exponential function $f(x)$ is all real numbers.

The **range** is all possible values of $f(x)$. In the basic function $f(x) = a^x$, the range is $(0, \infty)$.

The **zeros** are the values of x that produce a value of 0 for $f(x)$.

The **asymptotes** of the graph of the function $f(x)$ are the lines that the graph approaches but never touches. In the basic function $f(x) = a^x$, the horizontal asymptote is $y = 0$.

The **intercepts** of the graph are the points where the graph crosses the x- and y-axes.

The **intervals of increase or decrease** of the graph of the function $f(x)$ are the regions in which the graph is going up or going down.

The **end behavior** of the graph is what happens to the graph as x approaches negative infinity or infinity.

Increasing if $a > 1$

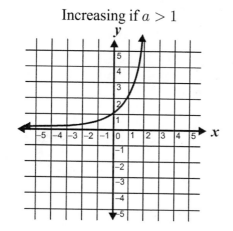

Decreasing if $a < 1$

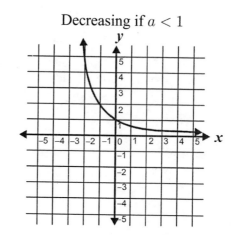

Example 1:   The graph of the function $f(x) = 5^x$ is shown. List the function's domain, range, and zeros, and the graph's asymptotes, intercepts, intervals of increase/decrease, and end behavior.

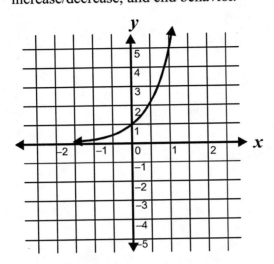

Domain: all real numbers
Range: Since $f(x)$ is always positive, the range of the function is $(0, \infty)$.
Zeros: The function doesn't have any zeros because it never crosses the x-axis.
Asymptotes: The graph of the function approaches the x-axis but never touches it, so the graph has an asymptote at $y = 0$.
Intercepts: The y-intercept is $(0, 1)$, and the graph doesn't have any x-intercepts.
Intervals: As x goes from negative infinity to infinity, the graph of the function is always going up, so it has interval of increase of $(-\infty, \infty)$, and there is no interval of decrease.
End Behavior: As x approaches negative infinity, $f(x)$ approaches 0, and as x approaches infinity, $f(x)$ approaches infinity.

Example 2:   Give an example of an exponential function whose graph passes through the point $(6, 1)$.

It is already known that the graph of an exponential function in the form $f(x) = a^x$ passes through the point $(0, 1)$ because if 0 is plugged in for x, the function becomes $f(x) = a^0 = 1$.
Therefore, for an exponential function's graph to pass through the point $(6, 1)$, if 6 is plugged into the function for x, $f(x)$ would have to equal 1.
An example of an exponential function that meets this condition is one in the form $f(x) = a^{x-6}$. If 6 is plugged into the function for x, the function becomes $f(x) = a^{6-6} = a^0 = 1$.
Since a can equal any real number, one example of an exponential function whose graph passes through the point $(6, 1)$ is $f(x) = 8^{x-6}$.

For each of the following exponential functions, list the function's domain, range, and zeros, and for the graph of the function list the asymptotes, intercepts, intervals of increase/decrease, and end behavior.

1. $f(x) = 3^x$

2. $f(x) = \left(\frac{1}{3}\right)^x$

3. $f(x) = -2^x$

4. $f(x) = 4^{-x}$

5. $f(x) = -3^{-x}$

6. $f(x) = \left(\frac{1}{3}\right)^{-x}$

7. $f(x) = -7^x$

8. $f(x) = \left(\frac{1}{4}\right)^x$

9. $f(x) = \left(\frac{1}{5}\right)^x$

10. $f(x) = 6^x$

11. $f(x) = (4)(2^x) - 7$

12. $f(x) = (3)(7^x) + 9$

Give an example of an exponential function that meets each of the following criteria.

13. The graph of the function passes through the point $(-3, 1)$.

14. The graph of the function has a y-intercept at $f(x) = 12$.

15. The graph of the function has a y-intercept at $f(x) = -9$.

16. The function has a range of $(-\infty, -7)$.

17. The function has a zero at $x = \frac{1}{2}$.

18. When x is approaching $-\infty$, $f(x)$ is approaching 5, and when x is approaching ∞, so is $f(x)$. Find the function that has a graph with this type of end behavior.

10.2   Determining the Rate of Change of Exponential Functions

The average rate of change of the exponential function $f(x)$ is the change in the function over a given interval of x. In exponential functions, the rate of change is not constant. The average rate of change for $f(x)$ from one value of x, x_1, to another, x_2, can be calculated:

$$\frac{f(x_1) - f(x_2)}{x_1 - x_2}$$

Example 3:   Calculate the average rate of change of the exponential function $f(x) = 2^x$ from $x = 1$ to $x = 3$.

Step 1:   Find $f(1)$ and $f(3)$ by plugging in $x = 1$ and $x = 3$ into the equation.

$$f(1) = 2^1 = 2$$
$$f(3) = 2^3 = 8$$

Step 2:   Find the difference between $f(1)$ and $f(3)$.

$$f(1) - f(3) = 2 - 8 = -6$$

Step 3:   Find the difference between 1 and 3. $1 - 3 = -2$

Step 4:   Divide the change in $f(x)$ by the change in x. $-6 \div -2 = 3$

The average rate of change of $f(x)$ from $x = 1$ to $x = 3$ is 3.

Find the average rate of change of each of the following exponential functions from $x = 1$ to $x = 4$.

1. $f(x) = 5^x$

2. $f(x) = \left(\frac{1}{2}\right)^{-x} - 6$

3. $f(x) = -4^x + 1$

4. $f(x) = 3^{x+1}$

5. $f(x) = -5^{x-1}$

6. $f(x) = -3^x + 8$

7. $f(x) = 4^{x+2} - 1$

8. $f(x) = -2^{x+3} + 9$

9. $f(x) = \left(\frac{1}{6}\right)^{-x} - 10$

10. $f(x) = -5^x - 3$

11. $f(x) = \left(\frac{1}{6}\right)^{2-x}$

12. $f(x) = 8^{x-1} + 4$

10.3   Graphing Functions as Transformations of $f(x) = a^x$

An exponential function $f(x) = a^x$ may be as complicated as $f(x) = ba^{c(x-d)} + k$.

An exponential function in this form may be graphed by transforming the graph of $f(x) = a^x$. Six types of transformations can occur:

1. If $b \neq 1$, then vertical stretching/shrinking of the graph occurs. Vertically stretch the graph if $|b| > 1$, and compress the graph if $|b| < 1$.

2. If b is negative, reflect the graph across the x-axis.

3. If $k \neq 0$, then a translation vertically will occur. Move the graph k units up if k is positive and k units down if k is negative.

4. If $c \neq 1$, then horizontal stretching/shrinking of the graph occurs. Horizontally stretch the graph if $|c| < 1$, and compress the graph if $|c| > 1$.

5. If c is negative, reflect the graph across the y-axis.

6. If $d \neq 0$, then a translation horizontally will occur. Move the graph d units to the right if d is positive and d units to the left if d is negative.

Note: It does not matter which type of transformation happens first.

Example 4:   Graph the exponential function $f(x) = (-4)(2^x) - 5$ as a transformation of the function $f(x) = 2^x$.

The graph of the function $f(x) = 2^x$ is graphed below.

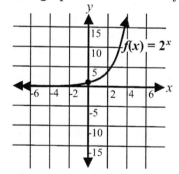

Step 1:   To transform the graph of the function $f(x) = 2^x$ into the graph of the function $f(x) = (-4)(2^x) - 5$, the first transformation that will be applied is a vertical stretch by a factor of 4. When this is done, the function becomes $f(x) = (4)(2^x)$.

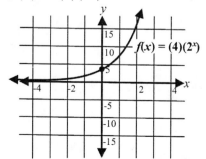

Step 2:   Next, a reflection across the x-axis will be applied. When this is done, the function becomes $f(x) = (-4)(2^x)$.

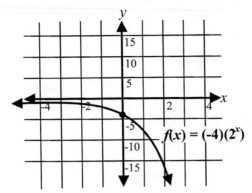

Step 3:   Finally, a translation of 5 units down will be applied. When this is done, the function becomes $f(x) = (-4)(2^x) - 5$.

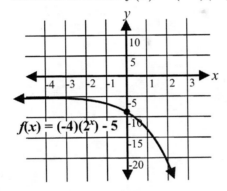

Graph each of the following exponential functions as transformations of $f(x) = 4^x$.

1. $f(x) = (-3)(4^x)$

2. $f(x) = (8)(4^x) + 2$

3. $f(x) = -4^x - 5$

4. $f(x) = (-9)(4^x)$

5. $f(x) = (7)(4^x) - 3$

6. $f(x) = (2)(4^x) + 9$

7. $f(x) = -4^x + 6$

8. $f(x) = (12)(4^x) - 1$

9. $f(x) = (-5)(4^x) + 4$

Graph each of the following exponential functions as transformations of $f(x) = \left(\frac{1}{2}\right)^x$.

10. $f(x) = \left(\frac{1}{2}\right)^{8x}$

11. $f(x) = \left(\frac{1}{2}\right)^{x-5}$

12. $f(x) = \left(\frac{1}{2}\right)^{-7x}$

13. $f(x) = \left(\frac{1}{2}\right)^{6(x+4)}$

14. $f(x) = \left(\frac{1}{2}\right)^{-9(x-2)}$

15. $f(x) = \left(\frac{1}{2}\right)^{3x+3}$

16. $f(x) = \left(\frac{1}{2}\right)^{10-x}$

17. $f(x) = \left(\frac{1}{2}\right)^{-4x+8}$

18. $f(x) = \left(\frac{1}{2}\right)^{12+6x}$

19. Graph the exponential function $f(x) = \left(-\frac{1}{5}\right)\left(10^{\frac{1}{2}(x+3)}\right)$ as a transformation of $f(x) = 10^x$.

10.4   Solving Simple Exponential Equations

The properties of exponents can be used to solve exponential equations.

Example 5:   Solve the exponential equation $4^{5(2+x)} = 1024$ for x.

Step 1:   Rewrite the equation, so that the bases on both sides of the equation are the same.
$$4^{5(2+x)} = 1024$$
$$4^{5(2+x)} = 4^5$$

Step 2:   If the bases on both sides of the equation are the same, then the exponents must be equal.
$$5\,(2 + x) = 5$$

Step 3:   Solve for x.
$$5\,(2 + x) = 5$$
$$2 + x = 1$$
$$x = -1$$

Example 6:   Solve the exponential equation $4^{x+1} = 32^{2x}$ for x.

Step 1:   Rewrite the equation, so that the bases on both sides of the equation are the same. Then simplify.
$$4^{x+1} = 32^{2x}$$
$$\left(2^2\right)^{x+1} = \left(2^5\right)^{2x}$$
$$2^{2(x+1)} = 2^{5(2x)}$$
$$2^{2x+2} = 2^{10x}$$

Step 2:   If the bases on both sides of the equation are the same, then the exponents must be equal.
$$2x + 2 = 10x$$

Step 3:   Solve for x.
$$2x + 2 = 10x$$
$$8x = 2$$
$$x = \tfrac{1}{4}$$

Solve each of the following exponential equations.

1. $2^x = 64$

2. $6^{x+5} = 216$

3. $3^{x-8} = 27$

4. $7^{2(x+6)} = 2,401$

5. $4^{1-x} = 512^{x-1}$

6. $5^{4x+1} = 625$

7. $2^{-3x-34} = 128^{2x}$

8. $10^{6-x} = 10,000$

9. $9^{-4(x+2)} = 6,561^{2x+1}$

10. $(3)(8^x) = 96$

11. $2^x = 4^{3x+2}$

12. $9^{x+7} = 27^{3x}$

10.5 Solving Simple Exponential Inequalities

Solving exponential inequalities is similar to solving exponential equations.

Example 7: Solve the inequality $9^x \leq 27^{2x-1}$ for x.

Step 1: Rewrite the inequality, so that the bases on both sides of the equation are the same. Then simplify.

$$9^x \leq 27^{2x-1}$$
$$(3^2)^x \leq (3^3)^{2x-1}$$
$$3^{2x} \leq 3^{3(2x-1)}$$
$$3^{2x} \leq 3^{6x-3}$$

Step 2: If the bases on both sides of the equation are the same, then the exponents must be equal.

$$3^{2x} \leq 3^{6x-3}$$
$$2x \leq 6x - 3$$

Step 3: Solve for x.

$$2x \leq 6x - 3$$
$$-4x \leq -3$$
$$x \geq \tfrac{3}{4}$$

The solution can also be written in interval notation as $\left[\tfrac{3}{4}, \infty\right)$.
Remember that (means to the point and] means including the point.

Solve each of the following exponential inequalities analytically.

1. $5^{2(x+5)} < 625$

2. $9^{x-10} \geq 27^{2x}$

3. $7^{4x} \leq 16,807^{x+2}$

4. $6^{7+x} > 7776$

5. $4^{x-3} < 1024$

6. $11^{3x-6} \geq 1331$

7. $2^{3(x-8)} \leq 512$

8. $3^{7x} > 243^{x-4}$

9. $8^{12-x} < 64$

10. $(14)(2^x) < 3584$

11. $3^{4x+2} \geq 9^x$

12. $7^x \leq 343$

13. $(7)(5^{x-2}) > 109,375$

14. $4^{2x} < 64$

15. $10^{3x} \geq 10,000^{x+2}$

16. $9^x \leq 27^{x+5}$

17. $8^x < 16^{2x+5}$

18. $6^x > 36^{2x-9}$

10.6   Solving Simple Exponential Equations Graphically

To solve a simple exponential equation graphically, consider one side of the equation as one function and the other side of the equation as another function. Then graph the two functions and see where they intersect.

Example 8:   Solve the equation $2^{3x} = 512$ graphically.

Step 1:   To solve the equation, the functions $f(x) = 2^{3x}$ and $g(x) = 512$ should be graphed.

Since the function $f(x) = 2^{3x}$ is in the form $f(x) = 2^{cx}$, with c equal to 3, the graph of the function $f(x) = 2^x$ should be horizontally compressed by a factor of $\frac{1}{3}$.

The graphs of $f(x) = 2^{3x}$ and $g(x) = 512$ are as follows:

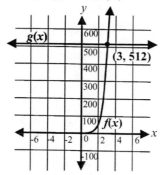

Step 2:   Find where the two functions intersect.

Here the functions intersect at the point $(3, 512)$. So, when $x = 3$ the equation is true.

Graph each of the following exponential equations to find the solution, then check your answer analytically.

1. $4^{x-2} = 256$

2. $5^{2x} = 3125$

3. $3^{2(x+5)} = 6561$

4. $7^{\frac{1}{4}(x-3)} = 2401$

5. $6^{4(x-6)} = \frac{1}{1296}$

6. $8^{-(x+1)} = 32,768$

7. $(3)(5^x) + 23 = 1898$

8. $\left(\frac{1}{4}\right)(2^x) - 31 = 225$

9. $(-8)(12^x) + 5 = -13,819$

10. $(7)(8^x) - 15 = 433$

11. $\left(\frac{1}{6}\right)(3^x) + \frac{35}{2} = 139$

12. $(10)(4^x) - 1 = -\frac{3}{8}$

13. $3^{x^2} = 81$

14. $5^{\sqrt{5x}} = 3125$

15. $4^{x^2-1} = 64$

16. $6^{\sqrt{7x+4}} = 7776$

17. $16^{\frac{1}{x}} = 4$

18. $2^{x^3} = 256$

19. Why doesn't the graph of the function $f(x) = 2^{\sqrt{x}}$ have any points on the negative side of the y-axis?

20. Why does the graph of the function $f(x) = 2^{\frac{1}{x}}$ get closer and closer to the y-axis but never touch it?

10.7   Solving Simple Exponential Inequalities Graphically

To solve a simple exponential inequality graphically, consider one side of the inequality as one function and the other side of the inequality as another function. Then graph the two functions, and see where they meet the conditions of the inequality.

Example 9:   Solve the exponential inequality $(5)(4^x) + 3 \leq 5123$ graphically.

Step 1:   First subtract 3 from both sides of the inequality, so it becomes $(5)(4^x) \leq 5120$, and then divide both sides of the inequality by 5 so that it becomes $4^x \leq 1024$. Then the inequality can be solved by graphing the functions $f(x) = 4^x$ and $g(x) = 1024$

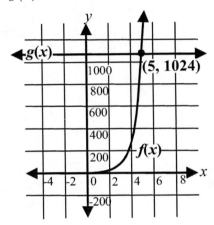

Step 2:   Find where the two functions intersect. Here the functions intersect at the point $(5, 1024)$.

Since the graph of $f(x)$ is below or intersecting with the graph of $g(x)$ when $x \leq 5$, the solution to the inequality is $x \leq 5$.

**Note: The solution can also be written in interval notation as $(-\infty, 5]$.

Graph each of the following exponential inequalities to find the solution, then check your answer analytically.

1. $4^{4x} \leq 4096$

2. $5^{x-8} \geq 15,625$

3. $2^{-(x+2)} < 2048$

4. $7^{5(x-3)} > 2401$

5. $3^{-5x} \geq 6561$

6. $6^{2(x+6)} < \frac{1}{36}$

7. $(16)(2^x) - 10 < 4086$

8. $\left(\frac{1}{20}\right)(5^x) + \frac{3}{4} \geq 782$

9. $(8)(4^x) + 9 \leq 8201$

10. $(9)(3^x) - \frac{82}{81} > -1$

11. $(56)(2^x) + 4 \geq 900$

12. $(-7)(6^x) + 1 < -\frac{1}{6}$

13. $64^{\frac{1}{x}} \leq 4$

14. $2^{\sqrt{4x}} > 1024$

15. $4^{x^2-9} \geq 16,384$

16. $16^{\frac{1}{x}} < 2$

17. $3^{x^3} \leq 6561$

18. $5^{x^2+2} > 125$

10.8   Relations That Can Be Represented by Functions

Real-life examples can be represented by functions. The most common functions are exponential growth and decay and half-life.

Example 10:   Atlanta, GA has a population of about 410,000 people. The U.S. Census Bureau estimates that the population will double in 26 years. If the population continues at the same rate, what will the population be in
a) 10 years?
b) 50 years?

Step 1:   Use the double growth equation $P = P_0(2^{t/d})$, where P = population at time t, P_0 = population at time $t = 0$, and d = double time.

Step 2:   Determine the variable of each of the facts given in the problem. In this case, $P_0 = 410,000$ people, $d = 26$ years, and $t = 10$ years for part a and $t = 50$ years for part b.

Step 3:   Plug all of the information into the given equation. Round to the nearest whole number.
a) $P = 410,000(2^{10/26}) = 410,000\,(1.3055) = 535,260$ people
b) $P = 410,000(2^{50/26}) = 410,000\,(3.7923) = 1,554,847$ people

Find the answers to the real-life problems by using the equations and variables given. Round your answer to the nearest whole numbers.

For questions 1 and 2, use the following half-life formula.

$A = A_0 \left(\frac{1}{2}\right)^{t/h}$
A = amount at time t
A_0 = amount at time $t = 0$
h is the half-life

1. If you have 6,000 atoms of hydrogen (H), and hydrogen's half-life is 12.3 years, how many atoms will you have left after 7 years?

2. Chlorine (Cl) has a half-life of 55.5 minutes. If you start with 200 milligrams of chlorine, how many will be left after 5 hours?

For questions 3 and 4, use the double growth formula.

$P = P_0(2)^{t/d}$

P = amount at time t

P_0 = amount at time $t = 0$

d is the half-life

3. There are about $3,390,000$ Girl Scouts in the United States. The Girl Scout Council says that there is a growth rate of $5 - 10\%$ per year, so they expect the Girl Scout population in the United States to double in 12 years. If the Girl Scout's organization expands as continuously as it has been, what will the population be

   (A) in 8 years?
   (B) next year?

4. Dr. Kellie noticed the bacteria growth in her laboratory. After observing the bacteria, she concluded that the double time of the bacteria is 40 minutes, and she started off with just $2,500$ bacteria. Assuming this information is accurate and constant, how many bacteria will be in Dr. Kellie's lab

   (A) in 5 minutes?
   (B) after 3 hours?

For questions 5 and 6, use the compound interest formula.

$A = P\left(1 + \dfrac{r}{k}\right)^{kt}$

A = amount at time, t

P = principle amount invested

k = how many times per year interest is compounded

r = rate

5. Lisa invested $\$1,000$ into an account that pays 6% interest compounded monthly. If this account is for her newborn boy, how much will the account be worth on his 21st birthday, which is exactly 21 years from now? Assume the interest rate stays the same.

6. Mr. Dumple wants to open up a savings account. He has looked at two different banks. Bank 1 is offering a rate of 5% compounded daily. Bank 2 is offering an account that has a rate of 8%, but it is only compounded semi-yearly. Mr. Dumple puts $\$5,000$ in an account and wants to take it out for his retirement in 10 years. Which bank will give him the most money back?

10.9   Exponential Growth and Decay

Many quantities experience exponential growth or decay under certain conditions. Examples include bacteria, populations, disease, money in a savings account that compounds interest, and radioisotopes. Exponential functions are those functions in which the independent variable is time, and time is an exponent (thus the name exponential function). For instance, the formula for growth of money in a savings account that compounds interest annually is:

$$A = P(1 + r)^t$$

where A is the value of the account after t years, P is the original amount of money in the account, and r is the annual interest rate.

Below are graphs of the general forms of exponential growth functions and exponential decay functions. Time is represented on the x-axis. Whatever is growing or decaying exponentially, such as population or money, is represented on the y-axis. Note that exponential function graphs are generally in Quadrant I since time and objects cannot be assigned negative values.

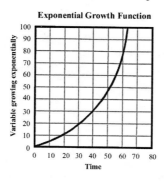
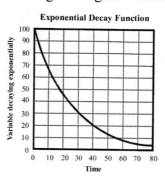

Example 11:   Mason deposited $2,000 into a savings account that pays an annual interest rate of 9% compounded annually. Using the formula $A = P(1 + r)^t$ determine the amount of money in the savings account after 1 year, 5 years, and 20 years. Using the calculated values, construct a graph.

Step 1:   Consider the known values. $P = 2,000$, and $r = 0.09$. The problem will have to be worked three times where $t = 1$, $t = 5$, and $t = 20$. A is the amount being calculated.

Step 2:
$$A = 2000(1 + 0.09)^1 \qquad A = 2000(1 + 0.09)^5 \qquad A = 2000(1 + 0.09)^{20}$$
$$A = 2000(1.09)^1 \qquad A = 2000(1.09)^5 \qquad A = 2000(1.09)^{20}$$
$$A = \$2,180 \qquad A = \$3,077.25 \qquad A = \$11,208.82$$

Step 3:   Use the calculated values to graph the function.

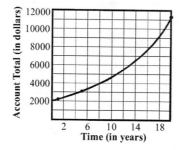

Copyright © American Book Company

Fill in the tables for the following functions. On the line under each table, label the given function as an exponential growth function or an exponential decay function. Round your answers to two decimal places. For extra practice, graph the functions.

1. $F(t) = 15(1.01)^t$

t	F(t)
1	
2	
3	
4	

_____

3. $M(t) = 1000(1.04)^t$

t	M(t)
2	
4	
6	
8	

_____

5. $C(t) = 5300(0.5)^t$

t	C(t)
5	
10	
15	
20	

_____

2. $S(t) = 350(0.85)^t$

t	S(t)
1	
3	
5	
7	

_____

4. $B(t) = 2(2.50)^t$

t	B(t)
1	
2	
3	
4	

_____

6. $R(t) = 80\left(\frac{1}{3}\right)^t$

t	R(t)
2	
4	
6	
8	

_____

Refer to the graph at right to answer questions 7–10.

7. Which town is experiencing exponential decay? growth?

8. Considering both towns A and B, what is changing exponentially with time?

9. Why would it not make sense to draw the graph of town B below the x-axis?

10. In what year does the population of town B reach 3,000?

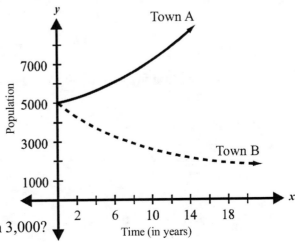

10.10   Geometric Sequences

A **geometric sequence** is a pattern where each term is multiplied by the same value to get the next term. The formula for finding the nth term in a geometric sequence is $t_n = t_1 r^{n-1}$, where t_1 is the first term in the series, and t_n is the nth term in the series. In the geometric series, r is the value multiplied by each term to reach the next term in the series. This means that r is a constant ratio in the geometric sequence. Therefore, geometric sequences are examples of exponential functions.

Example 12:   Below is a geometric sequence. Find the formula for the sequence. Then find the 8th term in the sequence.

$$27, 9, 3, 1, \frac{1}{3}, \ldots$$

Step 1:   The formula $t_n = t_1 r^{n-1}$ used to find the nth term in a geometric sequence is the same formula we will use to find the formula for the pattern. First, we need to find the missing variables t_1 and r. t_1 is the first term of the sequence, 27.

Step 2:   The variable r is the constant in the sequence. This is the number that each term is multiplied by to find the next term.

$9 \div 27 = \frac{1}{3}$

$3 \div 9 = \frac{1}{3}$

$1 \div 3 = \frac{1}{3}$

$\frac{1}{3} \div 1 = \frac{1}{3}$

Since each number is being multiplied by $\frac{1}{3}$ to get the next number in the sequence, $r = \frac{1}{3}$.

Thus, the formula for the sequence us $t_n = 27 \left(\frac{1}{3}\right)^{n-1}$.

Step 3:   To find the 8th term in the sequence, substitute 8 into the formula for n.

$$t_8 = 27 \left(\frac{1}{3}\right)^{8-1} = \frac{1}{81}$$

Find the formula for the sequences. Then find the 10th term in the sequence.

1. $1, \frac{1}{2}, \frac{1}{4}, \frac{1}{8}, \frac{1}{16}, \ldots$

2. $25, 5, 1, \frac{1}{5}, \ldots$

3. $100, 10, 1, \frac{1}{10}, \frac{1}{100}, \ldots$

4. $32, 8, 2, \frac{1}{2}, \frac{1}{8}, \ldots$

5. $-625, -125, -25, -5, \ldots$

6. $-9, -3, -1, -\frac{1}{3}, -\frac{1}{9}, \ldots$

7. $2, 4, 8, 16, 32, \ldots$

8. $3, 9, 27, 81, 243, \ldots$

Chapter 10 Review

For each of the following exponential functions, list the function's domain, range, and zeros, and for the graph of the function, list the asymptotes, intercepts, intervals of increase/decrease, and end behavior.

1. $f(x) = 9^x$

3. $f(x) = (8)(4^x) + 6$

5. $f(x) = (6)(5^x) - 11$

2. $f(x) = \left(\frac{1}{7}\right)^{-x}$

4. $f(x) = (-5)(3^x) - 1$

6. $f(x) = (-3)(12^x) + 2$

Find the average rate of change of each of the following functions from $x = 1$ to $x = 3$.

7. $f(x) = (16)(5^x) + 3$

8. $f(x) = \left(\frac{7}{10}\right)(2^x) - 5$

9. $f(x) = (-4)(3^x) + 2$

Graph each of the following exponential functions as transformations of $f(x) = 7^x$.

10. $f(x) = (-2)(7^x) - 3$

12. $f(x) = 7^{5(x+1)}$

14. $f(x) = (3)(7^{x+4})$

11. $f(x) = \left(\frac{1}{8}\right)(7^x) + 2$

13. $f(x) = 7^{\frac{1}{2}(x-7)}$

15. $f(x) = \left(\frac{2}{5}\right)(7^{6x})$

Solve each of the following exponential equations.

16. $10^{x+1} = 100$

20. $5^{x-2} = 25^{x+1}$

24. $11^x + 6 = 1337$

17. $5^{3(x-9)} = 125$

21. $10^{x+3} = 100$

25. $(6)(8^x) + \dfrac{253}{256} = 1$

18. $(-8)(6^x) = -288$

22. $9^{x-50} = 19{,}683^{3x}$

26. $343^{\frac{1}{x}} = 7$

19. $4^{x+8} = 32^{2x}$

23. $4^{4(x-2)} = 4096^{2x}$

27. $12^{\sqrt{-2x}} = 20{,}736$

Solve each of the following exponential inequalities.

28. $5^{x+11} \leq 625$

32. $8^{x-7} > 32^{2x}$

36. $(3)(2^x) + 6 < 12{,}294$

29. $10^{6x} > 1000^{x-3}$

33. $(5)(3^x) < 135$

37. $9^{x-13} \leq 243^{3x}$

30. $2^{x+9} \geq 32^{2x}$

34. $5^{-(x-8)} > 625$

38. $3^{x^2-18} > 2187$

31. $4^{x+3} < 128^{x-2}$

35. $3^{4x} \geq 729^{2x-1}$

39. $4^{\sqrt{2x}} \leq 4096$

Find the formula for the sequences. Then find the 8th term in the sequence.

40. $-32 + -16 + -8 + -4 + -2 + \ldots$

41. $27 + 9 + 3 + \frac{1}{3} + \frac{1}{9} + \ldots$

42. $64 + 48 + 36 + 27 + 20.25 + \ldots$

Chapter 10 Test

1. The solution to the exponential inequality $3^{5(x+2)} > \dfrac{1}{243}$ is $x > -3$. At what point do the graphs of the functions $f(x) = 3^{5(x+2)}$ and $g(x) = \dfrac{1}{243}$ intersect?

A. $\left(-3, \dfrac{1}{243}\right)$

B. $\left(-\dfrac{1}{243}, 3\right)$

C. $\left(\dfrac{1}{243}, 3\right)$

D. $\left(3, \dfrac{1}{243}\right)$

2. If $9^{2x-1} = 27^{3x}$, which of the following expressions is equivalent to x?

A. $3^{2x-1} = 3^{3x}$

B. $3^{4x-2} = 3^{3x}$

C. $3^{2x-1} = 3^{6x}$

D. $3^{4x-2} = 3^{9x}$

3. What transformations can be applied to the graph of the function $f(x) = 9^x$ to produce the graph of the function $f(x) = 9^{-(x+2)}$?

A. a translation of 2 units left then a reflection over the x-axis

B. a translation of 2 units left then a reflection over the y-axis

C. a translation of 2 units right then a reflection over the x-axis

D. a translation of 2 units right then a reflection over the y-axis

4. For which of the following exponential inequalities is the approximate solution $[-4, \infty)$?

A. $\left(\dfrac{1}{8}\right)(4^{-x}) \le 32$

B. $\left(\dfrac{1}{8}\right)(4^{x}) \le 32$

C. $(8)(4^{-x}) \le 32$

D. $(8)(4^{x}) \le 32$

5. To solve the exponential equation $4^{\sqrt{5x+9}} = 16,384$ graphically, a table of values was created to produce the graph of the function $f(x) = 4^{\sqrt{5x+9}}$. Which of the following points cannot be included in the table of values?

A. $(-1, 16)$
B. $(0, 64)$
C. $(4, 256)$
D. $(8, 16{,}384)$

6. Which of the following exponential equations can be solved with the graph shown?

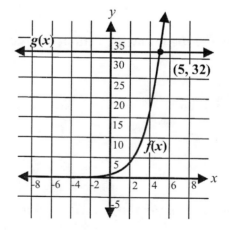

A. $2^x = 5$
B. $2^x = 32$
C. $5^x = 32$
D. $32^x = 5$

7. What is the average rate of change of the exponential function $f(x) = \left(\frac{1}{4}\right)^x + 5$ from $x = 1$ to $x = 3$?

A. $-\dfrac{15}{64}$

B. $-\dfrac{15}{128}$

C. $\dfrac{15}{128}$

D. $\dfrac{15}{64}$

8. What is the range of the exponential function $f(x) = \left(-\frac{3}{5}\right)(7^x) - 13$?

A. $(-\infty, -13)$

B. $\left(-\infty, -\frac{3}{5}\right)$

C. $(-\infty, 0)$

D. $(-\infty, 7)$

9. What transformations can be applied to the graph of the function $f(x) = 18^x$ to produce the graph of the function $f(x) = 18^{\frac{1}{3}x} + 7$?

A. a horizontal compression by a factor of $\frac{1}{3}$ and a translation of 7 units down

B. a horizontal compression by a factor of $\frac{1}{3}$ and a translation of 7 units up

C. a horizontal stretch by a factor of 3 and a translation of 7 units down

D. a horizontal stretch by a factor of 3 and a translation of 7 units up

10. What is the approximate solution to the exponential equation $\left(\frac{4}{3}\right)(3^{x+4}) = 324$?

A. $x = -1$

B. $x = 1$

C. $x = 2$

D. $x = 3$

11. In the graph shown, $f(x) = (9)(2^{x+5})$ and $g(x) = 2304$. Based on this information, what is the solution to the inequality $(-9)(2^{x+5}) \leq -2304$?

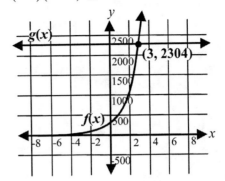

A. $x < 3$

B. $x \leq 3$

C. $x > 3$

D. $x \geq 3$

12. What is the approximate solution to the exponential inequality $8^{5x-1} < 32^x$?

A. $x > \frac{3}{10}$

B. $x > \frac{10}{3}$

C. $x < \frac{10}{3}$

D. $x < \frac{3}{10}$

13. Find the formula for the geometric sequence $3, 6, 12, 24, \ldots$

A. $t_n = 3(4)^{n-1}$

B. $t_n = (2)^{n-1}$

C. $t_n = 3(2)^{n-1}$

D. $t_n = (4)^{n-1}$

14. What is the 10th term in the sequence $400, 200, 100, 50, \ldots$?

A. $\frac{25}{2}$

B. 25

C. $\frac{25}{4}$

D. $\frac{25}{32}$

Chapter 11
Using Algebra for Data Analysis

This chapter covers the following Georgia Performance Standards:

MM2D	Data Analysis and Probability	MM2D2a
		MM2D2b
		MM2D2c
		MM2D2d

11.1   Writing an Equation From Data

Bivariate data are data that involve two variables that may be related to each other. Data is often written in a two-column format. If the increases or decreases in the ordered pairs are at a constant rate, then a linear equation for the data can be found.

Example 1:   Write an equation for the following set of data.

Dan set his car on cruise control and noted the distance he went every 5 minutes.

Minutes in operation (x)	Odometer reading (y)
5	28,490
10	28,494

Step 1:   Write two ordered pairs in the form (minutes, distance) for Dan's driving, $(5, 28490)$ and $(10, 28494)$, and find the slope.

$$m = \frac{28494 - 28490}{10 - 5} = \frac{4}{5}$$

Step 2:   Use the ordered pairs to write the equation in the form $y = mx + b$. Place the slope, m, that you found and one of the pairs of points as x_1 and y_1 in the following formula, $y - y_1 = m(x - x_1)$.

$y - 28490 = \frac{4}{5}(x - 5)$

$y - 28490 = \frac{4}{5}x - 4$

$y - 28490 + 28490 = \frac{4}{5}x - 4 + 28490$

$y + 0 = \frac{4}{5}x + 28486$

$y = \frac{4}{5}x + 28486$

166   Copyright © American Book Company

Write an equation for each of the following sets of data, assuming the relationship is linear.

1. **Doug's Doughnut Shop**

Years in Business	Total Sales
1	$55,000
4	$85,000

2. **Gwen's Green Beans**

Days Growing	Height in Inches
2	5
6	12

3. **At the Gas Pump**

Gallons Purchased	Total Cost
5	$18.25
7	$25.55

4. **Jim's Depreciation on his Jet Skis**

Years	Value
1	$4,500
6	$2,500

5. **Stepping on the Brakes**

Seconds	MPH
2	51
5	18

6. **Stepping on the Accelerator**

Seconds	MPH
4	35
7	62

7. **Aristotle's Closet**

Shirts	Price
3	$13.25
8	$32.00

8. **Rodriguez Family Vacation**

Hours Driven	Odometer Reading
1	263
3	423

9. **DJ's Dairy**

Gallons of Milk	Price
2	$7.58
4	$14.16

10. **Wall-to-Floor Decor**

Months in Business	Total Sales
4	$46,000
9	$84,000

11.2 Graphing Linear Data

Many types of data are related by a constant ratio. As you learned on the previous page, this type of data is linear. The slope of the line described by linear data is the ratio between the data. Plotting linear data with a constant ratio can be helpful in finding additional values.

Example 2: A department store prices socks per pair. Each pair of socks costs $0.75. Plot pairs of socks versus price on a Cartesian plane.

Step 1: Since the price of the socks is constant, you know that one pair of socks costs $0.75, 2 pairs of socks cost $1.50, 3 pairs of socks cost $2.25, and so on. Make a list of a few points.

Pair(s) x	Price y
1	0.75
2	1.50
3	2.25

Step 2: Plot these points on a Cartesian plane, and draw a ray through the points.

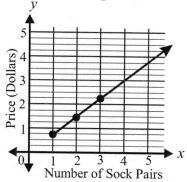

Example 3: What is the slope of the data in the example above? What does the slope describe?

Solution: You can determine the slope either by the graph or by the data points. For this data, the slope is 0.75. Remember, slope is rise/run. For every $0.75 going up the y-axis, you go across one pair of socks on the x-axis. The slope describes the price per pair of socks.

Example 4: Use the graph created in the above example to answer the following questions. How much would 5 pairs of socks cost? How many pairs of socks could you purchase for $3.00? Extending the line gives useful information about the price of additional pairs of socks.

Solution 1: The line that represents 5 pairs of socks intersects the data line at $3.75 on the y-axis. Therefore, 5 pairs of socks would cost $3.75.

Solution 2: The line representing the value of $3.00 on the y-axis intersects the data line at 4 on the x-axis. Therefore, $3.00 will buy exactly 4 pairs of socks.

Use the information given to make a line graph for each set of data, and answer the questions related to each graph.

1. The diameter of a circle compared with the circumference of a circle is a constant ratio. Use the data given below to graph a line to fit the data. Extend the line, and use the graph to answer the next question.

Circle

Diameter	Circumference
4	12.56
5	15.70

2. Using the graph of the data in question 1, estimate the circumference of a circle that has a diameter of 3 inches.

3. If the circumference of a circle is 3 inches, about how long is the diameter?

4. What is the slope of the line you graphed in question 1?

5. What does the slope of the line in question 4 describe?

6. The length of a side on a square and the perimeter of a square are constant ratios to each other. Use the data below to graph this relationship.

Square

Length of side	Perimeter
2	8
3	12

7. Using the graph from question 6, what is the perimeter of a square with a side that measure 4 inches?

8. What is the slope of the line graphed in question 6?

9. Conversions are often constant ratios. For example, converting from pounds to ounces follows a constant ratio. Use the data below to graph a line that can be used to convert pounds to ounces.

Measurement Conversion

Pounds	Ounces
2	32
4	64

10. Use the graph from question 9 to convert 40 ounces to pounds.

11. What does the slope of the line graphs for question 9 represent?

12. Graph the data below, and create a line that shows the conversion from weeks to days.

Time

Weeks	Days
1	7
2	14

13. About how many days are in $2\frac{1}{2}$ weeks?

11.3   Modeling Data with Linear Functions

When the dependent variable (y) changes at a constant rate in relation to the change in an independent variable (x), the relationship can be modeled with a linear function.

Example 5:   A gas-station owner has noticed that as the price of a gallon of gas has increased, the number of gallons of gas purchased at his station has decreased. The table below shows the average price of a gallon of gas at the station for the last 10 weeks and the number of gallons of gas purchased at the station during that week.

	Average Price	Gallons Purchased
Week 1	$2.40	3, 200
Week 2	$2.51	3, 145
Week 3	$2.69	3, 055
Week 4	$3.00	2, 900
Week 5	$3.14	2, 830
Week 6	$3.36	2, 720
Week 7	$3.59	2, 605
Week 8	$3.71	2, 545
Week 9	$4.01	2, 395
Week 10	$4.20	2, 300

Can the relationship between the average weekly price of a gallon of gas at the station and the number of gallons purchased for the last 10 weeks be modeled with a linear function? If so, plot the data and draw the line.

Step 1:   Determine if the relationship can be modeled with a linear function.

From the table, we see that for every $0.01 increase in the average weekly price of a gallon of gas, there has been a 5-gallon decrease in the number of gallons purchased per week. Since the dependent variable (the number of gallons purchased) decreases at a constant rate in relation to an increase in the independent variable (the average price of a gallon of gas), this is an inverse relationship that can be modeled with a linear function.

Step 2:   Plot the data and draw the line.
The average price of a gallon of gas is the independent variable (x), and the number of gallons purchased is the dependent variable y.

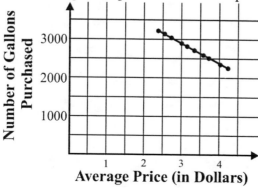

Example 6: A new barbershop has been open for 5 days, and the number of daily patrons to the barbershop has been increasing at a constant rate each day. The relationship between the number of days the barbershop has been open and the number of daily patrons can be modeled with a linear function as shown below. What is the equation of the linear function?

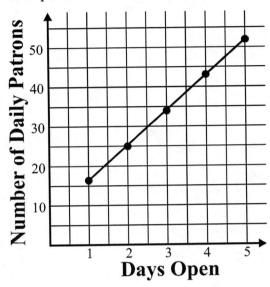

Step 1: Determine the slope of the equation of the line.

Looking at the graph, we can find two points. Two points on the line are $(1, 16)$ and $(3, 34)$. Calculate the slope.

$$\frac{\text{change in } y}{\text{change in } x} = \frac{34 - 16}{3 - 1} = 9.$$

So far, the equation of the line is $y = 9x + b$, where b is the y-intercept.

Step 2: Determine the y-intercept of the equation of the line.

The equation of the line is $y = 9x + b$, and one of the points on the line is $(1, 16)$. Using this information, substitute the point into the equation to solve for b.

$16 = 9(1) + b$

$16 = 9 + b$

$16 - 9 = b$

$b = 7$

The equation of the line is $y = 9x + 7$.

**Note: Even though the y-intercept of the equation of the line is 7, the line segment that is the model for this situation does not actually cross the y-axis, since the first day the barbershop had any patrons was day 1.

Determine whether or not each of the following situations can be modeled with a linear function.

1. For every $0.50 increase in the price of a loaf of bread, the number of loaves purchased per day is cut in half.

2. Every 5 minutes the number of cookies in a cookie jar decreases by 3.

3. Every time the number of fans in a stadium increases by 1, 000, the noise level increases by 10 percent.

4. For every mile a runner runs, she burns 100 calories.

5. For every new employee a company hires, it spends $4, 000 on training.

6. A car is travelling at 25 miles per hour.

7. The area of a square is equal to the length of a side of the square multiplied by itself.

8. The total number of visits to a website is quadrupling every month.

9. To produce a ton of paper, 24 trees must be cut down.

Find the equation of the linear function that can be used to model each situation.

10. (1 hr, 5 meters), (4 hrs, 41 meters)

11. ($1.50, 78 gallons), ($1.90, 54 gallons)

12. (26 people, 6 cans), (38 people, 9 cans)

13. (7 boxes, 44 lbs), (12 boxes, 79 lbs)

14. (88°, 70 customers), (95°, 56 customers)

15. (3 days, 120 clicks), (9 days, 200 clicks)

11.4   Making Scatter Plots

A scatter plot is a graph of the relationship between two variables.

Example 7:   Below is the height and weight of 14 people. Use this data to make a scatter plot.

height (in)	36	54	60	66	39	48	44	72	75	62	61	45	50	59
weight (lb)	40	104	107	150	48	77	62	195	205	115	112	65	85	106

Step 1:   To make a scatter plot, make a Cartesian plane and label the vertices using the two variables given in the table above.
Then plot the points on the grid.

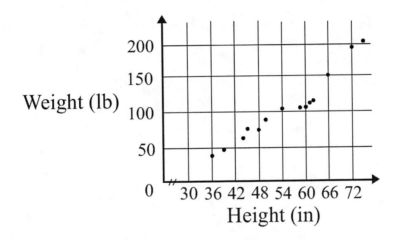

Step 2:   Determine the relationship between the two variables by looking at the graph. We can tell that as the height increases, weight increases.

Draw a scatter plot for the given data.

1.

Age	6	11	19	5	8	12	14	7	13	17	9
Height	46	56	64	42	52	56	63	51	60	63	54

2.

Gas Price	2.50	3.60	2.63	3.00	2.20	2.89	2.36	3.41	3.26
Dist. Driven/Week	250	75	225	175	300	200	280	125	150

3.

Height	62	70	76	65	74	75	73	71	77	66	72	63
Pts. Scored	21	10	15	30	40	6	11	22	14	17	18	26

11.5   Interpreting Data in Scatter Plots

You have already learned that scatter plots show the relationship between two variables. Now, you will learn to explain the relationship between variables.

Example 8:   The graph below shows the relationship between height and age.

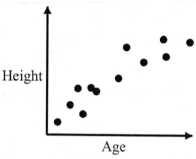

Although it isn't linear, there is clearly a positive relationship between age and height. This means that as age increases, height increases.

Example 9:   The graph below shows the relationship between price of an object and the number purchased by customers.

This illustrates a negative relationship. This means as price of an object increases, the number purchased decreases. In other words, if the price of an object goes up, fewer people will buy that object.

Example 10:   The graph below shows the relationship between number of points scored on a test and height

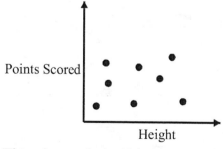

There is no relationship between height and points scored because there is no definable pattern. Therefore, height and number of points scored on a test are not correlated.

Explain the relationship between the variables in each of the following scatter plots.

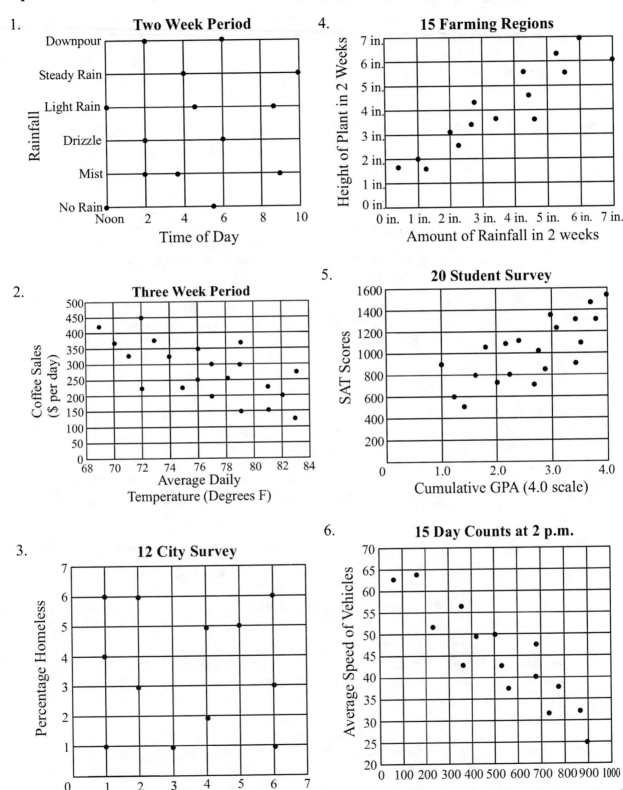

11.6   The Line of Best Fit

At this point, you now understand how to plot points on a Cartesian plane. You also understand how to find the data trend on a Cartesian plane. These skills are necessary to accomplish the next task, determining the line of best fit. The line of best fit is a straight line that demonstrates the relationship between two variables. The line does not necessarily divide the plotted points into two areas, but this sometimes is the best way to estimate the line of best fit.

To estimate the line of best fit, you must first draw a scatter plot of all data points. Once this is accomplished, draw an oval around all of the points plotted. Draw a line through the points in such a way that the line separates half the points from one another. You may now use this line to answer questions.

Example 11:   The following data set contains the heights of children between 5 and 13 years old. Make a scatter plot and draw the line of best fit to represent the trend. Using the graph, determine the height for a 14-year old child.

Age 5: 4'6",4'4",4'5"   Age 8: 4'8", 4'6", 4'7"   Age 11: 5'0", 4'10"
Age 6: 4'7", 4'5", 4'6"   Age 9: 4'9", 4'7", 4'10"   Age 12: 5'1", 4'11", 5'0", 5'3"
Age 7: 4'9", 4'7", 4'6", 4'8"   Age 10: 4'9", 4'8", 4' 10"   Age 13: 5'3", 5'2", 5'0", 5'1"

In this example, the data points lay in a positive sloping direction. To determine the line of best fit, all data points were circled, then a line of best fit was drawn. Half of the points lay below, half above the line of best fit drawn bisecting the narrow length of the oval. The is called "eye-balling."
To find the height of a 14–year old, simply continue the line of best fit forward. In this case, the height is 62 inches.

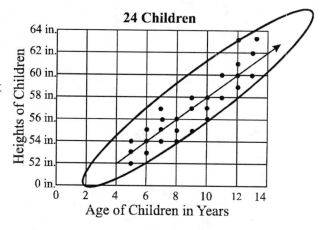

Plot the data sets below, then draw the line of best fit. Next, use the line to estimate the value of the next measurement.

1. Selected values of the Sleekster Brand Light Compact Vehicles: New Vehicle: $13,000$.
    1 year old: $12,000, $11,000, $12,500$ 3 year old: $8,500, $8,000, $9,000$
    2 year old: $9,000, $10,500, $9,500$ 4 year old: $7,500, $6,500, $6,000$
    5 year old: ?

2. The relationship between string length and kite height for the following kites:
    (L = 500 ft, H = 400 ft) (L = 250 ft, H = 150ft) (L = 100 ft, H = 75 ft)
    (L = 500ft, H = 350 ft) (L = 250 ft, H = 200 ft) (L = 100 ft, H = 50 ft)
    (L = 600 ft, H = ?)

11.7   More Lines of Best Fit

Relationships that can be modeled with linear functions usually are not exactly linear. In other words, the linear model is only an approximation, and there are points that do not lie exactly on the line. When this is the case, methods such as eyeballing (which we studied in the previous section) and finding the median-median line can be used to determine the equation of the linear model.

Example 12:   Jake rode his bicycle for a total of 240 minutes, and he travelled a total of 40 miles. However, he did not travel at a constant speed, so the graph representing his distance travelled as a function of time is not exactly linear. A scatter plot representing Jake's distance travelled in miles as a function of time passed in minutes is shown.

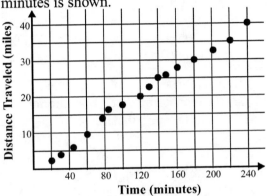

Use eyeballing to determine the equation of the linear function that can be used to model the relationship between the time passed and the distance travelled.

Step 1:   Determine the equation of a line that would be a good approximate representation of the relationship being modeled.
By looking at the points included in the scatter plot, it appears that if the line $y = \frac{1}{6}x$ were drawn, about the same number of points would be above the line as would be below the line. For this reason, the line $y = \frac{1}{6}x$ would be a good representation of the relationship between the time passed and the distance travelled.

Step 2:   Draw the line on the graph.

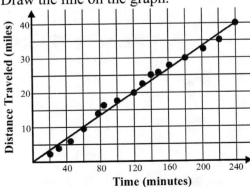

Since about the same number of points are, in fact, above the line as are below the line, the line $y = \frac{1}{6}x$ is an appropriate model.

Example 13:   Over the course of the last 9 months, a retail store has been increasing the amount of money it spends on advertising, and it has noticed that for the most part, the more money it spends, the more revenue is generated by its store. This is shown in the table below.

	Amount Spent on Advertising	Store Revenue
Month 1	$3,000.00	$30,000.00
Month 2	$4,500.00	$59,000.00
Month 3	$5,500.00	$55,000.00
Month 4	$7,000.00	$62,000.00
Month 5	$7,500.00	$31,000.00
Month 6	$9,500.00	$68,000.00
Month 7	$10,000.00	$75,000.00
Month 8	$11,500.00	$71,000.00
Month 9	$12,000.00	$77,000.00

Find the **median-median line** to determine the equation of the linear model that best represents the relationship between the amount of money spent on advertising and the amount of revenue generated by the store.

Step 1:   Divide the data into 3 groups.
Since there are 9 columns, the first group is the first 3 columns, the second group is the next 3 columns, and the third group is the last 3 columns.

Step 2:   Determine the summary point (median) for each group.

To determine the summary point for a group, the table should be written so that the x-coordinates of the data points are in order from least to greatest (this is already done).

Amount Spent on Advertising	Store Revenue
$3,000.00	$30,000.00
$4,500.00	$59,000.00
$5,500.00	$55,000.00
$7,000.00	$62,000.00
$7,500.00	$31,000.00
$9,500.00	$68,000.00
$10,000.00	$75,000.00
$11,500.00	$71,000.00
$12,000.00	$77,000.00

The x-coordinate of the summary point for the first group is the median of the first 3 x-coordinates in the first column, and the y-coordinate of the summary point for the first group is the median of the first three y-coordinates in the last column. Therefore, the summary point for the first group is ($4,500, $55,000). The summary points for the next two groups can be found in the same way, and are ($7,500, $62,000) and ($11,500, $75,000), respectively.

Step 3: Plot the three summary points, then draw a line through the first and last summary points.

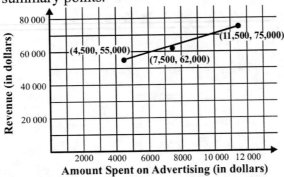

Step 4: Move the line one-third of the way toward the middle summary point to find the median-median line. The distance from all points below the line to the line should equal the distance from all points above the line to the line.

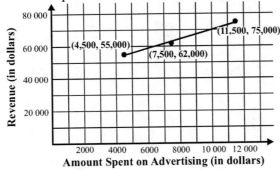

Step 5: Find the equation of the median-median line.
The slope of the median-median line equals the slope of the line that passes through the first and last summary points.

$$m = \frac{75000 - 55000}{11500 - 4500} = \frac{20000}{7000} \approx 2.86$$

Therefore, the equation of the median-median line is $y = 2.86x + b$.
The easiest way to find the y-intercept of the line is to extend the line all the way to the y-axis. The y-intercept is approximately $41,619$.
The equation of the linear model is $y = 2.86x + 41619$.
The line is graphed below along with all of the original data points.

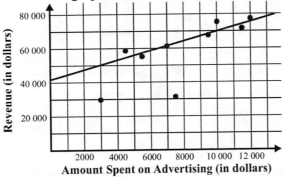

For each of the following groups of points, use eyeballing to determine the equation of the linear function that can be used to model the relationship in question.

1. ($1.50, $4.90), ($2.00, $6.00), ($2.50, $7.10), ($3.00, $8.10), ($3.50, $8.90)

2. (11.9 hr, 50 in), (13 hr, 56 in), (14.1 hr, 64 in), (15 hr, 72 in), (16 hr, 78 in)

3. (1 day, 8.2 km), (5 days, 9.8 km), (7 days, 11.3 km), (9 days, 11.7 km)

4. (6.3 gallons, 7 lbs), (8.7 gallons, 8 lbs), (12 gallons, 9.4 lbs), (15 gallons, 9.6 lbs)

5. (44 watts, $3.06), (52 watts, $3.20), (64 watts, $3.34), (76 watts, $3.60)

6. (5 yr, 22 mm), (6 yr, 26 mm), (7 yr, 33 mm), (8.3 yr, 37 mm), (8.7 yr, 42 mm)

7. (3 cars, 12.7 quarts), (4 cars, 20 quarts), (8 cars, 28 quarts), (9 cars, 35.3 quarts)

8. (2.1 wk, 1 cm), (3 wk, 2.1 cm), (4 wk, 2.9 cm), (5 wk, 4 cm), (5.9 wk, 5 cm)

9. ($2.75, 9 units), ($2.86, 19 units), ($2.95, 26 units), ($3.04, 42 units), ($3.15, 49 units)

Use the table below to answer questions 10–14.

Hours Studying	Points on Test
0.5	40
1.5	44
2	46
3	47
3.5	49
4	45
5	51
6	50
6.5	53
7.5	59
8	88
8.5	62
9	67
10	68
10.5	70
11	73
11.5	55
12	76
13	80
14	89
14.5	92

10. Determine the summary point for each of the three groups into which the data is divided.

11. Find the slope of the line that passes through the first and last summary points.

12. Find the slope of the median-median line.

13. Find the approximate y-intercept of the median-median line.

14. Find the equation of the linear model that best represents the situation.

11.8   Linear Regression

In the previous section, you saw how to estimate the line of best fit using a graph. The linear regression model for a set of data can be used to make predictions for other data values.

Example 14:   The following data set contains the length of a car trip that the Doran family has made and the number of stops that they made on each trip.

Length of trip	Number of Stops	Length of Trip	Number of Stops
2 hours	0 stops	8 hours	3 stops
5 hours	2 stops	5 hours	3 stops
4 hours	2 stops	11 hours	6 stops
10 hours	6 stops	9 hours	4 stops

The linear regression model for this set of data is $y = 0.608x - 0.857$. In other words, the line of best fit is: Stops $= (0.608 \times$ Length $) - 0.857$.

The slope means that for every hour longer the trip is, on average, they will stop 0.608 more times.

Let's consider how well the line predicts the data points at Length $= 5$ hours and Length $= 10$ hours.

$$y = 0.608 \times 5 - 0.857 = 2.183 \qquad y = 0.608 \times 10 - 0.857 = 5.223$$

The prediction for 5 hours was 2.183 stops, while the real observed values were 2 and 3, and the prediction for 10 hours was 5.223 stops, while the real observed value was 6. These are all quite close and show that this is a reasonable line of best fit.

Example 15:   Tabitha has to keep track of the number of minutes she reads each day and how far she gets into her book. Her observations from her most recent week of reading are graphed below.

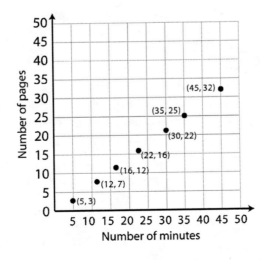

Which equation models these data points?

A. $y = -0.735x + 0.619$

B. $y = 0.266x - 2.619$

C. $y = 0.735x - 0.619$

D. $y = -0.266x + 2.619$

Step 1:   Eliminate choices that you can easily observe are wrong.
By looking at the graph we can see that the points are positively linear, so the choices A and D can be eliminated.

Step 2:   Test points from the scatterplot.
First, look at the line of best fit for choice B, $y = 0.266x - 2.619$.
Substitute one of the points from the scatterplot.
$(5, 3) : 3 = 0.266 \times 5 - 2.619$
$(5, 3) : 3 \neq -1.289$
Since $3 \neq -1.289$, the choice B is not the correct answer.
Look at the line of best fit for choice C, $y = 0.735x - 0.619$.
Substitute one of the points from the scatterplot.
$(5, 3) : 3 = 0.735 \times 5 - 0.619$
$(5, 3) : 3 = 3$
Since $3 = 3$, the choice C is the correct answer.

Use the linear regression model or data given to answer the following questions.

1. Using the scatterplot in example 15, and the linear regression model, $y = 0.735x - 0.619$, to answer the following question.
About how much of a page can she read per minute?

2. Dr. Silverstein charted 8 of his patients' candy consumption versus their number of cavities in a year. He also computed a linear regression model for his data: $y = 0.448x + 0.150$.

Patient	Candies Per Day	Cavities Per Year	Patient	Candies Per Day	Cavities Per Year
Kurt	1	1	Chris	2	0
Erin	4	2	Olivia	7	3
Sarah	4	3	Rimas	5	2
Brian	9	5	Tonya	10	4

How many cavities should Jessica have if she ate 8 candies per day? Use the linear regression model to determine your answer.

3. A group of 9 students in Mrs. Van Wyck's math class were given the assignment to determine if there was a strong relationship between the number of people in their household and the amount that their household spent on groceries (excluding pet food).
Their data points were as follows (Number of people in household, cost of groceries):
$(3, \$143), (4, \$156), (2, \$89), (2, \$127), (6, \$201), (5, \$180), (3, \$171), (3, \$152), (3, \$135)$
Using these data points, the students were able to calculate a linear regression model, although a few of the students calculated differents lines of best fit. Which equation models these data?

    A. $y = -\$21.18x + \$77.49$ C. $y = \$21.18x + \$77.49$
    B. $y = \$32.45x + \$63.71$ D. $y = \$32.45x - \$63.71$

4. Use the information in problem 3 to answer the following question. Mrs. Van Wyck has a household of 7 people. How many dollars would you estimate her grocery bill to be? Use the line of best fit to determine your answer.

For questions 5–9, use the data, linear regression models, and scatterplots to make predictions about the relationships or determine the appropriate line of best fit.

5. (10 years, 3.5 mm), (11 years, 9.2 mm), (13 years, 14.5 mm), (14 years, 22.8 mm),
   Linear Regression: $y = 4.39x - 40.18$
   What is the predicted height in millimeters after 16 years?

6. (2.2 min, 75 beats), (4 min, 149 beats), (6 min, 213 beats), (8.8 min, 298 beats)

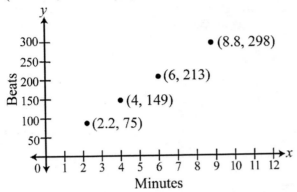

   Which equation models these data?

   A. $y = 33.4x + 8.39$

   B. $y = -15.77x + 8.39$

   C. $y = -33.4x + 8.39$

   D. $y = 33.4x - 8.39$

7. ($2.47, 11 pts), ($2.55, 16 pts), ($2.58, 19 pts), ($2.61, 20 pts), ($2.66, 27 pts),
   Linear Regression: $y = 80.91x - 189.67$
   What is the predicted number of points after spending $3.00.

8. (4 laps, 42 calories), (10 laps, 113 calories), (19 laps, 176 calories), (23 laps, 258 calories)
   Use the scatterplot to determine the line of best fit for the data.

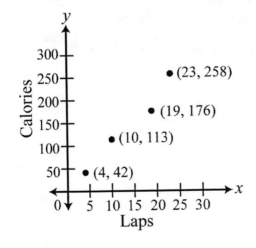

   Which equation models these data?

   A. $y = -10.5x - 0.31$

   B. $y = 12.75x + 0.31$

   C. $y = 10.5x + 0.31$

   D. $y = -10.5x + 0.51$

9. (2 carries, 9 yards), (3 carries, 21 yards), (7 carries, 28 yards), (8 carries, 43 yards),
   Linear Regression: $y = 4.46x + 2.94$
   What is the predicted number of yards for 10 carries?

11.9   Modeling Data with Quadratic Functions

When the change in a dependent variable changes at a constant rate in relation to the change in an independent variable, the relationship can be modeled with a quadratic function.

Example 16:   A backyard swimming pool originally containing 128 m^3 of water developed a small leak, so the amount of water in the swimming pool decreased with time. The table below shows the amount of water that was in the swimming pool after certain numbers of hours had passed since the leak began.

Hours Since Leak Began	Amount of Water in Pool in m^3
0	128
1	126
2	120
3	110
4	96
5	78
6	56
7	30
8	0

Can the relationship between the number of hours after the leak began and the amount of water in the pool be modeled with a quadratic function? If so, plot the data and draw the parabola.

Step 1:   Determine if the relationship can be modeled with a quadratic function.
From hour 1 to hour 2, the change in the amount of water in the pool was -6 m^3, from hour 2 to hour 3 it was -10 m^3, from hour 3 to hour 4 it was -14 m^3, and so on. The change in the amount of water in the pool is changing at a rate of -4 m^3 per hour. Since the change in the dependent variable decreases at a constant rate in relation to an increase in the independent variable, the relationship can be modeled with a quadratic function.

Step 2:   Plot the data and draw the line.
The number of hours after the leak began is the independent variable (x), and the amount of water in the pool is the dependent variable (y).

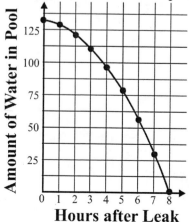

184   Copyright © American Book Company

Example 17:   A blog has been online for 5 days, and the change in the number of comments posted to the blog from one day to the next has been increasing at a constant rate. The relationship between the number of days the blog has been online and the total number of comments posted can be modeled with a quadratic function as shown below. What is the equation of the quadratic function?

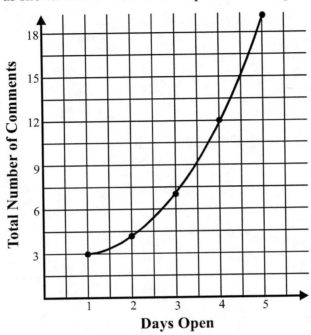

Days Open

Step 1:   Find the vertex of the parabola.

Looking at the graph, we see the right side of a parabola with a vertex of $(1, 3)$. If this is the case, the equation of the parabola is $y = a(x - 1)^2 + 3$, where a is a constant.

Step 2:   Substitute one point into the equation of the parabola and solve for a.

One point on the parabola is $(4, 12)$. Substitute and solve for a.

$12 = a(4 - 1)^2 + 3$

$12 = a(3)^2 + 3$

$12 = 9a + 3$

$12 - 3 = 9a + 3 - 3$

$9 = 9a$

$a = 1$

Since $a = 1$, the equation of the parabola is $y = 1(x - 1)^2 + 3$, or $y = (x - 1)^2 + 3$.
If all the other points on the parabola are tested, they all satisfy this equation, so the equation is, in fact, correct.

Determine whether or not each of the following situations can be modeled with a quadratic function.

1. Every month the number of checks in a check book decreases by 4.

2. For every $50 decrease in the price of a computer, the change in the number of computers sold increases by 12.

3. The total number of donations made to a charitable organization is increasing at a rate of 28 per day.

4. A person's heart is beating at a rate of 70 beats per minute.

5. For every hour that passes, the change in temperature decreases by 0.2 degrees.

6. For every week that passes, the total amount of rainfall increases by 0.1 inches.

7. Every day the change in the number of visitors to a park over the previous day increases by 18.

8. For every student a college accepts, it spends $50 on facility maintenance.

9. For every point won in a debate, the change in a politician's approval rating increases by 0.5 percent.

What is the equation of the quadratic function that can be used to model the situation with each of the following pairs of data points? Assume the first data point is the vertex of the parabola.

10. (3 years, 5 km), (8 years, 55 km)

11. (1 mile, 6 min), (9 miles, 70 min)

12. (3 signs, 10 people), (4 signs, 9 people)

13. ($3.90, 44 units), ($4.30, 60 units)

14. (2 games, 7 points), (6 games, 55 points)

15. (5 cases, $70.00), (7 cases, $58.00)

11.10   Curve of Best Fit

Sometimes, the trend of best fit is not best described by a line, but by some other kind of curve. Some questions will ask you to read this curve on a graph, predict missing values, and to interpret the meaning in real-life terms.

Example 18:   The great quarterback "Touchdown" Tofanelli played professional football for 12 years.
The following graph shows his touchdown passes each year in the league.

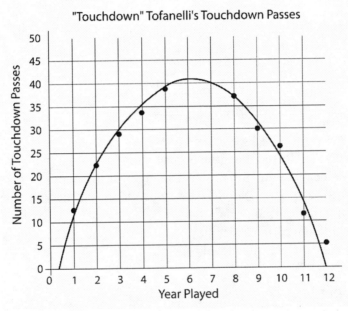

Year	1	2	3	4	5	6	7	8	9	10	11	12
Number of TD passes	12	22	29	33	39	?	?	37	30	26	11	3

Step 1:   Describe the curve of best fit, explaining in what periods (if any) there was a rapid increase, a rapid decrease, a slow increase, a slow decrease, or a steady level.

The curve of best fit is shaped like a parabola, with zeroes around Years 0 and 12. There is a rapid increase in TD passes per year from Years 1 to 3, a slow increase in TD passes per year from Years 4 to 6, a slow decrease in TD passes per year from Years 7 to 9, and a rapid decrease in TD passes from Years 10 to 12. In everyday terms, Tofanelli got better every year until he hit his "prime" around Years 3, played his best years in Years 6 and 7, and lost his effectiveness after Year 10.

Step 2:   According to the curve of best fit, how many touchdown passes should he have thrown in years 6 & 7?

The curve passes at Year = 6 passes through 41 TD passes or so, and Year = 7 clearly passes through 40 TD passes.

Answer the questions by looking at the curve of best fit graphs.

1.

Car Ads

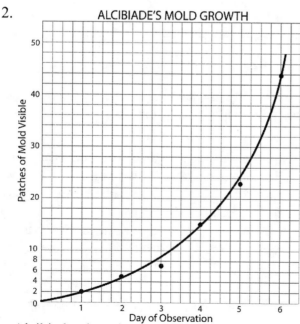

(A) A car executive wanted to see how much increasing his ad budget would affect sales. He plotted previous ad campaigns for similar cars against the number of sales. According to the curve of best fit, how much would their sales increase if they increased their ad budget from $10 million to $15 million?

(B) Explain how the amount of sales changes in comparison to the amount spent on advertising. Include an estimate of when sales level off.

2.

Alcibiade, the scientist, is testing the growth of a particular kind of mold. According to the curve of best fit, how many patches of mold should there be after 6 days?

11.11   Quadratic Regression

When a relationship is not exactly quadratic, quadratic regression can be used to determine the equation of the quadratic model.

Example 19:   A college has offered a course on computer graphics for the last 5 semesters, and the enrollment in the course has increased each semester. The college has found that as the enrollment in the course has increased, the number of textbooks on computer graphics sold in its bookstore also increased. The table below shows the enrollment in the course for each of the last 5 semesters and the number of textbooks on computer graphics sold in its bookstore during that semester.

	Students Enrolled in Course	Textbooks Sold
Semester 1	9	16
Semester 2	11	19
Semester 3	16	44
Semester 4	19	71
Semester 5	25	152

The quadratic regression for this situation is $y = 0.5x^2 - 8.5x + 52$.

Use the curve of best fit to predict the number of textbooks sold during the seventh semester when there are 30 students enrolled in the course.

Step 1:   Substitute $x = 30$ in the quadratic regression model.

$$y = 0.5x^2 - 8.5x + 52$$
$$y = 0.5\,(30)^2 - 8.5\,(30) + 52$$

Step 2:   Solve for y.

$$y = (0.5 * 900) - 255 + 52$$
$$y = 450 - 255 + 52$$
$$y = 247$$

Answer: We can predict that if there are 30 students enrolled in the course, there will be 247 textbooks sold.

Use the quadratic regression or scatterplot given to answer each of the following questions.

1. (1 hr, 3 liters), (2 hrs, 7 liters), (3.5 hrs, 27 liters), (4 hrs, 34 liters), (5 hrs, 51 liters),

   Quadratic Regression: $y = 1.9x^2 + 0.97x - 0.71$

   Predict the number of liters after 7 hours.

2. (1 day, 4 views), (3 days, 25 views), (4 days, 49 views), (5 days, 79 views), (6 days, 99 views)

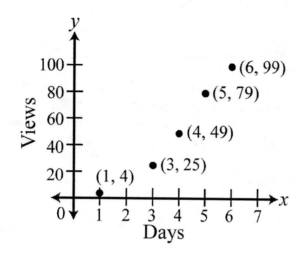

Which quadratic regression model represents the data in the scatterplot?

A. $y = -2.26x^2 + 4.06x - 3.51$

B. $y = -2.26x^2 - 4.06x - 3.51$

C. $y = 2.26x^2 - 4.06x + 3.51$

D. $y = 2.26x^2 + 4.06x - 3.51$

3. (2 people, $42), (6 people, $250), (8 people, $670), (12 people, $1250), (15 people, $1710)

Quadratic Regression: $y = 4.81x^2 + 51.75x - 115.92$

Predict how much it will cost for 17 people.

4. (2 min, 99 pgs), (4 min, 197 pgs), (7 min, 354 pgs), (8 min, 484 pgs), (9 min, 649 pgs)

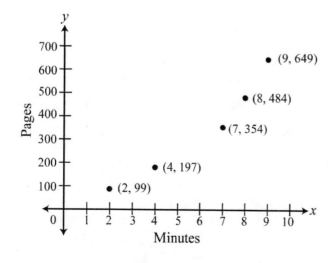

Which quadratic regression model represents the data in the scatterplot?

A. $y = 9.97x^2 + 36.13x + 146.83$

B. $y = 7.97x^2 + 36.13x + 149.83$

C. $y = 7.97x^2 - 36.13x + 146.83$

D. $y = 9.97x^2 - 36.13x + 146.83$

11.12   Misusing Lines and Curves of Best Fit

While the lines and curves of best fit are very helpful, you must be careful not to predict values too far outside the range of data.

Example 20:   Muddy Creek High School opened in 1997. In 1997, it taught only freshmen. In 1998, it taught freshmen and sophomores. Below is a graph of the number of students in each year.

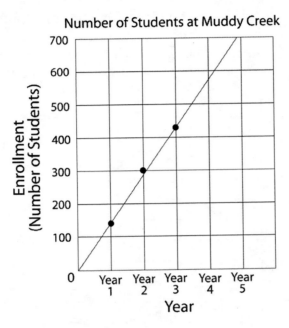

Number of Students at Muddy Creek

Year	1997	1998	1999	2000
Number of Students	140	302	435	?

About how many students should there be in the school in 2000 (year 4). Based on the line of best fit, how many students would we expect to be in the school by the year 2025 (year 29)? Is this number reasonable?

Step 1:   The exact line of best fit is $y = 147.5x - 2.67$. Whether or not this exact line is calculated, you can estimate that 140 or 145 are being added each year. The exact answer for the year 2000 is $y = 147.5 \times 4 - 2.67 = 587.33$, about 587 students. On the graph, you can see that it is between 580 and 600.

Step 2:   The same equation yields, for 2025, $y = 147.5 \times 29 - 2.67 = 4274.8$, roughly 4275 students. This number is not reasonable because the fast growth of the high school is a result of the introduction of an entirely new class each year. We have no way of knowing if and how much the high school will grow after the first four years.

11.13   Issues Between Two Variables

Some issues arise when using data to explore the relationship between two variables by creating a mathematical model. First, a mathematical model usually isn't perfect. Most of the time, there will be data that doesn't lie on the curve that is being used as a model. Also, if there is only a small amount of data, the wrong type of model might be chosen. A mathematical model can be used to determine a data point between two known data points, but it can't necessarily be used to predict future data points.

Example 21:   Since the release of the first version of its word processor, a computer software company has seen the sales of the word processor increase at a constant pace. The number of units sold in thousands as a function time in years since the release of the first version can be modeled with the linear function $y = 20x$ as shown.

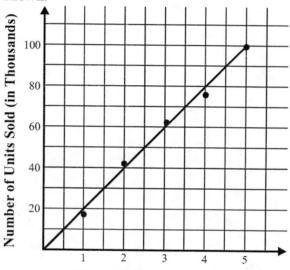

Years Since Release of First Version

If the trend continues, how many units does the mathematical model predict will be sold 10 years after the release of the first version? What could happen in the future to make the mathematical model's prediction inaccurate?

Step 1:   Calculate the mathematical model's prediction.

Since the linear function $y = 20x$ is being used as the mathematical model, the number of units sold in thousands 10 years after the release of the first version is $y = 20(10) = 200$. In other words, the mathematical model predicts that $200,000$ units will be sold 10 years after the release of the first version.

Step 2:   Identify reasons why the mathematical model's prediction may be inaccurate.

Many things could happen in the future to make the mathematical model's prediction inaccurate. For example, perhaps the word processor runs on only a certain operating system, and maybe that operating system will become obsolete. Also, perhaps a new competitor will emerge to cause the word processor to lose market share. There are an infinite number of possibilities that could make the mathematical model's prediction inaccurate.

Example 22:   Last April the change in the number of minutes remaining on Lucy's monthly cell phone plan decreased at a constant rate. The number of minutes remaining as a function of the number of days that had passed that month could be modeled with the quadratic function $y = -x^2 + 900$ as shown.

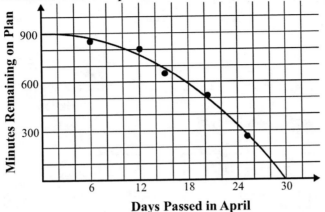

Days Passed in April

What is the domain of the mathematical model $y = -x^2 + 900$?

Step 1:   Determine the values of x for which the mathematical model doesn't make sense.
Since there are only 30 days in the month of April, any value for x less than 0 or greater than 30 doesn't make sense. Another reason why a value of x greater than 30 doesn't make sense is because it would cause a negative number of minutes to remain on Lucy's monthly cell phone plan, which isn't possible.

Step 2:   State the domain of the mathematical model.
The domain of the mathematical model is $0 \leq x \leq 30$.

The function provided was used to model each of the following relationships. Calculate the mathematical model's prediction for the time frame given, and provide one possible future event that could make the model's prediction inaccurate.

1. $y = 2x$; $y =$ the amount spent on milk in dollars, $x =$ number of weeks; the amount spent on milk after 257 weeks

2. $y = 7x + 6$; $y =$ number of visits to a newspaper's website, $x =$ number of days; the number of visits to the newspaper's website after 6123 days

3. $y = 55x$; $y =$ number of miles, $x =$ number of hours; the number of miles travelled by the car after 13 hours

4. $y = 120x + 27$; $y =$ number of trees in a park, $x =$ number of years; the number of trees in the park after 62 years

The function provided was used to model each of the following relationships. Determine the mathematical model's domain.

5. $y = -x^2 + 324$; the amount of air in a balloon in m^3 as a function of minutes passed

6. $y = 2x^2$; the number of e-mails received in May as a function of days passed that month

11.14   Correlation and Causation

When two variables in a relationship are correlated, a change in one variable suggests a change in the other. However, correlation does not imply causation. In other words, just because a change in variable x suggests a change in variable y, the change in x does not necessary cause the change in y. Both the change in x and the change in y could be caused by a third factor.

Example 23:   A study has shown that as the number of hours a person spends dancing increases, the probability that the person will experience hearing loss also increases. The relationship between hours spent dancing and probability of hearing loss is shown below:

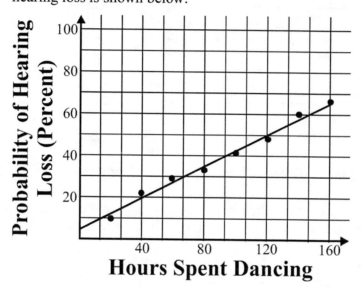

Because there is an obvious correlation between hours spent dancing and probability of hearing loss, the study concluded that dancing causes hearing loss. Is it likely that the study's conclusion is correct?

Step 1:   Determine if a third factor could cause a change in both variables.

What could cause both an increase in the number of hours spent dancing and an increase in the probability of hearing loss? How about loud music?

Step 2:   Decide if the relationship between the variables is likely one of causation, or if it is only a correlation.

Common sense dictates that loud music is much more likely to cause hearing loss than dancing. Therefore, the relationship between hours spent dancing and probability of hearing loss is only a correlation, and there is probably no causation involved.

Example 24:   Give an example of a variable that could be in correlation with the amount of hot cocoa a person consumes. Then explain whether or not this is an example of causation.

   Step 1:   Give an example.
   One possible example of a variable that could be in correlation with the amount of hot cocoa a person consumes is the probability that the person will experience frostbite. The more hot cocoa a person consumes, the more likely that person is to experience frostbite.

   Step 2:   Explain whether or not this correlation is an example of causation.
   Drinking hot cocoa probably doesn't cause frostbite. However, cold weather can cause both an increase in hot cocoa consumption and frostbite. Therefore, the correlation between hot cocoa consumed and frostbite is not an example of causation.

Decide if each of the following relationships is likely one of causation, or if it is only a correlation.

1. As a person's corrected vision improves, his reading ability improves.

2. The more umbrellas are in use, the greener the grass becomes.

3. The more a person types, the more likely the person is to experience carpal tunnel syndrome.

4. The more skiers are on the slopes, the more school days are cancelled.

5. As a person sits down more, he becomes more intelligent.

6. The windier it is, the more people are flying kites.

7. As the number of bicycles sold increases, the number of hybrid cars sold increases.

8. The noisier it is in a basketball area, the more hot dogs are sold in the arena.

9. As a person's income increases, the amount she pays in taxes increases.

Give an example of a variable that could be in correlation with each of the following variables. Then explain whether or not this is an example of causation.

10. a student's height

11. the number of bicycles on the road

12. the number of aspirin a person takes

13. the number of fires in a city

14. the number of children in a family

15. the number of teeth a toddler has

Chapter 11 Review

Determine whether or not each of the following situations can be modeled with a linear function.

1. For every page a writer writes, he gets paid $10.50.

2. The number of supporters of a candidate is increasing by 5 percent every month.

3. The perimeter of a square is equal to the length of a side of the square multiplied by 4.

4. The total number of signatures on a petition is tripling every week.

Find the equation of the linear function that can be used to model a situation with the following data points.

5. (5 yrs, 277 km), (9 yrs, 437 km)

6. (34 crates, $8.50), (41 crates, $7.66)

Determine whether or not each of the following situations can be modeled with a quadratic function.

7. Every minute the change in the amount of water in a bathtub decreases by 0.5 liters.

8. A company's debt increases by $500,000 every year.

9. The change in the number of people donating blood is increasing by 14 every quarter.

10. The number of mosquitoes is decreasing by 5 every minute.

Find the equation of the quadratic function that can be used to model a situation with the following data points. Assume the first data point is the vertex of the parabola.

11. (3 matches, 2 pts), (8 matches, 52 pts)

12. ($2.40, 12 bushels), ($6.90, 93 bushels)

Use the data below for questions 13–16.

(2 pages, 44 points), (9 pages, 48 points), (13 pages, 77 points), (16 pages, 53 points), (28 pages, 64 points), (41 pages, 51 points), (57 pages, 70 points), (58 pages, 73 points), (107 pages, 89 points)

13. Determine the summary point for each of the three groups into which the data is divided.

14. Find the slope of the median-median line.

15. Find the approximate y-intercept of the median-median line.

16. Find the equation of the linear model that best represents the situation.

For each of the following scatterplots, determine which equation models the data.

17.

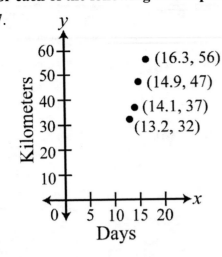

A. $y = 6.32x - 81.22$

B. $y = 8.04x - 74.56$

C. $y = -6.32x - 81.22$

D. $y = -8.04x + 74.56$

18.

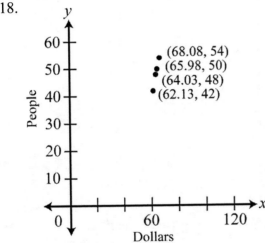

A. $y = -1.91x + 76.05$

B. $y = -1.91x - 76.05$

C. $y = 1.91x - 76.05$

D. $y = 1.91x + 76.05$

19.

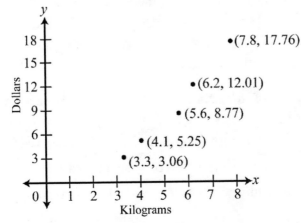

A. $y = 0.25x^2 + 0.55x - 1.34$

B. $y = 0.5x^2 + 0.25x - 1.25$

C. $y = -0.25x^2 + 0.55x - 1.34$

D. $y = -0.5x^2 + 0.25 + 1.25$

For each of the following groups of points, use the quadratic regression feature on a graphing calculator to determine the equation of the quadratic function that can be used to model the relationship in question.

20. (15 games, 30 errors), (25 games, 48 errors), (32 games, 60 errors), (40 games, 83 errors)
    Linear Regression: $y = 2.08x - 2.9$
    Predict how many errors there will be after 45 games.

21. (2 min, 58 gallons), (11 min, 79 gallons), (23 min, 91 gallons), (31 min, 125 gallons)
    Linear Regression: $y = 2.11x + 52.89$
    Predict how many gallons there will be after 40 minutes.

22. (4 hr, 2 pints), (8 hr, 13 pints), (10 hr, 35 pints), (15 hr, 78 pints), (19 hr, 141 pints)
    Quadratic Regression: $y = 0.51x^2 - 2.41x + 3.5$
    Predict how many pints there will be after 21 hours.

Explain the relationship between the variables in each of the following scatter plots.

23.
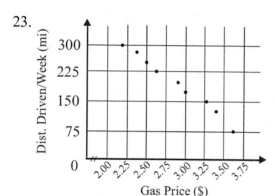

24.
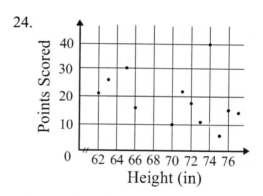

The function provided was used to model each of the following relationships. Calculate the mathematical model's prediction for the time frame given and provide one possible future event that could make the model's prediction inaccurate.

25. $y = 17,000x$; y = attendance of a hockey team, x = number of matches;
    the attendance of the hockey team after 66 matches

26. $y = 59x + 22$; y = number of pages printed by a laser printer, x = number of days;
    the number of pages printed by the laser printer after 713 days

The function provided was used to model each of the following relationships. Determine the mathematical model's domain.

27. $y = 4x$; the number of DVDs watched in a collection of 92 as a function of weeks passed

28. $y = -20x^2 + 1620$; a computer's value in dollars as a function of years passed

29. $y = 3x^2$; the number of online friends made in July as a function of days passed that month

30. $y = 0.2x$; the number of hours spent dusting as a function of the number of rooms cleaned

Decide if each of the following relationships is likely one of causation, or if it is only a correlation.

31. the more electricity is used, the more ice cream is eaten

32. the more gifts are given, the more carols are sung

33. as a person eats fewer sugary foods, he gets fewer cavities

34. the more fireworks are detonated, the more bratwursts are eaten

35. the more hours a wage-earner spends working, the more money he/she makes

36. as the grass becomes greener, more sunglasses are worn

Draw a scatter plot for the given data.

37.

Price of strawberries/lb	1.00	1.50	5.00	3.50	2.50	4.00	3.00
lbs purchased	75	65	20	40	52	30	47

38.

Height (in)	62	73	64	71	72	63	75	74	66	73	75
Homeruns hit	6	10	1	0	11	5	4	3	6	2	1

Answer the following questions about line and curve of best fit.

39. In 1870, Lonesome Dove was a prosperous Western town with 12,000 people when the railroad decided to change routes. The table below shows Lonesome Dove's population decline in subsequent decades:

Year	1870	1880	1890	1900	1910
Population of Lonesome Dove	12000	10300	8500	6900	5200

Find the exact line of best fit using a calculator, with 1870 as $x = 0$.

(A) According to the line of best fit, what was the population in 1896 (Year 26)?

(B) According to the line of best fit, what will the population be in 2010 (Year 140)? Is this number reasonable?

40. The graph below shows the median high temperature each month in Buenos Aires, Argentina.

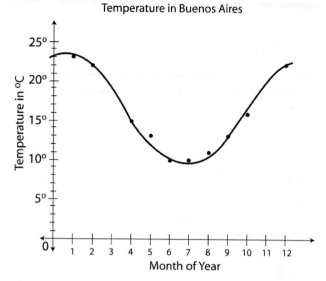

According to the curve of best fit, what should be the missing values for March and November?

Chapter 11 Test

1. Which of the following situations can best be modeled with a quadratic function?

   A. For every month that passes, the number of songs stored on an MP3 player increases by 22.
   B. The change in the number of students enrolled in a college over the previous semester is increasing by 58 each semester.
   C. The amount of yogurt consumed by citizens of a country is increasing by 25,000 ounces every month.
   D. The average number of minutes high school students sleep every night is decreasing by 3 minutes every 5 years.

2. Linear regression has been used to determine the equation of the linear function that models the situation that produces the points (6.2 minutes, 26 inches), (7.1 minutes, 34 inches), (7.9 minutes, 41 inches), and (9.3 minutes, 50 inches). What is the equation of the linear function?

   A. $y = -21.2x + 7.7$
   B. $y = -7.7x + 21.2$
   C. $y = 7.7x - 21.2$
   D. $y = 21.2x + 7.7$

3. The function $y = 0.1x + 74$ is being used to model the average life span of males in years as a function of the number of years from now. Which of the following future events would most likely make some of the mathematical model's predications inaccurate?

   A. a cure for the common cold
   B. advances in laser eye surgery
   C. a cure for gum disease
   D. less exercise and more calories consumed by the average male over time

4. A linear function is being used to model the number of daily visitors to a museum as a function of the admission price in dollars. If the slope of the line is -20, and if one of the points on the line is $(6, 780)$, what is the equation of the line?

   A. $y = -20x + 120$
   B. $y = -20x + 660$
   C. $y = -20x + 780$
   D. $y = -20x + 900$

5. Based on the data shown, which of the following is not a summary point used to find the median-median line that models the situation?

Times Played	Average Number of Points Scored on Video Game
1	444
2	478
4	497
6	530
7	522
8	545
10	468
13	582
17	619

   A. (7 time played, 530 points scored)
   B. (2 times played, 478 points scored)
   C. (7 times played, 522 points scored)
   D. (13 times played, 582 points scored)

6. If a change in variable x suggests a change in variable y, does the change in x cause the change in y?

   A. Always
   B. Sometimes
   C. Never
   D. Only if there is a direct relationship

7. Which of the following relationships is most likely one of causation?

  A. As the water temperature of a pond increases, the number of fish in the pond decreases.

  B. As the number of visits to a news website increases, the number of people evacuating a city increases.

  C. As credit-card usage increases, the unemployment rate increases.

  D. As the number of people snowboarding increases, the number of snowmen built increases.

8. Quadratic regression has been used to determine the equation of the quadratic function that models the situation that produces the points (5.3 kg, $90.55), (6.2 kg, $111.03), (7.5 kg, $151.63), (8.2 kg, $209.97), and (9.6 kg, $293.32). What is the equation of the quadratic function?

  A. $y = 10.9x^2 - 112.4x + 385.3$
  B. $y = 10.9x^2 + 385.3x - 112.4$
  C. $y = -60.4x^2 + 7.27x - 112.4$
  D. $y = 7.27x^2 - 60.4x + 205.44$

9. The number of people in a line as a function of minutes passed can be modeled with the quadratic function whose graph has a vertex of $(1, 14)$ as shown.

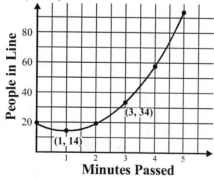

What is the quadratic function's equation?

  A. $y = 2(x - 1)^2 + 14$
  B. $y = 3(x - 1)^2 + 14$
  C. $y = 4(x - 1)^2 + 14$
  D. $y = 5(x - 1)^2 + 14$

10. Which of the following situations can best be modeled with a linear function?

  A. For every $0.15 decrease in the price of a carton of eggs, the number of cartons purchased increases by 10 percent.

  B. The total number of hot tamales sold is doubling every year.

  C. The area of a circle is equal to π times the radius squared.

  D. Every 3 months the number of potholes in the street increases by 5.

11. The change in the voltage of a car battery is decreasing at a constant rate. This can be modeled with the function $y = -x^2 + 9$. What is the domain of the model?

  A. $-9 \le x \le 9$
  B. $-3 \le x \le 3$
  C. $0 \le x \le 3$
  D. $0 \le x \le 9$

12. Heather and Robert each used eyeballing to determine the equation to model the data shown.

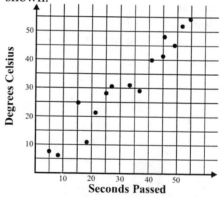

What of the following statements is true?

  A. Their equations will likely be the same because their data is the same.

  B. Their equations will likely be the same because the y-intercept of the mathematical model will obviously be 0.

  C. Their equations will likely be different because eyeballing is only an approximation.

  D. Their equations will only be different if one of them makes an error.

Practice Test 1

Part 1

You may use the formula sheet on page viii as needed.

1. Which is the graph of:
$$f(x) = \begin{cases} 2 & \text{if } x \leq 3 \\ 3+x & \text{if } 3 < x < 5 \\ \frac{1}{2}x & \text{if } x \geq 5 \end{cases}$$

A.

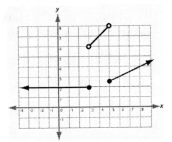

B.

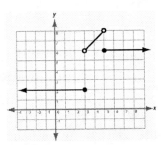

C.

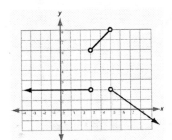

D.

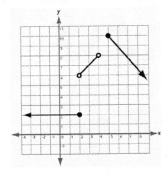

MM2A1b

2. What is the value of x?

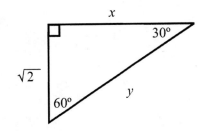

A. $\dfrac{\sqrt{2}}{3}$

B. 6

C. $2\sqrt{2}$

D. $\sqrt{6}$

MM2G1a

3. Find x.

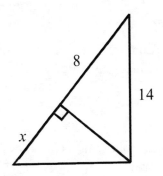

A. 24.4

B. 16.5

C. 22.7

D. 18.3

MM2G2b

4. Given the function $f(x) = 2x + 1$, what is its inverse?

A. $f^{-1}(x) = \dfrac{x+1}{2}$

B. $f^{-1}(x) = 2x - 1$

C. $f^{-1}(x) = \dfrac{x-1}{2}$

D. $f^{-1}(x) = 2(x-1)$

MM2A5b

5. Bobby is a fitness writer for a local magazine. He wants to know if men or women exercise more. To do this he gathered a random sample of men and a random sample of women. He asked both groups how many hours a week they spent exercising. What is the statistic being compared?

A. amount of total trips to the gym by each population

B. average number of hours spent in the gym each week by each population

C. amount of calories burned at gym by each population

D. average amount of water consumed each week by each population

MM2D1a

6. Which of the following is $\sqrt{-12}$ in imaginary form?

A. $2\sqrt{3}$

B. $-2i\sqrt{3}$

C. $2\sqrt{-3}$

D. $2i\sqrt{3}$

MM2N1a

7. To find the average number of hours spent playing video games each day by teenagers, the number of hours spent daily playing video games by each teenager of a large random sample of 1,750 teenagers was determined. The mean number of hours spent per day playing video games by teenagers in the sample was 7.5 hours, and the standard deviation of hours spent daily playing video games was 15. A smaller data sample was also observed. This smaller set consisted of 15 teenagers. The mean for this sample was 4 hours, and the standard deviation 17. What can you conclude from this data?

A. The larger sample has the higher standard deviation.

B. The smaller sample has the higher standard deviation.

C. The smaller sample has the higher mean.

D. The larger sample has the lower mean.

MM2D1d

8. If the length of $\overline{DE} = 8$, the length of $\overline{EC} = 11$, and $\overline{AD} = 10$, what is the length of $\overline{BC}$?

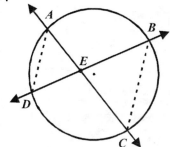

A. 7.27

B. 8.8

C. 13

D. 13.75

MM2G3a

9. What is the measure of $\angle B$?

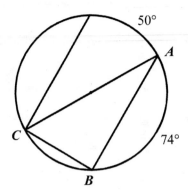

A. 25°

B. 37°

C. 50°

D. 90°

MM2G3b

10. For the equation $y = 3 \cdot 2^{x+2}$, what is the y-intercept and the asymptote?

A. $(0, 12)$; the x-axis

B. $(0, 0)$; the y-axis

C. $(0, 1)$; the x-axis

D. there is no y-intercept ; the y-axis

MM2A2b

11. A round clock measures 12 inches across the middle. What's the length of the minor arc formed along the edge of the clock when the hands are at 12:10?

A. 3.82 in

B. 6.28 in

C. 12.56 in

D. 18.84 in

MM2G3c

12. Which of the following is the solution to the inequality $|4x + 2| > 5$?

A. $x > \dfrac{3}{4}$ or $x < \dfrac{3}{4}$

B. $x < -\dfrac{7}{4}$ or $x > \dfrac{3}{4}$

C. $x < -7$ or $x > \dfrac{3}{4}$

D. $x > -\dfrac{7}{4}$ or $x < \dfrac{3}{4}$

MM2A1c

13. Caliyaah wants to see which high school basketball team scores the most points per game, Etowah High School or Woodstock High School. To do so, she went to six games at Etowah and six games at Woodstock. She recorded the final scores for each game in the chart below.

| EHS | 56 | 64 | 59 | 75 | 61 | 89 |
| WHS | 41 | 29 | 67 | 55 | 65 | 60 |

What can you conclude from the chart?

A. EHS has a higher mean by about 14.
B. WHS has a higher mean by about 14.
C. EHS has a higher mean by 2.
D. They have the same mean.

MM2D1c

14. Find the mean of the set of data. 50 points; 94 points; 80 points; 62 points; 106 points; 76 points; 83 points

A. 72.4 points
B. 88.6 points
C. 78.7 points
D. 92.5 points

MM2D1b

15. Find the mean of the set of data. 2 gallons; 7 gallons; 4 gallons; 12 gallons; 14 gallons; 9 gallons

A. 7 gallons

B. 8 gallons

C. 9 gallons

D. 10 gallons

MM2D1b

16. Find the mean of the set of data. $642; $988; $784; $282; $658; $844; $906; $476

A. $697.50

B. $797.14

C. $704.25

D. $654.83

MM2D1b

17. What is the approximate area of the shaded sector?

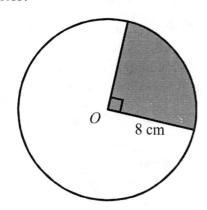

A. 12.56 cm^2

B. 25.12 cm^2

C. 50.24 cm^2

D. 200.96 cm^2

MM2G3c

18. The following graph was constructed to help solve the quadratic inequality $x^2 - x - 42 < 0$. Which of the following conclusions can be drawn?

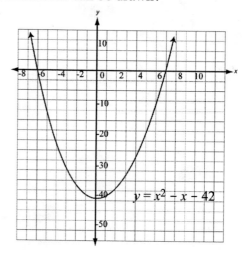

$$y = x^2 - x - 42$$

A. Because the parabola is below the x-axis between $x = -6$ and $x = 7$, the solution is $x < -6$ and $x > 7$.

B. Because the parabola is below the x-axis between $x = -6$ and $x = 7$, the solution is $-6 < x < 7$.

C. Because the parabola intersects the x-axis at $x = -6$ and $x = 7$, the solution is $x = -6$ and $x = 7$.

D. Because the parabola is above the x-axis when $x < -6$ and $x > 7$, the solution is $x < -6$ and $x > 7$.

MM2A4d

19. The measure of the sides of triangles are given below. Which of the following triangles is similar to a triangle with sides 2.4, 7, and 7.4?

A. $3, 8.75, 9$

B. $4, 8.4, 9.2$

C. $6, 17.5, 18.5$

D. $12, 14, 14.8$

MM2G2c

20. Using composition, determine which of the following are inverses of each other.

A. $f(x) = 2x + 1$ and $f^{-1}(x) = \frac{1}{2}x - \frac{1}{2}$

B. $f(x) = \frac{2}{3}x + 3$ and $f^{-1}(x) = \frac{2}{3}x - \frac{9}{2}$

C. $f(x) = -\frac{1}{2}x + 2$ and $f^{-1}(x) = 2x + 4$

D. $f(x) = -12x + 5$ and $f^{-1}(x) = \frac{x}{12} + \frac{5}{12}$

MM2A5d

21. A ski lift carries passengers 200 feet to the top of a slope. It's built at a 60° angle with the horizon. How far does the ski lift travel?

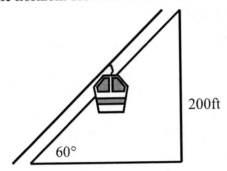

A. 400 ft

B. 231 ft

C. 173 ft

D. 346 ft

MM2G2c

22. Today at 10:00 AM there is 1 bacteria cell in a petri dish. This type of bacteria doubles every 20 minutes. How many bacteria will be in the dish after 3 hours?

A. 256

B. 512

C. 1024

D. 2048

MM2A2e

23. What is the value of x in the diagram below?

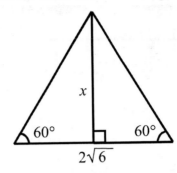

A. 12

B. $3\sqrt{2}$

C. $\frac{\sqrt{6}}{3}$

D. $2\sqrt{6}$

MM2G1a

24. Which of the following is $\sqrt{-20}$ in imaginary form?

A. $2i\sqrt{5}$

B. $-2i\sqrt{5}$

C. $2\sqrt{-5}$

D. $2\sqrt{5}$

MM2N1a

25. What is the measure $\angle ABD$?

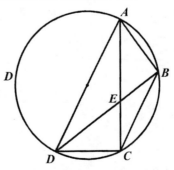

A. 30°

B. 60°

C. 90°

D. 120°

MM2G3b

26. The function $f(x)$ has the inverse $f^{-1}(x) = \sqrt[5]{6-x}$. What is $f(x)$?

   A. $f(x) = x^5 - 6$
   B. $f(x) = x^5 + 6$
   C. $f(x) = 6^5 - x^5$
   D. $f(x) = -x^5 + 6$

MM2A5b

27. Tina wants to divide a circle into 3 equal pie-shaped pieces. What will be the measure of each central angle?

   A. $30°$
   B. $60°$
   C. $90°$
   D. $120°$

MM2G3d

28. What is the range of the inverse of $y = x^2 - 8x + 7$?

   A. $-\infty < y < \infty$
   B. $-9 \le y < \infty$
   C. $-\infty < y \le 9$
   D. $9 \le y < \infty$

MM2A5a

29. What is the value of x?

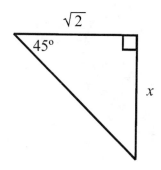

   A. 1
   B. 2
   C. $\sqrt{2}$
   D. $2\sqrt{2}$

MM2G1b

30. Given the equation $f(x) = x^2 - 4$, what are the zeros of the equation?

   A. $(0, -2)$ and $(0, 2)$
   B. $(-2, 0)$ and $(2, 0)$
   C. $(0, 4)$ and $(4, 0)$
   D. There are no zeros for this equation.

MM2A3c

31. Given: $\overline{AE} \parallel \overline{BD}$ and $\sin A = 0.6$. What is the measure of $\angle D$?

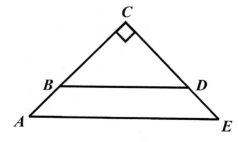

   A. $56°$
   B. $48°$
   C. $53°$
   D. $37°$

MM2G2a

32. Jeff was recently involved in a car wreck. Which of the following would most likely be the causing variable?

   A. slick tires
   B. the wetness of the roads
   C. the high volume on the stereo
   D. the car pulling out in front of Jeff's car

MM2D2d

33. Using the data points below, what is the equation of the linear function that can be used to model the situation?
(1 week, 4 miles), (8 weeks, 11 miles)

   A. $y = x - 3$
   B. $y = x + 3$
   C. $y = 2x + 3$
   D. $y = 2x - 3$

MM2D2a

34. Mark is collecting cans of food for a can drive. He wants to collect 1000 cans of food. He collects 64 cans every 60 minutes. Which equation best represents how many cans he has remaining to collect after a certain time? y = number of cans remaining to collect, t = time (in minutes)

time	cans
0	1000
60	936
120	872
180	808
240	744
300	680
360	616
420	552
480	488
540	424
600	360
660	296
720	232
780	168
840	104

A. $y = 1000 - 1\frac{1}{15}t$

B. $y = 60t$

C. $y = 5t - 1000$

D. None of the above

MM2D2a

35. A car executive wanted to see how much increasing his ad budget would affect sales. He plotted previous ad campaigns for similar cars against the number of sales. According to the curve of best fit below, how much would their sales increase if they increased their ad budget from \$10 million to \$15 million?

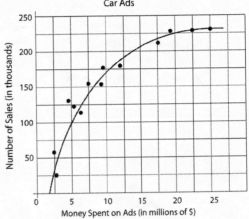

A. Their sales would increase by $40,000$.
B. Their sales would increase by $50,000$.
C. Their sales would increase by $60,000$.
D. Their sales will not increase.

MM2D2b

36. Use the scatterplot below to determine the equation of the quadratic function that can be used to model the relationship.

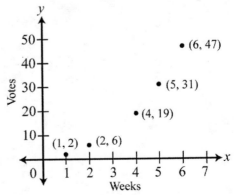

A. $y = 0.1x^2 - 8.1x + 9.5$
B. $y = 0.1x^2 + 8.1x + 9.5$
C. $y = 1.6x^2 - 2.4x + 3.36$
D. $y = 1.6x^2 + 2.4x + 3.36$

MM2D2c

Part 2

37. Compare the standard deviation of Louise and Thelma's bowling scores. Whose standard deviation is higher?

T	85	176	111	201	159	187	134
L	99	83	102	175	126	79	223

A. Thelma's standard deviation is higher.
B. Louise's standard deviation is higher.
C. Thelma and Louise have the same standard deviation.
D. Cannot be determined

MM2D1c

38. What is the value of x?

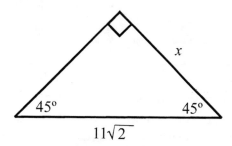

A. 2
B. 11
C. $2\sqrt{11}$
D. $\dfrac{11\sqrt{2}}{2}$

MM2G1b

39. Which of the following is the solution for $2x^2 + 5 = -13$?

A. $x = -3$
B. $x = \pm 3i$
C. $x = -9$
D. $x = \pm 9i$

MM2A4b

40. Sean is doing some research before moving into his first apartment. He is looking at two different areas, inside the city and outside the city. While doing his research he obtains prices for 8 apartments inside the city and 8 outside the city. How would Sean find the cheaper area to live in?

A. Add all of the apartment prices together and take an average of the total.
B. Take the range of the two populations and compare the two.
C. Take the mean of the two populations and compare the two.
D. Take the lowest priced apartment of the two areas and compare the two.

MM2D1a

41. $\overline{AB} \parallel \overline{DE}$ and $\cos D = 0.72$. What is the measure of $\angle A$?

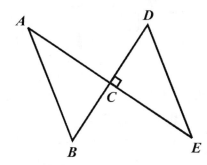

A. 44°
B. 46°
C. 37°
D. 43°

MM2G2a

42. Write $\sqrt{-5} + 6$ in standard form.

A. $-6 - i\sqrt{5}$
B. $6 + i\sqrt{5}$
C. $6 - i\sqrt{5}$
D. $i\sqrt{5} + 6$

MM2N1b

43. Simplify and write in standard form:

$$\frac{10i - 3}{5}$$

A. $2i - \dfrac{3}{5}$

B. $-\dfrac{3}{5} + 2i$

C. $-2i - \dfrac{3}{5}$

D. $\dfrac{3}{5} - 2i$

MM2N1d

44. Given that $\overline{PM}$ bisects $\angle NMQ$, $m\angle NMQ = 3x$, $m\angle MNQ = 2x$, and $m\angle NQM = 4x$, what is the measure of $\angle NAP$?

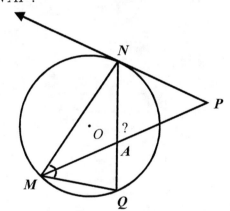

A. $70°$

B. $80°$

C. $30°$

D. $40°$

MM2G3a

45. Which of the following is the solution to $|6 - 3x| < 18$?

A. $-4 < x < 8$

B. $x < -4$ or $x > 8$

C. $x > -4$

D. $x < 4$

MM2A1c

46. What is the measure of an angle that the minute hand of a clock turns through between 4:30 p.m. and 5:20 p.m. of the same day?

A. $4620°$

B. $60°$

C. $300°$

D. $10°$

MM2G3c

47. Where is the vertex of the graph of $y = 2|x - 1| + 3$

A. $(1, -3)$

B. $(-1, 3)$

C. $(-1, -3)$

D. $(1, 3)$

MM2A1b

48. Tom wants to start planning a budget. To do this he added up all of his bills from month to month for the past 8 months. The results were as follows:

Month 1: $984.37   Month 5: $1,102.45
Month 2: $1,232.74   Month 6: $956.87
Month 3: $1,097.43   Month 7: $1,124.62
Month 4: $1,218.83   Month 8: $1,056.31

What is the average for Tom's monthly bills for the past 8 months?

A. $1,102.84

B. $1,096.70

C. $1,135.58

D. $1,059.44

MM2D1b

49. What is the approximate area of the shaded sector?

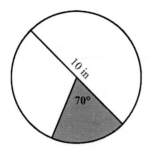

A. 3.05 in²
B. 6.1 in²
C. 15.26 in²
D. 61.05 in²

MM2G3c

50. Which of the following most accurately describes the translation from $f(x) = a^x$ to $f(x) = \frac{1}{4}a^x$?

A. The graph of $f(x) = a^x$ is shifted to the right $\frac{1}{4}$ unit.
B. The graph will be wider and flatter than $f(x) = a^x$.
C. The graph will be taller and narrower.
D. The graphs will be reflections of each other over the x-axis.

MM2A2c

51. Rosa has purchased a larger delivery van for her business.

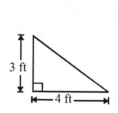 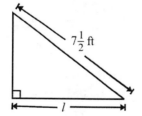

She intends to use a similar, larger logo sign on the new van. What will be the length (l) of the new logo sign?

A. 5 feet
B. 5$\frac{1}{4}$ feet
C. 6 feet
D. 10 feet

MM2G2a

52. If the graph below is the original relation, which of the following is the graph of its inverse relation?

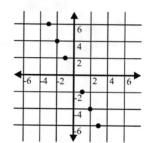

A.

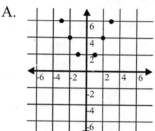

B.

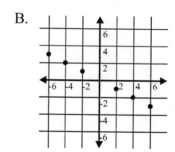

C.

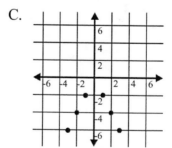

D.

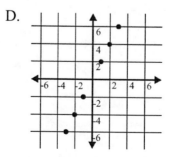

MM2A5c

Use the figure below to answer the next three questions.

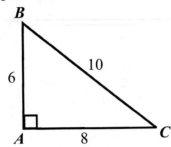

53. What is the tangent ratio of $\angle C$?

   A. $\dfrac{6}{10}$

   B. $\dfrac{8}{6}$

   C. $\dfrac{8}{10}$

   D. $\dfrac{6}{8}$

   MM2G2b

54. What is the sine of $\angle B$?

   A. $\dfrac{6}{10}$

   B. $\dfrac{8}{6}$

   C. $\dfrac{8}{10}$

   D. $\dfrac{6}{8}$

   MM2G2b

55. What is the cosine of $\angle C$?

   A. $\dfrac{8}{10}$

   B. $\dfrac{6}{10}$

   C. $\dfrac{10}{8}$

   D. $\dfrac{10}{6}$

   MM2G2b

56. What is the approximate volume of a sphere with a radius of 4 inches? Round your answer to the nearest hundredth.

   Use the formula $V = \dfrac{4}{3}\pi r^3$ $\pi \approx 3.14$

   A. 66.99 in^3

   B. 200.96 in^3

   C. 267.95 in^3

   D. 803.84 in^3

   MM2G4a

57. Solve $x^2 + 4x < 12$ algebraically. Which of the following is the correct solution?

   A. $x < 2$

   B. $x > -6$

   C. $-6 < x < 2$

   D. $x < -12$

   MM2A4d

58. Find the mean of the following set of data: 385 yards; 203 yards; 560 yards; 294 yards; 434 yards; 357 yards; 266 yards

   A. 416.5 yards

   B. 357 yards

   C. 312.4 yards

   D. 384 yards

   MM2D1b

59. Find the approximate length of an arc cut by a central angle of $36°$ in a circle with a radius of 5 inches.

   A. 3.14 in

   B. 6.28 in

   C. 1.57 in

   D. 12.56 in

   MM2G3c

Use the graph below to answer the next two questions.

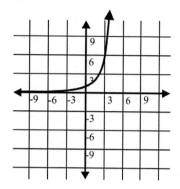

60. Which of the following best describes the asymptote of the graph?

    A. $x = 0$

    B. $x = 5$

    C. $y = 0$

    D. $y \to \infty$

    MM2A2b

61. Which of the following best describes the end behavior of the graph?

    A. as $x \to +\infty$, $f(x) \to +\infty$

    B. as $x \to +\infty$, $f(x) \to 0$

    C. as $x \to 0$, $f(x) \to -\infty$

    D. as $x \to +\infty$, $f(x) \to -\infty$

    MM2A2b

62. What is the range of the inverse of the following function?

    $y = x^2$

    A. $0 \le y < \infty$

    B. $0 \le x < \infty$

    C. $-\infty < y < \infty$

    D. $-\infty < x < \infty$

    MM2A5a

63. Which transformation can be applied to the graph of the quadratic function $f(x) = \frac{1}{2}x^2$ to produce the graph of the function $f(x) = -\frac{1}{2}x^2$?

    A. a translation down 1

    B. a reflection over the y-axis

    C. a reflection over the x-axis

    D. a vertical compression by a factor of $\frac{1}{2}$

    MM2A3c

64. In the diagram below, what is the measure of $\angle 3$?

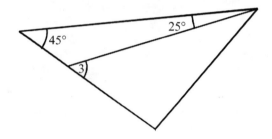

    A. $30°$

    B. $40°$

    C. $50°$

    D. $70°$

    MM2G2c

65. Given the equation $f(x) = -2x^2 - 12x - 14$, which of the following is the vertex form of the equation?

    A. $f(x) = 2(x - 3)^2 - 4$

    B. $f(x) = 2(-x - 3)^2 + 4$

    C. $f(x) = -2(x + 3)^2 + 4$

    D. $f(x) = -2(x^2 + 6x + 7)$ MM2A3a

66. Which of the following would be a causing variable in low test scores among high school students?

    A. Breakfast habits

    B. After school activities

    C. Social habits

    D. None of the above   MM2D2d

67. To find the average number of purses owned by women, the number of purses owned by each woman in a large random sample of $2,000$ women was determined. The mean number of purses owned by women in this population is 17 purses, and the standard deviation of the number of purses is 8. A smaller data sample was observed also. This smaller set consisted of 443 women. The mean for this sample was 28 purses, and the standard deviation was 7 purses. What can you conclude from this data?

A. The larger sample and the smaller sample have the same standard deviation.

B. The smaller sample has the higher standard deviation.

C. The larger sample has the lower standard deviation.

D. The larger sample has the higher standard deviation.

MM2D1d

68. The following table lists the amount Nathan charges for a certain number of car washes. Which equation below best represents the charges y for a given number if car washes?
x = number of car washes, y = charges in dollars

# of car washes (x)	Charges (y)
1	$10.00
2	$18.00
3	$26.00
4	$34.00

A. $y = 8x$

B. $y = 8x + 2$

C. $y = 8x + 10$

D. $y = 10x - 2$

MM2D2a

69. Selma saves a portion of her salary every month. The following graph is the amount she saves each month. Which equation best represents her monthly savings?
t = time (in months), y = monthly savings

A. $y = 10t$

B. $y = 10t + 40$

C. $y = 20t + 80$

D. $y = 2t + 4$

MM2D2a

70. Use the graph below for this question.

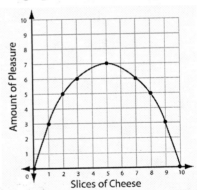

Thomas is fond of cheese. He is more pleased the more cheese he eats, until he eats too much and the cheese starts to make him feel sick. The graph above shows the number of slices that Thomas has eaten, and his amount of pleasure. What is the equation of this graph?

A. $f(x) = \frac{7}{25}(x - 5)^2 - 7$

B. $f(x) = \frac{7}{25}(x + 5)^2 - 7$

C. $f(x) = -\frac{7}{25}(x + 5)^2 + 7$

D. $f(x) = -\frac{7}{25}(x - 5)^2 + 7$

MM2D2a

71. Based upon the scatter plot below, about how many hours would Casey have to exercise to achieve 16% muscle tone?

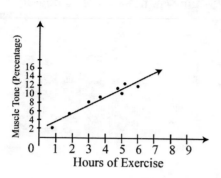

A. 9
B. 6.5
C. 7.5
D. 10

MM2D2b

72. Use the scatterplot below to determine the equation of the linear function that can be used to model the relationship.

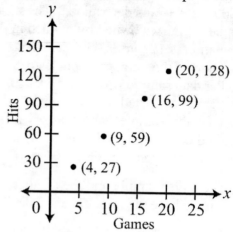

A. $y = -6.2x + 2.2$
B. $y = 6.2x + 2.2$
C. $y = -6.2x - 2.2$
D. $y = 6.2x - 2.2$

MM2D2c

Practice Test 2

Part 1

You may use the formula sheet on page viii as needed.

1. Ann is taking a survey for her statistics class. She wants to know the proportion of people who order water at a restaurant compared with people who order soda. To do this she visited two different local restaurants in order to get her results. What are the two populations being compared?

   A. people who drink soda and people who drink diet soda
   B. people who drink water
   C. people who drink soda and people who drink water
   D. people who drink tea and people who drink soda

   MM2D1a

2. What is the y-intercept of the quadratic function $f(x) = -\frac{1}{5}x^2 - 5$

   A. $(0, 5)$
   B. $(0, \frac{1}{5})$
   C. $(0, -\frac{1}{5})$
   D. $(0, -5)$

   MM2A3c

3. Sample: mean = 26 inches; standard deviation = 11 inches; Population size: 3,700; Range: 15 inches to 48 inches. What percent of the population falls within the given range?

   A. 47.5%
   B. 70%
   C. 82.5%
   D. 95%

   MM2D1d

4. If $\angle CDB = 36°$, what is the $m\angle A$?

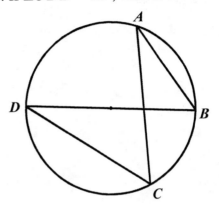

   A. 36°
   B. 64°
   C. 100°
   D. cannot be determined

   MM2G3b

5. A randomly-selected group of 8 people was formed. Each person was asked how many glasses of water they drank each week. Their answers were as follows:

   Person 1: 7 glasses   Person 5: 10 glasses
   Person 2: 12 glasses   Person 6: 2 glasses
   Person 3: 18 glasses   Person 7: 5 glasses
   Person 4: 9 glasses   Person 8: 15 glasses

   What is the standard deviation of this data sample?

   A. 6.45 glasses
   B. 5.23 glasses
   C. 5.69 glasses
   D. 4.74 glasses

   MM2D1b

6. The diameter of the circle below is 20 cm. What is the approximate length of arc *RS*?

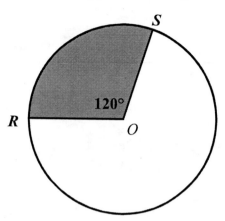

A. 5.23 cm

B. 10.46 cm

C. 20.93 cm

D. 104.66 cm

MM2G3c

7. What is the value of *x*?

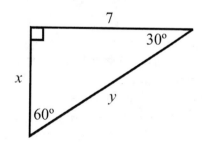

A. $\dfrac{7\sqrt{3}}{3}$

B. 14

C. $7\sqrt{3}$

D. $\dfrac{\sqrt{3}}{7}$

MM2G1a

8. A bank charges a $10 fee if the account balance is less than $200. If the balance is in between $200 and $500 there is a $5 fee. If at least $500 is in the account, there is no fee. Graph the fee schedule for different account balances.

A.

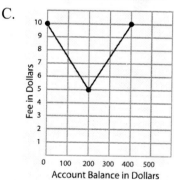

B.

C.

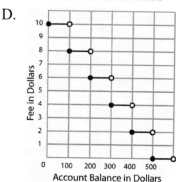

D.

MM2A1b

218

9. Nina wants to see whether doctors or nurses work more hours in a five day work week. She interviewed a random group of 5 nurses and asked them how many hours they worked in the last week. She then interviewed a random group of 5 doctors and asked them the same question. Looking at the chart below, which data set has the lower standard deviation?

Nurses	48	50	49	47	51
Doctors	53	54	53	51	52

A. They have the same standard deviation.
B. Not enough information
C. Nurses
D. Doctors

MM2D1c

10. Consider the quadratic equation $x^2 - 4x + 6 = 0$. Find the discriminant and give the numbers and type of solutions of the equation.

A. $(-4)^2 - (4)(1)(6) = -8$; two imaginary solutions
B. $(-4)^2 - (4)(1)(6) = 8$; two real solutions
C. $(4)^2 + (4)(1)(6) = 40$; two real solutions
D. $(6)^2 + (-4)(1)(6) = 12$; two real solutions

MM2A4c

11. What is the measure of y?

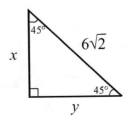

A. $3\sqrt{2}$
B. $\sqrt{2}$
C. 6
D. $3\sqrt{3}$

MM2G1b

12. Solve $6x^2 - 24x - 270 = 0$ using the quadratic formula.

A. $x = -5, 9$
B. $x = 6, 15$
C. $x = -7, 5$
D. $x = -9, 3$

MM2A4b

13. The sine of $\angle A$ equals the

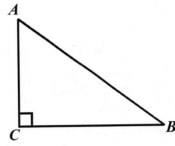

A. sine of $\angle B$.
B. tangent of $\angle C$.
C. cosine of $\angle A$.
D. cosine of $\angle B$.

MM2G2b

14. Write $\sqrt{-4} - 3$ in standard form.

A. $-3 + 2i$
B. $-3 - 2i$
C. $-2i + 3$
D. $-2i - 3$

MM2N1b

15. Simplify: $(-3)^3$

A. 27
B. -27
C. $27i$
D. $-27i$

MM2A2a

16. What is the length of $\overline{DA}$?

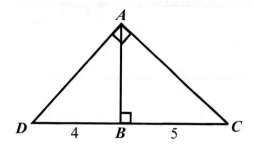

   A. 5
   B. 7
   C. $5\sqrt{2}$
   D. 6

MM2G2b

17. What is the length of x?

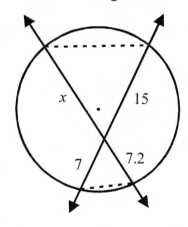

   A. 14.42
   B. 14.58
   C. 14.92
   D. 15.2

MM2G3a

18. The function $f(x)$ has the inverse $f^{-1}(x) = x - 8$. What is $f(x)$?

   A. $f(x) = x + 8$
   B. $f(x) = 8 - x$
   C. $f(x) = -x + 8$
   D. $f(x) = x - 8$

MM2A5b

19. Which of the following is the function of $y = |2x - 1| + 3$ written as a piecewise function?

   A. $f(x) = \begin{cases} 2x - 2 & \text{if } x \geq \frac{1}{2} \\ 2x + 4 & \text{if } x < \frac{1}{2} \end{cases}$

   B. $f(x) = \begin{cases} 2x - 1 + 3 & \text{if } x \geq 2 \\ 2x + 1 - 3 & \text{if } x < 2 \end{cases}$

   C. $f(x) = \begin{cases} 2x + 2 & \text{if } x \geq \frac{1}{2} \\ -2x + 4 & \text{if } x < \frac{1}{2} \end{cases}$

   D. $f(x) = \begin{cases} 2x + 1 & \text{if } x \geq 0 \\ 2x - 1 & \text{if } x < 0 \end{cases}$

MM2A1a

20. If arc AB is a semicircle, what is $m\angle BOC$?

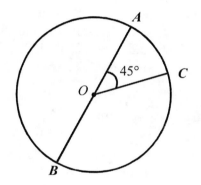

   A. 90°
   B. 180°
   C. 135°
   D. 235°

MM2G3b

21. Find the standard deviation for the following set of data: 45 degrees; 32 degrees; 53 degrees; 51 degrees; 62 degrees; 66 degrees; 62 degrees

   A. 9.72 degrees
   B. 12.44 degrees
   C. 11.83 degrees
   D. 10.72 degrees

MM2D1b

22. What is the length of x? Round your answers to the nearest tenth.

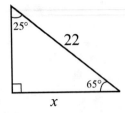

A. 10.3
B. 19.9
C. 52.1
D. 9.3

MM2G2b

23. Given the equation $f(x) = \frac{1}{2}(x-2)^2 + 1$, what is its vertex?

A. $(2, 1)$
B. $(2, -1)$
C. $(-2, 1)$
D. $(-2, -1)$

MM2A3c

24. The ratio of two similar spheres' radii is 1 to 3. What is the ratio of their volumes?

A. $\frac{2}{3}$

B. $\frac{1}{3}$

C. $\frac{1}{9}$

D. $\frac{1}{27}$

MM2G4b

25. Solve $x^2 + 6x - 7 = 0$ using a calculator.

A. $x = -7, 1$
B. $x = -1, 7$
C. $x = 1, 7$
D. $x = -1, -7$

MM2A4a

26. What is the value of b?

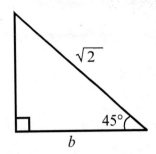

A. $\frac{\sqrt{2}}{2}$

B. 1

C. $2\sqrt{2}$

D. 4

MM2G1b

27. What is the axis of symmetry of the graph $y = -|x-1| + 3$?

A. $x = 1$
B. $x = -1$
C. $x = 3$
D. $x = -3$

MM2A1b

28. $\triangle ABC \sim \triangle EDF$

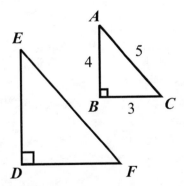

What is the measure of $\angle F$?

A. $55.33°$
B. $38.66°$
C. $36.87°$
D. $53.13°$

MM2G2a

29. What is the range of the inverse of the function $y = -x^2 + 1$?

A. $-\infty < y < \infty$
B. $-\infty < y \leq 0$
C. $-\infty < y \leq 1$
D. $1 \leq y < \infty$

MM2A5a

30. What is the value of the variable in the diagram below?

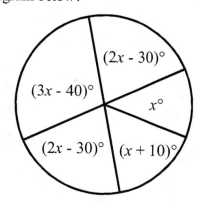

A. $x = 25$
B. $x = 30$
C. $x = 40$
D. $x = 50$

MM2G3d

31. A randomly selected group of people were asked how many miles they drove to and from work in one week. Their responses were as follows:

Person 1: 84 miles   Person 5: 79 miles
Person 2: 277 miles   Person 6: 92 miles
Person 3: 38 miles   Person 7: 137 miles
Person 4: 174 miles   Person 8: 206 miles

What is the average number of miles traveled by a member of the group each week?

A. 148.6 miles
B. 174.3 miles
C. 155.8 miles
D. 135.9 miles

MM2D1b

32. Jane has seen a rise in the purchasing of sunscreen since the beginning of summer. Is this correlation or causation?

A. Correlation
B. Causation
C. Both
D. Neither

MM2D2d

33. What is the equation of the graph below?

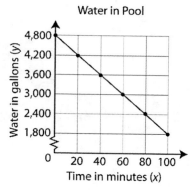

A. $y = 30x - 4800$
B. $y = -30x - 4800$
C. $y = -30x + 4800$
D. $y = 30x + 4800$

MM2D2a

34. Use the linear regression model and scatterplot below to predict the number of clicks when there are 10 ads.

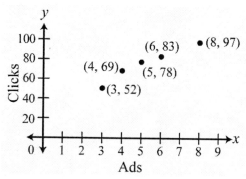

Linear Regression: $y = 8.5x + 31.8$

A. 115
B. 119
C. 117
D. 120

MM2D2c

35. Melissa is preparing to run a 5k race. She currently runs 1 mile each day. Each week Melissa adds 0.25 miles per day to her run. The following table shows the projected increase in her running schedule. Which function best represents the number of miles she runs during a specified week?

x = number of weeks, $f(x)$ = miles

Week	Miles
0	1.00
1	1.25
2	1.50
3	1.75
4	2.00
5	2.25
6	2.50
7	2.75
8	3.00

A. $f(x) = 2x + 1$

B. $f(x) = \frac{1}{4}x + 1$

C. $f(x) = \frac{1}{4}x - 1$

D. $f(x) = 2 - \frac{1}{2}x$

MM2D2a

36. The data set below displays the average weight for a Jack Russell Terrier. Using the line of best fit, determine the average weight of a Jack Russell when they are one year old?

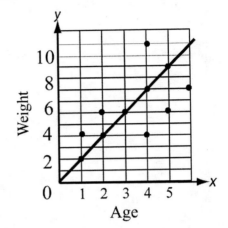

A 2 lbs

B 4 lbs

C 6 lbs

D 8 lbs

MM2D2b

Part 2

37. What is the value of x?

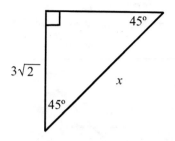

A. $9\sqrt{2}$
B. 18
C. 6
D. 12

MM2G1b

38. Compare the mean of Louise and Thelma's bowling scores. Whose average is higher?

T	85	176	111	201	159	187	134
L	99	83	102	175	126	79	223

A. Thelma's average is higher.
B. Louise's average is higher
C. Their averages are the same.
D. Cannot be determined.

MM2D1c

39. Given the equation $f(x) = (x+3)^2 - 2$, what is its vertex?

A. $(-3, 2)$
B. $(3, -2)$
C. $(3, 2)$
D. $(-3, -2)$

MM2A3c

40. Which of the following is the solution for $2x^2 + 16 = -48$?

A. $x = \pm 4$
B. $x = -4\sqrt{2}$
C. $x = 4\sqrt{2}$
D. $x = \pm 4i\sqrt{2}$

MM2A4b

41. Write $\sqrt{-2} - 4$ in standard form.

A. $-i\sqrt{2} + 4$
B. $i\sqrt{2} - 4$
C. $-4 + i\sqrt{2}$
D. $-4 - i\sqrt{2}$

MM2N1b

42. Given that $BD \parallel AE$ and $\tan D = \frac{4}{3}$, what is the measure of $\angle ABD$ to the nearest degree?

A. $37°$
B. $53°$
C. $127°$
D. $143°$

MM2G2a

43. Where is the vertex of the graph of
$$f(x) = \begin{cases} \frac{1}{2}x + \frac{3}{2} & \text{if } x < 1 \\ -x + 3 & \text{if } x \geq 1 \end{cases}$$

A. $(2, 1)$
B. $(3, 2)$
C. $(1, 2)$
D. $\left(\frac{1}{2}, -1\right)$

MM2A1b

224

44. If $\angle BDC = 35°$, what is the measure of $\angle C$?

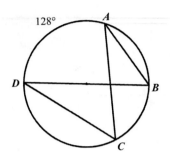

A. $35°$

B. $64°$

C. $81°$

D. $100°$

MM2G3b

45. Simplify: $x^2 \cdot x^{-4}$

A. x^{-2}

B. x^{-8}

C. $\dfrac{1}{x^2}$

D. $\dfrac{1}{x^8}$

MM2A2a

46. Find the value of the variable.

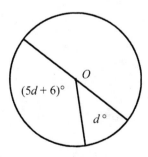

A. $d = 29$

B. $d = 59$

C. $d = 35$

D. $d = 19$

MM2G3d

47. Which of the following inequalities is represented by the graph shown below?

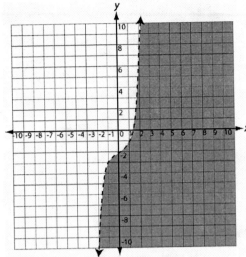

A. $y < x^2 - 2$

B. $y > x^2 - 2$

C. $y < x^3 - 2$

D. $y > x^3 - 2$

MM2A2d

48. Given that $\overline{DB} = 8$ and $\sin C = 0.8$, what is the length of $\overline{AD}$?

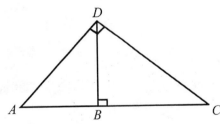

A. 13.3

B. 9.4

C. 10

D. 11.7

MM2G2a

49. What is the inverse of $f(x) = \frac{1}{4}x^2 - 3$?

A. $f^{-1}(x) = 4x + 12$

B. $f^{-1}(x) = \frac{1}{4}x^2 - 3$

C. $f^{-1}(x) = \pm\sqrt{4x + 12}$

D. $f^{-1}(x) = \pm\sqrt{4x + 3}$

MM2A5b

50. The Bernard High School football team has a record of 5-2 so far this season. What is the average number of yards completed per game so far this season?

Game 1: 385 yards   Game 5: 434 yards
Game 2: 203 yards   Game 6: 357 yards
Game 3: 560 yards   Game 7: 266 yards
Game 4: 294 yards

A. 416.5 yards
B. 357 yards
C. 312.4 yards
D. 384 yards

MM2D1b

51. What is the length of $\overline{AB}$?

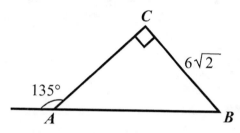

A. 12
B. $2\sqrt{6}$
C. 9
D. $3\sqrt{2}$

MM2G1b

52. For the function $y = x^3 + x^2$, what is the range of the function?

A. $-\infty < y < \infty$
B. $0 \le y < \infty$
C. $-\infty < y \le 0$
D. $-\infty < x < \infty$

MM2A5a

53. Which of the following is the solution to $3x^2 = -60$

A. $x = -\sqrt{20}$
B. $x = \pm 2\sqrt{5}$
C. $x = 2\sqrt{-5}$
D. $x = \pm 2i\sqrt{5}$

MM2A4b

54. Given that $\tan A = 1.6$, what is the length of $\overline{CD}$?

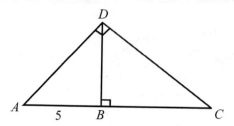

A. $2\sqrt{3}$
B. 15
C. 8
D. 13

MM2G2a

55. Given that $\overline{ED} \parallel \overline{AB}$ and $\cos B = 0.8$, what is the value of x?

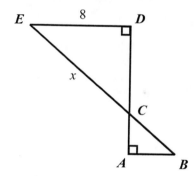

A. 14
B. 6.4
C. 10
D. 12

MM2G2a

56. What is the solution to the inequality $x^2 + 2x > 3$?

A. $x > 1$ or $x < -3$
B. $-3 < x < 1$
C. $x < -1$ or $x > 3$
D. $-1 < x < 3$

MM2A4d

57. What is the value of x?

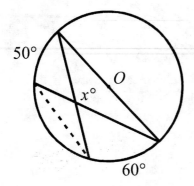

A. 100°

B. 120°

C. 125°

D. 140°

MM2G3a

58. What is the value of the variable in the diagram below?

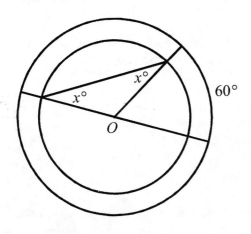

A. $x = 35$

B. $x = 60$

C. $x = 45$

D. $x = 30$

MM2G3d

59. Barry wants to attach a wire from the ground to the top of a wall that is perpendicular to the ground as shown. He positions the end of the wire 12 feet away from the bottom of the wall and such that $\tan \theta = \dfrac{3}{4}$. What length wire will he need for this project?

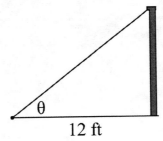

A. 12 feet

B. 15 feet

C. 16 feet

D. 20 feet

MM2G2c

60. Calculate the standard deviation of the following population set: 127, 140, 110, 103, 97, 156.

A. 122

B. 219

C. 438

D. 21

MM2D1b

61. Solve the equation $(x + 6)^2 = 169$

A. $x = 5, 13$

B. $x = -17, 3$

C. $x = -19, 7$

D. $x = -7, 7$

MM2A4b

62. What is the domain and range of the equation $y = 4^{x-1} + 3$?

A. domain: $-3 < x < 3$; range: all real numbers

B. domain: all real numbers ; range: $y > 0$

C. domain: all real numbers ; range: all real numbers

D. domain: all real numbers ; range: $y > 3$

MM2A2b

63. What is the value of b?

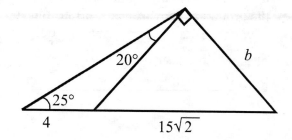

    A. 13

    B. $15\sqrt{3}$

    C. $\dfrac{15}{\sqrt{3}}$

    D. 15

MM2G1b

64. Find the inverse of $f(x) = \frac{1}{2}x^4 + 5$.

    A. $f^{-1}(x) = \pm\sqrt[4]{2x - 10}$

    B. $x = \pm\sqrt[4]{2y - 10}$

    C. $f^{-1}(x) = \frac{1}{16}x + 5$

    D. $x = \frac{1}{16}y + 5$

MM2A5b

65. Jake is a sports trainer. The past five years he has been working with high school track and field runners and cross country runners. He wants to know if paced long distance runners or aggressive short distance runners are more injury prone. To do this he has kept a record of visits by athletes and which sport they participate in. What is the difference between the two populations?

    A. the age of the runners

    B. the type of running

    C. the amount of water taken in by the runners

    D. the amount of practice each runner got

MM2D1a

66. To find the average number of hours spent playing video games each day by teenagers, the number of hours spent daily playing video games by each teenager of a large random sample of 1,750 teenagers was determined. The mean number of hours spent per day playing video games by teenagers in the sample was 7.5 hours, and the standard deviation of hours spent daily playing video games was 15. A smaller data sample was also observed. This smaller set consisted of 15 teenagers. The mean for this sample was 4 hours, and the standard deviation 17. What can you conclude from this data?

    A. The larger sample and the smaller sample have the same standard deviation.

    B. The larger sample has the higher mean.

    C. The larger sample has the higher standard deviation.

    D. The larger sample and the smaller sample have the same mean.

MM2D1d

67. Would a power outage and severe weather be causation or correlation?

    A. Correlation

    B. Causation

    C. Neither

    D. Both

MM2D2d

68. Using the data points below, what is the equation of the linear function that can be used to model the situation?
(2 boxes, $40.00), (10 boxes, $32.00)

    A. $y = 16x + 8$

    B. $y = -x + 42$

    C. $y = x + 42$

    D. $y = 7x - 8$

MM2D2a

69. Which of the following graphs most closely represents the graph of the function $f(x) = -x^2 + 3$?

A.

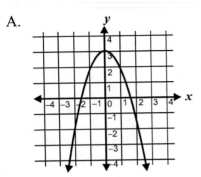

B.

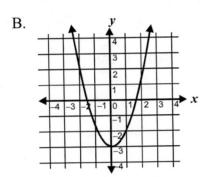

C.

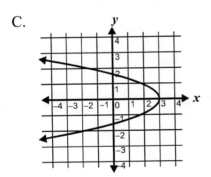

D.

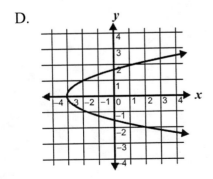

70. The information below is expressed by which linear function?

x	1	7	6	-2	-3
$f(x)$	15	3	5	21	23

A. $f(x) = -x + 21$

B. $f(x) = x + 15$

C. $2x = f(x) + 7$

D. $f(x) - 17 = -2x$

MM2D2a

71. Alcibiade, the scientist, is testing the growth of a particular kind of mold. According to the curve of best fit below, how many patches of mold should there be after 6 days?

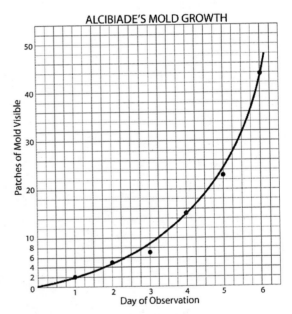

A. 38

B. 40

C. 42

D. 44

MM2D2a

MM2D2b

72. Use the quadratic regression and scatterplot below to predict the number of votes after 5 weeks.

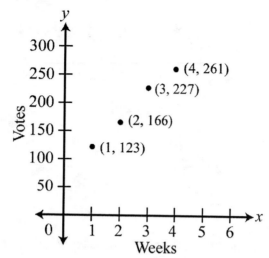

Quadratic Regression: $y = 47.5x + 75.5$

A. 312
B. 317
C. 313
D. 314

MM2D2c

Index